Nissan Owners Workshop Manual

Peter G Strasman
and John H Haynes Member of the Guild of Motoring Writers

Models covered

Nissan Sentra (B11 Series).
Sedan, Coupe and Wagon with 90.80 cu in (1488cc) and 97.45 cu in (1597cc) ohc engines

Covers automatic and 4- and 5-speed manual transmissions.
Does not cover diesel engined models

ISBN 1 85010 265 1

© Haynes Publishing Group 1984, 1986, 1987

All rights reserved. No part of this book may be reproduced or transmitted in any form or by any means, electronic or mechanical, including photocopying, recording or by any information storage or retrieval system, without permission in writing from the copyright holder.

ABCDE FGHIJ K

Printed in England *(1N3 — 982)*

Haynes Publishing Group
Sparkford Nr Yeovil
Somerset BA22 7JJ England

Haynes Publications, Inc
861 Lawrence Drive
Newbury Park
California 91320 USA

Library of Congress
Catalog card number
86-81875

Acknowledgements

Thanks are due to the Nissan Motor Company Limited of Japan for the provision of technical information and certain illustrations. The Champion Sparking Plug Company supplied the illustrations showing the various spark plug conditions, Castrol Limited provided lubrication data and Sykes-Pickavant supplied some of the workshop tools.

Thanks are also due to those people at Sparkford who helped in the production of this manual.

About this manual

Its aim

The aim of this manual is to help you get the best value from your vehicle. It can do so in several ways. It can help you decide what work must be done (even should you choose to get it done by a garage), provide information on routine maintenance and servicing, and give a logical course of action and diagnosis when random faults occur. However, it is hoped that you will use the manual by tackling the work yourself. On simpler jobs it may even be quicker than booking the car into a garage and going there twice, to leave and collect it. Perhaps most important, a lot of money can be saved by avoiding the costs a garage must charge to cover its labour and overheads.

The manual has drawings and descriptions to show the function of the various components so that their layout can be understood. Then the tasks are described and photographed in a step-by-step sequence so that even a novice can do the work.

Its arrangement

The manual is divided into thirteen Chapters, each covering a logical sub-division of the vehicle. The Chapters are each divided into Sections, numbered with single figures, eg 5; and the Sections into paragraphs (or sub-sections), with decimal numbers following on from the Section they are in, eg 5.1, 5.2, 5.3, etc.

It is freely illustrated, especially in those parts where there is a detailed sequence of operations to be carried out. There are two forms of illustration: figures and photographs. The figures are numbered in sequence with decimal numbers, according to their position in the Chapter – eg Fig. 6.4 is the fourth drawing/illustration in Chapter 6. Photographs carry the same number (either individually or in related groups) as the Section or sub-section to which they relate.

There is an alphabetical index at the back of the manual as well as a contents list at the front. Each Chapter is also preceded by its own individual contents list.

References to the 'left' or 'right' of the vehicle are in the sense of a person in the driver's seat facing forwards.

Unless otherwise stated, nuts and bolts are removed by turning anti-clockwise, and tightened by turning clockwise.

Vehicle manufacturers continually make changes to specifications and recommendations, and these, when notified, are incorporated into our manuals at the earliest opportunity.

Whilst every care is taken to ensure that the information in this manual is correct, no liability can be accepted by the authors or publishers for loss, damage or injury caused by any errors in, or omissions from, the information given.

Introduction to the Sunny and Sentra

This is the front wheel drive replacement for the very popular rear wheel drive vehicle. There is nothing about the vehicle which is other than conventional and the home mechanic should not be presented with any problems on how to tackle the dismantling of a unit or component.

Removal of certain components can require slightly more work than would normally be expected, and the transmission is somewhat complex in design. However, provided the procedures given are adhered to, no real problems should arise when undertaking any work on this range of vehicles.

The model range is wide enough to cater for all owner requirements, and the vehicle should prove reliable and economical in use.

Contents

Nissan Sunny Saloon

Nissan Sunny Estate

Nissan Sentra Sedan

Nissan Sentra Coupe

General dimensions, weights and capacities

Sunny B11 models

Dimensions

Overall length:	
Saloon and Coupe	4135.0 mm (162.8 in)
Estate	4255.0 mm (167.5 in)
Overall width	1620.0 mm (63.8 in)
Overall height:	
Saloon	1390.0 mm (54.7 in)
Coupe	1355.0 mm (53.3 in)
Estate	1360.0 mm (53.5 in)
Ground clearance	175.0 mm (6.9 in)
Wheelbase	2400.0 mm (94.5 in)
Front track	1395.0 mm (54.9 in)
Rear track	1375.0 mm (54.1 in)

Kerb weight

Typical values only. Add 20 kg (44 lb) for automatic transmission

1.3 litre models:	
Two-door	791 kg (1742 lb)
Four-door	801 kg (1764 lb)
1.5 litre models:	
Saloon	816 kg (1979 lb)
Coupe	861 kg (1896 lb)
Estate	886 kg (1951 lb)

Trailer weight (with brakes)

Typical values only. Refer to your dealer for precise weights

1.3 litre models	801 kg (1764 lb)
1.5 litre models:	
Saloon and Estate	1001 kg (2205 lb)
Coupe	1003 kg (2209 lb)

Trailer weight (without brakes)

Typical values only. Refer to your dealer for precise weights

1.3 litre models	450 kg (992 lb)
1.5 litre models	551 kg (1213 lb)

Roof rack capacity

All models	75 kg (165 lb)

Sunny N12 models

Dimensions

Overall length	3960.0 mm (155.9 in)
Overall width	1620.0 mm (63.8 in)
Overall height	1390.0 mm (54.7 in)
Ground clearance	170.0 mm (6.7 in)
Wheelbase	2415.0 mm (95.1 in)
Front track	1395.0 mm (54.9 in)
Rear track	1375.0 mm (54.1 in)

Kerb weight

1.3 litre models:	
Three-door	807 kg (1779 lb)
Five-door	818 kg (1804 lb)
1.5 litre models:	
Three-door	821 kg (1810 lb)
Five-door	832 kg (1813 lb)

Trailer weight (with brakes)

Typical values only. Refer to your dealer for precise weights

1.3 litre models	800 kg (1764 lb)
1.5 litre models	1000 kg (2205 lb)

Trailer weight (without brakes)

Typical values only. Refer to your dealer for precise weights

1.3 litre models	400 kg (882 lb)
1.5 litre models	550 kg (1213 lb)

Roof rack capacity

All models	75 kg (165 lb)

Sentra models

Dimensions

Overall length:	
Sedan and Coupe	4240.0 mm (116.9 in)
Wagon	4375.0 mm (172.5 in)
Overall width	1620.0 mm (63.8 in)
Overall height:	
Sedan	1385.0 mm (54.5 in)
Coupe	1355.0 mm (53.3 in)
Wagon	1360.0 mm (53.5 in)
Ground clearance	170.0 mm (6.7 in)
Front track	1395.0 mm (54.9 in)
Rear track	1375.0 mm (54.1 in)
Wheelbase	2400.0 mm (94.5 in)

Weights

Refer to the vehicle FMVSS certification label

All model variations

Capacities

Fuel tank	50 litres (11 Imp gals, 13.25 US gals)
Cooling system:	
Manual transmission	5.5 litres (9.7 Imp pints, 5.8 US qts)
Automatic transmission	6.0 litre (10.6 Imp pints, 6.3 US qt)
Cooling system expansion tank	0.7 litre (1.2 Imp pints, 0.75 US qt)
Engine oil (with filter change)	3.9 litres (6.9 Imp pints, 4.12 US qts)
Manual transmission:	
Four-speed	2.3 litres (4.0 Imp pints, 2.4 US qts)
Five-speed	2.7 litres (4.8 Imp pints, 2,8 US qts)
Automatic transmission	6.0 litres (10.6 Imp pints, 6.3 US qts)
Power steering system	1.0 litre (1.76 Imp pints, 1.06 US qts)

Use of English

As this book has been written in England, it uses the appropriate English component names, phrases, and spelling. Some of these differ from those used in America. Normally, these cause no difficulty, but to make sure, a glossary is printed below. In ordering spare parts remember the parts list may use some of these words:

English	American	English	American
Aerial	Antenna	Motorway	Freeway, turnpike etc
Accelerator	Gas pedal	Number plate	License plate
Anti-roll bar	Stabiliser or sway bar	Paraffin	Kerosene
Bonnet (engine cover)	Hood	Petrol	Gasoline (gas)
Boot (luggage compartment)	Trunk	Petrol tank	Gas tank
Bulkhead	Firewall	'Pinking'	'Pinging'
Cam follower or tappet	Valve lifter or tappet	Propeller shaft	Driveshaft
Carburettor	Carburetor	Quarter light	Quarter window
Catch	Latch	Retread	Recap
Choke/venturi	Barrel	Reverse	Back-up
Circlip	Snap-ring	Rocker cover	Valve cover
Clearance	Lash	Saloon	Sedan
Crownwheel	Ring gear (of differential)	Seized	Frozen
Disc (brake)	Rotor/disk	Side indicator lights	Side marker lights
Drop arm	Pitman arm	Side light	Parking light
Drop head coupe	Convertible	Silencer	Muffler
Dynamo	Generator (DC)	Spanner	Wrench
Earth (electrical)	Ground	Sill panel (beneath doors)	Rocker panel
Engineer's blue	Prussian blue	Split cotter (for valve spring cap)	Lock (for valve spring retainer)
Estate car	Station wagon	Split pin	Cotter pin
Exhaust manifold	Header	Steering arm	Spindle arm
Fault finding/diagnosis	Trouble shooting	Sump	Oil pan
Float chamber	Float bowl	Tab washer	Tang; lock
Free-play	Lash	Tappet	Valve lifter
Freewheel	Coast	Thrust bearing	Throw-out bearing
Gudgeon pin	Piston pin or wrist pin	Top gear	High
Gearchange	Shift	Trackrod (of steering)	Tie-rod (or connecting rod)
Gearbox	Transmission	Trailing shoe (of brake)	Secondary shoe
Halfshaft	Axleshaft	Transmission	Whole drive line
Handbrake	Parking brake	Tyre	Tire
Hood	Soft top	Van	Panel wagon/van
Hot spot	Heat riser	Vice	Vise
Indicator	Turn signal	Wheel nut	Lug nut
Interior light	Dome lamp	Windscreen	Windshield
Layshaft (of gearbox)	Countershaft	Wing/mudguard	Fender
Leading shoe (of brake)	Primary shoe		
Locks	Latches		

Miscellaneous points

An 'oil seal', is also fitted to components lubricated by grease!

A 'damper' is a 'shock absorber', it damps out bouncing, and absorbs shocks of bump impact. Both names are correct, and both are used haphazardly.

Note that British drum brakes are different from the Bendix type that is common in America, so different descriptive names result. The shoe end furthest from the hydraulic wheel cylinder is on a pivot; interconnection between the shoes as on Bendix brakes is most uncommon. Therefore the phrase 'Primary' or 'Secondary' shoe does not apply. A shoe is said to be 'Leading' or 'Trailing'. A 'Leading' shoe is one on which a point on the drum, as it rotates forward, reaches the shoe at the end worked by the hydraulic cylinder before the anchor end. The opposite is a 'Trailing' shoe and this one has no self servo from the wrapping effect of the rotating drum.

Buying spare parts and vehicle identification numbers

Buying spare parts

Spare parts are available from many sources, for example: Nissan garages, other garages and accessory shops, and motor factors. Our advice regarding spare part sources is as follows:

Officially appointed Nissan garages – This is the best source of parts which are peculiar to your vehicle and are otherwise not generally available (eg complete cylinder heads, internal gearbox components, badges, interior trim etc). It is also the only place at which you should buy parts if your vehicle is still under warranty: non-standard components may invalidate the warranty. To be sure of obtaining the correct parts it will always be necessary to give the storeman your vehicle's engine and chassis number, and if possible, to take the 'old' parts along for positive identification. Remember that some parts are available on a factory exchange scheme – any parts returned should always be clean! It obviously makes good sense to go straight to the specialists on your vehicle for this type of part for they are best equipped to supply you.

Other garages and accessory shops – These are often very good places to buy materials and components needed for the maintenance of your vehicle (eg spark plugs, bulbs, drivebelts, oils and greases, touch-up paint, filler paste, etc). They also sell general accessories, usually have convenient opening hours, charge lower prices and can often be found not far from home.

Motor factors – Good factors will stock all of the more important components which wear out relatively quickly (eg clutch components, pistons, valves, exhaust systems, brake cylinders/pipes/hoses/seals/shoes and pads etc). Motor factors will often provide new or reconditioned components on a part exchange basis – this can save a considerable amount of money.

Vehicle identification numbers

The chassis number is located on a plate in the rear corner of the engine compartment (photo). The number is repeated on the bulkhead upper panel into which it is stamped (photo).

The engine number is stamped into a machined inclined surface on the crankcase just below the distributor mounting (photo).

On North American models, an emission control information label is located under the bonnet, and an emission decal is on the rear door pillar.

An FMVSS certification label is located on the centre (B) pillar.

Tyre pressures are also shown on a label attached to the centre (B) pillar (photo).

Vehicle identification plate

Vehicle chassis number on bulkhead

Engine number

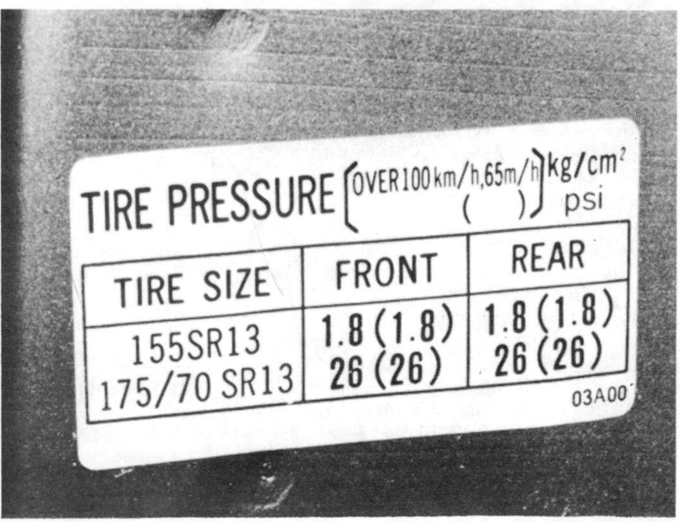

Tyre pressure label

Tools and working facilities

Introduction

A selection of good tools is a fundamental requirement for anyone contemplating the maintenance and repair of a motor vehicle. For the owner who does not possess any, their purchase will prove a considerable expense, offsetting some of the savings made by doing-it-yourself. However, provided that the tools purchased are of good quality, they will last for many years and prove an extremely worthwhile investment.

To help the average owner to decide which tools are needed to carry out the various tasks detailed in this manual, we have compiled three lists of tools under the following headings: *Maintenance and minor repair, Repair and overhaul,* and *Special.* The newcomer to practical mechanics should start off with the *Maintenance and minor repair* tool kit and confine himself to the simpler jobs around the vehicle. Then, as his confidence and experience grow, he can undertake more difficult tasks, buying extra tools as, and when, they are needed. In this way, a *Maintenance and minor repair* tool kit can be built-up into a *Repair and overhaul* tool kit over a considerable period of time without any major cash outlays. The experienced do-it-yourselfer will have a tool kit good enough for most repair and overhaul procedures and will add tools from the *Special* category when he feels the expense is justified by the amount of use to which these tools will be put.

It is obviously not possible to cover the subject of tools fully here. For those who wish to learn more about tools and their use there is a book entitled *How to Choose and Use Car Tools* available from the publishers of this manual.

Maintenance and minor repair tool kit

The tools given in this list should be considered as a minimum requirement if routine maintenance, servicing and minor repair operations are to be undertaken. We recommend the purchase of combination spanners (ring one end, open-ended the other); although more expensive than open-ended ones, they do give the advantages of both types of spanner.

Combination spanners - 10, 11, 12, 13, 14 & 17 mm
Adjustable spanner - 9 inch
Engine sump/gearbox drain plug key
Spark plug spanner (with rubber insert)
Spark plug gap adjustment tool
Set of feeler gauges
Brake bleed nipple spanner
Screwdriver - 4 in long x $\frac{1}{4}$ in dia (flat blade)
Screwdriver - 4 in long x $\frac{1}{4}$ in dia (cross blade)
Combination pliers - 6 inch
Hacksaw (junior)
Tyre pump
Tyre pressure gauge
Oil can
Fine emery cloth (1 sheet) or wet and dry abrasive paper
Wire brush (small)
Funnel (medium size)

Repair and overhaul tool kit

These tools are virtually essential for anyone undertaking any major repairs to a motor vehicle, and are additional to those given in the *Maintenance and minor repair* list. Included in this list is a comprehensive set of sockets. Although these are expensive they will be found invaluable as they are so versatile - particularly if various drives are included in the set. We recommend the $\frac{1}{2}$ in square-drive type, as this can be used with most proprietary torque wrenches. If you cannot afford a socket set, even bought piecemeal, then inexpensive tubular box spanners are a useful alternative.

The tools in this list will occasionally need to be supplemented by tools from the *Special* list.

Sockets (or box spanners) to cover range in previous list
Reversible ratchet drive (for use with sockets)
Extension piece, 10 inch (for use with sockets)
Universal joint (for use with sockets)
Torque wrench (for use with sockets)
'Mole' wrench - 8 inch
Ball pein hammer
Soft-faced hammer, plastic or rubber
Screwdriver - 6 in long x $\frac{5}{16}$ in dia (flat blade)
Screwdriver - 2 in long x $\frac{5}{16}$ in square (flat blade)
Screwdriver - $1\frac{1}{2}$ in long x $\frac{1}{4}$ in dia (cross blade)
Screwdriver - 3 in long x $\frac{1}{8}$ in dia (electricians)
Pliers - electricians side cutters
Pliers - needle nosed
Pliers - circlip (internal and external)
Cold chisel - $\frac{1}{2}$ inch
Scriber
Scraper
Centre punch
Pin punch
Hacksaw
Valve grinding tool
Steel rule/straight-edge
Allen keys
Selection of files
Wire brush (large)
Axle-stands
Jack (strong scissor or hydraulic type)

Special tools

The tools in this list are those which are not used regularly, are expensive to buy, or which need to be used in accordance with their manufacturers' instructions. Unless relatively difficult mechanical jobs are undertaken frequently, it will not be economic to buy many of these tools. Where this is the case, you could consider clubbing together with friends (or joining a motorists' club) to make a joint purchase, or borrowing the tools against a deposit from a local garage or tool hire specialist.

The following list contains only those tools and instruments freely available to the public, and not those special tools produced by the vehicle manufacturer specifically for its dealer network. You will find occasional references to these manufacturers' special tools in the text of this manual. Generally, an alternative method of doing the job without the vehicle manufacturers' special tool is given. However, sometimes, there is no alternative to using them. Where this is the case and the relevant tool cannot be bought or borrowed, you will have to entrust the work to a franchised garage.

Valve spring compressor (where applicable)
Piston ring compressor
Balljoint separator
Universal hub/bearing puller
Impact screwdriver
Micrometer and/or vernier gauge
Dial gauge
Stroboscopic timing light

Dwell angle meter/tachometer
Universal electrical multi-meter
Cylinder compression gauge
Lifting tackle (photo)
Trolley jack
Light with extension lead

Buying tools

For practically all tools, a tool factor is the best source since he will have a very comprehensive range compared with the average garage or accessory shop. Having said that, accessory shops often offer excellent quality tools at discount prices, so it pays to shop around.

Remember, you don't have to buy the most expensive items on the shelf, but it is always advisable to steer clear of the very cheap tools. There are plenty of good tools around at reasonable prices, so ask the proprietor or manager of the shop for advice before making a purchase.

Care and maintenance of tools

Having purchased a reasonable tool kit, it is necessary to keep the tools in a clean serviceable condition. After use, always wipe off any dirt, grease and metal particles using a clean, dry cloth, before putting the tools away. Never leave them lying around after they have been used. A simple tool rack on the garage or workshop wall, for items such as screwdrivers and pliers is a good idea. Store all normal wrenches and sockets in a metal box. Any measuring instruments, gauges, meters, etc, must be carefully stored where they cannot be damaged or become rusty.

Take a little care when tools are used. Hammer heads inevitably become marked and screwdrivers lose the keen edge on their blades from time to time. A little timely attention with emery cloth or a file will soon restore items like this to a good serviceable finish.

Working facilities

Not to be forgotten when discussing tools, is the workshop itself. If anything more than routine maintenance is to be carried out, some form of suitable working area becomes essential.

It is appreciated that many an owner mechanic is forced by circumstances to remove an engine or similar item, without the benefit of a garage or workshop. Having done this, any repairs should always be done under the cover of a roof.

Wherever possible, any dismantling should be done on a clean, flat workbench or table at a suitable working height.

Any workbench needs a vice: one with a jaw opening of 4 in (100 mm) is suitable for most jobs. As mentioned previously, some clean dry storage space is also required for tools, as well as for lubricants, cleaning fluids, touch-up paints and so on, which become necessary.

Another item which may be required, and which has a much more general usage, is an electric drill with a chuck capacity of at least $\frac{5}{16}$ in (8 mm). This, together with a good range of twist drills, is virtually essential for fitting accessories such as mirrors and reversing lights.

Last, but not least, always keep a supply of old newspapers and clean, lint-free rags available, and try to keep any working area as clean as possible.

Spanner jaw gap comparison table

Jaw gap (in)	Spanner size
0.250	$\frac{1}{4}$ in AF
0.276	7 mm
0.313	$\frac{5}{16}$ in AF
0.315	8 mm
0.344	$\frac{11}{32}$ in AF; $\frac{1}{8}$ in Whitworth
0.354	9 mm
0.375	$\frac{3}{8}$ in AF
0.394	10 mm
0.433	11 mm
0.438	$\frac{7}{16}$ in AF
0.445	$\frac{3}{16}$ in Whitworth; $\frac{1}{4}$ in BSF
0.472	12 mm
0.500	$\frac{1}{2}$ in AF
0.512	13 mm
0.525	$\frac{1}{4}$ in Whitworth; $\frac{5}{16}$ in BSF
0.551	14 mm
0.563	$\frac{9}{16}$ in AF
0.591	15 mm
0.600	$\frac{5}{16}$ in Whitworth; $\frac{3}{8}$ in BSF
0.625	$\frac{5}{8}$ in AF
0.630	16 mm
0.669	17 mm
0.686	$\frac{11}{16}$ in AF
0.709	18 mm
0.710	$\frac{3}{8}$ in Whitworth; $\frac{7}{16}$ in BSF
0.748	19 mm
0.750	$\frac{3}{4}$ in AF
0.813	$\frac{13}{16}$ in AF
0.820	$\frac{7}{16}$ in Whitworth; $\frac{1}{2}$ in BSF
0.866	22 mm
0.875	$\frac{7}{8}$ in AF
0.920	$\frac{1}{2}$ in Whitworth; $\frac{9}{16}$ in BSF
0.938	$\frac{15}{16}$ in AF
0.945	24 mm
1.000	1 in AF
1.010	$\frac{9}{16}$ in Whitworth; $\frac{5}{8}$ in BSF
1.024	26 mm
1.063	$1\frac{1}{16}$ in AF; 27 mm
1.100	$\frac{5}{8}$ in Whitworth; $\frac{11}{16}$ in BSF
1.125	$1\frac{1}{8}$ in AF
1.181	30 mm
1.200	$\frac{11}{16}$ in Whitworth; $\frac{3}{4}$ in BSF
1.250	$1\frac{1}{4}$ in AF
1.260	32 mm
1.300	$\frac{3}{4}$ in Whitworth; $\frac{7}{8}$ in BSF
1.313	$1\frac{5}{16}$ in AF
1.390	$\frac{13}{16}$ in Whitworth; $\frac{15}{16}$ in BSF
1.417	36 mm
1.438	$1\frac{7}{16}$ in AF
1.480	$\frac{7}{8}$ in Whitworth; 1 in BSF
1.500	$1\frac{1}{2}$ in AF
1.575	40 mm; $\frac{15}{16}$ in Whitworth
1.614	41 mm
1.625	$1\frac{5}{8}$ in AF
1.670	1 in Whitworth; $1\frac{1}{8}$ in BSF
1.688	$1\frac{11}{16}$ in AF
1.811	46 mm
1.813	$1\frac{13}{16}$ in AF
1.860	$1\frac{1}{8}$ in Whitworth; $1\frac{1}{4}$ in BSF
1.875	$1\frac{7}{8}$ in AF
1.969	50 mm
2.000	2 in AF
2.050	$1\frac{1}{4}$ in Whitworth; $1\frac{3}{8}$ in BSF
2.165	55 mm
2.362	60 mm

A Haltrac hoist and gantry in use during a typical engine removal sequence

Jacking, wheel changing and towing

Jacking

The jack supplied with the vehicle should only be used for emergency roadside wheel changing.

Chock the roadwheels on the side opposite to that from which the wheel is being removed. Engage the jack in one of the two cut-outs at the base of the sill, either front or rear according to which wheel is being removed (photo).

When carrying out overhaul or repair work use a trolley jack or a hydraulic bottle or screw jack. Locate the jack under the vehicle only at the positions indicated and **always** supplement the jack with axle stands placed under the side-members.

To avoid repetition, the procedure for raising the vehicle in order to carry out work under it is not included before each operation described in this Manual. It is to be preferred, and is certainly recommended, that the vehicle is positioned over an inspection pit or raised on a lift. Where these facilities are not available, use ramps or jack up the vehicle and supplement with axle stands, as described earlier.

Wheel changing

The removal and refitting of a roadwheel should be carried out in the following way.

Prise off the centre trim (where fitted) from the roadwheel. Unscrew the roadwheel nuts just enough to release them. On roadwheels having a small plastic centre cap, twist it through a quarter turn and remove it (photo). Raise the roadwheel from the ground and then remove the nuts completely and lift the roadwheel from the studs.

Refit the roadwheel, tighten the nuts as tightly as possible while the wheel is held against rotation with the foot. Lower the vehicle and tighten the nuts fully (95 Nm, 70 lbf ft). Fit the cap/trim to the centre of the roadwheel.

Towing

The front and rear towing hooks may be used in an emergency. On vehicles with manual transmission, restrict the towing speed to below 80 kph (50 mph) and the distance towed to 80 km (50 miles). On vehicles with automatic transmission, restrict the speed to 30 kph (20 mph) and the distance towed to 30 km (20 miles).

If the transmission has a fault, then the front wheels of the vehicle must be raised and placed on a dolly.

Never tow a vehicle with automatic transmission by raising the rear wheels and leaving the front wheels in contact with the road.

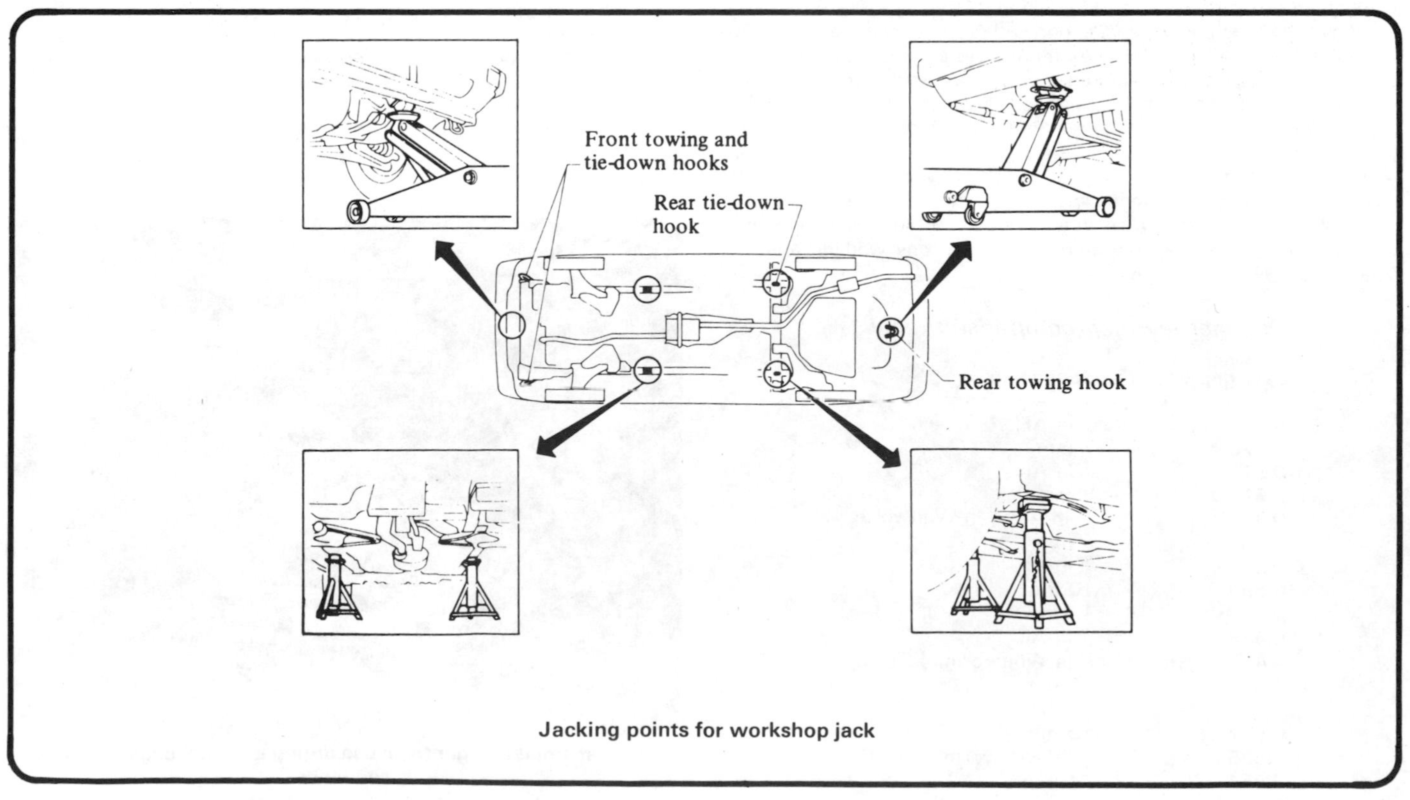

Jacking points for workshop jack

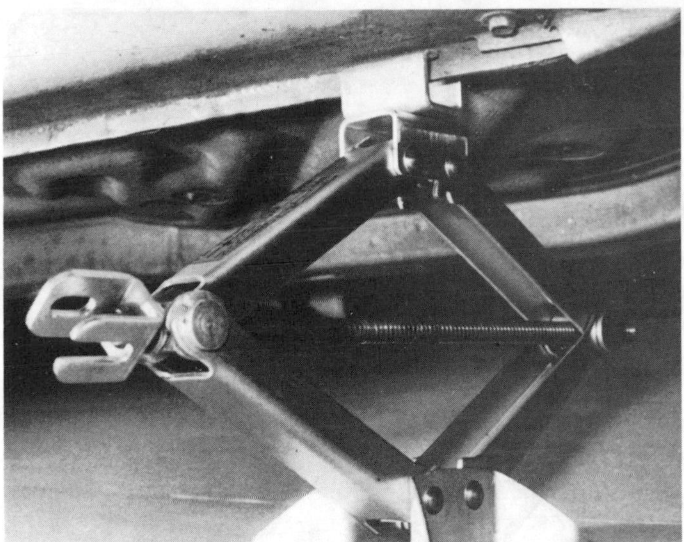

Vehicle tool kit jack

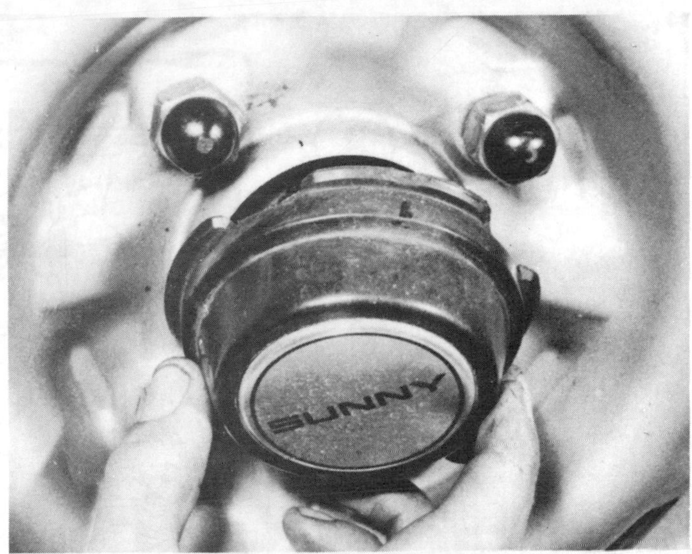

Removing roadwheel centre cap

Spare wheel and tool stowage (Saloon)

Emergency towing eye

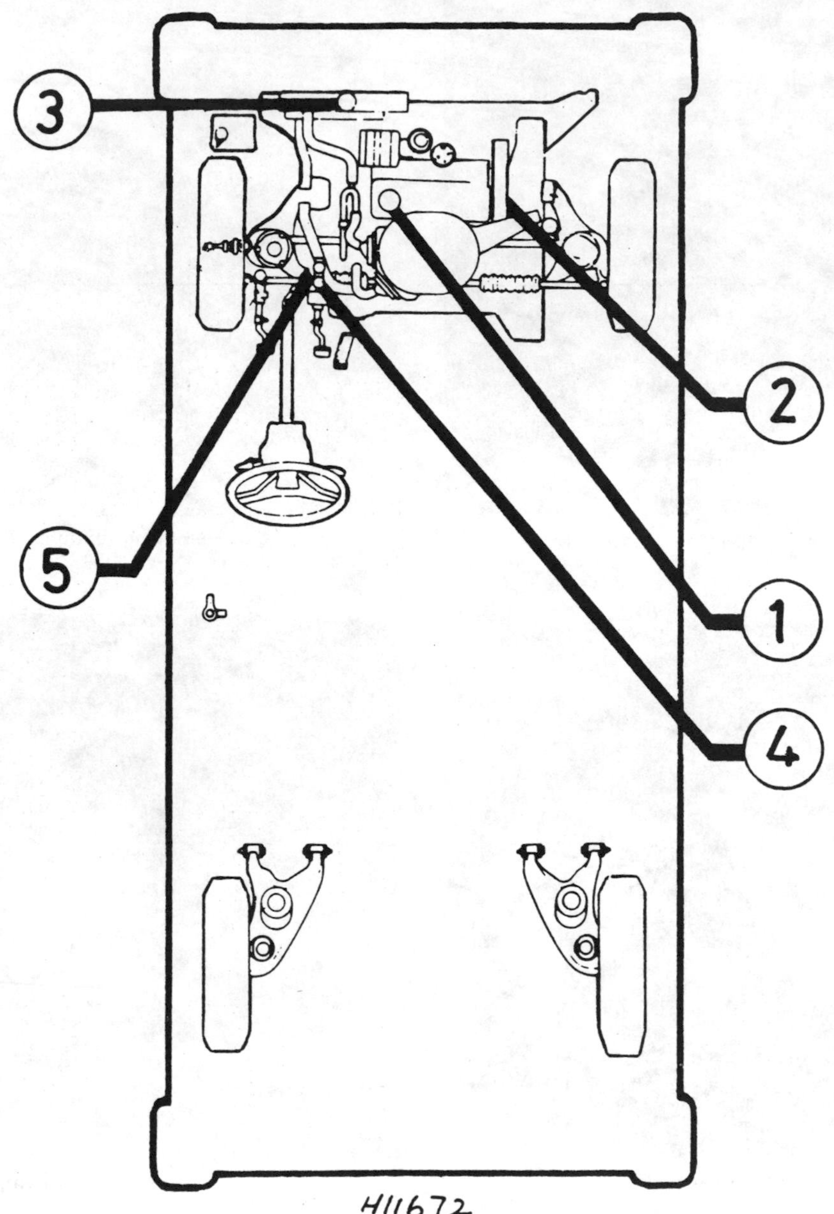

Recommended lubricants and fluids

Component or system	Lubricant type or specification	Castrol product
Engine 1	API SE or SF – SAE 10W/30, 10W/40 or 10W/50	**Castrol GTX**
Manual transmission 2	API GL-4	**Castrol Hypoy Light EP80W**
Automatic transmission 2	Dexron type fluid	**Castrol TQ Dexron R2**
Antifreeze 3	Ethylene glycol based	**Castrol Anti-freeze**
Brake fluid 4	DOT 3	**Castrol Girling Universal Clutch and Brake Fluid**
Power-assisted steering 5	Dexron type fluid	**Castrol TQ Dexron R2**

Note: *The above recommendations are general and are intended for guidance only. Lubrication requirements vary from territory to territory and depend upon vehicle usage. If in doubt, consult the operator's handbook supplied with the vehicle.*

Safety first!

Regardless of how enthusiastic you may be about getting on with the job at hand, take the time to ensure that your safety is not jeopardized. A moment's lack of attention can result in an accident, as can failure to observe certain simple safety precautions. The possibility of an accident will always exist, and the following points should not be considered a comprehensive list of all dangers. Rather, they are intended to make you aware of the risks and to encourage a safety conscious approach to all work you carry out on your vehicle.

Essential DOs and DON'Ts

DON'T rely on a jack when working under the vehicle. Always use approved jackstands to support the weight of the vehicle and place them under the recommended lift or support points.
DON'T attempt to loosen extremely tight fasteners (i.e. wheel lug nuts) while the vehicle is on a jack — it may fall.
DON'T start the engine without first making sure that the transmission is in Neutral (or Park where applicable) and the parking brake is set.
DON'T remove the radiator cap from a hot cooling system — let it cool or cover it with a cloth and release the pressure gradually.
DON'T attempt to drain the engine oil until you are sure it has cooled to the point that it will not burn you.
DON'T touch any part of the engine or exhaust system until it has cooled sufficiently to avoid burns.
DON'T siphon toxic liquids such as gasoline, antifreeze and brake fluid by mouth, or allow them to remain on your skin.
DON'T inhale brake lining dust — it is potentially hazardous (see *Asbestos* below)
DON'T allow spilled oil or grease to remain on the floor — wipe it up before someone slips on it.
DON'T use loose fitting wrenches or other tools which may slip and cause injury.
DON'T push on wrenches when loosening or tightening nuts or bolts. Always try to pull the wrench toward you. If the situation calls for pushing the wrench away, push with an open hand to avoid scraped knuckles if the wrench should slip.
DON'T attempt to lift a heavy component alone — get someone to help you.
DON'T rush or take unsafe shortcuts to finish a job.
DON'T allow children or animals in or around the vehicle while you are working on it.
DO wear eye protection when using power tools such as a drill, sander, bench grinder, etc. and when working under a vehicle.
DO keep loose clothing and long hair well out of the way of moving parts.
DO make sure that any hoist used has a safe working load rating adequate for the job.
DO get someone to check on you periodically when working alone on a vehicle.
DO carry out work in a logical sequence and make sure that everything is correctly assembled and tightened.
DO keep chemicals and fluids tightly capped and out of the reach of children and pets.
DO remember that your vehicle's safety affects that of yourself and others. If in doubt on any point, get professional advice.

Asbestos

Certain friction, insulating, sealing, and other products — such as brake linings, brake bands, clutch linings, torque converters, gaskets, etc. — contain asbestos. *Extreme care must be taken to avoid inhalation of dust from such products since it is hazardous to health.* If in doubt, assume that they *do* contain asbestos.

Fire

Remember at all times that gasoline is highly flammable. Never smoke or have any kind of open flame around when working on a vehicle. But the risk does not end there. A spark caused by an electrical short circuit, by two metal surfaces contacting each other, or even by static electricity built up in your body under certain conditions, can ignite gasoline vapors, which in a confined space are highly explosive. Do not, under any circumstances, use gasoline for cleaning parts. Use an approved safety solvent.

Always disconnect the battery ground (–) cable *at the battery* before working on any part of the fuel system or electrical system. Never risk spilling fuel on a hot engine or exhaust component.

It is strongly recommended that a fire extinguisher suitable for use on fuel and electrical fires be kept handy in the garage or workshop at all times. Never try to extinguish a fuel or electrical fire with water.

Fumes

Certain fumes are highly toxic and can quickly cause unconsciousness and even death if inhaled to any extent. Gasoline vapor falls into this category, as do the vapors from some cleaning solvents. Any draining or pouring of such volatile fluids should be done in a well ventilated area.

When using cleaning fluids and solvents, read the instructions on the container carefully. Never use materials from unmarked containers.

Never run the engine in an enclosed space, such as a garage. Exhaust fumes contain carbon monoxide, which is extremely poisonous. If you need to run the engine, always do so in the open air, or at least have the rear of the vehicle outside the work area.

If you are fortunate enough to have the use of an inspection pit, never drain or pour gasoline and never run the engine while the vehicle is over the pit. The fumes, being heavier than air, will concentrate in the pit with possibly lethal results.

The battery

Never create a spark or allow a bare light bulb near the battery. The battery normally gives off a certain amount of hydrogen gas, which is highly explosive.

Always disconnect the battery ground (–) cable *at the battery* before working on the fuel or electrical systems.

If possible, loosen the filler caps or cover when charging the battery from an external source. Do not charge at an excessive rate or the battery may burst.

Take care when adding water and when carrying a battery. The electrolyte, even when diluted, is very corrosive and should not be allowed to contact clothing or skin.

Always wear eye protection when cleaning the battery to prevent the caustic deposits from entering your eyes.

Household current

When using an electric power tool, inspection light, etc., which operates on household current, always make sure that the tool is correctly connected to its plug and that, where necessary, it is properly grounded. Do not use such items in damp conditions and, again, do not create a spark or apply excessive heat in the vicinity of fuel or fuel vapor.

Secondary ignition system voltage

A severe electric shock can result from touching certain parts of the ignition system (such as the spark plug wires) when the engine is running or being cranked, particularly if components are damp or the insulation is defective. In the case of an electronic ignition system, the secondary system voltage is much higher and could prove fatal.

Routine maintenance

The routine maintenance instructions listed are basically those recommended by the vehicle manufacturer. They are sometimes supplemented by additional maintenance tasks proven to be necessary.

The maintenance intervals recommended are those specified by the manufacturer. They are necessarily something of a compromise, since no two vehicles operate under identical conditions. The DIY mechanic, who does not have labour costs to consider, may wish to shorten the service intervals. Experience will show whether this is necessary.

Where the vehicle is used under severe operating conditions (extremes of heat or cold, dusty conditions, or mainly stop-start driving), more frequent oil changes may be desirable. If in doubt consult your dealer.

Weekly or before a long journey

Check engine oil level
Check operation of all lights, direction indicators, horn, wipers and washers
Check engine coolant level
Check colour of battery test indicator
Check washer fluid level
Check type pressures (cold) including the spare
Check brake fluid level
Check automatic transmission fluid level

After the first 1000 km (600 miles)

Check torque of cylinder head bolts (cold)
Adjust valve clearances
Check idle speed and mixture settings

Every 10 000 km (6000 miles) or six months, whichever occurs first

Check tyres for wear and damage
Check condition of steering rack bellows
Check condition of driveshaft bellows
Check level of power-assisted steering fluid
Check condition of exhaust system
Change engine oil and renew filter
Check idle speed and mixture
Check condition of contact breaker points and renew if necessary
Check dwell angle and ignition timing (mechanical breaker only)
Clean and re-gap spark plugs
Check transmission oil level
Check front disc pads for wear
Check brake hydraulic system for leaks
Lubricate controls, hinges and locks
Check brake and clutch pedals for height setting, stroke and free movement

Every 20 000 km (12 000 miles) or annually, whichever occurs first

Check and adjust valve clearances
Check drivebelts for condition and tension
Check coolant hoses for condition
Renew spark plugs (except MPG models)
Clean PCV system hoses and valve
Check for wear in steering and suspension
Check rear brake shoe linings for wear
Check front wheel alignment
Check condition of seat belts

Every 30 000 km (18 000 miles) or eighteen months, whichever occurs first

Emission control system
Check air induction valve filter (except MPG and Californian models)
Check exhaust gas sensor (MPG and Californian models)
Check fuel filler cap valve for operation

Every 40 000 km (24 000 miles) or two years, whichever occurs first

Renew fuel filter
Renew air cleaner filter element
Check condition of ignition leads
Check condition of brake servo hoses and operation of vacuum hose one-way valve
Check hub bearings for adequate lubrication
Renew charcoal canister filter (evaporative emission control system)
Check condition of evaporative emission control system hoses
Check operation of spark timing control system wiring and hoses (N American models)
Renew engine coolant
Renew brake hydraulic fluid by bleeding

Every 50 000 km (30 000 miles) or thirty months, whichever occurs first

Renew manual transmission oil
Renew automatic transmission fluid
Renew spark plugs (MPG models)

Every four years

Grease steering rack and rack end balljoints
Renew brake servo air filter

Engine compartment (air cleaner removed)

1 *Wiper arm*
2 *Air intake grille*
3 *Strut top mounting*
4 *Brake fluid reservoir (master cylinder)*
5 *Servo brake hose non-return valve*
6 *Fuel filter*
7 *Wiper linkage*
8 *Windscreen wiper motor*
9 *Heater hoses*
10 *Carburettor*
11 *Alternator*
12 *Engine oil filler cap*
13 *Engine mounting*
14 *Air cleaner hot air collector*
15 *Rocker cover*
16 *Distributor*
17 *Radiator cap*
18 *Battery*
19 *Washer fluid reservoir*
20 *Ignition coil*
21 *Ignition system ballast resistor*
22 *Intake manifold*
23 *Clutch release lever*

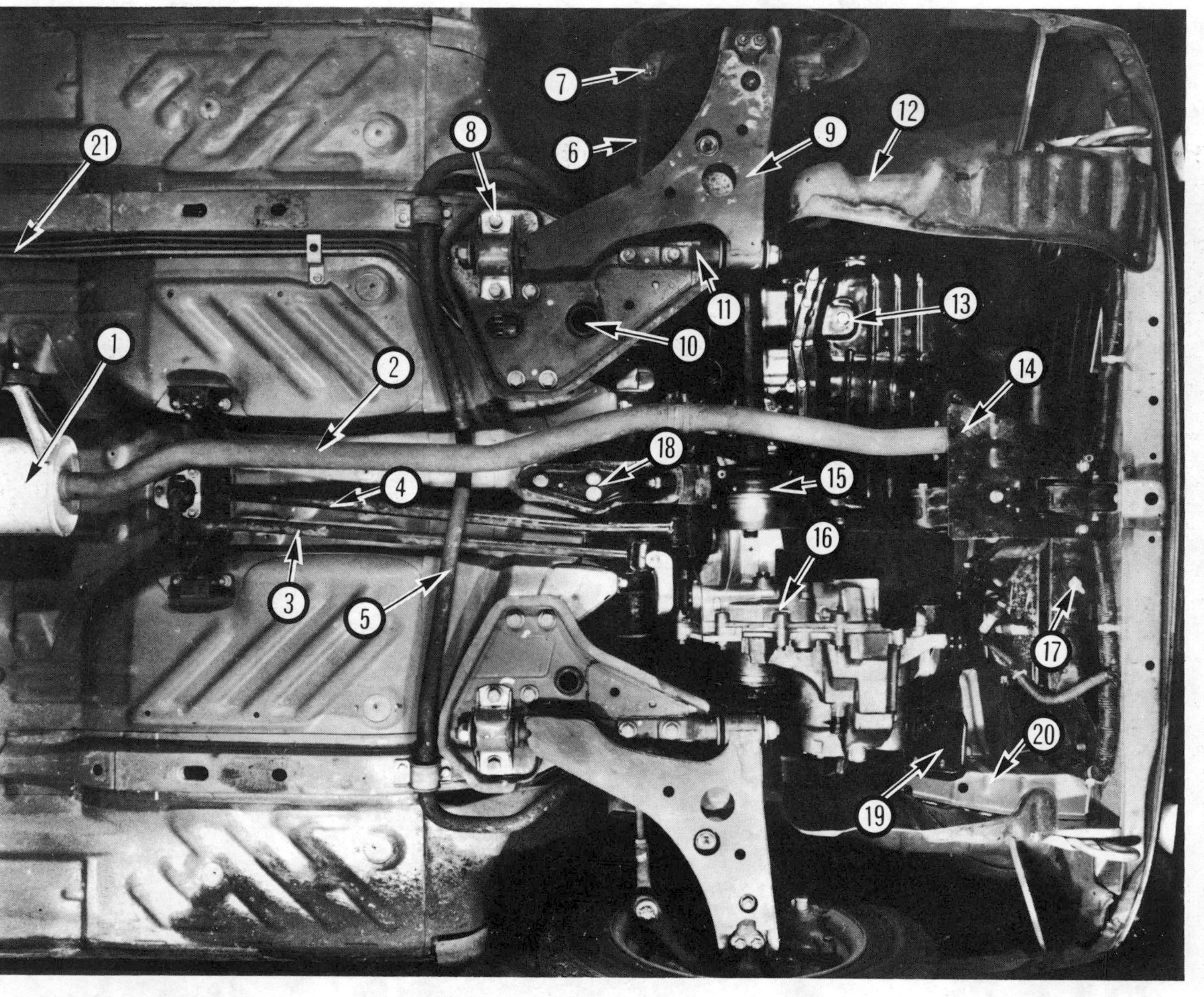

Front end viewed from underneath

1 *Exhaust expansion box*
2 *Exhaust front pipe*
3 *Gearchange rod*
4 *Gearchange stabiliser rod*
5 *Anti-roll bar*
6 *Tie-rod*
7 *Tie-rod end balljoint*
8 *Suspension arm clamp*
9 *Suspension arm*
10 *Support plate*
11 *Suspension arm pivot*
12 *Right-hand engine shield*
13 *Engine sump pan plug*
14 *Engine front mounting plate*
15 *Driveshaft inboard joint*
16 *Transmission*
!7 *Radiator drain plug*
18 *Engine rear mounting*
19 *Engine left-hand mounting*
20 *Left-hand engine shield*
21 *Brake and fuel lines*

Rear end viewed from underneath

1 *Handbrake cable equaliser*
2 *Trailing arm*
3 *Exhaust*
4 *Fuel tank*
5 *Fuel filler pipe*
6 *Fuel vent pipe*
7 *Fuel drain plug*
8 *Fuel feed pipe*

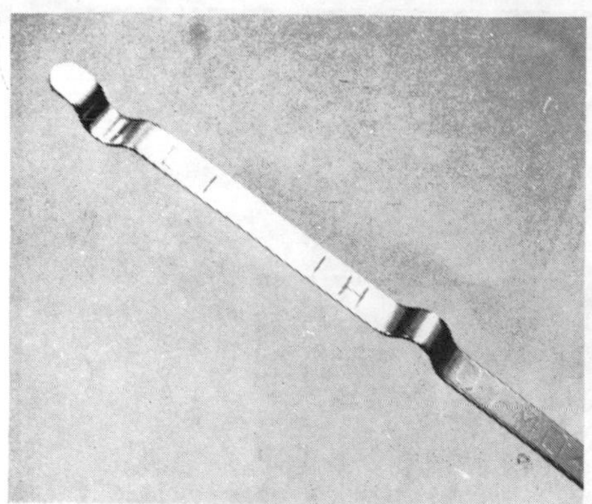
Engine oil dipstick markings

Topping-up with engine oil

Topping-up cooling system (without expansion tank)

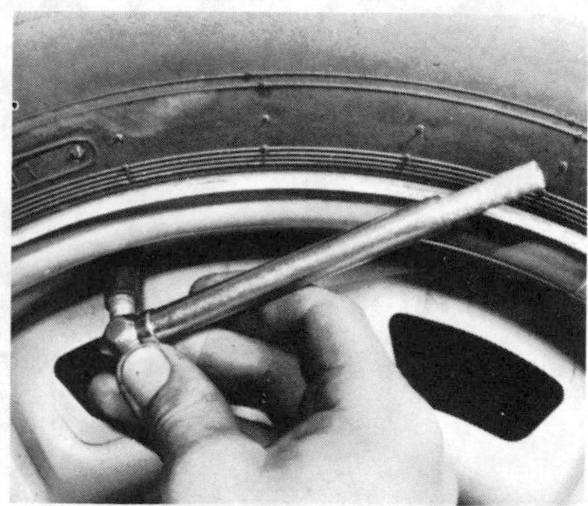
Checking tyre pressure

Checking tyre tread depth

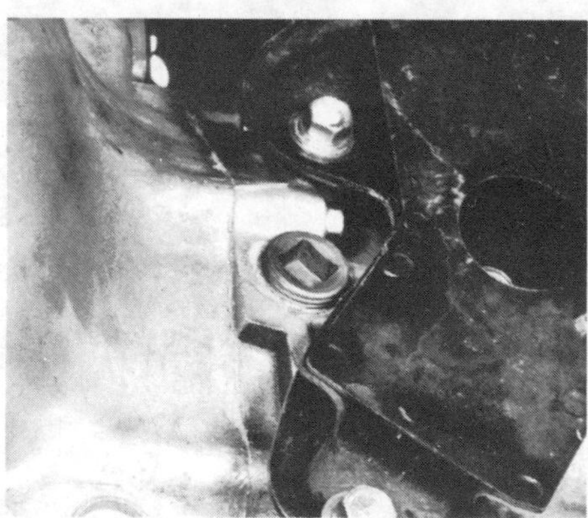
Manual transmission filler/level plug

Topping-up manual transmission

Fault diagnosis

Introduction

The vehicle owner who does his or her own maintenance according to the recommended schedules should not have to use this section of the manual very often. Modern component reliability is such that, provided those items subject to wear or deterioration are inspected or renewed at the specified intervals, sudden failure is comparatively rare. Faults do not usually just happen as a result of sudden failure, but develop over a period of time. Major mechanical failures in particular are usually preceded by characteristic symptoms over hundreds or even thousands of miles. Those components which do occasionally fail without warning are often small and easily carried in the vehicle.

With any fault finding, the first step is to decide where to begin investigations. Sometimes this is obvious, but on other occasions a little detective work will be necessary. The owner who makes half a dozen haphazard adjustments or replacements may be successful in curing a fault (or its symptoms), but he will be none the wiser if the fault recurs and he may well have spent more time and money than was necessary. A calm and logical approach will be found to be more satisfactory in the long run. Always take into account any warning signs or abnormalities that may have been noticed in the period preceding the fault – power loss, high or low gauge readings, unusual noises or smells, etc – and remember that failure of components such as fuses or spark plugs may only be pointers to some underlying fault.

The pages which follow here are intended to help in cases of failure to start or breakdown on the road. There is also a Fault Diagnosis Section at the end of each Chapter which should be consulted if the preliminary checks prove unfruitful. Whatever the fault, certain basic principles apply. These are as follows:

Verify the fault. This is simply a matter of being sure that you know what the symptoms are before starting work. This is particularly important if you are investigating a fault for someone else who may not have described it very accurately.

Don't overlook the obvious. For example, if the vehicle won't start, is there petrol in the tank? (Don't take anyone else's word on this particular point, and don't trust the fuel gauge either!) If an electrical fault is indicated, look for loose or broken wires before digging out the test gear.

Cure the disease, not the symptom. Substituting a flat battery with a fully charged one will get you off the hard shoulder, but if the underlying cause is not attended to, the new battery will go the same way. Similarly, changing oil-fouled spark plugs for a new set will get you moving again, but remember that the reason for the fouling (if it wasn't simply an incorrect grade of plug) will have to be established and corrected.

Don't take anything for granted. Particularly, don't forget that a 'new' component may itself be defective (especially if it's been rattling round in the boot for months), and don't leave components out of a fault diagnosis sequence just because they are new or recently fitted. When you do finally diagnose a difficult fault, you'll probably realise that all the evidence was there from the start.

Electrical faults

Electrical faults can be more puzzling than straightforward mechanical failures, but they are no less susceptible to logical analysis if the basic principles of operation are understood. Vehicle electrical wiring exists in extremely unfavourable conditions – heat, vibration and chemical attack – and the first things to look for are loose or corroded connections and broken or chafed wires, especially where the wires pass through holes in the bodywork or are subject to vibration.

All metal-bodied vehicles in current production have one pole of the battery 'earthed', ie connected to the vehicle bodywork, and in nearly all modern vehicles it is the negative (–) terminal. The various electrical components – motors, bulb holders etc – are also connected to earth, either by means of a lead or directly by their mountings. Electric current flows through the component and then back to the battery via the bodywork. If the component mounting is loose or corroded, or if a good path back to the battery is not available, the circuit will be incomplete and malfunction will result. The engine and/or gearbox are also earthed by means of flexible metal straps to the body or subframe; if these straps are loose or missing, starter motor, generator and ignition trouble may result.

Assuming the earth return to be satisfactory, electrical faults will be due either to component malfunction or to defects in the current supply. Individual components are dealt with in Chapter 10. If supply wires are broken or cracked internally this results in an open-circuit, and the easiest way to check for this is to bypass the suspect wire temporarily with a length of wire having a crocodile clip or suitable connector at each end. Alternatively, a 12V test lamp can be used to verify the presence of supply voltage at various points along the wire and the break can be thus isolated.

If a bare portion of a live wire touches the bodywork or other earthed metal part, the electricity will take the low-resistance path thus formed back to the battery: this is known as a short-circuit. Hopefully a short-circuit will blow a fuse, but otherwise it may cause burning of the insulation (and possibly further short-circuits) or even a fire. This is why it is inadvisable to bypass persistently blowing fuses with silver foil or wire.

Spares and tool kit

Most vehicles are supplied only with sufficient tools for wheel changing; the *Maintenance and minor repair* tool kit detailed in *Tools and working facilities,* with the addition of a hammer, is probably sufficient for those repairs that most motorists would consider attempting at the roadside. In addition a few items which can be fitted without too much trouble in the event of a breakdown should be carried. Experience and available space will modify the list below, but the following may save having to call on professional assistance:

Spark plugs, clean and correctly gapped
HT lead and plug cap – long enough to reach the plug furthest from the distributor
Distributor rotor, condenser and contact breaker points
Drivebelt(s) – emergency type may suffice
Spare fuses
Set of principal light bulbs
Tin of radiator sealer and hose bandage
Exhaust bandage
Roll of insulating tape
Length of soft iron wire
Length of electrical flex
Torch or inspection lamp (can double as test lamp)
Battery jump leads
Tow-rope
Ignition waterproofing aerosol
Litre of engine oil
Sealed can of hydraulic fluid
Worm drive clips
Tube of filler paste

If spare fuel is carried, a can designed for the purpose should be used to minimise risks of leakage and collision damage. A first aid kit and a warning triangle, whilst not at present compulsory in the UK, are obviously sensible items to carry in addition to the above.

When touring abroad it may be advisable to carry additional spares which, even if you cannot fit them yourself, could save having to wait while parts are obtained. The items below may be worth considering:

Clutch and throttle cables
Cylinder head gasket
Alternator brushes
Tyre valve core

One of the motoring organisations will be able to advise on availability of fuel etc in foreign countries.

Engine will not start

Engine fails to turn when starter operated
Flat battery (recharge, use jump leads, or push start)
Battery terminals loose or corroded
Battery earth to body defective
Engine earth strap loose or broken
Starter motor (or solenoid) wiring loose or broken
Automatic transmission selector in wrong position, or inhibitor switch faulty
Ignition/starter switch faulty
Major mechanical failure (seizure)
Starter or solenoid internal fault (see Chapter 10)

Starter motor turns engine slowly
Partially discharged battery (recharge, use jump leads, or push start)
Battery terminals loose or corroded
Battery earth to body defective
Engine earth strap loose
Starter motor (or solenoid) wiring loose
Starter motor internal fault (see Chapter 10)

Starter motor spins without turning engine
Flat battery
Flywheel gear teeth damaged or worn
Starter motor mounting bolts loose

Engine turns normally but fails to start
Damp or dirty HT leads and distributor cap (crank engine and check for spark)
Dirty or incorrectly gapped distributor points (mechanical breaker distributor)
No fuel in tank (check for delivery at carburettor)
Excessive choke (hot engine) or insufficient choke (cold engine)
Fouled or incorrectly gapped spark plugs (remove, clean and regap)
Other ignition system fault (see Chapter 4)
Other fuel system fault (see Chapter 3)
Poor compression (see Chapter 1)
Major mechanical failure (eg camshaft drive)

Engine fires but will not run
Insufficient choke (cold engine)
Air leaks at carburettor or inlet manifold
Fuel starvation (see Chapter 3)
Ballast resistor defective, or other ignition fault (see Chapter 4)

Engine cuts out and will not restart

Engine cuts out suddenly – ignition fault
Loose or disconnected LT wires
Wet HT leads or distributor cap (after traversing water splash)
Coil or condenser failure (check for spark)
Other ignition fault (see Chapter 4)

Engine misfires before cutting out – fuel fault
Fuel tank empty
Fuel pump defective or filter blocked (check for delivery)
Fuel tank filler vent blocked (suction will be evident on releasing cap)
Carburettor needle valve sticking
Carburettor jets blocked (fuel contaminated)
Other fuel system fault (see Chapter 3)

Engine cuts out – other causes
Serious overheating
Major mechanical failure (eg camshaft drive)

Engine overheats

Ignition (no-charge) warning light illuminated
Slack or broken drivebelt – retension or renew (Chapter 2)

Ignition warning light not illuminated
Coolant loss due to internal or external leakage (see Chapter 2)
Thermostat defective
Low oil level
Brakes binding
Radiator clogged externally or internally
Electric cooling fan not operating correctly
Engine waterways clogged
Ignition timing incorrect or automatic advance malfunctioning
Mixture too weak

Note: *Do not add cold water to an overheated engine or damage may result*

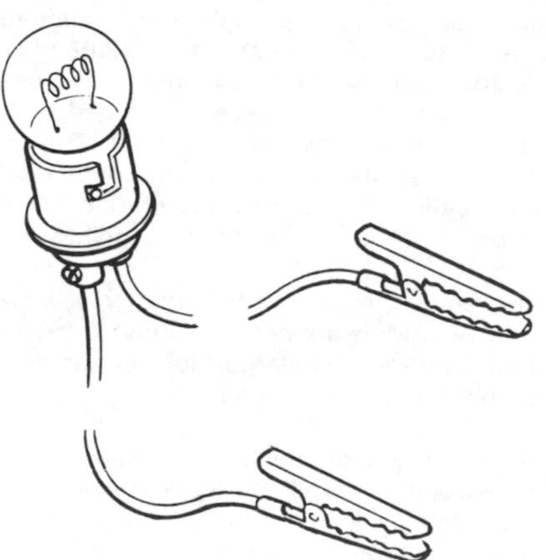

A simple test lamp is useful for tracing electrical faults

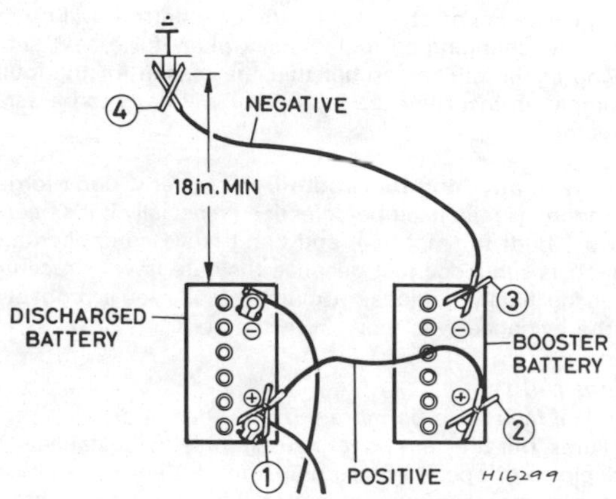

Jump start lead connections for negative earth vehicles – connect leads in the order shown

Low engine oil pressure

Gauge reads low or warning light illuminated with engine running

Oil level low or incorrect grade
Defective gauge or sender unit
Wire to sender unit earthed
Engine overheating
Oil filter clogged or bypass valve defective
Oil pressure relief valve defective
Oil pick-up strainer clogged
Oil pump worn or mountings loose
Worn main or big-end bearings

Note: *Low oil pressure in a high-mileage engine at tickover is not necessarily a cause for concern. Sudden pressure loss at speed is far more significant. In any event, check the gauge or warning light sender before condemning the engine.*

Engine noises

Pre-ignition (pinking) on acceleration

Incorrect grade of fuel
Ignition timing incorrect
Distributor faulty or worn
Worn or maladjusted carburettor
Excessive carbon build-up in engine

Whistling or wheezing noises

Leaking vacuum hose
Leaking carburettor or manifold gasket
Blowing head gasket

Tapping or rattling

Incorrect valve clearances
Worn valve gear
Worn timing belt
Broken piston ring (ticking noise)

Knocking or thumping

Unintentional mechanical contact
Worn drivebelt
Peripheral component fault (generator, coolant pump etc)
Worn big-end bearings (regular heavy knocking, perhaps less under load)
Worn main bearings (rumbling and knocking, perhaps worsening under load)
Piston slap (most noticeable when cold)

Chapter 1 Engine

Refer to Chapter 13 for Specifications and information on later models

Contents

Specifications

General

Type	Four-cylinder, in-line overhead cam, transversely mounted
Designation and capacity:	
E13	1269 cc (77.43 cu in)
E15	1488 cc (90.80 cu in)
E16	1597 cc (97.45 cu in)
Bore	76.0 mm (2.992 in)
Stroke:	
E13	70.0 mm (2.756 in)
E15	82.0 mm (3.228 in)
E16	88.0 mm (3.46 in)
Compression ratio:	
E13	9.0:1
E15 (excluding MPG models)	9.0:1 or 9.8:1 – depending upon operating territory
E15 (MPG models)	9.3:1
E16	9.4:1
Compression pressure:	
Normal	12.45 bar (181 lbf/in^2) at cranking speed
Minimum	9.81 bar (142 lb/in^2) at cranking speed
Power output:	
E13 (DIN)	60 bhp at 5600 rpm
E15 (DIN)	75 bhp at 5600 rpm
E15 (SAE)	67 bhp at 5200 rpm
E16 (SAE)	67 bhp at 5200 rpm
Maximum torque:	
E13 (DIN)	74 lbf ft at 3600 rpm
E15 (DIN)	89 lbf ft at 2800 rpm
E15 (SAE)	85 lbf ft at 3200 rpm
E16 (SAE)	85 lbf ft at 3000 rpm
Firing order	1–3–4–2 (No 1 cylinder at timing belt end)

Cylinder block

Material	Cast iron
Maximum bore out-of-round	0.02 mm (0.0008 in)
Maximum taper of bore	0.02 mm (0.0008 in)

Crankshaft

Number of main bearings	5
Main journal diameter	49.940 to 49.964 mm (1.9661 to 1.9671 in)
Crankpin diameter	39.954 to 39.974 mm (1.5730 to 1.5738 in)
Maximum journal and crankpin out-of-round	0.01 mm (0.0004 in)
Endfloat	0.05 to 0.18 mm (0.0020 to 0.0071 in)
Wear limit	0.30 mm (0.0118 in)
Main bearing running clearance:	
All models except MPG:	
Nos 1 and 5	0.031 to 0.076 mm (0.0012 to 0.0030 in)
Nos 2, 3 and 4	0.031 to 0.092 mm (0.0012 to 0.0036 in)
Wear limit	0.10 mm (0.0039 in)
MPG models:	
Nos 1, 3 and 5	0.047 to 0.076 mm (0.0019 to 0.0030 in)
Nos 2 and 4	0.031 to 0.092 mm (0.0012 to 0.0036 in)
Wear limit	0.10 mm (0.0039 in)
Big-end bearing clearance:	
E13	0.034 to 0.079 mm (0.0013 to 0.0031 in)
Wear limit	0.12 mm (0.0047 in)
E15 and E16	0.030 to 0.060 mm (0.0012 to 0.0024 in)
Wear limit	0.12 mm (0.0047 in)
Bearing undersizes:	
Main	0.25 mm (0.0098 in), 0.50 mm (0.0197 in) and 0.75 mm (0.0295 in)
Big-end	0.08 mm (0.0031 in), 0.25 mm (0.0098 in), 0.50 mm (0.0197 in) and 0.75 mm (0.295 mm)

Connecting rods

Gudgeon pin bore diameter (small-end)	18.962 mm to 18.978 mm (0.7465 to 0.7472 in)
Connecting rod side-play	0.1 to 0.37 mm (0.004 to 0.0146 in)
Wear limit	0.5 mm (0.020 in)

Gudgeon pin

Outside diameter	18.995 to 19.000 mm (0.7478 to 0.7480 in)
Gudgeon pin to piston clearance	0.008 to 0.012 mm (0.0003 to 0.0005 in)
Interference fit in connecting rod small-end	0.017 to 0.038 mm (0.0007 to 0.0015 in)

Pistons

Piston diameter	75.967 to 76.017 mm (2.9908 to 2.9928 in)
Oversizes	0.02 mm (0.0008 in) and 0.5 mm (0.020 in)
Gudgeon pin hole diameter	19.003 to 19.012 mm (0.7481 to 0.7485 in)
Piston clearance in cylinder block	0.023 to 0.043 mm (0.0009 to 0.0017 in)

Piston rings

Type	Two compression and one oil control
Clearance in groove:	
Top compression	0.040 to 0.073 mm (0.0016 to 0.0029 in)
2nd compression	0.030 to 0.063 mm (0.0012 to 0.0025 in)
Oil control	0.050 to 0.145 mm (0.0020 to 0.0057 in)
End gap:	
Top compression	0.20 to 0.35 mm (0.0079 to 0.0138 in)
2nd compression	0.15 to 0.30 mm (0.0059 to 0.0118 in)
Oil control	0.30 to 0.90 mm (0.0118 to 0.0354 in)

Jack shaft

Journal running clearance	0.020 to 0.098 mm (0.0008 to 0.0039 in)
Journal diameter:	
Front	31.987 to 32.000 mm (1.2593 to 1.2598 in)
Rear	25.587 to 28.600 mm (1.1255 to 1.1260 in)
Shaft bearing inside diameter:	
Front	32.020 to 32.085 mm (1.2606 to 1.2632 in)
Rear	28.620 to 26.685 mm (1.1268 to 1.1293 in)
Shaft endfloat	0.045 to 0.105 mm (0.0018 to 0.0041 in)
Fuel pump cam height	27.8 to 27.9 mm (1.094 to 1.098 in)

Camshaft

Journal diameter:	
Nos 1, 3 and 5	41.949 to 41.965 mm (1.6515 to 1.6522 in)
Nos 2 and 4	41.906 to 41.922 mm (1.6498 to 1.6505 in)
Bearing inside diameter	42.000 to 42.025 mm (1.6535 to 1.6545 in)
Camshaft running clearance:	
Nos 1, 3 and 5	0.035 to 0.076 mm (0.0014 to 0.0030 in)
Wear limit	0.15 mm (0.0059 in)
Nos 2 and 4	0.078 to 0.119 mm (0.0031 to 0.0047 in)
Wear limit	0.20 mm (0.0079 in)

Cam height:	
Intake	
E13	35.71 to 35.96 mm (1.4059 to 1.4157 in)
E15 and E16	35.884 to 36.134 mm (1.4128 to 1.4226 in)
Exhaust:	
E13	35.43 to 35.68 mm (1.3949 to 1.4047 in)
E15 and E16	35.64 to 35.89 mm (1.4031 to 1.4130 in)
Wear limit	0.2 mm (0.008 in)

Cylinder head

Material	Aluminium alloy
Surface out-of-true (limit)	0.1 mm (0.004 in)

Valves

Clearance (hot), intake and exhaust	0.28 mm (0.011 in)
Intake valve (E13 and E15):	
Head diameter	37.0 mm (1.46 in)
Length:	
Except N America	119.4 to 119.8 mm (4.7008 to 4.7165 in)
N America	118.5 to 118.9 mm (4.6653 to 4.6811 in)
Stem diameter	6.970 to 6.985 mm (0.2744 to 0.2750 in)
Valve seat angle:	
Except N America	29° 15′ to 29° 45′
N America	45° 15′ to 45° 45′
Exhaust valve (E13 and E15):	
Head diameter:	
Except N America	31.0 mm (1.22 in)
N America	30.0 mm (1.18 in)
Length:	
Except N America	119.65 to 120.05 mm (4.7106 to 4.7264 in)
N America	117.85 to 118.25 mm (4.6398 to 4.6555 in)
Stem diameter	6.945 to 6.960 mm (0.2734 to 0.2740 in)
Valve seat angle:	
Except N America	44° 15′ to 44° to 45′
N America	45° 15′ to 45° 45′
Intake valve (E16):	
Head diameter	37.0 mm (1.457 in)
Length	116.4 to 117.0 mm (4.58 to 4.61 in)
Stem diameter	6.970 to 6.985 mm (0.2744 to 0.2750 in)
Valve seat angle	45° 15′ to 45° 45′
Exhaust valve (E16):	
Head diameter	30.0 mm (1.181 in)
Length	115.75 to 116.35 mm (4.56 to 4.58 in)
Stem diameter	6.945 to 6.960 mm (0.2734 to 0.2740 in)
Valve seat angle	45° 15′ to 45° 45′
All models:	
Valve spring free length	46.70 mm (1.8386 in)

Valve guides

Outside diameter:	
Standard	12.033 to 12.044 mm (0.4737 to 0.4742 in)
Oversize	12.256 to 12.274 mm (0.4825 to 0.4832 in)
Inside diameter (reamed)	7.005 to 7.020 mm (0.2758 to 0.2764 in)
Guide hole in cylinder head:	
Diameter for standard guide	11.970 to 11.988 mm (0.4713 to 0.4720 in)
Diameter for oversize guide	12.200 to 12.211 mm (0.4803 to 0.4807 in)
Interference fit in cylinder head	0.045 to 0.074 mm (0.0018 to 0.0029 in)
Valve stem to guide clearance:	
Intake	0.015 to 0.045 mm (0.0006 to 0.0018 in)
Exhaust	0.045 to 0.075 mm (0.0018 to 0.0030 in)
Wear limit	0.1 mm (0.004 in)

Lubrication

Engine oil capacity (including oil change)	3.9 litres (6.9 Imp pts, 4.12 US qts)
Oil pressure (hot)	2.0 bar (28 lbf/in^2) at 1050 rpm

Torque wrench settings

	Nm	lbf ft
Alternator bracket bolt	12	9
Alternator link bolt	20	15
Engine mounting bracket to cylinder block	35	26
Manifold nuts	20	15
Oil pump to crankcase	12	9
Power-assisted steering pump bracket	30	22
Power-assisted steering pump fixing bolt	40	30
Spark plug	25	18

Coolant pump bolt	5	4
Coolant pump pulley bolt	5	4
Air conditioner compressor bracket bolt	30	22
Fuel pump fixing bolts	12	9
Crankshaft pulley bolt	140	104
Thermostat housing bolt	5	4
Camshaft pulley bolt	8	6
Connecting rod cap nut	35	26
Cylinder head bolts (cold):		
Stage 1	40	30
Stage 2	70	52
Cylinder head front cover	5	4
Flywheel bolts (manual transmission)	85	63
Driveplate bolts (automatic transmission)	100	74
Timing belt cover bolts	5	4
Jack shaft pulley bolt	8	6
Main bearing cap bolt	55	40
Sump pan bolts and nuts	5	4
Oil pick-up fixing bolts	8	6
Rocker shaft bolts	20	15
Belt tensioner locknut	20	15
Rocker cover nut	8	6
Rocker arm adjuster screw locknut	20	15
Bellhousing to engine	20	15
Oil pump pressure regulating valve cap	45	33
Oil pump cover bolts	5	4
North American models:		
EGR valve to pipe	50	37
Air injection pipe union	50	37
Front suspension top mounting nut	23	17
Suspension lower balljoint to track control arm	61	45
Caliper mounting bolts	61	45
Roadwheel nuts	95	70

1 General description

The engine is of four cylinder, in-line overhead camshaft type.

The cylinder block is of cast iron construction while the cylinder head, which is of cross-flow design, is made of light alloy.

A five bearing crankshaft is used.

The camshaft runs in bearings which are machined directly into the cylinder head.

Valve clearances are adjusted in the conventional way by means of a screw and locknut on the rocker arms.

2 Engine oil and filter

1 At weekly intervals, check the engine oil level. Do this by withdrawing the dipstick, wiping it clean, reinserting it and withdrawing it for the second time.

2 The oil level should be between the L and H marks. Top up if necessary.

3 At the intervals specified in Routine Maintenance, the oil should be drained when hot by removing the oil filler cap and the sump drain plug (photo). Use a large bowl to catch the oil.

4 Using a suitable filter removal tool, unscrew the cartridge type oil filter which is located on the cylinder block just to the rear of the alternator. Be prepared for some spillage of oil.

5 Wipe the filter mating face on the cylinder block clean and smear the rubber sealing ring of the new filter with a little grease. Screw on the filter hand-tight only (photo).

6 Refit the sump drain plug.

7 Refill with the correct quantity and type of engine oil. Refit the oil filler cap.

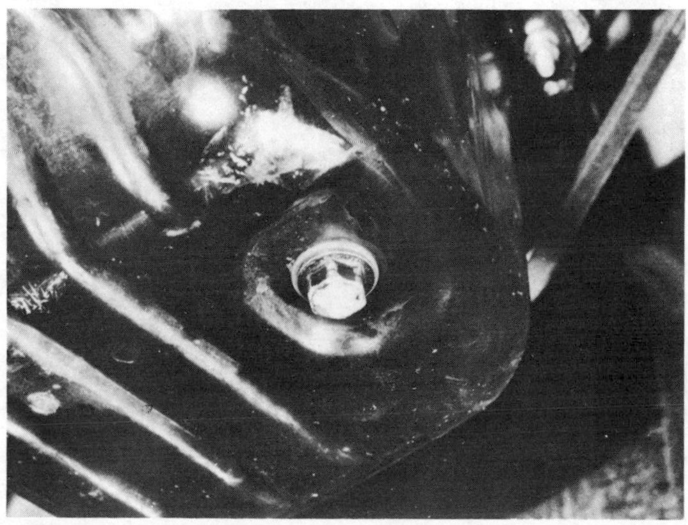

2.3 Engine sump pan drain plug

2.5 Oil filter

3 Major operations possible without removing engine from the vehicle

The following operations may be carried out with the engine in position in the vehicle.

Removal and refitting of the cylinder head
Adjustment of the valve clearances
Removal and refitting of the timing belt
Removal and refitting of the oil pump
Removal and refitting of the sump
Renewal of piston rings and big-end bearings

4 Cylinder head – removal and refitting

1 Disconnect the battery.
2 Disconnect the HT leads from the spark plugs and the ignition coil. Disconnect all negative LT leads from the coil.
3 Unbolt and remove the distributor (Chapter 4).
4 Remove the air cleaner (Chapter 3).
5 Drain the cooling system, retaining the coolant if suitable for further use.
6 Remove the rocker cover.
7 Unbolt and remove the hot air collector from the exhaust manifold.
8 Disconnect the exhaust downpipe from the exhaust manifold.
9 Refer to Chapter 2 and remove the drivebelts from the alternator, power steering pump and air conditioning compressor (where fitted). Remove the alternator adjuster link.
10 Disconnect the emission control hoses, pipes and leads as necessary to clear the cylinder head (refer to Chapter 3).
11 Disconnect the throttle and choke controls from the carburettor.
12 Disconnect the fuel hoses from the carburettor.
13 On models with an automatic choke, disconnect the electrical lead from the terminal on the automatic choke housing.
14 Unbolt and remove the intake manifold, complete with carburettor.
15 The belt covers must now be removed. Access to the screws can only be obtained after first removing the pulley from the coolant pump and the pulley from the crankshaft. To remove the latter, prise out the plug from the plastic shield which is directly in line with the crankshaft pulley bolt. Pass a socket with extension driver through the hole to unscrew the bolt (photo). Removal of the front right-hand roadwheel will make the job easier. In order to prevent the crankshaft rotating as the pulley bolt is unscrewed, engage second gear and have an assistant depress the foot brake.
16 Release the nut on the timing belt tensioner pulley.
17 Note the rotational direction of the belt. Original belts are marked with an arrow. Unmarked belts should be marked. Remove the belt.
18 Loosen the cylinder head bolts progressively in reverse order to that shown in the tightening sequence diagram (Fig. 1.1).
19 If the cylinder head is to be dismantled or decarbonised, refer to Section 15.
20 Before refitting the cylinder head make quite sure that the mating surfaces of the cylinder head and block are perfectly clean and free from carbon or old pieces of gasket.
21 Mop out the oil from the cylinder head bolt holes in the block, clean the bolt threads and oil lightly.
22 Release the rocker arm adjuster screw locknuts and unscrew the screws a few turns.
23 Turn the crankshaft, by means of the pulley bolt until the timing mark on the crankshaft sprocket is at its lowest point.
24 Turn the camshaft sprocket until the timing marks are approximately in alignment according to engine type. This will eliminate the possibility of the valves digging into the piston crowns when the cylinder head is lowered onto the block.
25 Place a new gasket on top of the cylinder block (photo).
26 Lower the cylinder head carefully onto the block (photo).
27 Screw the cylinder head bolts down finger tight. The shorter bolts go on the exhaust side. The longest bolt of all also goes on the exhaust side, at the timing belt end.
28 Tighten the cylinder head bolts in the sequence shown in Fig. 1.1 in two stages to the specified torque setting (photo).
29 Using a new gasket, bolt on the exhaust manifold and reconnect the downpipe (photos).

4.15 Using socket and extension to undo crankshaft pulley bolt

4.25 Cylinder head gasket

4.26 Lowering cylinder head into position

4.28 Tightening cylinder head bolts

4.29A Exhaust manifold gasket

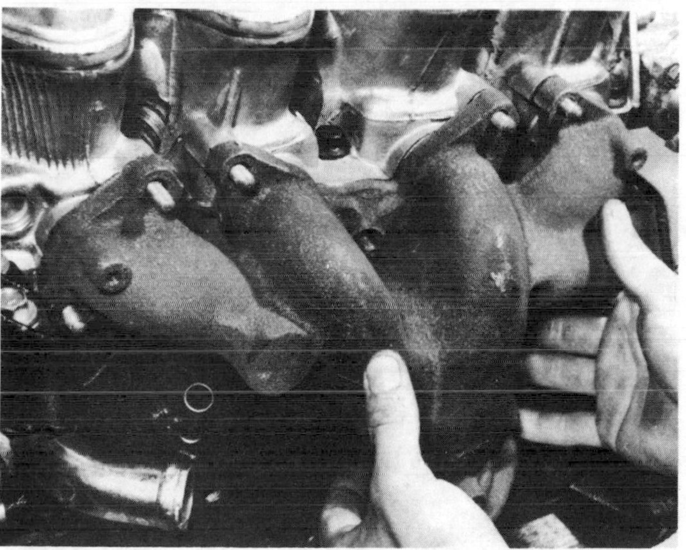

4.29B Exhaust manifold

4.30 Intake manifold with carburettor

4.31A Camshaft sprocket timing marks

4.31B Crankshaft sprocket timing marks

4.31C Adjusting belt tensioner (timing belt removed for clarity)

4.31D Timing belt fitted and tensioned

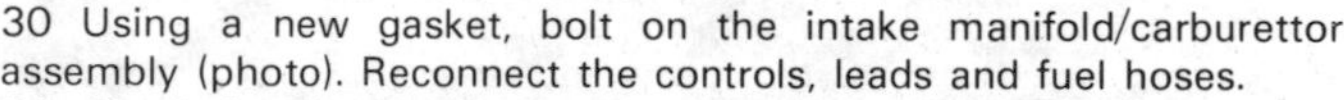

30 Using a new gasket, bolt on the intake manifold/carburettor assembly (photo). Reconnect the controls, leads and fuel hoses.
31 Check that the camshaft and crankshaft timing marks are correctly aligned and then engage the timing belt with them (photos).
32 With the belt tensioner pulley nut released, tension the belt. The belt is correctly tensioned when it can just be twisted through 90° holding it between finger and thumb at the centre of its longest run. Tighten the tensioner nut.
33 Refit the timing belt covers.
34 Refit any emission control components which were removed or disconnected.
35 Refit the alternator adjuster link.
36 Refit the drivebelts, tensioning them as described in Chapter 2.
37 Refit the hot air collector to the exhaust manifold (photo). This is held by two manifold bolts.
38 Refit the distributor (Chapter 4).
39 Reconnect the HT and LT ignition leads.
40 Adjust the valve clearances, as described in Section 5.
41 Using a new gasket, refit the rocker cover.
42 Refit the air cleaner.
43 Reconnect the battery.
44 Refill the cooling system (Chapter 2).
45 Check and top up the engine oil.
46 Check and adjust the valve clearances after the engine has reached normal operating temperature.
47 It is recommended that after the first 960 km (600 miles) the cylinder head bolt torque setting is checked. Do this with the engine cold. Unscrew the first bolt in the specified sequence through one quarter of a turn and then retighten to torque. Repeat one at a time on each of the remaining bolts.
48 Check the valve clearances (hot) on completion.

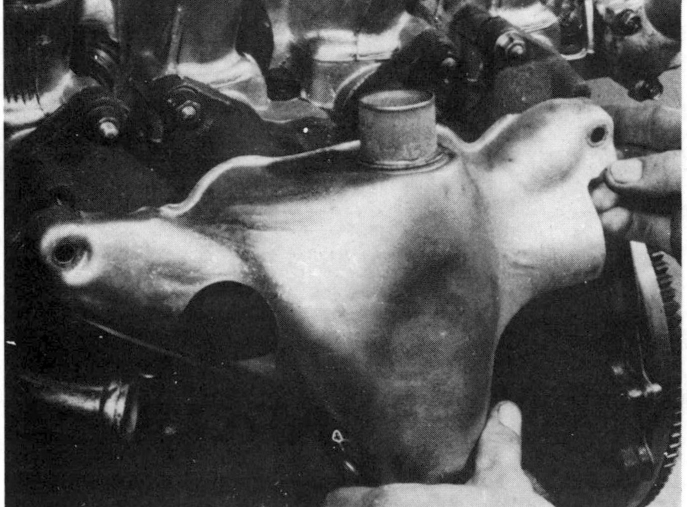

4.37 Exhaust manifold hot air collector

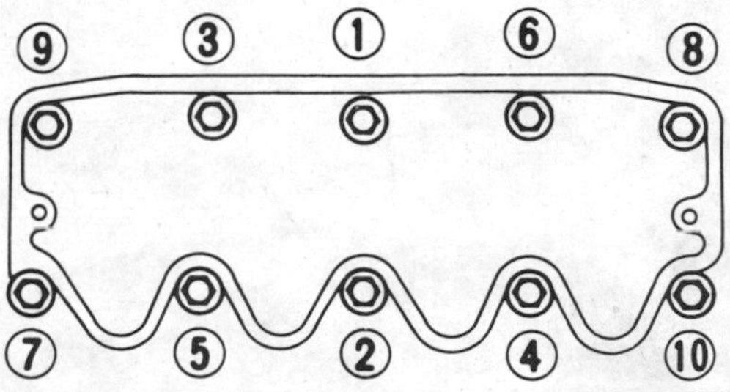

Fig. 1.1 Cylinder head bolt tightening sequence (Sec 4)

5 Valve clearance – adjustment

1 When this adjustment is being carried out at routine servicing, the engine should be at normal operating temperature.
2 Remove the air cleaner and the rocker cover, also the spark plugs.
3 Using a socket wrench on the crankshaft pulley bolt, turn the crankshaft until No 1 piston (at timing belt end of engine) is at TDC. This can be ascertained if a finger is placed over No 1 cylinder spark plug hole and the compression felt as it is being generated as the piston rises. The notch on the crankshaft pulley should be opposite the O mark on the timing scale.
4 Using a feeler blade of specified thickness check that it is a stiff sliding fit between the end of the valve stem and the ball end of the rocker arm adjuster screw on valves 1, 2, 3 and 6 (Fig. 1.2).
5 Where the clearance is not as specified, release the rocker arm adjuster screw locknut and turn the screw. Once the correct clearance is established, tighten the locknut without allowing the adjuster screw to turn (photo).
6 Now set No 4 piston at TDC on its compression stroke and repeat the operations on valves 4, 5, 7 and 8.
7 Check that the rocker cover gasket is in good order, refit the rocker cover, air cleaner and spark plugs.
8 The valve clearances are the same for both intake and exhaust valves.

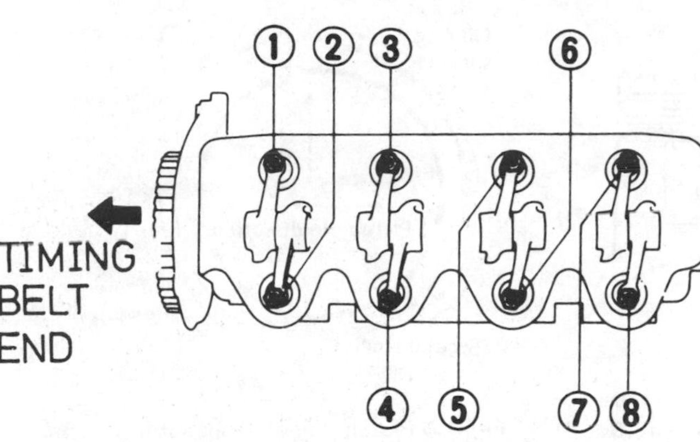

Fig. 1.2 Valve arrangement (Sec 5)

...efitting

...ning belt is renewed after 50 000 ...red.

...ng operations are as described in ...

...ng

...ed in Chapter 10, and move it to ...

... switch.

...ear, refer to Examination and ...

...se a new gasket and clean the ...

8 Sump pan – removal and refitting

1 Drain the engine oil.
2 Unbolt the reinforcement strut from the rear corner of the sump and transmission.
3 Disconnect the exhaust downpipe from the manifold and release the exhaust pipe front mounting. Remove the sump pan undershield.
4 Unscrew and remove the sump pan bolts and nuts. The nut nearest the transmission is very inaccessible and will require the use of a universally-jointed drive extension and socket to remove it.
5 Remove the sump pan by pulling the exhaust pipe downwards.
6 Remove and discard the old gaskets.
7 Before fitting the sump pan, stick new side gaskets and end sealing strips in position with gasket cement. Make sure that the ends of the sealing strips overlap the side gaskets. Cover the seam with a generous blob of cement.
8 Screw in the sump bolts and fit the nuts, tightening them evenly.
9 Reconnect the exhaust pipe.
10 Fill the engine with oil.

9 Piston rings and big-end bearing shells – renewal

1 The renewal of piston rings or substitution with special proprietary rings may be decided upon as a means of reducing heavy oil consumption without incurring the heavy cost of reboring and new oversize pistons.
2 Remove the cylinder head and the sump pan, as described in earlier Sections.
3 Note that the connecting rod big-end caps are numbered with matching numbers on adjacent machined surfaces on the connecting rod. Note to which side of the crankcase the numbers face, usually towards the jack shaft.
4 Unbolt and remove the oil pick-up pipe from within the crankcase.
5 Unscrew the big-end cap bolts and remove the caps. If the cap shell bearings are to be used again, tape them to their caps.
6 Using the wooden handle of a hammer, applied to the big-end of each connecting rod push the piston/rod assemblies out of the top of the cylinder block. If the cylinder bores are severely worn, and a wear ring can be felt at the top of the bores, the rings may have to be reduced by careful scraping before the piston rings will ride over it. Retain the bearing shells with their respective rods if they are to be used again.
7 To remove the piston rings, slide three old feeler blades behind the top ring and position them at equidistant points. The ring can now be slid upwards off the piston using a twisting motion. Repeat on the remaining rings.
8 Clean the piston ring grooves completely free from carbon and other deposits. A piece of old piston ring makes an ideal tool for the purpose.
9 Check that the rings supplied have the correct groove clearance (photo) and end gap (see Specifications). Check the end gap by pushing the ring a little way down the cylinder bore, set it squarely and use a feeler blade to check the gap.
10 Fit the rings to the piston by reversing the removal operations. The rings are marked on their top surfaces. The top compression ring has a chamfer on both edges.

9.9 Checking piston ring groove clearance

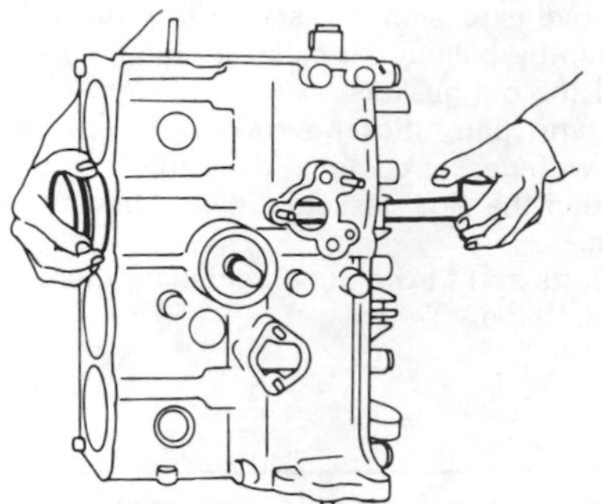

Fig. 1.3 Removing a piston/connecting rod (Sec 9)

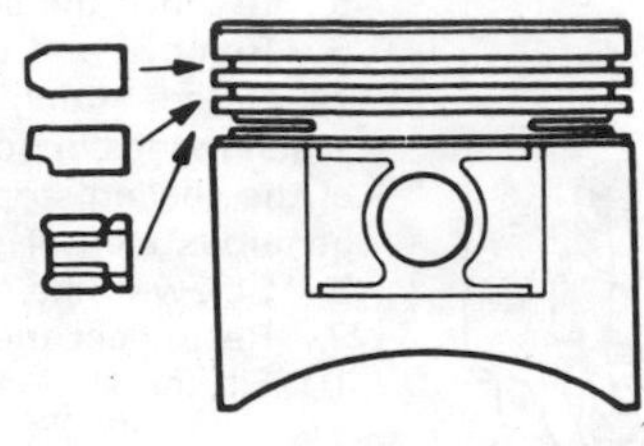

Fig. 1.4 Piston ring arrangement (Sec 9)

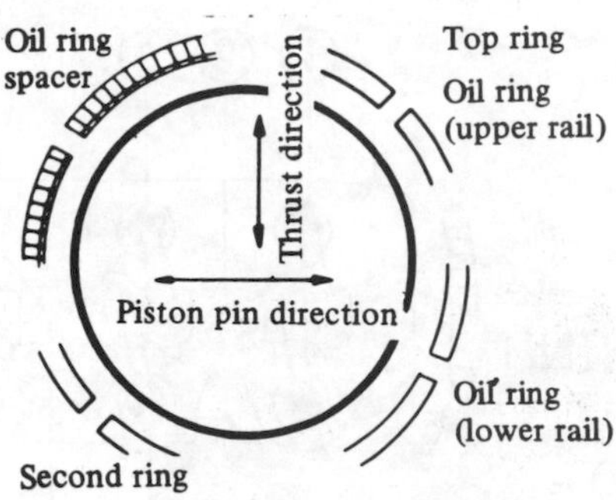

Fig. 1.5 Piston ring end gap setting diagram (Sec 9)

11 If new rings are fitted then, to ensure rapid bedding in, the cylinder bores must have their hard glaze removed. This can be done using a rotary abrasive flap wheel. Alternatively, use fine glasspaper, rubbing it up and down at approximately 45° to the bore.

12 Stagger the piston ring gaps at equidistant points of a circle, oil the rings liberally and fit a piston ring compressor. These are available at most accessory stores. Oil the cylinder bores.

13 Insert the first piston/rod assembly into its original bore so that the bottom edge of the compressor rests on the top face of the cylinder block and the mark on the piston crown is facing the timing belt end of the engine (photos).

14 Again applying the wooden handle of a hammer, this time to the piston crown, push the piston rod assembly into the cylinder bore. The ring compressor will be released. Repeat on the remaining pistons.

15 Draw the connecting rod of the first piston down to connect with the crankshaft crankpin. Make sure that the crankpins have been liberally oiled and the bearing shells are returned to their original positions (photo). Unless the shells are in excellent condition, without any signs of the copper underlay showing through the white bearing material, they should be renewed with ones of identical size. The size is stamped on the back of the shell. Standard shells are unmarked or stamped STD or 0-00. If not standard it will be stamped with the undersize, for example 0.25 mm.

16 Fit the big-end cap with its shell so that the matching numbers are adjacent (photo) and towards the jack shaft.

17 Insert and tighten the cap bolts to the specified torque (photo).

18 Repeat on the remaining three piston/rods assemblies.

19 Refit the cylinder head and the sump pan, as described in earlier Sections.

20 Refill the engine with oil and coolant.

10 Engine removal – method and precautions

The engine should be removed from the vehicle as a unit complete with transmission. The help of an assistant will definitely be required.

For vehicles with air conditioning

If components of the air conditioning system obstruct the overhaul of the engine and cannot be moved sufficiently within the limits of

9.13A Piston ring clamp

9.13B Piston crown front marking (arrowed)

9.15 Connecting rod shell bearing

9.16 Connecting rod and cap markings

9.17 Tightening big-end cap nut

their flexible hoses to avoid such obstruction the system should be discharged by your dealer or a competent refrigeration engineer.

As the system must be completely evacuated before recharging, the necessary vacuum equipment to do this is only likely to be held by your dealer.

The refrigerant fluid is Freon 12 and, although harmless under normal conditions, contact with eyes or skin must be avoided. If Freon comes into contact with a naked flame a poisonous gas is created which is injurious to health.

11 Engine/manual transmission – removal and separation

Refer to Chapter 6 where necessary

1 With the help of an assistant, unbolt and remove the bonnet (see Chapter 12).

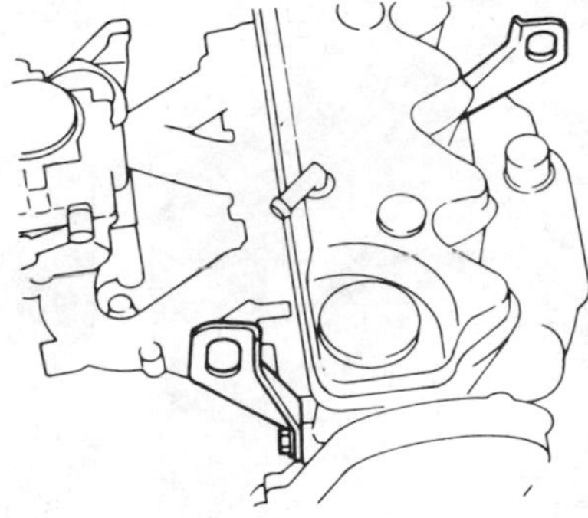

Fig. 1.6 Engine lifting eyes (Sec 11)

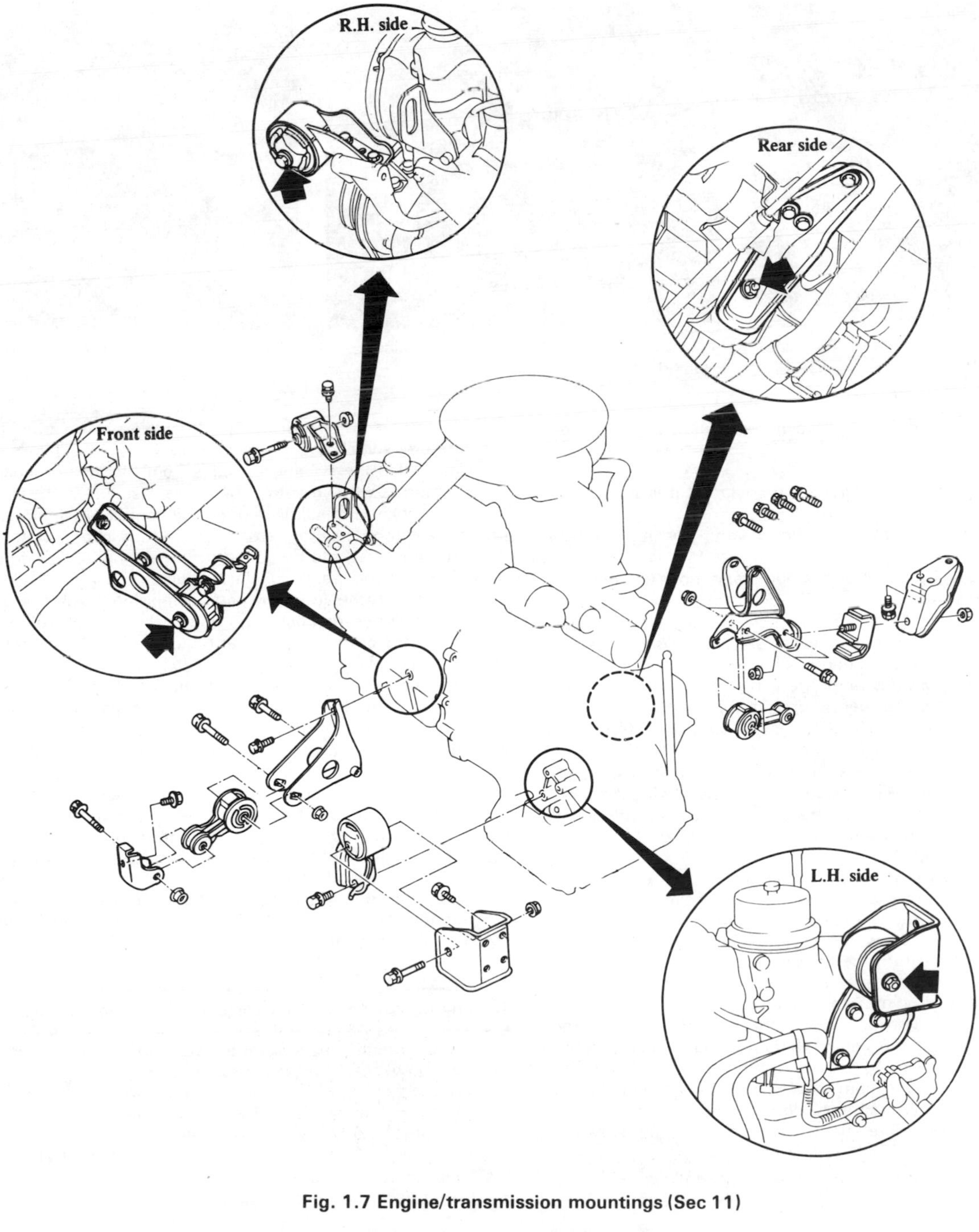

Fig. 1.7 Engine/transmission mountings (Sec 11)

11.8A Exhaust downpipe at manifold

11.8B Exhaust front mounting

11.17 Speedo cable connection at transmission

11.21 Pulling out wiring harness

11.23A Engine mounting (rear centre lower bracket)

11.23B Engine mounting (rear centre)

2 Disconnect the battery and remove it together with its support bracket.
3 Remove the air cleaner.
4 Drain the cooling system, retaining the coolant if it is suitable for further use.
5 Remove the radiator complete with electric cooling fan (see Chapter 2).
6 If power steering is fitted, unbolt the pump and move it to one side of the engine compartment.
7 If air conditioning is fitted, unbolt the compressor and belt tensioner pulley and move them aside. *Do not disconnect the refrigerant circuit pipelines* (see Chapter 2).
8 Disconnect the exhaust downpipe from the manifold (photo) and the mounting bracket near the fuel pump (photo).
9 Unbolt and disconnect the gearchange control rod and its stabiliser rod from the transmission.
10 Support the vehicle under its side-member and then disconnect the front suspension lower balljoints. Do this by unscrewing the three nuts which hold the balljoint to the suspension arm. It is recommended that new nuts are used at reassembly.
11 Remove the front roadwheels.
12 Drain the engine and transmissions oils.
13 Unbolt the disc calipers and tie them up out of the way.
14 Unscrew, but do not remove, the nuts at the front suspension strut top mountings. This is to allow movement of the struts when the driveshafts are withdrawn from the transmission.
15 To disconnect a driveshaft, insert a large screwdriver or suitable lever behind the inboard joint flange and prise to overcome the resistance of the joint circlip. Take care not to damage the transmission oil seal and do not pull on the outer end of the driveshaft or the joints may come apart. Insert a rod into the side gears in the transmission casing to prevent them moving into the differential case.
16 Disconnect the clutch operating cable from the release lever.
17 Disconnect the speedometer drive cable from the transmission (photo).
18 Disconnect the throttle and choke cables from the carburettor.
19 Disconnect the fuel hoses from the fuel pump and plug them.
20 Disconnect all electrical leads, including those from the coolant temperature switch, oil pressure switch, reverse lamp switch and alternator, also the HT and LT leads from the ignition coil.
21 On models with an automatic choke, disconnect the electrical lead from the choke terminal. Withdraw the complete wiring harness from under the intake manifold after releasing the clips (photo).
22 Lifting eyes should be bolted to the engine. Attach suitable lifting gear and take the weight of the engine.
23 Disconnect the four engine/transmission flexible mountings by unscrewing either the bush pivot bolt or the nut according to location. The bolt at the bottom of the rear mounting bracket must be removed as well (photos).
24 Lift the engine/transmission up and out of the engine compartment (photo). Take care not to damage adjacent components or the wiring surface.
25 With the unit removed, clean away external dirt using a water soluble solvent or paraffin and a stiff brush.
26 To separate the engine from the transmission unbolt and remove the starter motor and then withdraw the bolts which connect the clutch bellhousing to the engine. Note that some of these bolts retain the upper coolant tube, the engine sump pan protective shield, the sump pan-to-bellhousing reinforcement tube and the transmission mounting brackets. Mark their positions for ease of refitting (photos).
27 Support the weight of the transmission and then withdraw it in a straight line from the engine.

12 Engine/automatic transmission – removal and separation

1 The operations for removal are very similar to those described for vehicles with manual transmission in the preceding Section but observe the following differences. Refer also to Chapter 7.
2 Ignore any reference to the clutch cable.
3 Remove the front wing protective shield.
4 Disconnect the speed selector cable from the transmission, also the inhibitor switch leads.
5 Disconnect and plug the oil cooler hoses.

11.23C Engine mounting (front left-hand)

11.23D Engine mounting (front right-hand)

11.23E Engine mounting (front centre)

11.24 Removing engine/transmission from car

11.26A Removing starter motor

11.26B Coolant tube at bellhousing

11.26C Protective shield

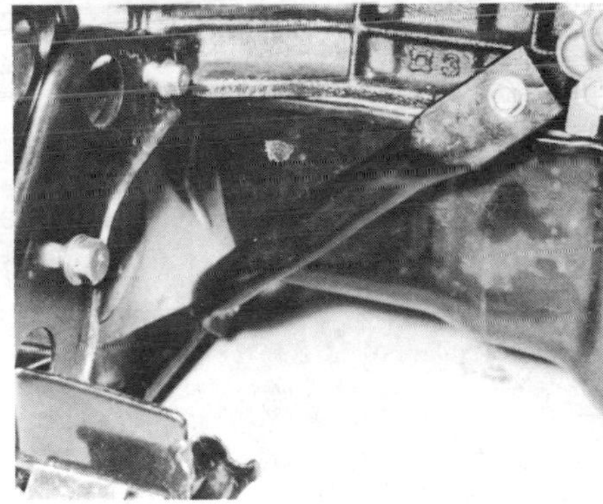
11.26D Reinforcement tube

11.26E Transmission mounting bracket

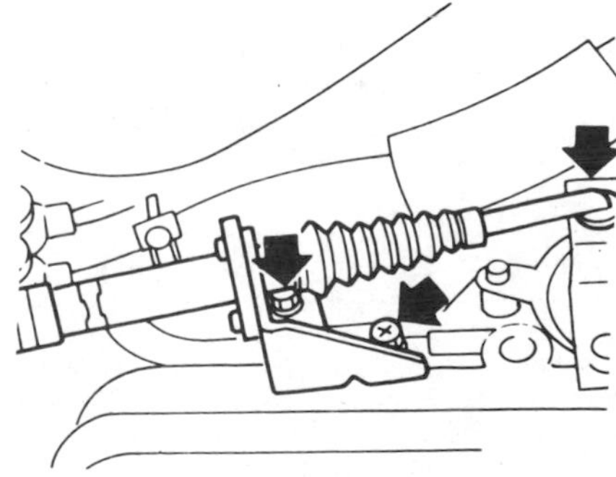
Fig. 1.8 Automatic speed selector control cable securing points (Sec 12)

6 To separate the engine from the automatic transmission first unbolt and remove the starter motor.

7 Mark the relationship of the torque converter to the driveplate using a dab of quick-drying paint.

8 Unscrew the torque converter-to-driveplate connecting bolts. The crankshaft will have to be turned to bring each bolt into view in the cut-out in the torque converter housing before a spanner or socket wrench can be used. Remove the engine-to-transmission connecting bolts.

9 Withdraw the automatic transmission, at the same time have an assistant hold the torque converter in full engagement with the oil pump driveshaft to avoid loss of transmission fluid.

13 Engine dismantling – general

1 Before commencing a major engine overhaul, make sure that you

have gathered together clean rags, brushes, freeing fluid and a good selection of tools – including a torque wrench.
2 A number of clean tins or other containers is useful to keep the various nuts and bolts safely. Mark the tins as a guide to where the fixings belong.
3 Have a pencil and paper handy to record sequences of assembly of small items, or to sketch an item which may present difficulty at reassembly or refitting.
4 Obtain all the necessary gaskets and oil seals in advance.
5 If it is known that only one component of the engine is worn or damaged the dismantling operations should only be pursued as far as is necessary to rectify the problem, the engine need not be completely dismantled.

14 Engine – complete dismantling

1 Place the engine in an upright position on the bench or, if there is no alternative, on a sheet of hardboard on the floor.
2 First remove any ancillary components such as the alternator

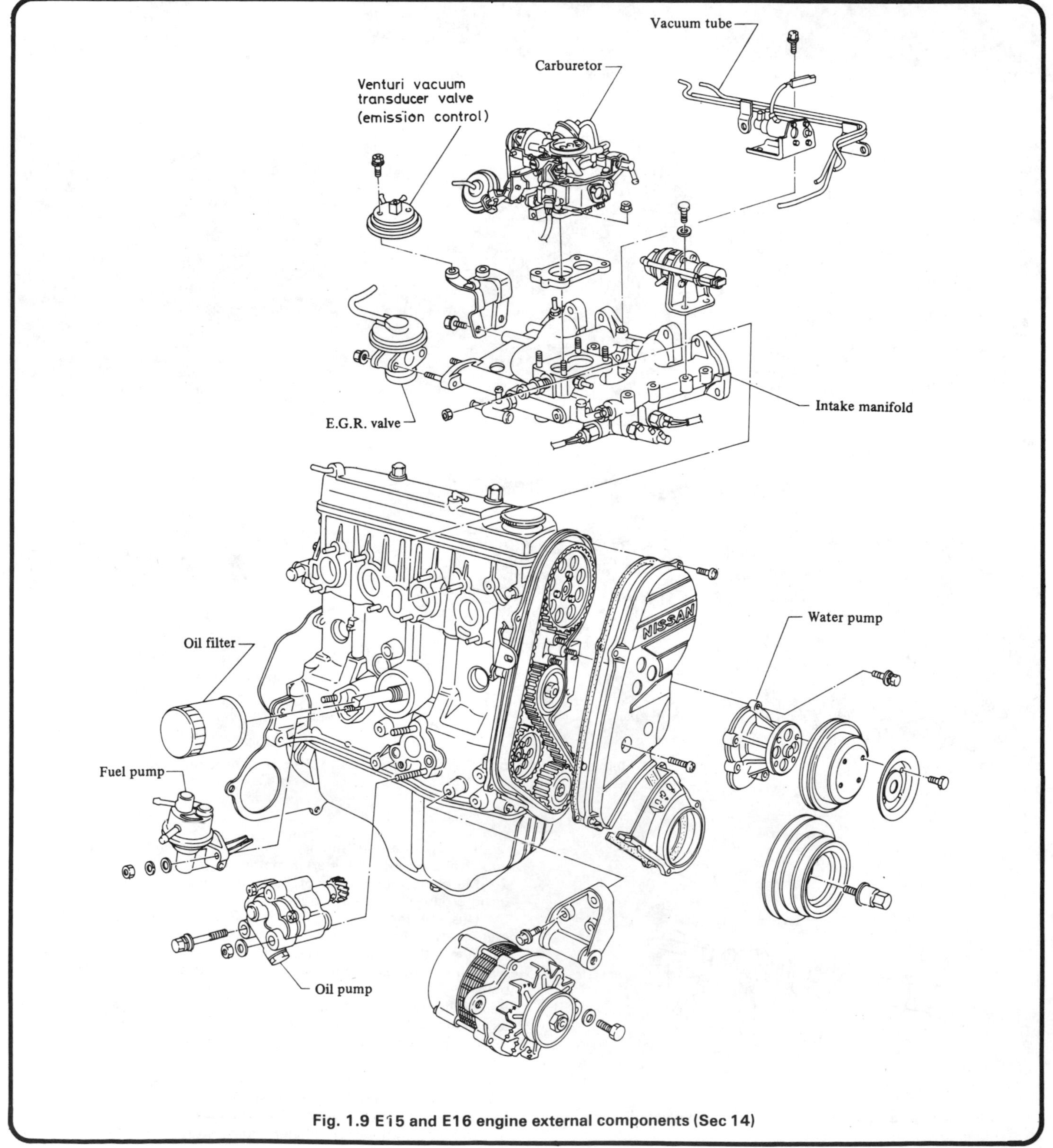

Fig. 1.9 E15 and E16 engine external components (Sec 14)

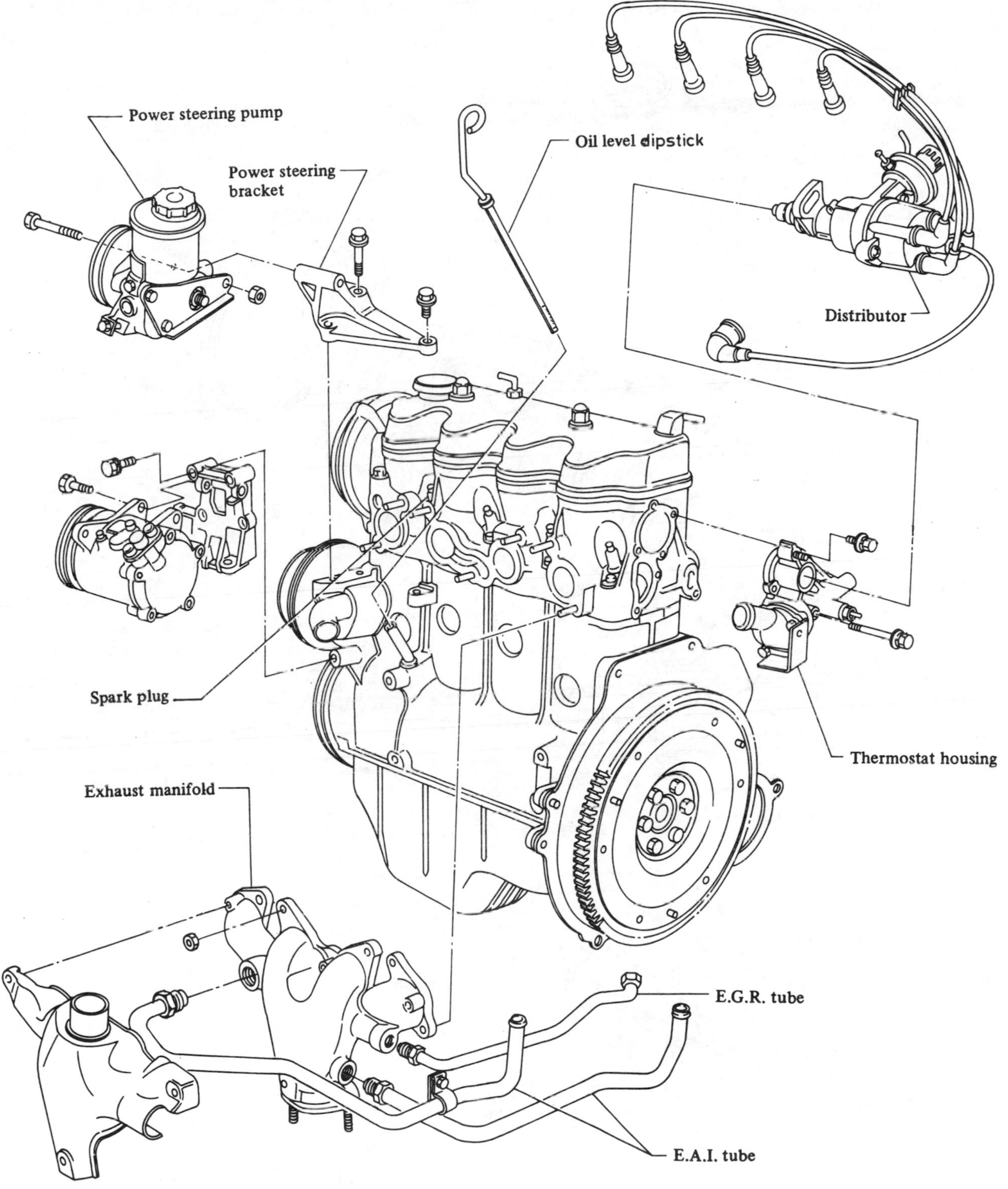

Fig. 1.10 E15 and E16 engine external components (Sec 14)

(Chapter 10), distributor (Chapter 4), fuel pump (Chapter 3), manifolds (Chapter 3) and clutch assembly (Chapter 5).

3 Unscrew and remove the oil filter. Be prepared for some loss of oil.

4 Remove the alternator mounting bracket and also those for the power steering pump and air conditioning compressor (where these are fitted).

5 Unbolt and remove the oil pump.

6 Unbolt and remove the thermostat housing.

7 Unbolt and remove the coolant pump pulley and then the coolant pump.

8 Carefully turn the engine onto its side and remove the sump pan (Section 8).

9 Using a piece of wood inserted between the crankcase and one of the crankshaft counterweights to prevent the crankshaft rotating, unscrew and remove the crankshaft pulley bolt and the pulley.

10 As the flywheel bolt holes are not offset, mark the relationship of

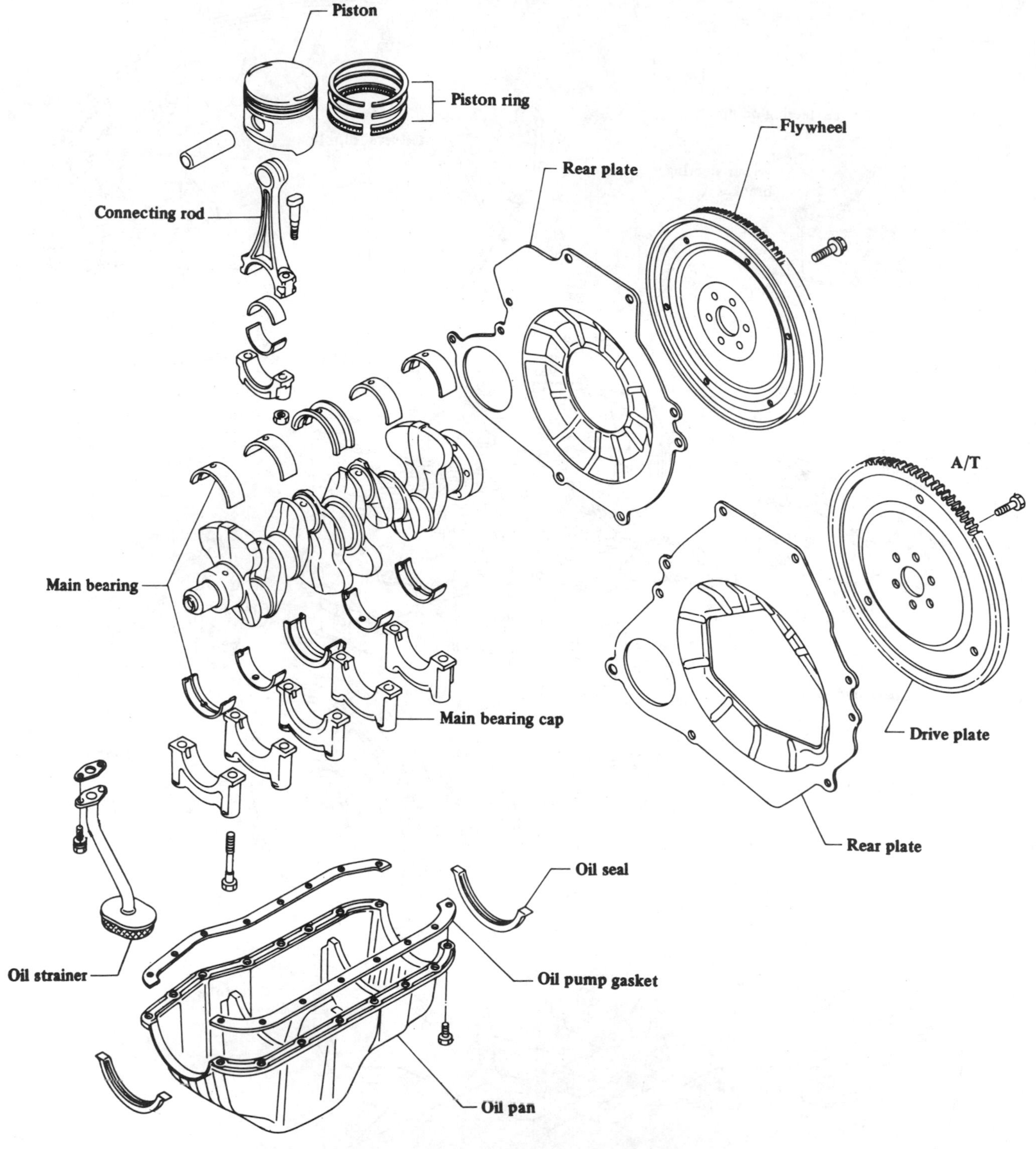

Fig. 1.11 Engine internal components (Sec 14)

the flywheel to the crankshaft hub. Unscrew the bolts and remove the flywheel. Take out the temporary wooden chock. Pull the engine endplate from the dowels.

11 Working at the timing belt end of the engine, remove the belt upper and lower covers. The cover screws are tight and may require the use of an impact driver.

12 Unbolt and remove the belt tensioner pulley.

13 Remove the timing belt, marking its rotational direction if it is to be used again.

14 Unbolt and remove the sprocket from the jack shaft. Unbolt the triangular mounting block used for attaching the alternator adjuster link.

15 Remove the crankshaft sprocket and the timing belt guide disc. If it is tight use a three-legged pulley, taking care not to damage the teeth.

16 Remove the rocker cover.

17 Unscrew and remove the cylinder head bolts and remove the cylinder head and gasket, as described in Section 4. Unbolt the timing belt lower backplate. Take the oil slinger from the end of the crankshaft.

18 Extract the securing screw and remove the jack shaft retaining plate. Withdraw the jack shaft.

19 From within the crankcase unbolt and remove the oil pick-up pipe and strainer.

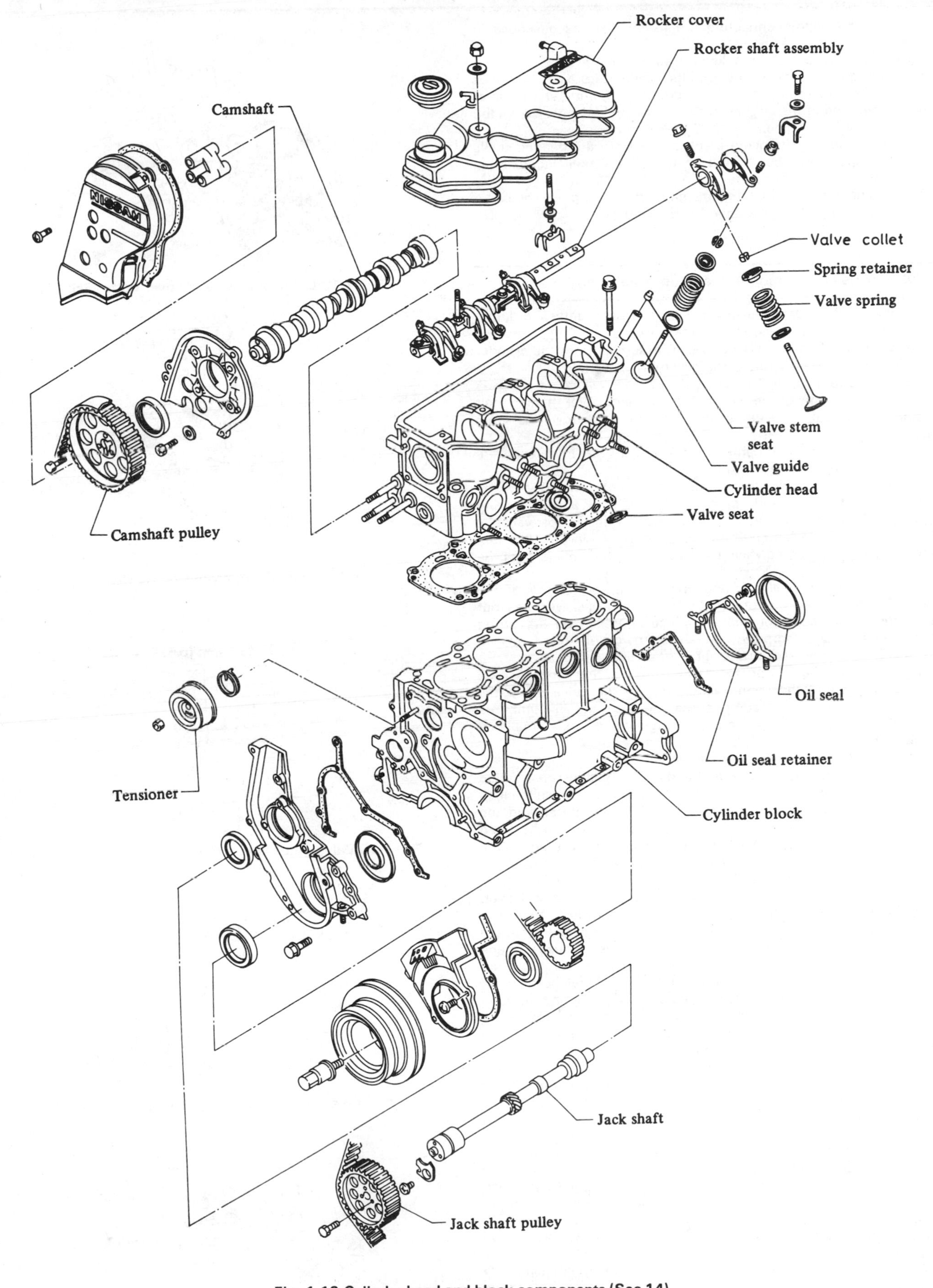

Fig. 1.12 Cylinder head and block components (Sec 14)

20 Remove the piston/connecting rod assemblies, as described in Section 9.
21 Unbolt and remove the crankshaft rear oil seal retainer.
22 Unscrew the main bearing cap bolts, working from the end ones towards the centre. The caps are numbered 1 to 5, number 1 being at the timing belt end of the engine, but the numbers are legible from the flywheel end of the engine.
23 Lift the crankshaft from the crankcase. Retain the bearing shells with their respective caps. Note that the centre shell incorporates thrust flanges to control endfloat.
24 The engine is now completely dismantled and all parts should be cleaned and examined, as described in Section 18.

15 Cylinder head – dismantling and decarbonising

1 The manifolds and rocker cover will have been detached during removal of the cylinder head (see Section 4).
2 Unscrew the bolts and lift the rocker assembly from the cylinder head. Identify which way round the assembly is located.
3 Unbolt and remove the camshaft pulley.
4 Unbolt and remove the cylinder head end cover (timing belt backplate). This retains the camshaft. Unscrew and remove the spark plugs.
5 Carefully withdraw the camshaft, taking care not to damage the bearings as the lobes pass through.
6 The valves and their associated components should now be removed. Due to the depth of the cylinder head a valve spring compressor having a long reach will be required. If this is not available, temporarily refit the rocker shaft and then make up a lever with a fork at one end to compress the valve spring by using the underside of the rocker shaft as a fulcrum.
7 Compress the first valve spring, extract the split cotters. If the valve spring refuses to compress, do not apply excessive force but remove the compressor and place a piece of tubing on the spring retainer and strike it a sharp blow to release the collets from the valve stem. Refit the compressor and resume operations.
8 Gently release the compressor, take off the spring retaining cap, the valve spring and the spring seat. Remove the valve. Keep the valves with its associated components together and in numbered sequence so that it can be refitted in its original position. A small box with divisions is useful for this purpose.
9 Remove the other valves in a similar way.
10 Bearing in mind that the cylinder head is of light alloy construction and is easily damaged use a blunt scraper or rotary wire brush to clean all traces of carbon deposits from the combustion spaces and the ports. The valve head stems and valve guides should also be freed from any carbon deposits. Wash the combustion spaces and ports down with a suitable solvent and scrape the cylinder head surface free of any foreign matter with the side of a steel rule, or a similar article.
11 If the engine is installed in the car, clean the pistons and the top of the cylinder bores. If the pistons are still in the block, then it is essential that great care is taken to ensure that no carbon gets into the cylinder bores as this could scratch the cylinder walls or cause damage to the piston and rings. To ensure this does not happen, first turn the crankshaft so that two of the pistons are at the top of their bores. Stuff rag into the other two bores or seal them off with paper and masking tape. The waterways should also be covered with small pieces of masking tape to prevent particles of carbon entering the cooling system and damaging the coolant pump.
12 Press a little grease into the gap between the cylinder walls and the two pistons which are to be worked on. With a blunt scraper carefully scrape away the carbon from the piston crown, taking great care not to scratch the aluminium. Also scrape away the carbon from the surrounding lip of the cylinder wall. When all carbon has been removed, scrape away the grease which will now be contaminated with carbon particles, taking care not to press any into the bores. To assist prevention of carbon build-up the piston crown can be polished with a metal polish. Remove the rags or masking tape from the other two cylinders and turn the crankshaft so that the two pistons which were at the bottom are now at the top. Place rag in the cylinders which have been decarbonised, and proceed as just described.
13 Examine the head of the valves for pitting and burning, especially the heads of the exhaust valves. The valve seatings should be examined at the same time. If the pitting on the valve and seat is very

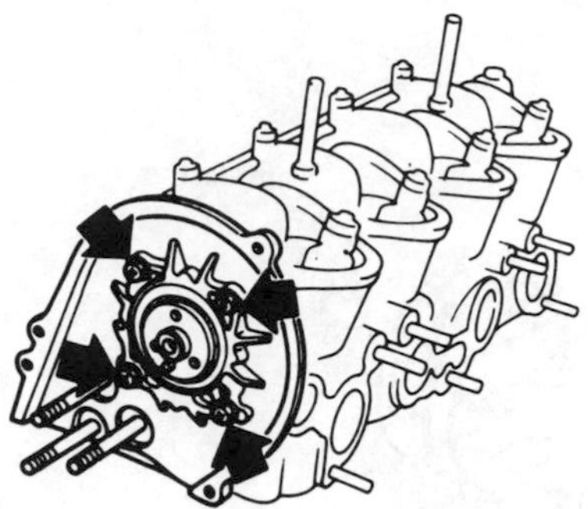
Fig. 1.13 Cylinder head end cover bolts (Sec 15)

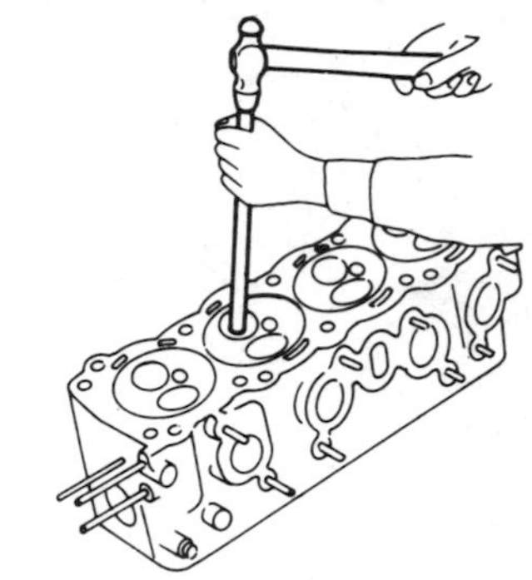
Fig. 1.14 Removing a valve guide (Sec 15)

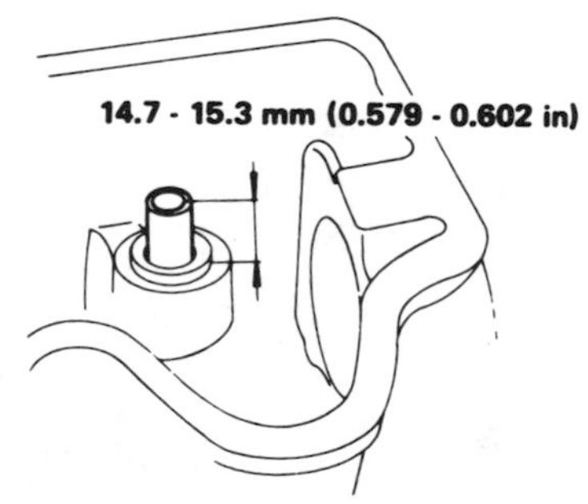

Fig. 1.15 Valve guide projection from cylinder head (Sec 15)

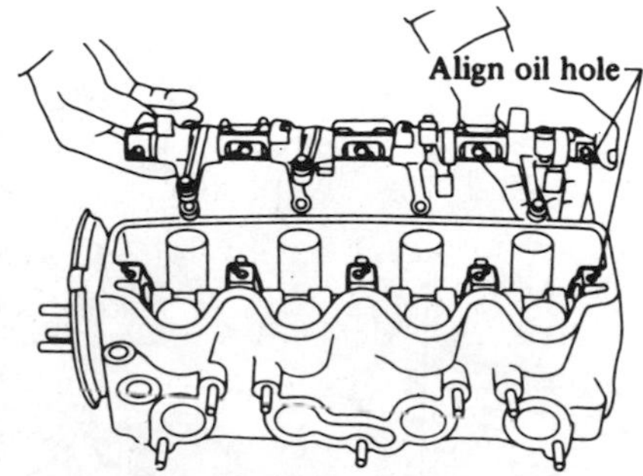

Fig. 1.16 Rocker shaft oil hole alignment (Sec 15)

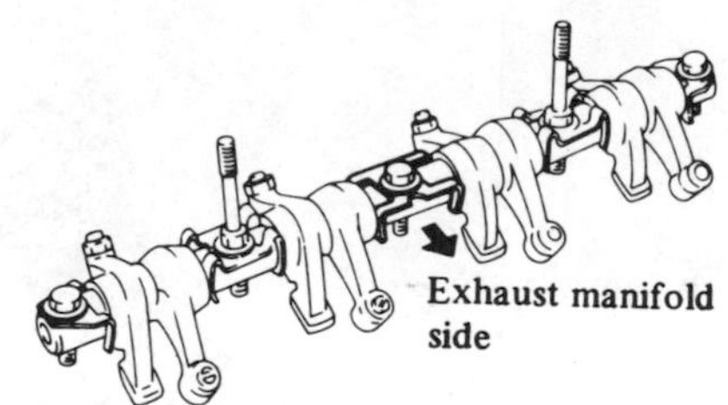

Fig. 1.17 Rocker assembly fitting direction (Sec 15)

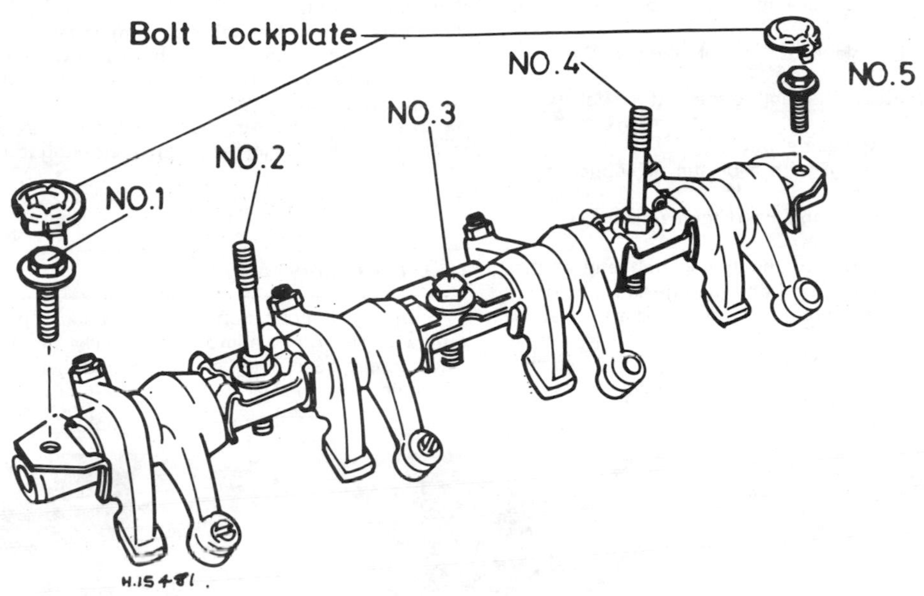

Fig. 1.18 Rocker shaft bolt lockplates (Sec 15)

slight, the marks can be removed by grinding the seats and valves together with coarse, and then fine valve grinding paste.

14 Where bad pitting has occurred to the valve seats it will be necessary to recut them and fit new valves. This latter job should be entrusted to the local agent or engineering works. In practice it is very seldom that the seats are so badly worn. Normally it is the valve that is too badly worn for refitting, and the owner can easily purchase a new set of valves and match them to the seats by valve grinding.

15 Valve grinding is carried out as follows. Smear a trace of coarse carborundum paste on the seat face and apply a suction grinding tool to the valve head. With a semi-rotary motion, grind the valve head to its seat, lifting the valve occasionally to redistribute the grinding paste. When a dull matt even surface is produced on both the valve seat and the valve, wipe off the paste and repeat the process with fine carborundum paste, lifting and turning the valve to redistribute the paste as before. A light spring placed under the valve head will greatly ease this operation. When a smooth unbroken ring of light grey matt finish is produced on both valve and valve seat faces, the grinding operation is complete. Carefully clean away every trace of grinding compound, take great care to leave none in the ports or in the valve guides. Clean the valves and valve seats with a solvent-soaked rag, then with a clean rag, and finally, if an air line is available, blow the valves, valve guides and valve ports clean.

16 Check that all valve springs are intact. If any one is broken, all should be renewed. Check the free height of the springs against new ones. If some springs are not within specifications, replace them all. Springs suffer from fatigue and it is a good idea to renew them even if they look serviceable.

17 Check that the oil supply holes in the rocker arms are clear.

18 The cylinder head can be checked for warping either by placing it on a piece of plate glass or using a straight-edge and feeler blades. If there is any doubt or if its block face is corroded, have it re-faced by your dealer or motor engineering works.

19 Test the valves in their guides for side-to-side rock. If this is any more than almost imperceptible new guides must be fitted. This, as with valve seat renewal, is really a job for your dealer as the cylinder head must be warmed and the old guide driven out. New guides should be pressed in to protrude 15.0 mm (0.59 in) above the cylinder head and then reamed using a 12.2 mm (0.480 in) reamer.

20 Renew the valve stem oil seals (photo).

21 Commence reassembly by oiling the stem of the first valve and pushing it into its guide (photo).

15.20 Valve stem oil seal

15.21 Fitting a valve into its guide

22 Fit the spring seat (photo), the valve spring (photo) and the spring cap (photo). The closer coils of the valve spring must be towards the cylinder head.
23 Compress the valve spring and locate the split collets in the valve stem cut-outs (photo).
24 Gently release the compressor, checking to see that the collets are not displaced.
25 Fit the remaining valves in the same way.
26 Tap the end of each valve stem with a plastic or copper-faced hammer to settle the components.
27 Lubricate the camshaft bearings and insert the camshaft into the cylinder head (photo).
28 Fit the cylinder head end cover to the timing belt end of the cylinder head, complete with new oil seal and new gasket (photos).
29 Bolt on the camshaft sprocket (photo). The bolt holes are offset so it will only go on one way.
30 Before refitting the rocker gear, check the shaft for wear and the rocker arms for general condition (photo). Renew any worn components, but make sure when reasembling that they are kept in their original order.
31 The oil hole in the rocker shaft must face downwards and the cut-out in the centre retainer must be towards the exhaust manifold side.
32 With the rocker arm adjuster screws fully released, bolt the rocker gear to the cylinder head.
33 The rocker shaft fixing bolts on later models incorporate lockplates to eliminate the possibility of them working loose (photo).

16 Lubrication system

1 The engine lubrication system depends upon oil contained in the sump pan being drawn into an externally mounted oil pump, which is driven from a gear on the jack shaft, and then pressurised to supply all the engine working parts.

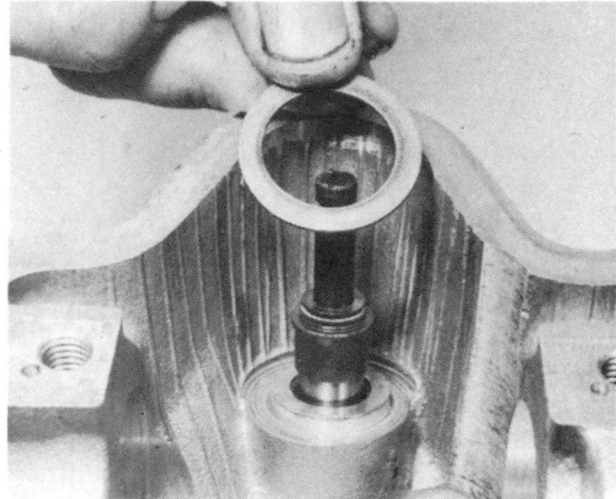
5.22A Valve spring seat

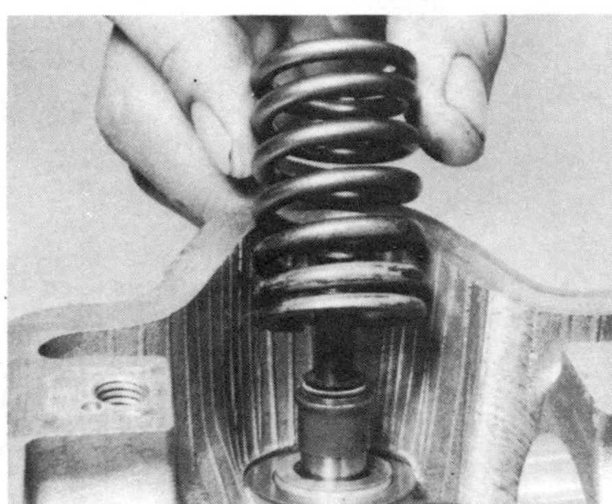
15.22B Valve spring

15.22C Valve spring cap

15.23 Compressing valve spring and locating collets

15.27 Inserting camshaft into cylinder head

15.28A Cylinder head end cover gasket

15.28B Cylinder head end cover

15.28C Tightening cylinder head end cover bolts

15.29 Camshaft sprocket

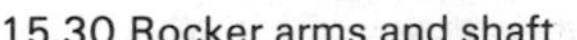
15.30 Rocker arms and shaft

15.33 Rocker shaft bolt lockplate (arrowed)

16.5 Pressure relief valve

2 Oil from the pump passes through an externally mounted full-flow disposable type oil filter.

3 An oil pressure regulator valve is incorporated in the oil pump and an oil pressure switch is located close to the filter which actuates a warning lamp if pressure loss occurs.

4 Intermittent flickering of the oil pressure warning lamp may occur when the engine is idling after a long high speed run. This should be ignored as long as the lamp goes out immediately the engine speed is increased.

5 A pressure relief valve is located in the oil filter mounting base (photo). Should it be seen to be cracked or broken when the oil filter is removed, the valve may be prised out with a screwdriver and a new one tapped into position. The purpose of this valve is to open and bypass the filter should the filter become clogged.

17 Crankcase ventilation system (PCV)

1 This is of positive, dual-line type which returns blow-by gas (which has passed the piston rings) from the crankcase to either the air cleaner or the intake manifold, according to manifold vacuum.

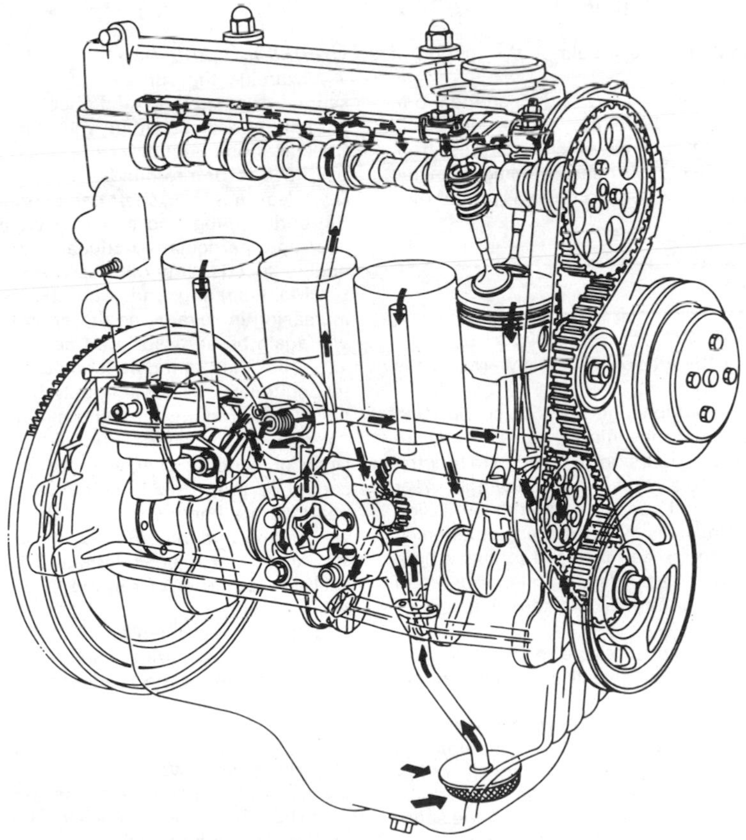

Fig. 1.19 Engine lubrication circuit (Sec 16)

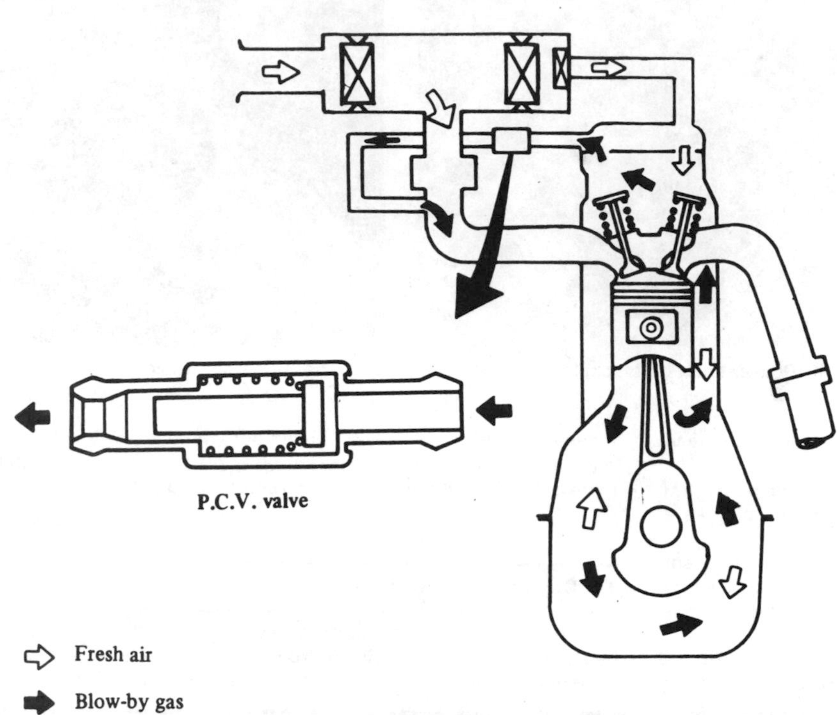

Fig. 1.20 Crankcase emission control system (Sec 17)

P.C.V. valve

To intake manifold

Fig. 1.21 PCV (Positive Crankcase Ventilation) valve (Sec 17)

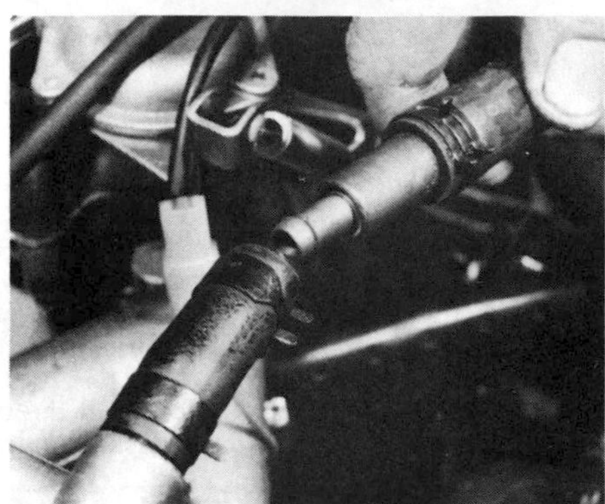

17.1 Crankcase vent hose and PCV valve

According to engine load conditions a valve regulates the routing of the gas (photo).

2 Check the system connecting hoses regularly and clean them out.

3 To test the operation of the valve, have the engine idling and disconnect the hose from the side of the valve which is furthest from the intake manifold. Vacuum hiss should be heard coming from the open end of the valve and a strong suction felt if a finger is placed over it. If this is not so, renew the valve.

18 Examination and renovation

Cylinder block and crankcase

1 Examine the castings carefully for cracks, especially around the bolt holes and between cylinders.

2 The cylinder bores must be checked for taper, ovality, scoring and scratching. Start by examining the top of the cylinder bores. If they are at all worn, a ridge will be felt on the thrust side. This ridge marks the top of piston travel. The owner will have a good indication of bore wear prior to dismantling by the quantity of oil consumed and the emission of blue smoke from the exhaust, especially when the engine is cold.

3 An internal micrometer or dial gauge can be used to check bore wear and taper against Specifications, but this is a pointless operation if the engine is obviously in need of reboring – indicated by excessive oil consumption.

4 Your engine reconditioner will be able to rebore the block for you and supply the correct oversize pistons to give the correct running clearance.

5 If the engine has reached the limit for reboring cylinder liners can be fitted, but here again this is a job for your engine reconditioner.

6 To rectify minor bore wear it is possible to fit proprietary oil control rings, as described in Section 9. A good way to test the condition of the engine is to have it at normal operating temperature with the spark plugs removed. Screw a compression tester (available from most motor accessory stores) into the first plug hole. Hold the accelerator fully depressed and crank the engine on the starter motor for several revolutions. Record the reading. Zero the tester and check the remaining cylinders in the same way. All four compression figures should be approximately equal and within the tolerance given in Specifications. If they are all low, suspect piston ring or cylinder bore wear. If only one reading is down, suspect a valve not seating.

Crankshaft and bearings

7 Examine the surfaces of the crankpins and journals for signs of scoring or scratching, and check for ovality or taper. If the crankpin or journals are not within the dimensional tolerances given in the Specifications Section at the beginning of this Chapter the crankshaft will have to be reground.

8 Wear in a crankshaft can be detected while the engine is running. Big-end bearing and crankpin wear is indicated by distinct metallic knocking, particularly noticeable when the engine is pulling from low engine speeds. Low oil pressure will also occur.

9 Main bearing and journal wear is indicated by engine rumble increasing in severity as the engine speed increases. Low oil pressure will again be an associated condition.

10 Crankshaft grinding should be carried out by specialist engine reconditioners who will supply the matching undersize bearing shells to give the required running clearance.

11 Inspect the connecting rod big-end and main bearing shells for signs of general wear, scoring, pitting and scratching. The bearings should be matt grey in colour. If a copper colour is evident, then the bearings are badly worn and the surface material has worn away to expose the underlay. Renew the bearings as a complete set.

12 At time of major overhaul it is worthwhile renewing the bearing shells as a matter of routine even if they appear to be in reasonably good condition.

13 Bearing shells can be identified by the marking on the back of the shell. Standard sized shells are usually marked STD or 0.00. Undersized shells are marked with the undersize, such as 0.25 mm.

Connecting rods

14 Check the alignment of the connecting rods visually. If you suspect distortion, have them checked by your dealer or engine reconditioner on the special jig which he will have.

15 The gudgeon pin is an interference fit in the connecting rod small-end and removal or refitting and changing a piston is a job best left to your dealer or engine reconditioner due to the need for a press and jig.

Pistons and piston rings

16 If the engine is rebored then new oversize pistons with rings and

gudgeon pins will be supplied. Have the supplier fit the pistons to the rods so that the oil hole in the connecting rod is located as shown with reference to the front facing mark on the piston crown (see Fig. 1.22).
17 Removal and refitting of piston rings is covered in Section 9.

Flywheel

18 Check the clutch mating surface of the flywheel. If it is deeply scored (due to failure to renew a worn driven plate) then it should be renewed. Slight roughness may be smoothed with fine emery cloth.
19 If lots of tiny cracks are visible on the surface of the flywheel this will be due to overheating caused by slipping the clutch or 'riding' the clutch pedal.
20 With a pre-engaged type of starter motor it is rare to find the teeth of the flywheel ring gear damaged or worn, but if they are the ring gear will have to be renewed.
21 To remove the ring gear, drill a hole between the roots of two teeth, taking care not to damage the flywheel, and then split the ring with a sharp cold chisel.
22 The new ring gear must be heated to between 180 and 220°C (356 and 428°F) which is very hot, so if you do not have facilities for obtaining these temperatures, leave the job to your dealer or engine reconditioner.

Driveplate (automatic transmission)

23 Should the starter ring gear on the driveplate require renewal, the driveplate should be renewed complete.

Camshaft

24 Examine the camshaft bearings for wear, scoring or pitting. If evident then the complete cylinder head will have to be renewed as the bearings are machined directly in it.
25 The camshaft itself should show no marks or scoring on the journal or cam lobe surfaces. Where marks are evident, renew the camshaft or have it reprofiled by a specialist reconditioner.
26 Check the teeth of the camshaft sprocket for wear. Renew the sprocket if necessary.

Timing belt and tensioner

27 Examine the belt for cracking or fraying and tooth wear. If any of these conditions is evident or if the belt has been in service for 80 000 km (50 000 miles) it is recommended that it is renewed.
28 The tensioner should not be noisy or shaky when turned, and have good spring action. Where these conditions are not met with, renew the tensioner complete (photo).

Jack shaft

29 The jack shaft journals should be smooth – without scoring or scratches. Wear can be checked using a micrometer.
30 The bearings are renewable, but make sure that the lubrication holes line up with those in the crankcase as the new bearings are pressed in.
31 When refitting the jack shaft end plug (removed to extract the bearings) coat the edges with a suitable sealant.

Oil pump

32 To dismantle the oil pump, remove the cover screws and take off the cover.
33 Lift out the outer rotor (photo). The inner rotor with drivegear cannot be separated from the pump casing.
34 Clean and dry the pump components and refit the outer rotor. Using a feeler blade check the following clearances (photos):

Rotor tip clearance	0.12 mm (0.0047 in) maximum
Outer rotor to pump body clearance	0.15 to 0.21 mm (0.0059 to 0.0083 in)

35 Using a straight-edge across the top of the outer rotor check the following clearances, again using a feeler blade:

Oil pump body to straight edge	0.02 mm (0.0008 in) maximum
Inner rotor endfloat	0.05 mm (0.002 in) maximum

36 If, after these checks, the pump proves to be worn, renew it.
37 The pressure regulator components are seldom found to be faulty,

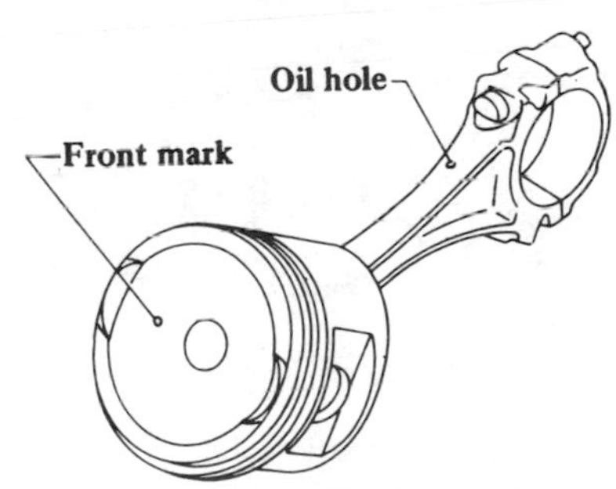

Fig. 1.22 Connecting rod/piston alignment (Sec 18)

18.28 Belt tensioner and spring

18.33 Oil pump rotors (note directional mark for correct refitting)

18.34A Checking rotor tip clearance

18.34B Checking rotor outer clearance

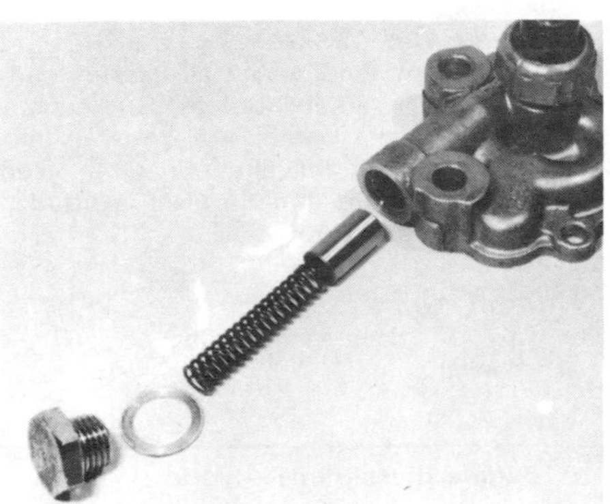

18.37 Oil pump pressure regulating valve

18.38A Prising out an oil seal

18.38B Using a socket to fit oil seal

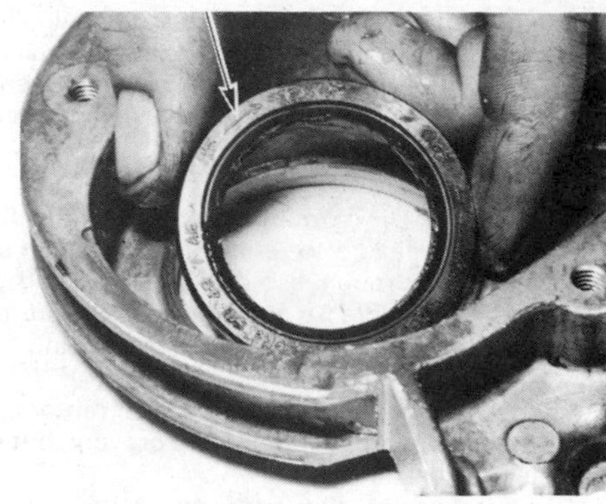

18.38C Fitting an oil seal (note shaft directional arrow)

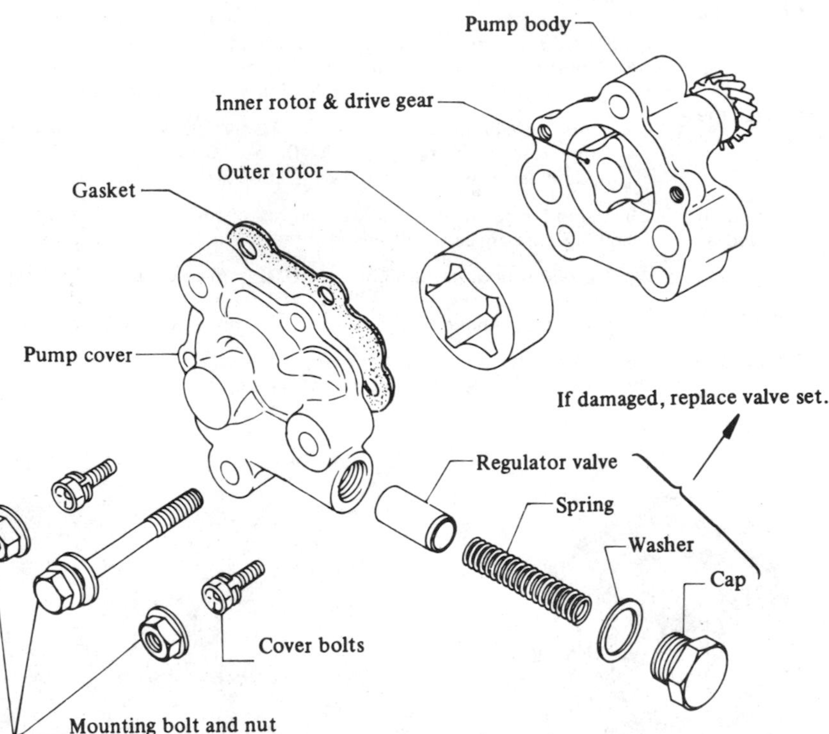

Fig. 1.23 Exploded view of oil pump (Sec 18)

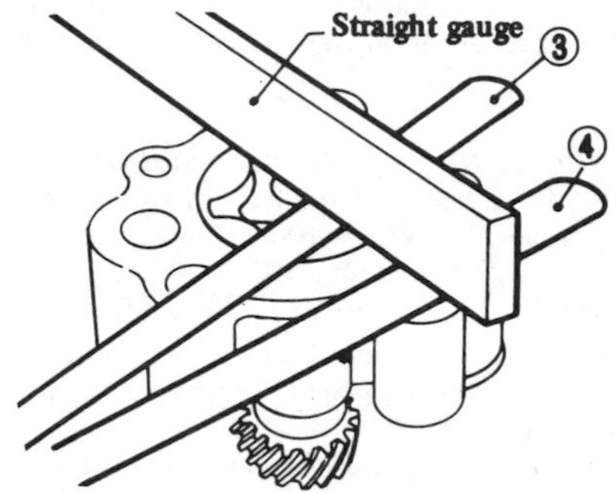

Fig. 1.24 Checking oil pump clearances (Sec 18)

3 *Inner rotor endfloat*
4 *Oil pump body to straight-edge*

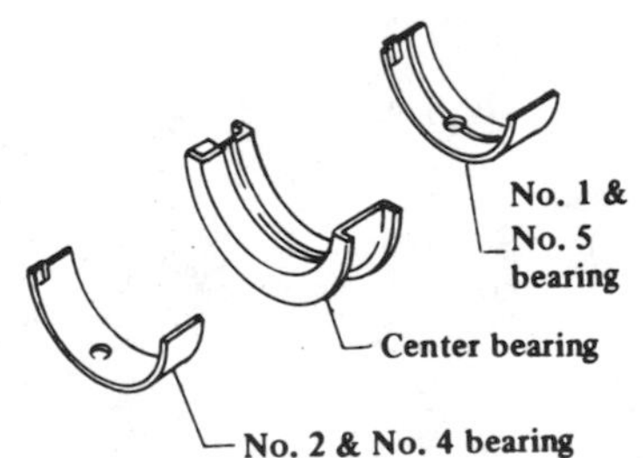

Fig. 1.25 Main bearing shell identification (Sec 20)

but if they are to be inspected, unscrew the cap and extract the spring and valve plunger (photo). When refitting, remember to fit the sealing washer and tighten the cap to the specified torque.

Oil seals and gaskets

38 It is recommended that all gaskets and oil seals are renewed at major engine overhaul (photo). Sockets are useful for removing or refitting oil seals (photo). An arrow is moulded onto the seals to indicate the rotational direction of the component which it serves (photo). Make sure that the seal is fitted the correct way round to comply with the arrow.

Cylinder head

39 This is covered in Section 15, during dismantling and decarbonising.

19 Engine reassembly – general

1 To ensure maximum life with minimum trouble from a rebuilt engine, not only must everything be correctly assembled, but everything must be spotlessly clean, all the oilways must be clear, locking washers and spring washers must always be fitted where indicated and all bearing and other working surfaces must be thoroughly lubricated during assembly.

2 Before assembly begins renew any bolts or studs, the threads of which are in any way damaged, and whenever possible use new spring washers.

3 Apart from your normal tools, a supply of clean rag, an oil can filled with engine oil (an empty plastic detergent bottle thoroughly cleaned and washed out, will do just as well), a new supply of assorted spring washers, a set of new gaskets, and a torque wrench, should be collected together.

20 Engine – reassembly

1 Stand the cylinder block in an inverted position on the bench.

2 Clean the shell bearing recesses in the crankcase free from all grit and dirt and fit the bearing shells. The centre shell is of thrust flange type (photo), Nos 1 and 5 are of grooved type (photo) and Nos 2 and 4 are plain.

20.2A Main bearing centre shell bearing with thrust flanges

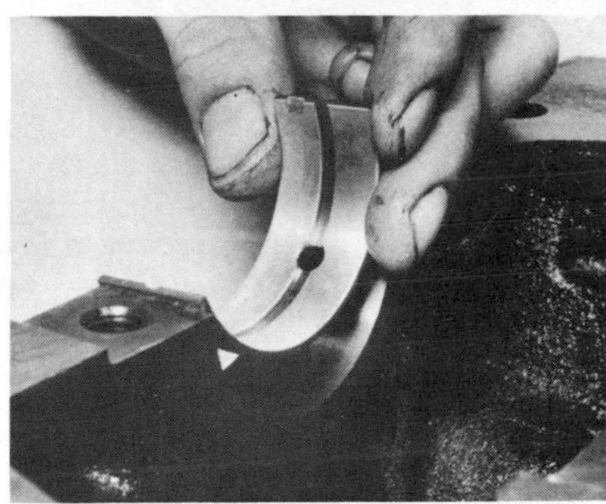
20.2B Main bearing cap shell

20.3A Oiling crankcase main bearing shells

20.3B Lowering crankshaft into position

20.5 Fitting centre main bearing cap

20.6 Tightening main bearing cap bolt

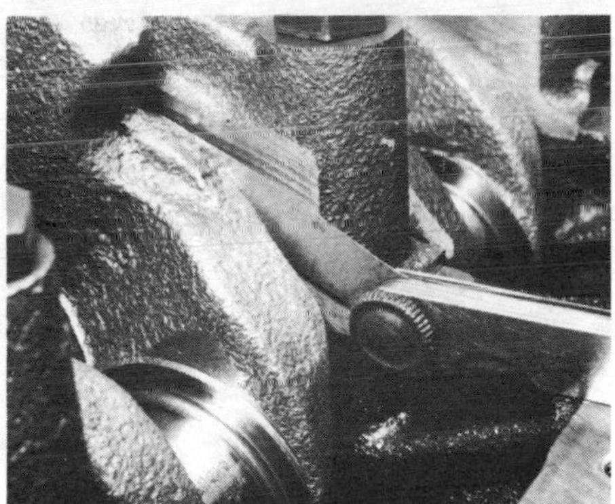
20.7 Checking crankshaft endfloat

20.8A Crankshaft oil seal retainer gasket

20.8B Crankshaft oil seal and retainer

3 Oil the shells and lower the crankshaft into position (photos).

4 Clean the recesses in the main bearing caps free from grit and dirt and fit the bearing shells to match those already fitted to the crankcase. Oil the shells.

5 Fit the main bearing caps in their numbered sequence so that the numbers can be read from the flywheel end. Cap No 1 is at the timing belt end. The caps will only seat one way round (photo).

6 Insert and tighten the cap bolts to the specified torque – working from the centre ones towards each end (photo).

7 Now check the crankshaft endfloat using either a dial gauge or feeler blades inserted between the flange of the centre bearing and the machined shoulder of the crankshaft (photo). Make sure that the crankshaft is pushed fully in one direction and then the other when measuring. If the endfloat is excessive (see Specifications) and new bearing shells have been fitted then it can only be due to an error at regrinding.

8 Bolt on the crankshaft oil seal retainer complete with a new oil seal and gasket (photos). Apply grease to the oil seal lips before pushing it over the flywheel mounting flange and check that the lip of the seal is not doubled under. Cut the ends of the gasket flush (photo).

9 Oil the cylinder bores and fit the piston/connecting rods (complete with bearing shells) into their respective cylinders, as described in Section 9. Make sure that the front mark on the piston crown is towards the timing belt end of the engine.

10 Oil the crankpins.

11 Wipe out the recesses in the big-end caps and fit the bearing shells. Oil the shells.

12 Draw the connecting rods down onto the crankpins, fit the caps (numbers adjacent) and screw in and tighten the bolts to the specified torque (photo).

13 Oil the jack shaft journals, insert the jack shaft into its bearings and fit the retaining plate and screw, having applied locking fluid to the threads (photos).

14 Fit the cylinder head, as described in Section 4.

20.8C Cutting oil seal retainer gasket flush

20.12 Main and big-end caps

20.13A Inserting jack shaft into crankcase

20.13B Jack shaft retaining plate

20.13C Jack shaft retaining plate screw

20.15 Crankshaft oil slinger

20.16A Timing belt lower backplate gasket

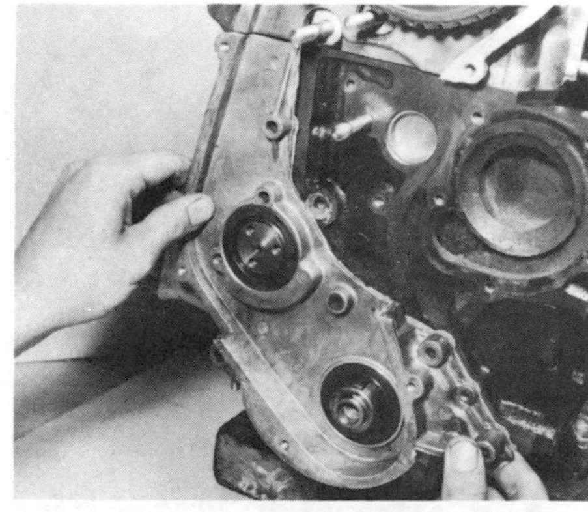
20.16B Timing belt lower backplate

20.17A Timing belt guide disc

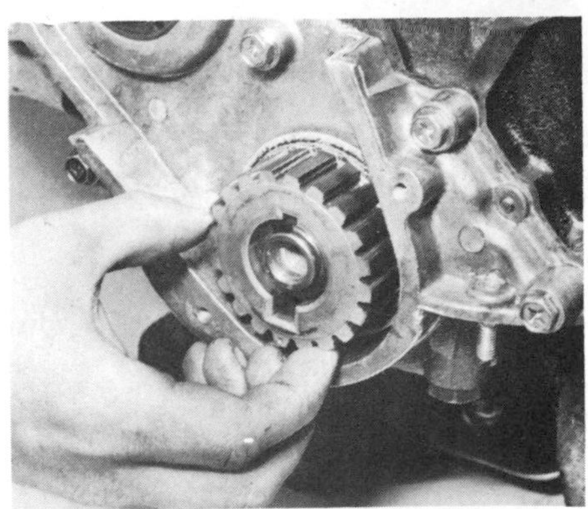
20.17B Crankshaft sprocket

20.18 Jack shaft sprocket

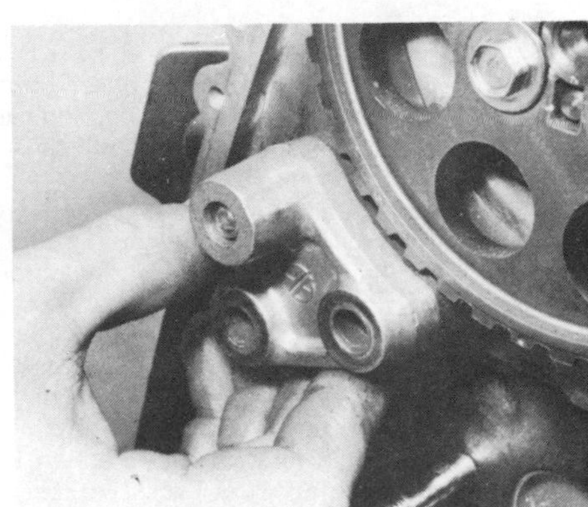
20.19 Alternator adjuster link mounting block

15 Fit the oil slinger to the front end of the crankshaft (photo).
16 Fit the timing belt lower backplate using a new gasket and oil seals (photos). Note that the two longer bolts go into the lower holes.
17 Refit the timing belt guide disc to mate with the concave side of the crankshaft sprocket which should now be fitted (photos).
18 Bolt the sprocket to the jack shaft (photo). This sprocket does not go in any special position.
19 Fit the triangular mounting block for the alternator adjuster link (photo).
20 The camshaft sprocket will normally have been fitted during reassembly of the cylinder head. If not, fit it now.
21 Fit and tension the timing belt, as described in Section 6. Bolt on the oil pick-up pipe, using a new gasket (photo).
22 Stick new gaskets and seals to the sump pan mating flange of the crankcase. Apply a bead of gasket sealant to the joints of the gasket strips and sealing strips before locating the sump pan (photos). Screw in the bolts progressively – do not over tighten (photo).
23 Fit the timing belt upper and lower covers using new sealing strips (photos). Fit the reinforcement plate (photo).
24 Fit the engine endplate to its dowels at the flywheel end of the engine (photo).
25 Fit the flywheel, aligning the marks made before removal (photo).
26 Apply thread locking fluid to the bolt threads and tighten them to the specified torque (photo). Jam the flywheel starter ring teeth to prevent the flywheel from turning as the bolts are tightened.
27 Fit the crankshaft pulley and tighten to the specified torque, again jamming the flywheel teeth (photo).
28 Refit the coolant pump and pulley (Chapter 2).
29 Refit the thermostat housing using a new gasket (photos).
30 Using a new gasket bolt on the oil pump (photo).
31 Refit the alternator mounting bracket.
32 Where an air conditioner or power-assisted steering is fitted, bolt on the compressor and pump brackets.
33 Fit a new oil filter, as described in Section 2.

20.21 Oil pick-up pipe and gasket

20.22A Sump pan gasket and sealing strip overlap

20.22B Locating sump pan

20.22C Tightening sump pan bolt

20.23A Timing belt lower cover

20.23B Timing belt upper cover

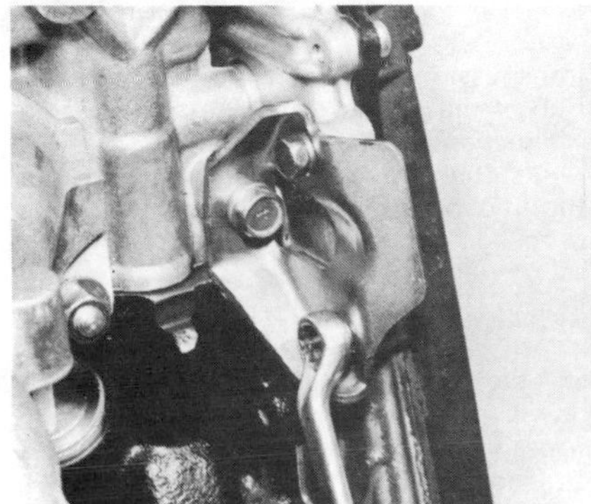
20.23C Cylinder head/crankcase reinforcement plate

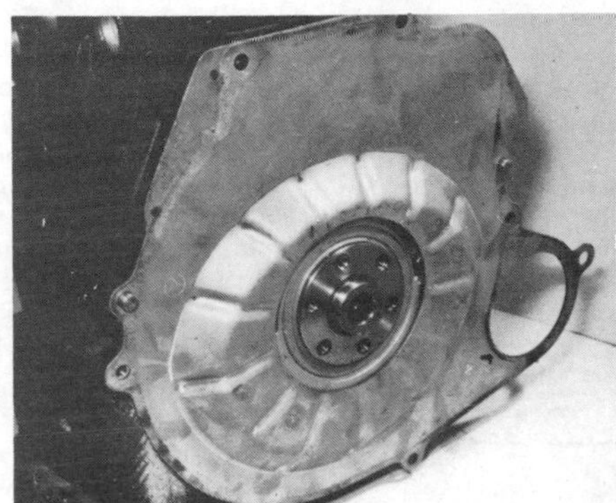
20.24 Engine endplate

20.25 Fitting flywheel

20.26 Tightening flywheel bolts

20.27 Tightening crankshaft pulley bolt

20.29A Thermostat housing gasket

20.29B Thermostat housing (coolant temperature switch arrowed)

20.30 Oil pump and gasket (oil pressure switch arrowed)

20.35A Fitting rocker cover

20.35B Tightening rocker cover nuts

21.9A Distributor connections
A LT (coil negative) *B Earth*

21.9B Cylinder head earth connection

34 Refit the ancillary items including the alternator, the distributor, the fuel pump, the manifolds and the clutch. Use new gaskets and refer to the appropriate Chapter for specific details.
35 Adjust the valve clearances (Section 5), fit a new gasket to the rocker cover and tighten the domed nuts (photos).
36 Screw in the spark plugs and connect the ignition leads.

21 Engine/manual transmission – reconnection and refitting to vehicle

Reconnection

Refer also to Chapter 6

1 Refer to Chapter 5 and make sure that the clutch driven plate has been centralised.
2 Apply a smear of molybdenum disulphide grease to the input shaft splines and then offer the transmission to the engine. As the input shaft splines pass into the hub of the driven plate, the transmission may require turning in either direction to align the splines.
3 Insert and tighten the flange connecting bolts, but remember to locate the coolant tube, the mounting brackets, the sump pan undershield and the sump-to-bellhousing reinforcement strut.
4 Bolt on the starter motor.

Refitting

5 Connect the hoist to the lifting lugs, then raise the engine/transmission and lower it carefully into the engine compartment. On RHD vehicles pass the alternator under the brake master cylinder as the engine is lowered.
6 Engage the flexible mountings and fit the connecting bolts. The bracket plate at the rear lower mounting incorporates a cut-out with a locating pin which may require the careful use of a jack under the sump pan to engage it.

21.11 Reverse lamp switch leads (arrowed)

21.13 Rocker cover vent hose

7 Remove the hoist.
8 Reconnect the alternator leads and the lead to the automatic choke (where fitted).
9 Reconnect the ignition HT and LT leads, and the earth leads to the side of the cylinder head (photos). Note that the wiring harness is located in a protective sleeve and is routed under the intake manifold. It is held in position by plastic straps on the underside of the manifold.
10 Reconnect the lead to the oil pressure switch.
11 Reconnect the leads to the coolant temperature switch and reverse lamp switch (photo).
12 Reconnect the fuel hoses to the fuel pump.
13 Reconnect the throttle cable and choke operating cables and the rocker cover vent hose (photo).
14 Reconnect the speedometer drive cable to the transmission.
15 Reconnect the clutch operating cable to the release lever. Adjust the clutch cable, as described in Chapter 5.
16 Remove the temporary side gear locating rods and then reconnect the inboard ends of the driveshafts with the final drive. Take care not to damage the oil seals. Use new circlips on the driveshafts and push the splined ends of the shafts into the transmission as far as they will go. Strike the weld bead of the joint cover to drive the shaft fully home. Test that the circlip has locked in its groove by pulling on the joint cover.
17 Using new nuts, reconnect the suspension bottom balljoints.
18 Tighten the suspension top strut mounting nuts to the specified torque.
19 Refit the disc calipers.
20 Refit the front roadwheels, lower the vehicle.
21 Reconnect the gearchange rod and its stabiliser rod.
22 Reconnect the exhaust downpipe to the manifold.
23 Refit the air conditioner compressor and the power steering pump (if fitted).
24 Refit the radiator and electric fan. Reconnect the fan and thermal switch leads.
25 Refit the air cleaner.
26 Refit and reconnect the battery.
27 Refit the bonnet.
28 Fill the cooling system, and the engine and transmission with the specified oil.
29 Refit the drivebelts and tension them, as described in Chapter 2.

22 Engine/automatic transmission – reconnection and refitting to vehicle

Reconnection

Refer also to Chapter 7

1 The operations are very similar to those described in the preceding Section, but the following special points should be noted.
2 Before connecting the driveplate to the torque converter, check to see that the converter is pushed fully home. This can be determined if dimension A is not less than specified (see Fig. 1.26).
3 Align the marks on the driveplate and torque converter (made before dismantling). Apply thread locking fluid to the clean threads of the connecting bolts and tighten them to the specified torque. Bolt on the starter motor.

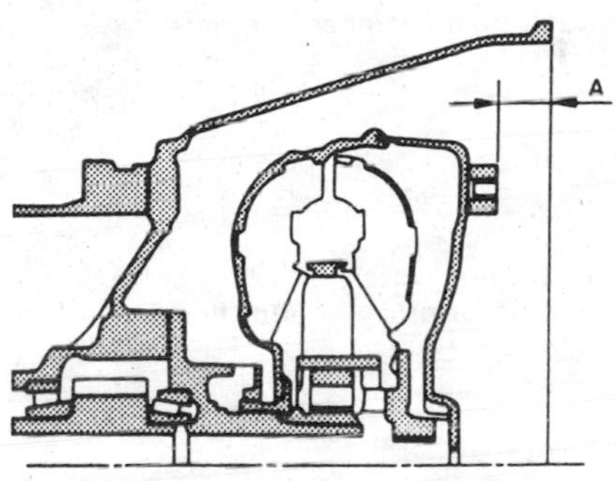

Fig. 1.26 Torque converter installed fully into housing (Sec 22)

A = Not less than 21.1 mm (0.831 in)

Refitting

4 Reconnect the speed selector control cable and adjust it, if necessary.
5 Reconnect the inhibitor switch leads.
6 Reconnect the oil cooler hoses.
7 Refit the front wing protective shield.
8 Top up the automatic transmission fluid.

23 Initial start-up after major overhaul

1 Set the idle speed screw to a higher setting than normal to offset the drag caused by new engine components.
2 Start the engine. This may take rather longer than usual as the fuel pump has to fill the carburettor with fuel.
3 Once the engine starts, allow it to warm up without racing and then check for oil leaks.
4 There will be some odd smells caused by oil and grease burning off metal surfaces.
5 Treat the engine as a new unit for the first few hundred miles by restricting speed and load.
6 Once the engine is run-in after 1000 km (600 miles), check the idle speed, the valve clearances and the tightening torque of all engine nuts and bolts. Change the engine oil and filter at the same time.

24 Fault diagnosis – engine

Symptom	Reason(s)
Engine fails to turn when starter control operated	
No current at starter motor	Flat or defective battery Loose battery leads Defective starter solenoid or switch or broken wiring Engine earth strap disconnected
Current at starter motor	Jammed starter motor drive pinion Defective starter motor
Engine turns but will not start	
No spark at spark plug	Ignition leads or distributor cap damp or wet Ignition leads to spark plugs loose Shorted or disconnected low tension leads Dirty, incorrectly set, or pitted contact breaker points* Faulty condenser* Defective ignition switch Ignition leads connected wrong way round Faulty coil Contact breaker point spring earthed or broken*
No fuel at carburettor float chamber or at jets	No petrol in petrol tank Vapour lock in fuel line (in hot conditions or at high altitude) Blocked float chamber needle valve Fuel pump filter blocked Choked or blocked carburettor jets Faulty fuel pump
Engine stalls and will not restart	
Excess of petrol in cylinder or carburettor flooding	Too much choke allowing too rich a mixture or wet plugs Float damaged or leaking or needle not seating Float lever incorrectly adjusted
No spark at spark plug	Ignition failure – sudden Ignition failure – misfiring precedes total stoppage Ignition failure – in severe rain or after traversing water splash
No fuel at jets	No petrol in petrol tank Petrol tank breather choked Sudden obstruction in carburettor Water in fuel system
Engine misfires or idles unevenly	
Intermittent spark at spark plug	Ignition leads loose Battery leads loose on terminals Battery earth strap loose on body attachment point Engine earth lead loose Low tension leads on coil loose Low tension lead to distributor loose Dirty or incorrectly gapped plugs Dirty, incorrectly set, or pitted contact breaker points* Tracking across inside of distributor cover Ignition too retarded Faulty coil Slack timing belt
Fuel shortage at engine	Mixture too weak Air leak in carburettor Air leak at inlet manifold to cylinder head, or inlet manifold to carburettor
Lack of power and poor compression	
Mechanical wear	Burnt out valves Sticking or leaking valves Weak or broken valve springs Worn valve guides or stems Worn pistons and piston rings

** Applies only to ignition systems with a mechanical contact breaker*

Chapter 2 Cooling, heating and air conditioning

Refer to Chapter 13 for Specifications and information on later models

Contents

Specifications

System type
Radiator, thermostat, belt-driven pump and electric cooling fan

Radiator cap pressure
0.89 bar (13 lbf/in^2)

Thermostat

Opening temperature:	
Temperate climate	82°C (180°F)
Cold climate	88°C (190°F)
Tropical climate	76.5°C (170°F)
Fully open temperature:	
Temperate climate	95°C (203°F)
Cold climate	100°C (212°F)
Tropical climate	90°C (194°F)

Coolant temperature switch

Operating temperature	90°C (194°F)

Coolant capacity

Manual transmission	5.5 litres (9.7 Imp pts, 5.8 US qts)
Automatic transmission	6.0 litres (10.6 Imp pts, 6.3 US qts)

Drivebelt tension

Deflection is measured with moderate thumb pressure applied at the centre of the belt's longest run. The tension of a new drivebelt should be checked after the vehicle's first operating period.

Component:	Deflection (old belt)	Deflection (new belt)
Alternator	13.0 to 17.0 mm (0.51 to 0.67 in)	10.0 to 14.0 mm (0.39 to 0.55 in)
Compressor	9.0 to 11.0 mm (0.35 to 0.43 in)	7.0 to 9.0 mm (0.28 to 0.35 in)
Power steering pump	7.0 to 9.0 mm (0.28 to 0.35 in)	6.5 to 8.5 mm (0.256 to 0.335 in)

Torque wrench settings

	Nm	lbf ft
Coolant pump bolts	14	10
Thermostat housing cover bolts	11	8

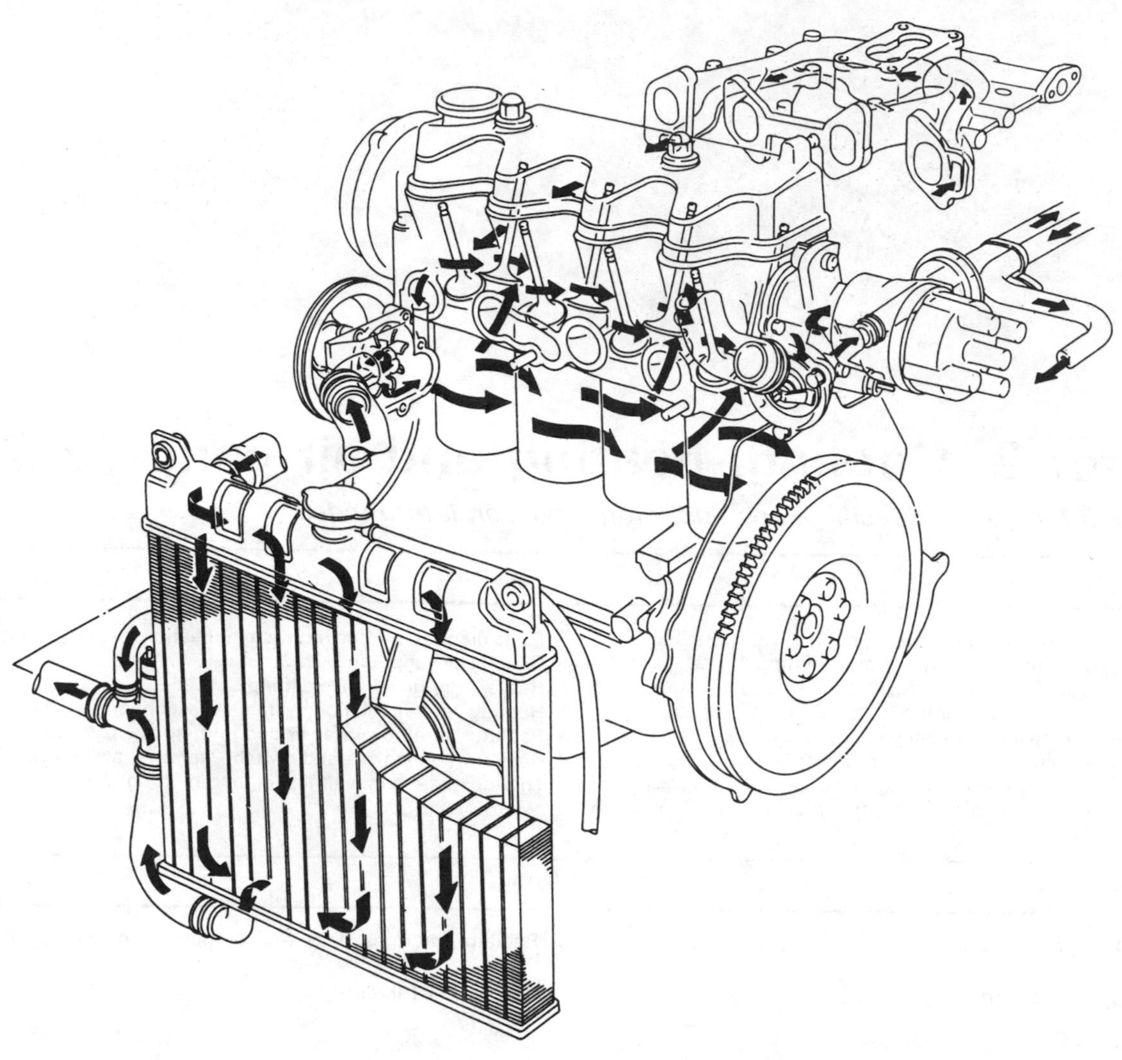

Fig.2.1 Cooling system flow diagram (Sec 1)

1 General description

The cooling system comprises a front-mounted radiator, a belt-driven coolant pump and an electric radiator cooling fan.

Some models have a remotely-sited expansion tank which accepts displaced coolant when the engine is hot. When the engine cools down, excess coolant is drawn back into the radiator, so eliminating the need for regular topping-up.

Coolant from the engine cooling system is used for the vehicle interior heater and also to warm the intake manifold at the base of the carburettor.

2 Cooling system – maintenance

1 Regularly check the condition and security of the cooling system hoses. Renew any which have hardened or are splitting.

2 On vehicles without a coolant expansion tank, check the coolant level in the radiator every week. This should be done when the engine is cold. Remove the radiator cap and check that the coolant level is between 20.0 and 30.0 mm (0.79 and 1.18 in) below the top surface of the header tank. If topping-up is required, use a mixture containing antifreeze made up in similar proportions to the original mixture.

3 If the coolant level is to be checked when the engine is hot, cover the radiator cap with a cloth and turn the cap to its first stop to allow any steam to escape, otherwise there is a risk of scalding.

4 On vehicles which have an expansion tank, check visually that the coolant level in the tank is between the MIN and MAX marks when the engine is cold. Topping-up should very rarely be required. The need for frequent topping-up to the expansion tank will indicate an internal (gasket) or external leak somewhere in the system. Whenever you have to top up the expansion tank, always use an antifreeze mixture made up in silimar proportions to the original coolant.

3 Cooling system – draining, flushing and refilling

1 Preferably drain the cooling system when the engine is cold. Set the heater control to HOT, removo the radiator cap or expansion tank cap and then unscrew the drain tap at the base of the radiator (photo).

2 If the system has been well maintained the coolant should run clear to the last drop, in which case the radiator tap may be closed and the system refilled immediately with fresh antifreeze mixture.

3 If the system has been neglected, and the coolant is badly contaminated with rust and sediment, flush it through by inserting a cold water hose in the radiator filler neck.

4 In severe cases of neglect it may be necessary to remove the radiator, invert it and reverse flush it, or even use a cleaning and descaling fluid in accordance with the manufacturer's instructions.

5 To refill the system on vehicles without an expansion tank, fill the radiator to its specified level and then run the engine for a few minutes with the radiator cap removed. Switch off and top up if necessary. Refit the radiator cap.

6 To refill the system on vehicles with an expansion tank, fill the

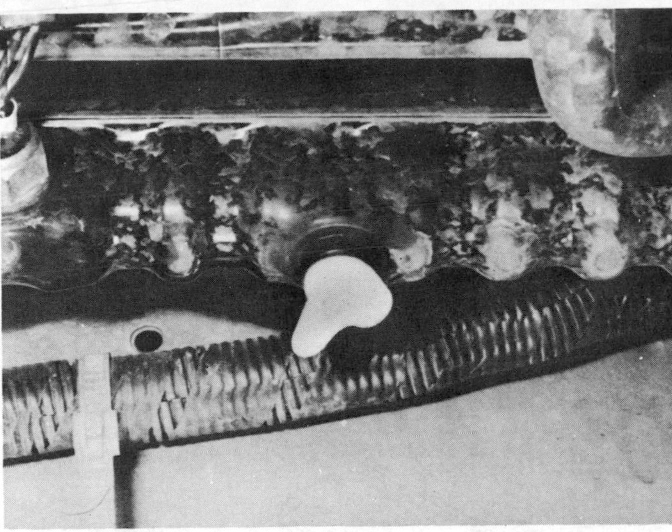

3.1 Radiator drain tap

radiator brim full and fit the cap. Fill the expansion tank to the MAX mark. Run the engine for a few minutes and top up the expansion tank if necessary.
7 A cylinder block drain plug is not fitted.

4 Coolant mixtures

1 It is essential to keep the cooling system filled with antifreeze mixture instead of plain water. Apart from the obvious protection against damage caused by low temperatures, suitable antifreeze liquids contain an inhibitor against corrosion which, of course, works all year round.
2 Antifreeze should be mixed in accordance with the manufacturer's instructions on the container and the proportion of liquid to water should be chosen to meet the local weather conditions although a 50/50 mixture will ensure maximum protection against freezing and corrosion.
3 Before filling the system with antifreeze mixture check that all the hoses are in sound condition and that all hose clips are tight. Antifreeze has a searching action and will leak more readily than plain water.
4 Renew the coolant mixture every 2 years, as the inhibitor in the solution will by then be of little value. When it is necessary to top up the cooling system, use a mixture of the same strength as that in the system.
5 Always buy a top quality antifreeze of glycol base. Other cheaper antifreeze products usually contain chemicals which evaporate during service and soon provide little protection.
6 If the car is operating in climatic conditions which do not require antifreeze, always use a corrosion inhibitor to prevent corrosion of the system, particularly its light alloy content.

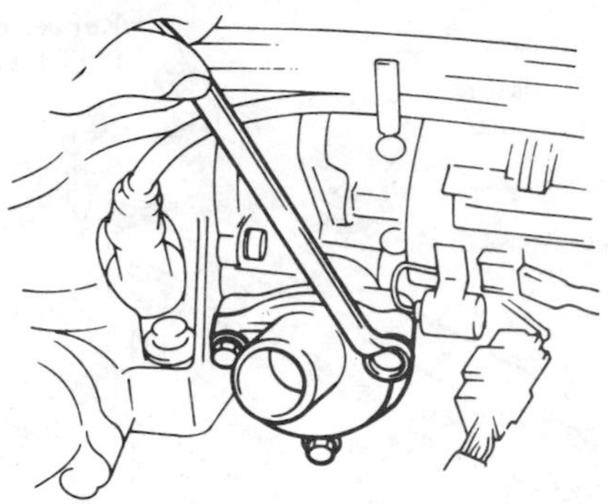

Fig. 2.2 Unscrewing thermostat housing cover bolts (Sec 5)

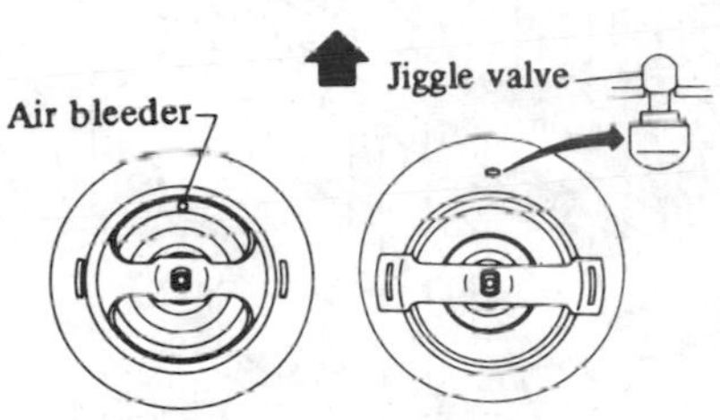

Fig. 2.3 Location of thermostat bleed hole and jiggle valve (Sec 5)

5 Thermostat – removal, testing and refitting

1 Drain sufficient coolant (2 litres) to bring the coolant level below the thermostat housing.
2 Disconnect the coolant hose from the thermostat housing (photo).
3 On North American models, release the exhaust air injection tube clamp bolts.
4 Unbolt and remove the thermostat housing cover, discard the gasket and withdraw the thermostat (photo). If the thermostat is stuck tight, do not lever it out by inserting a screwdriver under its bridge piece, but cut around the edge of its rim using a sharp knife.
5 To check the thermostat, suspend it in water at a temperature near that of the opening temperature of the unit. Observe that it opens fully as the temperature of the water is increased. Allow the thermostat to cool, when it should be fully closed.
6 If a thermostat is seized in the closed position leave it out until a replacement can be obtained.
7 Refit the thermostat into a clean seat with its air bleed hole or jiggle pin uppermost. Use a new gasket, fit the cover (photo) and tighten the bolts securely, but do not overtighten them.
8 Reconnect the hose and refill the cooling system.

5.2 Hose at thermostat housing

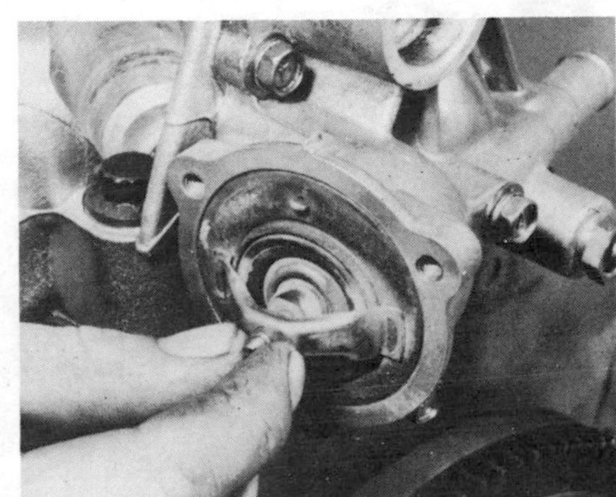

5.4 Removing thermostat

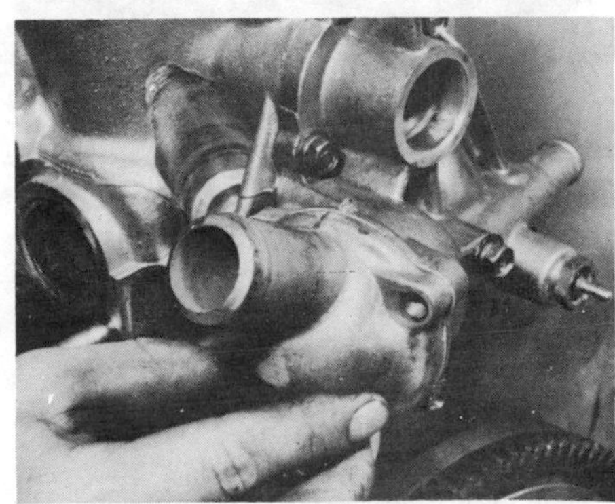

5.7 Thermostat housing cover

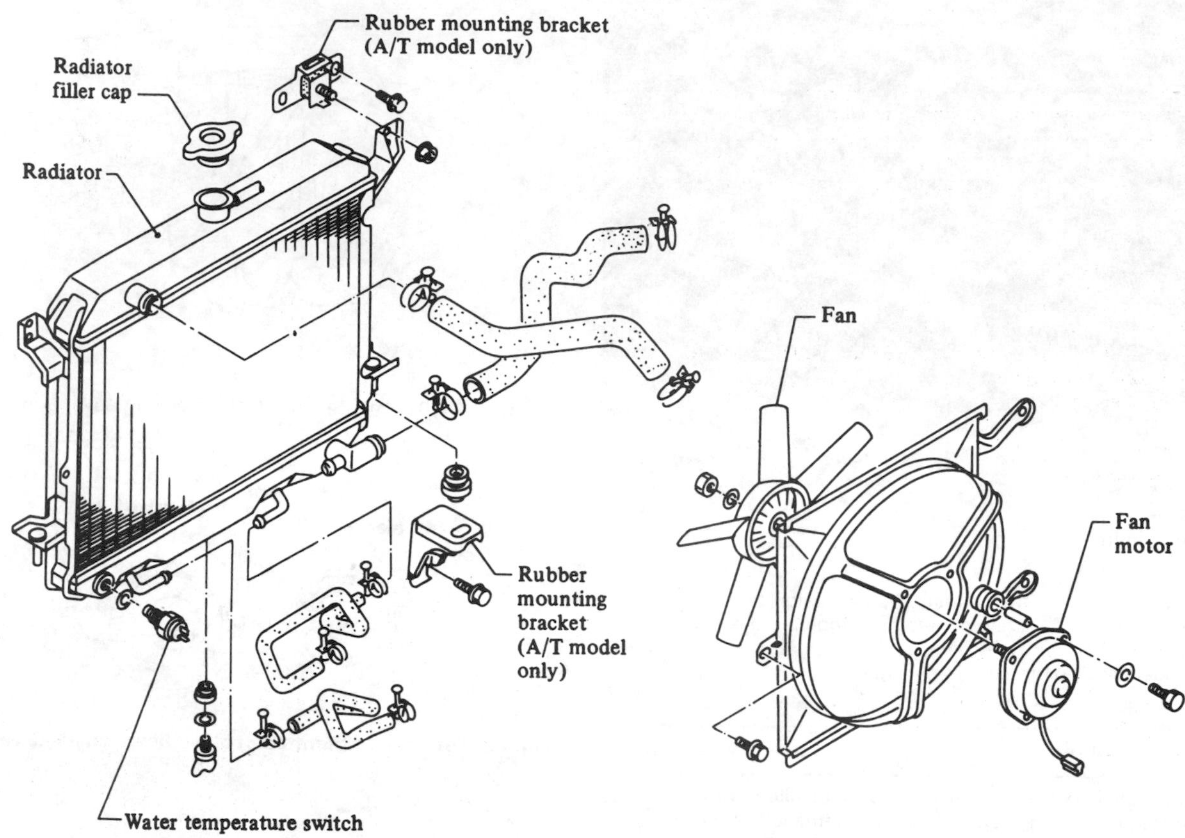

Fig. 2.4 Radiator and fan components (Sec 6)

6 Radiator cooling fan and switch – removal and refitting

Fan

1 Open the bonnet

2 Disconnect the leads from the fan motor.

3 Unbolt the fan mounting struts and lift the assembly from the engine compartment.

Switch

4 The thermostatic switch can only be unscrewed from the base of the radiator if the cooling system is drained first.

5 Disconnect the switch leads and unscrew the switch.

6 The switch can be tested using a simple test bulb and battery if it is lowered into water and the temperature raised to the specified operational level.

7 Refitting is a reversal of removal, use a new sealing washer under the radiator switch.

7 Radiator – removal, repair and refitting

1 Drain the cooling system, as described in Section 3. Retain the coolant if required for further use.

2 Disconnect the radiator hoses (photo).

3 Disconnect the leads from the thermostatic switch at the base of the radiator and from the fan.

4 On vehicles equipped with automatic transmission, disconnect the fluid cooler lines from the radiator and plug them.

5 Unbolt the radiator top and side mountings (photo) and lift the radiator from the engine compartment, complete with cooling fan (photo).

6 If the radiator was removed because of a leak, it is best to leave its repair to the professional radiator repairer, although it may be possible to use fibreglass or a similar product to seal it.

7 Loss of coolant may sometimes be caused by a defective radiator pressure cap. Your dealer can test this for you.

7.2 Radiator lower hose and coolant tube connection

7.5A Unscrewing radiator mounting bolt

7.5B Removing radiator/fan assembly

8 Refitting is a reversal of removal, fill the cooling system as described in Section 3.

8 Drivebelts – removal, refitting and tensioning

1 The number of drivebelts fitted and their configuration will depend upon the units with which the particular vehicle is equipped. These include:

Power steering
Air conditioning

2 An alternator is fitted to all models.
3 If the vehicle is equipped with air conditioning and power steering then the compressor belt will have to be removed first, followed by the one for the power steering pump, in order to be able to reach the inner belt which drives the alternator.

Compressor belt

4 Release the idler pulley locknut and the adjuster nuts on the eye bolt.
5 Fully slacken the adjustment until the belt can be slipped off the pulley.
6 Fit the belt and tension in accordance with the table in Specifications.

Power steering pump belt

7 Remove the air conditioner compressor belt (if fitted) and then release the power steering pump bracket lockbolt. Turn the adjuster bolt to fully slacken the belt and then slip it off the pulley.
8 Fit the belt and tension in accordance with the table in Specifications.

Alternator belt

9 Remove the air conditioner compressor and power steering pump drivebelts, as previously described.
10 Release the alternator mounting and adjuster link bolts and push the alternator in towards the engine until the belt can be slipped off the pulleys.
11 Fit the belt and tension in accordance with the table in Specifications.

General

12 Never overtension a drivebelt, or the coolant pump or alternator bearings may be damaged.

9 Coolant temperature switch and gauge

1 The coolant temperature switch can only be removed from its thermostat housing location after the cooling system has been partially drained (2.0 litres).
2 To test a coolant temperature switch requires the use of an ohmmeter, so this is a job best left to your dealer or auto-electrician.
3 Faulty indication of the temperature gauge may be caused by the switch-to-gauge lead earthing due to damaged insulation, check this first.
4 Immediate indication of maximum temperature when the ignition is switched on will be due to a fault in either the gauge or the switch.

10 Coolant pump – removal and refitting

1 The need for renewal of a coolant pump will normally be due to leakage from around the driving spindle, or noisy operation, indicating worn bearings.
2 Drain the cooling system, as described in Section 3. Disconnect the coolant hose from the pump (photo).
3 Remove the alternator drivebelt, see Section 8.
4 Unbolt and remove the coolant pump pulley bolts. To hold the pulley from rotating place a bar between two of the bolt heads which are not being unscrewed (photo).

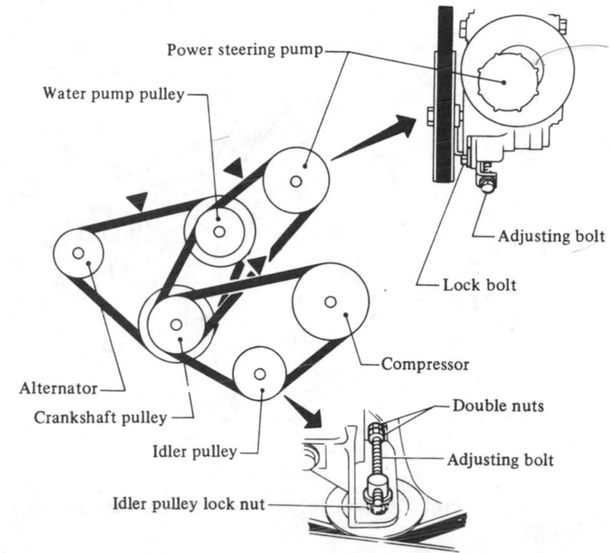

Fig. 2.5 Drivebelt arrangement (Sec 8)

10.2 Hose connection at coolant pump

10.4 Coolant pump pulley

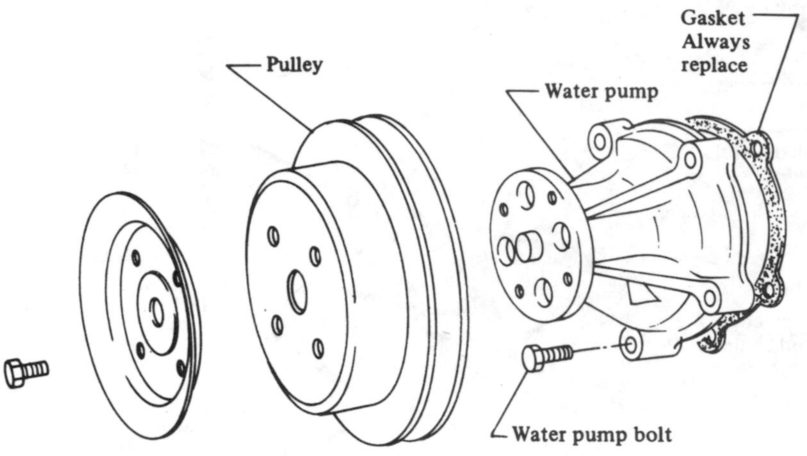

Fig. 2.6 Coolant pump components (Sec 10)

Fig. 2.7 Unscrewing coolant pump bolts (Sec 10)

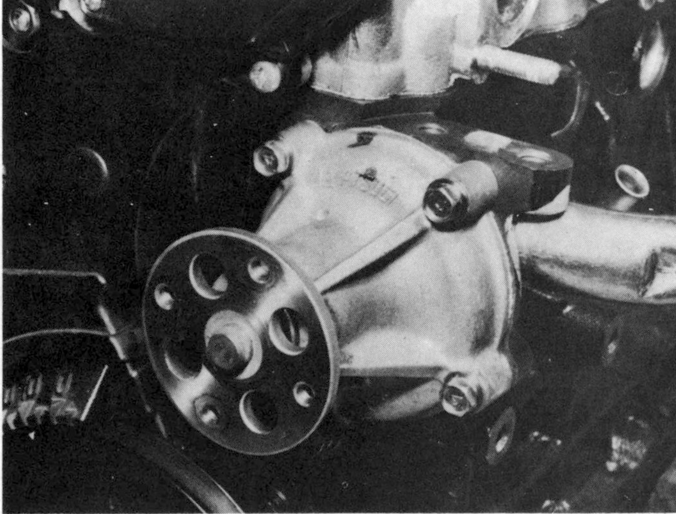

10.5A Coolant pump with pulley removed

10.5B Coolant pump gasket

5 Unbolt and remove the coolant pump and discard the gasket (photos).

6 The coolant pump cannot be overhauled, as new seals and internal components are not available. A new pump will therefore have to be obtained if the original one is worn or leaking.

7 Refitting is a reversal of removal, but use a new gasket and tighten the bolts to the specified torque.

8 Tension the drivebelts (Section 8).

9 Refill the cooling system.

11 Heating and ventilation system – description

1 The heater incorporates a matrix which is fed with hot coolant from the engine cooling system (photo).

2 A booster (blower) is used to force air through the matrix when the vehicle is stationary or moving too slowly for the normal ram effect of the air to be available.

3 Temperature levels and airflow are controlled from levers on a facia-mounted control panel. Heated air can be supplied to the vehicle interior through centre or side ducts, or to the windscreen for demisting or defrosting purposes.

4 Fresh air ventilation is supplied through facia-mounted grilles, air being drawn in through the grille at the base of the windscreen. Stale

11.1 Heater hose connections at bulkhead

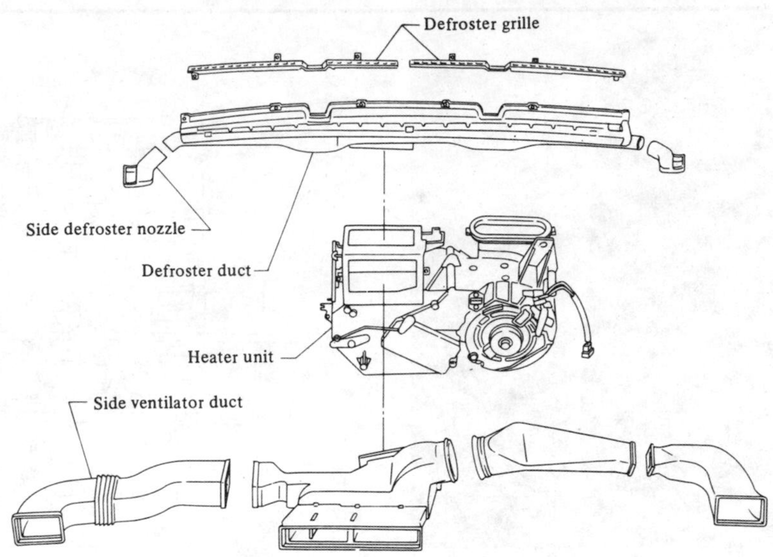

Fig. 2.8 Heater – LHD models (Sec 11)

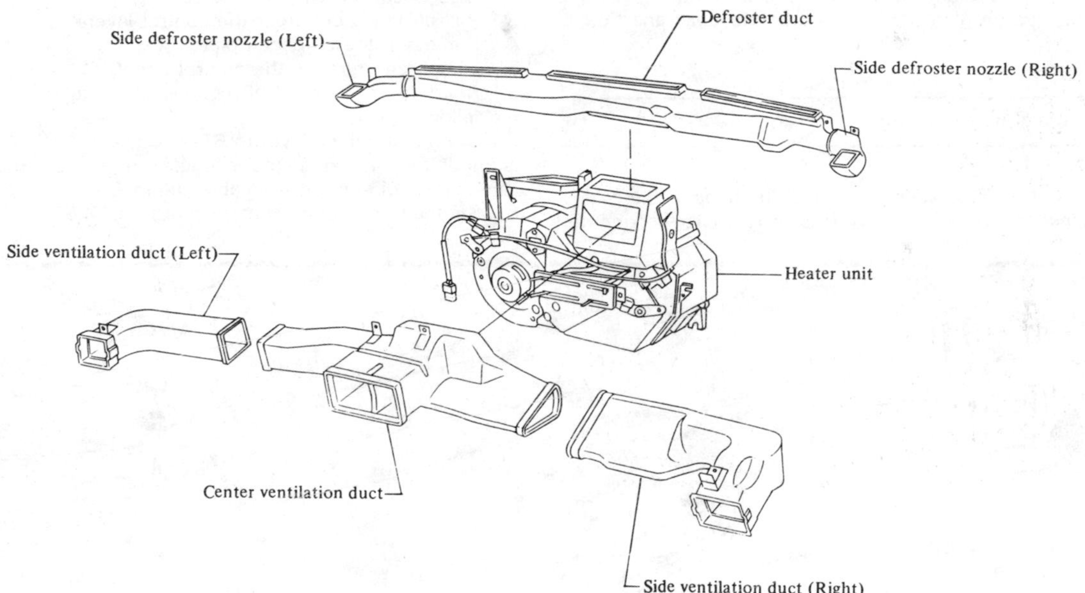

Fig. 2.9 Heater – RHD models (Sec 11)

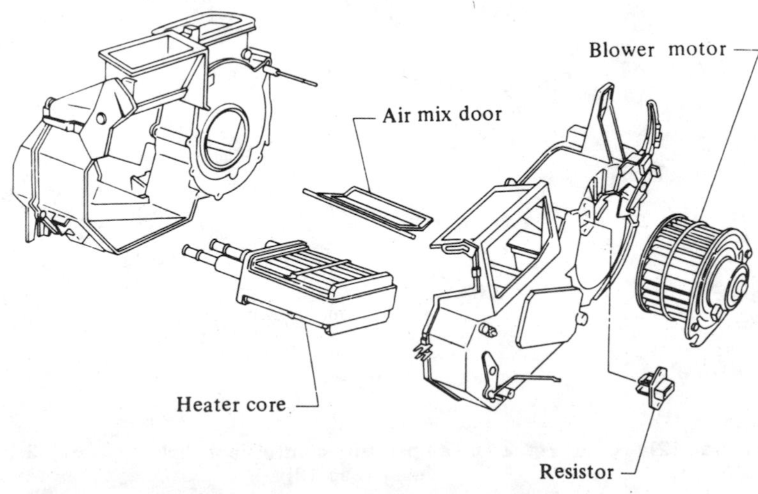

Fig. 2.10 Components of the heater assembly (Sec 11)

11.4 Stale air exhaust (Saloon and Estate)

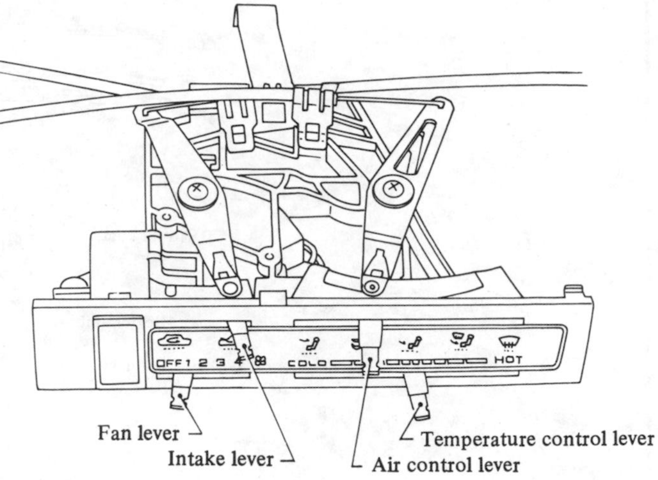

Fig. 2.11 Heater control assembly (Sec 12)

air is exhausted through grilles just forward of the rear lamp clusters on the rear corners of Saloon and Estate versions (photo), or from outlets at the rear quarter panels or pillars on Hatchback and Coupe models.

12 Heater – removal and refitting

Control panel

1 Release the control cable clamps and slip the ends of the cables from the pivot pins on the airflow flaps. It is worthwhile marking the position of the clamps in relation to the cables for ease of refitting.

2 Disconnect the wiring harness plug.

3 Pull off the knobs from the control levers.

4 Remove the escutcheon plate.

5 Unbolt and remove the control panel.

6 Refitting is a reversal of removal, but adjust the control cables in the following way.

7 Set the air intake lever to RECIRC (MAX A/C if an air conditioner is fitted). Set the flap at the recirculation position. Engage the control cable on its pin and fit the cable clamp.

8 Set the temperature control lever to MAX COLD. Move the air mix

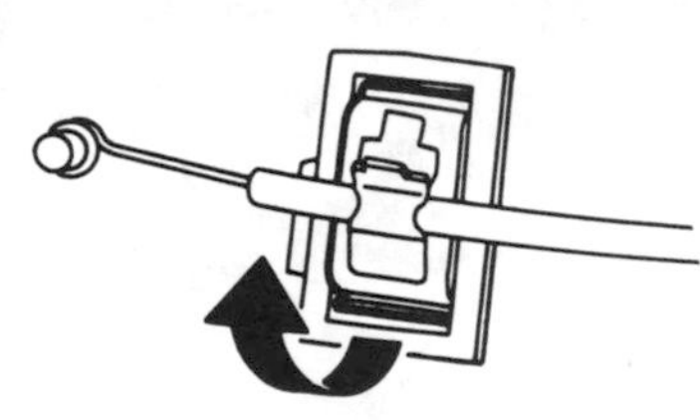

Fig. 2.12 Heater outer cable clamp (Sec 12)

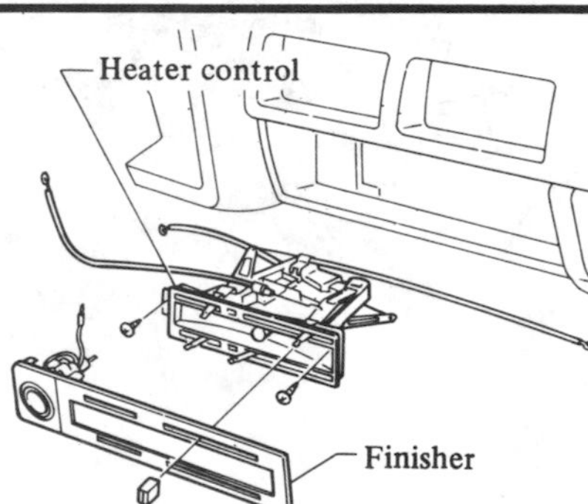

Fig. 2.13 Heater control – B11 models (Sec 12)

Fig. 2.14 Heater control – N12 models (Sec 12)

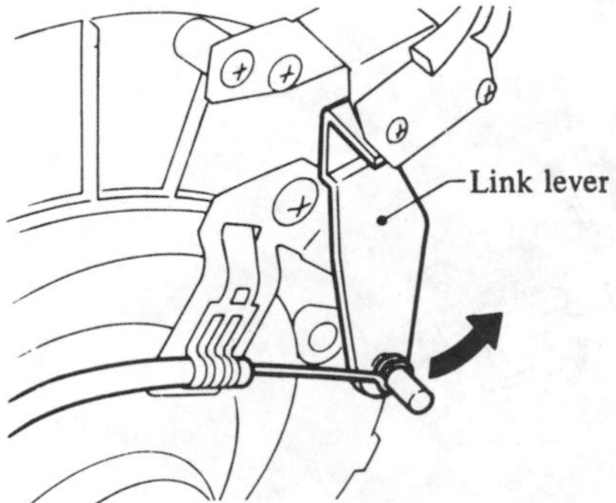

Fig. 2.15 Air intake link lever (Sec 12)

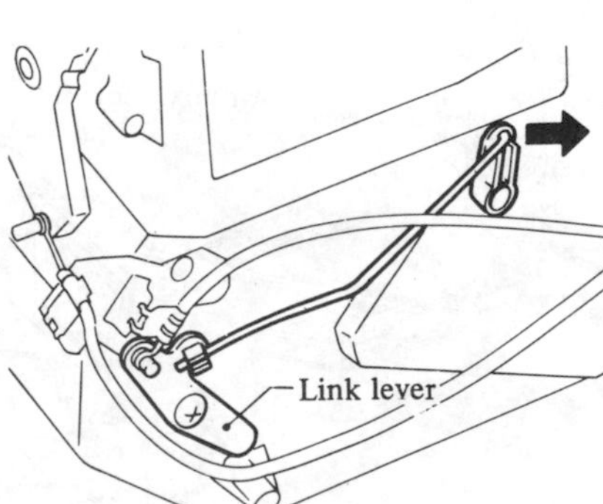

Fig. 2.16 Temperature control cable link lever (Sec 12)

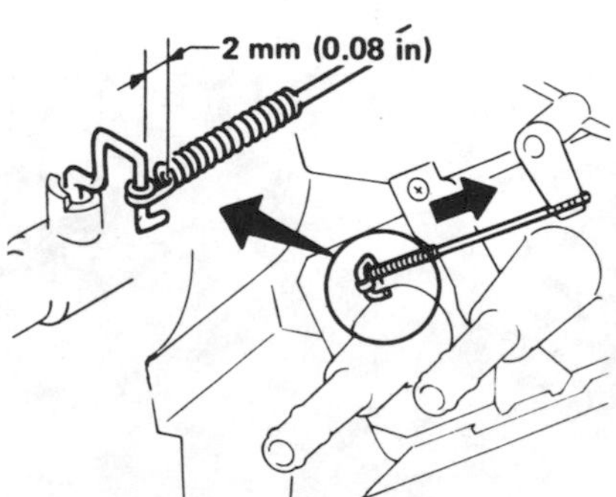

Fig. 2.17 Setting the coolant valve control rod (Sec 12)

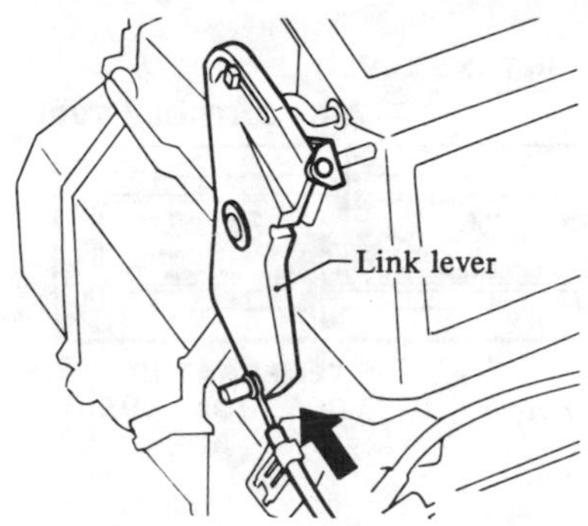

Fig. 2.18 Air control link lever (Sec 12)

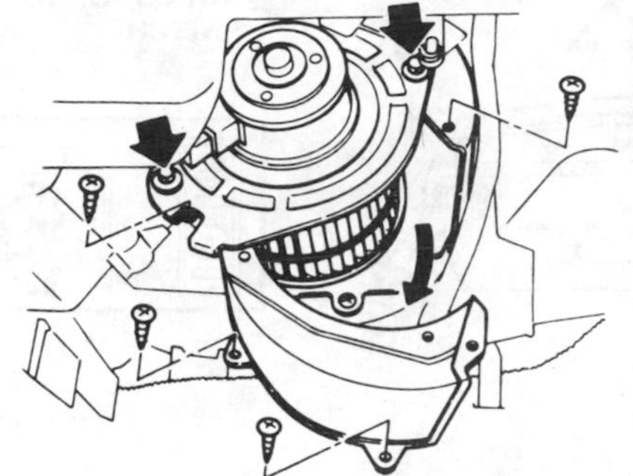

Fig. 2.19 Blower motor removal (Sec 12)

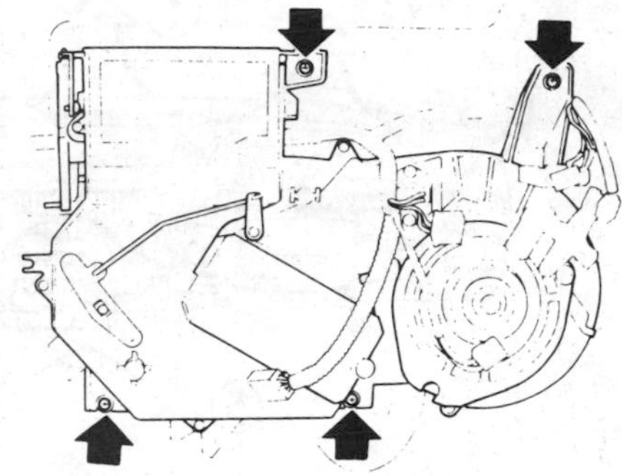

Fig. 2.20 Heater mounting screws (Sec 12)

flap lever in the direction of the arrow (Fig. 2.16) and connect the control rod to the link lever. Hold these positions, engage the control cable with its pin and then clamp the outer cable.

9 Pull the control rod of the coolant valve in the direction of the arrow (Fig. 2.17) until there is a clearance of 2.0 mm (0.08 in) between the end of the rod and the link lever. Connect the rod to the flap lever.

10 Set the air control lever in the DEF position, then move the link lever in the direction of the arrow (Fig. 2.18). Connect the end of the control cable to the link lever and then clamp the outer cable.

Blower motor

11 Remove the lower cover from the facia panel (see Chapter 12).
12 Disconnect the blower motor wiring harness.
13 Extract the screws from the heater lower casing and pull the casing downwards.
14 Extract the blower motor mounting screws and remove the motor. Refitting is a reversal of removal.

Heater (complete unit)

15 Drain the cooling system, as described in Section 3.
16 Disconnect the heater hoses within the engine compartment.
17 Refer to Chapter 10 and remove the instrument panel.
18 Remove the heater control panel, as described earlier in this Section. Unscrew the heater mounting bolts.
19 Withdraw the heater assembly, taking care to protect the carpets against coolant spillage.
20 Refitting is a reversal of removal. Refill the cooling system as described in Section 3.

13 Air conditioner – operation and precautions

1 An air conditioner with combined heater is an option on certain models.

2 The refrigerant fluid used in the system is odourless and non-poisonous. It is not corrosive nor inflammable.

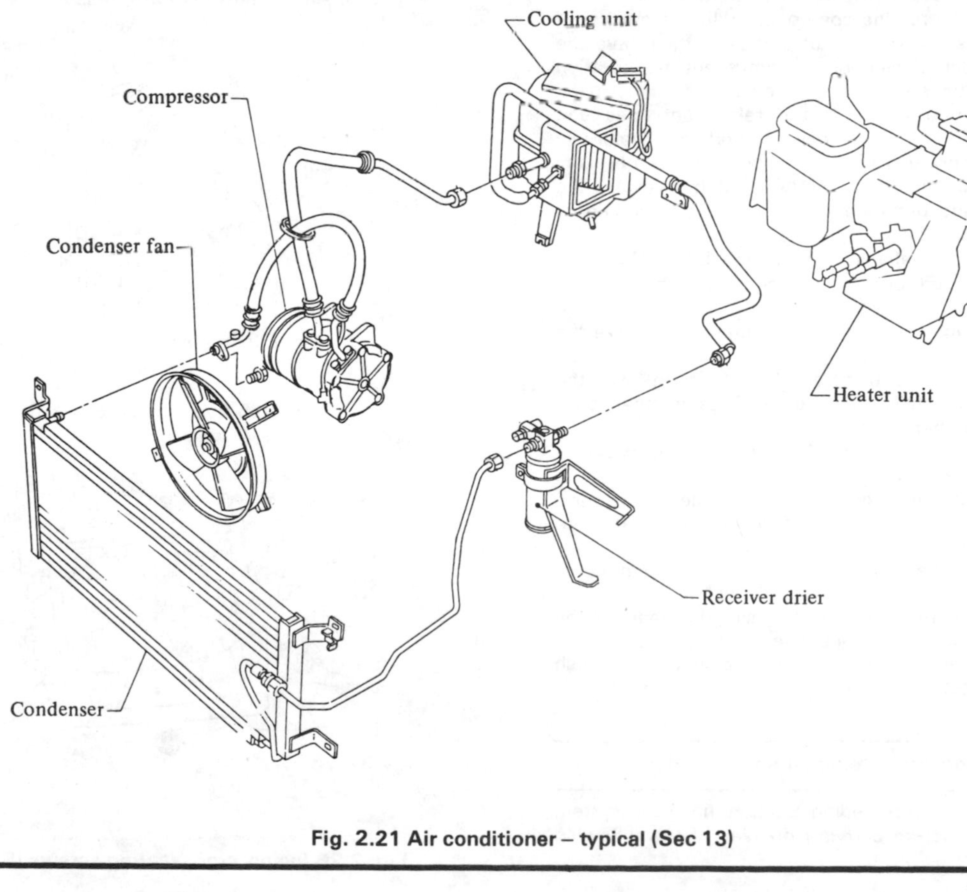

Cooling unit
Compressor
Condenser fan
Heater unit
Receiver drier
Condenser

Fig. 2.21 Air conditioner – typical (Sec 13)

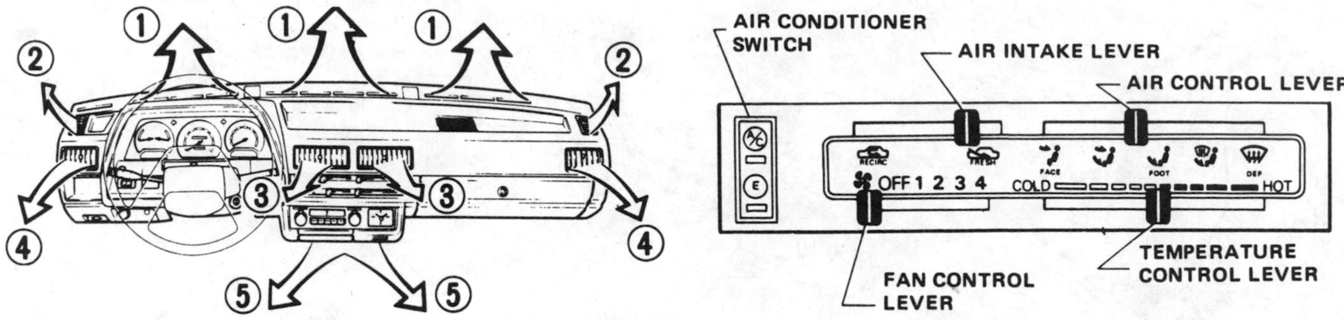

Fig. 2.22 Air conditioner control panel (Sec 13)

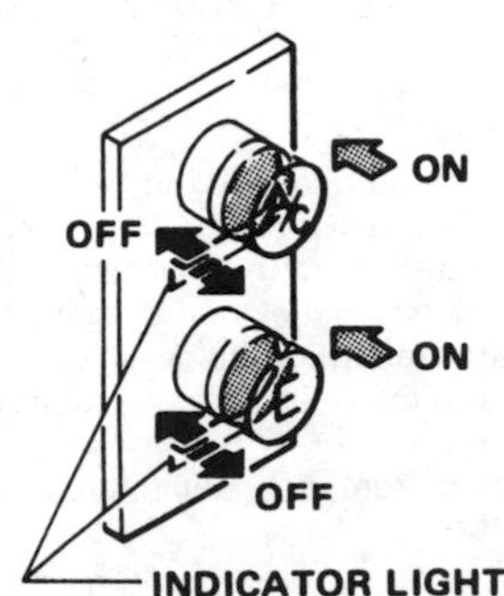

Fig. 2.23 Air conditioner ON/OFF and MAX/ECONOMY switches (Sec 13)

3 Leaks are not dangerous unless the fluid or vapour comes into contact with a naked flame when a poison gas is created.

4 Refrigerant fluid is dangerous to the eyes and skin and contact should be avoided.

5 If overhaul operations require the removal of any part of the system, try and move the obstructing component within the limits of its flexible connecting hoses, if this is not sufficient then have the system discharged by your dealer or a competent refrigeration engineer. He should also be employed to recharge the system on completion. It is most important that the refrigerant lines and components are kept free from internal moisture and your dealer will use a vacuum pump to ensure this after the circuit has been broken.

6 To operate the air conditioner, push the A/C switch to ON and the fan control lever to a setting between 1 and 4. The air conditioner warning lamp will come on.

7 Two further settings are available – MAX and ECONOMY. The MAX setting should be selected for rapid cooling in very hot or humid conditions.

8 To obtain the best results from your air conditioner, observe the following points.

9 If the vehicle has been parked in the sun for a long time with the windows closed, open them fully for two or three minutes after switching on the air conditioner.

10 Under normal conditions, keep all windows and ventilators closed when the air conditioner is working.

11 During the summer, if the air conditioner has not been used for a week, turn the fan control lever on and off several times at three second intervals with the engine idling.

12 During the winter, run the system for ten minutes at monthly intervals.

13 If the vehicle is being steam cleaned, avoid using the steam on the system components, particularly the condenser.

14 Periodically brush or hose flies and dirt from the condenser which might otherwise restrict its airflow.

14 Air conditioner components – removal and refitting

1 As already explained in the preceding Section, have the system discharged by your dealer before carrying out any of the following operations.

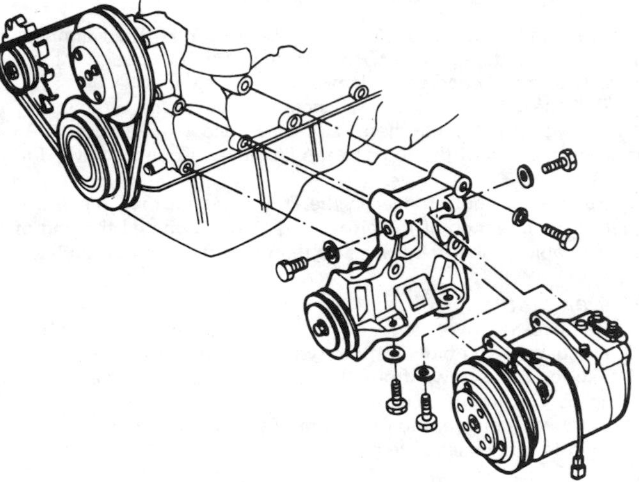

Fig. 2.24 Air conditioner compressor (Sec 14)

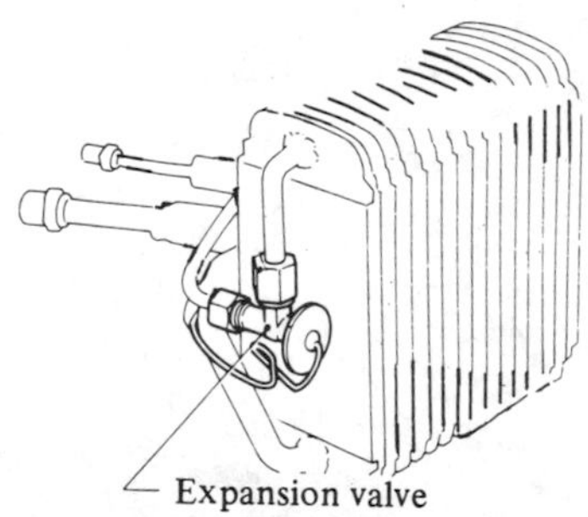

Fig. 2.25 Evaporator (Sec 14)

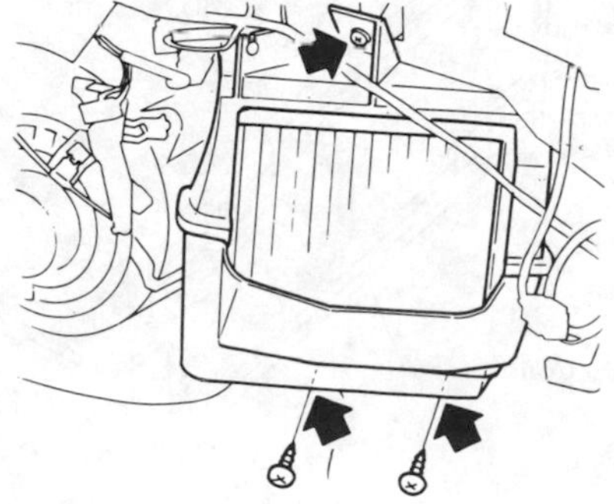

Fig. 2.26 Evaporator securing screws (Sec 14)

Switch ①
Switch ②
Flap valve
control cable
Link lever

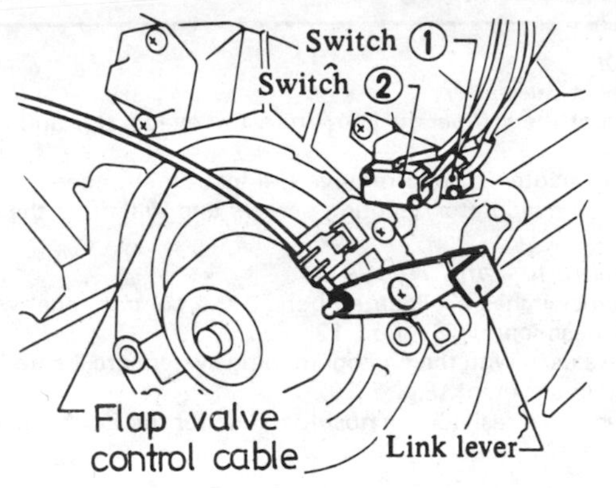

Fig. 2.27 Air conditioner microswitch arrangement (Sec 14)

Intake lever
Microswitch-2
Mircoswitch-1
Link lever

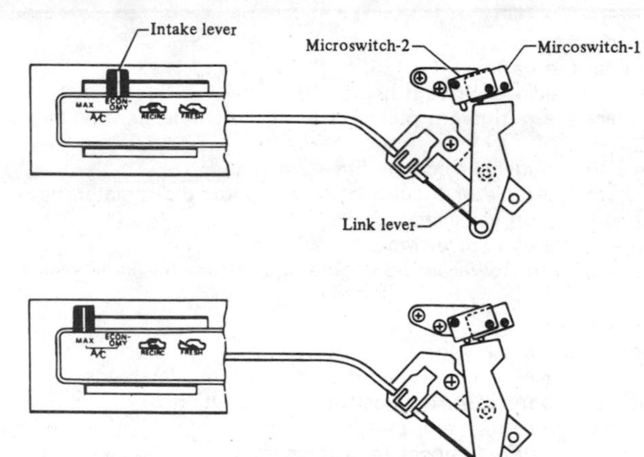

Fig. 2.28 Microswitch details (Sec 14)

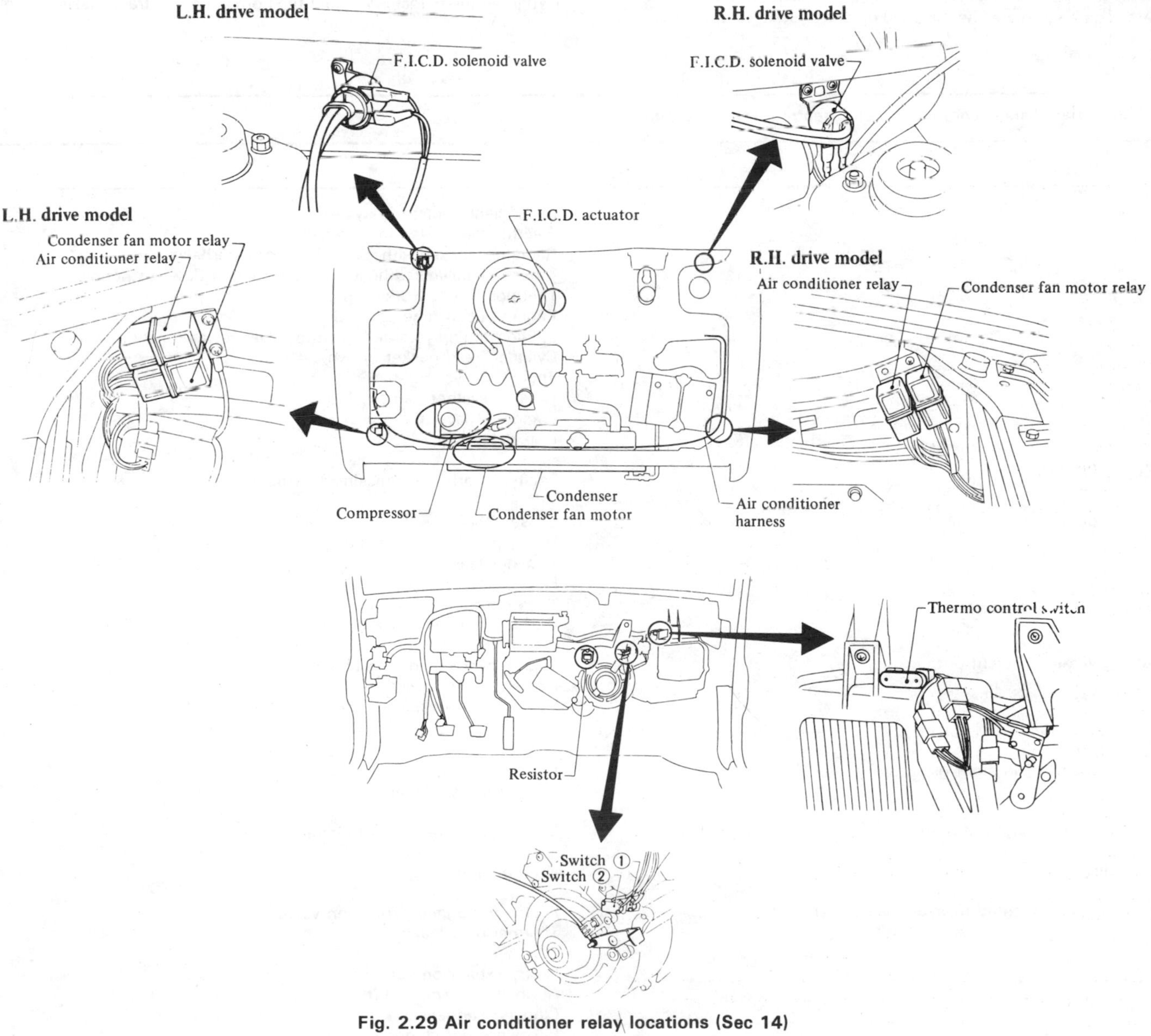

L.H. drive model
F.I.C.D. solenoid valve
R.H. drive model
F.I.C.D. solenoid valve
L.H. drive model
Condenser fan motor relay
Air conditioner relay
F.I.C.D. actuator
R.H. drive model
Air conditioner relay
Condenser fan motor relay
Compressor
Condenser
Condenser fan motor
Air conditioner
harness
Thermo control switch
Resistor
Switch ①
Switch ②

Fig. 2.29 Air conditioner relay locations (Sec 14)

FICD Fast idle control device

Condenser

2 Disconnect the battery.
3 Remove the radiator grille (Chapter 12).
4 Disconnect the refrigerant pipelines from the condenser and cap them.
5 Remove the condenser cooling fan.
6 Disconnect the radiator mountings and support the radiator, not allowing it to hang on its hoses.
7 Disconnect the condenser mountings.
8 Push the radiator towards the engine and lift out the condenser.

Compressor

9 Disconnect the battery.
10 Raise the front of the vehicle and support it on axle stands.
11 Remove the compressor drivebelt (refer to Section 8).
12 Disconnect the compressor clutch harness.
13 Disconnect the flexible hoses from the compressor and cap them.
14 Remove the compressor after disconnecting its mounting and adjuster bolts.
15 Keep the compressor in its 'in car' attitude, otherwise oil could enter the low pressure chambers. Should this happen, the compressor pulley must be turned through several revolutions when refitted to the vehicle in order to expel the oil. Failure to do this could result in internal damage once the air conditioning system is operated.

Evaporator

16 Disconnect the battery.
17 Disconnect the refrigerant lines from the evaporator and cap the pipes.
18 Refer to Chapter 10 and remove the instrument panel.
19 Extract the evaporator securing screws and withdraw the unit.

Control switches and relays

20 The microswitches are located behind the control panel which is removed as described in Section 12.
21 The relays used with the air conditioning system are located within the engine compartment (Fig. 2.29).
22 Switches and a resistor are positioned under the facia panel inside the vehicle.

Refitting

23 Refitting of all components is a reversal of removal, but observe the following points.
24 Use new O-ring seals when reconnecting pipelines and hoses.
25 Once the compressor is refitted with the drivebelt correctly tensioned, release the bolts which secure the flexible mounting knuckles to the engine front left and the rear mounting brackets. Retighten them again with just the normal engine/transmission weight on them.

15 Fault diagnosis – cooling system, heating and air conditioning

Symptom	Reason(s)
Overheating	Insufficient coolant in system Electric cooling fan inoperative Radiator blocked either internally or externally Kinked or collapsed hose causing coolant flow restriction Thermostat not working properly Engine out of tune Ignition timing retarded or auto-advance malfunction Cylinder head gasket blown Engine not yet run-in Exhaust system partially blocked Engine oil level too low Brakes binding
Engine running too cool	Faulty, incorrect or missing thermostat
Loss of coolant	Loose hose clips Hoses perished or leaking Radiator leaking Filler/pressure cap defective Blown cylinder head gasket Cracked cylinder block or head
Heater gives insufficient output	Engine overcooled (see above) Heater matrix blocked Heater controls maladjusted or broken
Air conditioner	
Bubbles observed in sight glass of receiver drier	Leak in system Low refrigerant level
Mist observed in sight glass of receiver drier	Major leak in refrigerant circuit
No cooling	No refrigerant
Expansion valve frosted over on evaporator	Faulty or clogged expansion valve Thermal bulb leaking
Insufficient cooling	Faulty expansion valve Air in refrigerant circuit Clogged condenser Receiver drier clogged Faulty compressor Compressor overfilled with oil

Chapter 3 Fuel and emission control systems

Refer to Chapter 13 for Specifications and information on later models

Contents

Specifications

General

System type	Rear-mounted fuel tank, mechanical fuel pump, dual barrel downdraught carburettor. Emission control system
Fuel tank capacity	50.0 litres (11.0 Imp gal, 13.25 US gal)
Fuel octane:	
Except N America:	
High compression	97 RON
Low compression	88 RON
N America (unleaded)	91 RON
Fuel pump pressure	0.167 to 0.235 bar (2.4 to 3.4 lbf/in^2)

Carburettor

Type	Nikki dual barrel downdraught

All models except N America

Idle speed:	
Manual transmission	650 to 750 rpm
Automatic transmission (in N)	700 to 800 rpm
Idle mixture CO content in exhaust gas	1.0 to 2.0%
Fast idle (automatic choke):	
Manual transmission:	
E13 engine	1900 to 2300 rpm
E15 engine	2000 to 2400 rpm
Automatic transmission:	
E15 engine	2200 to 2600 rpm
Dashpot (automatic transmission):	
Dashpot in contact with stop lever	
Engine speed:	
E13 engine	1700 to 2100 rpm
E15 engine	1800 to 2200 rpm

N American models

Idle speed:	
All manual transmission models except MPG	700 to 800 rpm
MPG models	650 to 750 rpm
Automatic transmission (in D)	600 to 700 rpm
Idle mixture CO content in exhaust gas	1.0 to 3.0%
Fast idle (automatic choke):	
On 2nd step of cam	
E15 engine (MPG models)	2400 to 3200 rpm
E16 engine (USA):	
Manual	2400 to 3200 rpm
Automatic	2700 to 3500 rpm
E16 engine (California):	
Manual	2600 to 3400 rpm
Automatic	2900 to 3700 rpm
E16 engine (Canada):	
Manual	1900 to 2700 rpm
Automatic	2400 to 3200 rpm
Dashpot (automatic transmission):	
Dashpot in contact with stop lever	
Engine speed (Canadian models)	2300 to 2500 rpm

Accelerator pump

Fuel ejected per stroke	0.3 to 0.5 cc (0.018 to 0.031 cu in)
Stroke limiter gap (US models)	1.07 to 1.47 mm (0.0421 to 0.0579 in)

Torque wrench settings

	Nm	lbf ft
Solenoid fuel cut-off valve	22	16
Fuel pump nuts	12	9
Manifold nuts	20	15
Thermal vacuum valve	22	16
Neutral switch	22	16
Catalytic converter end flange bolts	40	30
Converter shield bolts	8	6
Carburettor mounting nuts	20	15
Fuel tank mounting bolts	40	30
Exhaust downpipe to manifold	24	18

1 General description

The fuel system includes a temperature-controlled air cleaner, a fuel pump actuated by a cam on the engine jack shaft and a dual barrel carburettor.

The fuel tank is mounted at the rear of the vehicle.

The carburettor may be of manual or automatic choke type, depending upon vehicle model and operating territory.

All models have emission control systems, but those destined for operation in N America have a very comprehensive arrangement with modified carburettors and other components.

2 Air cleaner – servicing, removal and refitting

1 At the intervals specified in Routine Maintenance remove the air cleaner cover, take out the air cleaner element and discard it (photos).

2 Wipe out the interior of the air cleaner casing, fit a new element and replace the cover so that the arrows are in alignment (photo).

3 On North American models, two additional filter elements are located within the air cleaner casing, these include one for the crankcase PCV intake and one for the air induction valve (refer to Section 16).

4 Depending upon the model, the air cleaner may be fitted with one of the following devices:

Idle compensator (photo). This is basically a thermostatic valve which at high under-bonnet temperatures when the engine is idling admits extra air to weaken the excessively rich mixture. The idle compensator can be assumed to be functioning correctly if a distinct hiss can be heard when it opens.

Temperature sensor. This is used to monitor the temperature of the intake air.

Air control valve. A flap valve to vary the source of intake air, either hot from around the exhaust manifold or cold from the front of the engine compartment. Its operation may be checked by using a mirror

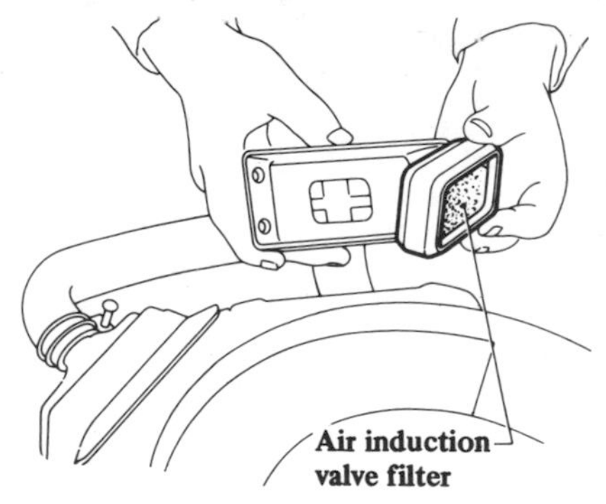

Fig. 3.1 Air induction valve filter (Sec 2)

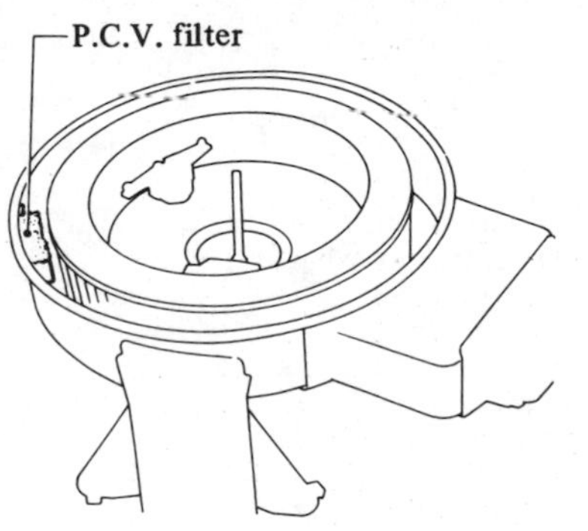

Fig. 3.2 Crankcase ventilation filter (Sec 2)

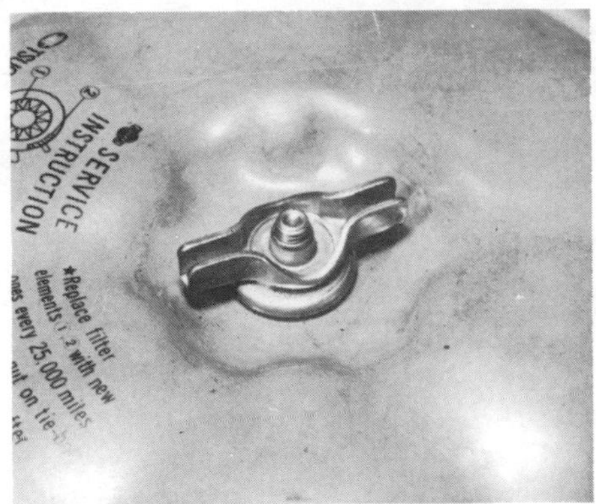

SERVICE INSTRUCTION
★Replace filter elements
every 25,000 miles
2.1A Air cleaner cover wing nut

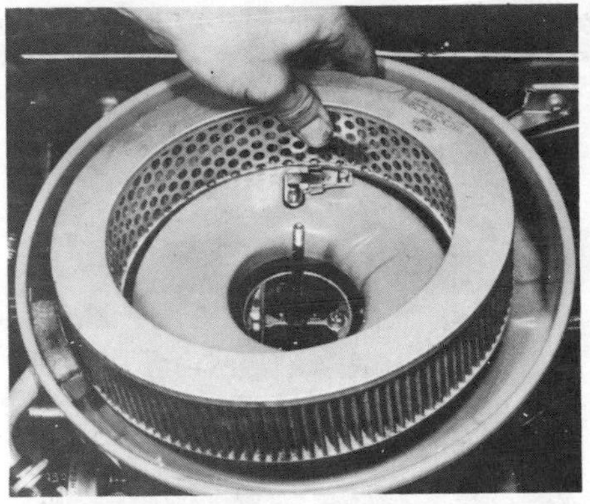

2.1B Removing air cleaner element

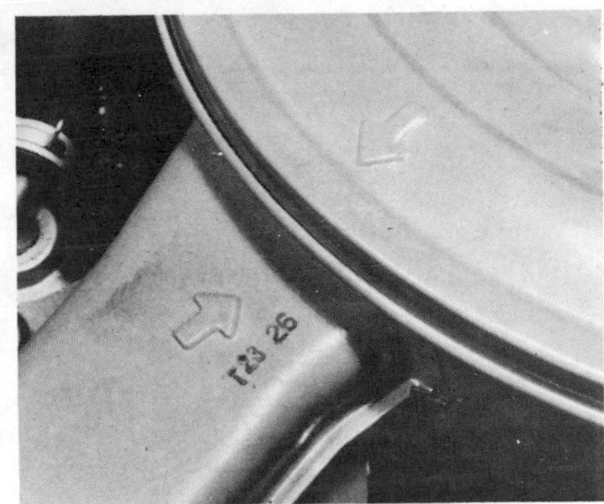

T23 26
2.2 Air cleaner alignment arrows

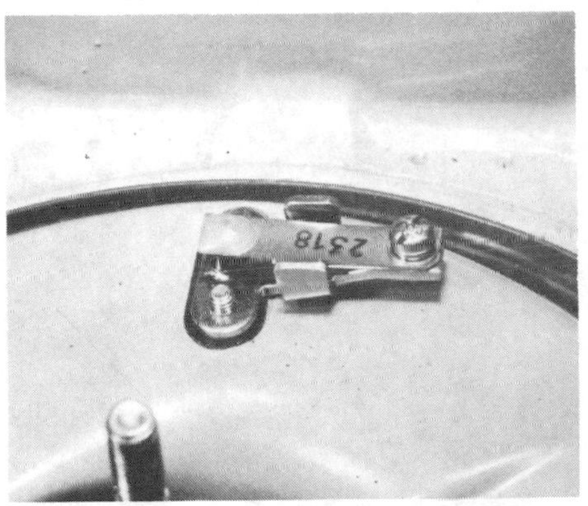

2518
2.4 Air cleaner idle compensator

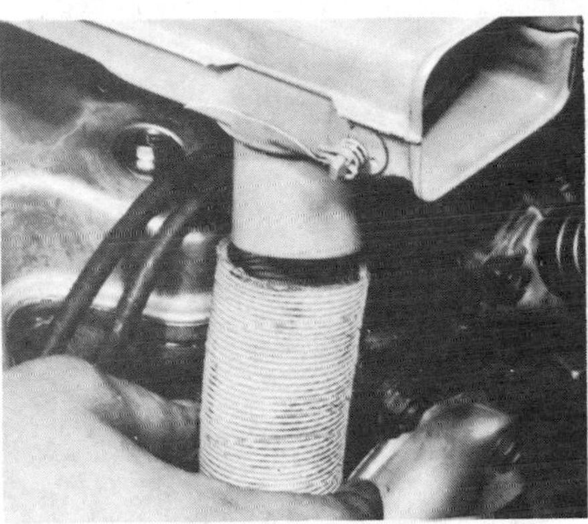

2.8 Air cleaner hot air duct

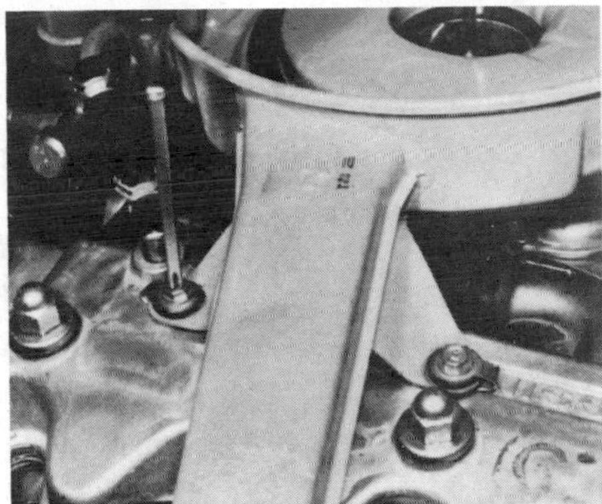

2.9 Air cleaner mounting screws

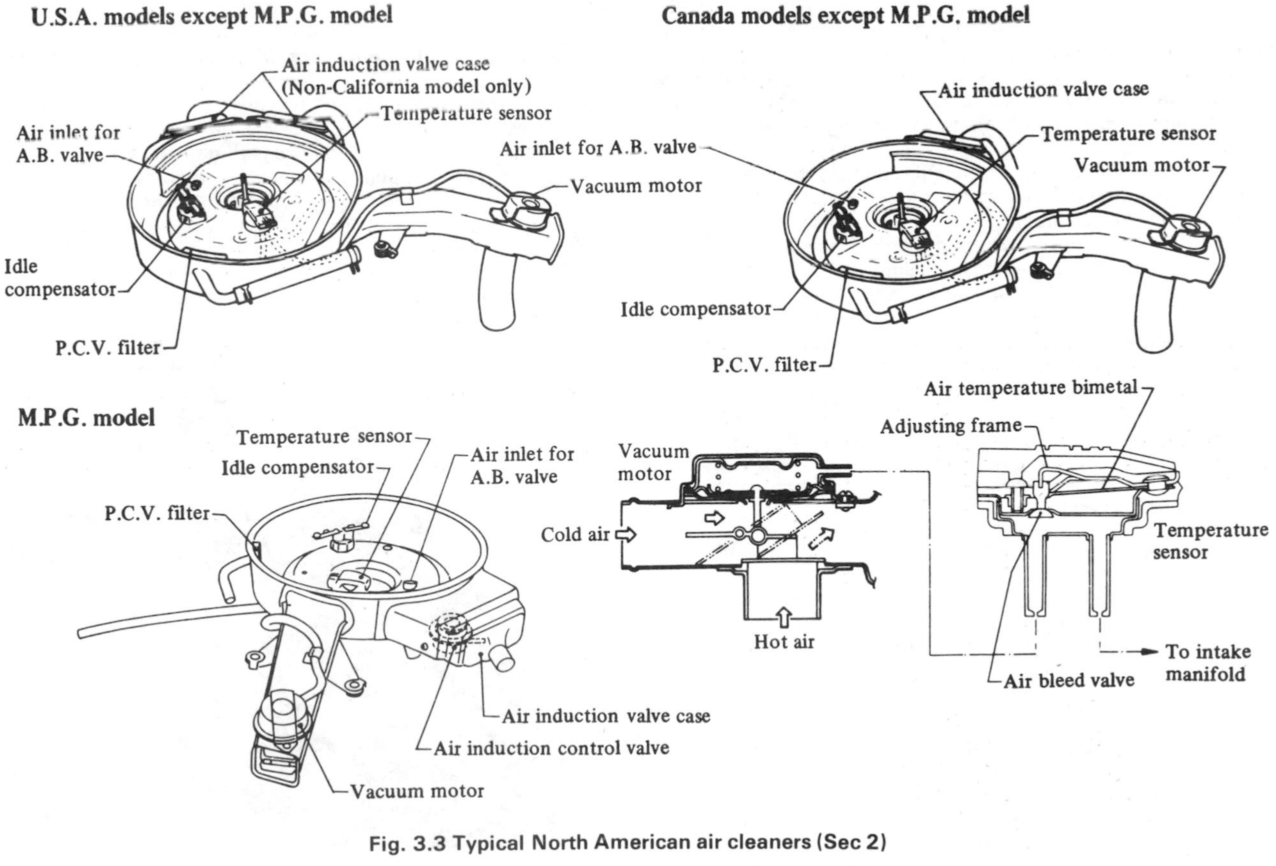

U.S.A. models except M.P.G. model
Air induction valve case (Non-California model only)
Temperature sensor
Air inlet for A.B. valve
Vacuum motor
Idle compensator
P.C.V. filter
Canada models except M.P.G. model
Air induction valve case
Temperature sensor
Air inlet for A.B. valve
Vacuum motor
Idle compensator
P.C.V. filter
M.P.G. model
Temperature sensor
Idle compensator
P.C.V. filter
Air inlet for A.B. valve
Air induction valve case
Air induction control valve
Vacuum motor
Vacuum motor
Cold air
Hot air
Air temperature bimetal
Adjusting frame
Temperature sensor
Air bleed valve
To intake manifold

Fig. 3.3 Typical North American air cleaners (Sec 2)

AB anti-backfire *PCV Positive crankcase ventilation*

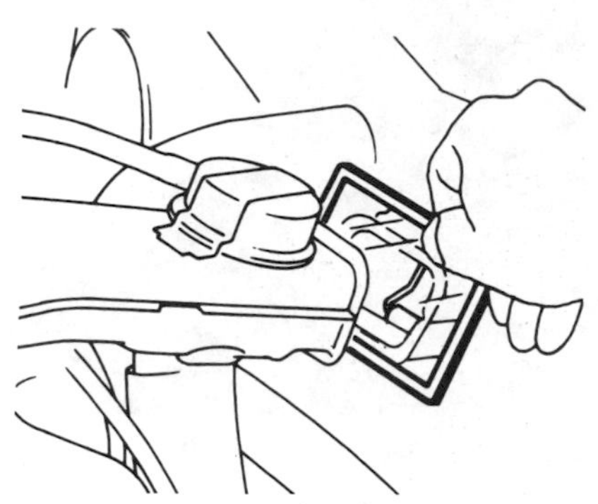

Fig. 3.4 Using a mirror to check position of air cleaner flap valve (Sec 2)

2.10 Air cleaner intake air control lever

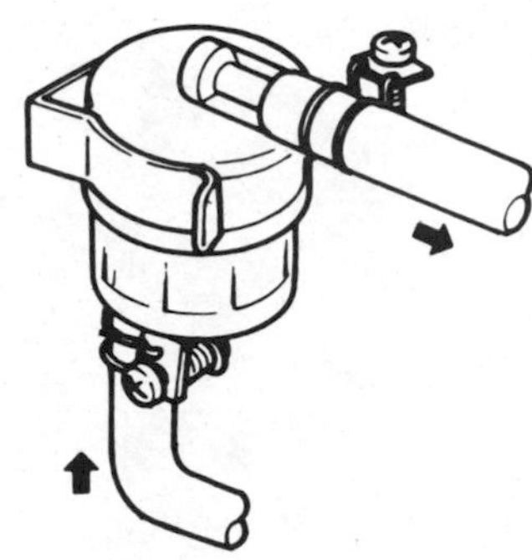

Fig. 3.5 In-line fuel filter (Sec 3)

3.1 Fuel filter

4.3 Fuel pump insulator

4.5 Fitting fuel pump

to see if the flap is closed to cold air entry when the engine is cold, or open to cold air when the engine is at normal operating temperature.
Vacuum capsule. This is used also to vary the setting of the air intake control valve, but its operation is controlled by engine vacuum which varies with engine load.
5 To remove the air cleaner casing, disconnect the hot air duct (photo) and identify and disconnect the other flexible hoses. Remove the cover and the filter element.
6 Extract the casing strut screws (photo) and lift the air cleaner from the carburettor. Refitting is a reversal of removal.
7 On models which have an air cleaner without automatic temperature control, the intake air deflector lever should be moved to the Winter or Summer position according to season (photo). In the Winter setting, warmed air is drawn in from the space between the exhaust manifold and the hot air collector plate.

3 Fuel filter – renewal

1 An in-line type of fuel filter is used (photo).
2 At the intervals specified in Routine Maintenance disconnect the fuel hoses from the filter, remove the filter from its securing clip and discard it.
3 Fit the new filter, start the engine and check for leaks.

4 Fuel pump – removal and refitting

1 The mechanically-operated fuel pump is of rocker arm type, actuated by an eccentric cam on the jack shaft.
2 Disconnect the fuel hoses from the pump, and plug them to prevent loss of fuel.
3 Unscrew and remove the pump mounting nuts and washers and lift the pump from the crankcase. Discard the joint gaskets, but retain the insulator, if fitted (photo).
4 The fuel pump is of sealed type and, if clogged or faulty, will have to be renewed, cleaning and repair is not possible.
5 Clean the pump and crankcase mating faces, use new joint gaskets and bolt the pump into position (photo).
6 Reconnect the fuel hoses (photo), run the engine and test for leaks.

4.6 Connecting fuel hose to pump

5 Fuel level transmitter and gauge – removal and refitting

1 To remove the transmitter, first drain the tank by unscrewing the drain plug from the base of the tank. Drain the fuel into a closed container.
2 Working inside the luggage compartment, extract the screws and remove the transmitter cover plate (photo).
3 Disconnect the wiring harness plug.
4 Disconnect the fuel supply and return hoses.
5 Twist the sender unit mounting plate by placing a large screwdriver or flat piece of metal across the plate to engage against two tags.
6 Withdraw the transmitter carefully, taking care not to bend or damage the float.
7 The fuel gauge can be removed after withdrawing the instrument panel, as described in Chapter 10.
8 Refitting is a reversal of removal, but make sure that the transmitter O-ring is in good order.

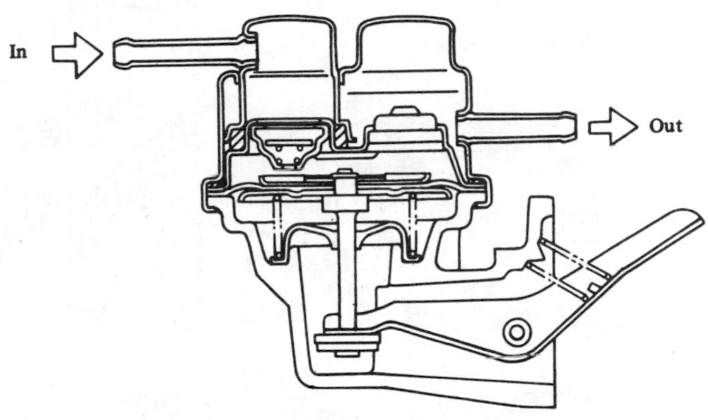

Fig. 3.6 Sectional view of fuel pump (Sec 4)

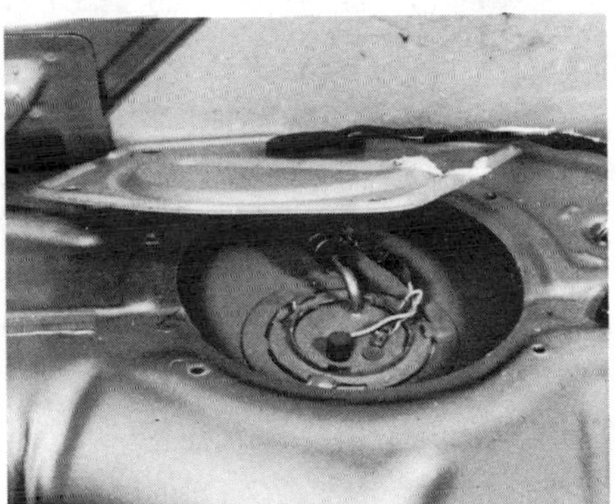

5.2 Fuel tank transmitter

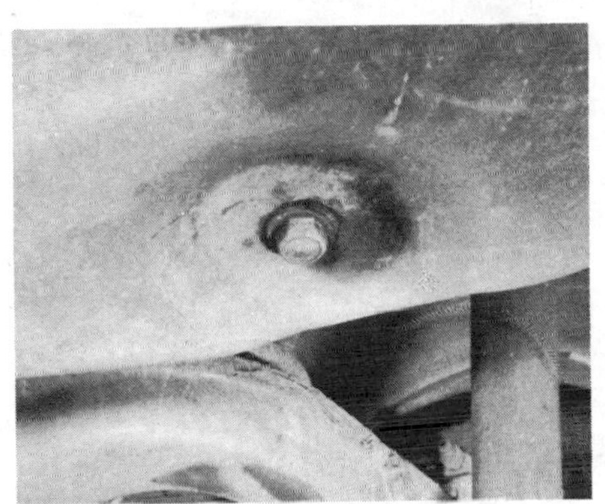

6.1 Fuel tank drain plug

6.3 Fuel tank filler and vent hoses

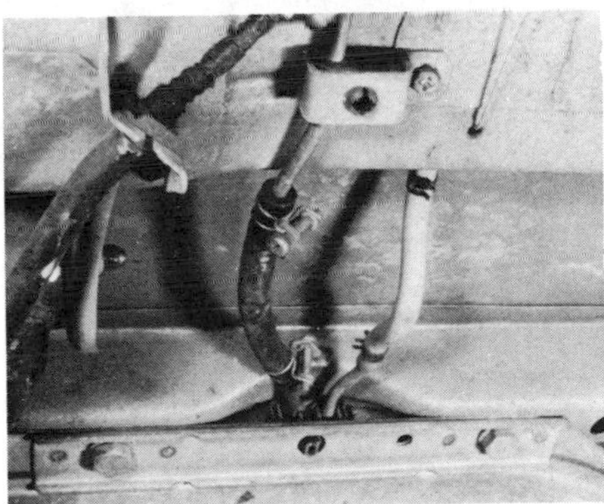

6.4 Fuel tank feed and return hoses

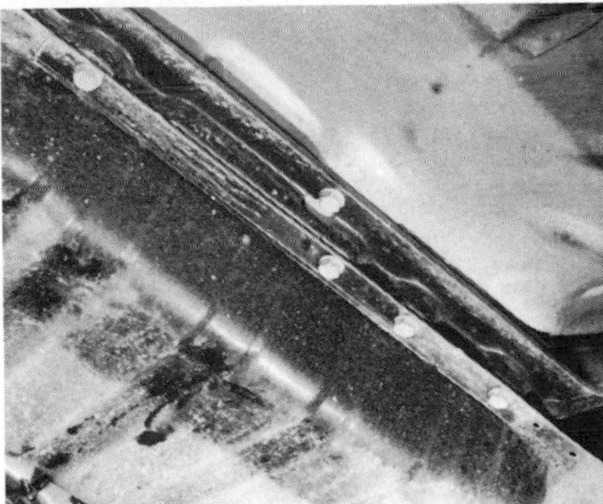

6.5 Fuel tank mounting bolts

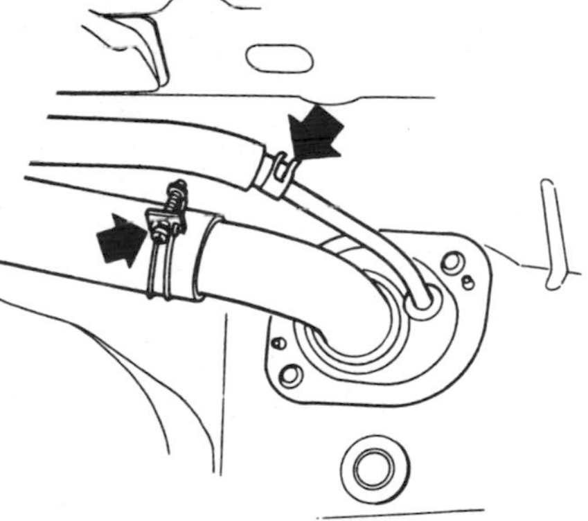

Fig. 3.7 Fuel filler and vent hose retaining clips (Sec 6)

6 Fuel tank – removal, repair and refitting

1 Drain the fuel by unscrewing the drain plug from the base of the tank (photo).
2 Working within the luggage compartment, remove the cover plate from the tank transmitter unit and then disconnect the wiring harness plug.
3 Working under the rear wing, disconnect the fuel filler and ventilation hoses (photo). Stuff a piece of rag into the openings to prevent the entry of dirt.
4 Working at the front of the fuel tank, disconnect the fuel flow and return hoses (photo), and the evaporation control system hoses.
5 Support the tank and then unscrew and remove the six mounting bolts from the tank flange (photo). Lower and remove the tank from the vehicle.
6 A leak in a fuel tank can be sealed using one of the several products available at motor accessory stores. For a permanent repair the tank will have to be soldered or brazed, but *on no account attempt to do this work yourself* due to the risk of explosion unless the tank has been steamed out thoroughly. Radiator repairers can usually undertake fuel tank repair work.
7 Removal of sediment, water or sludge can be carried out after first having removed the tank transmitter unit. Pour in some paraffin, or petrol, and shake the tank vigorously. Empty the tank and repeat the operations as many times as is necessary to clean it and then give a final rinse with clean fuel.
8 Refitting is a reversal of removal.

7.3 Carburettor fuel cut-off valve (arrowed)

7 Carburettor – description

1 The carburettor on all models is of dual barrel downdraught type, but the calibration, ancillary devices and whether it is of manual choke or automatic choke type depends upon the particular vehicle model and operating territory.

2 **Automatic choke.** This is of bi-metal spring type, the heating being carried out electrically. A relay is located within the engine compartment for operating the automatic choke.

3 **Fuel cut-off solenoid valve.** The purpose of this valve (photo) is to prevent the engine running on when the ignition is switched off. This is done by cutting off the fuel supply to the idle circuit.

4 **Secondary throttle vacuum diaphragm.** This is actuated by vacuum conditions in the carburettor venturi. The diaphragm is linked to the secondary throttle in order to open it after the primary throttle valve plate has opened through an angle of 48°.

5 **Dashpot.** On certain models equipped with automatic transmission, a dashpot is fitted to the carburettor to prevent the engine stalling during sudden braking or quick release of the accelerator pedal.

6 **Choke unloader.** This device opens the choke valve plate slightly when increasing the engine speed during the warm-up period to provide a suitable fuel/air mixture which would otherwise be too rich.

7 **Vacuum break diaphragm.** This is a double-acting type

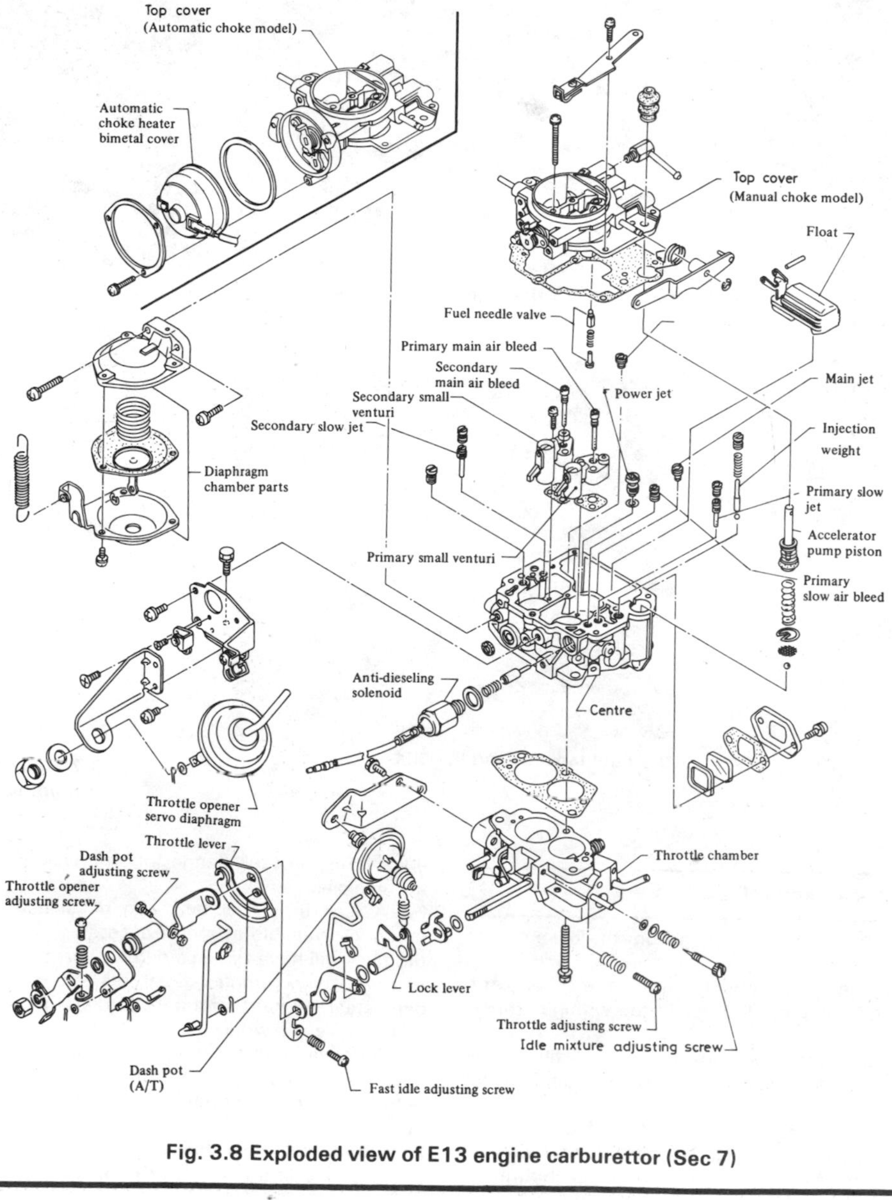

Fig. 3.8 Exploded view of E13 engine carburettor (Sec 7)

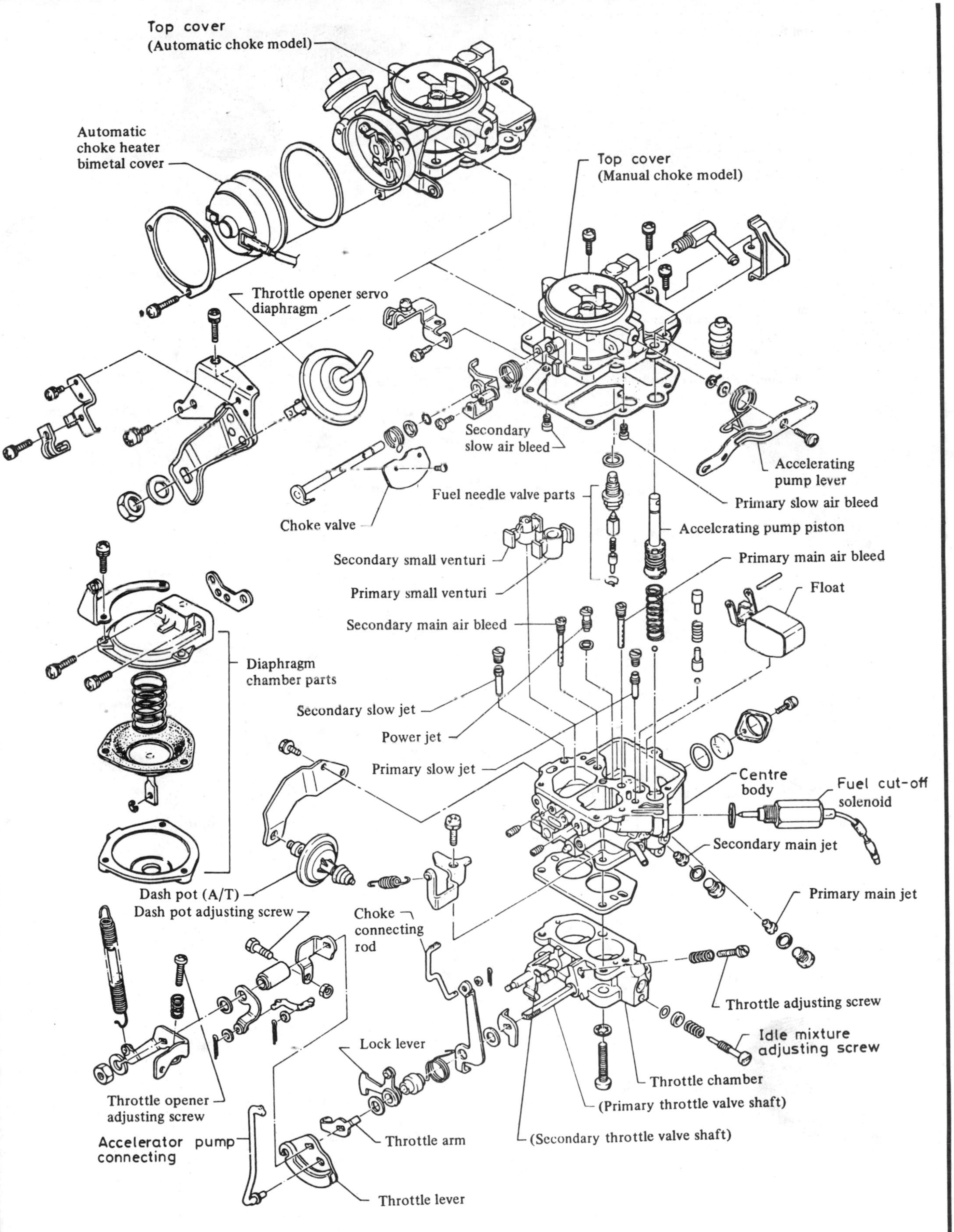

Top cover
(Automatic choke model)
Automatic
choke heater
bimetal cover
Top cover
(Manual choke model)
Throttle opener servo
diaphragm
Secondary
slow air bleed
Accelerating
pump lever
Fuel needle valve parts
Primary slow air bleed
Choke valve
Accelcrating pump piston
Secondary small venturi
Primary main air bleed
Float
Primary small venturi
Secondary main air bleed
Diaphragm
chamber parts
Secondary slow jet
Power jet
Primary slow jet
Centre
body
Fuel cut-off
solenoid
Secondary main jet
Dash pot (A/T)
Dash pot adjusting screw
Primary main jet
Choke
connecting
rod
Throttle adjusting screw
Idle mixture
adjusting screw
Lock lever
Throttle chamber
Throttle opener
adjusting screw
(Primary throttle valve shaft)
Accelerator pump
connecting
Throttle arm
(Secondary throttle valve shaft)
Throttle lever

Fig. 3.9 Exploded view of E15 engine carburettor (Sec 7)

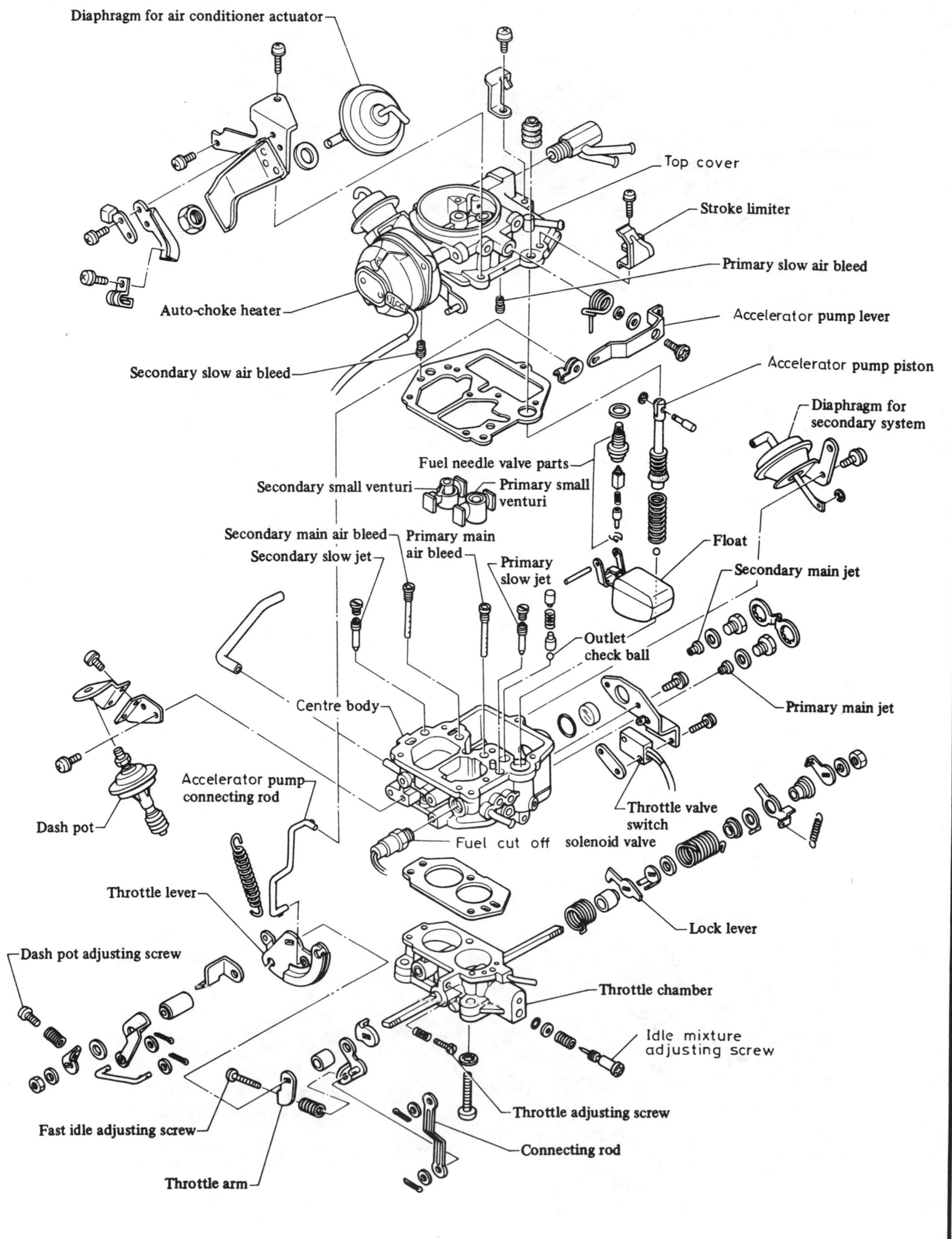

Fig. 3.10 Exploded view of N. American carburettor – except California and MPG models (Sec 7)

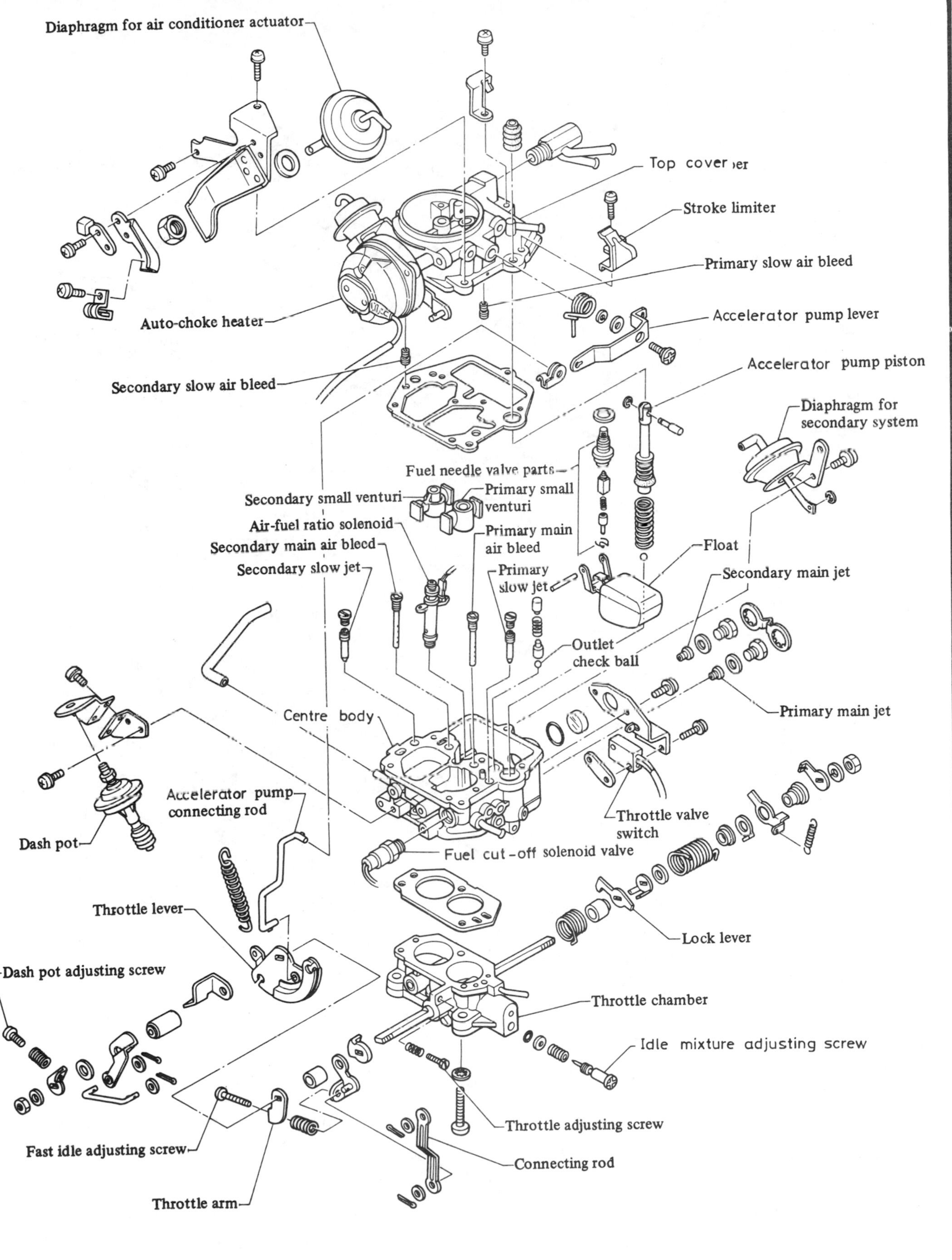

Fig. 3.11 Exploded view of carburettor for Californian models (Sec 7)

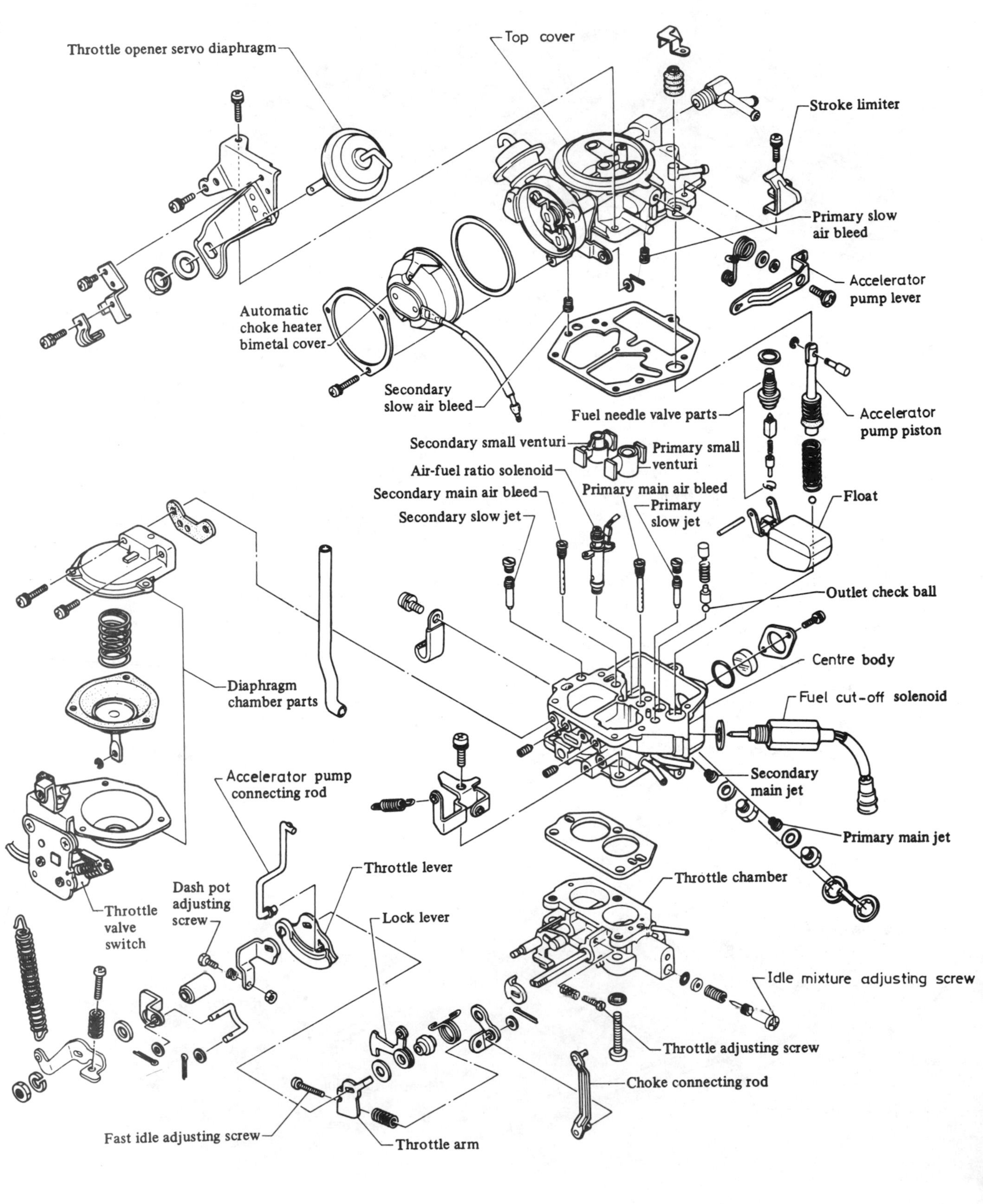

Fig. 3.12 Exploded view of carburettor for MPG models (Sec 7)

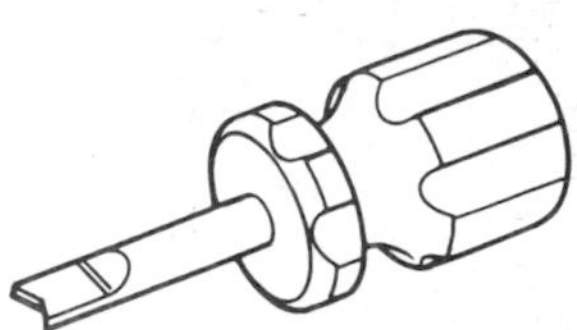

Fig. 3.13 Special screwdriver used to turn idle mixture screw (Sec 8)

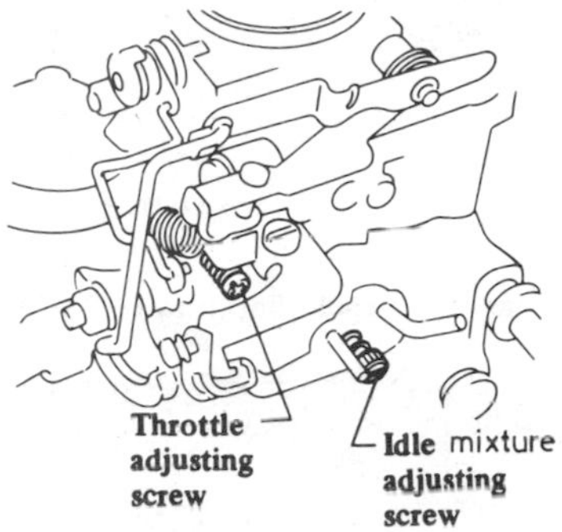

Fig. 3.14 Carburettor adjustment screws (Sec 8)

8.2 Idle mixture screw with limiter cap

8.6 Throttle speed screw (arrowed)

diaphragm which opens the choke valve plate immediately after cold starting to create a suitable fuel/air mixture in accordance with the prevailing engine vacuum conditions.

8 **Altitude compensator.** The purpose of this device is to weaken the fuel/air mixture at high altitudes when it would otherwise be too rich. The compensator is a barometric pressure-sensitive bellows which opens and closes a needle type air bleed valve.

8 Carburettor – idle speed and mixture adjustment (except N American models)

1 The mixture is preset during production and should not normally require altering. However, adjustment may be necessary if the carburettor has been overhauled or after a high mileage when the engine characteristics may have changed slightly due to the build-up of carbon or wear in the engine components.

2 On most models, the idle mixture screw is fitted with a limiter cap (photo). The screw can be turned if a screwdriver blade is ground to a shape similar to that shown in Fig. 3.13.

3 Have the engine at normal operating temperature with the ignition timing and valve clearances correctly set.

4 Connect a tachometer to the engine in accordance with the manufacturer's instructions.

5 If an air conditioner is fitted, make sure that it is switched off.

6 With the engine idling turn the throttle speed screw (photo) as necessary to bring the speed within the range given in Specifications.

7 For accuracy, the idle mixture should be adjusted using a CO meter (exhaust gas analyser). Rev up the engine two or three times to clear it and then let it idle. Turn the idle mixture screw until the meter indicates a CO content within the specified tolerance. This adjustment should be carried out quickly. If it extends over more than two minutes, rev the engine again before resuming adjustment.

8 If an exhaust gas analyser is not available, carry out the following alternative method of adjusting the idle mixture. Turn the idle mixture screw until the engine speed is at its highest level and does not increase any further. Make sure that the engine is idling smoothly and then readjust the throttle speed screw to bring the idle speed within the specified range.

9 If the territory in which the vehicle is being used is subject to strict emission regulations the idle mixture CO content should **always** be checked with an exhaust gas analyser.

10 If the idle mixture screw has been removed during carburettor overhaul, a starting point for mixture adjustment can be established if the screw is turned in very gently until it just seats and then unscrewed two full turns.

9 Carburettor – idle speed and mixture adjustment (N American models)

1 The operations are similar to those described in the preceding Section, but observe the following special points.

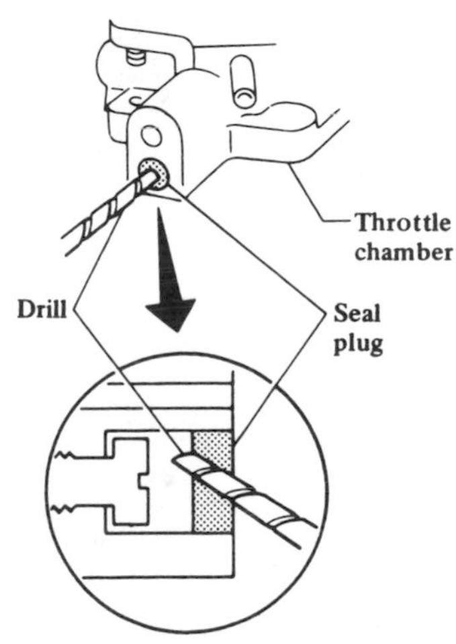

Fig. 3.15 Idle mixture screw plug removal (Sec 9)

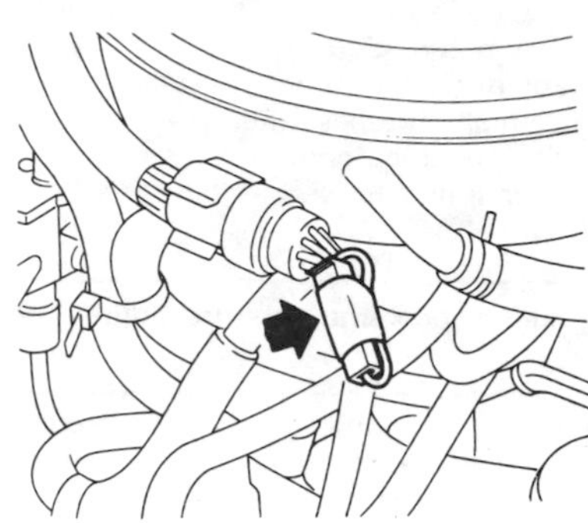

Fig. 3.16 Fuel/air ratio solenoid wiring harness disconnected (Sec 9)

2 To remove the idle mixture screw plug, drill a hole in it and prise it out using a thin rod or screwdriver.
3 Make sure that all electrical accessories are switched off. If the radiator cooling fan comes on during adjustment, wait until it switches off before continuing.
4 On California and MPG models, disconnect the fuel/air ratio solenoid wiring harness.
5 Fit a new sealing plug to the mixture screw hole on completion.

10 Carburettor – in car adjustments (except N American models)

Fast idle (automatic choke)

1 Bring the engine to normal operating temperature. Remove the choke housing cover.
2 Set the fast idle lever on the second step of the fast idle cam.

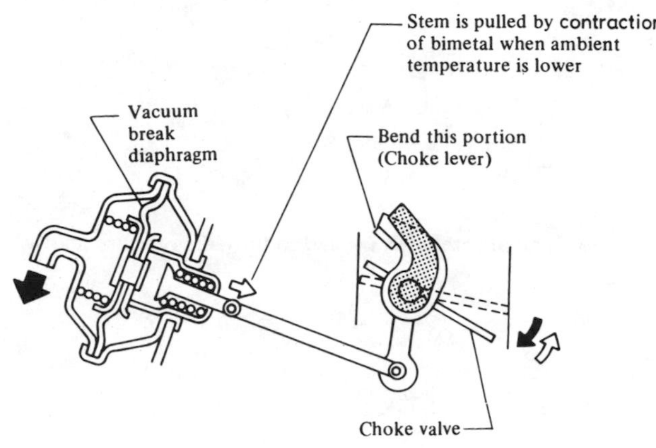

Fig. 3.17 Vacuum break diaphragm (Sec 10)

3 Check that the fast idle engine speed is as given in the Specifications. If it is not, turn the fast idle screw as necessary.

Vacuum break

4 With the engine cold, remove the air cleaner and close the choke valve plate.
5 Depress the diaphragm rod fully and then check the clearance R is as specified (see Fig. 3.18). The clearance is measured between the edge of the valve plate and the wall of the carburettor. Where necessary, bend the choke lever.

Choke unloader (automatic choke)

6 With the engine cold remove the air cleaner and automatic choke housing cover, and close the choke valve plate.
7 Turn the throttle lever until the primary throttle valve is fully open. If it is not, bend the tongue of the unloader. The clearance C should be as specified (see Fig. 3.19).

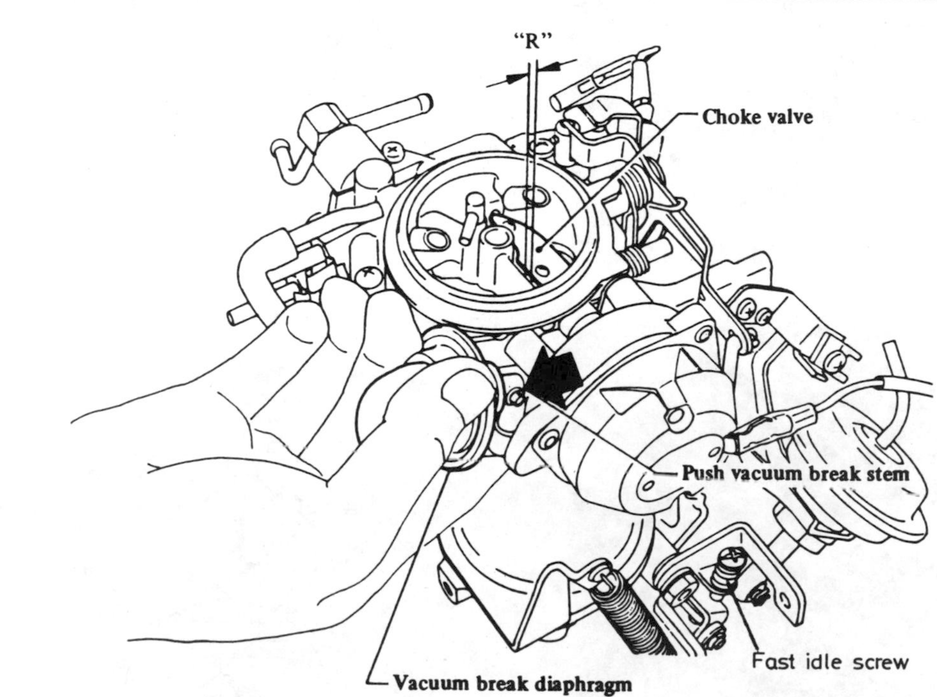

Fig. 3.18 Checking vacuum break adjustment (Sec 10)

R (E13 engine) = 1.27 to 1.45 mm (0.05 to 0.06 in) *R (E15 engine) = 1.18 to 1.36 mm (0.046 to 0.054 in)*

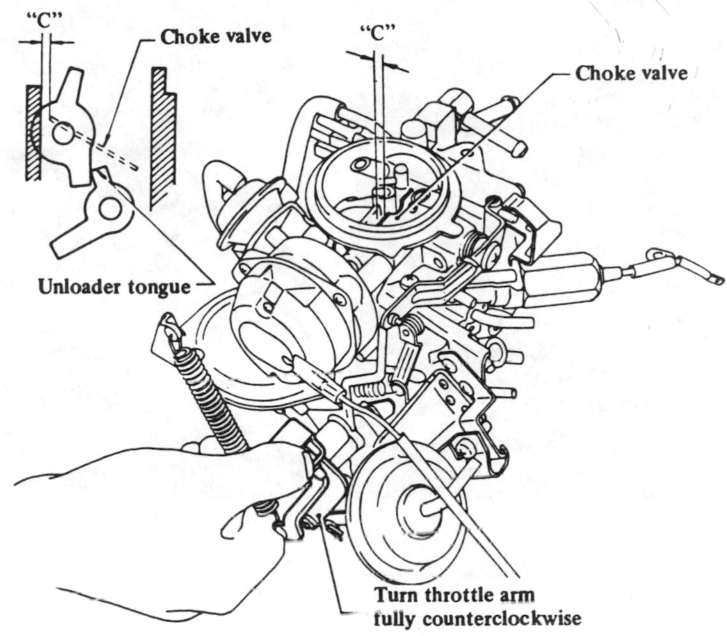

Fig. 3.19 Checking setting of choke unloader (Sec 10)

C (E13 engine) = 1.74 mm (0.0685 in) *C (E15 engine) = 2.01 mm (0.0791 in)*

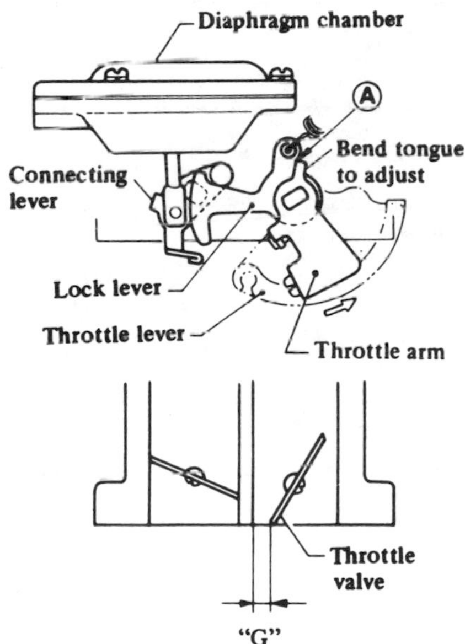

Fig. 3.20 Valve plate interlock setting diagram (Sec 10)

G (E13 engine) = 5.84 to 5.90 mm (0.230 to 0.232 in)
G (E15 engine) = 5.80 to 5.86 mm (0.228 to 0.231 in)

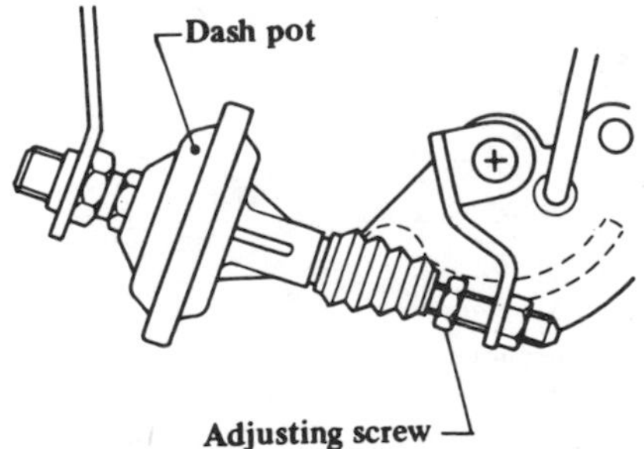

Fig. 3.21 Dashpot (Sec 10)

Primary and secondary valve plate interlock

8 Turn the throttle lever until the throttle arm contacts the lock lever at point A (see Fig. 3.20).

9 Check that the clearance G is as specified. If it is not, bend the tongue on the throttle arm as necessary.

Dashpot (automatic transmission)

10 Have the engine at normal operating temperature and idling.

11 Turn the throttle lever on the carburettor by hand and have an assistant record the engine speed shown on the tachometer at the point where the dashpot just makes contact with the stop lever. If the speed is not as specified, release the locknut and turn the dashpot rod.

12 Tighten the locknut and make sure that the engine speed drops from 2000 to 1000 rpm in three seconds.

11 Carburettor – in car adjustments (N American models)

1 Most of the adjustments are described in the preceding Section, but use the appropriate figures specified for these models.

2 An additional adjustment operation is as follows.

Automatic choke

3 The correct setting of the choke housing cover is for its mark to be opposite the centre mark on the housing scale.

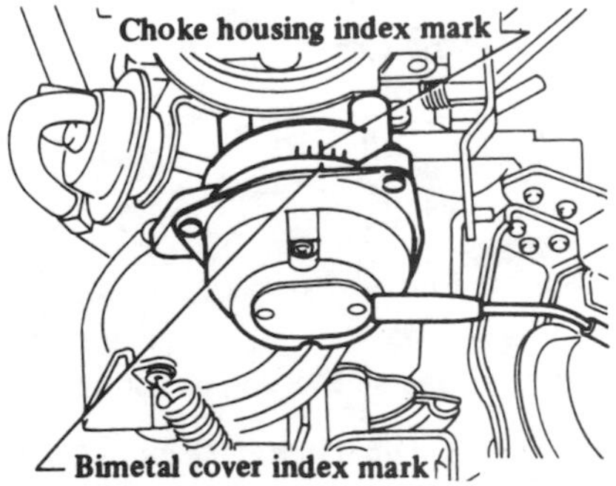

Fig. 3.22 Automatic choke housing and cover markings (Sec 11)

12.3 Choke cable at carburettor

12.6 Disconnecting the fuel pump from the carburettor

12 Carburettor – removal and refitting

1 Remove the air cleaner.
2 Disconnect the accelerator control cable from the carburettor.
3 Disconnect the choke control cable (photo) or the electrical lead (automatic choke).
4 Disconnect the lead from the fuel cut-off solenoid valve.
5 Where fitted (see Section 16) disconnect the leads from the terminals of the mixture heating system.
6 Disconnect and plug the fuel hoses (photo).
7 Unbolt and remove the carburettor from the intake manifold. Take care not to drop the mounting nuts into the carburettor intake.
8 Refitting is a reversal of removal, but always use a new gasket at the manifold joint.

13 Carburettor – overhaul

1 With the carburettor removed from the engine, clean away all external dirt and grease.
2 The need for complete dismantling of a carburettor seldom occurs.

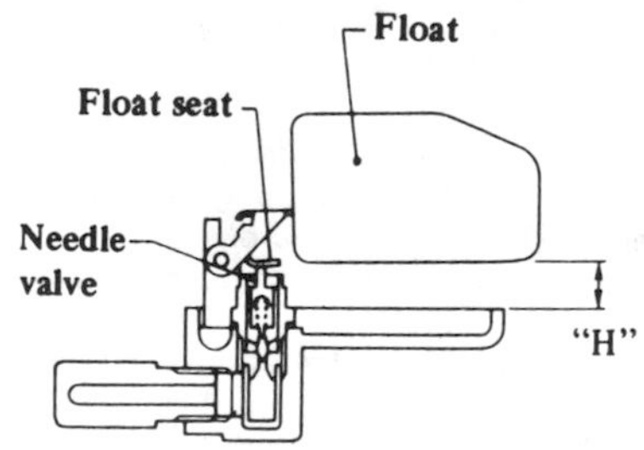

Fig. 3.23 Float setting diagram (Sec 13)

H (E13 engine) = 15.0 mm (0.59 in)
H (E15 engine) = 12.0 mm (0.47 in)

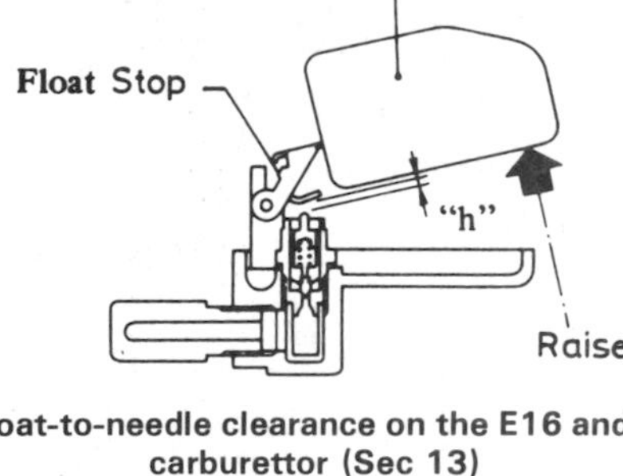

Fig. 3.24 Float-to-needle clearance on the E16 and E15 engine carburettor (Sec 13)

h = 1.3 to 1.7 mm (0.051 to 0.067 in)

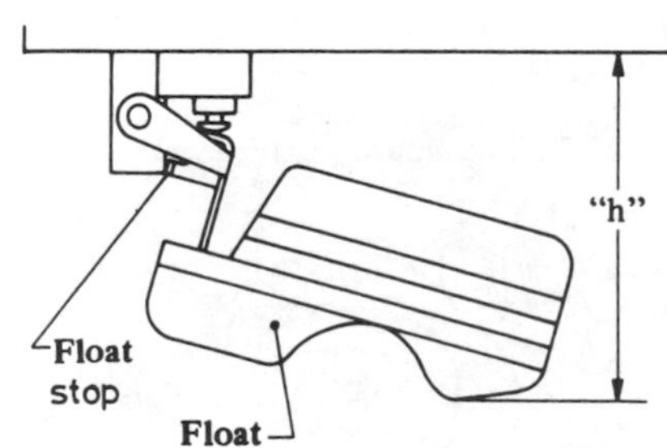

Fig. 3.25 Float stroke on E13 engine carburettor (Sec 13)

h = 45.0 mm (1.77 in)

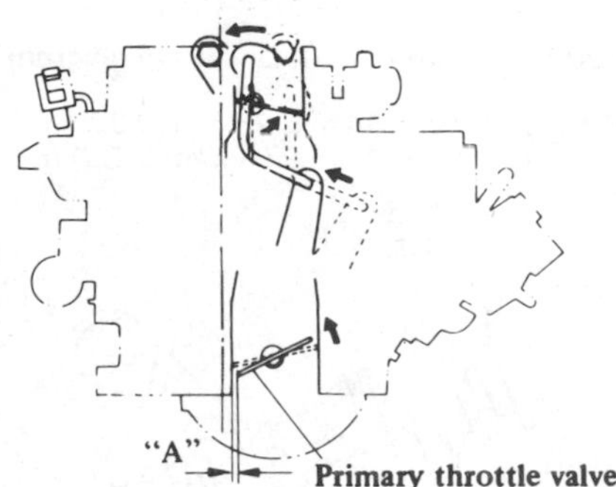

Fig. 3.26 Fast idle adjustment – manual choke (Sec 13)

A (E13 engine) = 1.37 to 1.51 mm (0.0539 to 0.0595 in)
A (E15 engine) = 1.42 to 1.56 mm (0.559 to 0.0614 in)

13.13 Carburettor fuel bowl sight glass

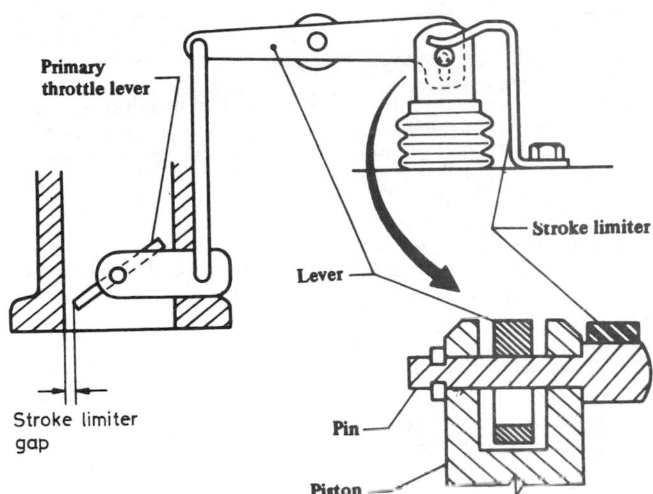

Fig. 3.27 Accelerator pump – North American models (Sec 13)

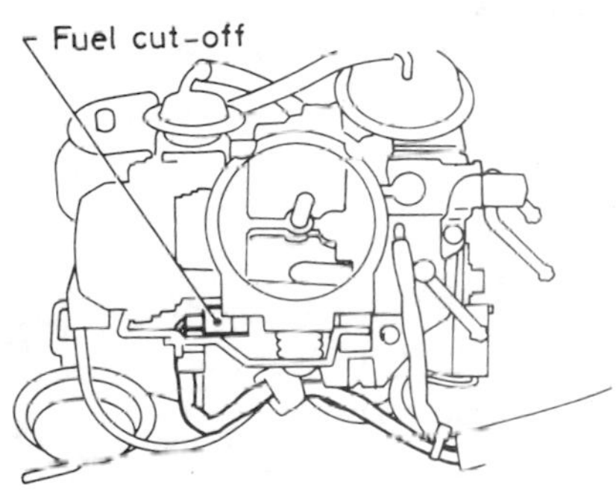

Fig. 3.28 Fuel cut-off valve – E16 engine (Sec 13)

Fig. 3.29 Fuel cut-off valve – MPG model (Sec 13)

The usual reason is to clean the jets and fuel bowl and to check the adjustments described later in this Section. In fact, where the major components of the carburettor are worn, such as the throttle or choke valve plate spindles or bushes, and the unit has seen long service, it will almost certainly be more economical to purchase a new or factory-reconditioned carburettor.

3 Extract the retaining screws and take off the top cover (choke chamber).

4 The float and the fuel inlet needle valve can be removed once the float arm pivot pin is pushed out.

5 Clean out the float chamber and clean the jets and bleed holes by applying air pressure from a tyre pump. If the jets are badly clogged or are suspected of being the wrong ones they should be unscrewed. *Never probe a jet with wire,* but if air pressure fails to clear it use a nylon bristle. The jets can be checked for size by quoting the carburettor index number to your dealer's parts department.

6 To remove the throttle block from the carburettor main body, disconnect the choke linkage, invert the carburettor and extract the fixing screws.

7 Obtain a repair kit for your carburettor which will contain all the necessary gaskets, seals and other renewable items.

8 Reassemble by reversing the dismantling operations, but as work progresses check the following adjustments and settings. A twist drill is useful when measuring valve plate clearances, as the precise diameter will serve as a gauge.

Float setting

9 Invert the carburettor cover so that the float arm rests on the fuel inlet needle valve under its own weight. Measure the distance H between the surface of the float and the face of the top cover (see Fig. 3.23).

10 If this is not as specified, carefully bend the float seat.

11 On E15 and E16 engined models, check the clearance H between the float seat and the end of the fuel inlet needle valve (see Fig. 3.24). If it is not as specified, bend the float stop.

12 On E13 engined models the float stroke should be measured (see Fig. 3.25). If not as specified, bend the float stop.

13 With the carburettor in the vehicle, the fuel level can be checked through the sight glass on the fuel bowl (photo).

Fast idle (manual choke)

14 Close the choke valve plate and then check the gap A between the edge of the primary throttle valve plate and the wall of the carburettor (see Fig. 3.26). Adjust the clearance to specification by turning the fast idle screw.

Accelerator pump

15 To check the volume of fuel ejected from the fuel pump, pour fuel into the float chamber and then turn the throttle lever from fully closed to fully open ten times. Hold the lever in the fully open position for a period of three seconds between strokes.

16 Catch the ejected fuel in a measuring glass and then divide the total volume by ten to obtain the volume of fuel ejected per stroke. if this is not as specified, check the pump linkage for wear or distortion.

17 On US models a pump stroke limiter is fitted. To check the setting, actuate the accelerator pump rod until the pump lever just comes into contact with the piston pin. Now measure the gap between the edge of the primary throttle valve plate and the carburettor throat wall (see Fig. 3.27). If it is not as given in Specifications, bend the stroke limiter.

18 If the solenoid fuel cut-off valve was removed, screw it in, using a new sealing washer, to the specified torque setting.

14 Emission control systems – general

All models are equipped with some kind of emission control system. On North American versions, more sophisticated and complex systems are used.

It must be appreciated that keeping the ignition and fuel systems correctly set and the valve clearances precisely adjusted all contribute to the general reduction in the emission of noxious exhaust gases.

15 Emission control systems – description and maintenance (except N American models)

Crankcase ventilation system (PCV)

1 This is described in Chapter 1.

Temperature controlled air cleaner

2 This is described in Section 2 of this Chapter.

Spark timing control system (TCS)

3 This is a supplementary vacuum advance system which varies the ignition advance according to prevailing engine conditions as a means of reducing the emission of noxious gases from the exhaust.

4 The system includes the following components:

Vacuum switching valve – varies the vacuum passage connecting with the distributor to alter the advance setting.

Coolant temperature switch – for monitoring and signalling the engine coolant temperature.

Top, neutral and overdrive switches – for relaying the transmission mode according to gear lever position. Relays for these switches are located on the bracket within the engine compartment.

Clutch switch – actuated by the pedal arm to cut off current to the vacuum switching valve when the pedal is depressed.

5 Check the system electrical connections and hoses regularly for security and condition. Connect a stroboscope to the engine when it is cold and check that the following conditions are met.

Coolant temperature	Thermal vacuum valve	Ignition spark
Below 10°C (50°F)	*Closed*	*Full advance*
Between 10° and 50°C (50° to 122°F)	*Open*	*Partial advance*
Above 50°C (122°F)	*Closed*	*Full advance*

6 If the advance does not operate as specified and indicated by the stroboscopic timing lamp, check the thermal vacuum valve.

7 Drain some coolant from the cooling system, remove the valve and apply suction to the port nearest the top of the valve. Immerse the valve in water and check the operation of the valve as the water temperature is raised. **Do not allow water to enter the valve.**

Below 10°C (50°F) the valve should be closed
Between 10° and 50°C (50° and 122°F) the valve should be open
Above 50°C (122°F) the valve should be closed

8 Renew the valve if it does not perform satisfactorily.

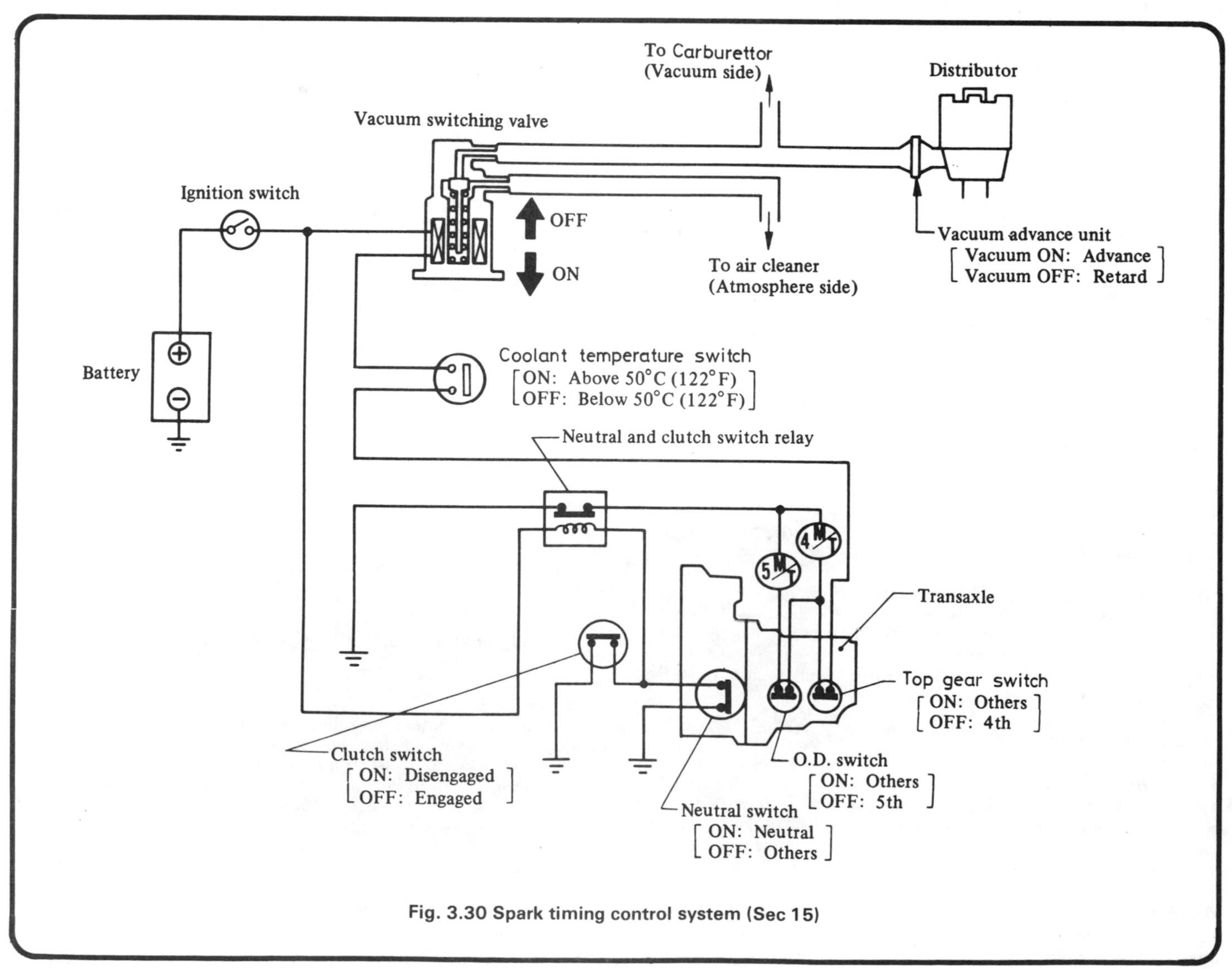

Fig. 3.30 Spark timing control system (Sec 15)

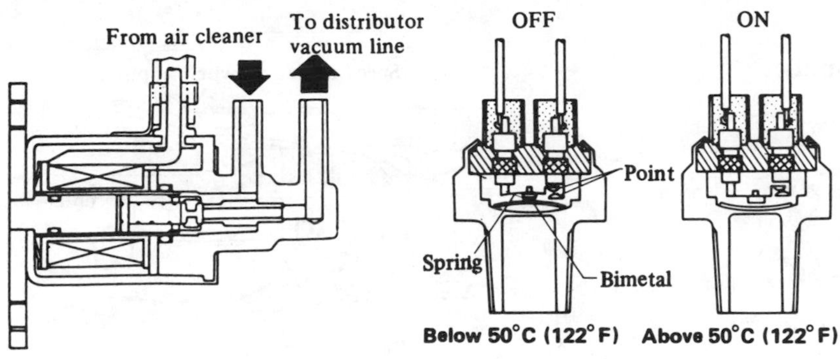

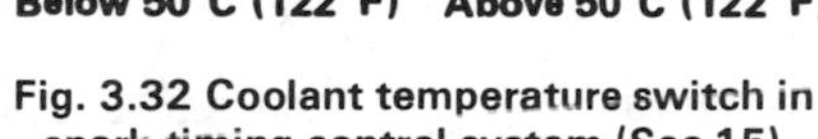

Fig. 3.31 Vacuum switching valve in spark timing control system (Sec 15)

Fig. 3.32 Coolant temperature switch in spark timing control system (Sec 15)

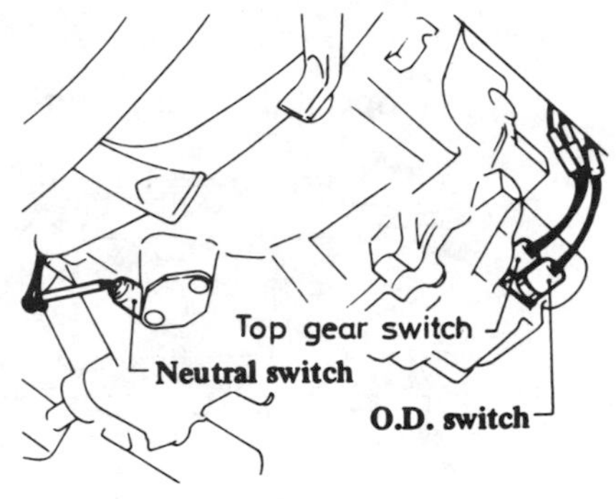

Fig. 3.33 Transmission switches in spark timing control system (Sec 15)
OD Overdrive

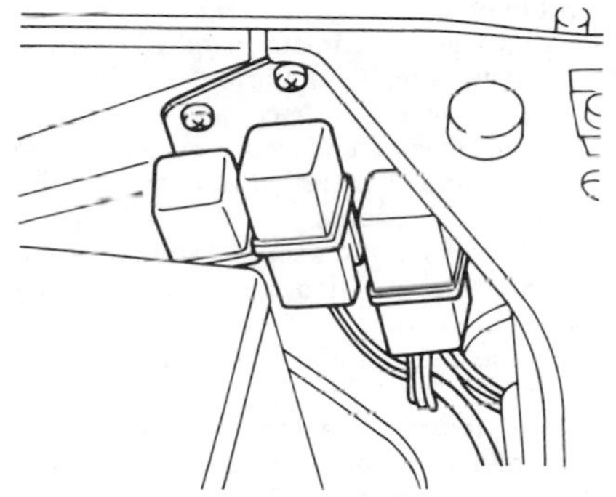

Fig. 3.34 Neutral and clutch switch relays in spark timing control system (Sec 15)

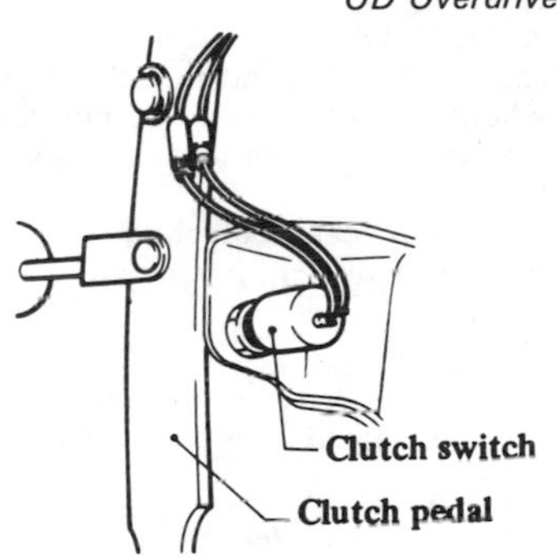

Fig. 3.35 Clutch switch in spark timing control system (Sec 15)

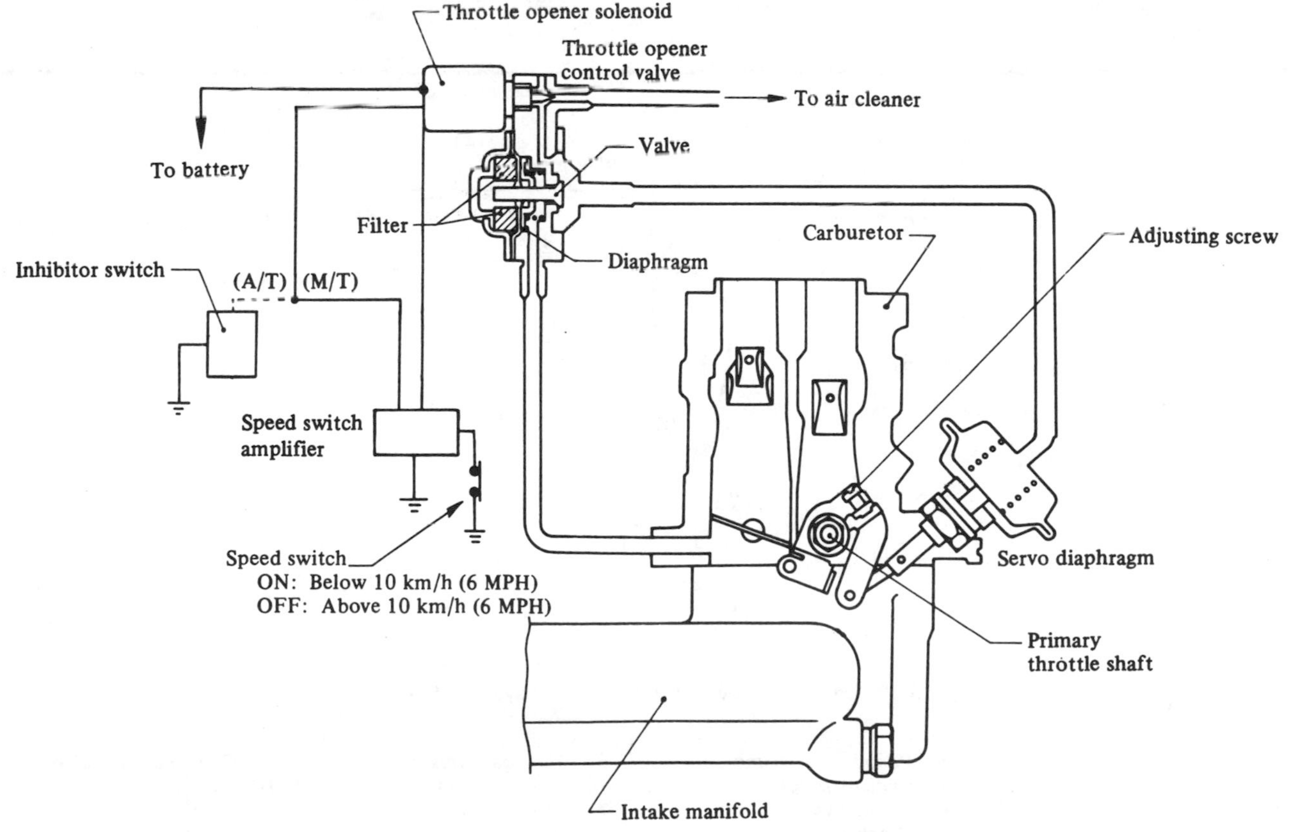

Fig. 3.36 Throttle opener control system (Sec 15)

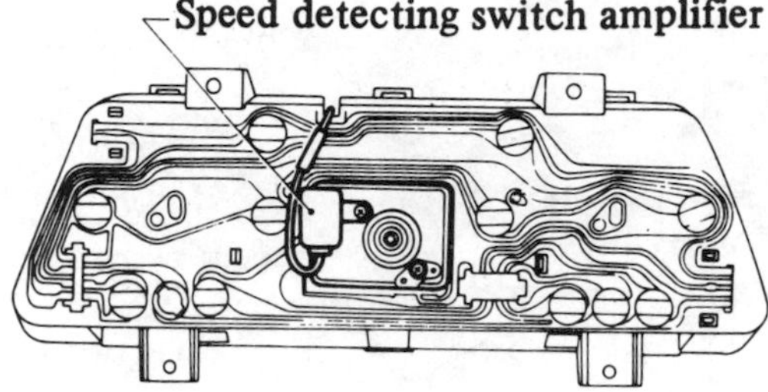

Fig. 3.37 Speed detecting switch – B11 models (Sec 15)

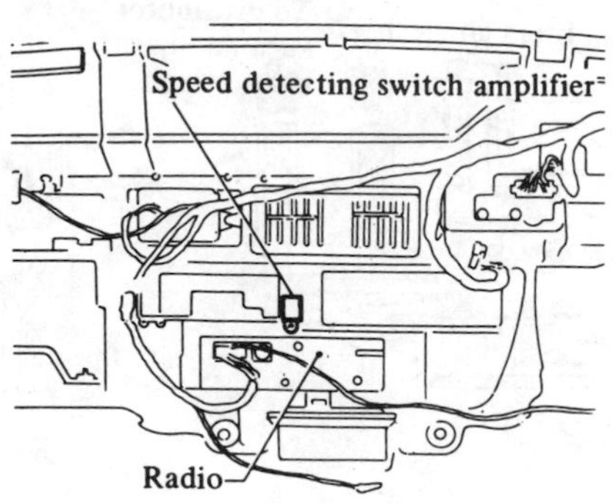

Fig. 3.38 Speed detecting switch – N12 models (Sec 15)

Throttle opener control system

9 This system is designed to open the throttle valve plate slightly during deceleration, when manifold vacuum is high but the mixture volume for normal combustion is small and excessive hydrocarbons are emitted.

10 The system incorporates a speed detecting switch and amplifier, vacuum control and solenid valves and a vacuum diaphragm unit.

Hoses – general

11 Emission control system hoses are colour coded and their significance should be appreciated when removing or connecting them.

Yellow	*Vacuum line to distributor*
Green	*Intake manifold line*
Pink	*Atmospheric pressure line*

Evaporative emission control system

12 This system prevents fuel vapour being released to atmosphere from the fuel tank.

13 When the engine is not running, vapour from the fuel tank passes through a vent line to a canister filled with activated charcoal where it is stored until the engine is started.

14 Once the engine is started and running, a purge control valve opens and the canister and vent line are cleared of vapour which is drawn into the intake manifold and then burned during the normal engine combustion process.

15 Periodically check the security and condition of all system hoses.

16 At the intervals specified in Routine Maintenance label the hoses connected to the carbon canister and disconnect them.

17 Remove the canister and extract the filter. If contaminated, renew it.

18 As the fuel tank is of sealed type, it is important that the vent hose is never crushed and that the check (non-return) valve is kept in good order, otherwise vacuum conditions could occur within the tank and cause the tank to collapse. To test the check valve, remove it and blow through it from the fuel tank side. Some air should pass against the pressure of the coil spring. Now blow from the engine side – the airflow should be unrestricted.

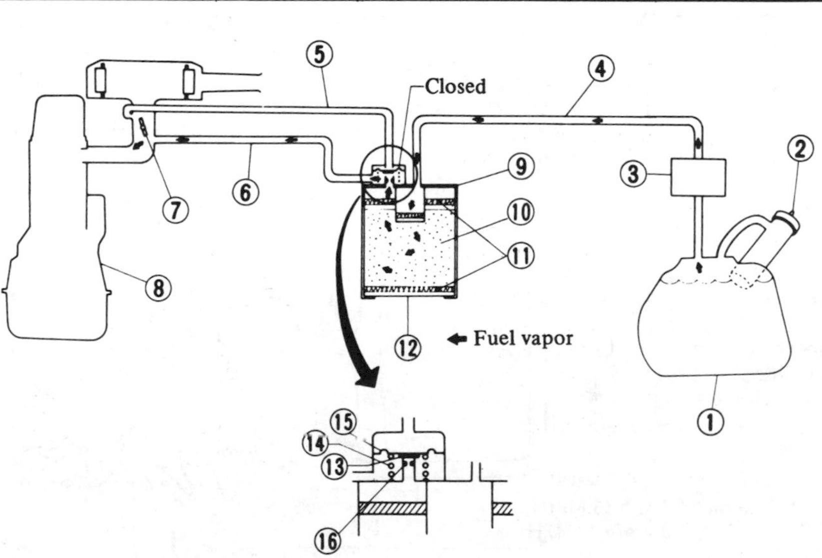

Fig. 3.39 Fuel evaporative emission control system (Sec 15)

1 Fuel tank
2 Fuel filler cap
3 Fuel check valve
4 Vapour vent line
5 Vacuum signal line
6 Canister purge line
7 Throttle valve
8 Crankcase
9 Charcoal canister
10 Activated charcoal
11 Screen
12 Filter
13 Purge control valve
14 Diaphragm spring
15 Diaphragm
16 Orifice

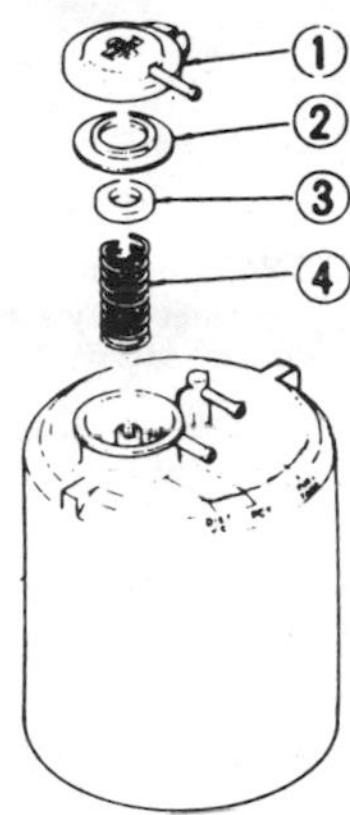

Fig. 3.40 Charcoal canister (Sec 15)

1 Cover
2 Diaphragm
3 Retainer
4 Diaphragm spring

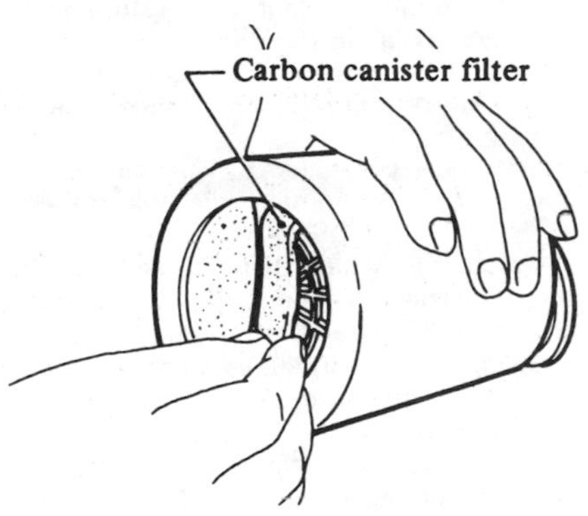

Fig. 3.41 Removing canister filter (Sec 15)

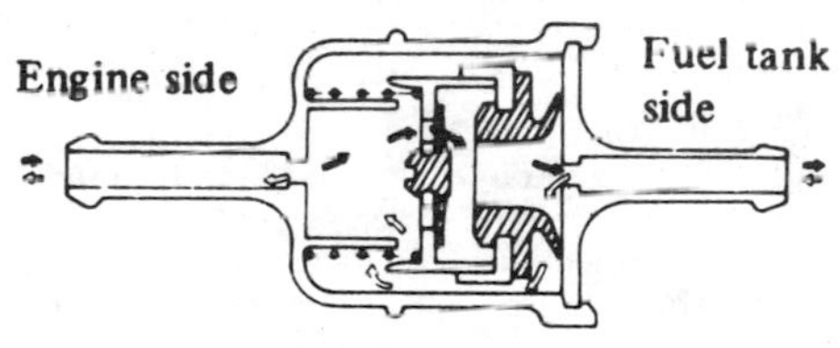

Fig. 3.42 Check valve in evaporative control system (Sec 15)

16 Emission control systems – description and maintenance (N American models)

Crankcase emission control system

1 This is described in Chapter 1.

Temperature controlled air cleaner

2 This is described in Section 2 of this Chapter.

Spark timing control system (TCS)

3 The purpose of this system is as described in the preceding Section, but the circuit and components vary slightly as will be seen from the diagram (Fig. 3.44).

Air induction system (AIS)

4 This system, which is not used on Californian models, is designed to inject air into the exhaust manifold in order to dilute the CO and HC content of the exhaust gas.

5 Pressure within the exhaust manifold changes to partial vacuum at regular intervals due to the opening and closing of the exhaust valves. The volume of injected air is directly proportional to the vacuum pressure created.

6 Maintenance consists of periodically checking the security and condition of the hoses and renewing the air induction valve filter (refer to Section 2).

7 The purpose of the system on MPG models is similar to that just described, but, as a catalytic converter is used on these models, the AIS system is only brought into operation when the engine is cold.

Exhaust gas recirculation system (EGR)

8 This system arranges the return of a proportion of the exhaust gas to the combustion chamber in order to reduce the flame temperature during combustion. This reduces the level of nitrogen oxide in the exhaust gas.

9 The system varies, as shown in the diagram, according to vehicle operating temperature (see Fig. 3.47).

10 Components of the system include the following:

Control valve – controls the volume of exhaust gas admitted to the intake manifold by responding to the degree of vacuum caused by the position of the carburettor throttle valve plate.

Venturi vacuum transducer (VVT) – monitors exhaust pressure and carburettor venturi vacuum which in turn influences the EGR control valve setting according to engine conditions and load.

Thermal vacuum valve (three port type) – sensitive to engine coolant temperatures, it controls the opening of the air passage from the air cleaner. This valve also serves the catalyst warm-up system and the fuel evaporative emission control system.

Thermal vacuum valve (two port type) – mounted on the intake

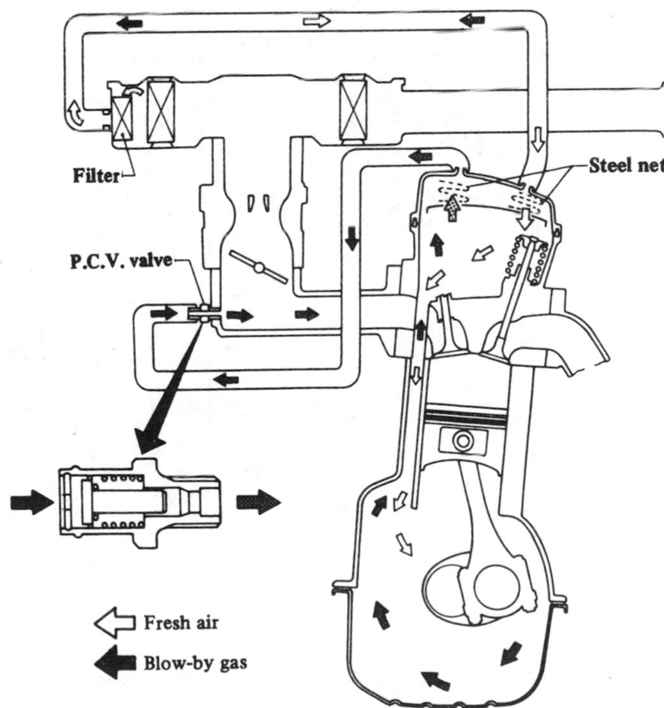

Fig. 3.43 Crankcase emission control system on North American models (Sec 16)

PCV Positive crankcase ventilation

manifold, it is sensitive to engine coolant temperature and controls the opening of the vacuum passage in the thermal vacuum valve.

Vacuum delay valve (VDV) – fitted in the vacuum control line to the EGR valve, it reduces the rate of vacuum change when the throttle valve is opened rapidly.

Vacuum switching valve – controlled by current from the vacuum switch, it supplies vacuum from the reservoir tank to the EGR control valve.

Vacuum switch – actuated when there is an increase in intake manifold vacuum during deceleration and interrupts the electrical signal to the vacuum switching valve.

One-way valve – designed to retain the vacuum in the reservoir tank.

11 Check the security of the system pipe connections at regular intervals. After a high mileage, the EGR control valve should be removed for cleaning of deposits or renewal. To do this, disconnect the hose and remove the mounting nuts. Take the opportunity to clean deposits from the connecting pipe and manifold port. Use a new gasket when refitting the valve.

12 If the thermal vacuum valve must be removed for any reason, treat it carefully as it is of plastic construction. Drain about 1.0 litre (1.76 Imp pts, 1.057 US qts) of coolant before attempting to unscrew the valve.

Air/fuel ratio control system

13 This system operates through a closed-loop or open-loop control, depending upon engine conditions such as coolant temperature, speed and the signal from the exhaust gas sensor (see paragraph 15). The purpose of the system is to precisely control the air/fuel ratio to enable the catalyst in the catalytic converter to reduce the emissions of CO, HC and NOx to the lowest possible levels.

14 Main components of the system include a control unit and a solenoid valve. If the solenoid valve must be removed during overhaul of the carburettor, remove the top cover from the carburettor and invert it. Extract the enrichment jet and retaining screw, and withdraw the solenoid valve.

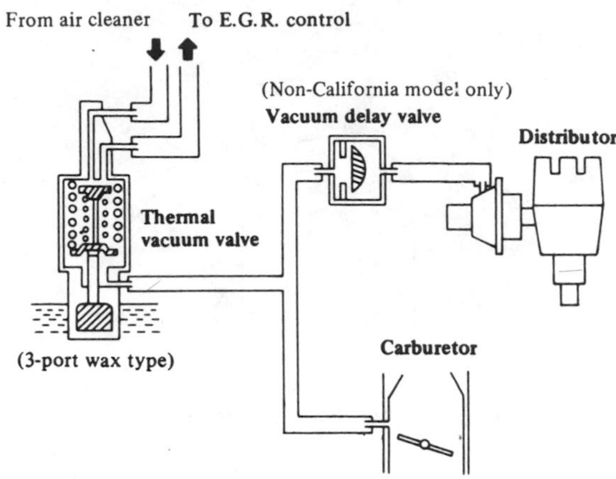

Fig. 3.44 Spark timing control system – North American models (Sec 16)

EGR Exhaust gas recirculation

Exhaust gas sensor

15 This is fitted into the exhaust manifold and monitors the oxygen content in the exhaust gas. A warning lamp is fitted which illuminates after 50 000 km (30 000 miles) as a reminder to inspect and possibly renew the sensor.

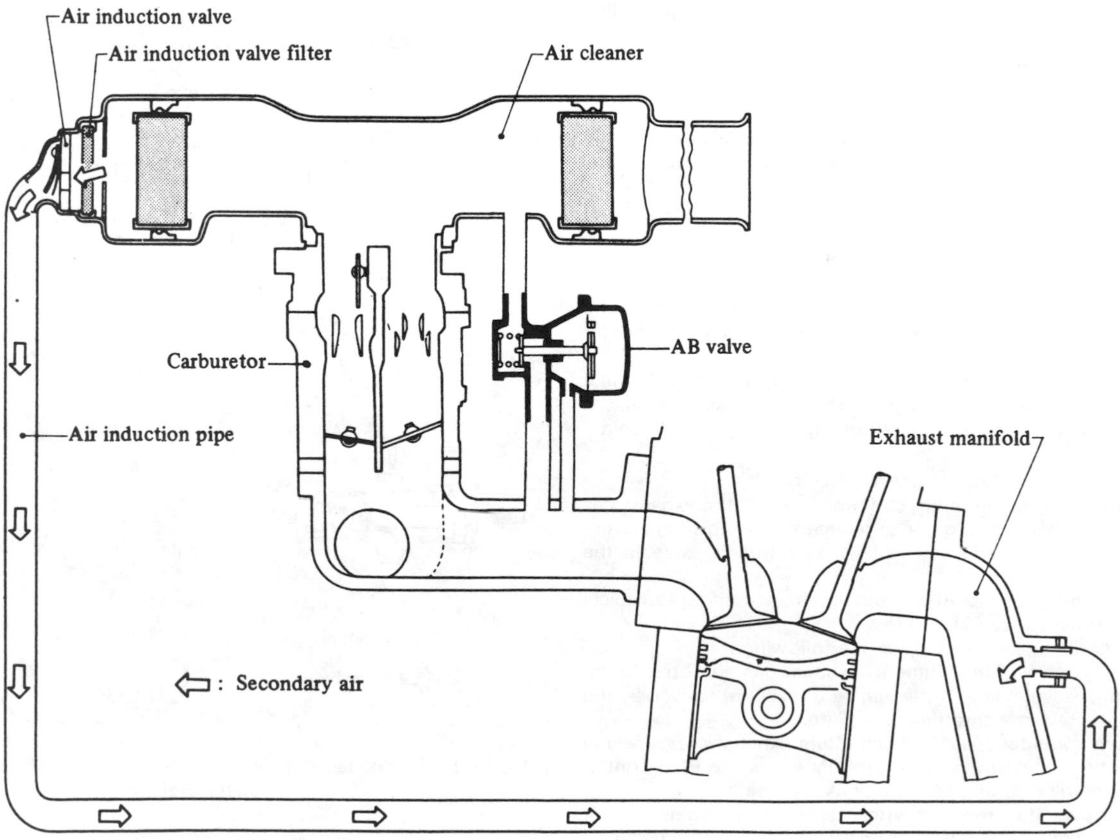

Fig. 3.45 Air induction system – except MPG (Sec 16)

AB Anti-backfire

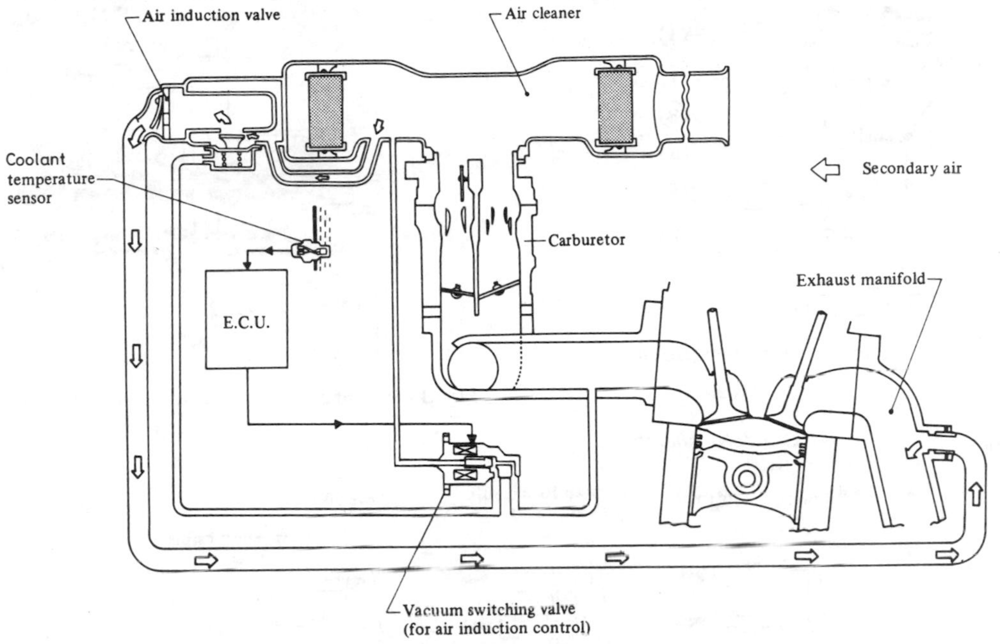

Fig. 3.46 Air induction system MPG models (Sec 16)

ECV Electronic control unit

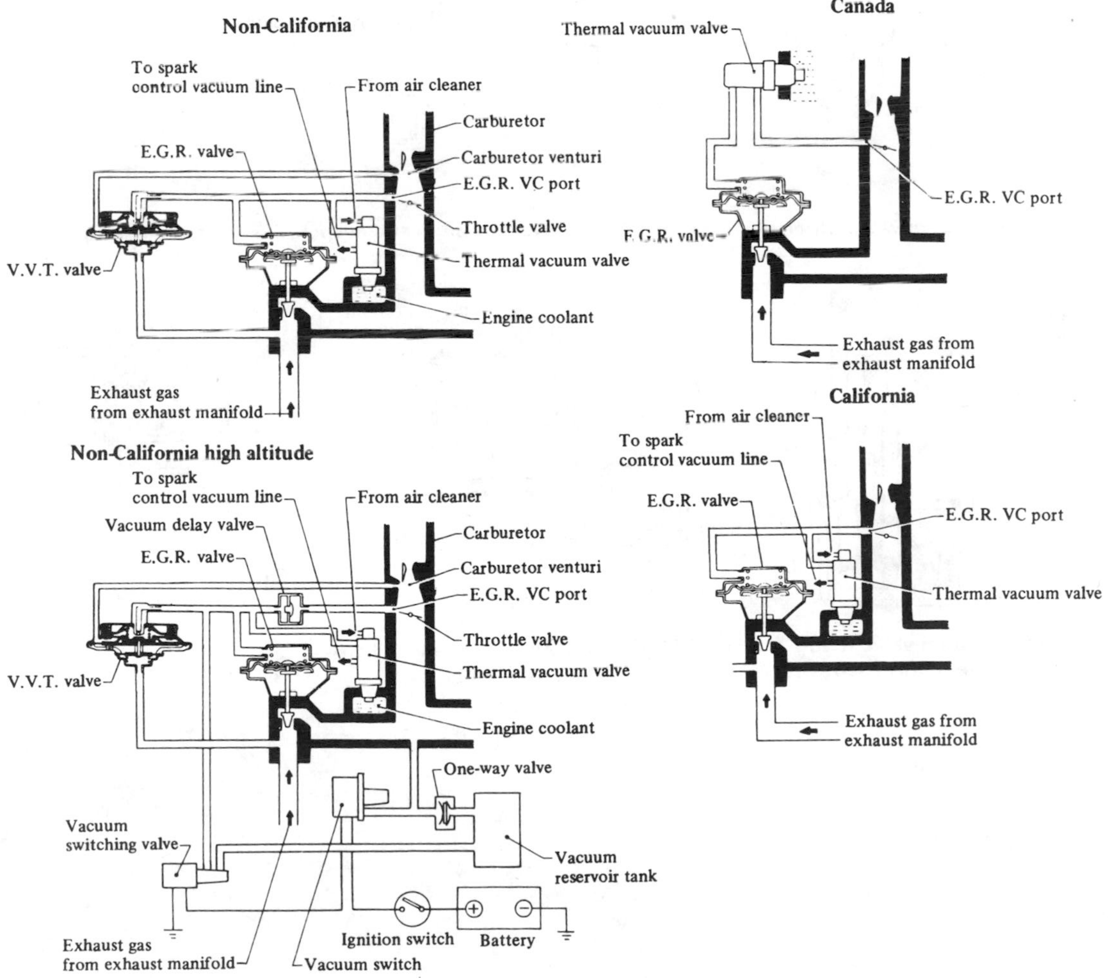

Fig. 3.47 Exhaust gas recirculation system (Sec 16)

VVT Venturi vacuum transducer

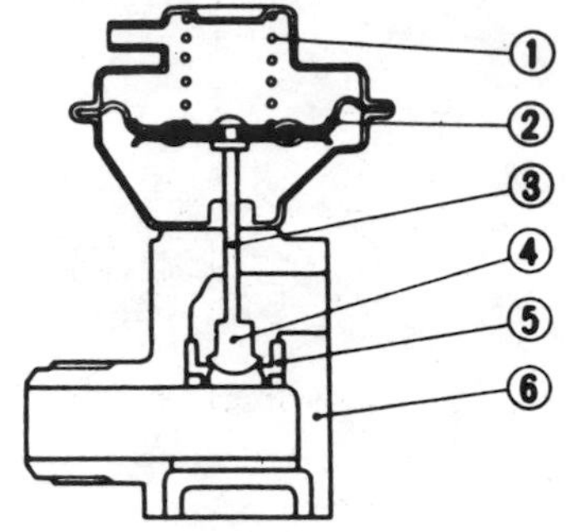

Fig. 3.48 EGR system control valve (Sec 16)

1 Diaphragm spring
2 Diaphragm
3 Valve shaft
4 Valve
5 Valve seat
6 Valve chamber

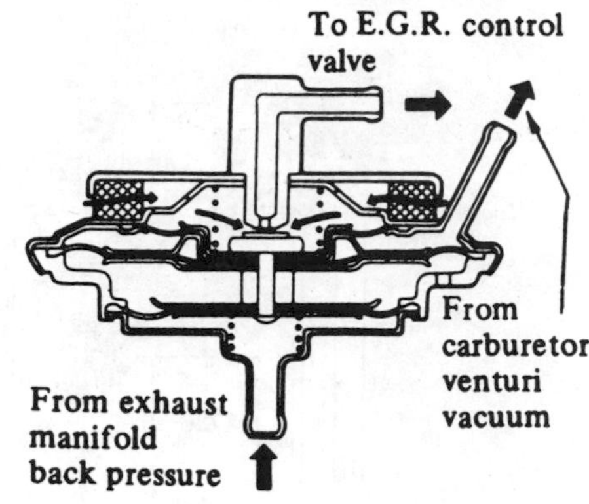

Fig. 3.49 Venturi vacuum transducer – EGR system (Sec 16)

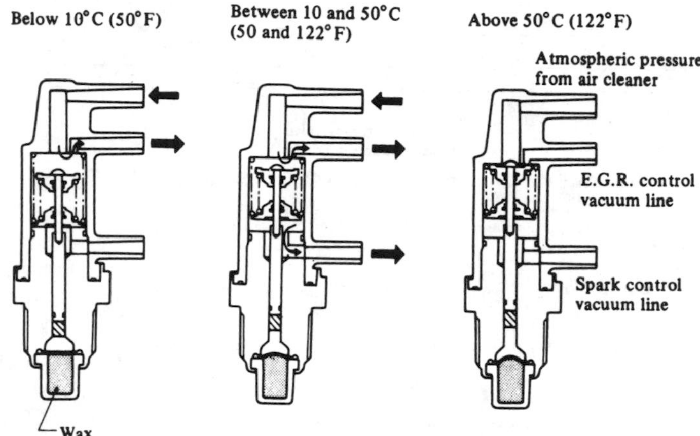

Fig. 3.50 Thermal vacuum valve (three part type) in EGR, catalyst warm-up and evaporative emission control systems (Sec 16)

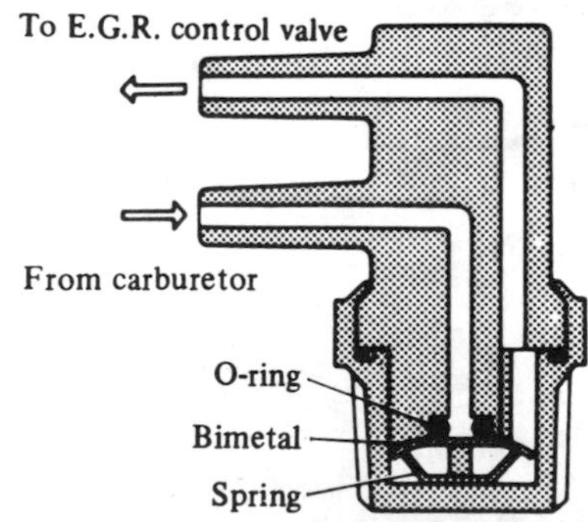

Fig. 3.51 Thermal vacuum valve (two-port type) in EGR system only (Sec 16)

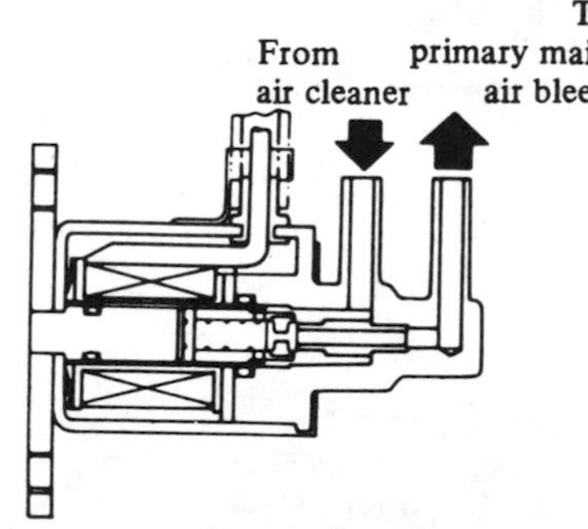

Fig. 3.52 Vacuum switching valve – EGR system (Sec 16)

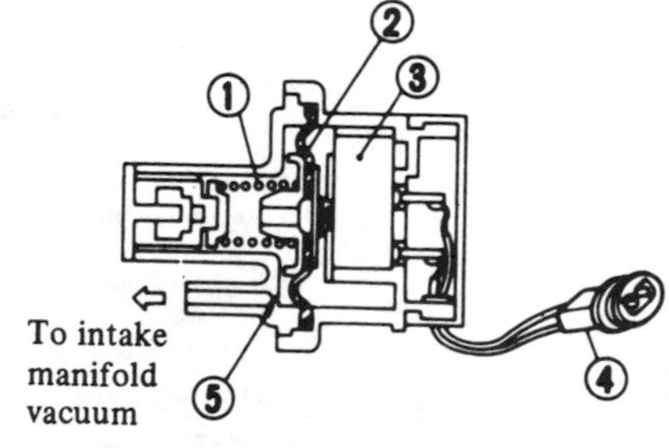

Fig. 3.53 Vacuum switch – EGR system (Sec 16)

1 Spring
2 Diaphragm
3 Microswitch
4 Wiring connector
5 Orifice

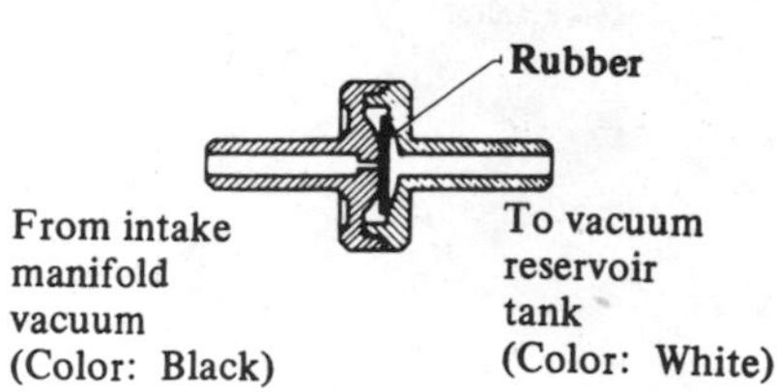

Fig. 3.54 One-way (non-return) valve in EGR system (Sec 16)

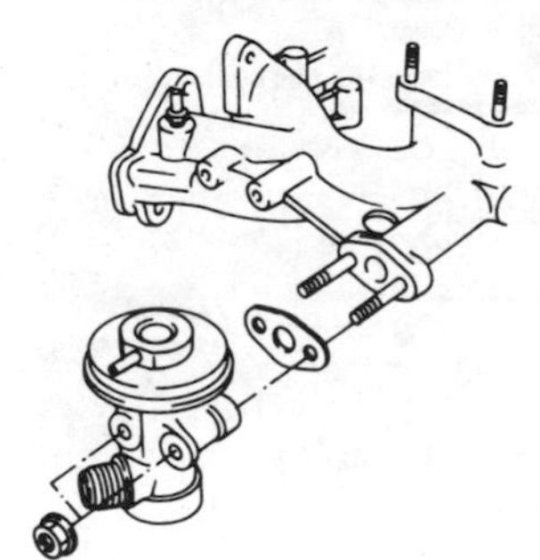

Fig. 3.55 EGR valve removed (Sec 16)

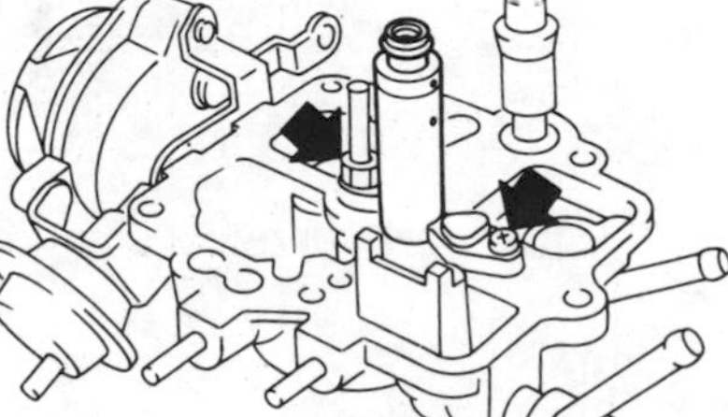

Fig. 3.56 Air fuel ratio control system solenoid valve and enrichment jet (Sec 16)

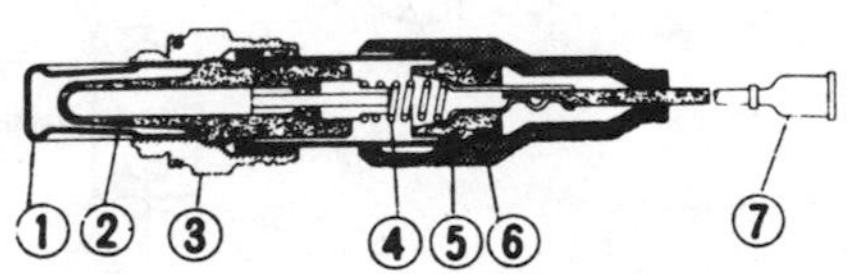

Fig. 3.57 Exhaust gas sensor (Sec 16)

1 Louvre
2 Zirconia tube
3 Holder
4 Spring
5 Terminal support
6 Protective boot
7 Wiring connector

Exhaust manifold
Exhaust gas sensor
Air induction hose

Fig. 3.58 Location of exhaust gas sensor (Sec 16)

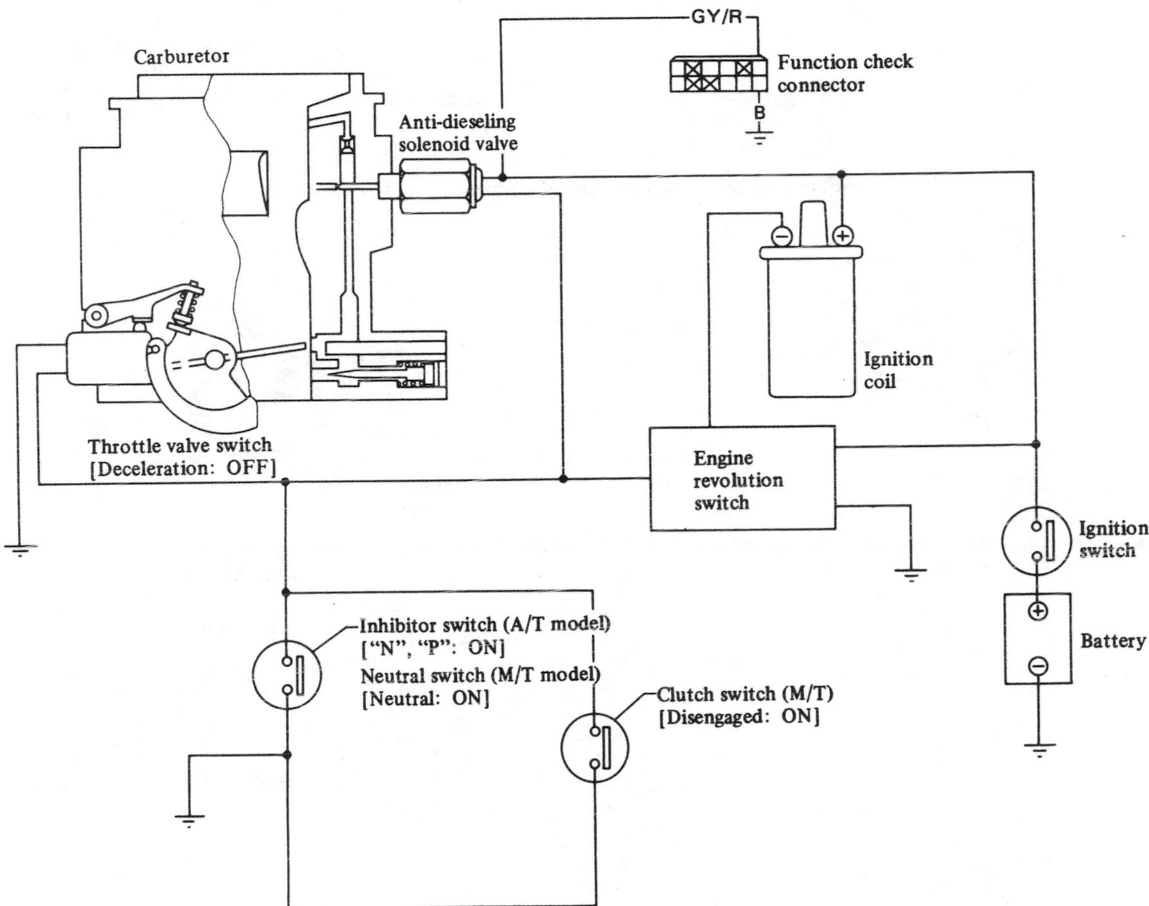

Fig. 3.59 Fuel cut-off system – except Californian and MPG models (Sec 16)

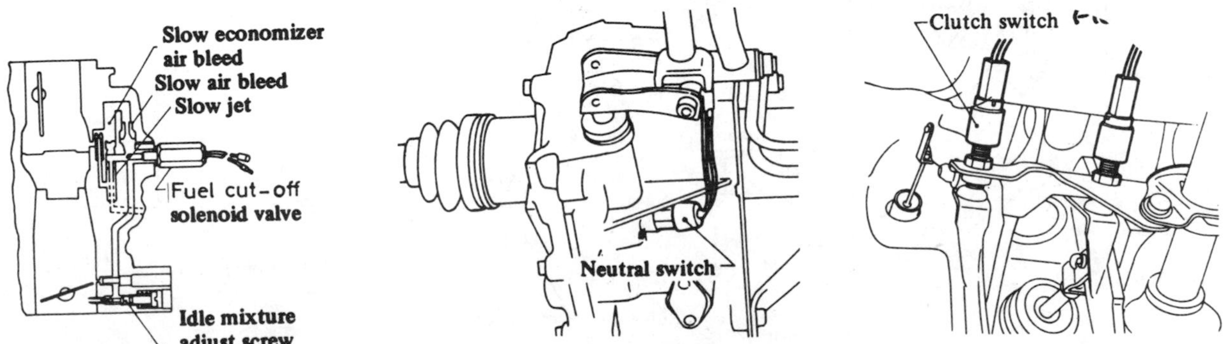

Fig. 3.60 Fuel cut-off solenoid valve (Sec 16)

Fig. 3.61 Transmission neutral switch – fuel cut-off system (Sec 16)

Fig. 3.62 Clutch switch – fuel cut-off system (Sec 16)

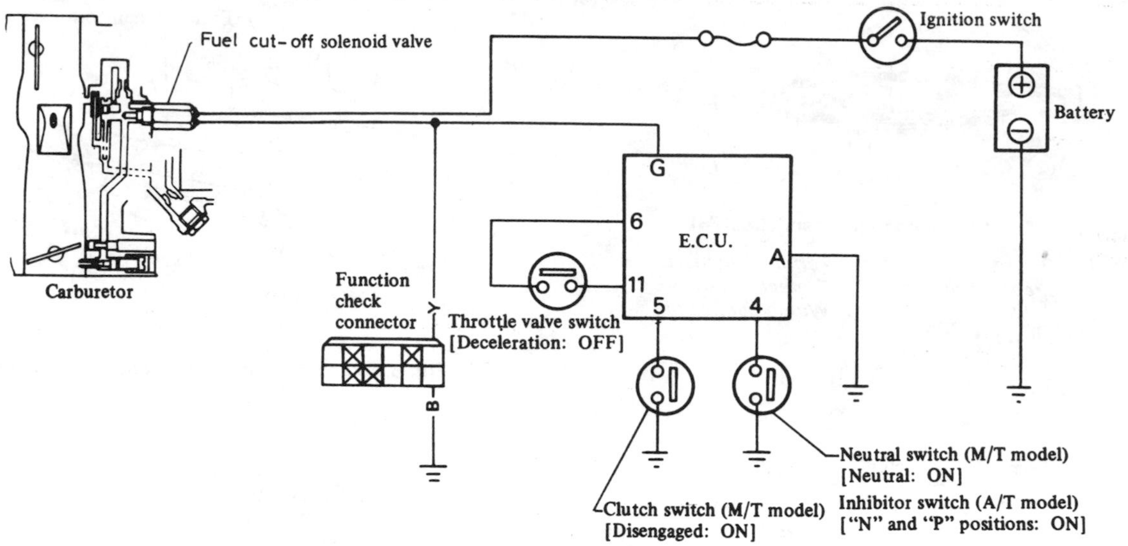

Fig. 3.63 Fuel cut-off system – Californian models (Sec 16)

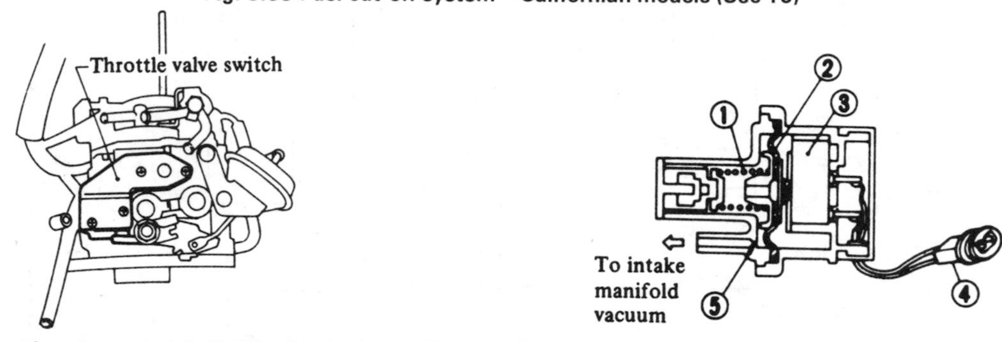

Fig. 3.64 Throttle valve switch in Californian fuel cut-off system (Sec 16)

Fig. 3.65 Vacuum switch in Californian fuel cut-off system (Sec 16)

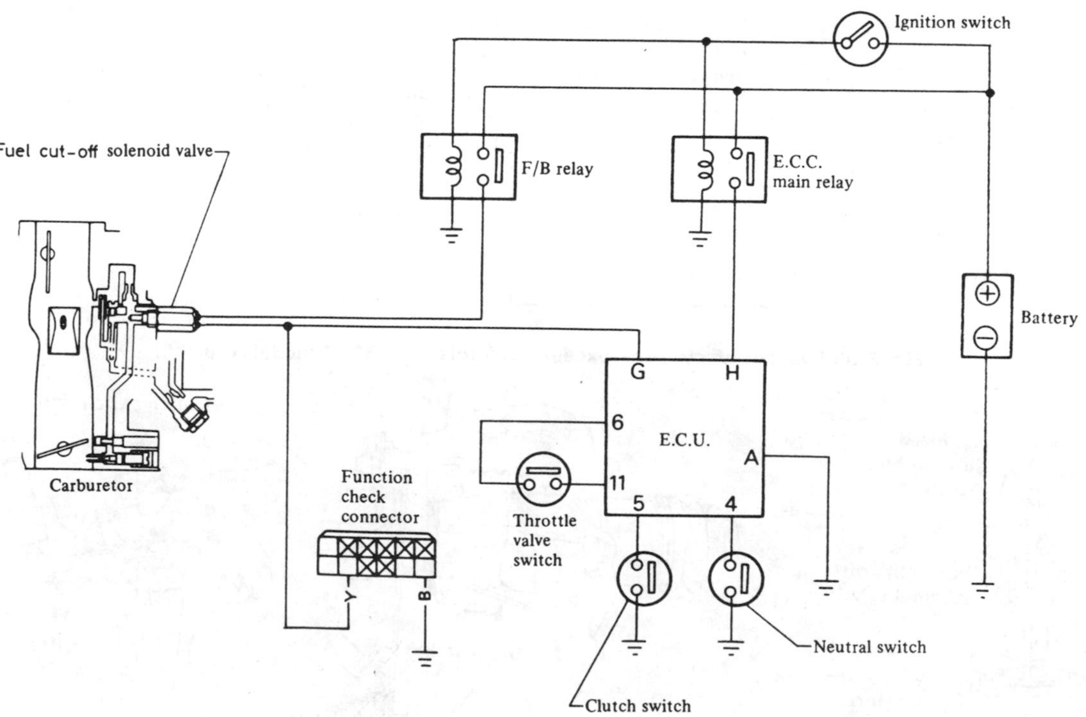

Fig. 3.66 Fuel cut-off system – MPG models (Sec 16)

ECC Electronically controlled carburettor ECU Electronic control unit

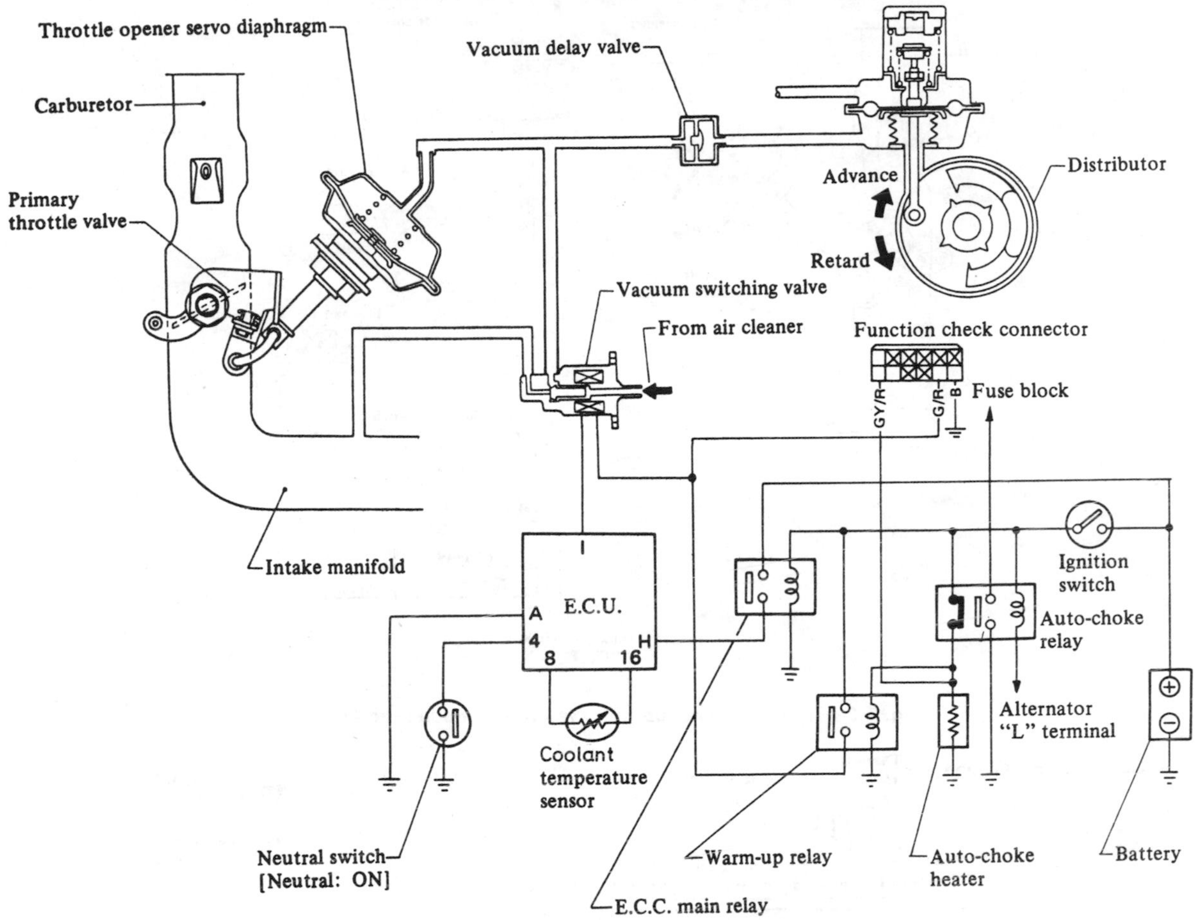

Throttle opener servo diaphragm
Vacuum delay valve
Carburetor
Primary throttle valve
Advance
Distributor
Retard
Vacuum switching valve
From air cleaner
Function check connector
GY/R
G/R
B
Fuse block
Intake manifold
I
E.C.U.
A
4
8
16
H
Ignition switch
Auto-choke relay
Alternator "L" terminal
Coolant temperature sensor
Neutral switch
[Neutral: ON]
Warm-up relay
Auto-choke heater
Battery
E.C.C. main relay

Fig. 3.67 Catalyst warm-up system – MPG models (Sec 16)

ECC Electronically controlled carburettor *ECU Electronic control unit*

Secondary side
Mixture heater
Primary side
Carburetor insulator

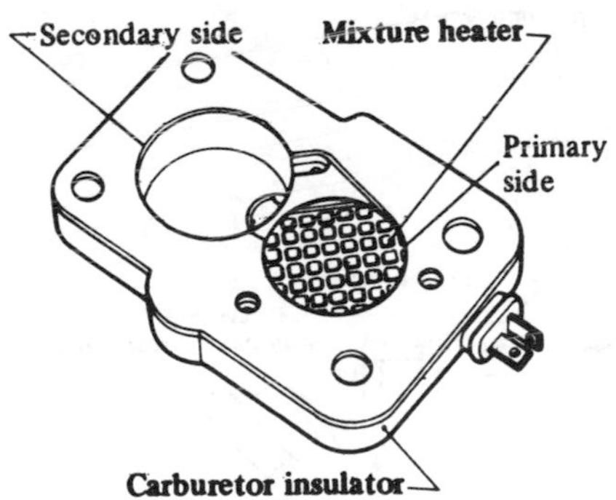

Fig. 3.68 Mixture heating element (Sec 16)

Engine speed switch and relay (MPG models)

16 Designed to protect the catalytic converter from extremely high temperatures during high engine speeds. The system also includes a relay mounted on the fuse block.

Fuel cut-off system (except Californian and MPG)

17 The system is designed to cut off the fuel supply during deceleration at high speeds and also to prevent running on when the ignition is switched off.
18 Components of the system include:
Solenoid valve. The valve is open to allow fuel to flow into the carburettor idling circuit only when the ignition is switched on.
Neutral switch. This energises the vacuum switch when the transmission is in neutral.
Clutch switch. This energises the vacuum switch when the clutch pedal is depressed.
Engine speed switch. This detects the engine speed when the fuel shut-off system comes into operation.

Fuel cut-off system (Californian models)

19 This system differs from that described in earlier paragraphs in respect of some of the components used.
Throttle valve switch. This is connected to the electronic control unit (ECU), it operates according to the position of the throttle valve plate.
Vacuum switch. When intake manifold vacuum increases during deceleration, the switch actuates to interrupt the electrical signal to the vacuum switching valve.

Fuel cut-off system (MPG models)

20 This system differs from other versions by not operating when the engine is cold, nor under no-load conditions, in order to prevent the engine from stalling.

Catalyst warm-up system (MPG models)

21 This is designed to warm up the catalytic converter quickly in order to improve its conversion efficiency at the earliest possible moment.

Mixture heating system (except California and MPG)

22 This is a method of heating the carburettor beneath the throttle block by an electric element during the warm-up period. The heater is switched off by the coolant temperature switch as engine temperature rises.

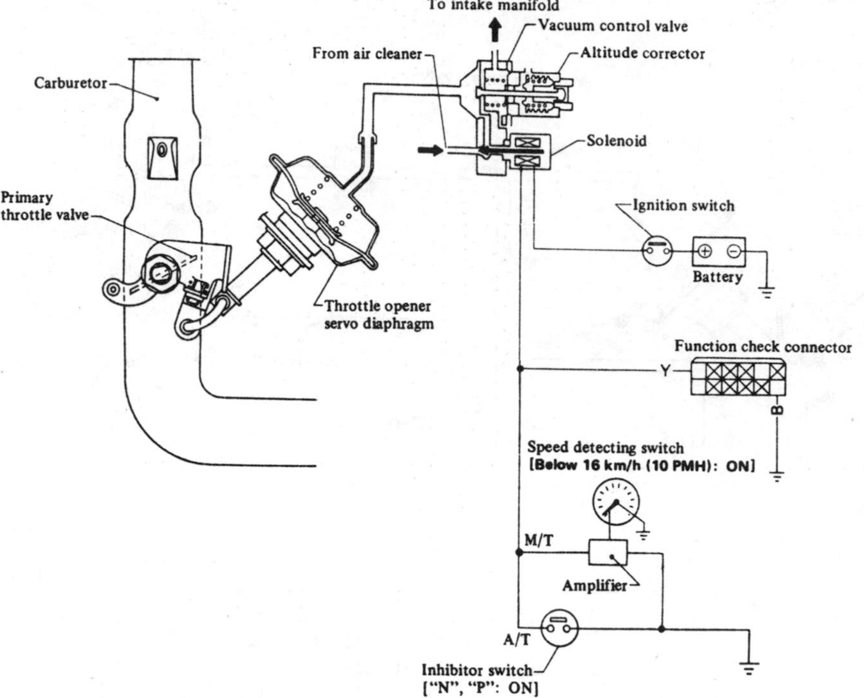

Fig. 3.69 Throttle opener control system – Canada (Sec 16)

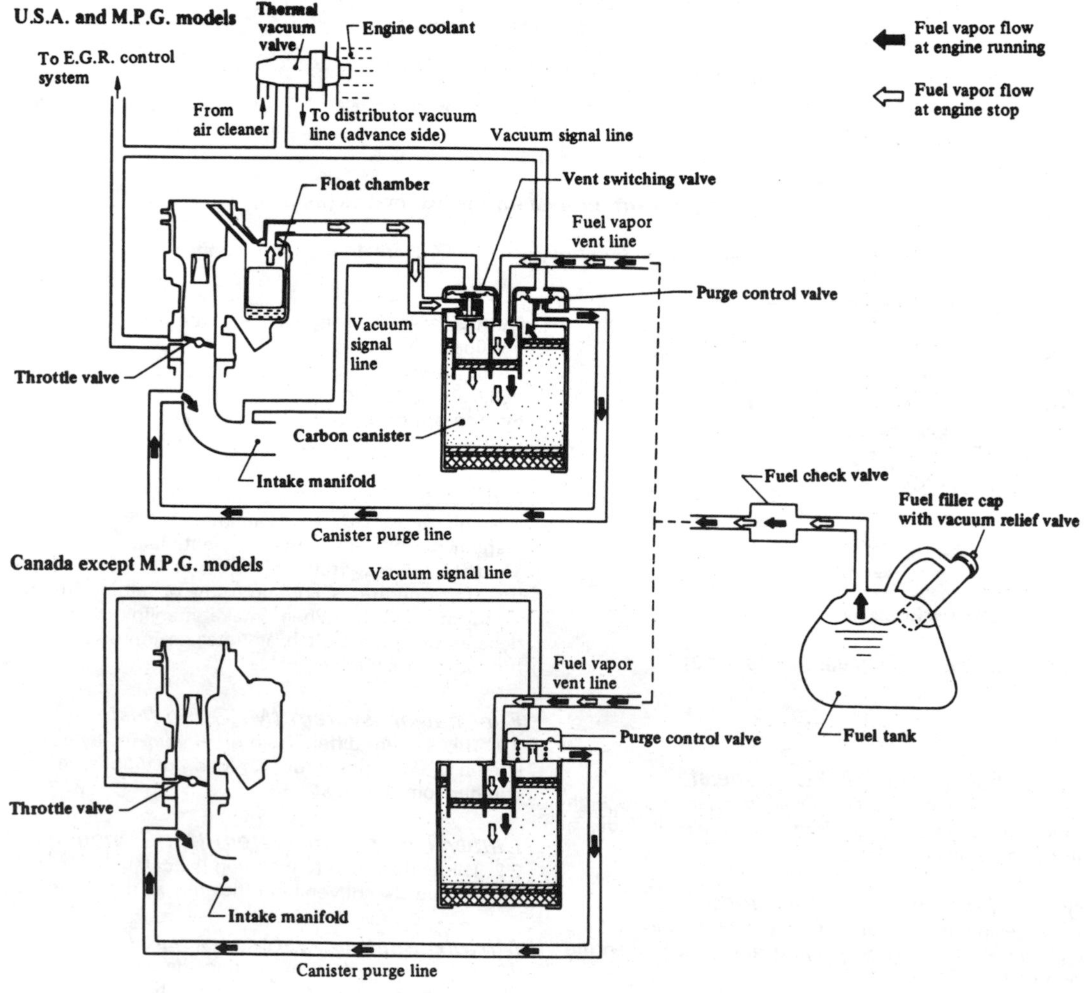

Fig. 3.70 Fuel evaporative emission control system (Sec 16)

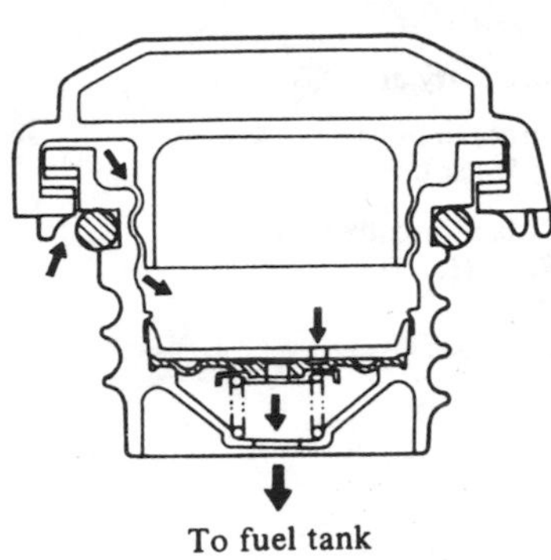

Fig. 3.71 Fuel tank filler cap with vacuum relief valve (Sec 16)

Throttle opener control system (TOCS) – Canada

23 Designed to open the throttle valve plate slightly during deceleration to prevent excessive emissions of unburned HC.

Evaporative control system

24 The purpose of the system is as described in Section 15, but evaporation from the carburettor float chamber is also routed into the system circuit.

25 Additional components are incorporated in the circuit and these include a vent switching valve, a thermal vacuum valve and a fuel tank filler cap fitted with a vacuum relief valve.

Emission control system modifications on vehicles operating at high altitudes

26 An altitude compensator has been added for the carburettor, its purpose being as described in Section 7.

27 On vehicles equipped with automatic transmission, the EGR system is modified to include a vacuum tank, a vacuum delay valve, a vacuum switching valve and a vacuum switch.

17 Catalytic converter

1 This device is fitted into the exhaust system of North American vehicles. It is basically a container for a catalyst which, as exhaust gases pass through it, becomes oxidised and changes the gas to harmless water and carbon dioxide.

2 If the exhaust system is being dismantled, take care not to damage the catalytic converter when removing its shield or flange connecting bolts.

3 On vehicles fitted with this device, certain precautions should be taken:

Do not allow the engine to idle for excessive lengths of time
Use only unleaded fuel
Avoid running out of fuel
Do not park over long grass or other combustible material

4 The catalytic converter may become very hot after the vehicle has descended a long gradient, keep the vehicle interior well ventilated.

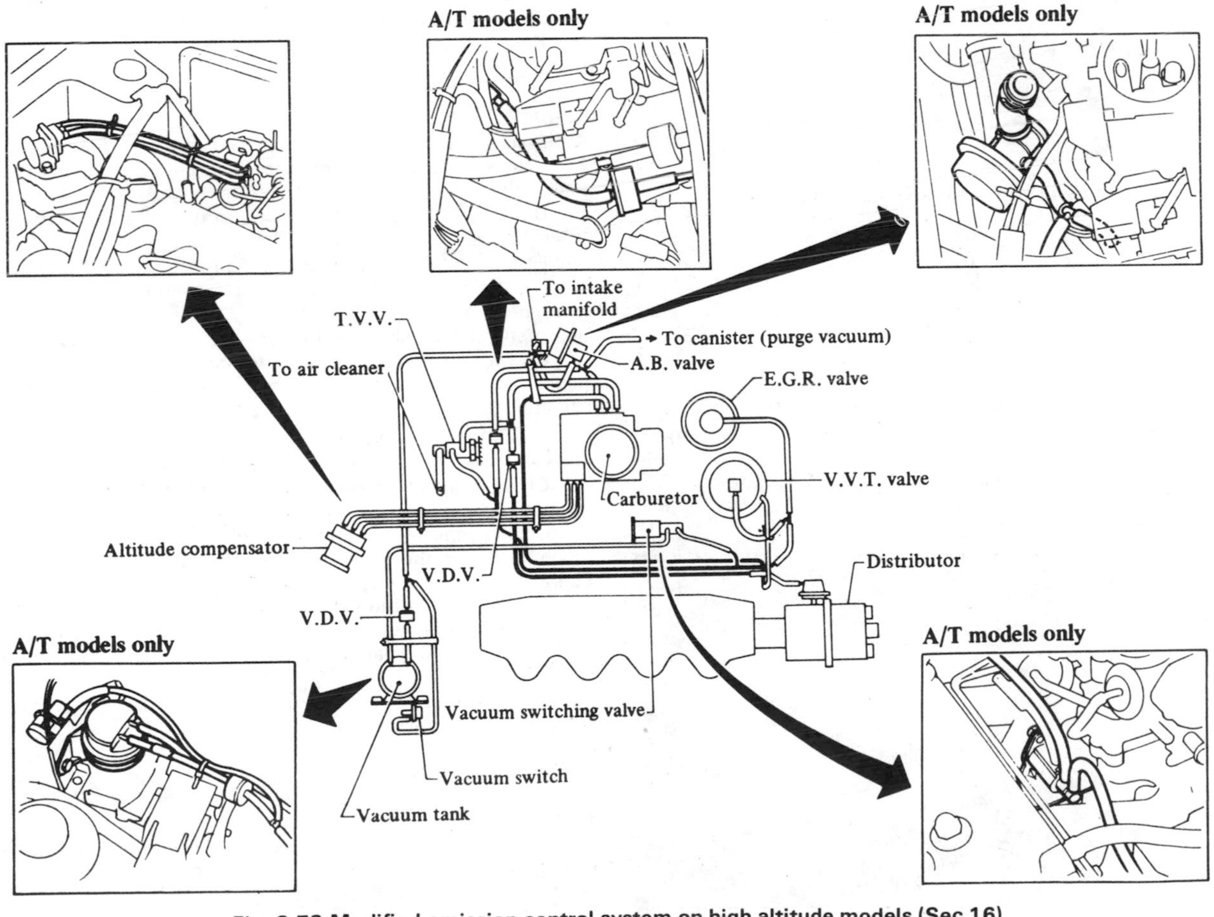

Fig. 3.72 Modified emission control system on high altitude models (Sec 16)

TVV Thermal vacuum valve *VDV vacuum delay valve*

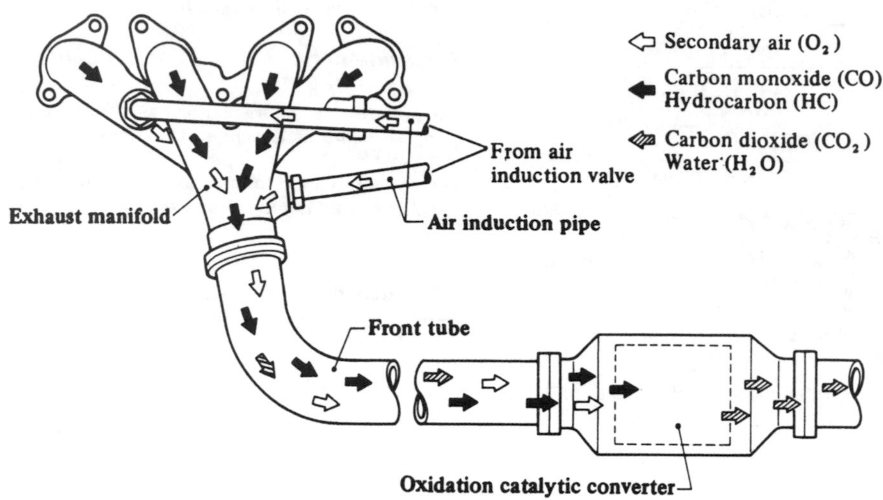

Fig. 3.73 Catalytic converter installation (Sec 17)

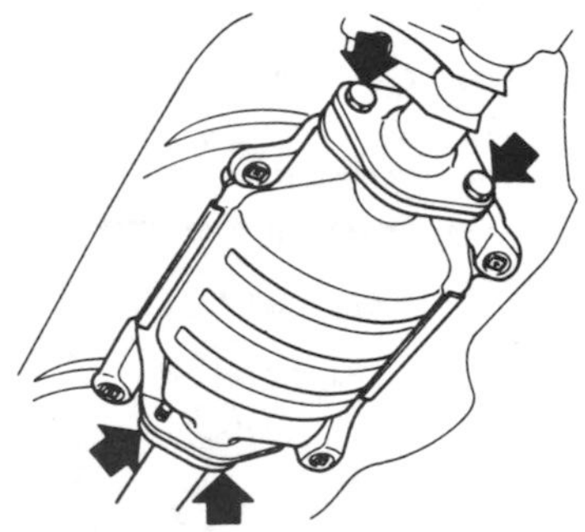

Fig. 3.74 Catalytic converter connections (Sec 17)

Fig. 3.75 Accelerator cable connection to pedal arm (Sec 18)

18.6 Carburettor throttle cable quadrant

18 Accelerator pedal and cable – removal, refitting and adjustment

Pedal

1 Release the cable from the top of the pedal arm.

2 Extract the E-clip from the pedal pivot shaft, disengage the return spring and remove the pedal.

3 Refitting is a reversal of removal, but apply grease to the moving parts.

Cable

4 Disconnect the cable from the top of the pedal arm.

5 Release the plastic grommet at the engine compartment rear bulkhead.

6 Disconnect the cable at the carburettor (photo) and then withdraw it into the engine compartment.

7 Fit the new cable by reversing the removal operations. Adjust it by moving the position of the outer cable clamp to give the correct free movement at the pedal pad (see Fig. 3.77). Make sure that the automatic choke valve plate is fully open before adjusting the cable.

8 On vehicles equipped with automatic transmission, check that the pedal can be depressed fully into the kickdown position (also refer to Chapter 7).

19 Choke control cable – removal and refitting

1 Remove the air cleaner from the carburettor, release the cable pinch screw on the trunnion at the carburettor and the cable clamp screw.

2 Working inside the vehicle at the facia panel, unscrew the choke control knob bezel nut and withdraw the cable into the vehicle interior. If a choke warning lamp switch is fitted, disconnect the electrical leads.

3 Refitting is a reversal of removal. Make sure that the bulkhead cable grommet makes a good seal.

4 With the cable in position, do not tighten the pinch screw until the choke control knob has been pulled out by about 3.0 mm (0.12 in) and the choke valve plate has been checked as being in the fully open position.

5 Finally check that with the control pulled right out, the valve plate is fully closed. Adjust the position of the outer cable in the clamp if necessary to achieve this.

20 Manifolds and exhaust system

1 The manifolds are located on opposite sides of the engine. As the

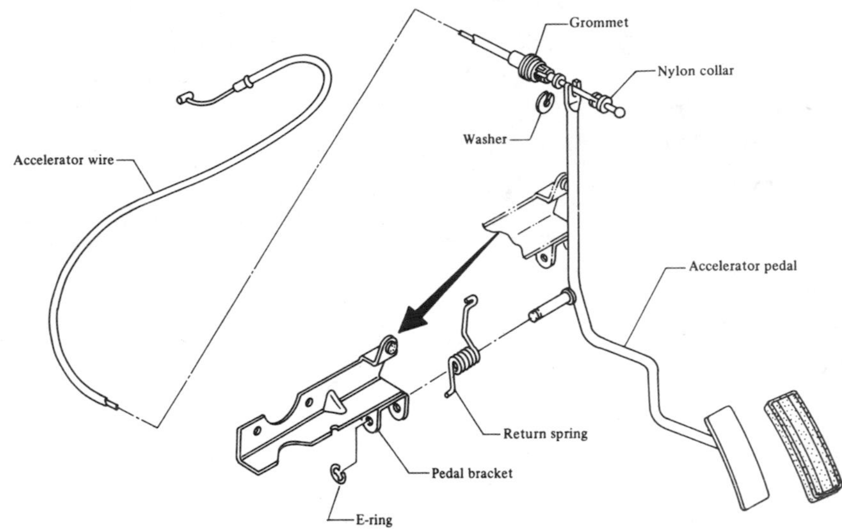

Fig. 3.76 Typical accelerator control (Sec 18)

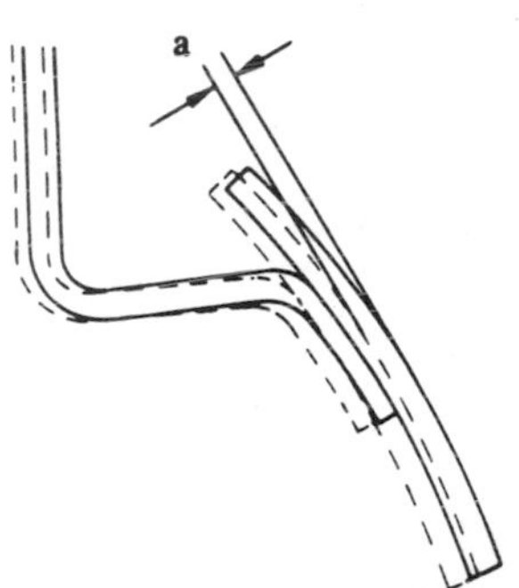

Fig. 3.77 Accelerator pedal free play (Sec 18)

a = 1.0 to 2.0 mm (0.04 to 0.08 in)

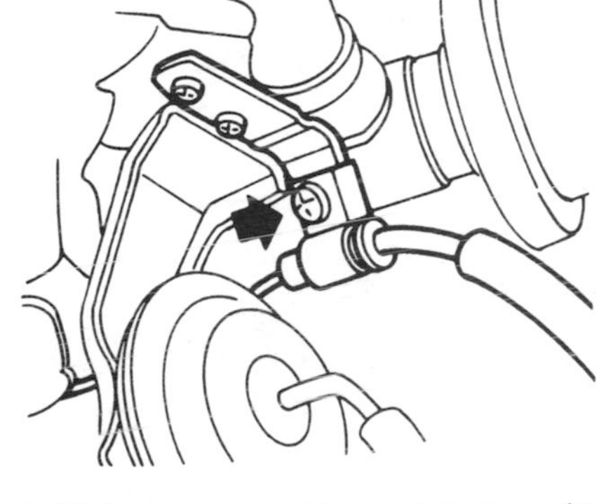

Fig. 3.78 Accelerator cable conduit clamp (Sec 18)

20.4A Exhaust expansion box rubber mounting

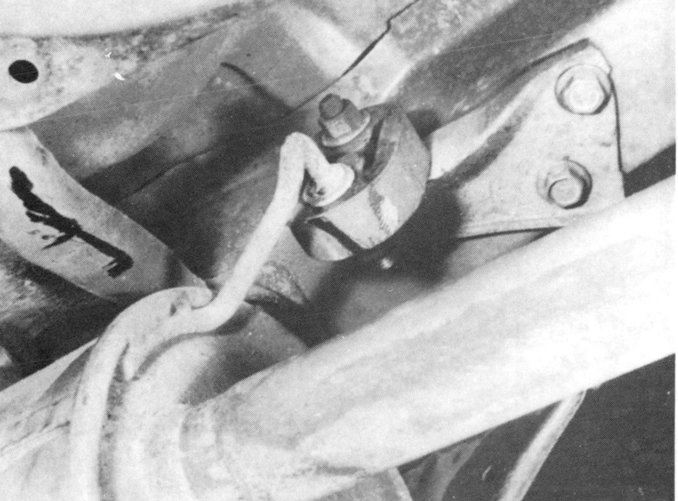

20.4B Exhaust silencer rubber mounting

intake manifold is coolant heated, the cooling system must be drained before it can be removed.

2 Always use new gaskets when refitting the manifolds and tighten all nuts and bolts to the specified torques.

3 The exhaust system may have one or two downpipes, depending upon whether it has a low or high compression engine. On models without a catalytic converter, the system incorporates an expansion box and a silencer.

4 The exhaust system is suspended on flexible mountings (photos).

5 When any one section of the exhaust system needs renewal it often follows that the whole lot is best replaced.

6 It is most important when fitting exhaust systems that the bends

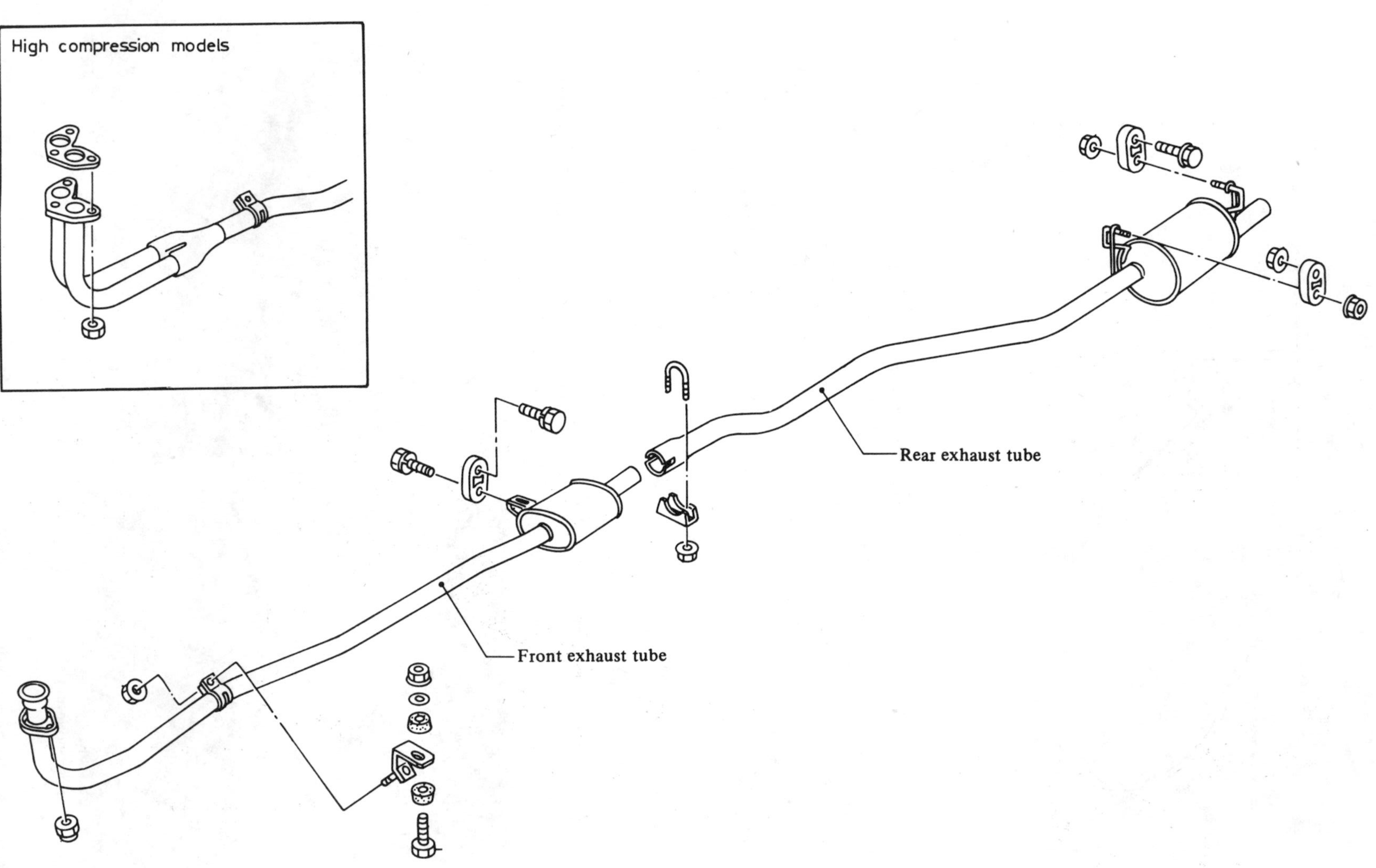

Fig. 3.79 Typical exhaust system (Sec 20)

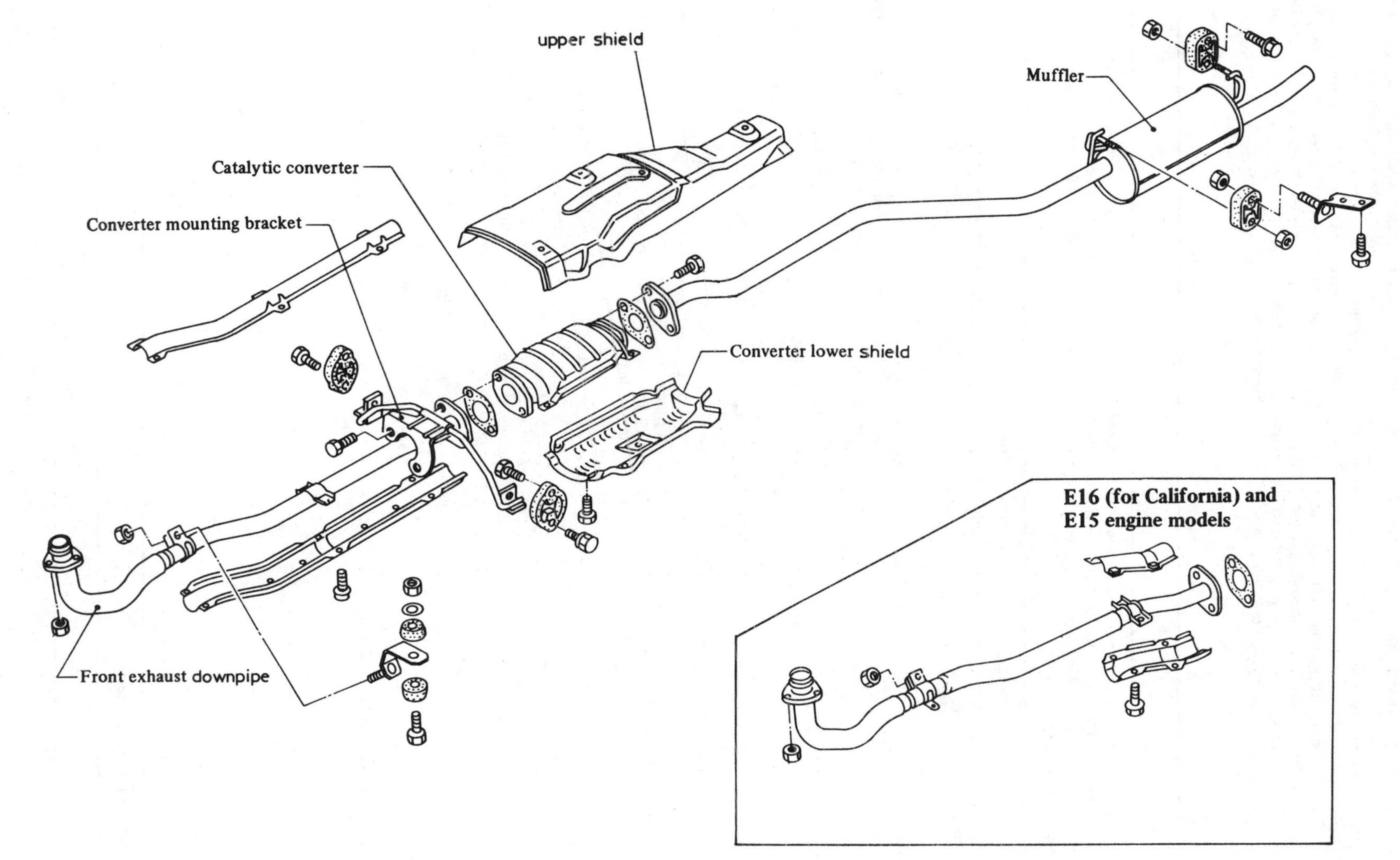

Fig. 3.80 Typical exhaust system incorporating catalytic converter (Sec 20)

and contours are carefully followed and that each connecting joint overlaps the correct distance. Any stresses or strain imparted in order to force the system to fit the hanger rubbers, will result in early fractures and failures.

7 When fitting a new part of a complete system it is well worth removing ALL the system from the car and cleaning up all the joints so that they fit together easily. The time spent struggling with obstinate joints whilst flat on your back under the car is eliminated and the likelihood of distorting or even breaking a section is greatly reduced. Do not waste a lot of time trying to undo rusted and corroded clamps and bolts. Cut them off. New ones will be required anyway if they are that bad.

8 Use an exhaust joint sealant when assembling pipe sections to ensure that the respective joints are free from leaks.

9 When fitting the new system, only semi-tighten the retainers initially until the complete system is fitted, then when you have checked it for satisfactory location, tighten the securing bolts/nuts. If the hangers are stretched, perished or broken they must be renewed, otherwise the system will vibrate, leading to leaks, premature wear or even factures.

21 Fault diagnosis – fuel system

Unsatisfactory engine performance and excessive fuel consumption are not necessarily the fault of the fuel system or carburettor. In fact they more commonly occur as a result of ignition and timing faults. Before acting on the following it is necessary to check the ignition system first. Even though a fault may lie in the fuel system it will be difficult to trace unless the ignition is correct. The faults below, therefore, assume that this has been attended to first (where appropriate).

Symptom	Reason(s)
Smell of fuel when engine is stopped	Leaking fuel lines or unions Leaking fuel tank
Smell of fuel when engine is idling	Leaking fuel line unions between pump and carburettor Overflow of fuel from float chamber due to wrong level setting, ineffective needle valve or punctured float
Excessive fuel consumption for reasons not covered by leaks or float chamber faults	Worn jets Over-rich setting Sticking mechanism Dirty air cleaner element Sticking air cleaner thermostatic mechanism
Difficult starting, uneven running, lack of power, cutting out	One or more jets blocked or restricted Float chamber fuel level too low or needle valve sticking Fuel pump not delivering sufficient fuel Faulty solenoid fuel shut-off valve (if fitted) Induction leak
Difficult starting when cold	Choke control or automatic choke maladjusted Automatic choke not cocked before starting
Difficult starting when hot	Automatic choke malfunction Accelerator pedal pumped before starting Vapour lock (especially in hot weather or at high altitude)
Engine does not respond properly to throttle	Faulty accelerator pump Blocked jet(s) Slack in accelerator cable
Engine idle speed drops when hot	Defective temperature compensator Overheated fuel pump

22 Fault diagnosis – emission control system

Symptom	Reason(s)
Excessive HC or CO in exhaust gas	Air cleaner clogged Float level too high Faulty spark control system Faulty throttle opener control system Leaking intake manifold gasket

Symptom	Reason(s)
Excessive HC, CO and NOx in exhaust gas	Worn piston rings Incorrect valve clearances Faulty thermostat Blown cylinder head gasket Clogged PCV valve Incorrect idle mixture Clogged fuel filter Faulty idle compensator Choke not fully off Incorrect ignition settings Malfunction of emission control system component

HC Hydrocarbons
CO Carbon monoxide
NOx Oxides of nitrogen

Chapter 4 Ignition system

Contents

Specifications

General

System type:
- All models except N America .... Mechanical breaker distributor
- N America .... Electronic system with breakerless distributor

Firing order .... 1-3-4-2 (No 1 cylinder at timing belt end)

Distributor

Mechanical breaker system

Rotor rotation .... Anti-clockwise
Contact points gap .... 0.45 to 0.55 mm (0.018 to 0.022 in)
Dwell angle .... 49 to 55°
Cap carbon brush minimum length .... 10.0 mm (0.39 in)

Breakerless system

Rotor rotation .... Anti-clockwise
Air gap .... 0.3 to 0.5 mm (0.012 to 0.020 in)
Cap carbon brush minimum length .... 10.0 mm (0.39 in)

Ignition timing

All models except N America

At idle speed with the vacuum pipe disconnected and plugged

E13 engine .... 0 to 4° BTDC
E15 engine .... 2 to 6° BTDC

N America

At idle speed with the vacuum pipe disconnected and plugged. Refer also to the vehicle decal

E15 and E16 engines (1982 models):
- All models except MPG:
  - Manual transmission .... 0 to 4° ATDC
  - Automatic transmission .... 4 to 8° ATDC
- MPG models .... 0 to 2° ATDC

E15 and E16 engines (1983 models):
- All models except MPG:
  - Manual transmission .... 3 to 7° ATDC
  - Automatic transmission .... 3 to 7° ATDC
- MPG models .... 0 to 2° ATDC

Ignition coil

Mechanical breaker system

Type	C6R-206
Primary resistance	1.35 to 1.65 ohms
Secondary resistance	6800 to 10 200 ohms

Breakerless system

Type	C1T-72
Primary resistance	1.04 to 1.27 ohms
Secondary resistance	7300 to 11 000 ohms

Spark plugs

Type	NGK BPR5ES or equivalent
Electrode gap	0.8 to 0.9 mm (0.031 to 0.035 in)

Torque wrench settings

	Nm	lbf ft
Spark plugs	25	18

1 General description

On models other than those destined for operation in N America a conventional mechanical contact breaker type ignition system is fitted. On N American models, an electronic (breakerless) system is used.

Mechanical breaker type ignition

In order that the engine can run correctly it is necessary for an electrical spark to ignite the fuel/air mixture in the combustion chamber at exactly the right moment in relation to engine speed and load. The ignition system is based on feeding low tension voltage from the battery to the coil where it is converted to high tension voltage. The high tension voltage is powerful enough to jump the spark plug gap in the cylinders many times a second under high compression, providing that the system is in good condition and that all adjustments are correct.

The ignition system is divided into two circuits, low tension and high tension.

The low tension circuit (sometimes known as the primary) consists of the battery, lead to the ignition switch, lead from the ignition switch to the low tension or primary coil windings, and the lead from the low tension coil windings to the contact breaker points and condenser in the distributor.

The high tension circuit consists of the high tension or secondary

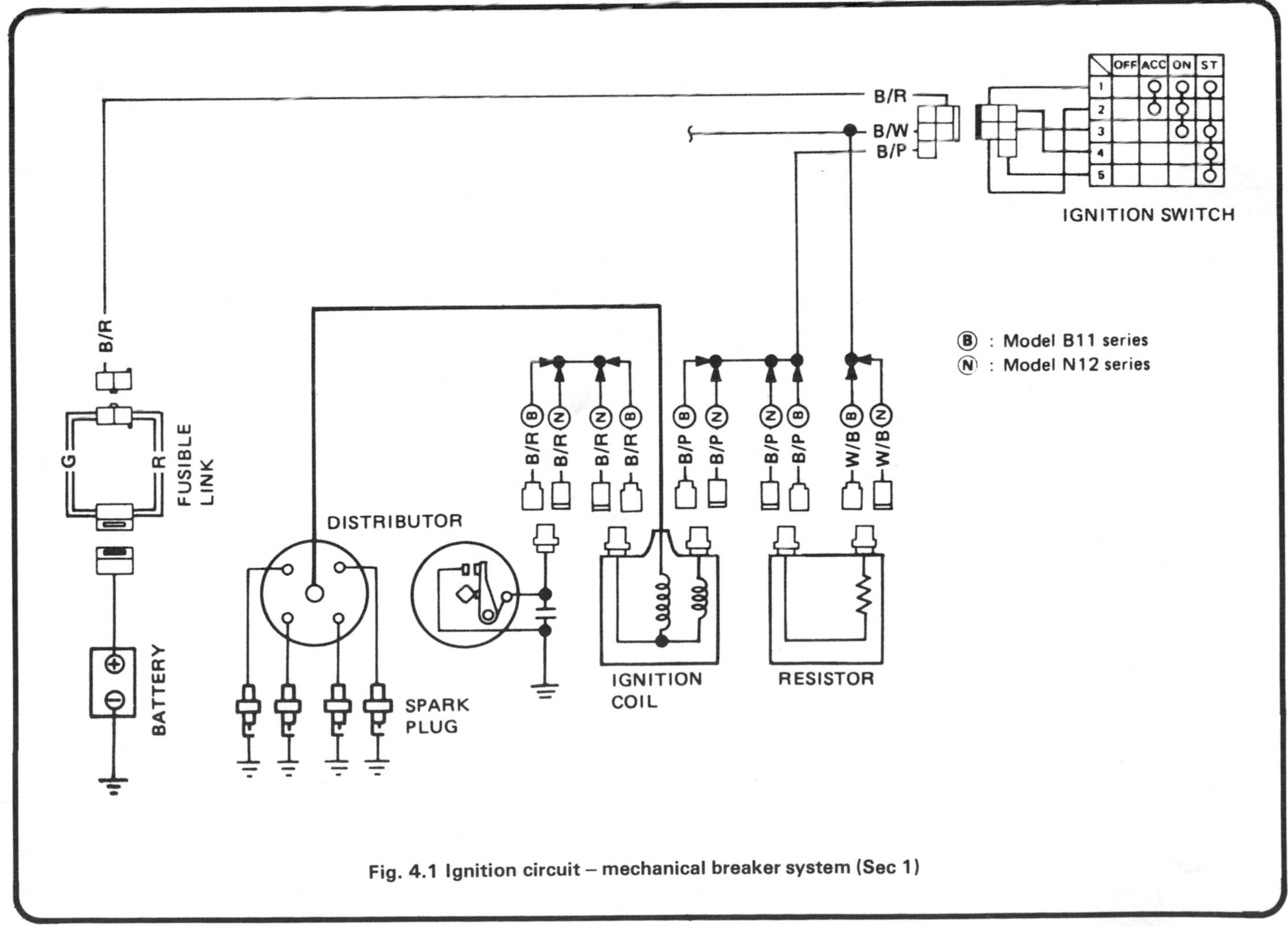

Fig. 4.1 Ignition circuit – mechanical breaker system (Sec 1)

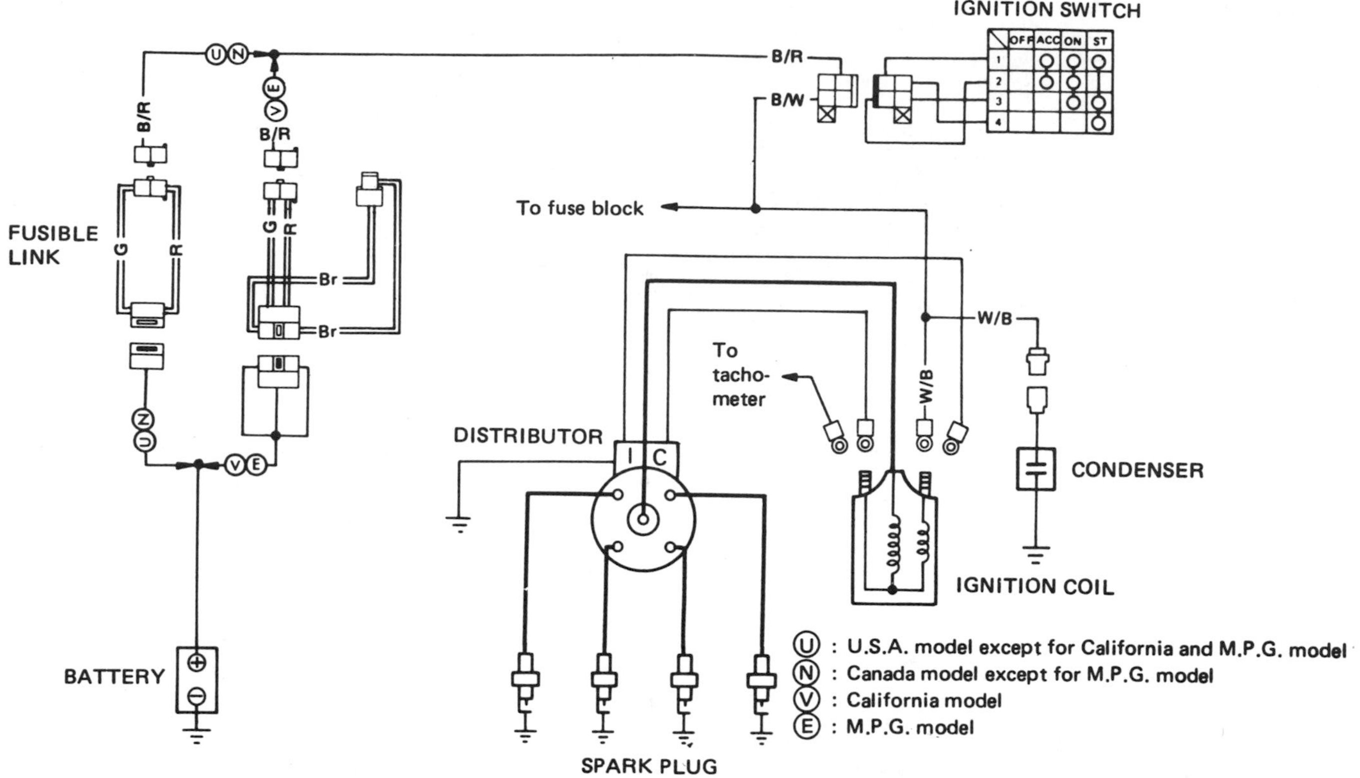

Fig. 4.2 Ignition circuit – breakerless system (Sec 1)

coil winding, the heavy ignition lead from the centre of the coil to the centre of the distributor cap, the rotor arm, and the spark plug leads and spark plugs.

The system functions in the following manner. Low tension voltage is changed in the coil into high tension voltage by the opening and closing of the contact breaker points in the low tension circuit. High tension voltage is then fed via the carbon brush in the centre of the distributor cap (photo), to the rotor arm of the distributor, and each time it comes in line with one of the four metal segments in the cap, which are connected to the spark plug leads, the opening and closing of the contact breaker points causes the high tension voltage to build up, jump the gap from the rotor arm to the appropriate metal segment and so via the spark plug lead to the spark plug, where it finally jumps the spark plug gap to earth.

The ignition is advanced and retarded automatically, to ensure that the spark occurs at just the right instant for the particular load at the prevailing engine speed.

The ignition advance is controlled both mechanically and by a vacuum operated system. The mechanical governor comprises two weights, which move out from the distributor shaft as the engine speed rises due to centrifugal force. As they move outwards they rotate the cam relative to the distributor shaft, and so advance the spark. The weights are held in position by two light springs and it is the tension of the springs which is largely responsible for correct spark advancement.

The vacuum control consists of a diaphragm, one side of which is connected via a small bore tube to the carburettor, and the other side to the contact breaker plate. Depression in the inlet manifold and carburettor, which varies with engine speed and throttle opening, causes the diaphragm to move, so moving the contact breaker plate, and advancing or retarding the spark.

A ballast resistor in the low tension feed to the coil keeps the coil voltage down to 6V during normal running. The wire is bypassed when the starter motor is operating, to compensate for reduced battery voltage.

Breakerless type ignition

The main components comprise a distributor and special coil and condenser.

1.6 Interior of distributor cap – carbon brush arrowed

Instead of the conventional contact breaker points, a reluctor and pick-up unit are used to change low tension (LT) voltage into high tension (HT) voltage.

In view of the high voltage used in this system *care must be taken in handling leads and components when the engine is running.* This is particularly important to anyone equipped with a cardiac pacemaker.

2 Mechanical breaker distributor – servicing contact points

1 At the intervals specified in Routine Maintenance open the bonnet, prise back the clips which secure the distributor cap and move the cap complete with HT leads to one side.

2.4 Distributor with cap removed

A LT negative terminal
B Contact points
C Fixed arm
D C-clip
E Earth wire

2.13 Checking contact breaker points gap

2 Pull off the rotor.
3 Open the contact points by prising the spring contact arm with the thumb nail. If the faces of the points are dirty or severely eroded they must be removed.
4 To remove the contact breaker, disconnect the LT (negative) lead from the terminal on the distributor body (photo).
5 Release, *but do not remove,* the screws which hold the contact breaker to the distributor baseplate. Slide the contact breaker out from under the screws.
6 To remove the spring contact arm, extract the C-clip and slide the arm off the pivot post.
7 If only slight surface pitting or build-up is evident on the faces of the contact points this may be removed by using abrasive paper or rubbing squarely on an oilstone.
8 If the points faces are severely eroded, or there is a large pip on one face, do not attempt to dress them as an excessive amount of metal will have to be removed. Renew them instead.
9 Wipe the faces of new contact points with solvent to remove any protective grease.
10 Apply a drop of oil to the pivot, fit the spring contact arm and the C-clip.
11 Fit the contact breaker assembly to the distributor baseplate, but leave the screws just finger tight. Connect the earth lead.
12 The crankshaft must now be turned until the plastic heel of the spring contact arm is positioned on one of the cam peaks of the distributor shaft.
13 Adjust the fixed contact arm until, using feeler blades, the points gap is as specified – with the feeler blade a stiff sliding fit (photo). A cut-out is provided in the fixed contact arm with a fulcrum pin so that a small screwdriver can be used to lever the arm and control its movement.
14 Once the gap is correct, tighten the fixed contact screws. Recheck the points gap.
15 Apply a smear of high melting-point grease to the distributor shaft cams.
16 Apply two drops of oil to the felt pad in the recess at the top of the distributor shaft. On some models, a felt pad is not used, in which case just oil the screw.
17 Fit the rotor and distributor cap.
18 Setting the points as just described should be regarded as a basic setting only, the dwell angle should now be checked, as described in the next Section.

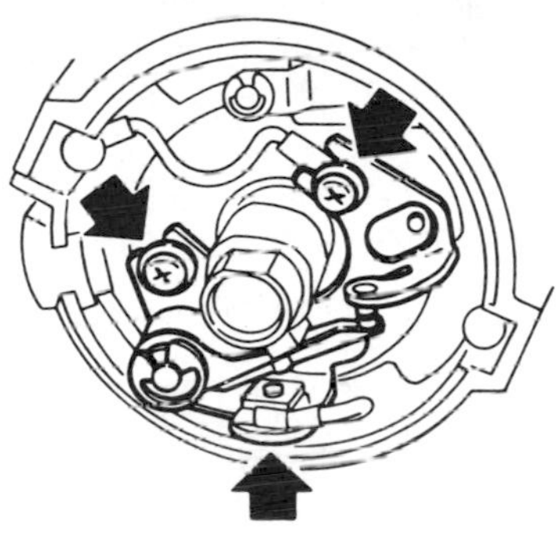

Fig. 4.3 Contact breaker securing screws and LT terminal (Sec 2)

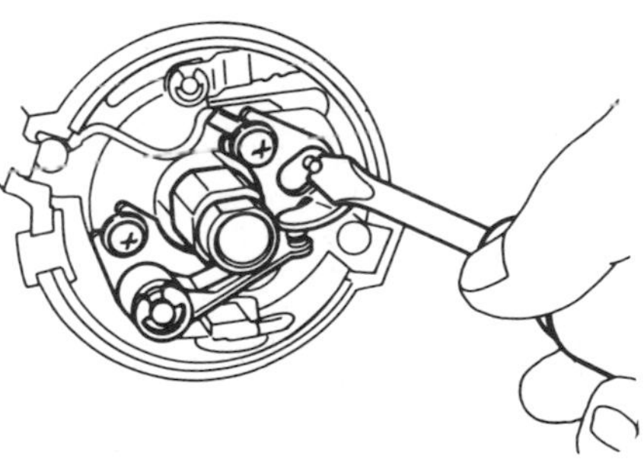

Fig. 4.4 Adjusting contact breaker points gap (Sec 2)

3 Dwell angle – checking

1 On modern engines, setting the contact breaker gap in the distributor using feeler gauges must be regarded as a basic adjustment only. For optimum engine performance, the dwell angle must be checked. The dwell angle is the number of degrees through which the distributor cam turns during the period between the instance of closure and opening of the contact breaker points. Checking the dwell angle not only gives a more accurate setting of the contact breaker gap but also evens out any variations in the gap which could be caused by wear in the distributor shaft or its bushes, or difference in height of any of the cam peaks.
2 The angle should be checked with a dwell meter connected in accordance with the maker's instructions. Refer to the Specifications for the correct dwell angle. If the dwell angle is too large, increase the points gap, if too small, reduce the points gap.
3 The dwell angle should always be adjusted before checking and adjusting the ignition timing.

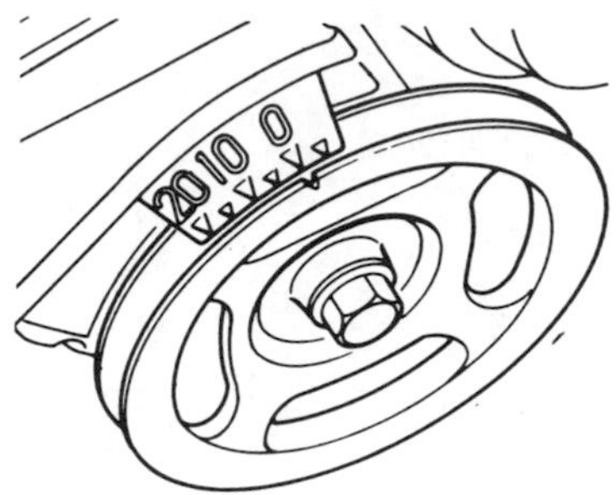

Fig. 4.5 Typical ignition timing marks (Sec 4)

4 Ignition timing

1 The following procedure applies to vehicles equipped with either a mechanical or electronic type ignition system.
2 Have the engine at normal operating temperature with the vacuum hose disconnected from the distributor and plugged.
3 Connect a stroboscope (timing lamp) in accordance with the manufacturer's instructions.
4 With the engine idling, point the timing lamp at the index above the crankshaft pulley. The notch in the pulley rim should be in alignment with the mark on the index which applies to your particular vehicle (see Specifications).
5 If the marks are not in alignment, release the distributor clamp plate nut and turn the distributor in either direction as necessary to align the marks.
6 Tighten the nut, switch off the engine, reconnect the vacuum hose and remove the timing lamp.
7 Any difficulty experienced in seeing the timing marks clearly can be overcome by applying a spot of white paint to the pulley notch and the specified timing mark on the index.

5 Condenser – removal, testing and refitting

1 The purpose of the condenser (sometimes known as the capacitor) is to ensure that when the contact breaker points open there is no sparking across them which would waste voltage and cause wear.
2 The condenser is mounted on the outside of the distributor body. If it develops a short-circuit it will cause ignition failure as the points will be prevented from interrupting the low tension circuit.
3 If the engine becomes very difficult to start or begins to miss after several miles running and the breaker points show signs of excessive burning, then the condition of the condenser must be suspect. A further test can be made by separating the points by hand with the ignition switched on. If this is accompanied by a strong blue flash it is indicative that the condenser has failed in the open circuit mode.
4 Without special equipment the only sure way to diagnose condenser trouble is to replace a suspected unit with a new one and note if there is any improvement.
5 To remove the condenser from the distributor take off the distributor cap and rotor arm.
6 Release the terminal nut and disconnect the condenser lead from the terminal.
7 Remove the LT lead connecting the coil to the distributor, from the ignition coil.
8 Undo and remove the screw securing the condenser assembly to the distributor case. Note that the condenser is supplied complete with the LT lead to the coil and the LT spade tag and mounting grommet. Refitting of the condenser follows the reverse procedure to removal.

6 Distributor – removal and refitting

1 The distributor is driven from the flywheel end of the camshaft. It is located in a recess in the thermostat housing.
2 The distributor drive coupling is of offset tongue type so that removal and refitting is simply a matter of disconnecting the leads and vacuum pipe (photo), unscrewing the clamp plate nut and withdrawing the distributor from the cylinder head (photo).

6.2A Distributor vacuum hose

6.2B Removing distributor

3 Provided the offset tongue on the distributor shaft is aligned with the slot in the end of the camshaft, the distributor can be pushed fully home in its seat.
4 Turn the distributor until, on mechanical breaker distributors, the points are just about to open when the engine timing marks are in alignment. On breakerless systems, turn the distributor until a peak on the reluctor is aligned with the stator prong.
5 Check and adjust the ignition timing, as described in Section 4.

7 Distributor (mechanical breaker type) – overhaul

1 With the distributor removed from the engine (Section 6), clean away external dirt.
2 Prise off the spring clips and take off the cap.
3 Pull off the rotor.
4 Extract the fixing screws and remove the vacuum advance capsule. It will need tilting in order to release the link rod from the pivot on the baseplate once the E-clip has been prised off the pivot.
5 Extract the two screws and remove the baseplate.
6 Remove the contact breaker from the baseplate.
7 If the contact breaker fixing screws are removed, take care that the anti-friction balls are not lost as the baseplate upper and lower sections separate.

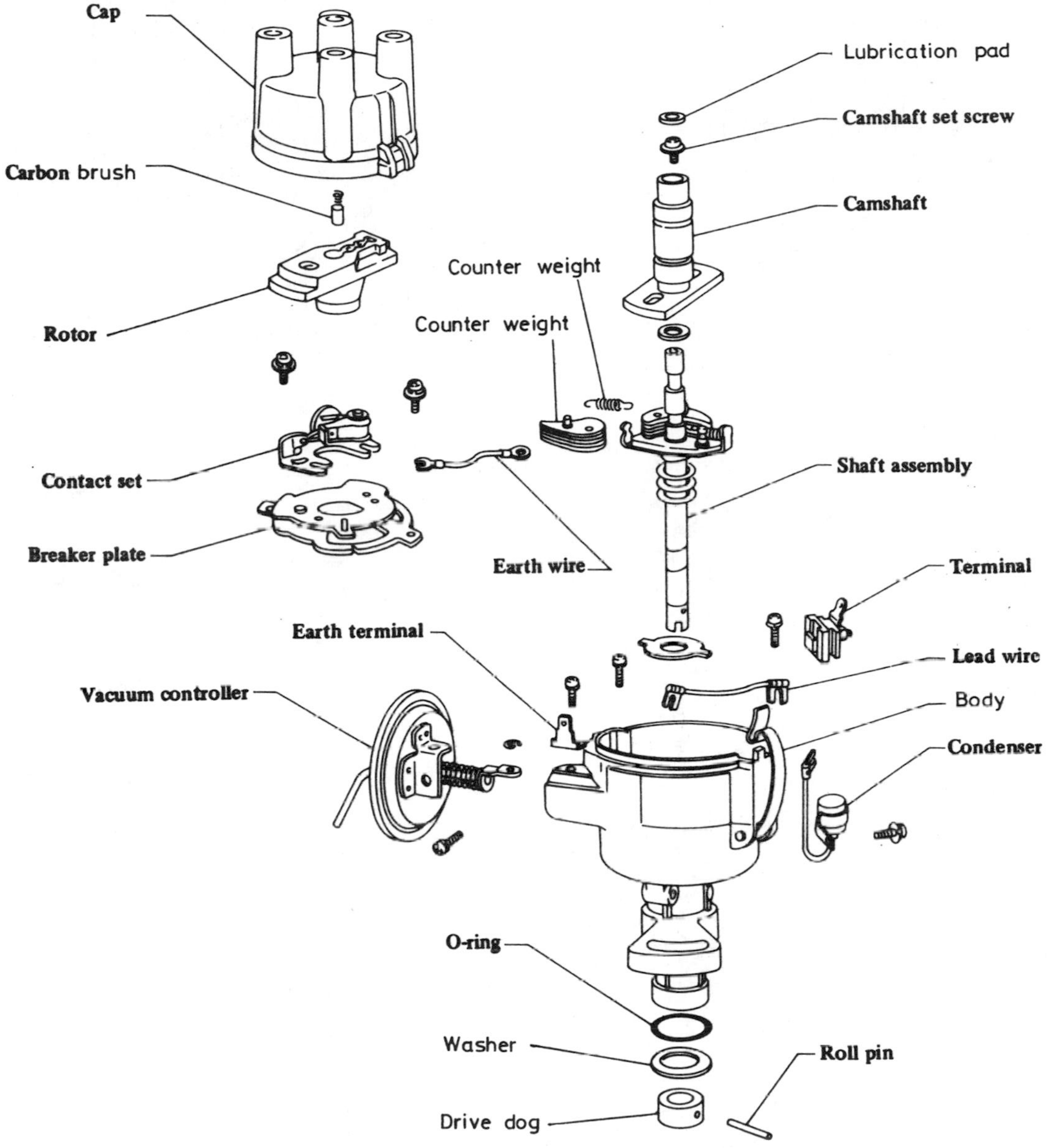

Cap
Lubrication pad
Camshaft set screw
Carbon brush
Camshaft
Counter weight
Rotor
Counter weight
Shaft assembly
Contact set
Breaker plate
Earth wire
Terminal
Earth terminal
Lead wire
Vacuum controller
Body
Condenser
O-ring
Washer
Roll pin
Drive dog

Fig. 4.6 Exploded view of distributor – mechanical breaker type (Sec 7)

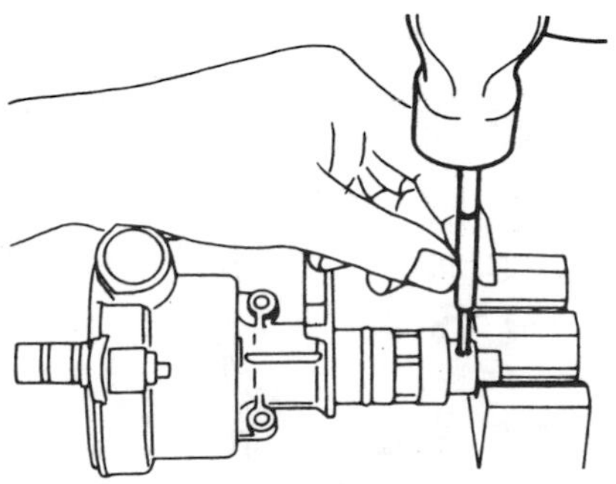

Fig. 4.7 Removing drive dog pin (Sec 7)

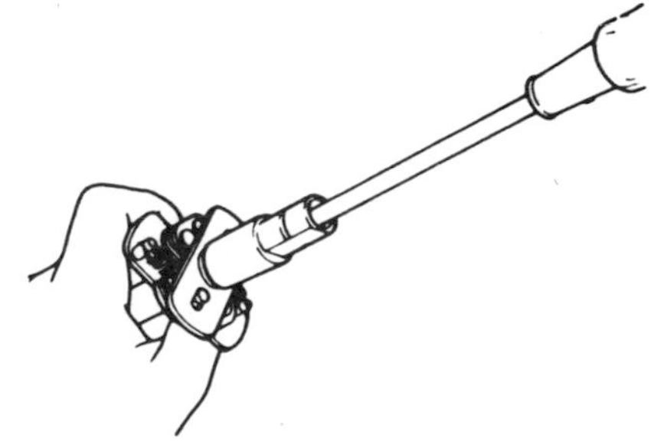

Fig. 4.8 Extracting distributor shaft screw (Sec 7)

1
2
3
4
5

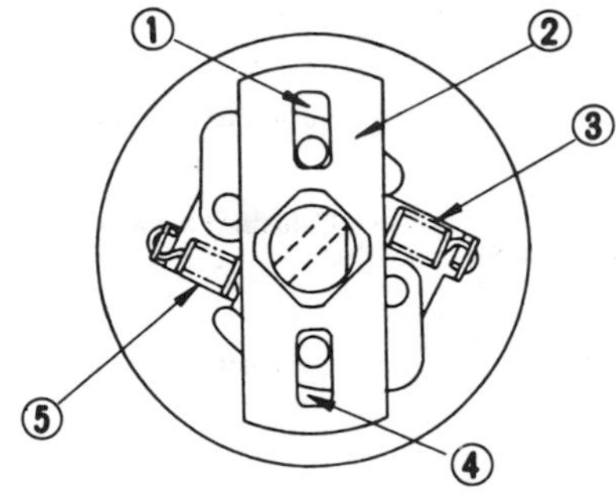

Fig. 4.9 Counterweight spring locations (Sec 7)

1 *Short rectangular hole*
2 *Cam*
3 *Spring with rectangular hooked end*
4 *Long rectangular hole*
5 *Spring with circular hooked end*

Camshaft cutout portion
Drive dog tongue off set

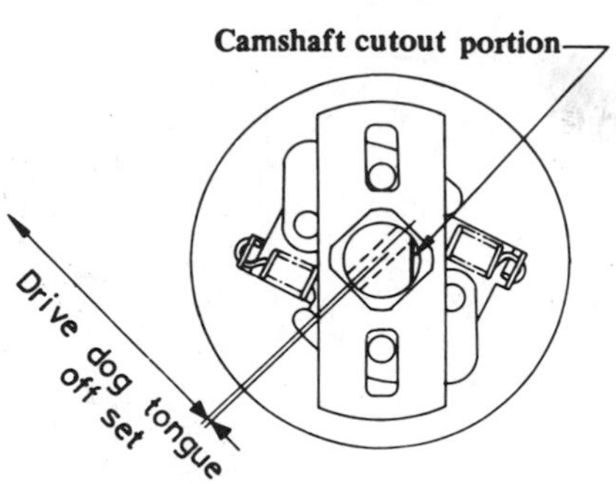

Fig. 4.10 Distributor shaft cut-out in relation to offset drive dog tongue (Sec 7)

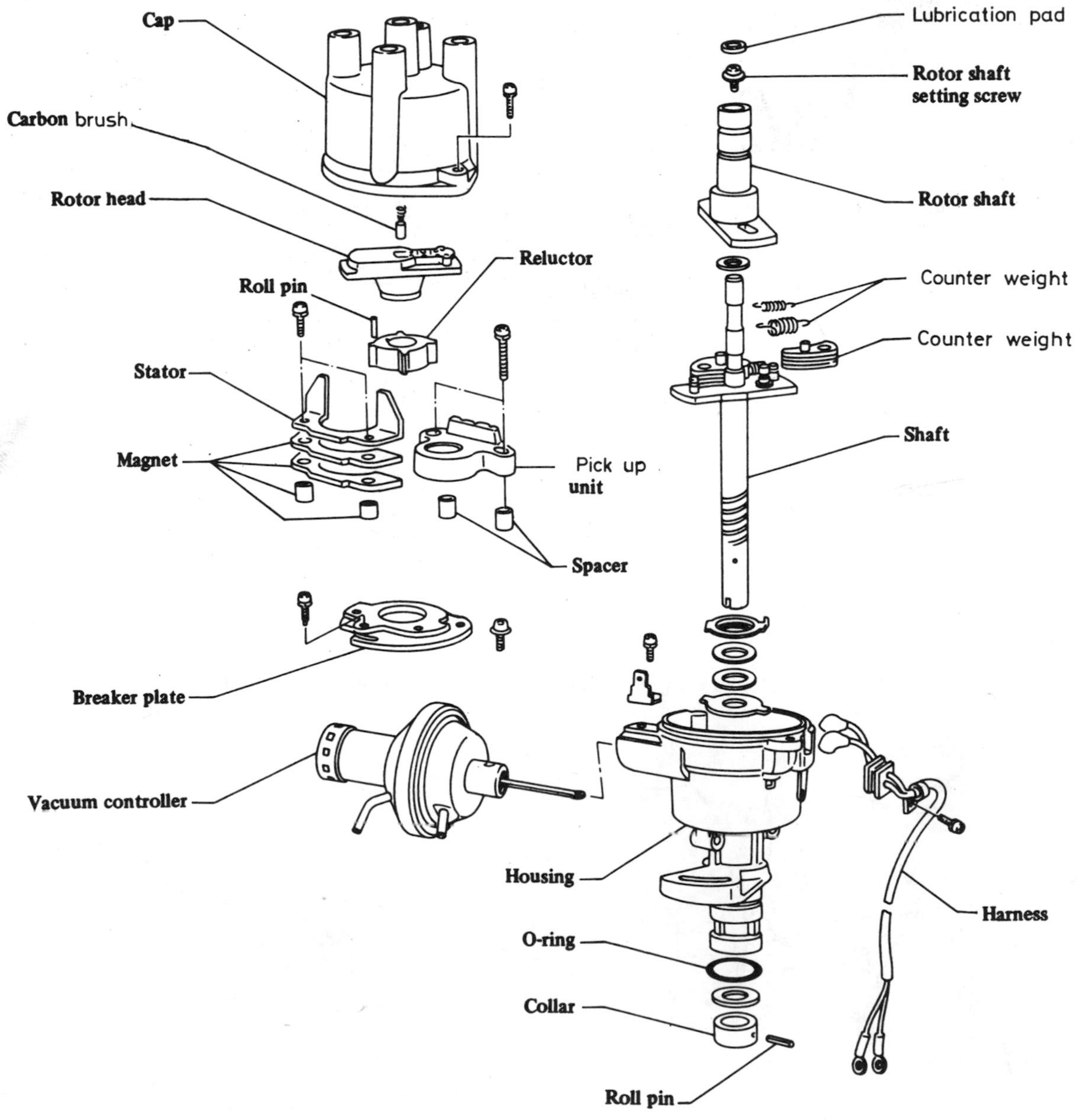

Cap
Carbon brush
Rotor head
Roll pin
Reluctor
Stator
Magnet
Pick up unit
Spacer
Breaker plate
Vacuum controller
Lubrication pad
Rotor shaft setting screw
Rotor shaft
Counter weight
Counter weight
Shaft
Housing
O-ring
Collar
Roll pin
Harness

Fig. 4.11 Exploded view of breakerless type distributor (Sec 8)

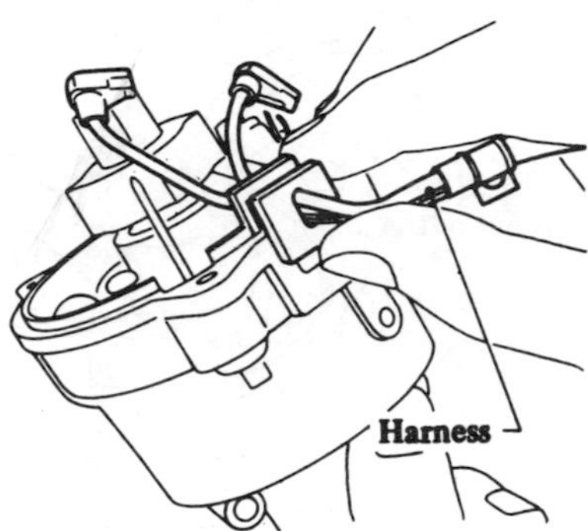

Fig. 4.12 Removing wiring harness/insulator block (Sec 8)

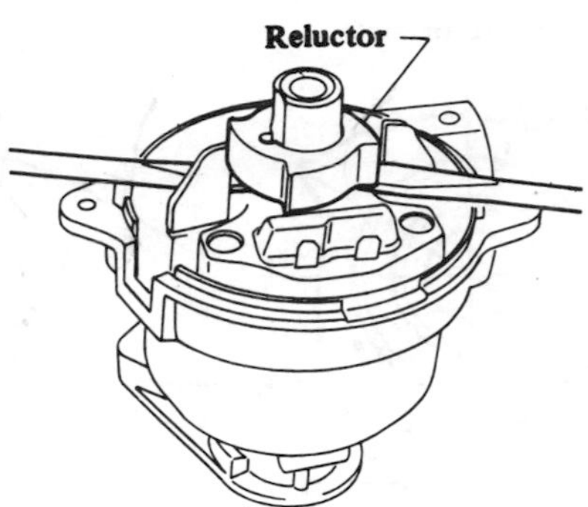

Fig. 4.13 Removing reluctor (Sec 8)

8 Mark the drive dog with respect to tongue offset to shaft, and drive out the retaining pin.
9 Withdraw the shaft from the distributor body.
10 Extract the felt lubrication pad from the recess in the top of the shaft and remove the screw which is exposed.
11 Mark the relationship of cam assembly to shaft and separate them.
12 If the cam counter weights and springs must be dismantled, make quite sure that the springs are marked with a dab of quick drying paint so that they can be reconnected in their original positions.
13 With the distributor dismantled, clean and examine all components for wear. If the shaft bushes and other items are worn, it may well be more economical to purchase a new distributor complete.
14 Take the opportunity to carefully examine the cap and rotor for tiny cracks. These can cause conductance paths and prevent starting or be responsible for erratic running. Renew these components if necessary, particularly the rotor if the metal contact is eroded or the carbon brush inside the cap is worn to the specified minimum.
15 Reassembly is a reversal of dismantling, apply light grease to all components as work proceeds and make quite sure that they are aligned with each other in their original positions.

8 Distributor (breakerless type) – overhaul

1 With the distributor removed from the engine (Section 6), clean away external dirt.
2 Remove the cap.
3 Pull off the rotor.
4 Extract the fixing screws and remove the vacuum advance capsule. It will need tilting to release the link rod from the pivot on the baseplate once the E-clip has been prised off the pivot.
5 Disconnect the wiring harness by sliding the insulator block out of the cut-out in the distributor body.
6 Using two screwdrivers as levers, prise the reluctor carefully from the distributor shaft.
7 Extract the fixing screws and remove the baseplate.
8 Extract the screws and remove the pick-up unit and spacers.
9 Remove the magnet and stator from the baseplate.
10 Mark the relative position of the drive dog tongue to the distributor shaft and drive out the connecting pin.
11 Withdraw the shaft from the distributor body.
12 Extract the felt lubrication pad from the recess in the top of the shaft and remove the screw now exposed. Separate the rotor shaft from the mainshaft.
13 If necessary, disconnect the springs and remove the counter-weights, but mark the location of the springs with a dab of quick-drying paint.
14 Clean and inspect all components. The reluctor and stator should be unscratched and not distorted, otherwise renew them. If the carbon brush is worn down to its specified minimum length, renew the cap.
15 Apply grease to all friction and bearing surfaces as work proceeds.
16 Reassembly is a reversal of dismantling, but observe the following points.
17 When reconnecting the counterweight springs, fit the smaller diameter spring first.
18 Set the relative position of the rotor shaft cut-out to the mainshaft offset drive dog tongue as shown in Fig. 4.15.

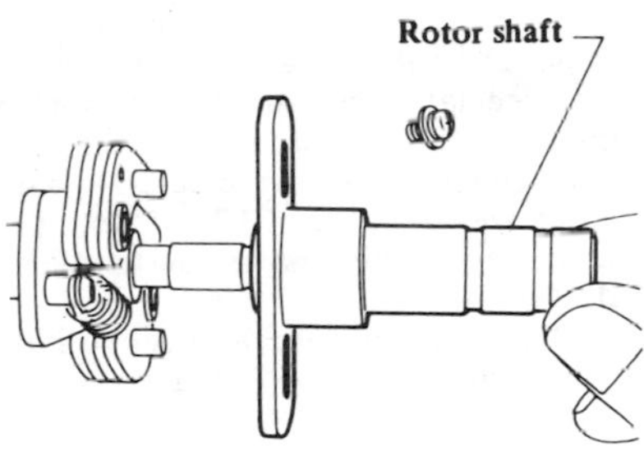

Fig. 4.14 Removing rotor shaft from mainshaft (Sec 8)

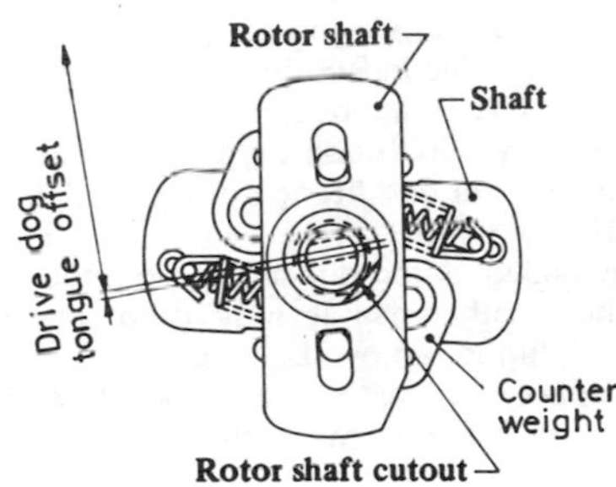

Fig. 4.15 Relationship of rotor shaft cut-out to offset drive dog tongue (Sec 8)

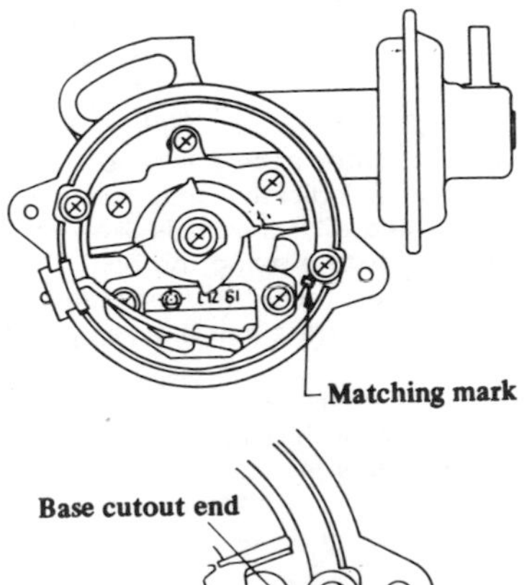

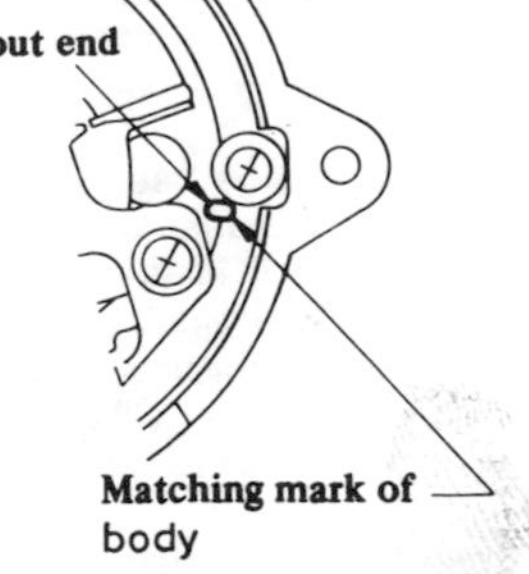

Fig. 4.16 Baseplate to distributor body marks (Sec 8)

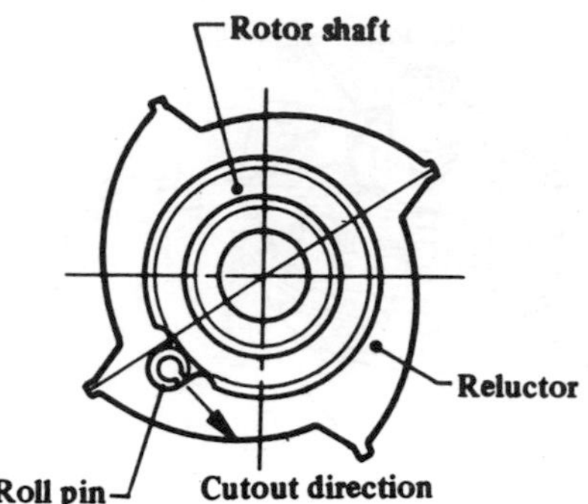

Fig. 4.17 Reluctor roll pin slit location (Sec 8)

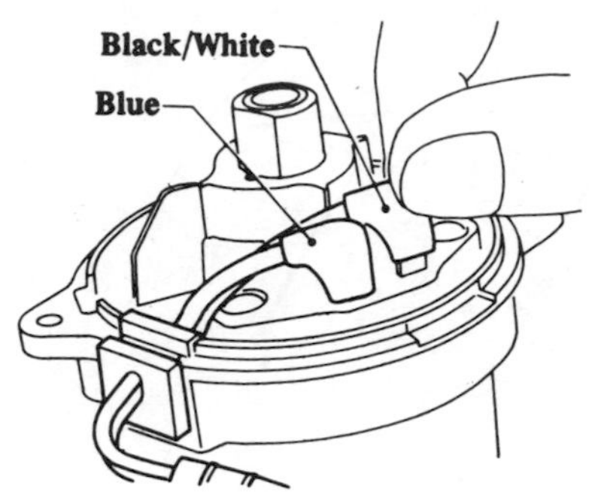

Fig. 4.18 Wiring harness connection to distributor (Sec 8)

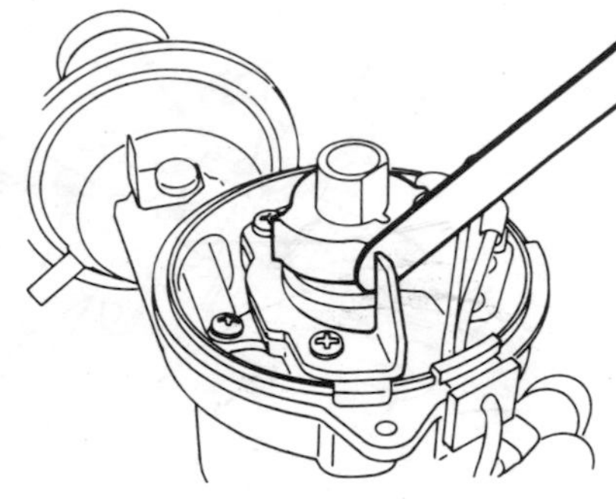
Fig. 4.19 Checking air gap (Sec 8)

19 Use a new roll pin to fix the drive dog to the shaft.
20 When fitting the baseplate make sure that its mark is in alignment with the one on the distributor body.
21 If the roll pin was removed from the reluctor, fit a new one so that its slit is positioned as shown in Fig. 4.17.
22 Make sure that the wiring harness spade terminals are correctly located (Fig. 4.18).
23 Finally, set the reluctor air gap (reluctor peak to stator prong edge) to the specified dimension using a feeler blade (Fig. 4.19).

9 Spark plugs and HT leads – general

1 The correct functioning of the spark plugs is vital for economical running and efficiency of the engine.
2 At the intervals specified in Routine Maintenance the plugs should be removed, cleaned and re-gapped.
3 To remove the plugs, first open the bonnet and pull the HT leads from them. Grip the rubber end fitting not the lead, otherwise the lead connection may be fractured.
4 Brush out any accumulated dirt or grit from the spark plug recess in the cylinder head otherwise it may drop into the combustion chamber when the plug is removed.
5 Unscrew the spark plugs with a deep socket or a box spanner. Do not allow the tool to tilt, otherwise the ceramic insulator may be cracked or broken.
6 Examination of the spark plugs will give a good indication of the condition of the engine
7 If the insulator nose of the spark plug is clean and white, with no deposits, this is indicative of a weak mixture, or too hot a plug (a hot plug transfers heat away from the electrode slowly, a cold plug transfers heat away quickly).
8 The plugs fitted as standard are specified at the beginning of this Chapter. If the top and insulator nose are covered with hard black-looking deposits, then this is indicative that the mixture is too rich. Should the plug be black and oily, then it is likely that the engine is fairly worn, as well as the mixture being too rich.
9 If the insulator nose is covered with light tan to greyish brown deposits, then the mixture is correct and it is likely that the engine is in good condition.
10 If there are any traces of long brown tapering stains on the outside of the white portion of the plug, the plug will have to be renewed, as this shows that there is a faulty joint between the plug body and the insulator, and compression is being allowed to leak away.
11 Before cleaning a spark plug, wash it in a suitable solvent to remove oily deposits.
12 Although a wire brush can be used to clean the electrode end of the spark plug this method can cause metal conductance paths across the nose of the insulator and it is therefore to be preferred that an abrasive powder cleaning machine is used. Such machines are available quite cheaply from motor accessory stores or you may prefer to take the plugs to your dealer who will not only be able to clean them but also to check the sparking efficiency of each plug under compression.
13 The spark plug gap is of considerable importance, as, if it is too large or too small, the size of the spark and its efficiency will be seriously impaired. For the best results the spark plug gap should be set in accordance with the Specifications at the beginning of this Chapter.
14 To set it, measure the gap with a feeler gauge, and then bend open, or close, the outer electrode until the correct gap is achieved. The centre electrode should never be bent as this may crack the insulation and cause plug failure if nothing worse.
15 Special spark plug electrode gap adjusting tools are available from most motor accessory stores.
16 Before refitting the spark plugs, wash each one thoroughly again in order to remove all trace of abrasive powder and then apply a trace of grease to the plug threads.
17 Screw each plug in by hand. This will make sure that there is no chance of cross threading (photo).
18 Tighten to the specified torque. If a torque wrench is not available, just nip up each plug. **It is better to slightly undertighten rather than overdo it and strip the threads from the light alloy cylinder head.**
19 When reconnecting the spark plug leads, make sure that they are refitted in their correct order, 1-3-4-2, No 1 cylinder being at the timing belt end of the engine.
20 The plug leads require no routine attention other than being kept clean and wiped over regularly. At intervals however, pull each lead off the plug in turn and remove it from the distributor. Water can seep down into the joints giving rise to a white corrosive deposit which must be carefully removed from the end of each cable. A smear of petroleum jelly applied to the end fitting of the cables will help to eliminate this problem.

9.17 Fitting a spark plug

Measuring plug gap. A feeler gauge of the correct size (see ignition system specifications) should have a slight 'drag' when slid between the electrodes. Adjust gap if necessary

Adjusting plug gap. The plug gap is adjusted by bending the earth electrode inwards, or outwards, as necessary until the correct clearance is obtained. Note the use of the correct tool

Normal. Grey-brown deposits, lightly coated core nose. Gap increasing by around 0.001 in (0.025 mm) per 1000 miles (1600 km). Plugs ideally suited to engine, and engine in good condition

Carbon fouling. Dry, black, sooty deposits. Will cause weak spark and eventually misfire. Fault: over-rich fuel mixture. Check: carburettor mixture settings, float level and jet sizes; choke operation and cleanliness of air filter. Plugs can be re-used after cleaning

Oil fouling. Wet, oily deposits. Will cause weak spark and eventually misfire. Fault: worn bores/piston rings or valve guides; sometimes occurs (temporarily) during running-in period. Plugs can be re-used after thorough cleaning

Overheating. Electrodes have glazed appearance, core nose very white – few deposits. Fault: plug overheating. Check: plug value, ignition timing, fuel octane rating (too low) and fuel mixture (too weak). Discard plugs and cure fault immediately

Electrode damage. Electrodes burned away; core nose has burned, glazed appearance. Fault: pre-ignition. Check: as for 'Overheating' but may be more severe. Discard plugs and remedy fault before piston or valve damage occurs

Split core nose (may appear initially as a crack). Damage is self-evident, but cracks will only show after cleaning. Fault: pre-ignition or wrong gap-setting technique. Check: ignition timing, cooling system, fuel octane rating (too low) and fuel mixture (too weak). Discard plugs, rectify fault immediately

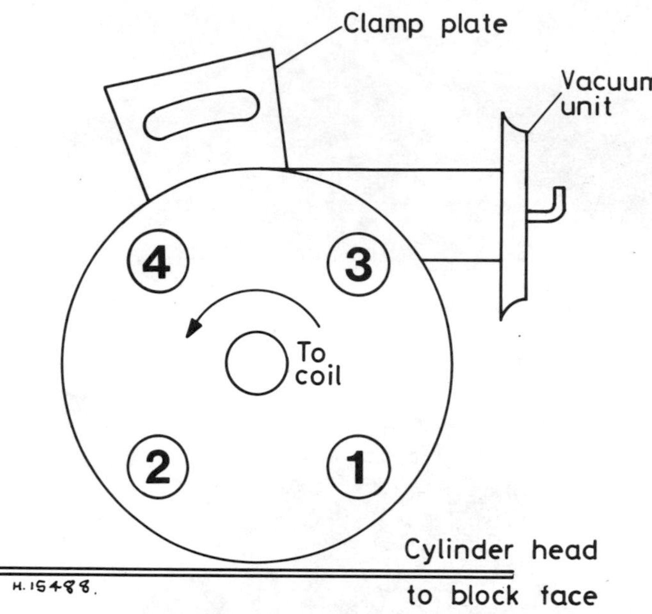

Fig. 4.20 Plug lead connecting diagram (Sec 9)

10 Coil – general

1 The coil is an auto-transformer and has two sets of windings wound around a core of soft iron wires. The resistance of the windings is given in Specifications at the beginning of this Chapter.
2 If the coil is suspect then the resistance may be checked by an auto-electrician and if faulty it may readily be renewed after undoing the mounting bolts.
3 A ballast resistor is mounted adjacent to the coil, (photo).

11 Ignition switch/steering lock – removal and refitting

1 Disconnect the battery, turn the ignition switch to OFF (photo).
2 Remove the lower shroud from the upper part of the steering column and the steering wheel, both as described in Chapter 11.
3 Disconnect the switch wiring harness plug.
4 The switch/lock clamp is held by two ordinary and two shear-head screws. The latter must be drilled out or a proprietary bolt removing tool employed to extract them.
5 The ignition switch section may be separated from the lock section after removal of the two securing screws.
6 Use two new shear-head screws when refitting the assembly, but do not fully tighten the screws to break off their heads until the operation of the lock has been checked. The lock tongue should pass smoothly into the cut-out in the steering column shaft. If it does not, slightly reposition the lock.

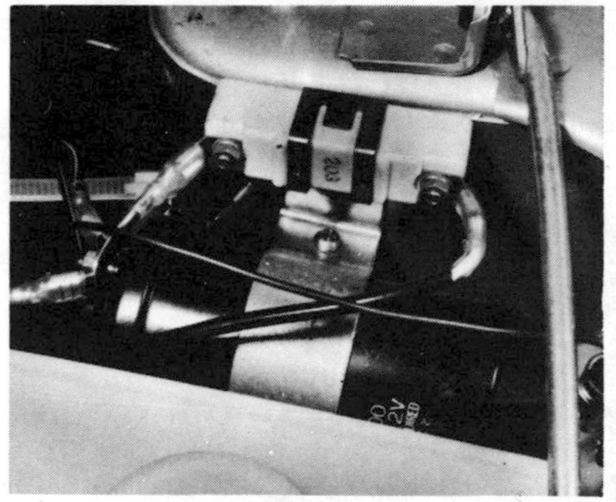

10.3 Coil ballast resistor

11.1 Ignition/steering lock key positions

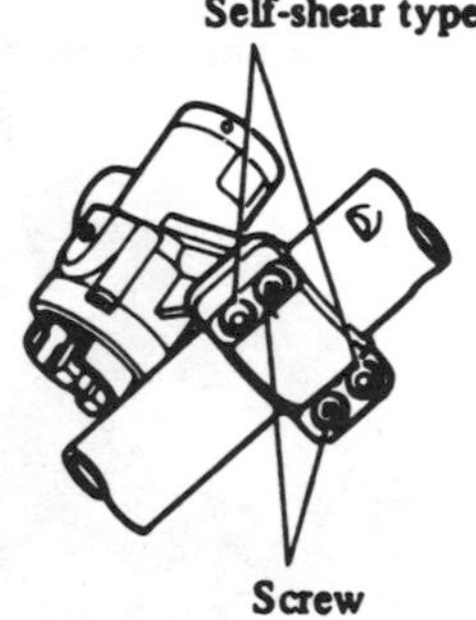

Fig. 4.21 Ignition switch/steering lock screws (Sec 11)

12 Fault diagnosis – mechanical breaker system

Symptom	Reason(s)
Engine fails to start	Loose battery connections Discharged battery Oil on contact points Disconnected ignition leads Faulty condenser
Engine starts and runs but misfires	Faulty spark plug Cracked distributor cap Cracked rotor arm Worn advance mechanism Incorrect spark plug gap Incorrect contact points gap Faulty condenser Faulty coil Incorrect ignition timing Poor engine/transmission earth connections

Engine overheats, lacks power	Seized distributor weights Perforated vacuum pipe Incorrect ignition timing
Engine 'pinks'	Timing too advanced Advance mechanism stuck in advanced position Broken distributor weight spring Low fuel octane rating Upper cylinder oil used in fuel Excessive oil vapour from crankcase ventilation system (worn piston rings)

Fault diagnosis – breakerless system

Symptom	Reason(s)
Starter turns, but engine will not start	Faulty or disconnected leads Faulty spark plug Air gap incorrect Fault in ignition coil Fault in pick-up/stator unit
Engine starts, but runs erratically	Incorrect timing Fouled spark plug Incorrectly connected HT leads Crack in distributor cap or rotor Poor battery, engine and earth connections

Chapter 5 Clutch

Contents

Specifications

Type	Single dry plate with diaphragm spring. Sealed ball release bearing. Cable actuated

Driven plate

Outside diameter	180.0 mm (7.09 in)
No of torsion springs	6

Pedal

Clutch pedal height above floorpan:	
RHD	201.0 to 207.0 mm (7.91 to 8.15 in)
LHD	191.0 to 197.0 mm (7.52 to 7.76 in)
Pedal free play	11.0 to 21.0 mm (0.43 to 0.83 in)

Torque wrench settings	**Nm**	**lbf ft**
Cover bolts	21	16
Bellhousing-to-engine bolts	40	30

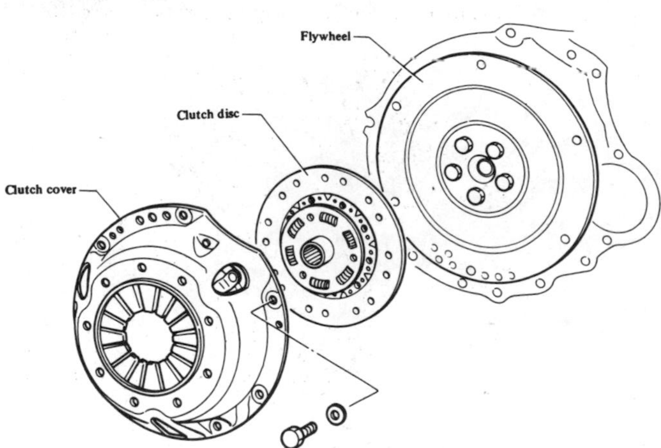

Fig. 5.1 Clutch components (Sec 1)

1 General description

The clutch is of single dry plate type with a diaphragm spring.

Clutch operation is controlled by a cable connected to a pendant type foot pedal.

The release bearing is of sealed ball type.

2 Clutch – adjustment

1 At the intervals specified in Routine Maintenance, check the clutch pedal height setting and the pedal free movement.

2 The distance between the upper surface of the pedal pad and the surface of the protective coating of the floor pan should be as specified:

3 If adjustment is required, release the two locknuts on the pedal arm stop bolt and adjust their position.

4 Now check the pedal free play by depressing the pedal with the fingers until firm resistance is felt. The distance through which the pedal has travelled to this point when measured should be within the

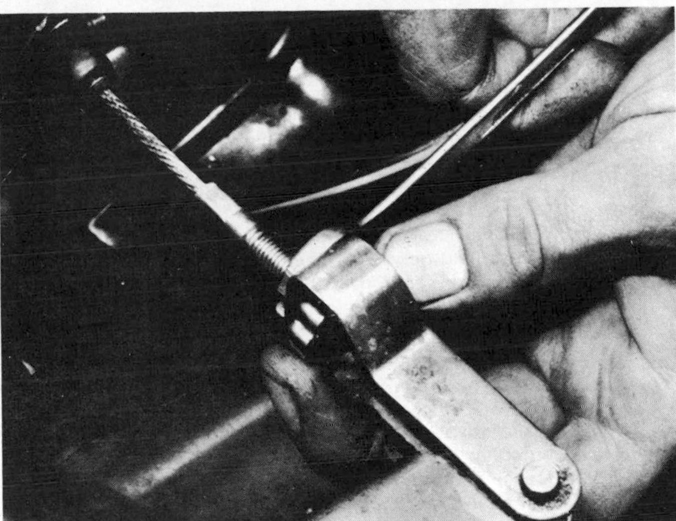

2.4 Adjusting the clutch cable

specified tolerances. If it is not, release the locknut on the cable at the clevis fork on the end of the release lever and adjust the cable length by turning the knurled adjuster wheel (photo). Tighten on completion.

3 Clutch cable – renewal

1 Remove the cover from under the facia panel.
2 Release the nuts at the end of the cable at the release lever and disconnect the cable from the lever (photo).
3 Working inside the vehicle, remove the clevis pin and disconnect the cable from the clutch pedal arm.
4 Unscrew the two nuts which retain the cable grommet to the bulkhead and withdraw the cable from the vehicle.
5 Refit the new cable by reversing the removal operations, and then carry out the adjustments described in Section 2.

4 Clutch pedal – removal and refitting

1 Remove the cover from under the facia panel.
2 Disconnect the cable from the pedal arm.
3 Extract the E-clip from the end of the pivot shaft.
4 Unhook the pedal return spring and slide the pedal off the pivot shaft.

3.2 Disconnecting the clutch cable from the release lever

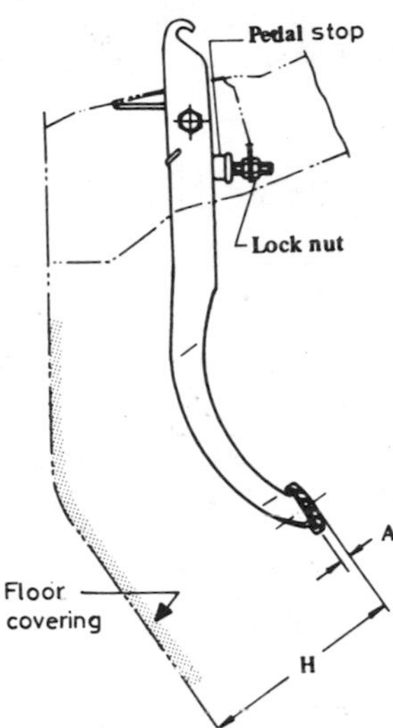

Fig. 5.2 Clutch pedal adjustment (Sec 2)

A Pedal free play B Pedal height

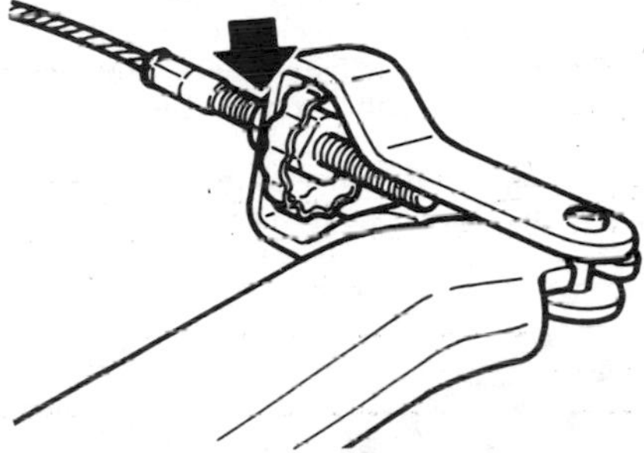

Fig. 5.3 Cable adjuster at release lever (Sec 2)

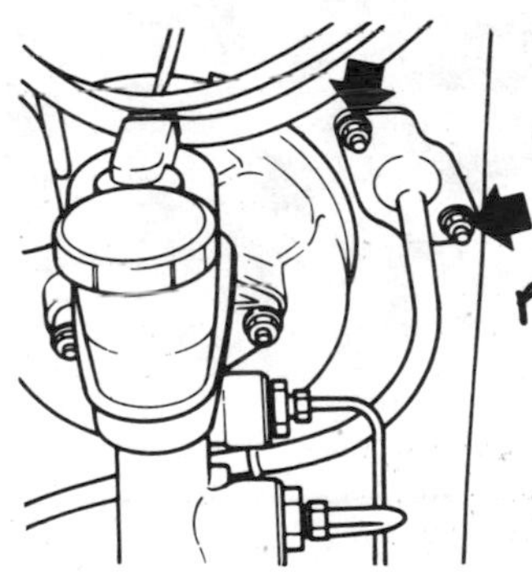

Fig. 5.4 Clutch cable grommet retaining nuts at bulkhead (Sec 3)

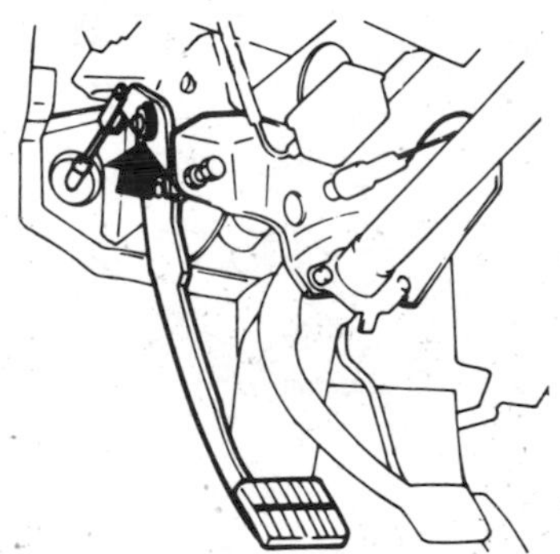

Fig. 5.5 Clutch pedal E-clip (Sec 4)

5 The pivot bushes may be renewed.
6 Refitting is a reversal of removal, apply grease to the pivot shaft and bushes.
7 Adjust the pedal height and free movement, as described in Section 2.

5 Clutch – removal

1 Access to the clutch is obtained by removing the transmission, as described in Chapter 6.
2 Unscrew each of the clutch cover bolts progressively a turn at a time until the pressure of the diaphragm spring is relieved. If the flywheel tends to turn as the bolts are unscrewed, jam the teeth of the starter ring gear using a large screwdriver or similar blade.
3 Remove the clutch cover, catching the driven plate as it is released from the flywheel.
4 The clutch cover bolts are offset so it can only be refitted in one position.

6 Clutch – inspection

1 Examine the driven plate. If the friction linings are worn down to, or nearly down to the rivet heads, the plate should be renewed. Do not attempt to re-line the plate yourself, it is unlikely to prove satisfactory.
2 If the linings are good for further service, check the torsion springs and the hub for cracks.
3 Examine the splines in the driven plate hub for wear.
4 Check the clutch pressure plate cover assembly. If any parts show evidence of cracking or severe rusting, or if the fingers of the diaphragm spring are worn or stepped by contact with the release bearing, renew the assembly. Do not attempt to dismantle the pressure plate cover.
5 Check the friction surfaces of both the pressure plate and the flywheel. If grooved, or showing signs of very fine surface cracking, the flywheel may be machined – subject to certain limitations described in Chapter 1 – but the pressure plate assembly will have to be renewed complete.
6 If the clutch components are oil-stained or the inside of the clutch bellhousing is covered in oil, suspect a faulty oil seal on the transmission input shaft or crankshaft rear end. Renew the defective oil seal before installing new components.
7 A pilot bearing is not fitted in the centre of the crankshaft rear mounting flange for the flywheel.

7 Clutch release bearing – removal, inspection and refitting

1 Whenever the transmission is removed for clutch overhaul, check the release components and renew the bearing as a matter of routine.
2 Disconnect the springs from the release bearing, slide the release bearing off the bearing mounting sleeve (photo).
3 Check that the release control shaft bushes are not worn. If they are, the fork-to-cross-shaft retaining pins will have to be driven out (photo), the return spring is released as the shaft is withdrawn. The pins can only be driven out if the cross-shaft is turned to allow the pins to pass out into the small cavities in the bellhousing.
4 Reassembly is a reversal of dismantling, apply grease to the cross-shaft bushes and to the release bearing recess.
5 Smear a little molybdenum disulphide grease onto the release bearing mounting sleeve and the input shaft splines. Make sure that the release bearing is pushed fully home until the retaining spring clips are heard to click (photo).
6 When correctly reassembled, the numbers moulded onto the release fork should be visible.

7.2 Removing the release bearing

7.3 Release fork roll pin

7.5 Release bearing spring clips fully engaged

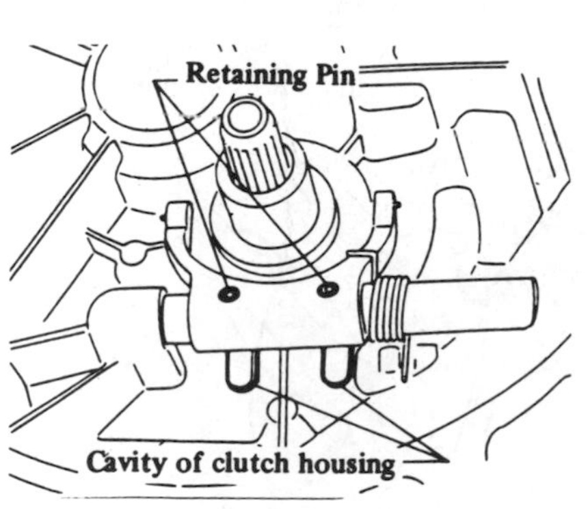

Fig. 5.6 Release lever cross-shaft pins (Sec 7)

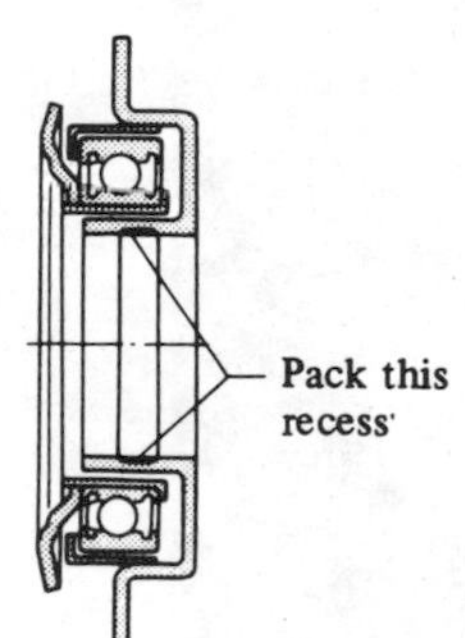

Fig. 5.7 Grease recess in clutch release bearing (Sec 7)

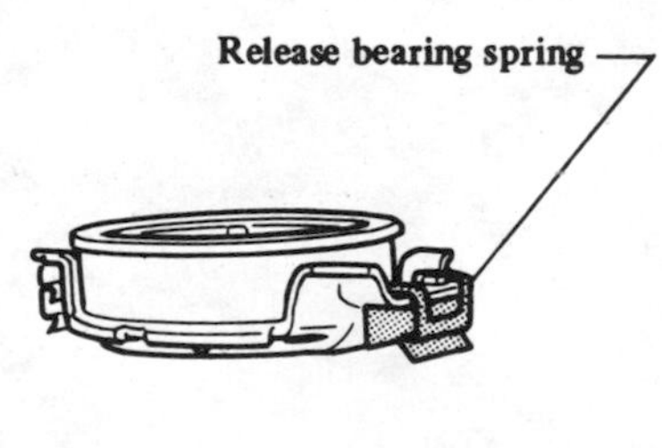

Fig. 5.8 Release bearing spring clip (Sec 7)

8.2 Locating driven plate

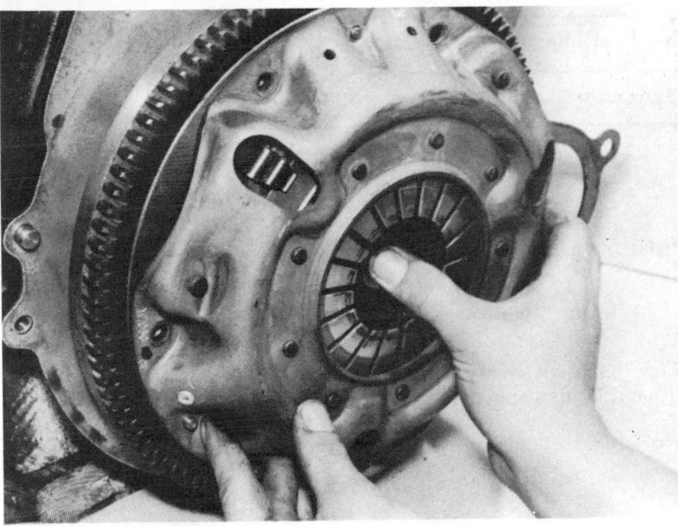
8.3 Locating clutch cover

8.4 Alignment tool

8.5 Clutch driven plate centralised

8 Clutch – refitting

1 Make sure that the flywheel and pressure plate friction surfaces are clean, and free from protective grease.

2 Place the driven plate against the flywheel so that its hub has the greater projecting side away from the flywheel (photo).

3 Offer up the clutch cover (photo) and screw in the bolts finger tight. The mounting dowels are offset so the cover can only be fitted one way.

4 The driven plate must now be centralised. To do this, a conventional clutch alignment tool cannot be used due to the fact that a pilot bush is not fitted in the centre of the flywheel mounting flange. The splined hub of the driven plate should therefore be centralised within the tips of the diaphragm spring fingers visually or, more accurately, by cutting a cardboard disc of outside diameter equal to the outside diameter of the diaphragm spring fingers. Now punch a hole centrally in the cardboard disc and then push a bar or rod through the hole in the disc and engage it in the splined hub of the driven plate (photo). The diameter of the bar or rod should be such that it provides a sliding fit in the hub. A bar of incorrect diameter can be adjusted to suit by winding tape around it.

5 The driven plate should now be moved in the appropriate direction to centralise the cardboard disc (photo). Tighten the cover bolts and remove the tool.

Fault diagnosis overleaf

9 Fault diagnosis – clutch

Symptom	Reason(s)
Judder when taking up drive	Loose engine or gearbox mountings Badly worn friction linings or contaminated with oil Worn splines on gearbox input shaft or driven plate hub
*Clutch spin (failure to disengage) so that gears cannot be meshed	Incorrect release bearing to pressure plate clearance Rust on splines (may occur after vehicle standing idle for long periods) Damaged or misaligned pressure plate assembly Cable stretched or broken
Clutch slip (increase in engine speed does not result in increase in vehicle road speed – particularly on gradients)	Incorrect release bearing to pressure plate finger clearance Friction linings worn out or oil contaminated
Noise evident on depressing clutch pedal	Dry, worn or damaged release bearing Incorrect pedal adjustment Weak or broken pedal return spring Excessive play between plate hub splines and input shaft splines
Noise evident as clutch pedal released	Distorted driven plate Broken or weak drive plate cushion coil springs Incorrect pedal adjustment Weak or broken clutch pedal return spring Distorted or worn input shaft Release bearing loose on retainer hub

**This condition may also be due to the driven plate being rusted to the flywheel or pressure plate. It is possible to free it by applying the handbrake, engaging top gear, depressing the clutch pedal, and operating the starter motor. If really badly corroded, then the engine will not turn over, but in the majority of cases the driven plate will free. Once the engine starts, rev it up and slip the clutch several times to clear the rust deposits.*

Chapter 6 Manual transmission

Refer to Chapter 13 for Specifications and information on later models

Contents

Specifications

General

Type	Transversely mounted with four or five forward speeds and reverse. Synchromesh on all forward gears, floor-mounted gearchange	
Designation:		
Four-speed	RN4F30A	
Five-speed	RS5F30A	

Ratios

Four-speed transmission:		
1st	3.333:1	
2nd	1.955:1	
3rd	1.286:1	
4th	0.902:1	
Reverse	3.417:1	
	Excluding MPG models	**MPG models**
Five-speed transmission:		
1st	3.333:1	3.06:1
2nd	1.955:1	1.71:1
3rd	1.286:1	1.33:1
4th	0.902:1	0.81:1
5th	0.756:1	0.68:1
Reverse	3.417:1	3.55:1
Final drive ratios:		
E13 engine	3.895:1	
E15 engine – excluding MPG models	3.550:1	
E15 engine – MPG models	2.42:1	
E16 engine	3.550:1	
Oil capacity		
Four-speed	2.3 litres (4.0 Imp pts, 2.4 US qts)	
Five-speed	2.7 litres (4.8 Imp pts, 2.8 US qts)	

Gear endfloat

1st gear	0.18 to 0.31 mm (0.0071 to 0.0122 in)
2nd, 3rd and 4th gear	0.20 to 0.40 mm (0.0079 to 0.0157 in)
5th gear	0.18 to 0.41 mm (0.0071 to 0.0161 in)

Torque wrench settings

	Nm	lbf ft
Clutch bellhousing to engine	40	30
Clutch bellhousing to casing	20	15
Circular cover to transmission casing	8	6
Bearing retainer screws	20	15
5th/Reverse detent plug	25	18
Crownwheel bolts	80	59
Oil filler/level plug	30	22
Oil drain plug	30	22
Reverse lamp switch	25	18
Neutral switch (seat belt)	25	18
Left-hand mounting bracket	35	26
Rear mounting to bodyframe	35	26
Rear mounting to transmission	35	26
Gearchange support rod to transmission	12	9
Gearchange control rod to transmission	8	6
Front mounting bracket to transmission	20	15
Front suspension strut top mounting nuts	23	17
Suspension lower balljoint to track control arm	61	45
Caliper mounting bolts	61	45
Roadwheel nuts	95	70

1 General description

The manual transmission is of four or five-speed type, depending upon the model. On both transmissions top gear is of overdrive type.

Synchromesh is provided on all forward gears and gear selection is by means of a floor-mounted control lever.

The transmission is mounted transversely in line with the engine. Power is transmitted from the clutch through an input shaft and mainshaft to the final drive/differential which is incorporated within the transmission casing.

The four and five-speed units are so similar that their overhaul is not described separately in this Chapter as it is assumed that owners of four-speed models will be able to ignore reference to a 5th gear in the operations listed.

2 Transmission – lubrication

1 At the intervals specified in Routine Maintenance check the oil level in the transmission, preferably when the oil is cold – having stood for at least one hour.

2 Unscrew and remove the combined filler/level plug (photo). The oil should be level with the bottom of the hole and just starting to dribble out. If not, top it up as necessary.

3 Although the vehicle manufacturers do not specify changing the transmission oil, as it is regarded as a 'sealed for life' unit, we recommend that it is changed at the intervals specified in Routine Maintenance, particularly if the vehicle is used for towing or regular load carrying. The additives contained in the oil gradually lose their characteristics with age.

4 Drain the oil hot, after coming in off the road. This will ensure that any abrasive dirt or metal swarf held in suspension will be flushed out. The drain plug takes a $\frac{1}{2}$ in square drive extension.

5 Clean the magnetic drain plug before refitting, and then fill with the correct quantity and grade of oil to the level of the filler plug. Refit the plug.

2.2 Using $\frac{1}{2}$ in drive adaptor to remove filler/level plug

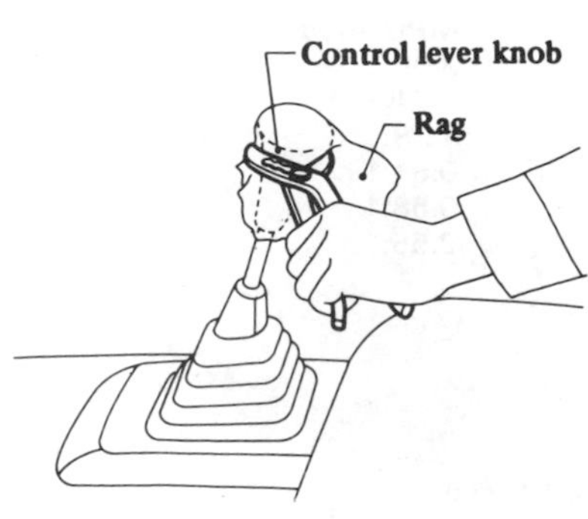

Fig. 6.1 Twisting off gearchange lever knob (Sec 3)

Fig. 6.2 Gearchange control and support rod securing nuts (Sec 3)

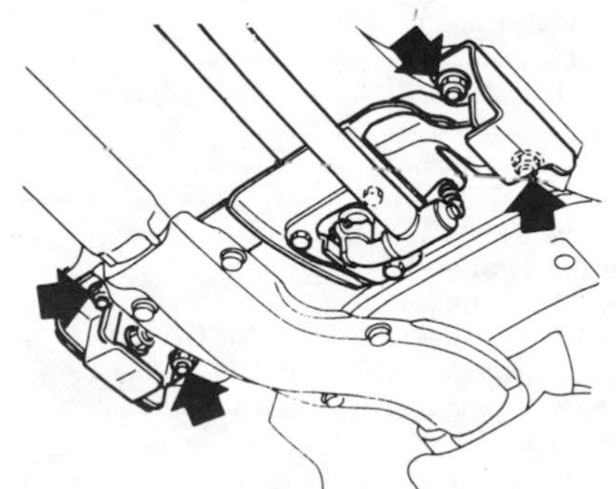

Fig. 6.3 Gearchange control rod bracket retaining nuts (Sec 3)

3.3 Gearchange control rod bracket

3 Gearchange lever and rods – disconnection, reconnection and adjustment

1 Twist off the gearchange lever knob. It may be necessary to protect the knob and then use grips to remove it.
2 Remove the nuts and separate the control and support rods from the transmission.
3 Unbolt the control rod bracket (photo) and lift away the control assembly.
4 Reconnect by reversing the operations just described.
5 Release, but do not remove, the selector stop plate bolts.
6 Move the control lever to 1st gear position.
7 Move the stop plate until a 1.0 mm (0.039 in) gap is visible between the stop and the gearchange lever.
8 Tighten the stop plate bolts. Check the movement and selection of all gears.

4 Gearchange control rods – dismantling and reassembly

1 Disconnect the control and support rods, as described in the preceding Section.
2 Remove the control lever bracket, the set spring ring, the bearing set seat and the bearing set spring.

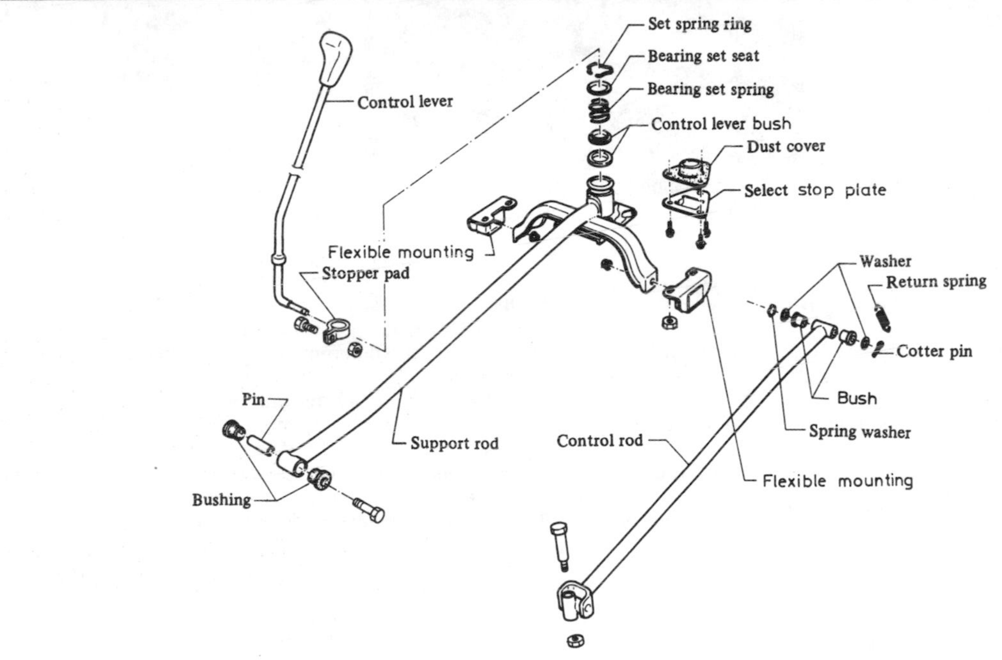

Fig. 6.4 Gearchange control components (Sec 4)

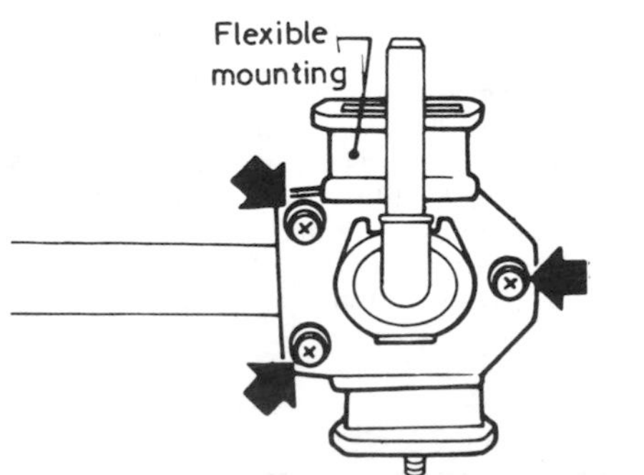

Fig. 6.5 Gearchange control flexible mounting (Sec 4)

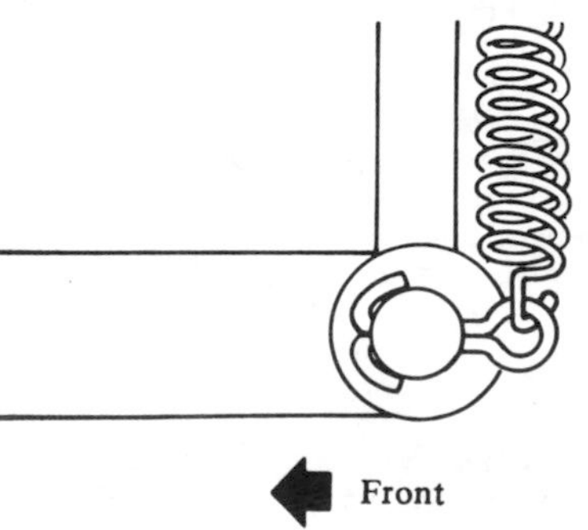

Fig. 6.6 Gearchange control rod cotter pin (Sec 4)

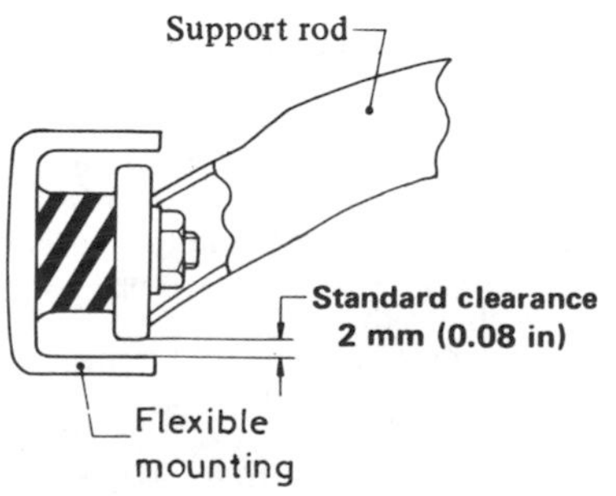

Fig. 6.7 Gearchange control flexible mounting clearance (Sec 4)

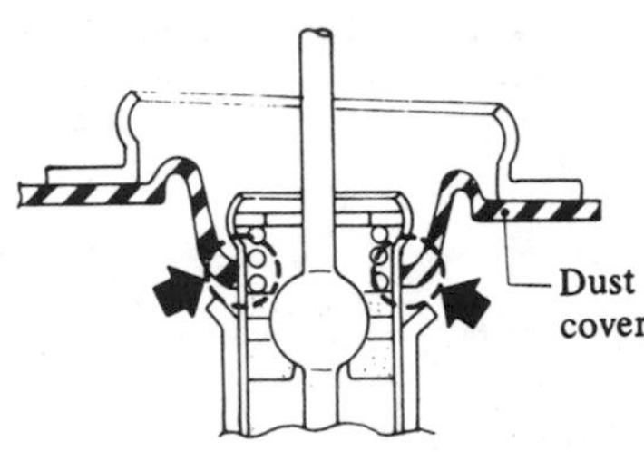

Fig. 6.8 Gearchange lever dust cover (Sec 4)

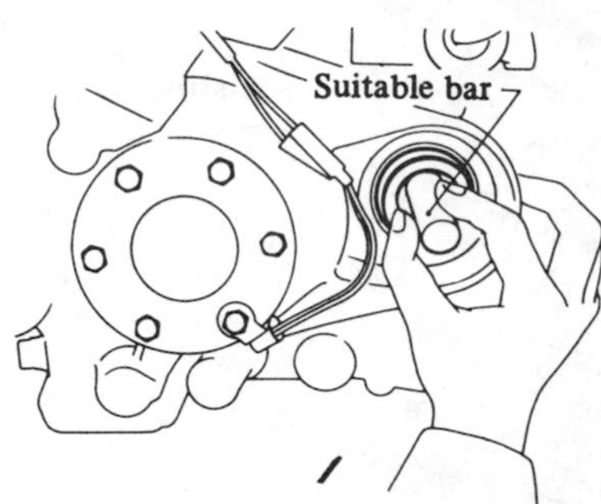

Fig. 6.9 Fitting temporary bar into side gear (Sec 5)

Fig. 6.10 Front wing inner panel fixing bolts (Sec 5)

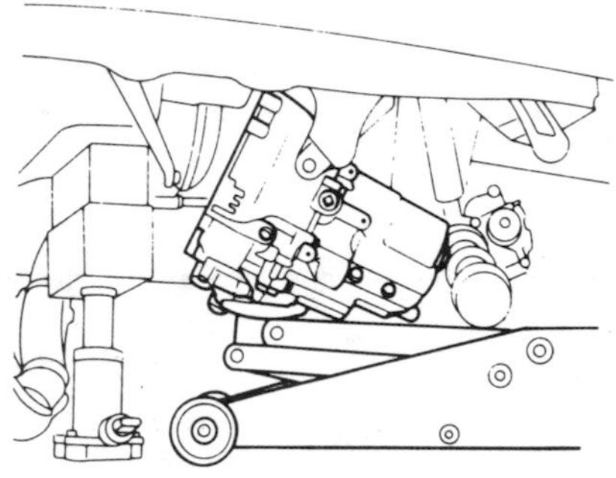

Fig. 6.11 Withdrawing manual transmission (Sec 5)

5.13 Gearchange control rods at transmission

5.16 Transmission cover plate earth terminal

3 Remove the flexible mountings, the dust cover and control lever bearing.
4 The control rod flexible bushes may be drawn out using a bolt, nut, washers and a distance piece. Fit new bushes after having smeared them with hydraulic fluid.
5 Reassembly is a reversal of dismantling, apply grease to the pivot and friction surfaces.
6 Always use a new cotter pin at the end of the control rod and make sure that its ends are bent round as shown (Fig. 6.6).
7 Adjust the clearance between the support rod and the flexible mounting backplate (see Fig. 6.7).
8 Fit the dust cover securely.

5 Transmission – removal and refitting

1 Open the bonnet and remove the battery and its retaining clamp.
2 Release the cooling system expansion tank from its retainer and move it out of the way.
3 Drain the transmission oil.
4 Disconnect the driveshafts from the transmission using the following procedure.
5 Support the vehicle under its side-members and then disconnect the front suspension lower balljoints. Do this by unscrewing the three nuts which hold the balljoint to the suspension arm. It is recommended that new nuts are used at reassembly.
6 Remove the front roadwheels.
7 Unbolt the disc calipers and tie them up out of the way; it is not necessary to disconnect the hydraulic lines.
8 Unscrew, but do not remove, the nuts at the suspension strut top mountings. This is to provide flexibility of the struts when the driveshafts are withdrawn from the transmission.
9 To disconnect a driveshaft, insert a large screwdriver or other suitable lever behind the inboard joint flange and then prise to overcome the resistance of the joint circlip.
10 Take care not to damage the transmission oil seal and do not pull on the outer end of the driveshaft or the joints may come apart.
11 Once the driveshafts have been disconnected, insert a short bar into each of the side gears as it is possible for the side gears to rotate and to fall into the differential case. Alternatively, a U-shaped piece of wire may be used.
12 Unbolt and remove the front wing inner protective panel.
13 Disconnect the gearchange control and support rods from the transmission (photo).
14 Disconnect the clutch operating cable from the release lever.
15 Disconnect the speedometer cable from the transmission.
16 Disconnect the leads from the reverse lamp switch and the cover plate earth terminal (photo).
17 Support the engine and the transmission on jacks with blocks of wood as insulators.
18 Disconnect the transmission mountings.
19 Unscrew and remove the bolts which hold the transmission bellhousing to the engine. Note the location of the coolant tube, lower protective shield and the sump-to-transmission reinforcement tube held by some of the bolts.
20 Withdraw the transmission from under the vehicle. It will be found easier to do this if a trolley jack is used.
21 Refitting is a reversal of removal, but observe the following points. Apply a smear of molybdenum disulphide grease to the input shaft splines. If the clutch has been dismantled, make sure that the driven plate has been centralised (Chapter 5).
22 Tighten all bolts and nuts to the specified torques, and reconnect the driveshafts, as described in Chapter 8.
23 Check the clutch adjustment and refill the transmission with oil.

6 Transmission – dismantling

1 With the transmission removed from the vehicle, clean away external dirt using a water-soluble solvent, or paraffin, and a stiff brush. Remove the mounting brackets, noting their location.
2 Drain the transmission oil if not drained previously.
3 With the unit standing on the flange of the clutch bellhousing,

unscrew the casing-to-bellhousing bolts and withdraw the casing from the bellhousing. On five-speed units, tilt the casing slightly as it is withdrawn to prevent the selector fork jamming inside the casing. If the casing is stuck, tap it off carefully to break the joint using a plastic hammer.

Transmission casing

4 Unscrew and remove the reverse lamp switch.

5 Remove the oil trough.

6 If the input shaft rear bearing is to be renewed, remove the very small welch plug from the transmission casing. Do this by drilling a hole in the plug and then screw in a self-tapping screw. The screw will probably force out the plug or its head can be used to lever it out.

7 Unbolt the circular cover from the casing and take out the spacer and the mainshaft bearing adjusting shim. If the mainshaft bearing is to be renewed, drive out the old outer track and fit the new one.

8 If the differential side bearings are to be renewed, drive the bearing outer track from the transmission casing. A new oil seal will be required.

Clutch housing

9 The clutch housing will have been left standing with the geartrains projecting from it when the transmission casing was drawn off.

10 Withdraw the selector shaft out of the 3rd, 4th and 5th selector forks. Extract the coil spring from the end of the shaft.

11 Remove the 5th, 3rd and 4th selector forks. Retain the plastic slides from the forks. Do not lose the rectangular bushes located in the fork arm cut-outs.

12 Remove the control bracket with the 1st/2nd selector fork. Take care not to lose the small 5th speed detent ball and spring. Extract the

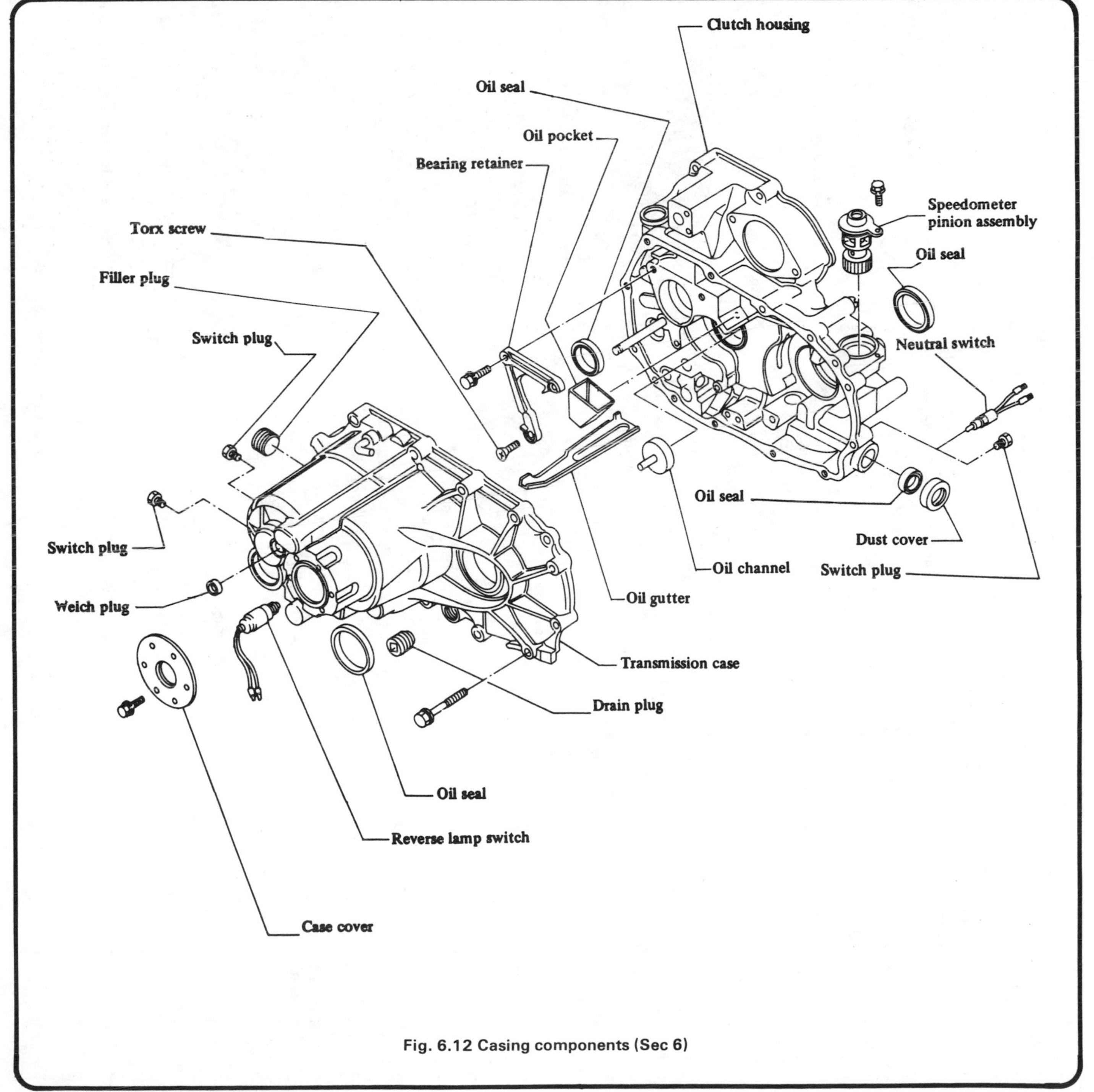

Fig. 6.12 Casing components (Sec 6)

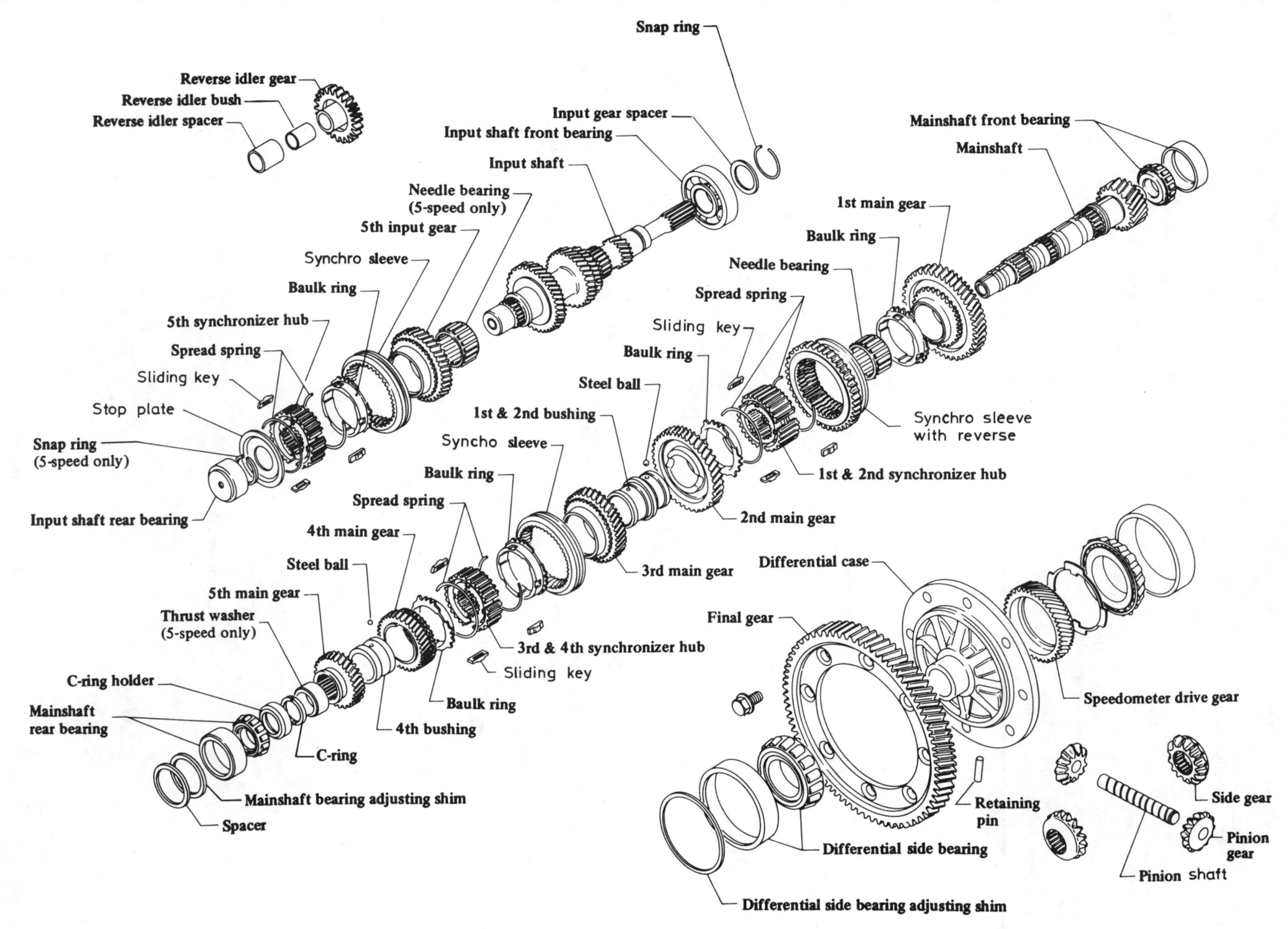

Fig. 6.13 Geartrains (Sec 6)

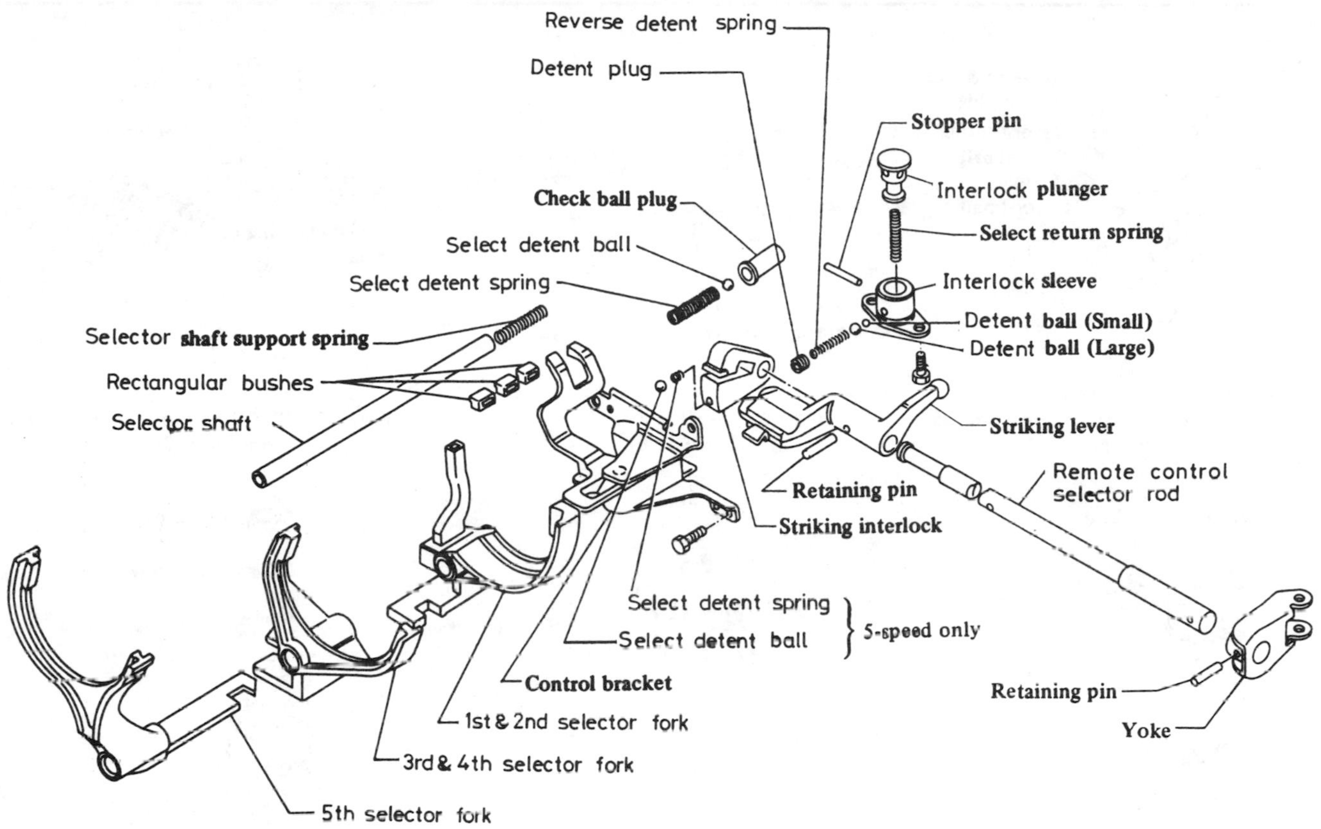

Reverse detent spring
Detent plug
Stopper pin
Interlock plunger
Check ball plug
Select return spring
Select detent ball
Select detent spring
Interlock sleeve
Detent ball (Small)
Detent ball (Large)
Selector shaft support spring
Rectangular bushes
Selector shaft
Striking lever
Remote control selector rod
Retaining pin
Striking interlock
Select detent spring
Select detent ball
5-speed only
Control bracket
Retaining pin
Yoke
1st & 2nd selector fork
3rd & 4th selector fork
5th selector fork

Fig. 6.14 Selector components (Sec 6)

Casing cover
Spacer
Mainshaft bearing adjusting shim

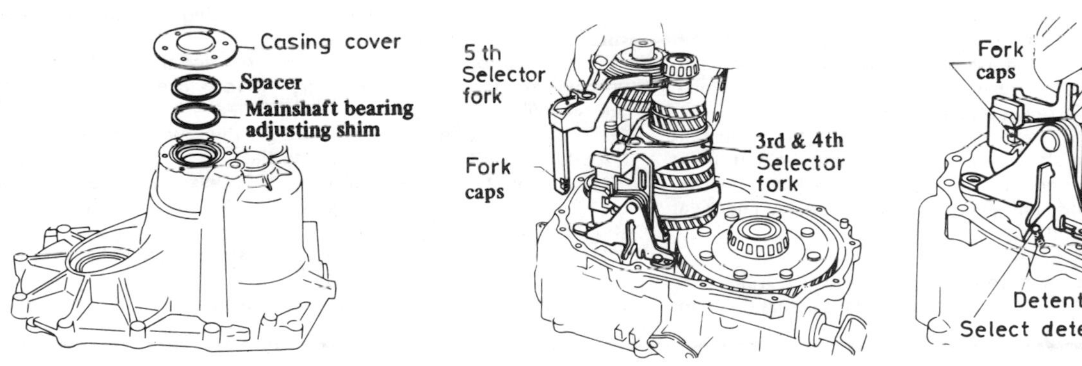

Fig. 6.15 Transmission casing circular cover (Sec 6)

5 th Selector fork
Fork caps
3rd & 4th Selector fork

Fig. 6.16 3rd/4th and 5th gear selector forks (Sec 6)

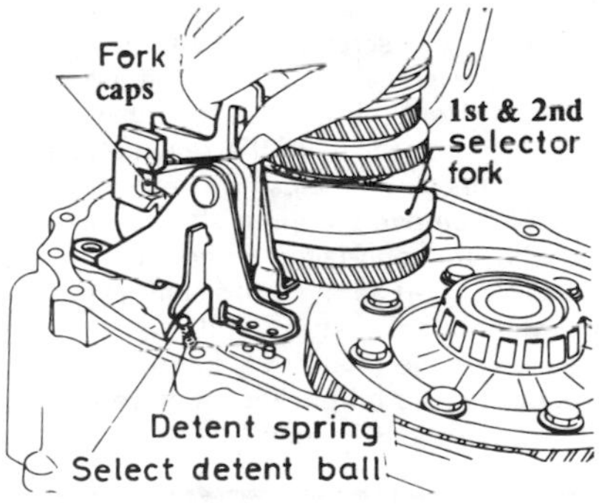

Fork caps
1st & 2nd selector fork
Detent spring
Select detent ball

Fig. 6.17 1st/2nd selector fork and control bracket (Sec 6)

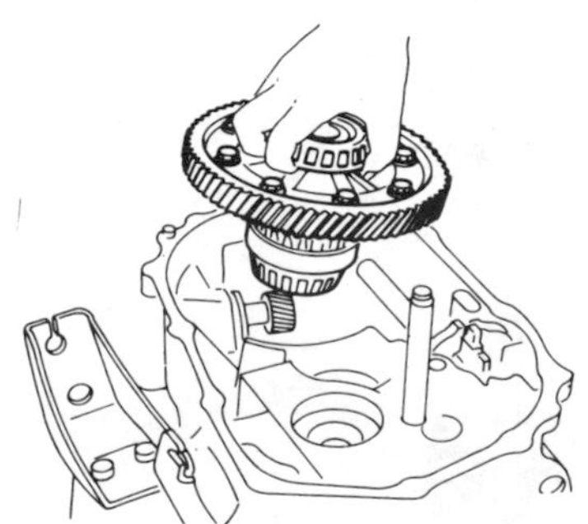

Fig. 6.18 Removing final drive/differential (Sec 6)

Check detent
Detent ball plug
Shift selector ball

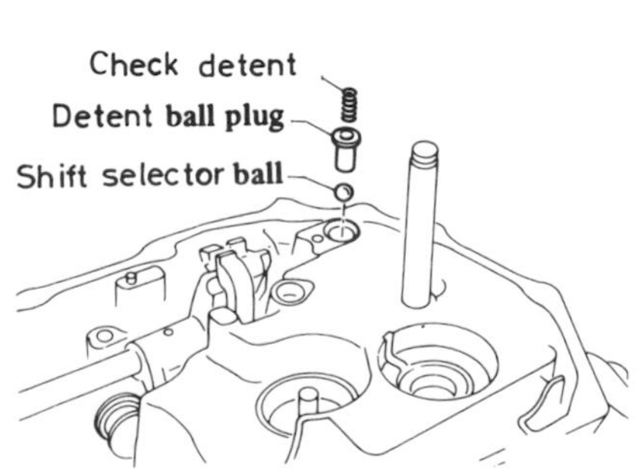

Fig. 6.19 Detent components (Sec 6)

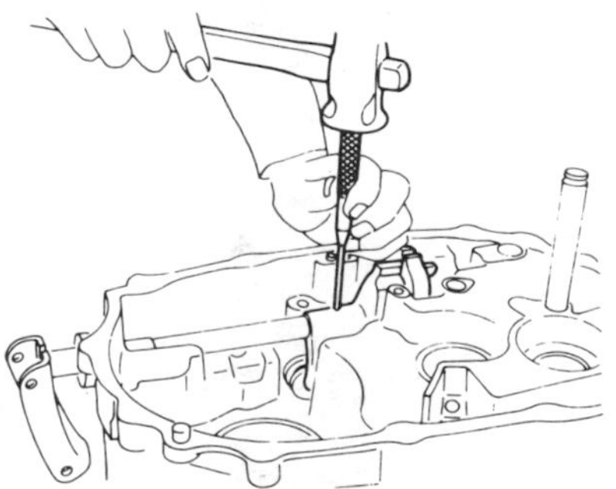

Fig. 6.20 Removing selector dog roll pin (Sec 6)

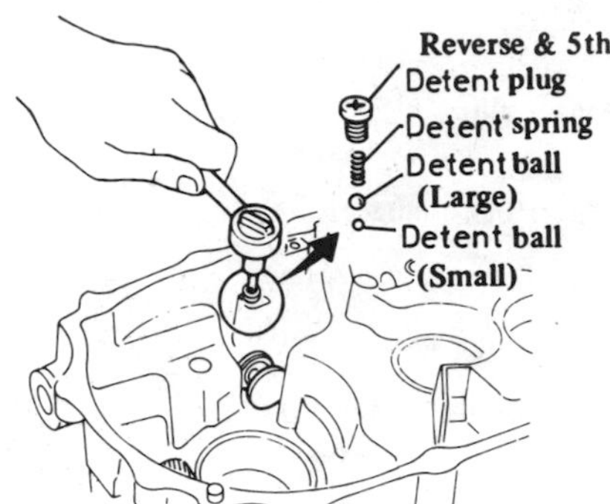

Fig. 6.21 5th/reverse detent components (Sec 6)

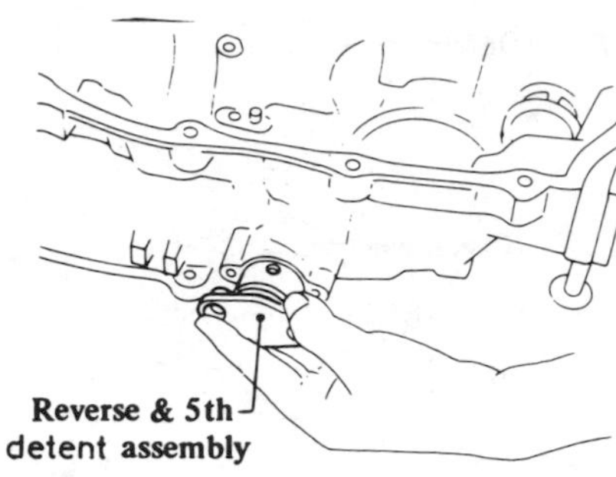

Fig. 6.22 5th/reverse interlock assembly (Sec 6)

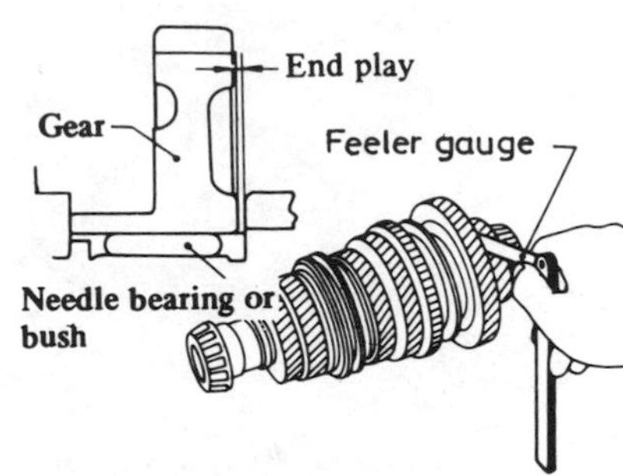

Fig. 6.23 Checking input shaft 5th gear endfloat (Sec 6)

Fig. 6.24 Input shaft 5th gear circlip and stop plate (Sec 6)

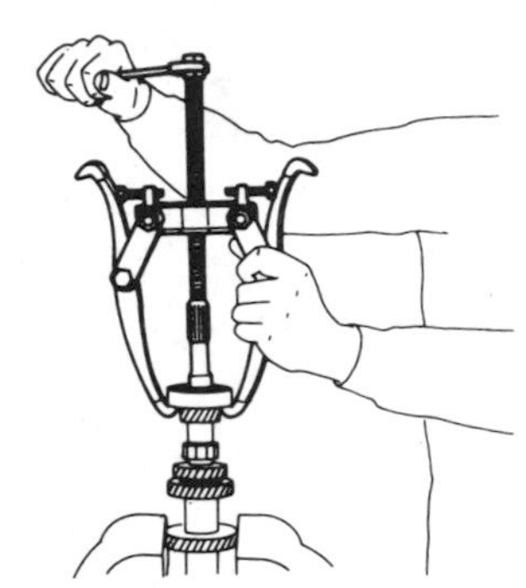

Fig. 6.25 Removing input shaft front bearing (Sec 6)

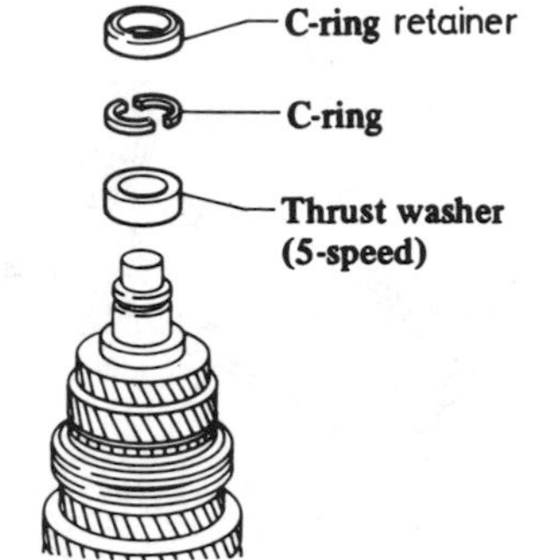

Fig. 6.26 5th gear thrust components on mainshaft (Sec 6)

larger coil spring and ball from the remote control selector rod hole.

13 Remove the screws from the triangular shaped bearing retainer. One of these screws is of Torx type and will require a special bit to unscrew it. Hold the reverse idler gear up while the screw is undone. Remove the spacer from the reverse idler shaft.

14 Turn the clutch housing on its side and remove the mainshaft assembly. Remove the input shaft assembly by tapping the end of the shaft with a plastic-faced or copper hammer. Reverse idler gear will come off its shaft as the input shaft is released, but mark the idler gear as to which way up it is fitted.

15 Take out the final drive/differential.

16 If the plastic oil pocket must be removed then the bearing outer track which retains it must first be drawn out using a suitable extractor with thin claws. Extract the small retaining bolt and remove the speedometer drivegear.

17 Drive the roll pin from the selector rod dog then withdraw the rod, dog and interlock. When removing the rod, take care not to damage the oil seal lips.

18 Unscrew 5th/reverse detent plug, which will require a Torx type bit, and then extract the spring and ball.

19 Remove 5th/reverse interlock plunger assembly, the screws again being of Torx type. Extract the smaller detent ball. The O-ring seal should be renewed at reassembly.

20 Remove the clutch release shaft, bearing and lever, as described in Chapter 5.

21 Remove the plastic oil channel from the transmission casing.

Fig. 6.27 Mainshaft 4th gear components (Sec 6)

Fig. 6.28 2nd and 3rd/4th gear components on mainshaft (Sec 6)

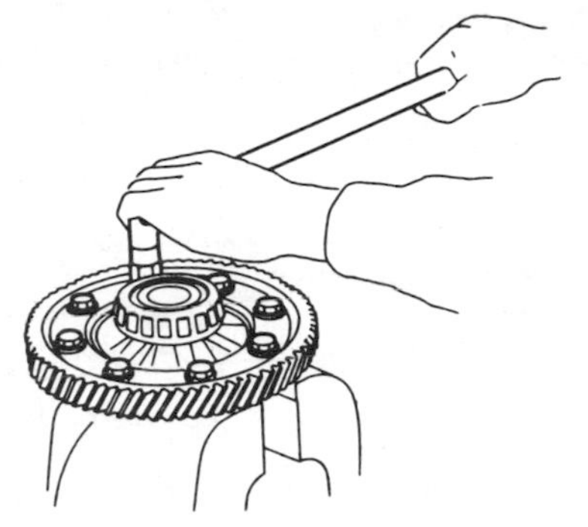

Fig. 6.29 Unbolting crownwheel (Sec 6)

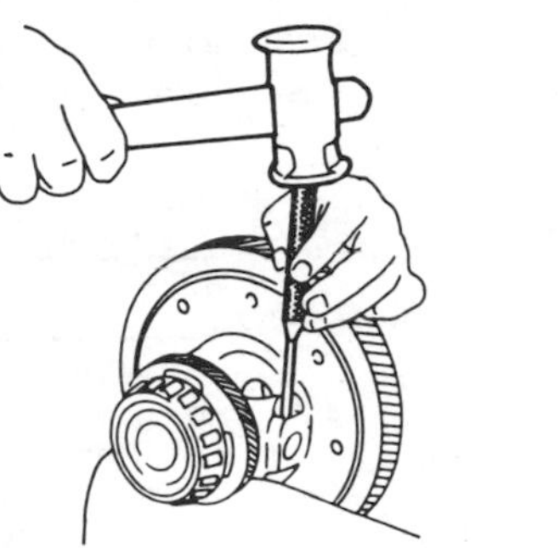

Fig. 6.30 Removing pinion shaft lockpin (Sec 6)

6.24 Input shaft with 5th gear and synchroniser removed

Input shaft

22 On five-speed units, measure and record the input shaft 5th gear endfloat. Extract the circlip and 5th gear stop plate.

23 Remove 5th gear with the synchroniser and the split needle bearing from inside the gear.

24 The input shaft (photo) cannot be dismantled further except to draw off the front bearing after having first extracted the retaining circlip and taken off the spacer. If a bearing puller is not available, support the bearing and drive the shaft from it.

Mainshaft

25 Before dismantling the mainshaft, compare the endfloat of the gears with the specified tolerances. Inspect the components with endfloat which is outside the limits very carefully before reassembly.

26 Remove the bearing inner races from the front and rear ends of the shaft. Use either a two-legged puller or press the shaft out of the bearings.

27 On five-speed units, remove the C-ring retainer, the C-rings and the thrust washer. Remove 5th gear, a puller will be required for this.

28 Remove 4th gear, the gear bush and steel locking ball.

29 Remove the baulk ring.

30 Remove 3rd/4th synchro unit.

31 Remove 3rd gear.

32 Remove 2nd and 3rd gear bush.

33 Remove the steel locking ball.

34 Remove 2nd gear.

35 Remove the baulk ring.

36 Remove 1st/2nd synchro unit with reverse gear (straight-cut teeth on synchro sleeve) together with 1st gear as an assembly. The synchro-hub is tight on the shaft and the best way to remove the assembly is to support under 1st gear and drive the shaft downwards, using a copper-faced hammer.

37 Remove 1st gear split needle bearing.

Differential/final drive

38 Unbolt the crownwheel from the differential case.

39 Using a punch, drive out the pinion shaft lockpin and withdraw the shaft.

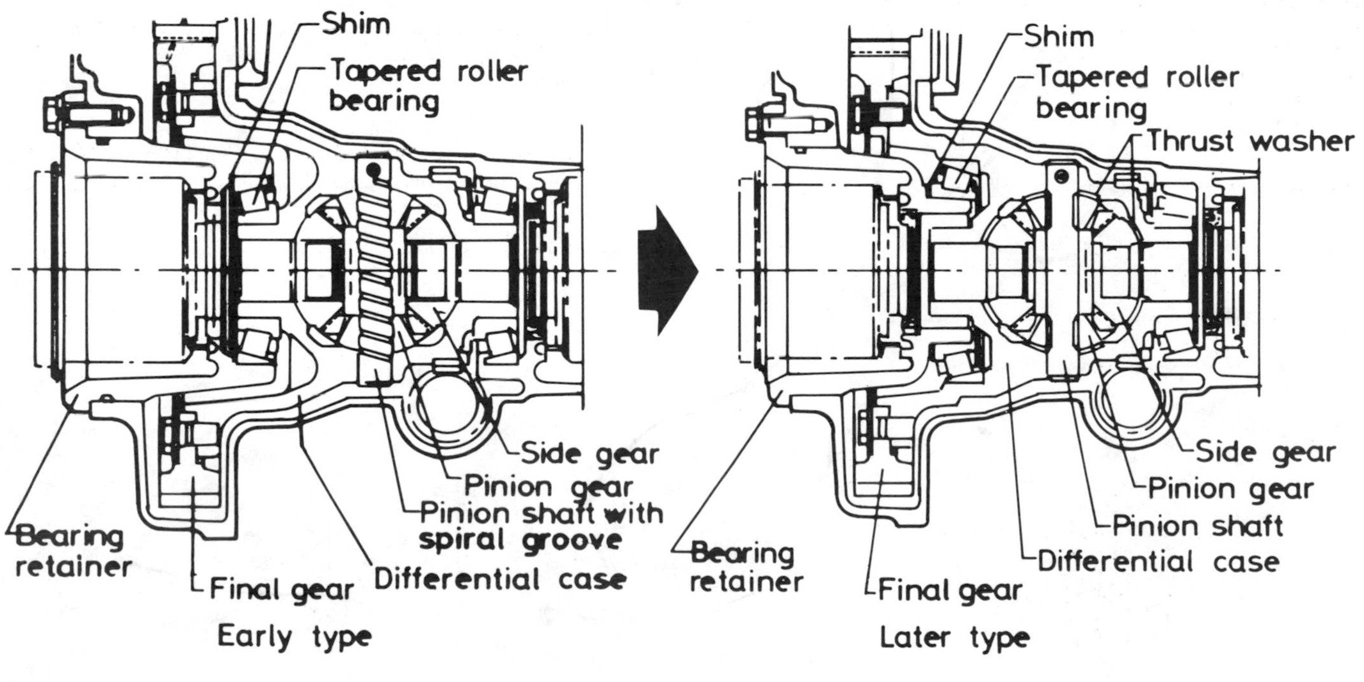

Fig. 6.31 Sectional views of early and later type final drive assemblies (Sec 6)

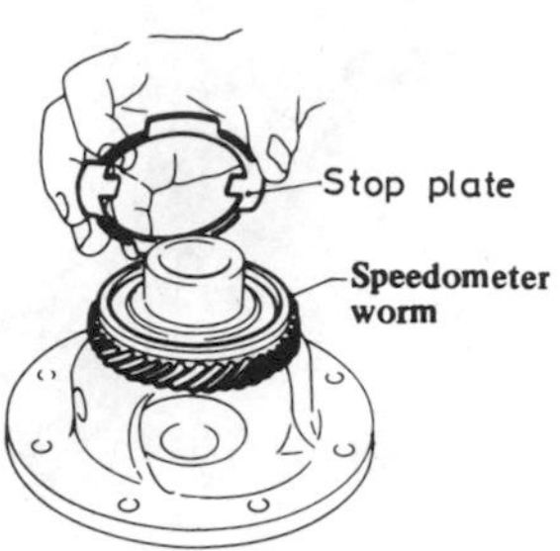

Fig. 6.32 Speedometer worm gear and stop plate (Sec 6)

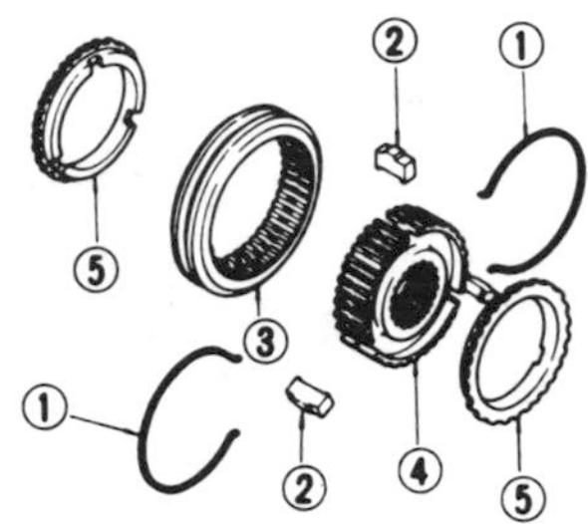

Fig. 6.33 Synchroniser components (Sec 7)
1 Spreader spring
2 Sliding key
3 Sleeve
4 Hub
5 Baulk ring

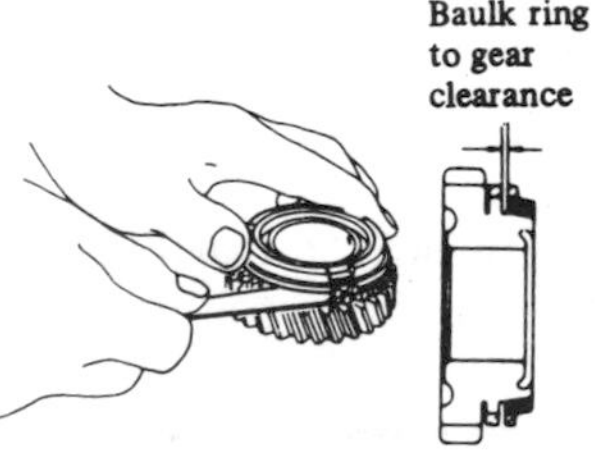

Fig. 6.34 Checking baulk ring-to-gear clearance (Sec 7)
Clearance = 0.7 mm (0.028 in)

Fig. 6.35 Synchro spring arrangement (Sec 7)

40 Remove the pinion and side gears.
41 Draw off the differential side bearing races, noting exactly how the taper of the rollers is set.
42 Remove the speedometer drivegear stop plate and the gear.

7 Transmission components – inspection

1 With the transmission completely dismantled, clean all components and inspect them for wear or damage.
2 Check the gears for chipped teeth and their bushes for wear.
3 Check the shafts for scoring or grooving.
4 Check the bearings for wear by spinning them with the fingers. If they shake or rattle then they must be renewed.
5 Wear in the synchronisers will usually be known about before dismantling, as a result of noisy gear changing or by the fact that the synchro action could be easily beaten during gear changing.
6 Even if the syncho is operating quietly, it is worthwhile checking the units in the following way at time of major overhaul.
7 Refer to Fig. 6.33. Extract the spreader springs, remove the sliding keys, and then push the hub from the sleeve, but not before having marked the components with quick-drying paint to ensure that their relative positions are maintained at reassembly.
8 Check the synchro components for wear or deformation. Place the baulk ring on its cone and twist it to ensure good contact between the surfaces. Using a feeler blade, check that the gap between gear and baulk ring is not less than specified (see Fig. 6.34). If it is, renew the baulk ring.
9 When reassembling the synchro units, make sure that the spreader springs run in opposite directions, when viewed from each side of the synchro, and that the spring ends do not engage in the same sliding key.
10 It is recommended that all oil seals are renewed at time of major overhaul (photos). These include those for the clutch cross-shaft, differential side bearings, gearchange control rod and the input shaft.
11 Should anything more than the slightest seepage of oil be observed during the normal operation of the vehicle the oil seals for the differential side bearings and the gearchange control rod can be renewed without having to remove the transmission from the vehicle.

8 Transmission – reassembly

Differential/final drive

1 Fit the speedometer worm drivegear and its stop plate to the differential case (photo).
2 Press or drive on the differential side gear inner races (photo).
3 Into the differential case fit the pinion gears with thrust washers (later models) and the pinion shaft (photo).
4 Drive in a new pinion shaft roll pin, making sure that it is flush with the differential case (photo).
5 Clean the threads of the crownwheel bolts and apply thread-locking fluid, then screw them in and tighten to the specified torque.

7.10A Interior of transmission casing

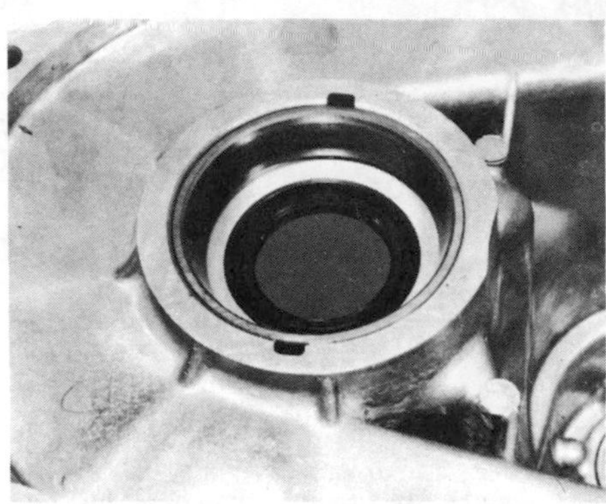

7.10B Differential bearing outer track and oil seal in transmission casing

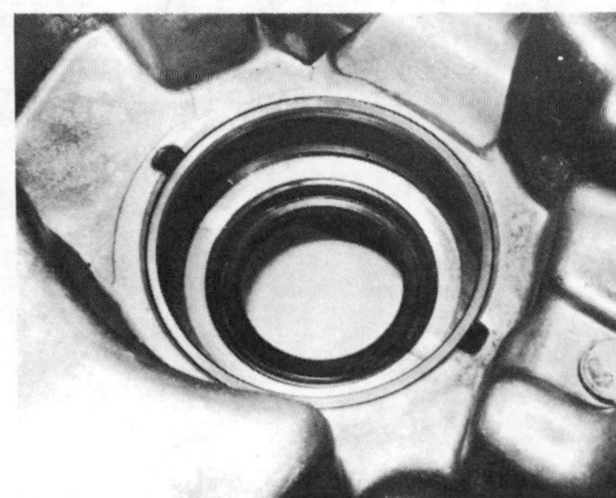

7.10C Differential bearing outer track and oil seal in clutch bellhousing

8.1 Differential case
1 *Tapered roller bearing*
2 *Stop plate*
3 *Speedometer worm drive gear*

8.2 Method of fitting differential bearing

8.3 Fitting differential pinion and gears

8.4 Pinion shaft roll pin

Mainshaft

6 Oil all components liberally as they are reassembled.

7 Fit 1st gear needle bearings to the mainshaft (photos).

8 Fit 1st gear (photo).

9 Fit 1st gear baulk ring (photo).

10 Fit 1st/2nd synchro unit with reverse (photo). Tap the synchro-hub down the mainshaft using a piece of tubing, but hold the synchro together with the hand in case the vibration makes it fall apart.

11 Locate the steel lock ball in its hole in the shaft. *On no account place the ball in the hole in the shaft groove* (photo).

12 Fit 2nd gear baulk ring (photo).

13 Fit 2nd gear (photo).

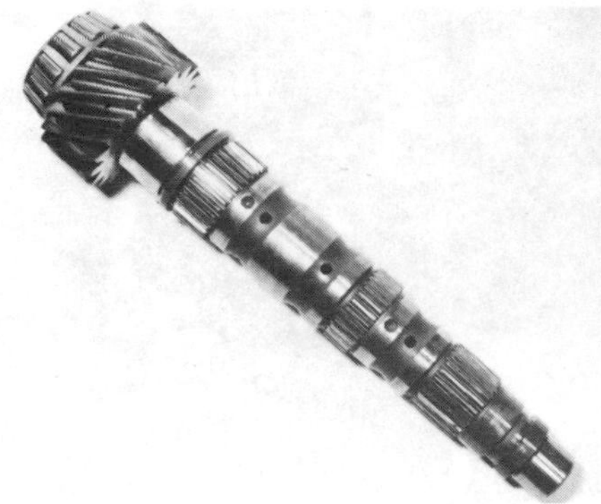
8.7A Mainshaft dismantled

8.7B 1st gear split needle bearing

8.8 1st gear

8.9 1st gear baulk ring

8.10 1st/2nd synchro with reverse gear

8.11 Steel lock ball for 2nd/3rd gear bush in correct hole

8.12 2nd gear baulk ring

8.13 2nd gear

8.14 2nd/3rd gear bush

8.15 3rd gear

8.16 Baulk ring

8.17 3rd/4th synchro unit

8.19 Lock ball (4th gear bush) and baulk ring

8.20 4th gear bush

8.21 4th gear

8.22A 5th gear

8.22B Driving 5th gear onto mainshaft

8.23 5th gear thrust washer

8.24 C-ring

8.25 C-ring retainer

8.26 Mainshaft bearing

8.27 Checking mainshaft gear endfloat

8.28 Input shaft split type needle roller bearing

8.29 Input shaft 5th gear

14 Fit 2nd/3rd gear bush, turning it slowly to engage its cut-out with the lock ball (photo).
15 Fit 3rd gear (photo).
16 Fit the baulk ring (photo).
17 Fit 3rd/4th synchro unit (photo) so that the engraved dashes in the sleeve are visible.
18 Using thick grease, stick the second (4th gear bush) lock ball in its shaft hole – *not the hole in the shaft groove.*
19 Fit the baulk ring (photo).
20 Fit 4th gear bush, turning it slowly to engage its cut-out with the lock ball (photo).
21 Fit 4th gear (photo).
22 If the transmission is of five-speed type, fit 5th gear (photo). Drive it onto the mainshaft using a piece of tubing (photo).
23 On five-speed models only, fit the thrust washer (photo).
24 Fit the C-ring (photo). These are supplied in various thicknesses to correct gear endfloat.
25 Fit the C-ring retainer (photo).
26 Press on new bearing inner races to both ends of the mainshaft (photo).
27 Using feeler blades check that the gear endfloat is within the specified tolerances (photo). If any endfloat measurements are outside the specified limits the shaft should be dismantled and the components re-examined.

Input shaft

28 Fit the split type needle roller bearing (photo).
29 Fit 5th gear (photo).
30 Fit the baulk ring (photo).
31 Fit the synchro unit (photo) so that the engraved dashes on the sleeve are visible.
32 To the synchro unit fit the stop plate and the circlip (photos). The circlips are available in various thicknesses to eliminate endfloat.
33 Press on a new shaft front bearing, fit the spacer and use a new circlip (photo).

8.30 5th gear baulk ring

8.31 5th gear synchro on input shaft

8.32A Input shaft synchro unit stop plate

8.32B Input shaft stop plate circlip

8.33 Input shaft front bearing circlip

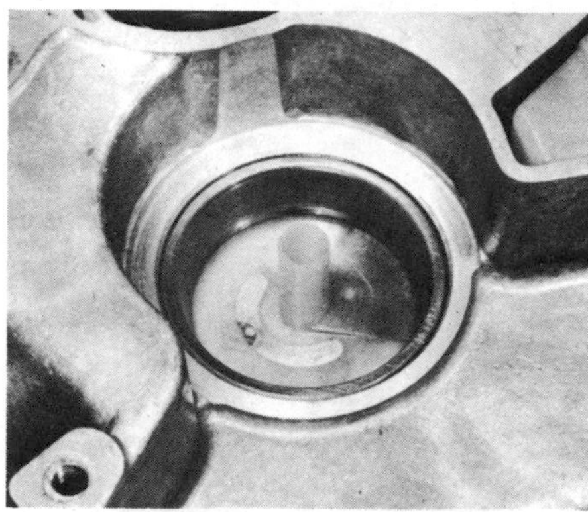
8.34 Oil channel

8.38A Using a magnet to fit the small reverse/5th detent ball

8.38B Using a magnet to fit the larger reverse/5th detent ball

8.38C Using a magnet to fit reverse/5th detent spring

8.38D Reverse/5th detent plug

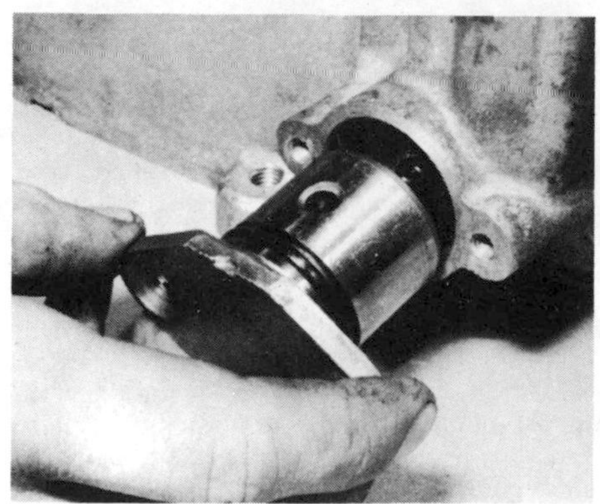
8.38E Interlock plunger assembly

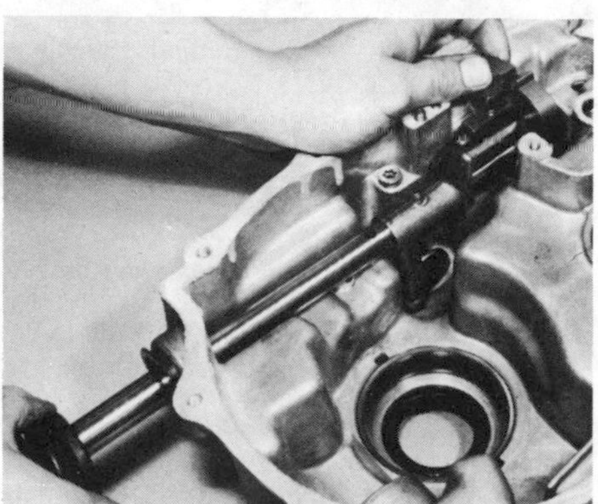
8.41A Assembling remote control rod, striking lever and interlock

8.41B Striking lever roll pin (outer)

8.41C Striking lever roll pin (inner)

8.42 Speedometer drivegear

8.43 Lowering differential/final drive into transmission casing

8.44 Method of retaining differential side gears

8.45 Fitting input shaft geartrain with reverse idler gear

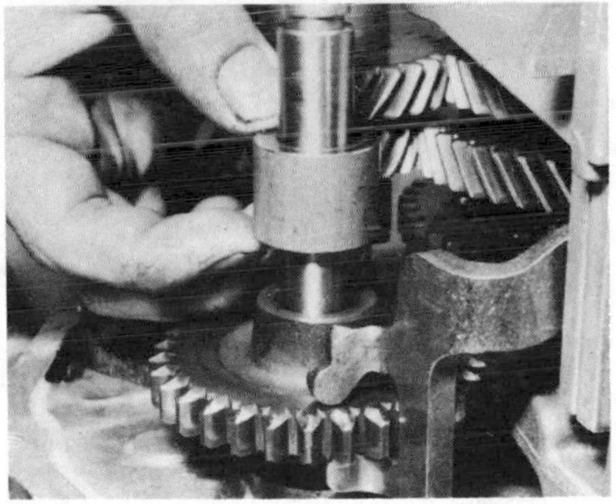
8.46 Reverse idler gear spacer

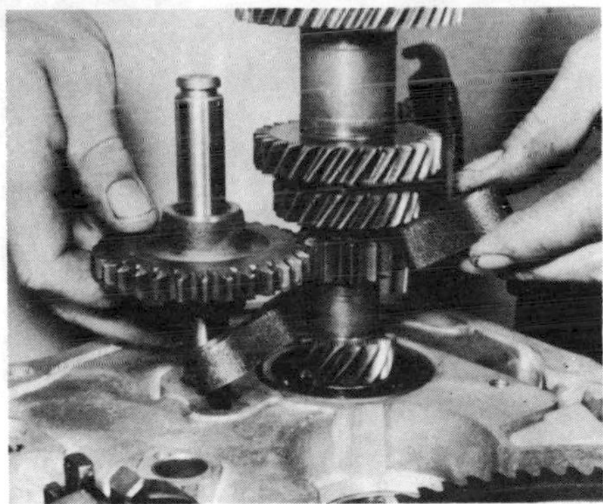
8.47A Fitting triangular shaped bearing retainer

8.47B Tightening bearing retainer screw

Clutch housing

34 Fit a new oil channel so that its relieved area is towards the oil pocket when installed (photo).

35 Press or drive the differential and mainshaft bearing outer tracks into their seats.

36 Remember that the mainshaft bearing outer track retains the oil pocket, so align the pocket correctly before fitting the bearing track.

37 Reassemble the clutch release mechanism (Chapter 5).

38 Refit the interlock plunger assembly (photo). Fit reverse/5th detent balls (small one first) the spring and plug (photos).

39 The force of the reverse detent should now be checked using a spring balance. On four-speed models the pull required to move against the detent should be between 5.4 and 7.7 kg (12 to 17 lb). On five speed models the pull should be between 7.2 and 9.1 kg (16 to 20 lb).

40 The detent force may be increased by changing the detent plug for one of greater length.

41 Using new double roll pins, refit the remove control rod, striking lever and interlock (photos). The notch in the control rod should be downwards.

42 Refit the speedometer drive gear and screw in the lockbolt (photo).

43 Fit the side gears and retain them with rods or a wire clip bent into a U-shape (photo). Some later models have side gear thrust washers.

44 Lower the differential/final drive into position (photo).

45 Fit the input shaft and reverse idler gear simultaneously (photo). The idler gear (marked before removal) should be refitted in its original position. Use a plastic-faced or copper hammer to tap the input shaft fully home in the clutch housing.

46 Fit the spacer to the reverse idler shaft (photo).

47 Fit the triangular shaped bearing retainer (photo). Apply thread

8.48 Fitting mainshaft/geartrain

8.49A Remote control housing bush

8.49B Remote control housing ball

8.49C Remote control housing spring

8.50A Detent spring (remote control interlock)

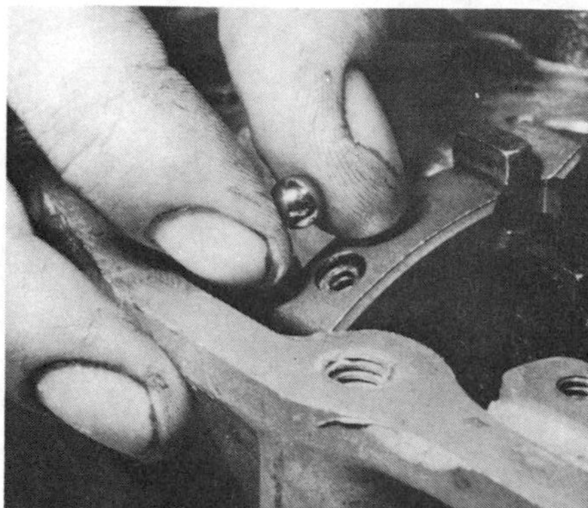
8.50B Detent ball (remote control interlock)

8.50C Remote control bracket (screws arrowed)

8.50D Remote control interlock detent ball correctly located (arrowed)

8.51A Selector forks
A 4th/5th *B 2nd/3rd*

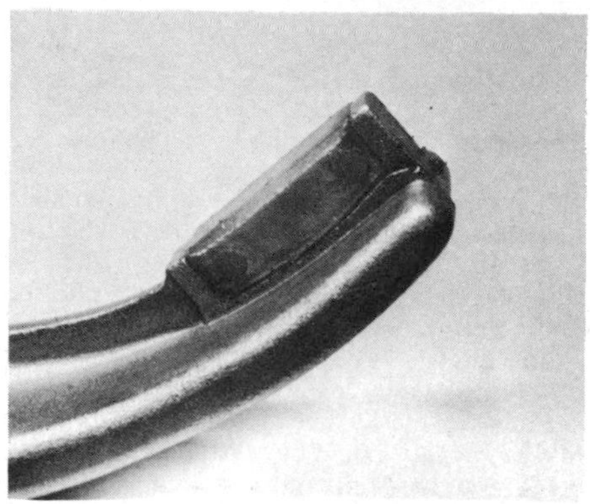
8.51B Selector fork plastic slide

8.51C Selector dog metal bushes

8.52A Fitting selector shaft into forks

8.52B Selector shaft coil spring

8.59 Fitting transmission casing

8.60 Tightening casing bolts

8.61A Mainshaft bearing adjusting shim

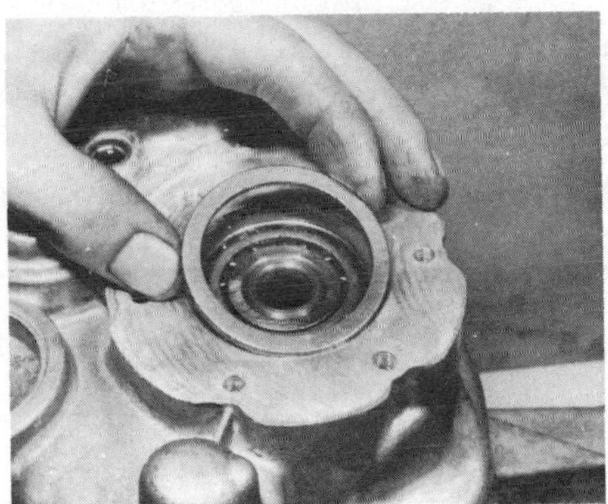
8.61B Mainshaft bearing spacer

8.62 Transmission casing circular cover

locking fluid to the screw threads and tighten them as tightly as possible (photo). Note the Torx type screw next to the idler.

48 Fit the mainshaft (photo) carefully meshing the gearteeth with those of the input shaft as the operation proceeds, push both synchro sleeves downwards and hold the reverse idler gear upwards.

49 Fit the bush, the ball and the large coil spring to the hole in the remote control rod housing (photos).

50 Fit the control bracket which incorporates reverse selector fork. Make sure that 1st/2nd selector fork is located under the bracket and 5th speed detent spring and ball are placed into the hole in the remote control interlock as the assembly operations progress (photos). Tighten the control bracket screws.

51 Locate the selector forks. The 2nd/3rd fork is the lower one and the 4th/5th fork the upper one (photo). Make sure that the plastic slides are in position in the fork arm cut-outs (photo) also the rectangular shaped metal bushes are in the selector dog cut-outs (photo).

52 Pass the selector shaft through the forks (photo), making sure that the coil spring is located in the recess in the lower end of the shaft (photo).

Transmission casing

53 If the differential side bearings were renewed, fit the new bearing outer track now with a new oil seal.

54 If the mainshaft bearing was renewed, fit the new track into the casing now.

55 If the input shaft rear bearing was renewed, tap a new small welch plug into the hole in the casing.

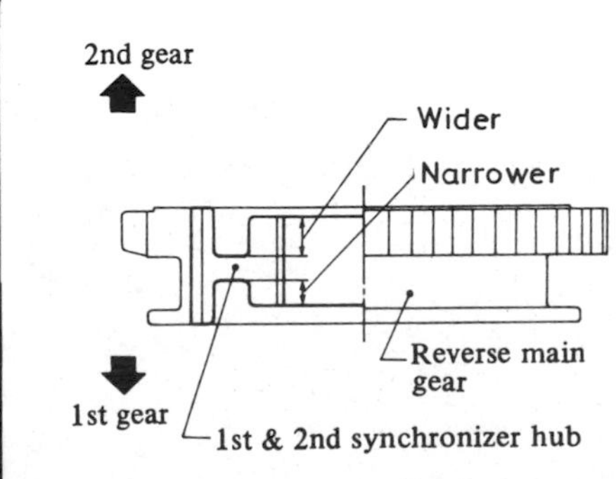

Fig. 6.36 1st/2nd synchro-hub to sleeve relationship (Sec 8)

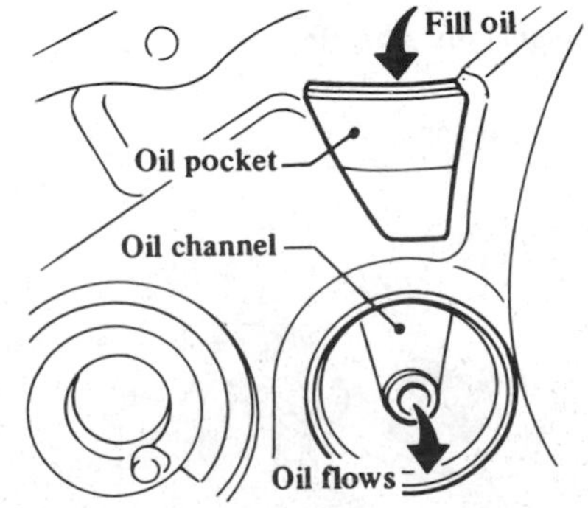

Fig. 6.37 Oil pocket/oil channel arrangement (Sec 8)

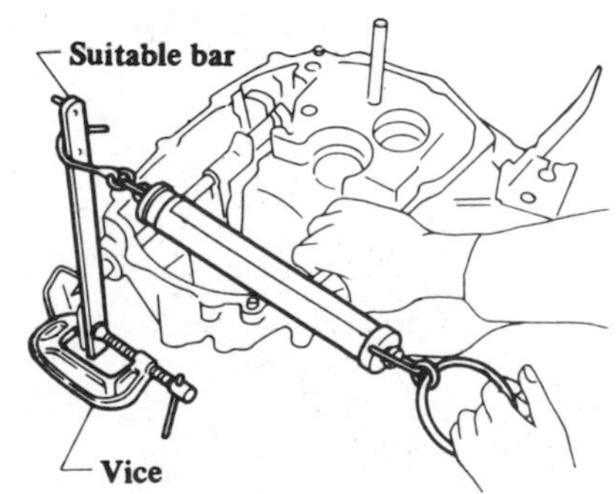

Fig. 6.38 Checking reverse detent resistance (Sec 8)

56 Fit the plastic oil trough.
57 Screw in the reverse lamp switch.
58 With the clutch housing standing on the bench with the geartrains vertical, apply jointing compound to the mating faces of the transmission casing and clutch housing.
59 Lower the casing into position over the geartrains (photo). On five-speed units, tilt the casing as necessary to clear the selector fork.
60 Fit the connecting bolts and tighten to the specified torque (photo).
61 If the mainshaft bearing has not been changed, fit the original adjusting shim and spacer (photos). If a new bearing has been fitted, refer to Section 10 for details of mainshaft bearing adjustment.
62 Apply jointing compound to the edges of the circular cover and bolt it into position on the transmission casing (photo).

9 Final drive – adjustment

1 If any of the following components of the transmission have been renewed during overhaul then you will have to take the assembly to your dealer for the final drive to be adjusted to ensure correct crownwheel-to-pinion meshing and the specified bearing preload.

Differential casing
Differential side bearing
Clutch housing
Transmission casing

2 Owing to the need for special tools, this work is not within the scope of the home mechanic.

10 Mainshaft bearing preload – adjustment

1 If any of the following components have been renewed during overhaul, then the mainshaft bearing preload must be checked and adjusted.

Mainshaft
Mainshaft bearings
Clutch housing
Transmission casing

2 Remove the circular cover from the transmission.
3 To carry out the adjustment, measure between the machined face of the transmission casing and the surface of the spacer. A shim should now be selected which is 0.2 mm (0.008 in) thicker than the dimension just taken.
4 Fit the spacer, the selected shim and the cover and check that the input shaft turns smoothly with 4th gear selected. A special tool is available from dealers (KV38105900) which engages in the side gears and gives a torque reading for rotation of the final drive when 4th gear is selected.
5 The correct turning torque should be between 7.4 and 10.8 Nm (5.5 to 7.8 lbf ft).

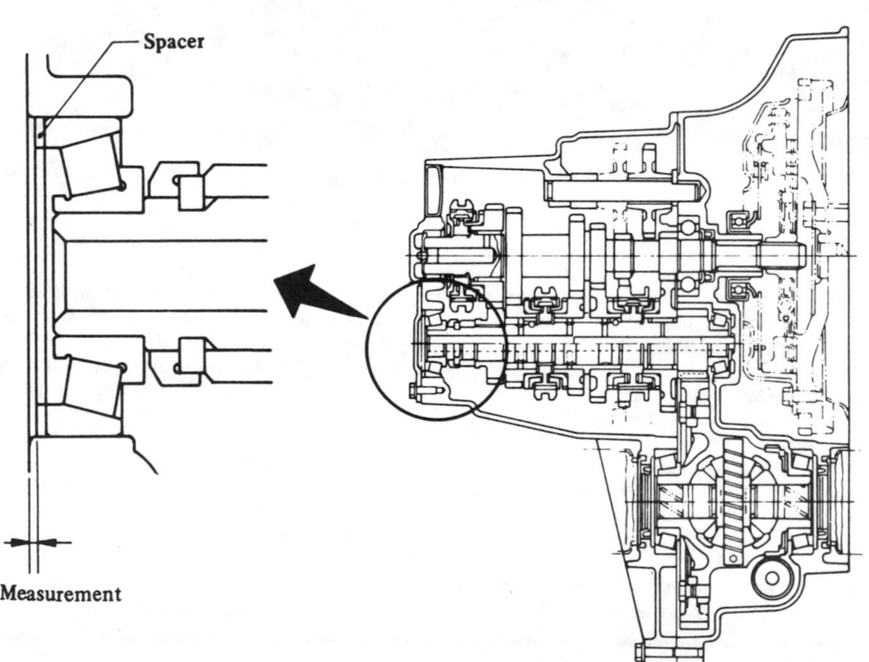

Fig. 6.39 Final drive bearing adjusting shim (Sec 10)

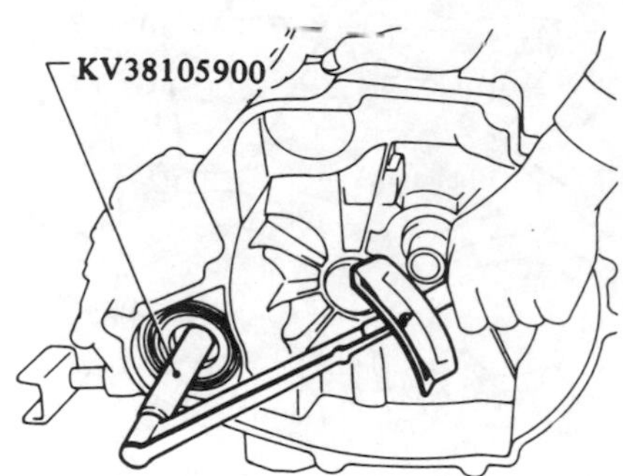

Fig. 6.40 Using special tool to check final drive turning torque (Sec 10)

11 Fault diagnosis – manual transmission

Symptom	Reason(s)
Weak or ineffective synchromesh	Synchro baulk rings worn, split or damaged Synchromesh units worn or damaged
Jumps out of gear	Gearchange mechanism worn Synchromesh units badly worn Selector fork badly worn
Excessive noise	Incorrect grade of oil in gearbox or oil level too low Gear teeth excessively worn or damaged Shaft thrust washers worn allowing excessive end play Worn bearings
Difficulty in engaging gears	Clutch pedal adjustment incorrect
Noise when cornering	Wheel bearing or driveshaft fault Differential fault

Note: *It is sometimes difficult to decide whether it is worthwhile removing and dismantling the gearbox for a fault which may be nothing more than a minor irritant. Gearboxes which howl, or where the synchromesh can be beaten by a quick gearchange, may continue to perform for a long time in this state. A worn gearbox usually needs a complete rebuild to eliminate noise because the various gears, if re-aligned on new bearings, will continue to howl when different wearing surfaces are presented to each other. The decision to overhaul, therefore, must be considered with regard to time and money available, relative to the degree of noise or malfunction that the driver has to suffer.*

Chapter 7 Automatic transmission

Refer to Chapter 13 for Specifications and information on later models

Contents

Specifications

Type	RL3F01A fully automatic, with three element torque converter and two planetary geartrains. Three forward speeds and reverse. Final drive is integral	
Ratios		
1st	2.826:1	
2nd	1.543:1	
3rd	1.000:1	
Reverse	2.364:1	
Final drive	3.364:1	
Fluid capacity	6.0 litres (10.6 Imp pts, 6.3 US qts)	
Torque wrnech settings	**Nm**	**lbf ft**
Drive plate to torque converter	60	44
Torque converter housing to engine	20	15
Sump pan bolts	7	5
Control valve body to transmission casing	9	7
Governor valve body to shaft	7	5
Oil cooler union nut at transmission casing	48	35
Reinforcement strut to engine crankcase	35	26
Reinforcement strut to transmission casing	20	15
Front suspension strut top mounting nuts	23	17
Suspension lower balljoints to track control arm	61	45
Caliper mounting bolts	61	45
Roadwheel nuts	95	70

1 General description

The automatic transmission incorporates a torque converter with planetary geartrains and the final drive/differential unit.

Six speed selector control lever positions are used:

P *Park – to lock up the transmission mechanically*
R *Reverse gear*
N *Neutral*
D *Forward speed – changing automatically up and down between 1st, 2nd and 3rd gear ratios*
2 *Second gear hold, will change between 1st and 2nd gears only*
1 *First (low) gear hold*

Kickdown in D is used for rapid acceleration during overtaking, it changes down to 2nd or 1st gear, depending upon roadspeed, when accelerator is fully depressed.

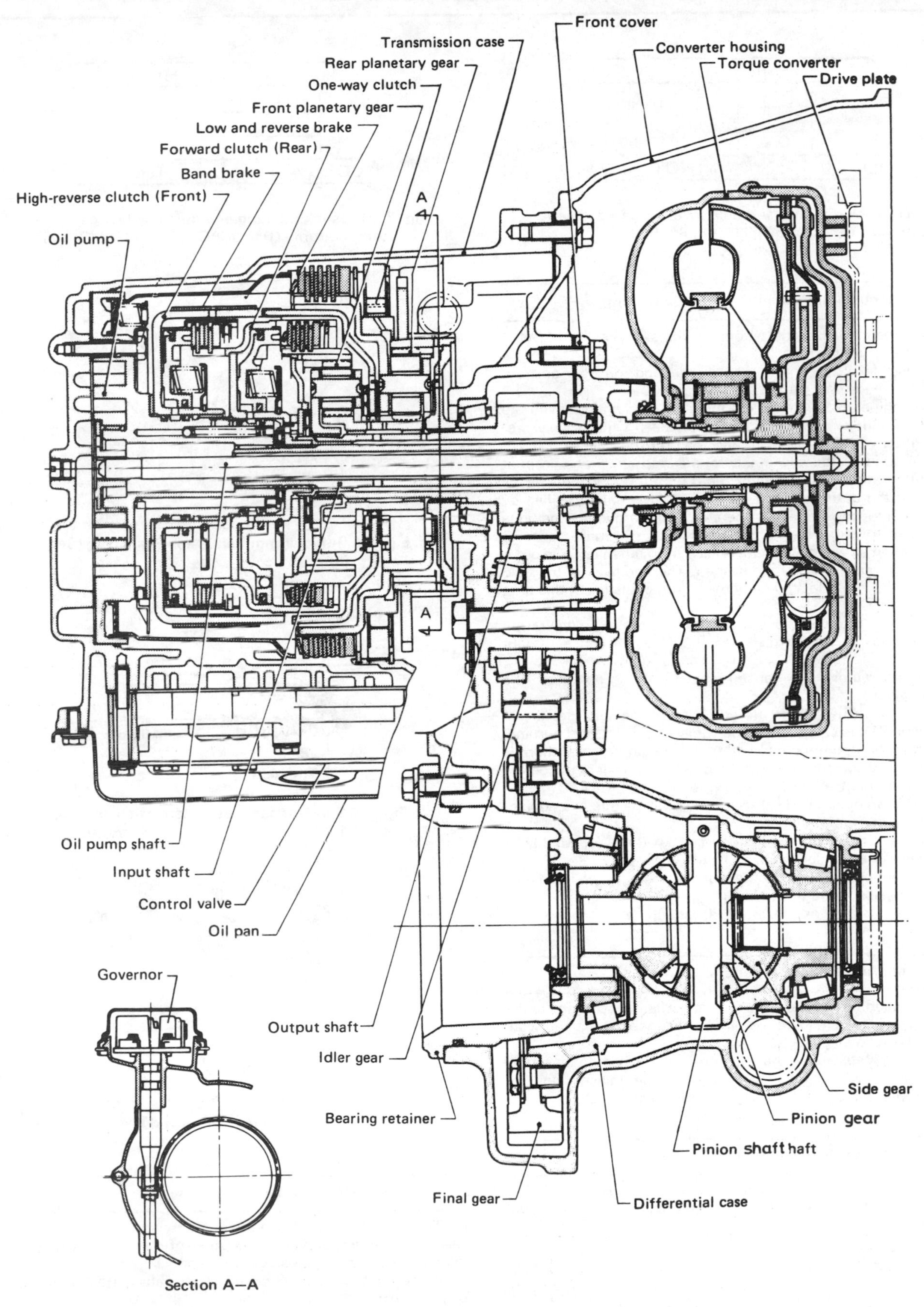

Fig. 7.1 Sectional view of the automatic transmission (Sec 1)

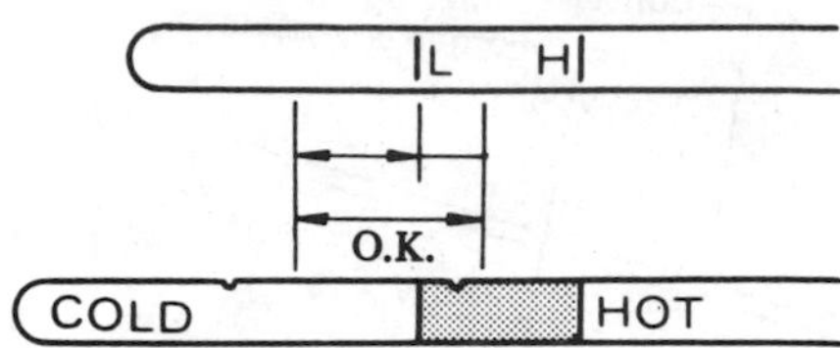

Fig. 7.2 Dipstick marking and fluid level range – ambient temperature 10 to 30°C (50 to 86°F) (Sec 2)

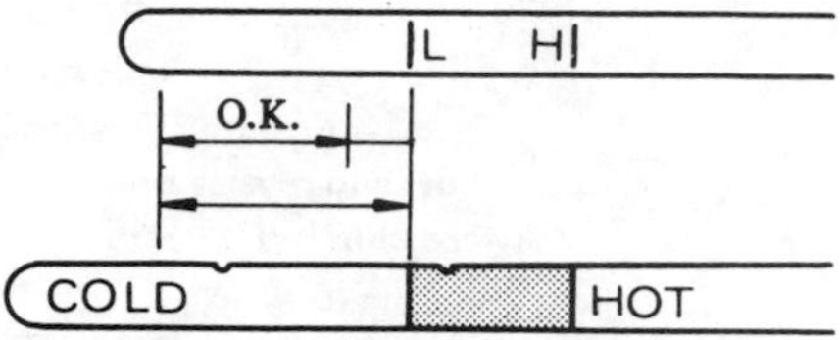

Fig. 7.3 Dipstick marking and fluid level range – ambient temperature -10 to 10°C (14 to 50°F) (Sec 2)

2 Fluid level – checking, topping-up and changing

1 It is recommended that the automatic transmission fluid level is checked at weekly intervals.
2 The precise level of the fluid will depend on the ambient temperature (see Figs. 7.2 and 7.3).
3 Start the engine and run it for ten minutes at a fast idle. With the engine idling, withdraw the transmission dipstick, wipe it clean, re-insert it and then withdraw it again and read off the fluid level.
4 If it is not as indicated in the illustrations, top up. On no account overfill the automatic transmission or run it with too low a fluid level.
5 Renewal of the automatic transmission fluid is only specified by the manufacturers if the vehicle is operated under arduous conditions – such as trailer towing. However, it would seem to make sense to change the fluid on all vehicles after a reasonably high mileage in order to remove any impurities from the system. The additives in the fluid will almost certainly have lost some of their characteristics by this time as well.
6 Before draining the fluid, have it at normal operating temperature by running on the road for a distance of at least five miles (eight kilometres).
7 Unscrew and remove the transmission drain plug and catch the fluid in a container.
8 The condition of the fluid is an indication of the serviceability of the transmission. If it is very dark or nearly black and smells of burning, suspect worn friction components within the transmission. If there is no odour then the discolouration may be due to a small leak of coolant coming from the fluid cooler within the radiator.
9 If the fluid is an opaque pink in colour this will be due to a coolant leak or flood water contamination.
10 If the fluid is dark brown in colour and sticky, this will probably be due to overheating by under or over filling.
11 Refit the drain plug, withdraw the dipstick and pour the fresh fluid into the transmission through the dipstick guide tube.
12 Check the fluid level, as previously described.

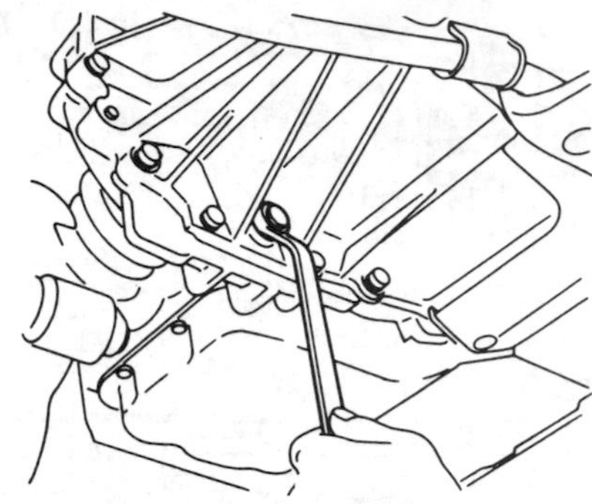

Fig. 7.4 Removing transmission drain plug (Sec 2)

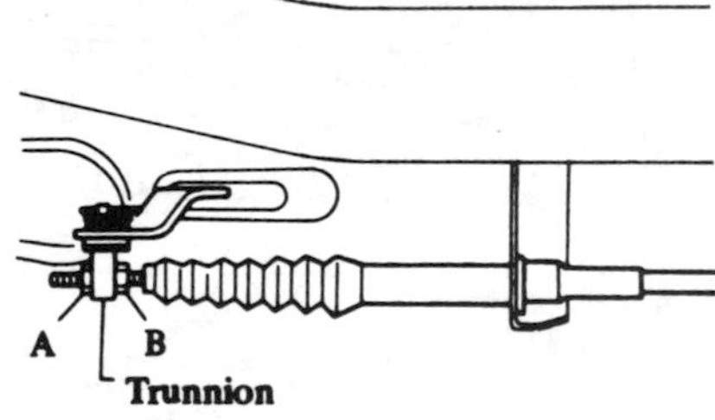

Fig. 7.5 Selector cable at transmission end (Sec 4)
A Locknut *B Locknut*

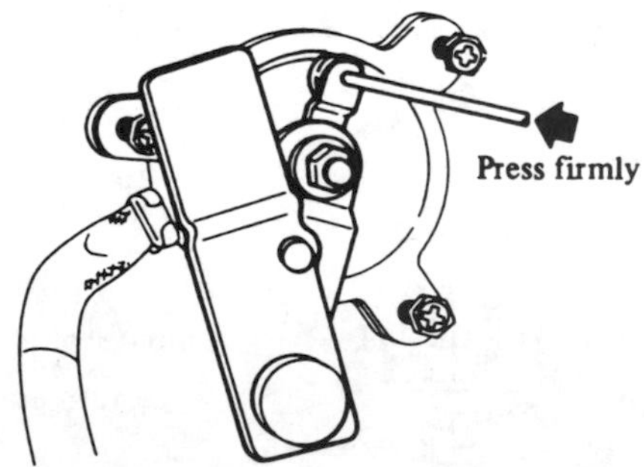

Fig. 7.6 Aligning inhibitor switch and lever holes (Sec 5)

3 Overhaul and adjustment – general

1 Due to the need for special tools and equipment, operations to the automatic transmission should be limited to the in-vehicle work described in the following Sections.
2 Where more extensive overhaul is required, it is best to leave this to your dealer or, where necessary, remove the transmission for professional repair or renewal, as described in Section 10.

4 Speed selector cable – adjustment

1 When the hand control lever is moved to all positions on the index, the individual detents should be positively felt. If this is not so, adjust in the following way.
2 Set the control lever to P.
3 Working at the selector lever on the transmission casing, disconnect the cable.
4 With the fingers, move the selector lever positively into its P detent.
5 Using the cable end fitting locknuts, adjust the cable until it applies no tension in either direction to the selector lever on the transmission. Tighten the locknuts.
6 Check that all selector positions are positively obtained.

5 Inhibitor switch – adjustment

1 The inhibitor switch controls the reversing lamps when R is selected, and also prevents operation of the starter when the hand control lever is in any position but P or N.
2 If the inhibitor switch does not operate correctly, adjust in the following way.
3 Loosen, but do not remove, the switch screws.
4 Set the hand control lever to N.
5 Push a 2.5 mm (0.098 in) diameter pin through the switch lever and switch body holes to align them. Hold the pin and tighten the switch screws. Remove the pin.

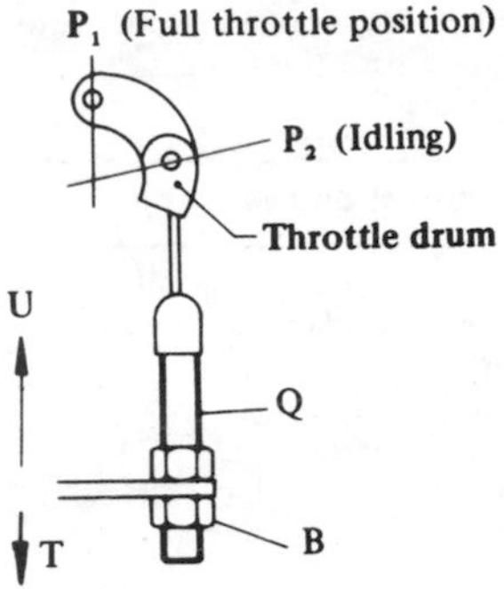

Fig. 7.7 Throttle cable end fitting at carburettor (Sec 6)

B Locknut
P1 Full throttle position
P2 Idle position
Q Cable end fitting
T Adjustment movement direction
U Adjustment movement direction

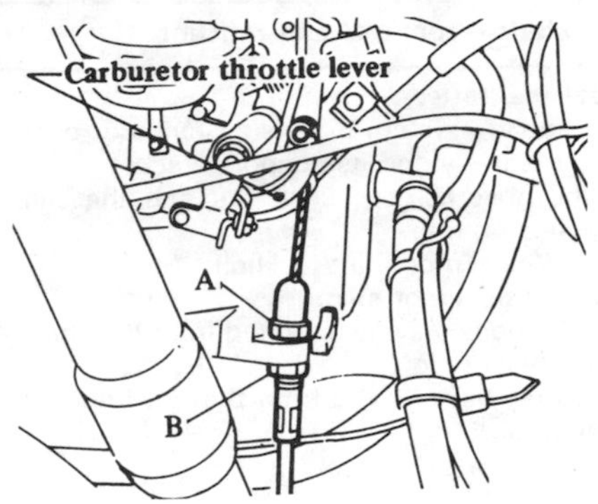

Fig. 7.8 Throttle cable at carburettor (Sec 6)

A Locknut
B Locknut

P_1 (Full throttle position)
P_2 (Idling)
Throttle drum
(P_1)
L
(P_2)

Fig. 7.9 Throttle cable movement diagram (Sec 6)

L = 27.4 to 31.4 mm (1.079 to 1.236 in)
P1 Full throttle position
P2 Idle position

6 Kickdown cable – adjustment and renewal

1 Release the cable locknuts at the carburettor.

2 With the throttle cable pulley held in the full throttle position move the cable and fitting in the direction T (see Fig. 7.7). Tighten nut B to eliminate any free movement.

3 Unscrew nut B between one and one and a half turns and secure it in this position by tightening nut A (see Fig. 7.8).

4 Check that the throttle cable end fitting movement L is within the specified tolerances (see Fig. 7.9).

5 To renew the cable, first remove the fluid sump pan and control valve assembly, as described in the next Section.

6 Disconnect the kickdown cable from the carburettor.

7 Disconnect the other end of the cable from the lever and then release the cable conduit from the casing by flattening the lockplate tab and unscrewing the nut.

8 Fit the new cable by reversing the removal operations. Bend up the locktab around the nut.

9 Adjust as previously described.

7 Brake band – adjustment

1 This will normally only be required if a fault develops, indicated by one of the following symptoms.

No change from 1st to 2nd
Speed changes direct from 1st to 3rd
Severe jerk on 1st to 2nd upshift
Poor acceleration
Maximum speed not obtained
No 3rd to 2nd downshift
No kickdown when in 3rd gear
Slip in 3rd to 2nd downshift
No manual 3rd to 2nd downshift
Transmission overheats

2 Drain the transmission fluid.

3 Remove the sump pan shield, the sump pan and the gasket from the transmission.

4 Unscrew the bolts evenly and progressively and withdraw the control valve assembly.

5 Release the brake band anchor pin locknut and then, using a torque wrench, tighten the pin to between 4.0 and 6.0 Nm (3 and 4 lbf ft).

6 Now unscrew the anchor pin through $2\frac{1}{2}$ complete turns. Hold the anchor pin stationary and tighten the locknut to between 16.0 and 22.0 Nm (12 and 16 lbf ft).

7 Refit the control valve, sump pan (using a new gasket) and the shield. Fill the transmission with the specified fluid (see the Recommended lubricants and fluids chart).

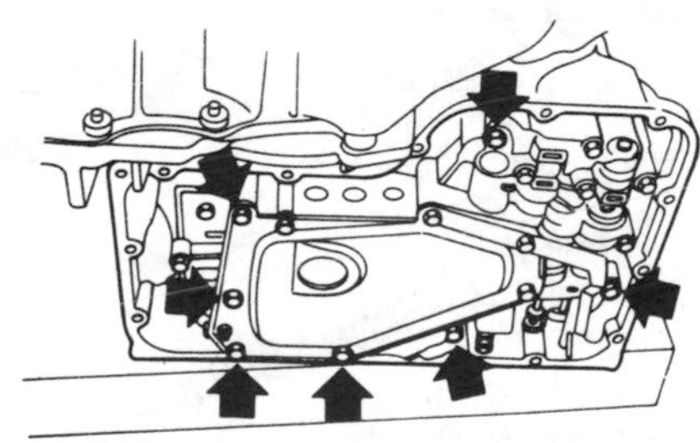

Fig. 7.10 Control valve assembly bolts (Sec 7)

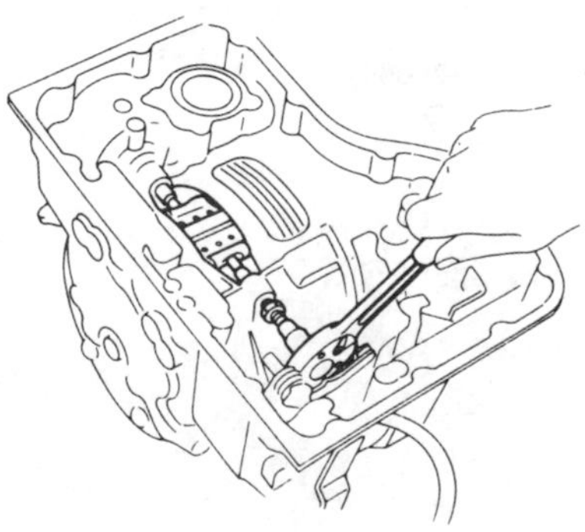

Fig. 7.11 Adjusting brake band anchor pin (Sec 7)

8 Governor shaft – removal and refitting

1 Disconnect the battery.
2 Move the cooling system expansion tank out of the way.
3 Remove the battery and its support bracket.
4 Release the governor cap snap retainer, the cap with breather hose, and the sealing ring.
5 Unscrew the governor shaft lockbolt.
6 Withdraw the governor shaft.
7 The governor body may be unbolted from the shaft, and scratched or worn components renewed.
8 The worm may be removed from the governor shaft after driving out the securing pin.
9 Refitting is a reversal of removal.

9 Differential bearing oil seals – renewal

1 Provided the driveshafts are disconnected from the transmission, as described in Chapter 8, the oil seals may be extracted using a two-legged puller.
2 Apply transmission fluid to the lips of the new oil seals before fitting them. A piece of tubing applied to the outer rim of the oil seal can be used to drive them into their seats.

10 Transmission – removal and refitting

1 Place the vehicle over an inspection pit or raise the front end and support it securely on axle stands positioned under the side-members.
2 Disconnect the battery.
3 Remove the left-hand roadwheel.
4 Drain the transmission fluid.
5 Remove the left-hand plastic wing shield.
6 Disconnect both driveshafts, as described in Chapter 6, Section 5, paragraphs 4 to 11.
7 Disconnect the speedometer cable from the transmission.
8 Disconnect the throttle cable from the carburettor and the leads from the inhibitor switch.
9 Disconnect the speed selector cable from the transmission lever, and the cable support bracket from the transmission casing.
10 Remove the dipstick guide/fluid filler tube.
11 Support the engine on a jack with a block of wood as an insulator.

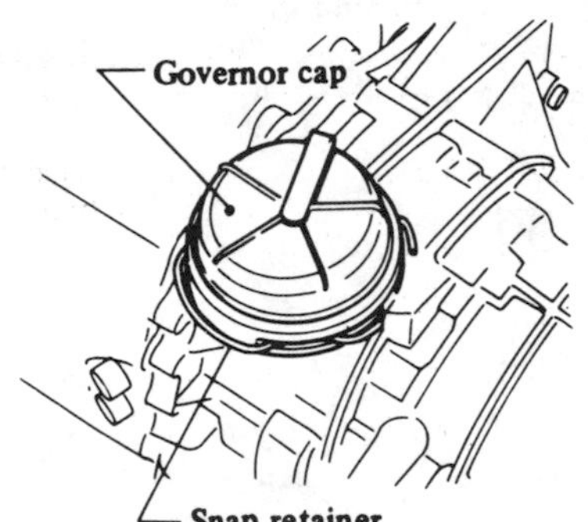

Fig. 7.12 Governor cap (Sec 8)

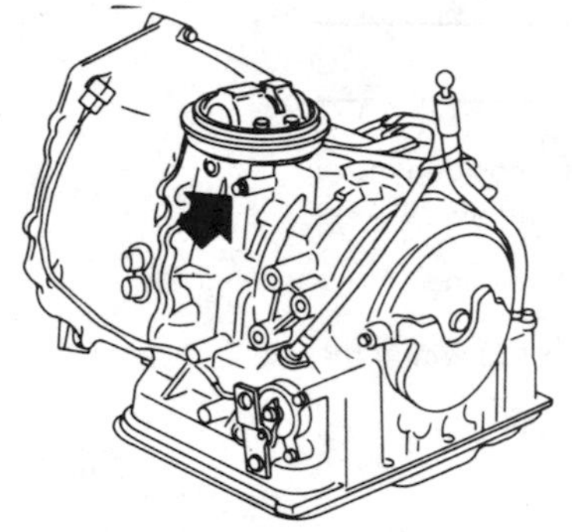

Fig. 7.13 Governor shaft lockbolt (Sec 8)

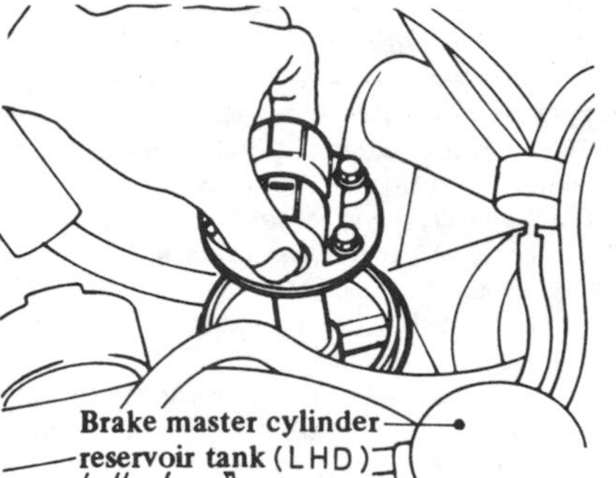

Fig. 7.14 Withdrawing governor shaft (Sec 8)

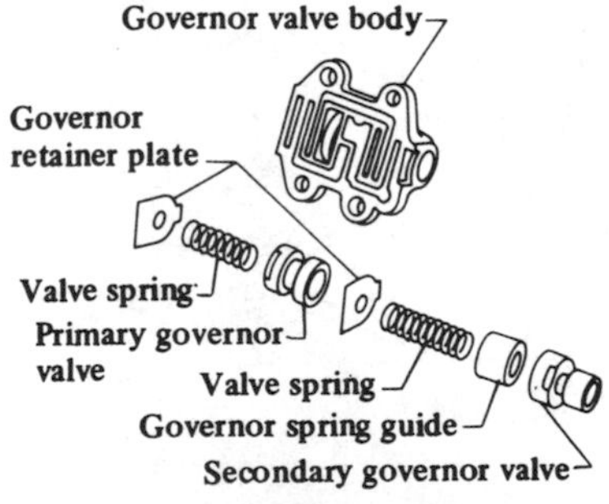

Fig. 7.15 Governor body components (Sec 8)

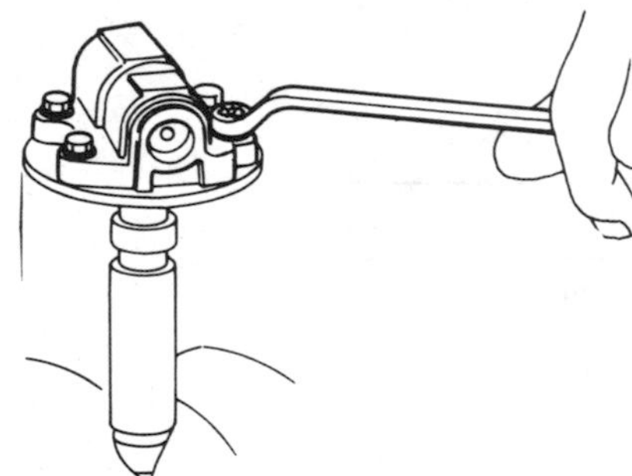

Fig. 7.16 Unscrewing governor body bolts (Sec 8)

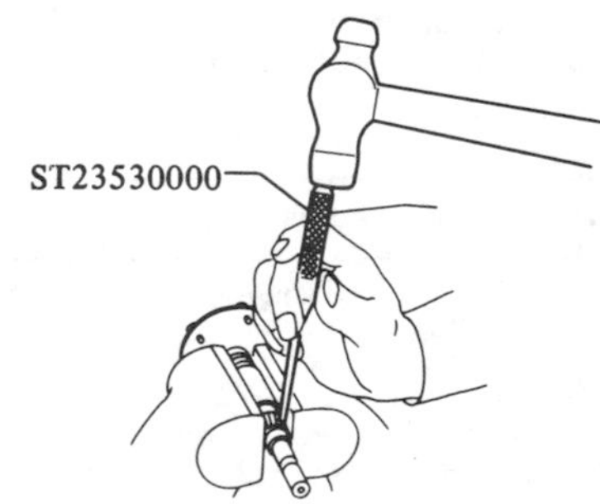

Fig. 7.17 Driving out governor shaft worm pin (Sec 8)

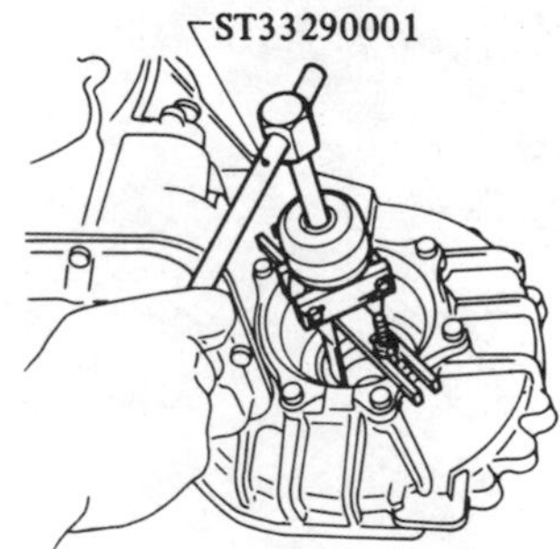

Fig. 7.18 Removing a differential bearing oil seal (Sec 9)

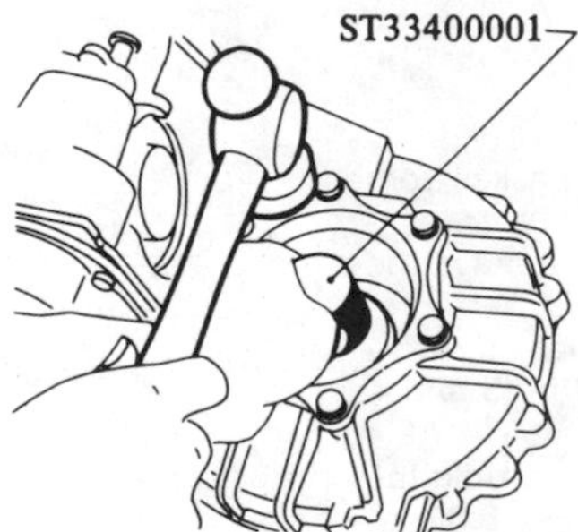

Fig. 7.19 Driving in a new differential oil seal (Sec 9)

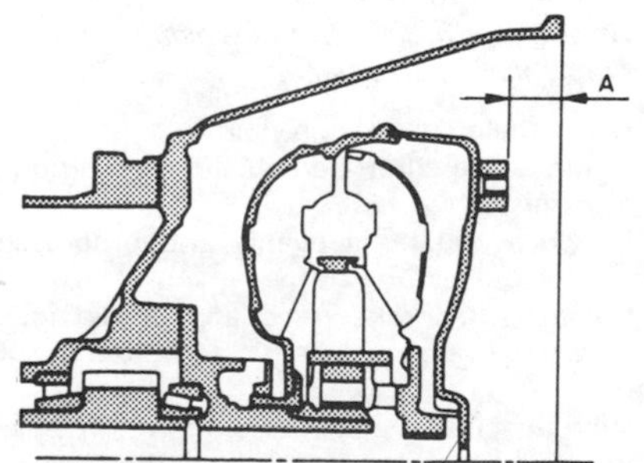

Fig. 7.20 Torque convertor fully installed (Sec 10)

A = Not less than 21.1 mm (0.831 in)

12 Support the transmission on a second jack – preferably of trolley type.
13 Disconnect and plug the oil cooler pipes.
14 Mark the relationship of the torque converter to the driveplate using a dab of quick-drying paint.
15 Unscrew the torque converter-to-driveplate connecting bolts. The crankshaft will have to be turned to bring each bolt into view within the cut-out of the torque converter housing before a spanner or socket wrench can be used.
16 Withdraw the automatic transmission flexible mounting pivot bolts.
17 Unbolt and remove the starter motor.
18 Unscrew and remove the torque converter housing-to-engine connecting bolts. Record the location of the coolant tube and mounting brackets held by some of these bolts. Unbolt the engine-to-transmission reinforcement strut.
19 Withdraw the transmission from under the front wing, having an assistant hold the torque converter in full engagement with the oil pump driveshaft to prevent loss of fluid.
20 If the transmission is being replaced with a new or rebuilt unit, check what is fitted to the new unit before parting with the original transmission. The parts not supplied can then be removed from the old unit.
21 Before offering up the transmission to the engine, check that the converter is pushed fully home. This can be determined if dimension A is not less than that specified (see Fig. 7.20).
22 Align the marks on the driveplate and torque converter (made before dismantling), apply thread locking fluid to clean bolt threads, and screw in and tighten the bolts to the specified torque.
23 Bolt on the starter motor.
24 Fit the engine-to-transmission connecting bolts, making sure to locate the coolant tube and mounting brackets under their correct bolts. Refit the mounting pivot bolts. Refit the reinforcement strut.
25 Reconnect the speed selector control cable, and adjust if necessary.
26 Reconnect the inhibitor switch leads.
27 Reconnect the fluid cooler hoses.
28 Refit the wing protective shield.
29 Refit the dipstick guide/fluid filler tube.
30 Reconnect the throttle cable.
31 Reconnect the speedometer drive cable.
32 Reconnect the driveshafts, as described in Chapter 8, Section 3.
33 Refit the left-hand roadwheel.
34 Reconnect the battery.
35 Check and top up the transmission fluid.

11 Fault diagnosis – automatic transmission

1 As has been mentioned elsewhere in this Chapter, no service repair work should be considered by anyone without the specialist knowledge and equipment required to undertake this work. This is also relevant to fault diagnosis. If a fault is evident, carry out the various adjustments previously described, and if the fault still exists consult the local garage or specialist.
2 Before removing the automatic transmission for repair, make sure that the repairer does not require to perform diagnostic tests with the transmission installed.
3 Most minor faults will be due to incorrect fluid level, incorrectly adjusted selector control or throttle cables and the internal brake band being out of adjustment (refer to Section 7).

Chapter 8 Driveshafts, hubs, roadwheels and tyres

Contents

Specifications

Driveshafts

Type	Open shaft with spider or ball and cage type joints at each end

Front hub bearings

Inner and outer tapered roller

Rear hub bearings

Inner and outer tapered roller

Roadwheels

Type	Pressed steel or light alloy
Size:	
Pressed steel	$4\frac{1}{2}$ J – 13
Alloy	5J – 13
Tyres:	
Type	Radial ply
Sizes	155 SR 13, 175/70 SR 13 (option)
Pressures:	
Front and rear	1.79 bar (26 lbf/in^2)

Refer also to the individual vehicle decal

Torque wrench settings

Torque wrench settings	Nm	lbf ft
Front suspension strut top mounting nuts	23	7
Stub axle carrier to base of front strut	80	59
Tie-rod balljoint taper pin	48	35
Suspension lower balljoint to track control arm	61	45
Driveshaft nut:		
E13 engine	149	110
E15, E16 engines	190	140
Brake disc to hub	34	25
Caliper mounting bolts	61	45
Roadwheel nuts	95	70
Rear hub retaining nut:		
Stage one	40	30
Stage two	Unscrew through 90°	

1 General description

The driveshafts are of open type, transmitting power from the final drive/differential within the transmission to the front roadwheels.

At the roadwheel end of the shaft, a Rzeppa (spider) or Birfield (ball and cage) joint is fitted. At the inboard end of the shaft either a spider or double offset ball type joint is fitted, depending upon the model.

None of the joints can be repaired or dismantled, but can only be renewed as assemblies after detaching them from the shaft.

The front hub bearings comprise inner and outer tapered roller races using a spacer to provide the specified bearing pre-load.

The rear hub bearings are of the usual inner and outer tapered roller bearing type, with pre-load adjustment being carried out by a nut and split pin.

The roadwheels may be of pressed steel or light alloy construction,

Drive shaft
Inboard oil seal
Stub axle carrier
Disc brake
Spacer
Outboard oil seal
Inboard Wheel bearing
Disc shield
Washer
Outboard Wheel bearing
Wheel hub
Nut retainer
Split pin

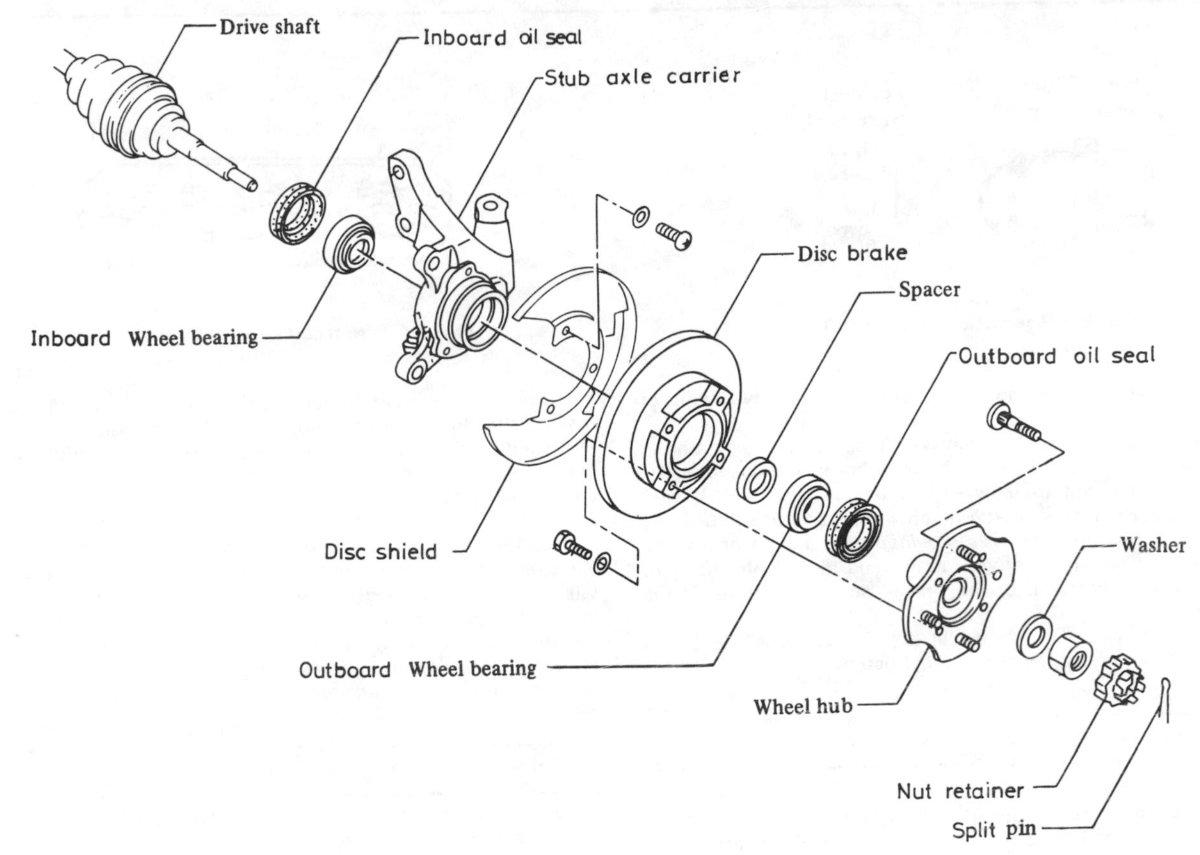

Fig. 8.1 Front hub components (Sec 1)

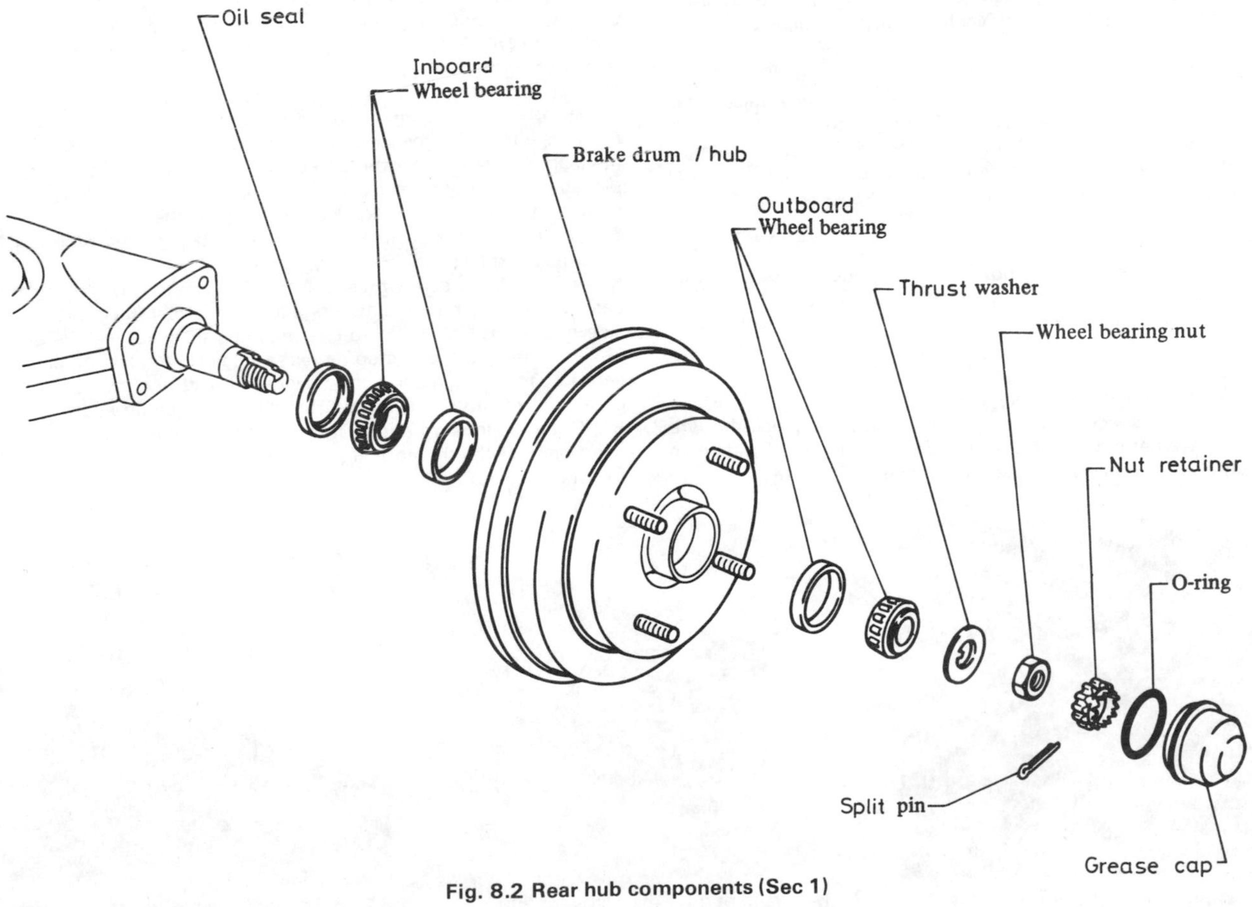

Oil seal
Inboard
Wheel bearing
Brake drum / hub
Outboard
Wheel bearing
Thrust washer
Wheel bearing nut
Nut retainer
O-ring
Split pin
Grease cap

Fig. 8.2 Rear hub components (Sec 1)

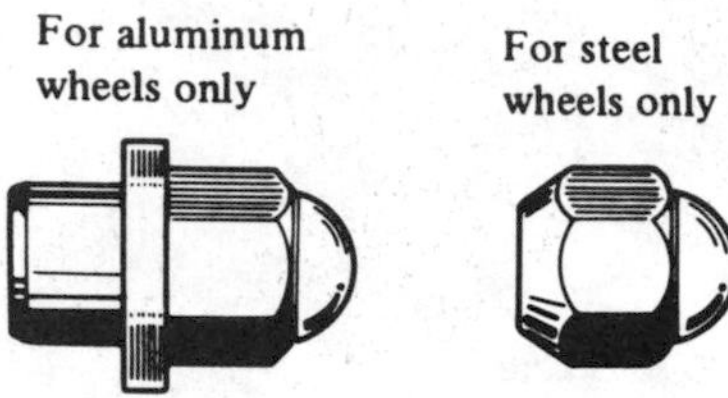

Fig. 8.3 Roadwheel nuts (Sec 1)

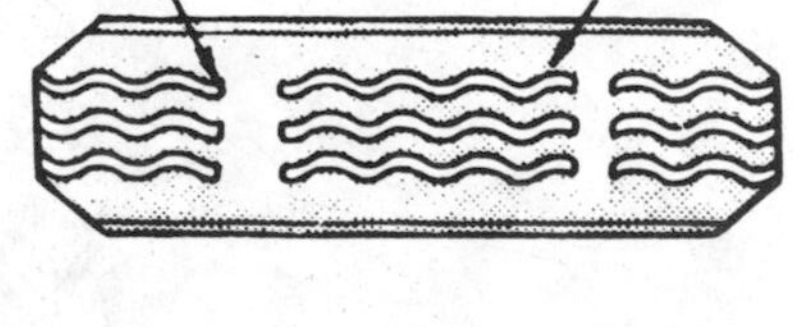

Fig. 8.4 Tyre tread wear indicators (Sec 2)

according to model. The securing nuts differ between the two types of roadwheel.

On North American models a lightweight spare tyre is located in the luggage area. This type of emergency tyre has so many limitations for use that it is difficult to think of any advantages for it over a conventional tyre. Remember that if a lightweight tyre has to be used in an emergency, *use only the nuts provided with it* – never use the nuts from alloy wheels. Restrict your roadspeed to 80 kph (50 mph) and avoid heavy applications of the brakes and sharp turns of the steering wheel.

On all models, except a few small engined versions for special territories, the tyres are of radial ply construction.

2 Maintenance

Driveshafts

1 Regularly inspect the driveshaft joint bellows for splits and the consequent leakage of lubricant. If evident, renew the bellows (see Section 6).

2 Grip the driveshaft and attempt to rotate it in each direction. Even the slightest movement (roadwheels held locked by application of the brakes) will indicate wear in the driveshaft joints or splines.

Hub bearings

3 At the intervals specified in Routine Maintenance raise each roadwheel in turn and, with the brakes off, grip the top and the bottom of the tyre and attempt to rock it. Anything more than an almost imperceptible movement will indicate the need for adjustment, or point to worn bearings (see Sections 7, 8 and 9).

Roadwheels

4 Keep the roadwheels clean, both on the inside and out, so that rust or corrosion can be quickly detected and eliminated.

5 Avoid rubbing against kerbs whether parking or at roadspeeds.

Tyres

6 Check the tyre pressures every week.

7 At the intervals specified in Routine Maintenance check the tyre treads for wear. Wear indicators are moulded into the tread and when these become visible the tyre must be renewed.

8 Examine the tread for cuts and remove flints and small nails, making sure that they have not penetrated the carcase.

9 Examine the inner and outer walls for splits, bulges or blisters. Evidence of these or punctures will make the services of a professional tyre repairer essential.

10 Tread wear may be evened out by moving the roadwheels between the front and rear – *but only on the same side of the vehicle.* With radial tyres, interchanging them diagonally or from side to side will upset the handling characteristics for some time. Roadwheels should only be moved if they have been balanced off the vehicle.

11 Always have new tyres balanced after fitting and have the roadwheels rebalanced should steering vibration or 'shimmy' occur when the tyres have become worn.

3 Driveshaft – removal and refitting

1 Raise the front of the vehicle, support it securely under the side-members and then remove the roadwheel.

2 Disconnect the front suspension lower balljoint. Do this by unscrewing the nuts which hold the balljoint to the suspension arm. It is recommended that new nuts are used at reassembly.

3 Unscrew, but do not remove, the nuts at the suspension strut top mounting. This is to provide flexibility to the strut when the driveshaft is withdrawn.

4 Extract the split pin, take off the nut retainer, and loosen the driveshaft-to-hub retaining nut. In order to hold the hub against rotation, either refit the roadwheel and lower the vehicle to the ground, have an assistant apply the brakes, or use a length of steel rod or bar placed between two roadwheel studs as a lever. Take steps to prevent damage to the stud threads by screwing on the nuts.

5 Unbolt the brake caliper and tie it up out of the way (photo). There is no need to disconnect the hydraulic line.

6 Insert a large screwdriver or other lever between the transmission casing and the inboard joint flange of the driveshaft. On the right-hand side of the casing an aperture is provided for inserting the lever.

7 Prise the joint to overcome resistance of the retaining circlip. Take care not to damage the transmission oil seal and do not pull on the outer end of the driveshaft as the joints may come apart.

8 Once the inboard end of the shaft has been disconnected, insert a short bar into the differential side gear as it is possible for the side gear to rotate and to fall into the differential case.

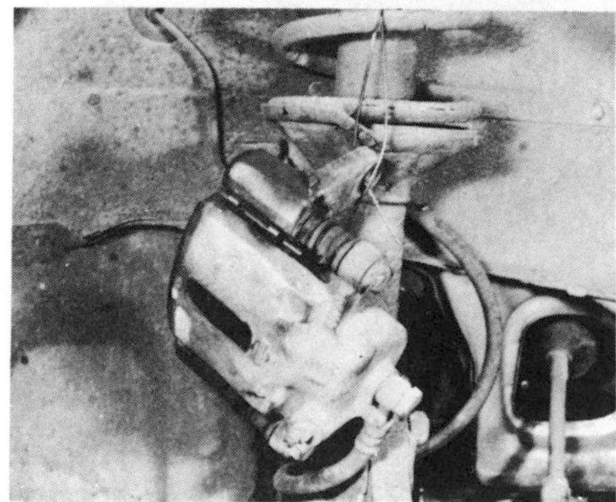

3.5 Brake caliper tied to suspension strut

3.11A Circlip at driveshaft inboard end

3.11B Fitting driveshaft to transmission

3.13A Front hub thrust washer

3.13B Screwing on driveshaft nut

3.13C Tightening driveshaft nut

3.13D Fitting nut retainer

3.13E Fitting split pin

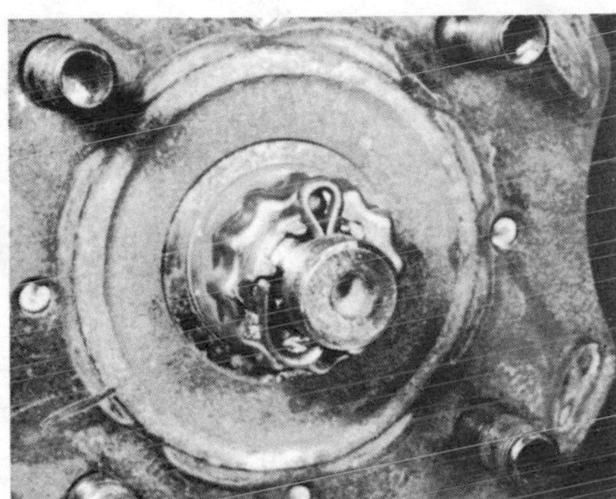

3.13F Split pin correctly fitted

9 Withdraw the driveshaft until the splined end of the shaft clears the transmission, and then lower the end of the shaft to the floor.
10 Working at the outboard end of the shaft, remove the driveshaft nut and washer and push the driveshaft out of the hub. If it is tight, use a two or three-legged puller to push it out.
11 Use a new circlip when fitting the inboard end of the driveshaft (photo). Push the shaft fully home in the side gear (photo) after having first removed the temporary gear retaining bar and having applied grease to the oil seal lips. Pull the joint cover to check that the circlip is positively engaged. The flange of the joint casing may be tapped with a plastic-faced hammer if necessary to drive the shaft fully home.
12 Smear the splines at the outboard end of the driveshaft with grease and insert the shaft into the hub.
13 Fit the washer (photo) and tighten the nut to the specified torque (photo). Fit the nut retainer and a new split pin (photos).
14 Fit the brake caliper.
15 Tighten the strut top mounting nuts to the specified torque.
16 Fit the roadwheel and lower the vehicle.
17 Apply the foot brake to position the disc pads.
18 Check the oil level in the transmission and top up if necessary.

4 Driveshaft outboard joint – removal and refitting

1 With the driveshaft removed, as described in the preceding Section, remove and discard the bellows securing bands.
2 Using quick-drying paint, put alignment marks on the shaft and joint.
3 Using a plastic or copper-faced hammer tap the outboard joint

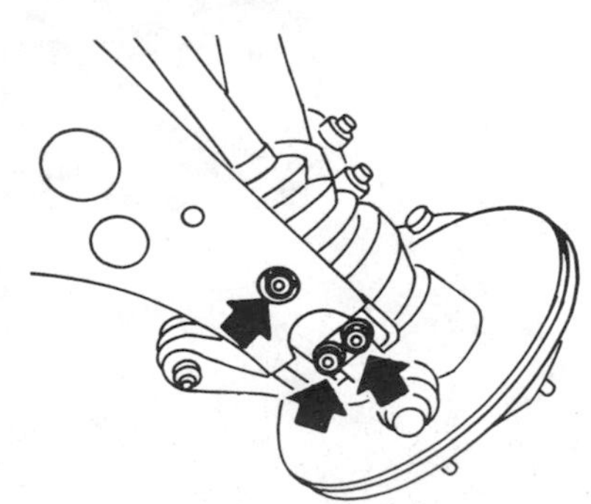

Fig. 8.5 Lower balljoint nuts (Sec 3)

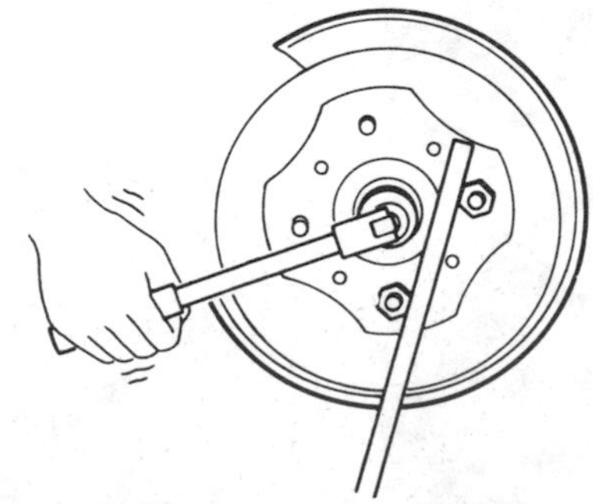

Fig. 8.6 Method of preventing roadwheel from rotating (Sec 3)

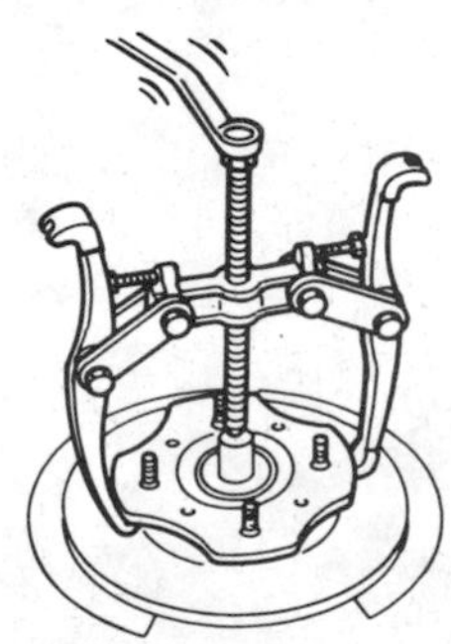

Fig. 8.7 Method of pushing driveshaft out of hub (Sec 3)

Joint assembly (road wheel side)
Bellows band (large)
Bellows (wheel side)
Bellows band (small)
Transaxle side
Double offset joint
Circlip
Drive shaft
Snap ring (large)
Inner race
Cage
Ball
Bellows band (small)
Bellows(transaxle side)
Bellows band (large)
Snap ring (small)
Road wheel side (rzeppa joint, birfield joint)
Tripod joint
Slide joint housing
Circlip
Spider assembly
Slide joint cover

Fig. 8.8 Driveshaft components (Sec 4)

Fig. 8.9 Driveshaft bellows securing bands (Sec 4)

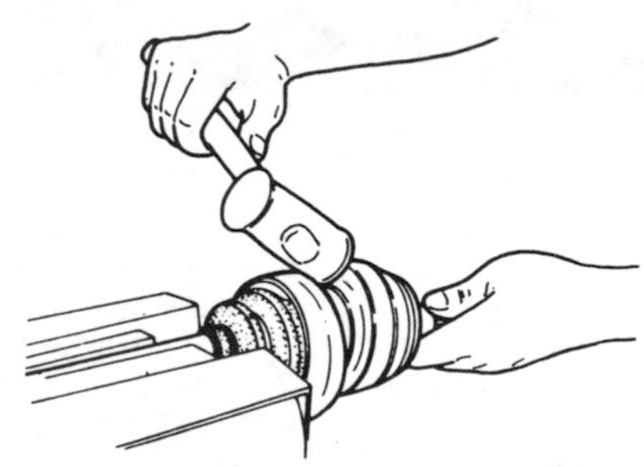

Fig. 8.10 Tapping outboard joint from driveshaft (Sec 4)

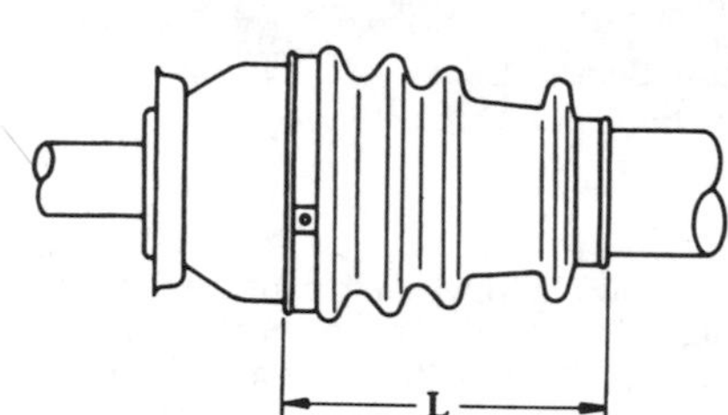

Fig. 8.11 Setting diagram for outboard joint bellows (Sec 4)

L (Rzeppa joint) = 100.0 mm (3.94 in)
L (Birfield joint) = 90.0 mm (3.54 in)

4.3 Removing driveshaft outboard joint

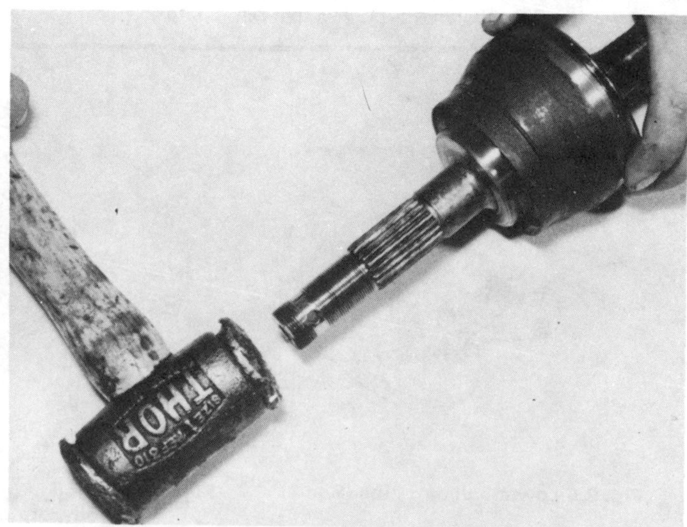

4.7 Refitting driveshaft outboard joint

assembly off the shaft against the resistance of the retaining circlip (photo). Quite heavy blows will be required to release it.

4 Withdraw the flexible bellows from the shaft.

5 If the joint is worn it can only be renewed as an assembly.

6 Commence refitting by sliding the bellows onto the shaft and fitting a new securing band to the narrower diameter.

7 If the original joint is being fitted, use a new retaining circlip and, having wiped away as much lubricant as possible, tap the joint onto the shaft until the circlip snaps home (photo). The marks made before removal should be in alignment.

8 If a new joint is being fitted, and it is of spider type, make sure that its spider is aligned as nearly as possible with the one at the opposite end of the shaft. This can be felt through the bellows.

9 Peel back the bellows and apply the specified quantity of the special grease which is supplied with each new joint. If the original joint is being refitted, Castrol MS3 grease can be used as an alternative.

Rzeppa joint	*110 g (3.88 oz)*
Birfield joint	*100 g (3.53 oz)*

10 It should be noted that the grease pack supplied with new joints differs between the inboard and outboard joints.

11 Set the bellows length (Fig. 8.11) and fit the securing bands.

5 Driveshaft inboard joint – removal and refitting

Spider type joint

1 With the driveshaft removed from the vehicle, grip it in a vice fitted with jaw protectors.

2 Remove the bellows retaining bands and discard them. Pull off the joint housing (photo).

3 Extract the joint circlip (photo).

4 If the original joint is to be refitted, mark the spider in relation to the shaft with a dab of quick-drying paint.

5 Support the spider and press the shaft from it. If a press is not available, the spider can be removed using a backing plate and a two or three-legged puller.

6 Slide the bellows from the shaft.

7 The slide joint cover can be removed by cutting slots in it with a hacksaw and bending the areas between the cuts outward.

8 Remove the cover O-ring and renew both the cover and O-ring at reassembly.

9 When reassembling, grease the O-ring and peen the rim of the new slide joint cover over its entire length and then seal the seam with RTV type sealant.

10 Fit the bellows to the shaft and locate a new securing band on the smaller diameter.

5.2 Driveshaft inboard joint

5.3 Driveshaft inboard joint spider and circlip

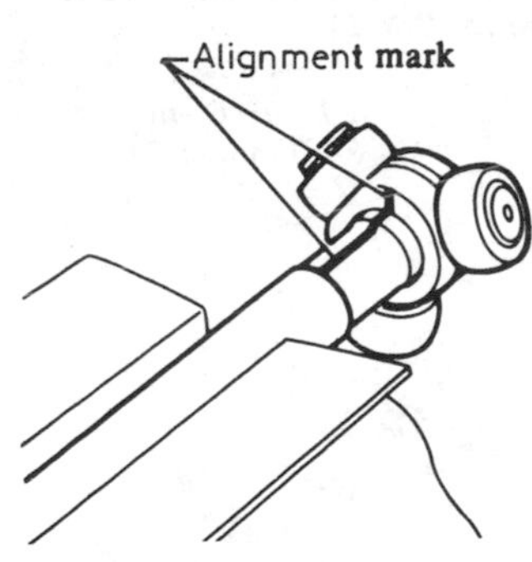

Fig. 8.12 Spider-to-shaft alignment mark (Sec 5)

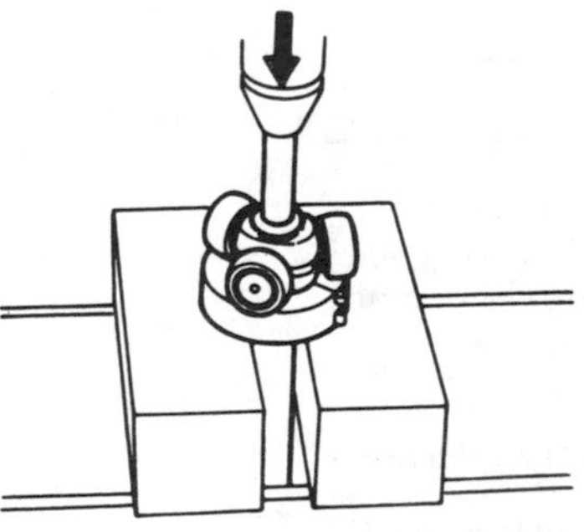

Fig. 8.13 Pressing shaft from spider (Sec 5)

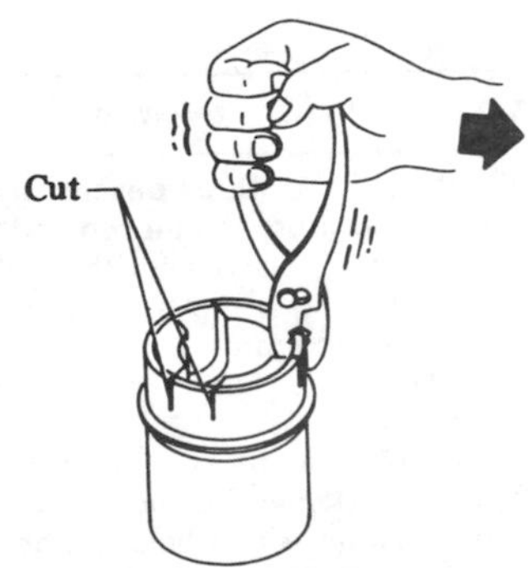

Fig. 8.14 Removing joint slide cover (Sec 5)

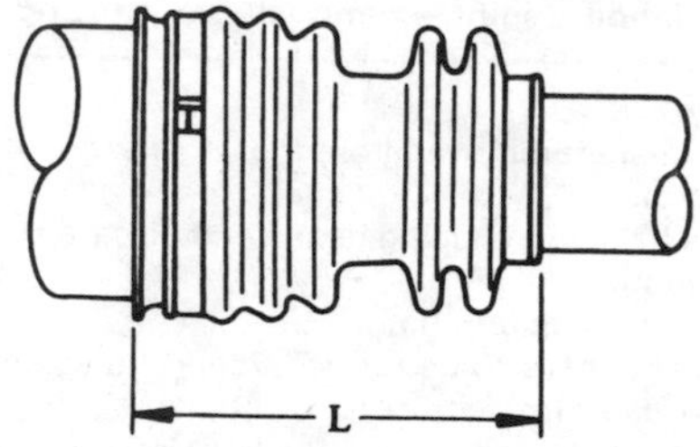

Fig. 8.15 Setting diagram for inboard joint bellows – spider type joint (Sec 5)

L = 112.0 mm (4.41 in)

11 Fit the spider to the shaft so that the marks made on removal are in alignment (original joint) or, if a new joint is being used, align the spider with the one at the opposite end of the shaft. This can be felt through the bellows.
12 Fit the spider to the shaft so that the chamfered face of the spider goes onto the shaft first. Drive the spider onto the shaft using a hammer and a piece of tubing.
13 Fit a new circlip so that its rounded side is towards the spider.
14 Pack the joint with 180 g (6.35 oz) of the specified grease (see Section 4).
15 Tighten the bellows into position and tighten the bellows securing bands when the end-to-end bellows dimension is as specified (see Fig. 8.15).

Double offset joint

16 With the driveshaft gripped in the jaws of a vice fitted with jaw protectors, remove the bellows retaining bands and discard them.
17 Pull back the bellows and prise out the large circlip now exposed.
18 Pull off the slide joint housing.
19 Wipe away the grease from the ball cage and remove the balls.
20 Turn the cage through half a turn and pull it from the inner race.
21 Extract the circlip and tap the inner race from the driveshaft.
22 Pull the bellows from the driveshaft.
23 Reassembly and refitting are reversals of dismantling and removal. Use new circlips and pack the joint with 100 g (3.53 oz) of the specified grease (see Section 4).
24 Fit new bellows bands and tighten them when the end-to-end length of the bellows is as specified (see Fig. 8.19).

6 Driveshaft flexible bellows – renewal

1 The renewal of split or damaged driveshaft flexible bellows can only be carried out after removal of the driveshaft and dismantling the joint, as described in earlier Sections of this Chapter.

7 Front hub bearings – renewal

1 Remove the driveshaft, as described in Section 3.
2 Unscrew the nut from the tie-rod end balljoint taper pin and, using a suitable splitter tool, disconnect the balljoint from the steering arm.
3 Unscrew and remove the two pinch-bolts from the clamp at the base of the suspension strut.
4 Prise the clamp open slightly and remove the stub axle carrier, hub and disc assembly.
5 The hub should now be separated from the stub axle carrier using a sliding hammer attached to the roadwheel studs.
6 Unscrew the nuts which hold the brake disc and rotor together.
7 Remove the bearing from the hub either by using a suitable bearing extractor or by supporting the bearing and pressing the hub from it.
8 Remove and discard the oil seal.
9 Remove the oil seal from the stub axle carrier and draw out the bearing tracks.
10 The hub bearings should be renewed in pairs (inner and outer), not singly.

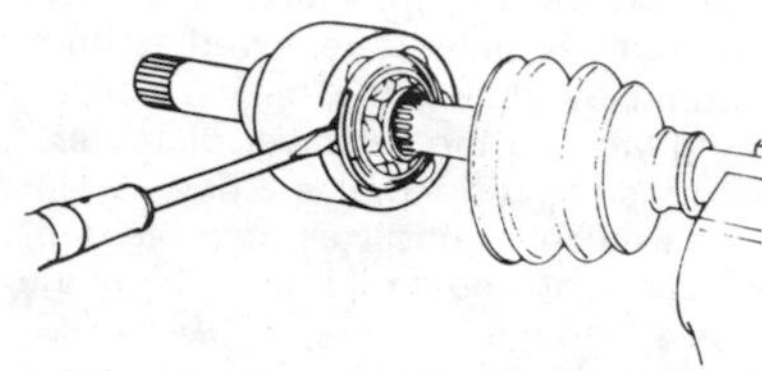

Fig. 8.16 Prising out circlip from double offset joint (Sec 5)

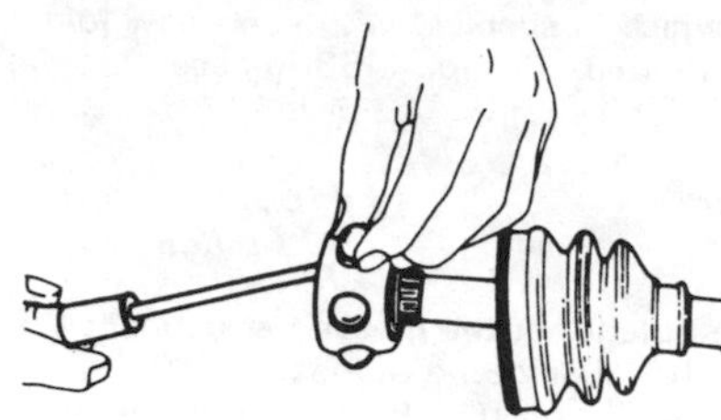

Fig. 8.17 Removing double offset joint balls (Sec 5)

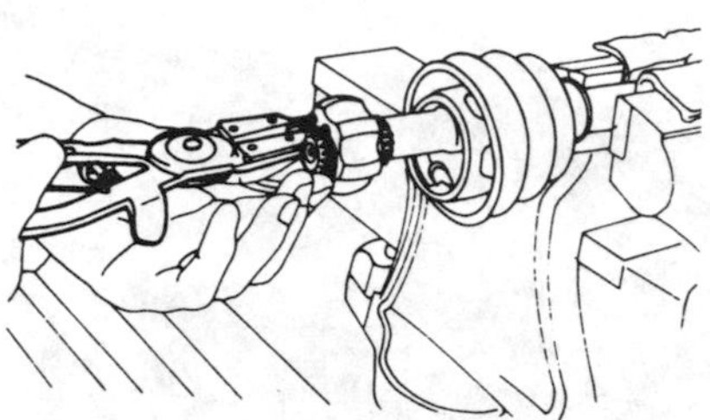

Fig. 8.18 Removing inner race circlip from double offset joint (Sec 5)

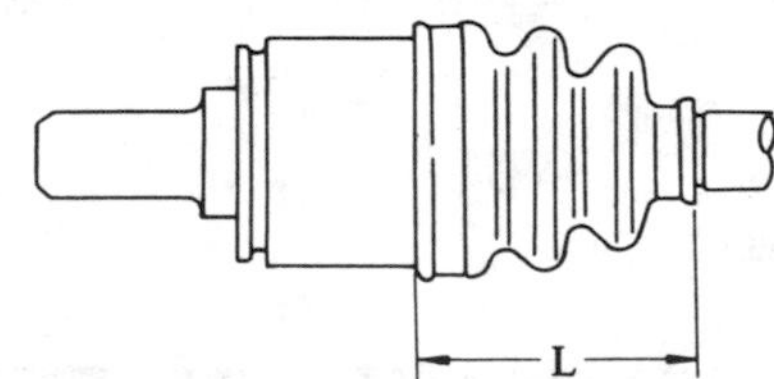

Fig. 8.19 Setting diagram for inboard joint bellows – double offset type joint (Sec 5)

L (E13 engine = 82.0 mm (3.23 in)

L (E15, E16 engines) = 84.0 mm (3.31 in)

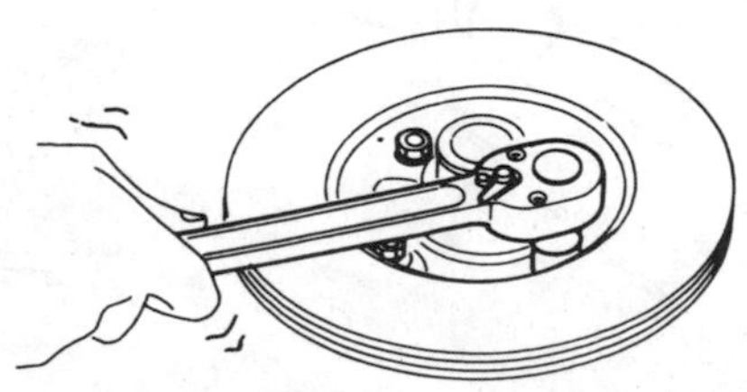

Fig. 8.20 Releasing hub-to-disc bolt (Sec 7)

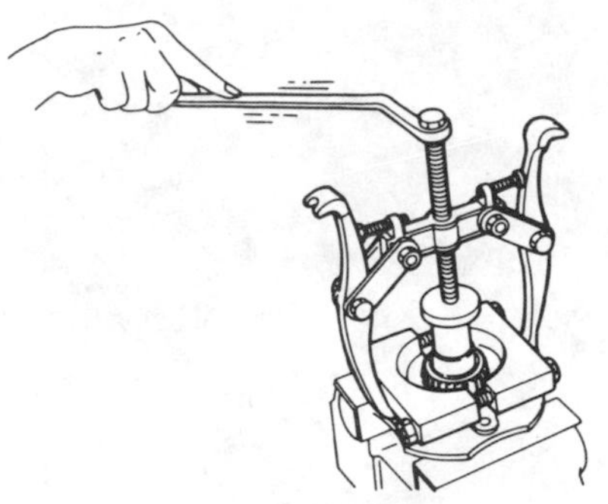

Fig. 8.21 Removing hub bearing (Sec 7)

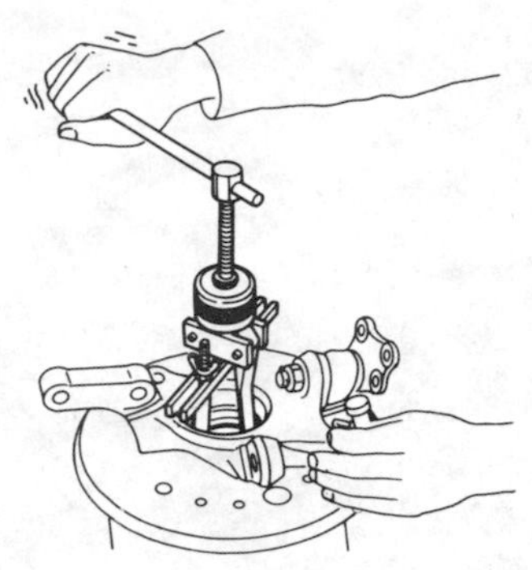

Fig. 8.22 Removing bearing outer track from stub axle carrier (Sec 7)

Fig. 8.23 Oil seal lip direction on front hub (Sec 7)

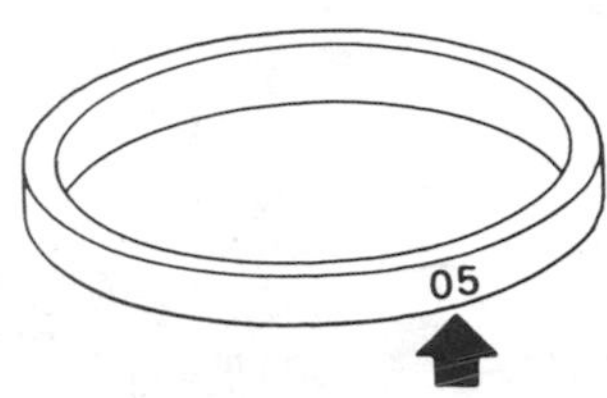

Fig. 8.24 Front hub bearing spacer and marking (Sec 7)

Fig. 8.25 Front hub/driveshaft nut split pin (Sec 8)

11 Clean the recesses in the stub axle carrier and drive in the new bearing outer tracks – using a piece of brass or copper tubing as a drift.
12 Fit the inboard bearing by applying a tubular drift to the bearing inner track.
13 Fit a new oil seal and then work grease into the bearing and the oil seal lips.
14 Fit the outboard bearing and oil seal, again using a tubular drift to fit the bearing to the hub.
15 Check that the oil seal lips are facing the correct way (see Fig. 8.23) and then apply grease to them.
16 Locate the spacer. If the original one is damaged, renew it with one which carries the same marking as the old one. The spacer thickness need only be changed if the stub axle carrier is renewed (see Chapter 11).
17 Fit the disc and hub together and tighten the connecting bolts to the specified torque.
18 Connect the hub with the stub axle carrier. Do this using a long bolt or length of studding with large washers and nuts to draw the hub fully into the carrier, but take great care not to damage the oils seals.
19 Clamp the stub axle carrier to the base of the suspension strut and tighten the pinch-bolts to the specified torque.
20 Reconnect the steering arm balljoint and refit the driveshaft, as described in Section 3.
21 Apply the footbrake once the caliper has been refitted to position the pads against the disc.
22 Refit the roadwheel and lower the vehicle.

8 Rear hub bearings – adjustment

1 At the regular inspection (see Routine Maintenance), check if the rear roadwheel can be rocked when jacked up by gripping the tyre at top and bottom. If so adjust the bearing preload in the following way. Chock the front wheels and release the handbrake.
2 With the roadwheel removed, prise off the grease cap, remove the split pin and nut retainer.
3 Unscrew the nut and remove the thrust washer.
4 Pull the brake drum towards you and catch the outboard bearing which will be displaced. Remove the drum.
5 If the bearings appear dry, work some multi-purpose grease into them.
6 Refit the brake drum (photo), the outboard bearing (photo), and thrust washer (photo) and screw on the nut finger tight.
7 Tighten the nut to the specified torque and then rotate the brake drum in both directions several revolutions to settle the bearings.

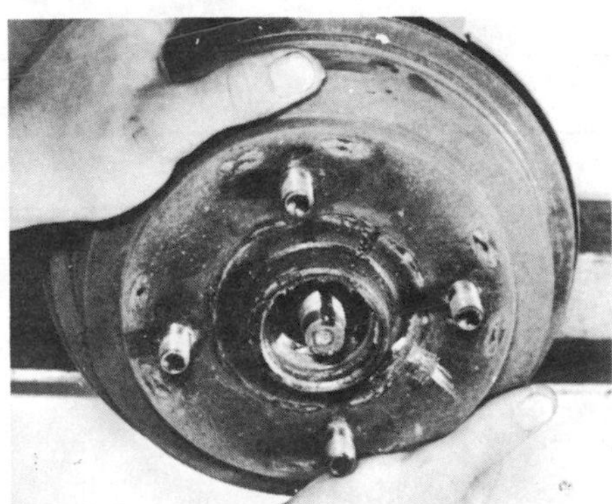

8.6A Fitting brake drum

8.6B Fitting rear hub outboard bearing

8.6C Fitting rear hub thrust washer

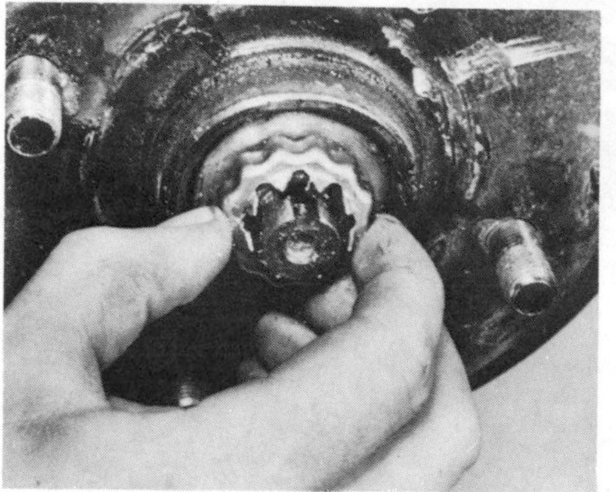
8.9 Rear hub nut retainer

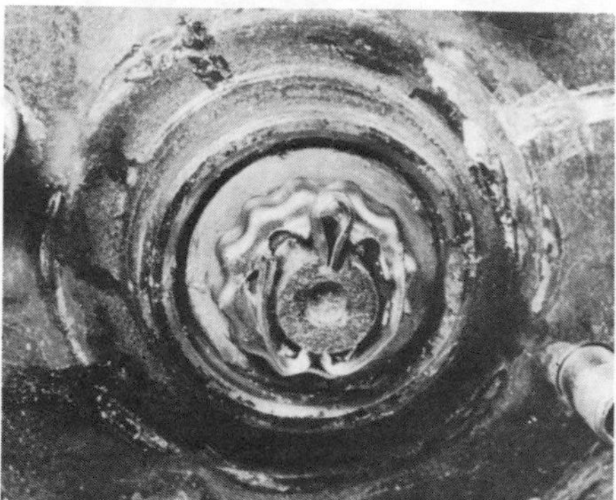
8.11 Rear hub nut split pin

8.12 Rear hub grease cap

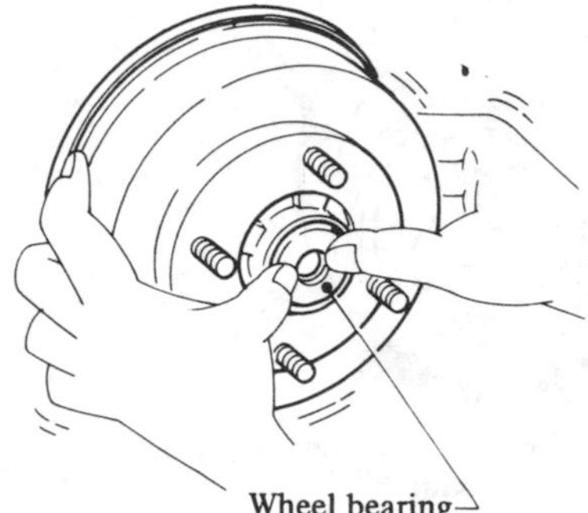

Fig. 8.26 Pulling off brake drum (Sec 9)

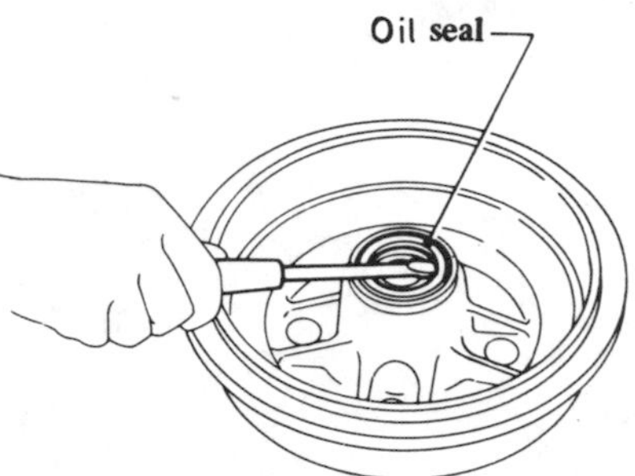

Fig. 8.27 Removing oil seal from brake drum (Sec 9)

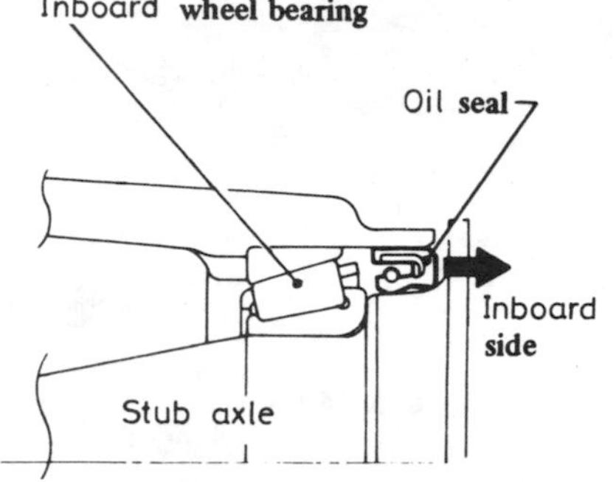

Fig. 8.28 Rear hub oil seal lip direction (Sec 9)

8 Check the tightness of the nut is still as specified and then unscrew it through 90°.

9 Fit the nut retainer so that its slots align with the split pin hole (photo) and fit a new split pin.

10 Check that the drum/hub turns smoothly without drag. There must not be any endfloat. If there is, and the adjustment has been carried out correctly, suspect worn bearings (see the next Section).

11 Bend the ends of the split pin around the nut retainer (photo).

12 Fill the grease cap only one third full with multi-purpose grease (photo), check that the O-ring is in good condition and tap the cap squarely into position.

9 Rear hub bearings – renewal

1 Worn rear hub bearings may be detected by noise, especially when cornering, or by failure to eliminate bearing endfloat during adjustment.

2 Raise the rear of the car, chock the front wheels, release the handbrake and remove the roadwheel.

3 Prise off the grease cap.

4 Extract the split pin, remove the nut retainer, unscrew the nut and remove the thrust washer.

5 Pull the brake drum towards you and catch the outboard bearing which will be displaced.

6 From the inner face of the drum prise out and discard the oil seal. Lift out the inner bearing.

7 Using a copper or brass drift, drive the bearing outer tracks from the drum.

8 The inner and outer bearings should be renewed at the same time.

9 Clean the recesses in the brake drum and drive the new bearing outer tracks squarely into them.

10 Fit the inboard bearing race and a new oil seal, having worked multi-purpose grease into the bearing rollers and fitted the oil seal lips.

11 Offer the drum onto the stub axle, taking care not to damage the lips of the oil seal with the shaft threads.

12 Work grease into the outboard bearing rollers and fit it onto the stub axle.

13 Fit the thrust washer and nut, finger tight.

14 Adjust the bearing preload and complete reassembly, as described in Section 8 paragraphs 7 to 12.

10 Fault diagnosis, hubs, roadwheels and tyres

Symptom	Reason(s)
Vibration	Driveshaft bent Worn universal joints Out-of-balance roadwheels
'Clonk' on taking up drive or on overrun	Worn universal joints Worn splines on shaft, hub carrier or differential side gears Loose driveshaft nut Loose roadwheel bolts
Noise or roar, especially when cornering	Worn hub bearings Incorrectly adjusted hub bearings

Chapter 9 Braking system

Refer to Chapter 13 for Specifications and information on later models

Contents

Specifications

System type

Dual-circuit, four wheel hydraulic with servo assistance. Mechanical handbrake on rear wheels

Front disc brakes

Disc diameter	240.0 mm (9.45 in)
Caliper cylinder diameter	48.1 mm (1.894 in)
Pad friction material minimum thickness	2.0 mm (0.079 in)
Disc minimum thickness after regrinding	10.0 mm (0.394 in)
Maximum run-out	0.07 mm (0.0028 in)

Rear drum brakes

Drum internal diameter	180.0 mm (7.09 in)
Maximum internal diameter after regrinding	181.0 mm (7.13 in)
Maximum out-of-round	0.03 mm (0.0012 in)
Shoe friction material minimum thickness	1.5 mm (0.059 in)
Wheel cylinder bore	17.46 mm (0.69 in)

Brake pedal free height

Right-hand drive:	
Manual transmission	201.0 to 207.0 mm (7.91 to 8.15 in)
Automatic transmission	203.0 to 209.0 mm (7.99 to 8.23 in)
Left-hand drive:	
Manual transmission	191.0 to 197.0 mm (7.52 to 7.76 in)
Automatic transmission	193.0 to 199.0 mm (7.60 to 7.84 in)

Torque wrench settings

	Nm	lbf ft
Bleed screws	9	7
Seat belt stalk bolt	31	23
Master cylinder to servo unit	11	8
Brake line union	18	13
Brake hose end fitting	20	15
Disc shield screws	4	3
Caliper mounting bracket	64	47
Caliper guide pin and lockpin	31	23
Disc-to-hub bolts	34	25
Rear backplate screws	33	24
Rear wheel cylinder screws	8	6

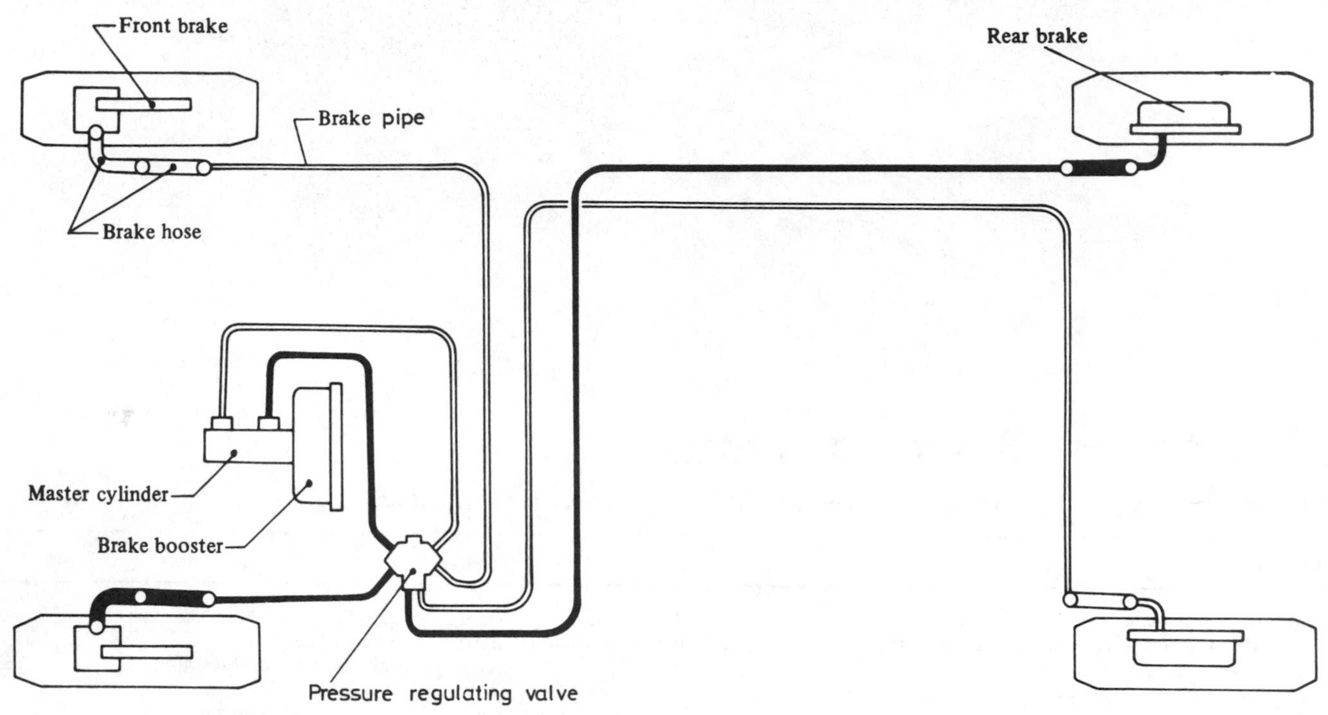

Fig. 9.1 Hydraulic circuits (Sec 1)

1 General description and maintenance

1 The braking system is of dual-line four wheel hydraulic type with servo assistance.
2 The hydraulic circuit is split diagonally.
3 A pressure regulating valve is incorporated in the hydraulic circuit to prevent the rear wheels locking up during heavy applications of the brake pedal.
4 The handbrake operates mechanically on the rear wheels and incorporates an 'on' warning lamp switch.
5 Maintenance consists of regularly checking the fluid level in the master cylinder reservoir (photo), even though a low-level warning lamp is fitted. The level should be maintained between the MIN and MAX marks on the reservoir. The fluid level will fall very slowly to compensate for wear in the brake friction material. If frequent topping-up is required, check for a leak in the system and rectify any immediately. Remember, if an external leak is not evident, fluid loss can occur through the rear of the master cylinder past defective rubber seals and into the vacuum servo unit.

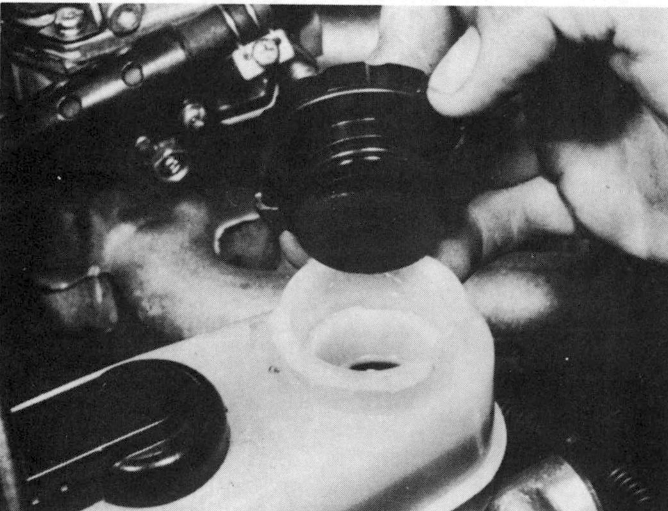

1.5 Master cylinder reservoir filler cap

6 Hydraulic fluid should be renewed by bleeding at regular intervals (see Routine Maintenance) in order to prevent corrosion within the brake components which is caused by the fact that brake fluid is hygroscopic (absorbs moisture from the air).
7 At the intervals specified in Routine Maintenance inspect the disc pads and brake shoes for wear of the friction material (refer to Sections 2 and 3).

2 Disc pads – inspection and renewal

1 Raise the front of the vehicle, support it securely, and remove the roadwheels.
2 Check the thickness of the friction material. This must not be less than that specified.
3 If the thickness is less than that figure the pads must be renewed as an axle set (four pads).
4 Unscrew and remove the caliper lower lockpin (photo).
5 Release the upper guide pin and swivel the cylinder body upwards (photo).
6 Remove the anti-squeal shims (photo).
7 Take out the pads (photo).
8 The retaining springs can be prised out, if required (photos), also the piston shims (photo).
9 Brush away dirt and dust. *Avoid inhaling it as it is injurious to health.* Do not depress the brake pedal while the pads are out of the caliper.
10 Smear a trace of high melting-point grease onto the pad backplates and then locate the pads (friction surface to disc), followed by the anti-squeal shims.
11 The piston must now be fully depressed into the cylinder in order to accommodate the increased thickness of the new pads. Depressing the piston will cause the fluid level to rise in the master cylinder reservoir, so anticipate this by syphoning out some fluid using a clean battery hydrometer or meat baster.

2.4 Releasing the caliper lower lockpin

2.5 Swivelling the caliper upwards

2.6 Caliper anti-squeal shim

2.7 Removing disc pad

2.8A Prising out pad retaining spring

2.8B Removing pad retaining spring

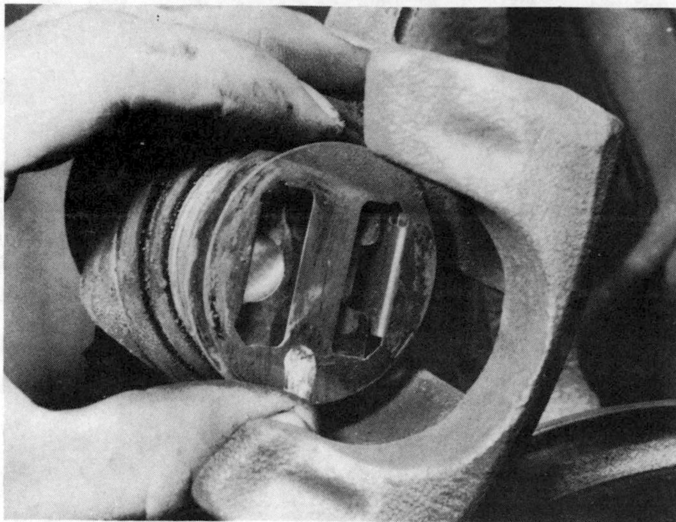

2.8C Removing piston shim

12 Swivel the cylinder body downwards, fit the lower lockpin and then tighten both pins to the specified torque.
13 Renew the pads on the opposite side, refit the roadwheels and lower the vehicle.
14 Apply the brakes hard to position the pads against the disc.
15 Check the fluid level, and top up the reservoir if necessary.

3 Rear brake linings – inspection and renewal

1 Chock the front wheels. Raise the rear of the vehicle, support it securely and remove the roadwheels. Release the handbrake.
2 Prise off the hub grease cap, extract the cotter pin, take off the nut retainer and unscrew and remove the nut.
3 Pull off the brake drum, catching the outboard bearing which will be displaced. It is possible for the brake drum to be held on the axle due to the brake shoes being locked in grooves which have been worn in the drum. Should this occur, prise the plug from the brake backplate and, using a screwdriver, lift the toggle lever from the automatic adjuster star wheel and turn the star wheel to contact the shoes.
4 Inspect the shoe linings. If their thickness is less than that specified the shoes must be renewed as an axle set (four shoes).
5 It is recommended that new shoes are purchased complete with

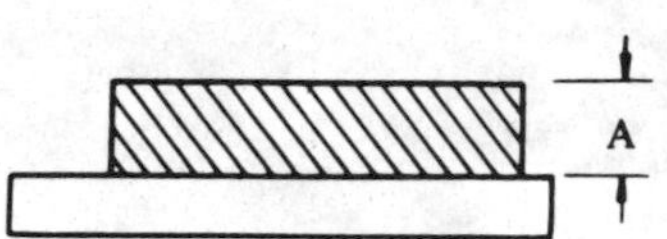

Fig. 9.2 Disc pad friction material wear limit (Sec 2)

A = 2.0 mm (0.079 in)

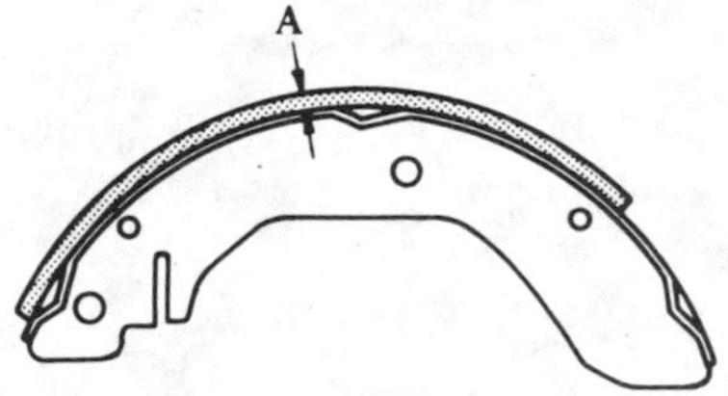

Fig. 9.3 Shoe friction material wear limit (Sec 3)

A = 1.5 mm (0.059 in)

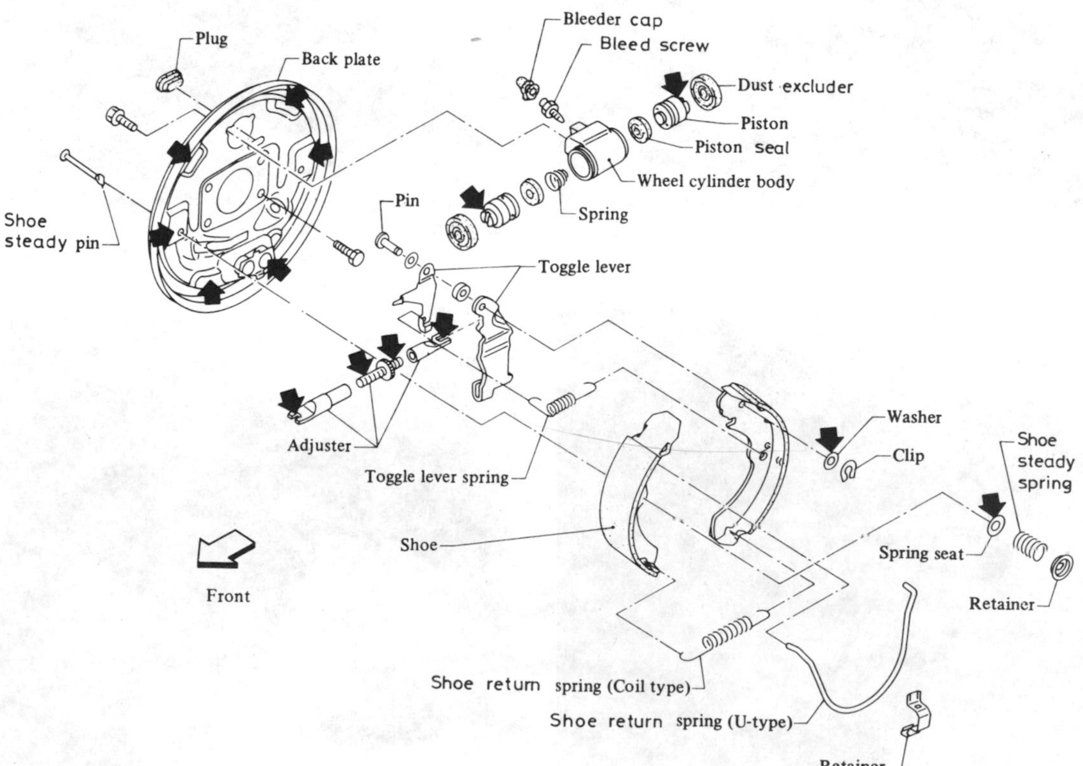

Fig. 9.4 Rear drum brake components (Sec 3)

3.7A Removing shoe steady spring cup

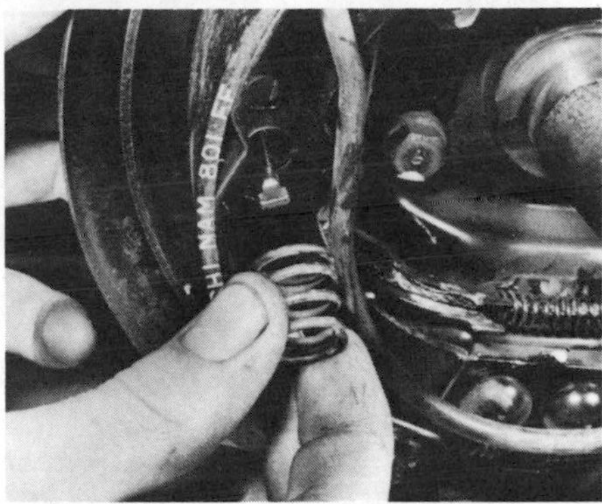
3.7B Removing shoe steady spring

3.8A Prising off shoe return spring clip

3.8B Prising off shoe return spring

3.9 Shoe automatic adjuster strut

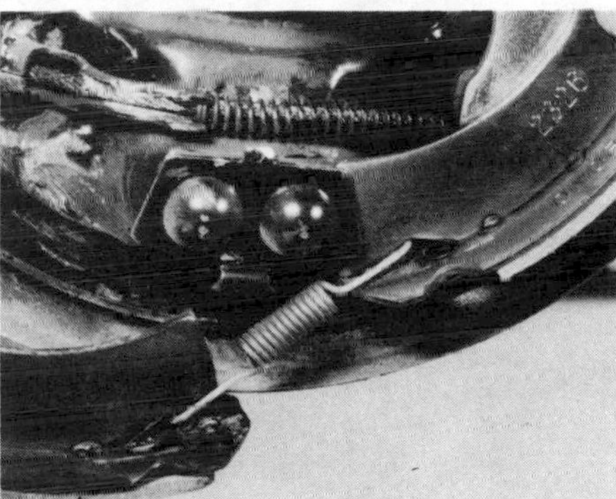
3.10 Shoe lower return spring

linings. Attempting to reline old shoes yourself seldom proves satisfactory.

6 If the old shoes appear oil stained, this will be due to a leaking wheel cylinder (defective seal) or to a faulty bearing oil seal.

7 Remove the shoe steady springs. To do this, grip the edges of the spring cup with a pair of pliers (photo), depress it against pressure of the coil spring and turn it through 90°. Release the spring cup and take off the spring (photo).

8 Prise off the shoe return spring clip (photo), and then release the shoe return spring. This is a U-shaped spring and one arm should be gripped and levered towards the other arm to release it from the hole in the shoe (photo). It is recommended that a rag is placed over the spring to prevent it flying out accidentally.

3.12 Handbrake and automatic adjuster toggle lever and spring

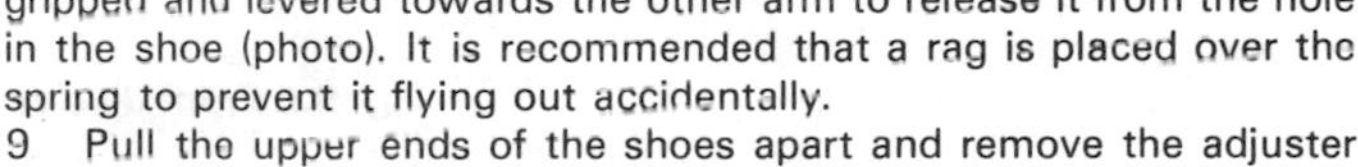

9 Pull the upper ends of the shoes apart and remove the adjuster strut (photo).

10 Disconnect the shoe lower return spring (photo).

11 Note the location of the shoes on the backplate with respect to the leading and trailing ends, as the lining material does not cover both ends of the shoes equally. Remove the shoes and, as they come away, disconnect the handbrake cable. Do not depress the brake pedal while the shoes are removed.

12 The handbrake and automatic adjuster toggle levers (photo) must be removed from the old shoe and fitted to the new one using the pin, washer, spring and U-shaped clip.

13 Apply a smear of grease to the shoe contact high spots on the brake backplate and to the ends of the wheel cylinder tappets.

14 Fit the new shoes by reversing the removal operations, but before fitting the automatic adjuster strut turn the star wheel to contact the strut fully.

15 Refit the brake drum and adjust the bearing preload, as described in Chapter 8.

16 Repeat the operations on the opposite brake.

17 Apply the handbrake several times to actuate the automatic adjuster and to position the shoe linings as close as possible to the drum.

18 Refit the roadwheels and lower the vehicle.

4 Caliper – removal, overhaul and refitting

1 Raise the front of the vehicle and support it securely. Remove the roadwheel. Disconnect the hydraulic hose from the caliper by unscrewing the hollow bolt from the banjo union. Note the copper washers, one each side of the union.

2 Unscrew the caliper mounting bolts and remove the caliper from the brake disc.

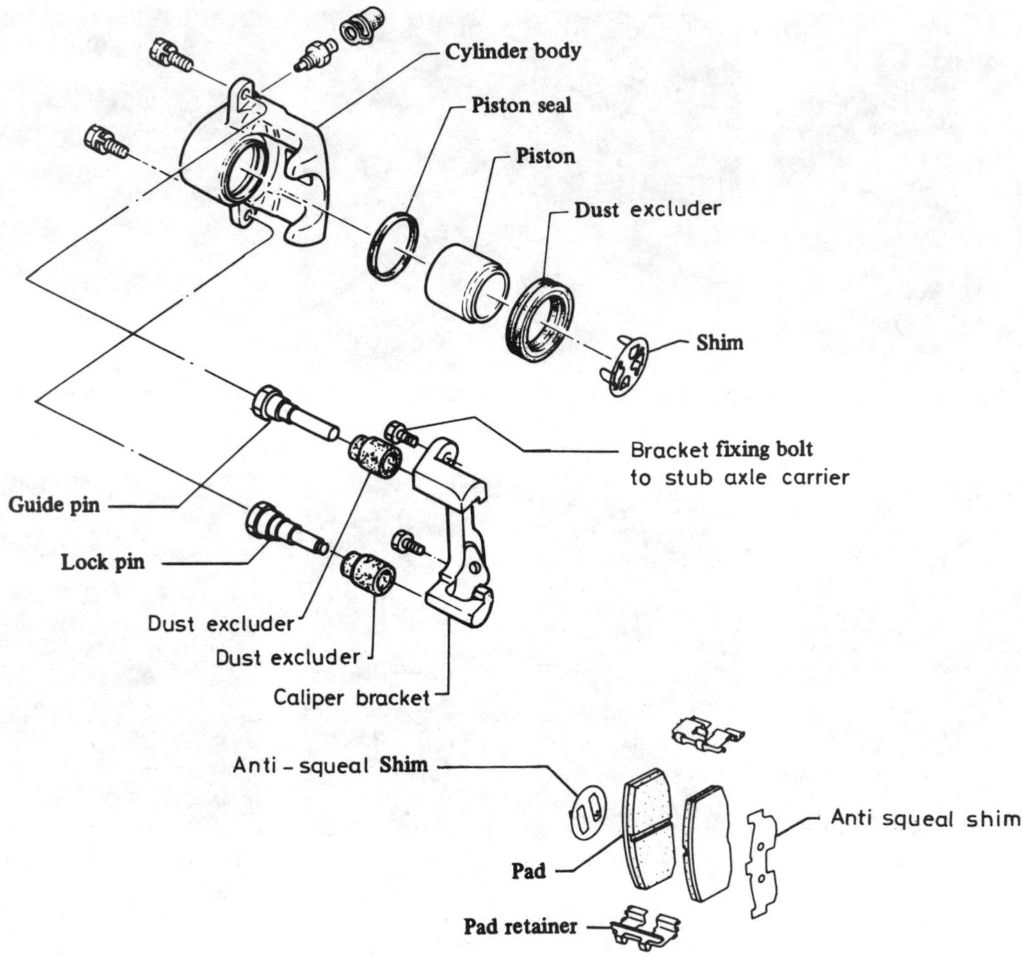

Fig. 9.5 Front disc caliper components (Sec 4)

3 Clean away external dirt, *avoiding inhaling any dust.* Remove the pads (Section 2).
4 Unscrew the guide pin and the lock pin, and separate the cylinder body from the caliper bracket.
5 Apply air pressure (such as is generated by a foot-operated pump) to the fluid entry hole in the caliper and eject the piston, dust excluder and retaining ring.
6 Inspect the surfaces of the piston and cylinder bore. If pitted or corroded, reassemble the caliper and renew it complete.
7 If the piston and cylinder are in good condition, use a sharp instrument to pick the piston seal out of its groove and discard it.
8 Wash all components in methylated spirits or clean hydraulic fluid and obtain a repair kit which will contain all the necessary new seals and other renewable items.

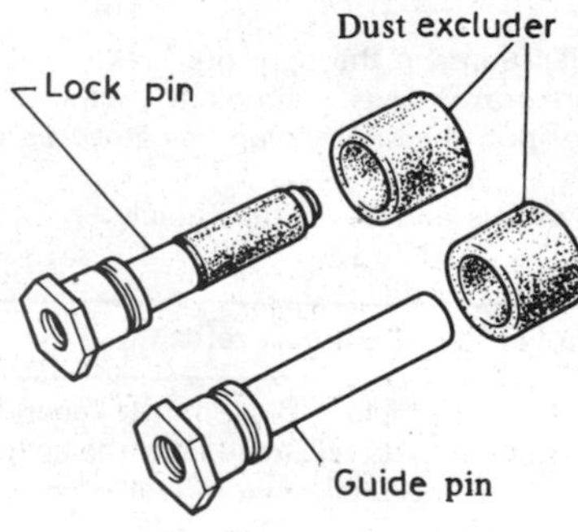

Fig. 9.6 Caliper guide pin and lockpin (Sec 4)

9 Commence reassembly by manipulating the new piston seal into its groove using the fingers only.
10 Push the piston part way into its bore, having first lubricated it with hydraulic fluid.
11 Fit the dust excluder and its retainer.
12 Smear the guide and lockpins with a little rubber grease and locate their dust covers, then connect the cylinder body to the caliper bracket. Tighten the pins to the specified torque.
13 Depress the piston fully, locate the pads, shims and springs and fit the caliper onto the discs.
14 Tighten the caliper mounting bolts to the specified torque.
15 Bleed the braking system, as described in Section 11.

5 Disc – inspection and renovation

1 Whenever the disc pads are inspected for wear, take the opportunity to examine the disc for deep scoring, grooving or cracks. Light scoring is normal.
2 The disc should not run out-of-true by more than the specified tolerance (see Specifications). This may be checked using a dial gauge or feeler blades between the disc and a fixed point as the disc is rotated.
3 Provided the thickness of the brake disc will not be reduced below the specified minimum, a scored disc may be reground for further use.
4 To remove the disc, refer to Chapter 8.

6 Rear wheel cylinder – removal and refitting

1 Remove the brake shoes, as described in Section 3.

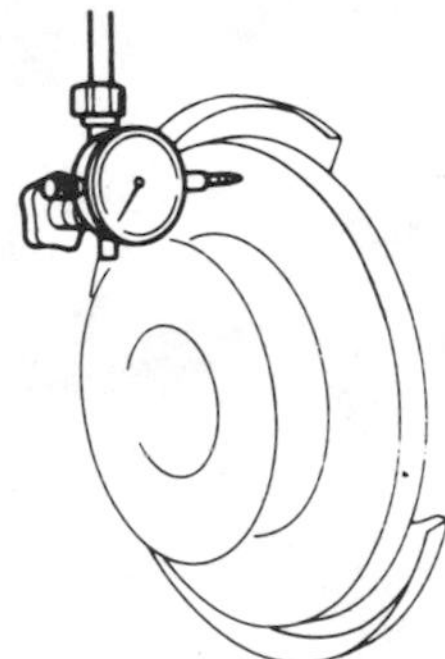

Fig. 9.7 Checking disc run-out with dial gauge (Sec 5)

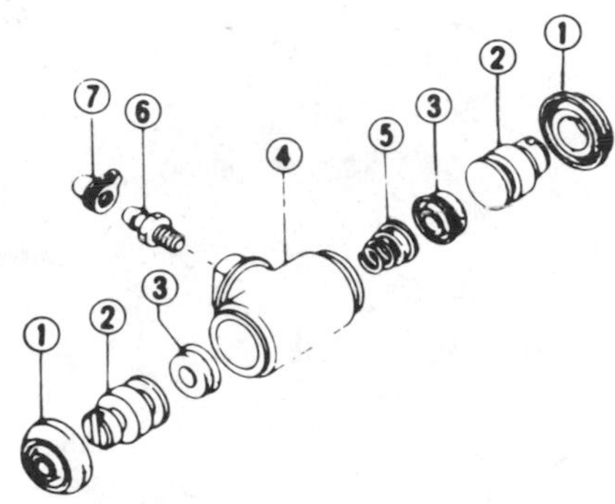

Fig. 9.8 Rear wheel cylinder components (Sec 6)

1 Dust excluder
2 Piston
3 Seal
4 Cylinder body
5 Spring
6 Bleed screw
7 Dust cap

2 Disconnect the hydraulic line from the cylinder.
3 Remove the wheel cylinder from the brake backplate (photo).
4 Clean away external dirt and pull off the dust covers.
5 Eject the internal components by tapping the cylinder on a block of wood or by applying air pressure from a foot operated tyre pump to the fluid entry hole. Note which direction the seal lips face.
6 Examine the surface of the piston and cylinder bore. If scored or corroded, renew the wheel cylinder complete.
7 If these components are in good condition, clean everything in either methylated spirits or hydraulic fluid, nothing else.
8 Discard the old seals and fit the new ones. These are contained in a repair kit, together with other renewable items.
9 Assemble the cylinder, applying hydraulic fluid as a lubricant as work progresses.
10 Refit the cylinder to the backplate, connect the fluid line and fit the brake shoes.
11 Bleed the brake circuit, as described in Section 11.

7 Brake drum – inspection and renovation

1 Whenever the brake drum is removed to inspect the wear of the shoe linings, take the opportunity to examine the interior friction surface of the drum.
2 If it is badly scored or grooved it is possible to have it machined, provided the internal diameter will not exceed the maximum specified dimension (see Specifications).

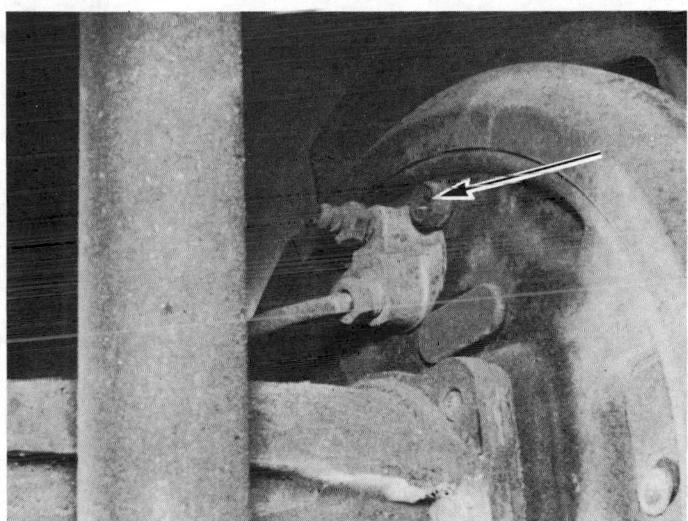

6.3 Rear wheel cylinder fixing bolt (arrowed)

8 Master cylinder – removal, overhaul and refitting

1 Disconnect the fluid lines from the master cylinder and allow the fluid to drain.
2 Unbolt the master cylinder from the front face of the vacuum servo unit (photo).
3 Withdraw the master cylinder, taking care not to spill hydraulic fluid on the paintwork.
4 Clean away external dirt.
5 Prise off the end cap and be prepared for the primary piston to be ejected.
6 Using a rod, slightly depress the secondary piston and unscrew and remove the stop screw.
7 Shake out the secondary piston. Note the direction in which all seal lips face.
8 Inspect the surfaces of the pistons and the cylinder bore. If they are scored or corroded, renew the master cylinder complete.
9 If these components are in good condition, clean them in either methylated spirits or hydraulic fluid, nothing else. Discard the seals, and obtain a repair kit which will contain all the necessary new seals and other renewable components. It should be noted that a primary piston of NABCO make is supplied as an assembly.
10 Manipulate the new seals into position with the fingers only.
11 Renew the reservoir seals. The valve assembly can be removed after extracting the circlip. Renew the valve O-ring.
12 As reassembly progresses, lubricate the components with clean hydraulic fluid.

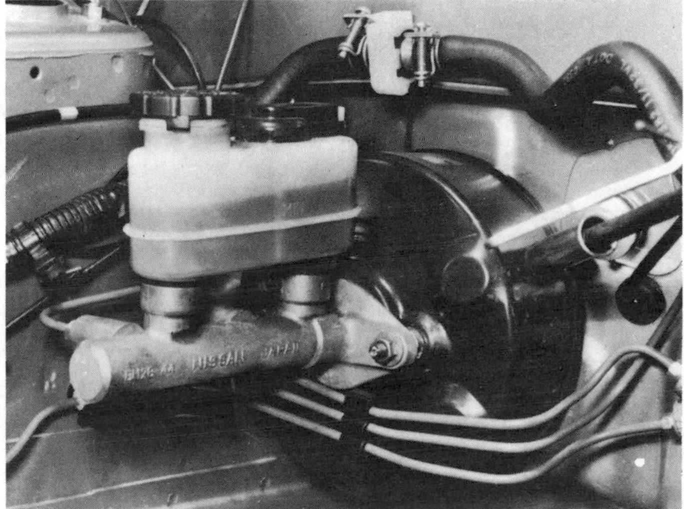

8.2 Master cylinder and servo unit

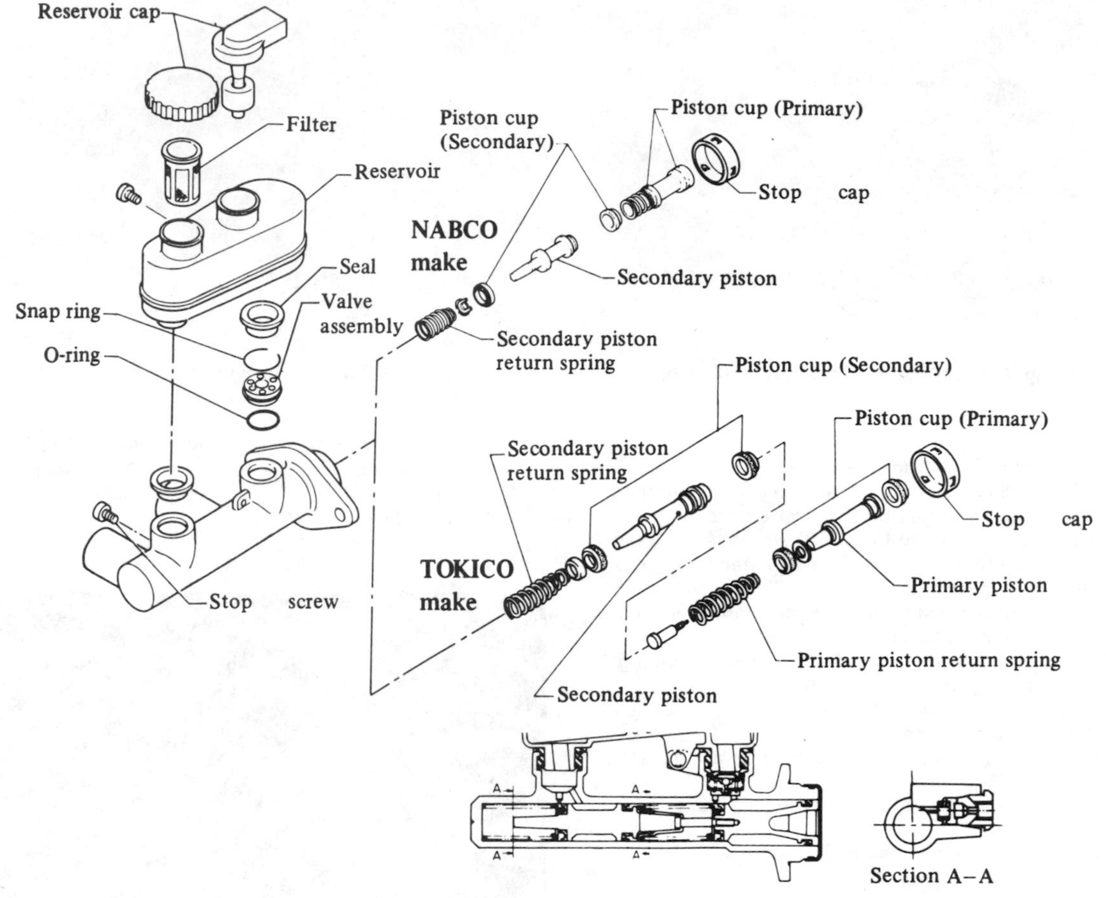

Fig. 9.9 Master cylinder components (Sec 8)

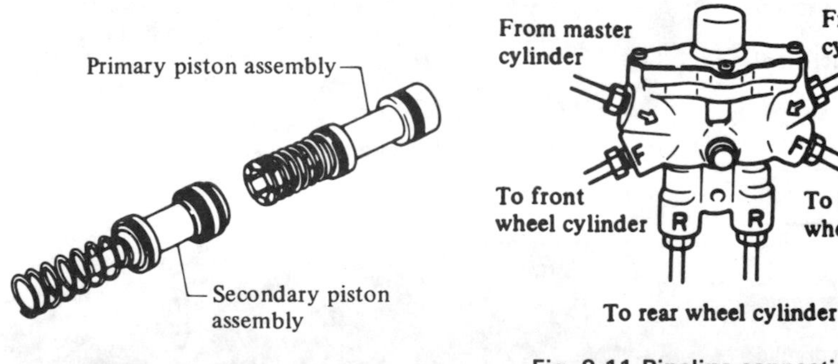

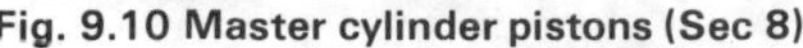

Fig. 9.10 Master cylinder pistons (Sec 8)

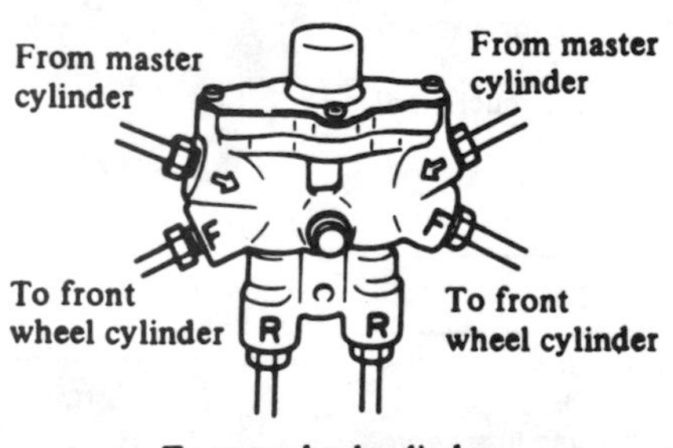

Fig. 9.11 Pipeline connections to pressure regulating valve (Sec 9)

9.1 Pressure regulating valve

13 Insert the secondary piston spring and then the assembled secondary piston into the cylinder.

14 Depress the secondary piston slightly with a rod and screw in the stop screw.

15 Fit the primary piston spring and the primary piston assembly and stake a new stop cap into position.

16 Fit the master cylinder to the front face of the vacuum servo unit.

17 Reconnect the fluid pipelines.

18 Bleed the complete system, as described in Section 11.

9 Pressure regulating valve

1 This valve is located on the engine compartment rear bulkhead.

2 Any fault can only be rectified by renewal of the valve, no repair being possible.

3 Removal is simply a matter of disconnecting the fluid lines and the central anchor bolt. Note the reconnection points for the individual pipelines to facilitate refitting.

4 Bleed the system on completion (Section 11).

10 Flexible and rigid hydraulic lines – inspection and renewal

1 Periodically inspect the condition of the flexible brake hoses. If they appear swollen, chafed or when bent double with the fingers tiny cracks are visible they must be renewed.

2 Always uncouple the rigid pipe from the flexible hose first, then release the end of the flexible hose from the support bracket (photo). To do this, pull out the lockplate using a pair of pliers.

3 Now unscrew the flexible hose from the caliper or connector. On calipers, a banjo type hose connector is used. When installing the hose, always use a new sealing washer.

4 When installation is complete, check that the flexible hose does

10.2 Flexible hose-to-rigid pipe connection

10.7 Brake pipes and fuel pipe in retaining clip

not rub against the tyre or other adjacent components. Its attitude may be altered to overcome this by pulling out the clip at the support bracket and twisting the hose in the required direction by not more than one quarter turn.

5 Bleed the hydraulic system (Section 11).

6 At regular intervals wipe the steel brake pipes clean and examine them for signs of rust or denting caused by flying stones.

7 Examine the fit of the pipes in their insulated securing clips and bend the tongues of the clips if necessary to ensure a positive fit (photo).

8 Check that the pipes are not touching any adjacent components or rubbing against any part of the vehicle. Where this is observed, bend the pipe gently away to clear.

9 Any section of pipe which is rusty or chafed should be renewed. Brake pipes are available to the correct length and fitted with end unions from most dealers and they can also be made to pattern by many accessory suppliers. When installing the new pipes use the old pipes as a guide to bending and do not make any bends sharper than is necessary.

10 The system will of course have to be bled when the circuit has been reconnected.

11 Hydraulic system – bleeding

1 The two independent hydraulic circuits are as follows:

(a) Front right-hand caliper and left rear wheel cylinder
(b) Front left-hand caliper and right rear wheel cylinder

2 If the master cylinder or the pressure regulating valve has been disconnected and reconnected then the complete system (both circuits) must be bled.

3 If a component of only one circuit has been disturbed then only the particular circuit need be bled.

4 Due to the design of the hydraulic system and pipeline layout, it will be found easier to bleed the system using a pressure bleeding kit. If the entire system is being bled, the sequence of bleeding should be carried out by starting at the bleed screw furthest from the master cylinder and finishing at the one nearest to it. Unless the pressure bleeding method is being used, do not forget to keep the fluid level in the master cylinder reservoir topped-up to prevent air from being drawn into the system which would make any work done worthless.

5 Before commencing operations, check that all system hoses and pipes are in good condition with all unions tight and free from leaks.

6 Take great care not to allow hydraulic fluid to come into contact with the vehicle paintwork as it is an effective paint-stripper. Wash off any spilled fluid immediately with cold water.

7 As the system incorporates a vacuum servo, destroy the vacuum by giving several applications of the brake pedal in quick succession.

Bleeding – two-man method

8 Gather together a clean glass jar and a length of rubber or plastic tubing which will be a tight fit on the brake bleed screws.

9 Engage the help of an assistant.

10 Push one end of the bleed tube onto the first bleed screw and immerse the other end in the glass jar which should contain enough hydraulic fluid to cover the end of the tube.

11 Open the bleed screw one half turn and have your assistant depress the brake pedal fully then slowly release it. Tighten the bleed screw at the end of each pedal downstroke to obviate any chance of air or fluid being drawn back into the system.

12 Wait between 20 and 40 seconds then repeat the operations as many times as is necessary until clean hydraulic fluid, free from air bubbles can be seen coming through into the jar.

13 Tighten the bleed screw at the end of a pedal downstroke and remove the bleed tube. Bleed from the remaining screws in a similar way.

Bleeding – using one-way valve kit

14 There are a number of one-man, one-way brake bleeding kits available from motor accessory shops. It is recommended that one of these kits is used wherever possible, rather than just a tube, as it will greatly simplify the bleeding operation and reduce the risk of air or fluid being drawn back into the system, quite apart from being able to do the work without the help of an assistant.

15 To use the kit, connect the tube to the bleed screw and open the screw one half turn.

16 Depress the brake pedal fully and slowly release it. The one-way valve in the kit will prevent expelled air from returning at the end of each pedal downstroke. Repeat this operation several times to be sure of ejecting all air from the system. Some kits include a translucent

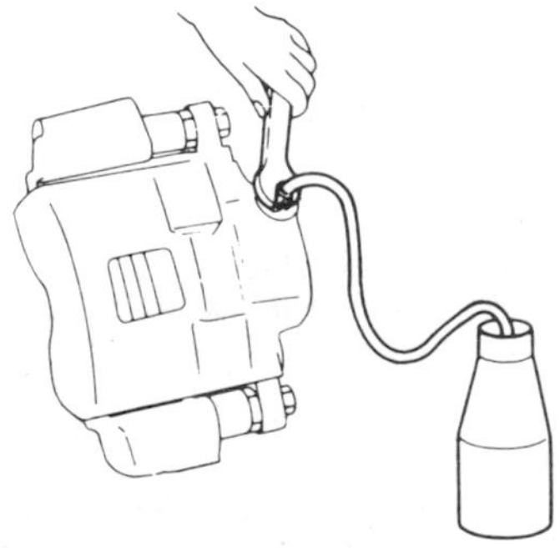

Fig. 9.12 Bleeding a caliper (Sec 11)

container which can be positioned so that the air bubbles can actually be seen being ejected from the system.
17 Tighten the bleed screw, remove the tube and repeat the operations in the remaining brakes.
18 On completion, depress the brake pedal. If it still feels spongy repeat the bleeding operations as air must still be trapped in the system.

Bleeding – using a pressure bleeding kit

19 These kits are available from motor accessory shops and are usually operated by air pressure from the spare tyre.
20 By connecting a pressurised container to the master cylinder fluid reservoir, bleeding is then carried out by simply opening each bleed screw in turn and allowing the fluid to run out, rather like turning on a tap, until no air is visible in the expelled fluid.
21 By using this method, the large reserve of hydraulic fluid provides a safeguard against air being drawn into the system during bleeding which often occurs if the fluid level in the reservoir is not maintained.
22 Pressure bleeding is particularly effective when bleeding 'difficult' systems or when bleeding the complete system at a time of routine fluid renewal.

All methods

23 When bleeding is completed, check and top up the fluid level in the master cylinder reservoir.
24 Check the feel of the brake pedal. If it feels at all spongy, air must still be present in the system and further bleeding is indicated. Failure to bleed satisfactorily after a reasonable repetition of the bleeding operations may be due to worn master cylinder seals.
25 Discard brake fluid which has been expelled. It is almost certain to be contaminated with moisture, air and dirt, making it unsuitable for further use. Clean fluid should always be stored in an airtight container as it absorbs moisture readily (hygroscopic) which lowers its boiling point and could affect braking performance under severe conditions.

12 Vacuum servo (booster) unit – description and maintenance

1 The vacuum servo unit is fitted into the brake hydraulic circuit in series with the master cylinder to provide assistance to the driver when the brake pedal is depressed. This reduces the effort required by the driver to operate the brakes under all braking conditions.
2 The unit operates by vacuum obtained from the induction manifold and comprises, basically, a booster diaphragm and check valve. The servo unit and hydraulic master cylinder are connected together so that the servo unit piston rod acts as the master cylinder pushrod. The driver's effort is transmitted through another pushrod to the servo unit piston and its built-in control system. The servo unit piston does not fit tightly into the cylinder, but has a strong diaphragm to keep its edges in constant contact with the cylinder wall, so assuring an airtight seal between the two parts. The forward chamber is held under vacuum conditions created in the inlet manifold of the engine and, during periods when the brake pedal is not in use, the controls open a passage to the rear chamber so placing it under vacuum conditions as well. When the brake pedal is depressed, the vacuum passage to the rear chamber is cut off and the chamber opened to atmospheric pressure. The consequent rush of air pushes the servo piston forward in the vacuum chamber and operates the main pushrod to the master cylinder.
3 The controls are designed so that assistance is given under all conditions and when the brakes are not required, vacuum in the rear chamber is established when the brake pedal is released. All air from the atmosphere entering the rear chamber is passed through a small air filter.
4 Under normal operating conditions the vacuum servo unit is very reliable and does not require overhaul except at very high mileages. In this case it is far better to obtain a service exchange unit, rather than repair the original unit.
5 It is emphasized that the servo unit assists in reducing the braking effort required at the foot pedal and, in the event of its failure, the hydraulic braking system is in no way affected except that the need for higher pedal pressure will be noticed.
6 Periodically inspect the condition of the vacuum hose in which is incorporated a non-return valve (photo). Renew the hose if it is split or has hardened.

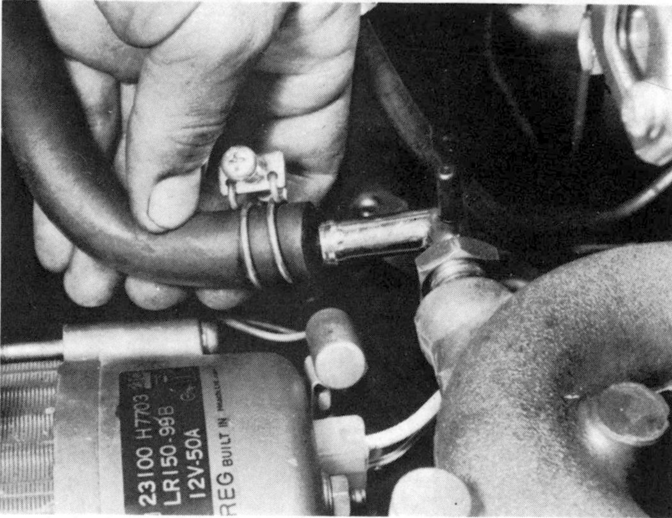

12.6 Servo hose at intake manifold

7 At the intervals specified in Routine Maintenance (or earlier in dusty climates) the air filter should be renewed.
8 To remove it from its location around the servo unit pushrod, peel back the dust excluder.
9 To save disconnecting the pushrod, the old filter may be cut away and removed.
10 Make a diagonal cut from the centre hole to the outside edge of the new filter and install it.
11 Refit the dust excluder.

13 Vacuum servo unit – removal and refitting

1 Remove the master cylinder, as described in Section 8.
2 Disconnect the vacuum hose from the servo unit.
3 Working inside the vehicle, disconnect the pushrod from the brake pedal.
4 Unbolt the brake servo unit from the bulkhead and remove it.
5 Refitting is a reversal of removal, but carry out the following checks before actually installing it.
6 Check the projection (A) of the pushrod which enters the master cylinder (see Fig. 9.13). The projection is set in production and the threads locked, so if it does not conform to specifications renew the complete unit.
7 Now check the length (B) of the pushrod which connects with the brake pedal (see Fig. 9.14). Adjust if necessary by turning the clevis fork after having released the locknut.

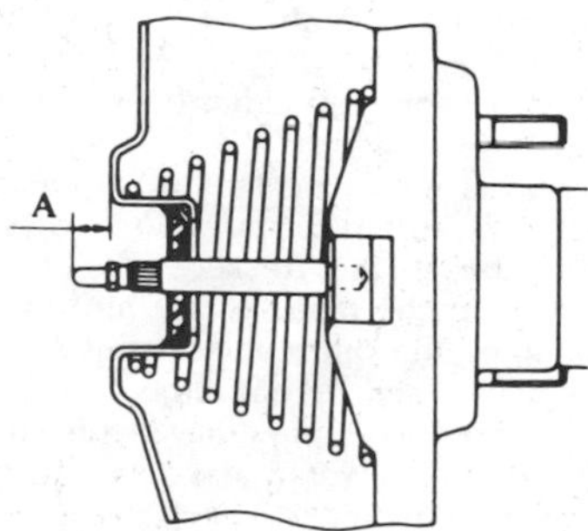

Fig. 9.13 Set length of servo unit-to-master cylinder pushrod (Sec 13)

A = 10.275 to 10.525 mm (0.4045 to 0.4144 in)

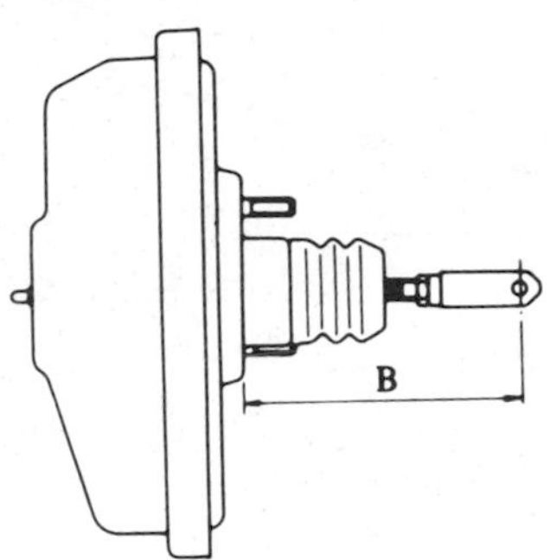

Fig. 9.14 Brake pedal pushrod setting diagram (Sec 13)

B = 150.0 mm (5.91 in)

14 Handbrake – adjustment

1 The handbrake is adjusted by the action of the rear shoe automatic adjuster and will require no further attention unless the cable stretches, normally only after a high mileage has been covered.

2 The handbrake should be fully applied with the rear wheels locked if the handbrake control lever is pulled up 6 to 7 notches (clicks) of the ratchet.

3 If the lever moves over an excessive number of notches, release the handbrake and adjust the cable by moving the locknuts at the cable stirrup which is adjacent to the equaliser under the vehicle (photo).

4 Keep the groove in the equaliser well greased at all times.

5 Working inside the vehicle, remove the centre console (see Chapter 12) and bend the handbrake warning switchplate down so that,with the ignition on, the warning lamp comes on when the lever is pulled up one notch.

15 Handbrake cables – renewal

Primary cable

1 Disconnect the secondary cable from the connecting stirrup which is adjacent to the equaliser under the vehicle (see photo 14.3). Do this by unscrewing the locknuts and then passing the cable end fitting through the groove in the equaliser.

2 Working inside the vehicle, remove the centre console, as described in Chapter 12.

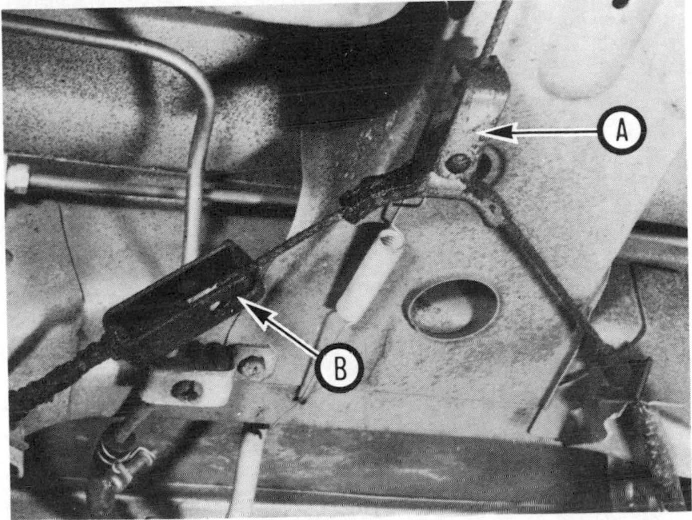

14.3 Handbrake cable adjustment

A Equaliser *B Adjuster stirrup*

3 Disconnect the lead from the handbrake warning switch (photo).

4 Remove the seat belt stalks.

5 Remove the hand control lever fixing screws and the cable bush fixing screws.

6 Withdraw the hand control lever with the primary cable attached into the vehicle interior.

7 To separate the primary cable from the control lever, drill out the connecting pin.

8 Refitting is a reversal of removal, a clevis pin and cotter pin are supplied for connecting the new cable to the hand control lever.

9 Adjust, as described in the preceding Section.

Secondary cable

10 Disconnect the cable at the stirrup which is adjacent to the equaliser under the vehicle.

11 Draw the longer cable through the groove in the equaliser.

12 Bend back the cable clips on the rear suspension arms (photo) and release the cables.

13 Raise the rear of the vehicle, support it securely and chock the front wheels. Remove both roadwheels and brake drums.

14 Unhook the handbrake cable end fittings from the handbrake lever on the brake shoes.

15.3 Handbrake control lever and warning switch (arrowed)

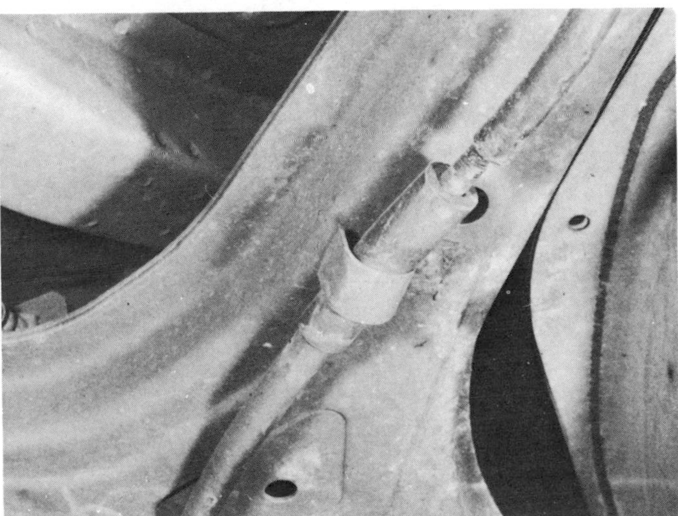

15.12 Handbrake cable clip on rear suspension trailing arm

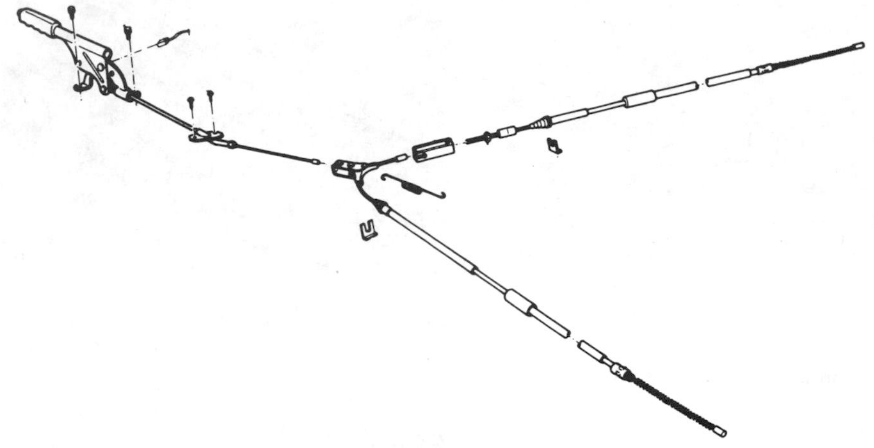

Fig. 9.15 Handbrake cables (Sec 15)

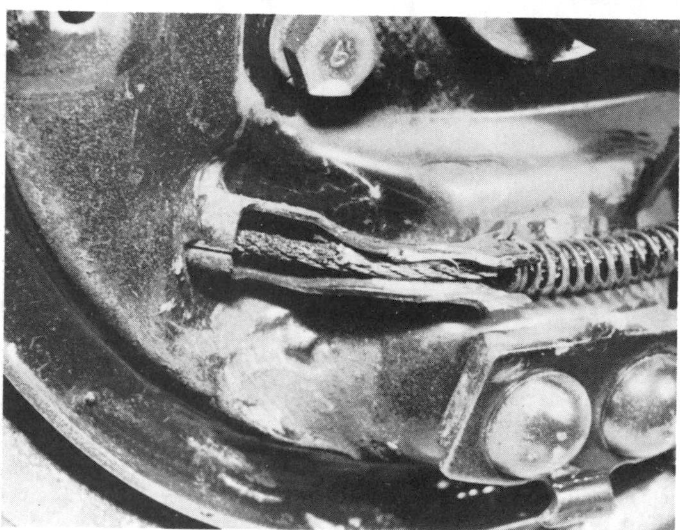

15.15 Handbrake cable at backplate

16.1 Control pedal arrangement

15 Remove both cables through the backplates (photo).
16 Fit the new cables by reversing the removal operations. Apply grease to the cable friction surfaces.
17 Refit the brake drums and adjust the bearings, as described in Chapter 8.
18 Refit the roadwheels.
19 Adjust the cables, as described in the preceding Section.

16 Brake pedal – removal, refitting and adjustment

1 Working within the vehicle, under the facia panel, disconnect the pushrod from the brake pedal arm (photo).
2 Extract the spring clip from the end of the pedal pivot shaft and unhook the pedal return spring.
3 Slide the pedal from the shaft.
4 The pivot bushes may be renewed.
5 Refitting is a reversal of removal, apply grease to the pivot shaft and bushes.
6 Measure from the metal surface of the floor to the top of the brake pedal pad. This dimension must be as given in the Specifications. If it is not, release the locknut and rotate the pushrod.
7 Once the pedal height has been set, depress the pedal fully and measure the distance between the upper surface of the pedal pad and the metal surface of the floor. This must not be less than 85.0 mm. (3.35 in). If it is, this indicates air is in the system which must be bled out immediately (Section 11).

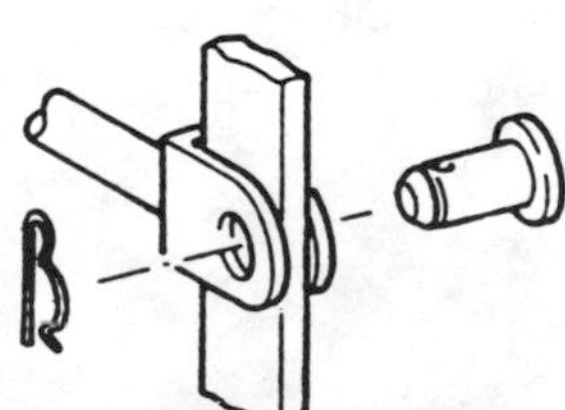

Fig. 9.16 Pushrod-to-brake pedal arm connecting components (Sec 16)

8 Finally, adjust the stop-lamp switch by means of its fixing nuts so that when the pedal arm is fully released there is a clearance (C) between the pedal stop pad and the end of the threaded part of the switch (see Fig. 9.18).
9 Tighten the locknuts without altering the setting of the switch.

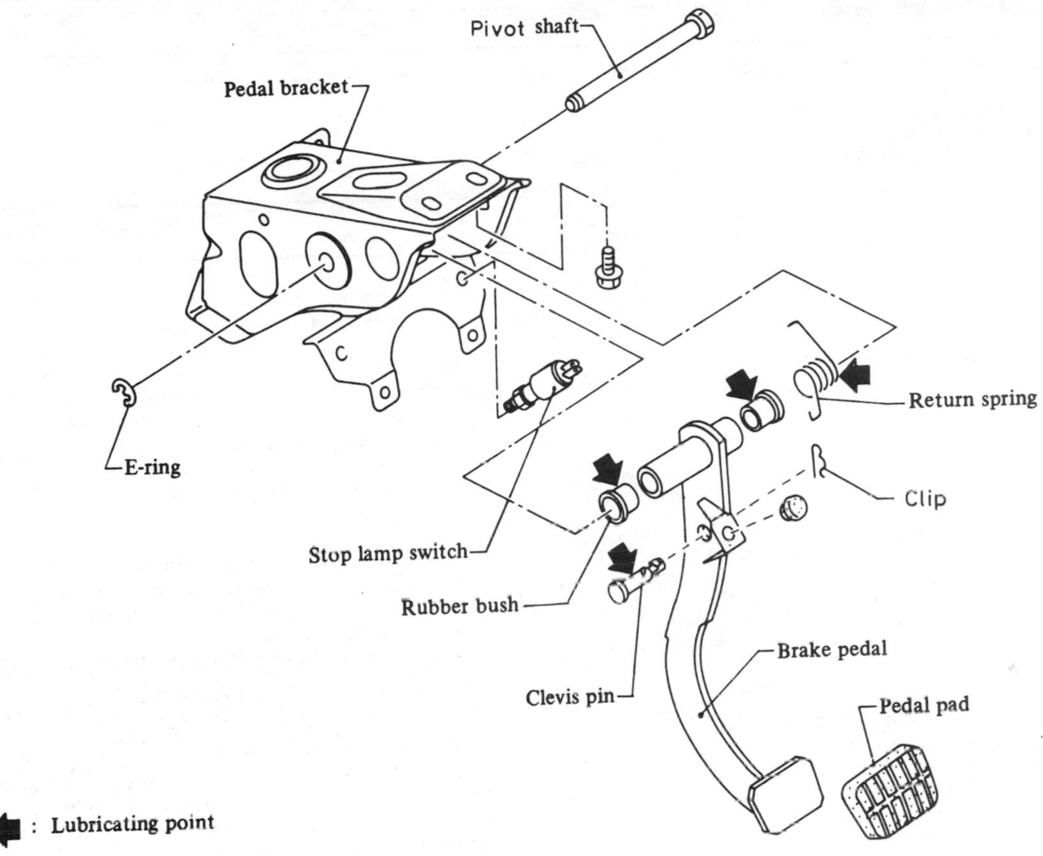

Fig. 9.17 Brake pedal components (Sec 16)

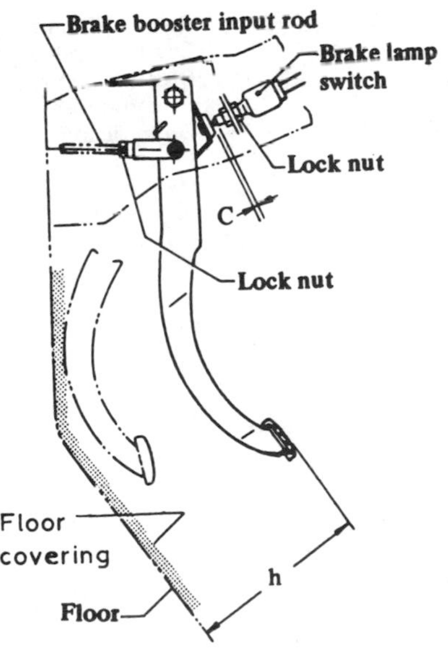

Fig. 9.18 Brake pedal height setting diagram (Sec 16)

C = 0 to 1.0 mm (0 to 0.04 in)
h See Specifications

17 Fault diagnosis – braking system

Before diagnosing faults from the following chart, check that any braking irregularities are not caused by:
Uneven and incorrect tyre pressures
Wear in the steering mechanism
Defects in the suspension and dampers
Misalignment of the bodyframe

Symptom	Reason(s)
Pedal travels a long way before the brakes operate	Incorrect pedal adjustment Brake shoes set too far from the drums (seized adjuster)
Stopping ability poor, even though pedal pressure is firm	Linings, discs or drums badly worn or scored One or more wheel hydraulic cylinders seized, resulting in some brake shoes not pressing against the drums (or pads against disc) Brake linings contaminated with oil Wrong type of linings fitted (too hard) Brake shoes wrongly assembled Servo unit not functioning
Car veers to one side when the brakes are applied	Brake pads or linings on one side are contaminated with oil Hydraulic wheel cylinder on one side partially or fully seized A mixture of lining materials fitted between sides Brake discs not matched Unequal wear between sides caused by partially seized wheel cylinders
Pedal feels spongy when the brakes are applied	Air is present in the hydraulic system
Pedal feels springy when the brakes are applied	Brake linings not bedded in (after fitting new ones) Master cylinder or brake backplate mounting bolts loose Severe wear in brake drums causing distortion when brakes are applied Discs out of true
Pedal travels right down with little or no resistance and brakes are virtually non-operative	Leak in hydraulic system resulting in lack of pressure for operating wheel cylinders If no signs of leakage are apparent the master cylinder internal seals are failing to sustain pressure
Binding, juddering, overheating	One or a combination of reasons given above Shoes installed incorrectly with reference to leading and trailing ends Broken shoe return spring Disc out-of-round Drum distorted Incorrect pedal adjustment
Lack of servo assistance	Vacuum hose disconnected or leaking Non-return valve defective or incorrectly fitted Servo internal defect

Chapter 10 Electrical system

Refer to Chapter 13 for Specifications and information on later models

Contents

Specifications

System type	12 volt negative earth battery, alternator and pre-engaged starter
Battery	30 to 60 Ahr according to model
Alternator	
Rating	35 or 50A according to model
Output voltage	14.4 to 15.0V at 20°C (68°F)
Minimum brush wear limit	7.0 mm (0.28 in)
Starter motor	
Minimum brush wear limit	11.0 mm (0.43 in)
Drive pinion-to-stop clearance (manual transmission starter)	0.3 to 2.5 mm (0.012 to 0.098 in)
Difference in idler gear height between solenoid and hand pressure activation (automatic transmission starter)	0.3 to 2.5 mm (0.012 to 0.098 in)
Bulbs	**Wattage**
Headlamp (sealed beam type)	65/55
Headlamp (bulb type)	45/40
Headlamp (Halogen bulb type)	60/55
Front direction indicator lamp:	
Except N. America	21
N America	27
Front sidelight:	
Except N America	5
N America	8
Front side indicator lamp:	
Except N America	5
N America	3.4
Rear side indicator lamp (N America)	3.4

Stop/tail lamp:	
Except N America	21/5
N America	27/8
Rear direction indicator lamp:	
Except N America	21
N America	27
Reversing lamp:	
Except N America	21
N America	27
Rear foglamp	21
Number plate lamp:	
Except N America	5
N America	10
Interior lamp	10
Luggage compartment lamp	5
Charge indicator	3
Warning and indicator lamps	1.2

Fuses (typical)

Circuit number	Circuit protected	Rating (amps)
1	Headlamp (RH)	10
2	Horn, hazard warning lamps	10
3	Stop-lamp	10
4	Rear wiper/washer, windscreen washer	10
5	Cigar lighter	10
6	Headlamp washer/wiper	10
7	Direction indicators, instruments, reversing lamps, seat belt	10
8	Headlamp (LH)	10
9	Radiator cooling fan	20
10	Clock, interior lamp	10
11	Tail lamp, rear number plate lamp, front sidelight	10
12	Windscreen wiper	10
13	Heater blower motor	20
14	Air conditioner	20
15	Auto-choke, fuel cut-off valve and catalyst warm-up system	20
16	Heated rear window or tailgate	20

Torque wrench settings

	Nm	lbf ft
Alternator bracket bolt	20	15
Alternator adjuster link bolt	12	9
Starter motor mounting bolts	40	30
Alternator pulley nut	40	30

1 General description

The major components of the 12 volt negative earth system consist of a 12 volt battery, an alternator (driven from the crankshaft pulley), and a starter motor.

The battery supplies a steady amount of current for the ignition, lighting and other electrical circuits and provides a reserve of power when the current consumed by the electrical equipment exceeds that being produced by the alternator.

The alternator has its own regulator which ensures a high output if the battery is in a low state of charge and the demand from the electrical equipment is high, and a low output if the battery is fully charged and there is little demand from the electrical equipment.

When fitting electrical accessories to cars with a negative earth system it is important, if they contain silicon diodes or transistors, that they are connected correctly, otherwise serious damage may result to the components concerned. Items such as radios, tape players, electronic ignition systems, electronic tachometer, automatic dipping etc, should all be checked for correct polarity.

2 Battery – maintenance

Low maintenance type

1 The battery fitted as original equipment is of the low maintenance or freedom type. The addition of water is not required with this type of battery.

2 Periodically wipe the top of the battery casing clean and apply petroleum jelly to the battery terminals to prevent build-up of corrosion.

3 The significance of the charge indicator on this type of battery should be understood (photo). If the indicator appears blue in colour, then the battery is fully charged.

4 If the indicator is colourless, then the battery is discharged.

5 Do not re-charge the battery at a rate of more than 10A. If the battery indicator does not change to blue after the charging period, then the battery must be considered to have reached the end of its useful life.

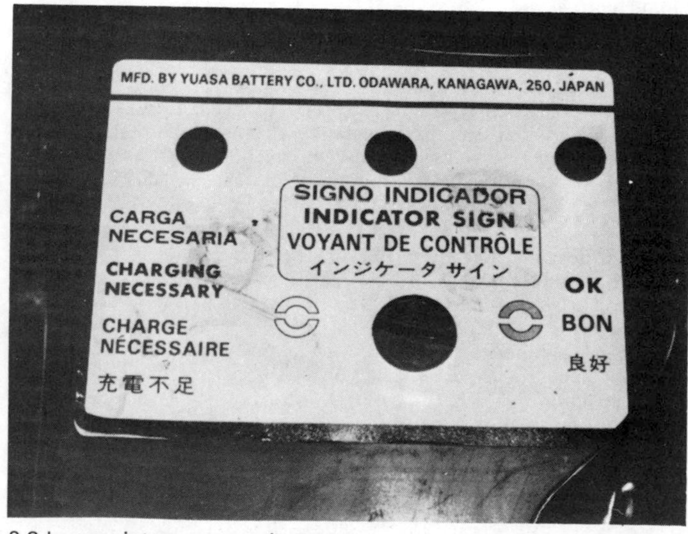

2.3 Low maintenance type battery

Standard type

6 If a replacement battery of conventional type is substituted for the original one, then carry out the following maintenance procedures.
7 Normal weekly battery maintenance consists of checking the electrolyte level of each cell to ensure that the separators are covered by 0.2 in (5 mm) of electrolyte. If the level has fallen, top up the battery using purified (distilled) water only. Do not overfill. If the battery is overfilled or any electrolyte spilled, immediately wipe away the excess as the electrolyte, which is dilute sulphuric acid, attacks and corrodes most metals it comes into contact with very quickly.
8 As well as keeping the terminals clean and covered with a light film of petroleum jelly, the top of the battery, and especially the top of the cells, should be kept clean and dry. This helps prevent corrosion and ensures that the battery does not become partially discharged by leakage through dampness and dirt.
9 Every three months remove the battery and inspect the support tray (photo), the battery clamp and the battery terminals for corrosion. This has the appearance of white fluffy deposits and if it exists it should be cleaned off using warm water to which a little ammonia or baking soda has been added. Treat the battery terminals with petroleum jelly and other metalwork with rust preventative paint.
10 If topping-up the battery becomes excessive and there has been no leakage of electrolyte then it is likely that the battery is being overcharged and it will have to be checked by an auto-electrician. An elderly battery may need more frequent topping-up than a new one because it will take a bigger charge. There is no need to worry about this provided that it gives good service.
11 With the battery on the bench at the three monthly interval check, measure the specific gravity of the electrolyte with a hydrometer to determine the state of charge and condition of the electrolyte. There should be very little variation between individual cells and, if a variation in excess of 0.025 exists it will be due to either:

(a) Loss of electrolyte from the battery at some time caused by spillage or a leak, resulting in a drop in the specific gravity of the electrolyte when the deficiency was made up with purified water instead of fresh electrolyte
(b) An internal short circuit caused by buckling of the plates or similar malady pointing to the likelihood of total battery failure in the near future.

12 The specific gravity of the electrolyte for fully charged and fully discharged conditions at different temperatures of the electrolyte is given below:

Fully discharged	Electrolyte temperature	Fully charged
1.098	38°C (100°F)	1.268
1.102	32°C (90°F)	1.272
1.106	27°C (80°F)	1.276
1.110	21°C (70°F)	1.280
1.114	16°C (60°F)	1.284
1.118	10°C (50°F)	1.288
1.122	4°C (40°F)	1.292
1.126	-1.5°C (30°F)	1.296

13 Do not attempt to add acid to a battery. If it is known that electrolyte has been spilled from a cell, leave the mixing of fresh electrolyte and replenishment to your dealer or service station.
14 If the vehicle is to be started from the battery in another vehicle, run one booster cable between the positive terminals of both batteries. Connect the remaining booster cable between the negative terminal of the rescue vehicle battery and the discharged vehicle's battery negative terminal or bodywork.
15 Disconnect the negative booster cable first.

2.9 Battery support tray

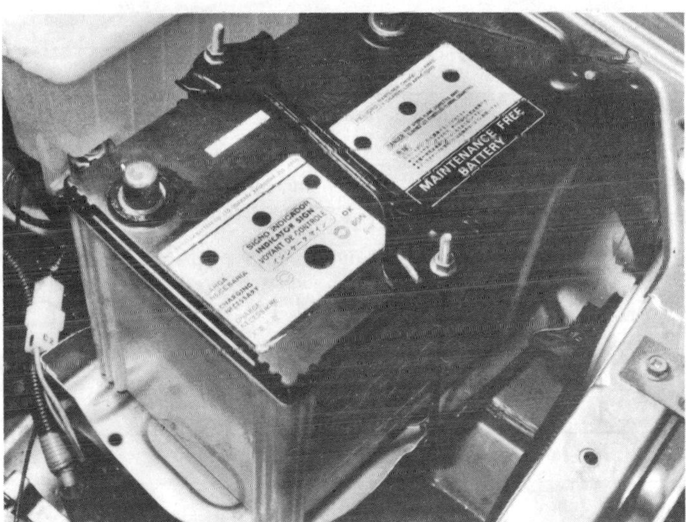

4.2 Battery retaining clamp

3 Battery – charging

1 The need for charging a battery from the mains has largely been eliminated with the advent of the alternator.
2 If short daily journeys are made, with much use of the starter and electrical accessories, it is still possible for the battery to become discharged as the alternator is not in use long enough to replace the current being used.
3 A trickle charger can safely be used overnight at a charging rate of 1.5A.
4 Specially rapid 'boost' charges which are claimed to restore the power of the battery in one to two hours should be avoided as they can cause serious damage to the battery plates through overheating.
5 While charging the battery note that the temperature of the electrolyte should never exceed 38°C (100°F) and remember that the gas produced in the cells contains hydrogen which is flammable and explosive, so do not smoke or bring naked lights near the top of the battery.
6 Always disconnect the battery leads before connecting the mains charger to the battery.

4 Battery – removal and refitting

1 Open the bonnet and disconnect the negative and then the positive battery leads.
2 Unscrew the nuts which hold the battery retainer in place (photo). Lift off the crossbar and unhook the clamp rods.
3 Lift out the battery, taking care not to tilt it.
4 Refitting is a reversal of removal, but make sure that it is located on the battery tray correctly with respect to the positive and negative lead connections to the battery.

6.2 Alternator rear terminals

6.9 Alternator mounting pivot showing location of washer

5 Alternator – description, maintenance and precautions

1 The alternator is mounted on the crankcase at the timing belt end of the engine.
2 The unit is driven by a belt from the crankshaft pulley. A voltage regulator is integral with the brush holder plate.
3 Keep the drivebelt correctly tensioned (see Chapter 2) and the electrical connections tight.
4 Keep the outside of the alternator free from grease and dirt.
5 It is important that the battery leads are always disconnected if the battery is to be charged. Also, if body repairs are to be carried out using electrical welding equipment, the alternator must be disconnected otherwise serious damage can be caused.
6 Do not stop the engine by pulling a lead from the battery.

6 Alternator – removal and refitting

1 Disconnect the battery.
2 Disconnect the leads from the rear of the alternator (photo).
3 Release the alternator mounting and adjuster link bolts, push the unit fully in towards the engine and slip the drivebelt off the pulley.

Left-hand drive versions

4 Remove the mounting and adjuster link bolts and lift the alternator from the engine.

Right-hand drive versions

5 Unscrew the nuts which hold the brake master cylinder to the face of the vacuum servo unit.
6 Remove the mounting and adjuster link bolts.
7 Tilt the brake master cylinder just enough to provide clearance for the alternator to be able to pass between the intake manifold and the master cylinder.
8 Remove the alternator from the engine.

Refitting

9 When refitting the alternator, note the position of the spacer washer on the pivot mounting (photo).
10 Tension the drivebelt, as described in Chapter 2, Section 8.

7 Alternator – overhaul

1 In the event of the charge (ignition) warning lamp not going out after the engine has started or if the battery is being overcharged, indicated by frequent topping-up or by undercharging, the following operations may be carried out to rectify worn brushes or a faulty voltage regulator. If more extensive overhaul is required, or if the alternator has had a long service life, it is recommended that a new or factory-rebuilt unit is obtained.
2 Remove the alternator and clean away external dirt.
3 Mark the relative position of the rear cover to the front (drive end) cover by scribing a line on them. Unscrew the tie-bolts.
4 Pull off the rear cover with the stator.
5 Unscrew the fixing nuts and separate the rear cover from the stator.
6 If the brush length is less than the specified minimum the brushes must be renewed. To do this, the brush leads must be unsoldered. The new brushes must be attached quickly to prevent the heat leaking away and damaging adjacent components. When locating the new brushes, note that the brushes must extend 11.0 mm (0.43 in) from their holders and the lead must be coiled in the terminal groove.
7 Unless the voltage regulator is faulty ignore the operations described in the next three paragraphs.
8 Remove the regulator securing rivets and unsolder the terminals.
9 Remove the bolts which retain the brush holder/regulator unit.
10 Refit the new regulator by reversing the disconnection and removal operations. Peen the rivets securely.
11 Before reassembling the rear cover/brush holder assembly to the motor/front cover, the brushes must be held in the raised position in order to be able to locate them on the slip rings. Do this by passing a thin rod through the hole provided in the alternator rear cover.
12 Align the marks made on the front and rear covers and join the sections of the alternator together.
13 Fit the tie-bolts, remove the temporary brush lift rod.
14 If for any reason the alternator pulley must be removed, the pulley retaining nut can be unscrewed if the rotor shaft is prevented from rotating by inserting a splined socket in the shaft recess.

8 Starter motor – description

1 The starter motor is of pre-engaged type.
2 When the starter switch is operated, current flows from the battery to the solenoid switch which is mounted on the starter body. The plunger in the solenoid moves inwards, so causing a centrally pivoted lever to push the drive pinion into mesh with the starter ring gear. When the solenoid plunger reaches the end of its travel, it closes an internal contact and full starting current flows to the starter field coils. The armature is then able to rotate the crankshaft, so starting the engine.
3 A special freewheel clutch is fitted to the starter drive pinion so that as soon as the engine fires and starts to operate on its own it does not drive the starter motor.

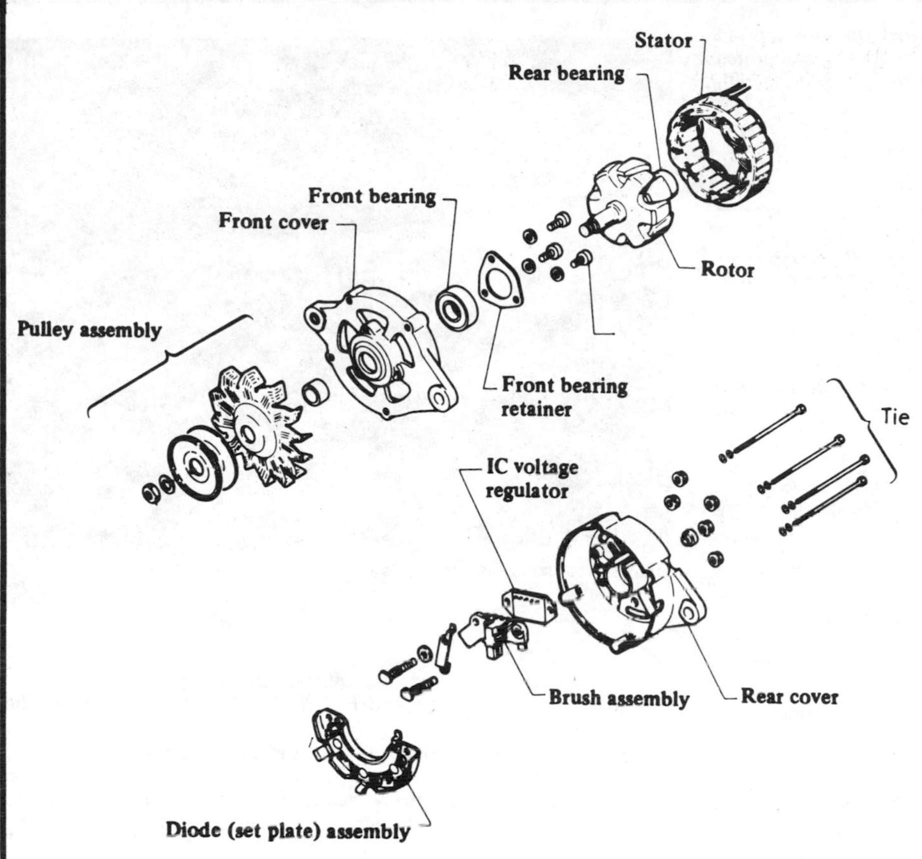

Fig. 10.1 Exploded view of the alternator (Sec 7)

Fig. 10.2 Alternator stator separated from rotor (Sec 7)

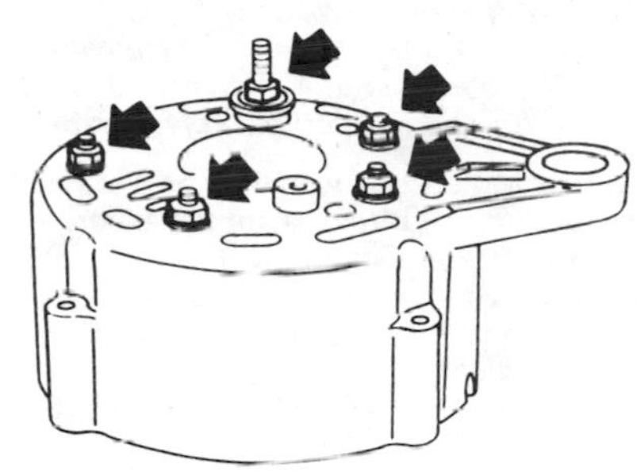

Fig. 10.3 Nuts retaining stator to alternator rear cover (Sec 7)

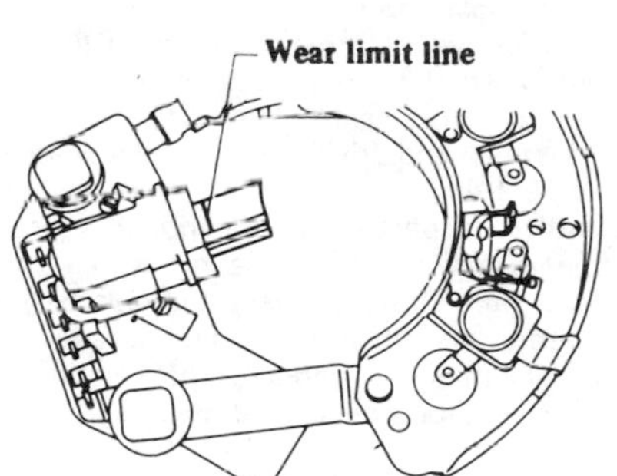

Fig. 10.4 Alternator brush wear limit line (Sec 7)

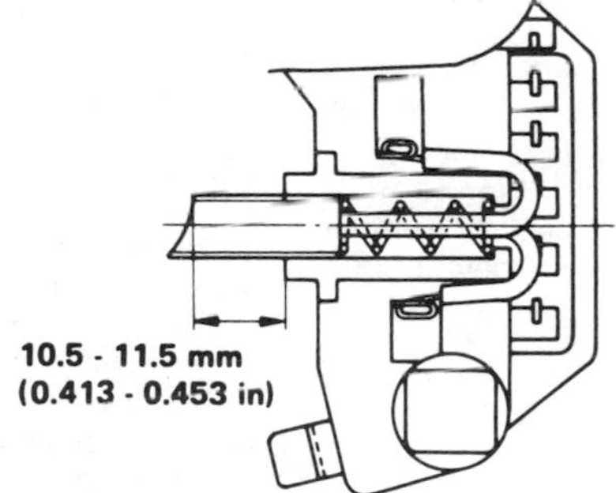

Fig. 10.5 Alternator brush positioning diagram (Sec 7)

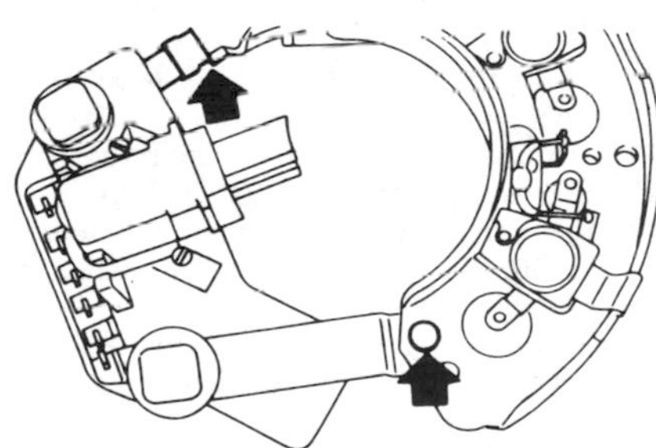

Fig. 10.6 Alternator brush holder/voltage regulator fixing points (Sec 7)

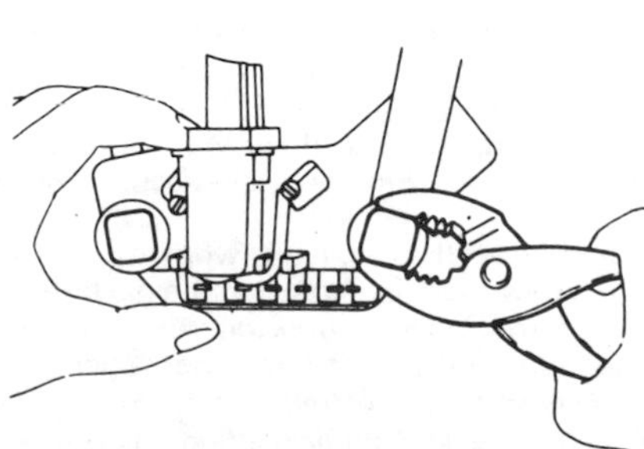

Fig. 10.7 Removing brush holder/regulator fixing bolt (Sec 7)

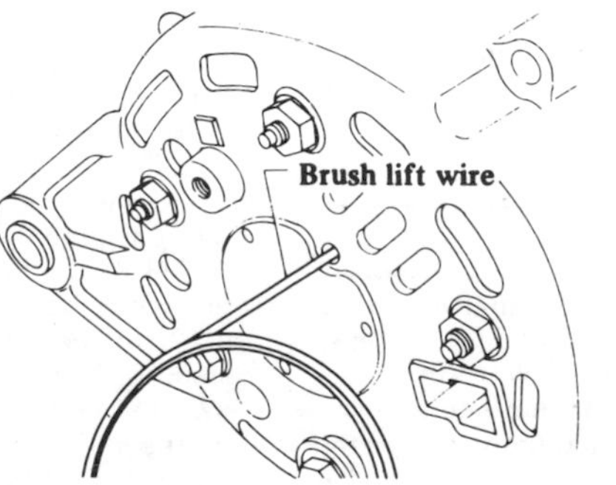

Fig. 10.8 Wire or rod used to retain alternator brushes in the retracted position (Sec 7)

4 When the starter switch is released, the solenoid is de-energised and a spring moves the plunger back to its rest position. This operates the pivoted lever to withdraw the drive pinion from engagement with the starter ring.
5 The starter motor used on vehicles equipped with automatic transmission incorporates an idler gear at the drive end.

9 Starter motor – testing in situ

1 If the starter motor fails to turn the engine when the switch is operated there are five possible causes:

(a) *The battery is faulty*
(b) *The electrical connections between the switch, solenoid, battery and starter motor are somewhere failing to pass the necessary current from the battery through the starter to earth*
(c) *The solenoid switch is faulty*
(d) *The starter motor is mechanically or electrically defective*
(e) *The starter motor pinion and/or flywheel ring gear is badly worn and in need of replacement*

2 To check the battery, switch on the headlights. If they dim after a few seconds the battery is in a discharged state. If the lights glow brightly, operate the starter switch and see what happens to the lights. If they dim then you know that power is reaching the starter motor but failing to turn it. If the starter turns slowly when switched on, proceed to the next check.
3 If, when the starter switch is operated, the lights stay bright, then insufficient power is reaching the motor. Remove the battery connections, starter/solenoid power connections and the engine earth strap and thoroughly clean them and refit them. Smear petroleum jelly around the battery connections to prevent corrosion. Corroded connections are the most frequent cause of electric system malfunctions.
4 When the above checks and cleaning tasks have been carried out, but without success, you will possibly have heard a clicking noise each time the starter switch was operated. This was the solenoid switch operating, but it does not necessarily follow that the main contacts were closing properly (if no clicking has been heard from the solenoid, it is certainly defective). The solenoid contact can be checked by putting a voltmeter or bulb across the main cable connection on the starter side of the solenoid and earth. When the switch is operated, there should be a reading or lighted bulb. If there is no reading or lighted bulb, the solenoid unit is faulty and should be renewed.
5 If the starter motor operates but doesn't turn the engine over then it is most probable that the starter pinion and/or flywheel ring gear are badly worn, in which case the starter motor will normally be noisy in operation.
6 Finally, if it is established that the solenoid is not faulty and 12 volts are getting to the starter, then the motor is faulty and should be removed for inspection.

10 Starter motor – removal and refitting

1 Disconnect the battery.
2 Disconnect the leads from the starter motor and solenoid terminals (photo).
3 Unscrew the starter motor fixing bolts and lift the unit from the engine.
4 Refitting is a reversal of removal.

11 Starter motor – overhaul

1 Such is the inherent reliability and strength of the starter motors fitted, it is very unlikely that a motor will need dismantling until it is totally worn out and in need of replacement as a whole.
2 If, however, the motor is only a couple of years old and a pinion carriage, solenoid system or brush fault is suspected then remove the motor from the engine and dismantle as described in the following paragraphs.
3 Extract the screws and remove the solenoid by tilting it to release its plunger from the shift lever. Retain the torsion spring and adjusting plate.

10.2 Starter solenoid terminals

4 Extract the screws and take off the rear cover.
5 Prise off the dust cap and E-ring (Fig. 10.11), and remove the thrust washers.
6 Remove the brush holder screws and the tie-bolts.
7 Remove the brush holder. To do this, pull the brush spring upwards and partially withdraw the brush. If the spring is now released it will apply pressure to the side of the brush and retain it in the partially withdrawn position.
8 Withdraw the yoke.
9 Withdraw the armature and shift lever from the drive end housing.
10 To remove the drive assembly from the armature shaft, tap the stop ring down the shaft to expose the circlip.
11 Prise the circlip from its groove, pull the stop ring off the shafts.
12 Remove the drive pinion assembly from the shaft.
13 On models with automatic transmission, remove the idler gear by prising out the E-ring and dust cap and driving out the idler shaft. Note which way round the gear is fitted.
14 With the motor dismantled, inspect all the components for wear.
15 If the commutator appears dirty or burned, clean it with a solvent-soaked rag and, if necessary, burnish it with very fine glasspaper.
16 If the segment insulators are flush with the surface of the segments, then the insulators must be undercut, as shown in Fig. 10.12. Use a thin hacksaw blade, or similar, and make sure that the undercut corners are square.
17 If an ohmmeter is available, test the armature for continuity between adjacent segments. The insulation can be tested by placing one probe of the test instrument on the armature shaft and the other on each segment in turn. If continuity is found to exist, the armature must be renewed.
18 Now check for continuity between the field coil positive terminal and the positive brush. If it does not exist, the field coils will have to be renewed.
19 Check the insulation by connecting one probe of the test instrument to the field coil positive terminal and the yoke. If continuity exists, the field coils must be renewed.
20 Renewal of starter motor field coils is a job best left to your dealer or auto-electrical agent due to the need for a pressure screwdriver and other equipment.
21 Check the brushes for wear. If they have worn down to the minimum specified length, renew them by removing the old brush lead and soldering on the new. Carry out the work quickly to avoid the spread of heat to the field coils, and do not allow the solder to seep down the lead or its flexibility will be impaired.
22 The brush holder can be checked for insulation breakdown by placing one probe of the tester on the positive side of the brush holder and the other one on the negative (baseplate) side. If continuity is indicated, renew the brush holder.
23 The solenoid switch can be checked for continuity by connecting the test instrument between the S terminal and the switch body. If no

continuity is indicated, renew the switch.
24 Now place the probes of the tester on the S and M terminals of the switch. If no continuity is indicated, renew the switch.
25 Finally check the teeth of the drive pinion and idler gear (automatic transmission). If they are worn or chipped renew the component. Test the pinion/clutch assembly for correct operation. It should turn smoothly in the drive direction and lock when turned in the reverse direction.
26 Reassemble by reversing the dismantling procedure. Lightly grease the friction surfaces, brushes, bearings and pivots as work proceeds.
27 On automatic transmission models, make sure that the idler gear is fitted the right way round with its collar opposite the groove in the pinion.
28 The pinion projection should now be checked by connecting the solenoid to a 12V battery to actuate it.
29 *On manual transmission models,* the clearance between the face of the pinion and the stop plate should be as specified in the Specifications at the beginning of this Chapter. If it is not, change the adjustment plate under the solenoid switch for one of different thickness. The plates are available in thicknesses of 0.5 mm (0.020 in) and 0.8 mm (0.031 in).
30 *On automatic transmission models,* with the solenoid actuated, measure the projection of the front face of the idler gear. Now measure again when the idler gear is pulled out by hand. The difference between the two measurements should be within the specified tolerance. If it is not, change the adjusting plate for one of suitable thickness.

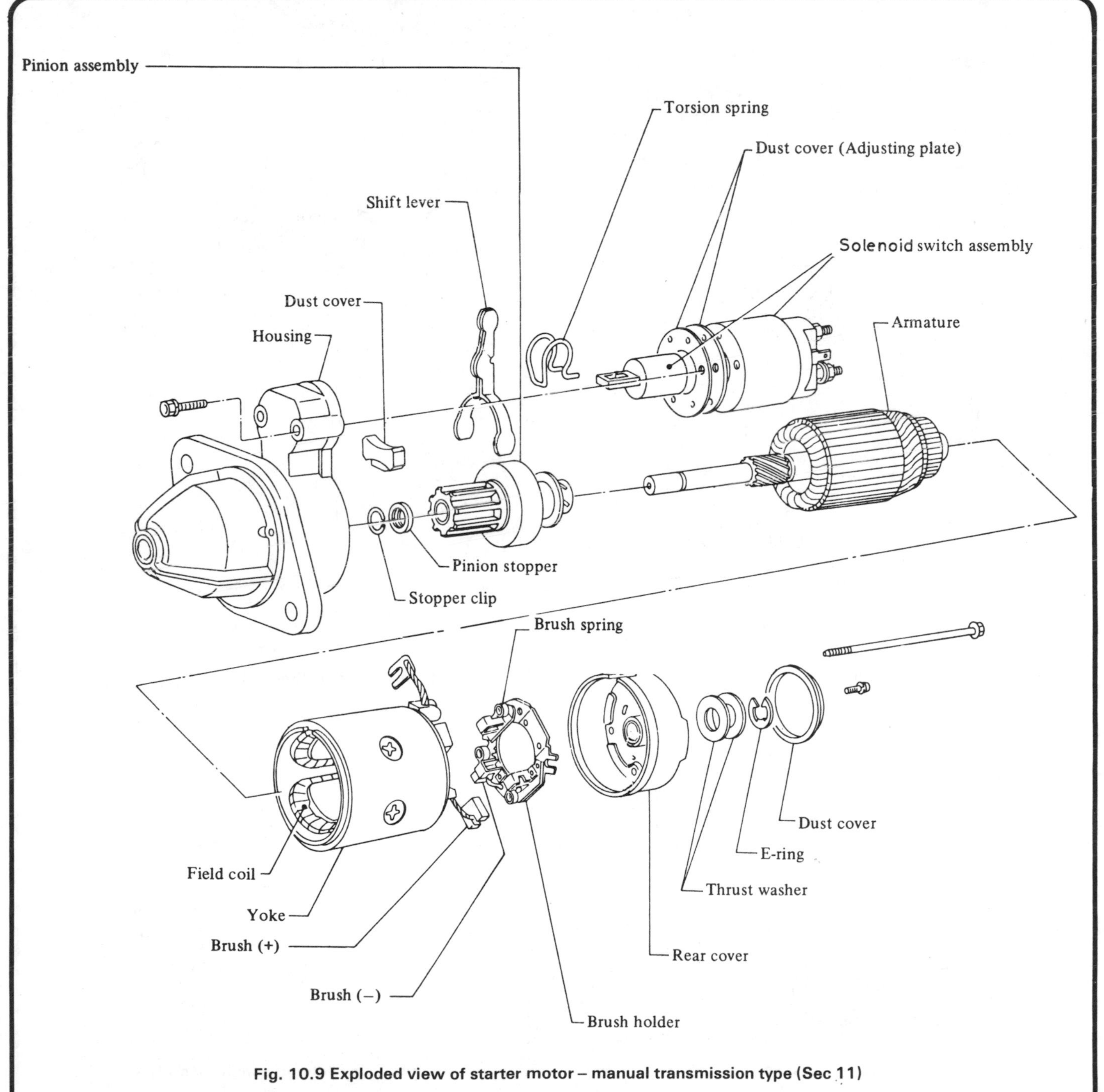

Fig. 10.9 Exploded view of starter motor – manual transmission type (Sec 11)

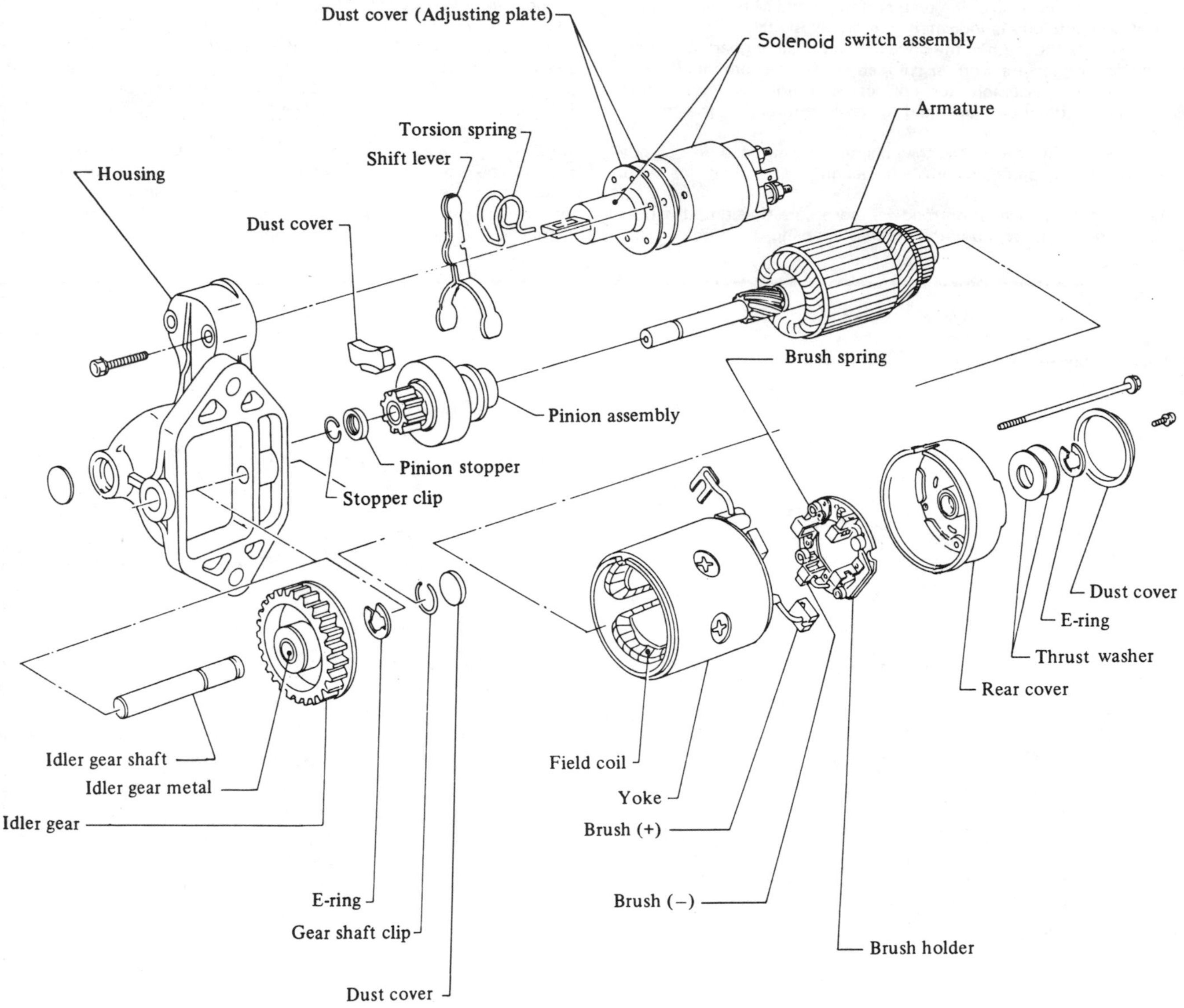

Dust cover (Adjusting plate)
Solenoid switch assembly
Armature
Torsion spring
Shift lever
Housing
Dust cover
Brush spring
Pinion assembly
Pinion stopper
Stopper clip
Dust cover
E-ring
Thrust washer
Rear cover
Idler gear shaft
Idler gear metal
Idler gear
Field coil
Yoke
Brush (+)
Brush (–)
Brush holder
E-ring
Gear shaft clip
Dust cover

Fig. 10.10 Exploded view of starter motor – automatic transmission type (Sec 11)

E-ring
Dust cover

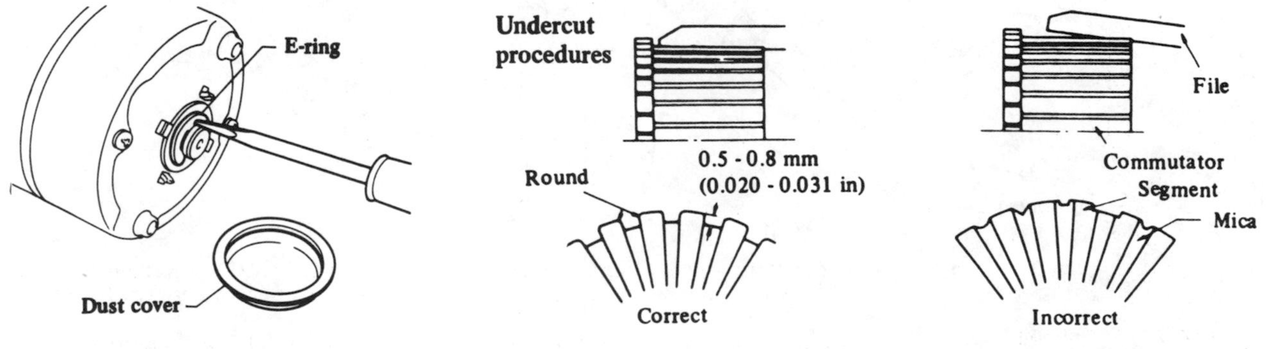

Fig. 10.11 Starter motor dust cap and E-ring (Sec 11)

Undercut procedures
File
0.5 - 0.8 mm
(0.020 - 0.031 in)
Round
Commutator
Segment
Mica
Correct
Incorrect

Fig. 10.12 Starter commutator insulator undercut (Sec 11)

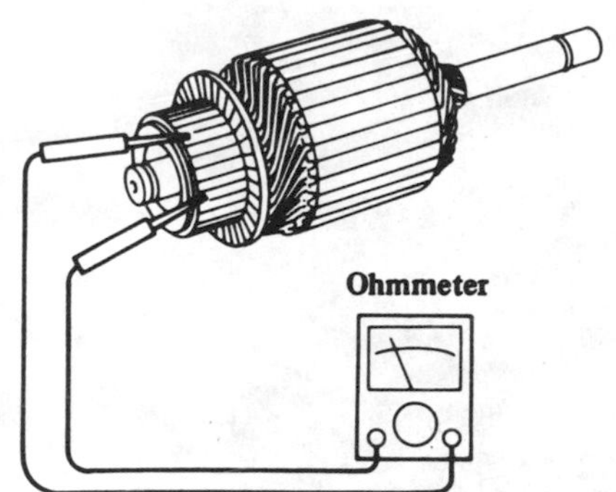

Fig. 10.13 Testing starter armature for continuity (Sec 11)

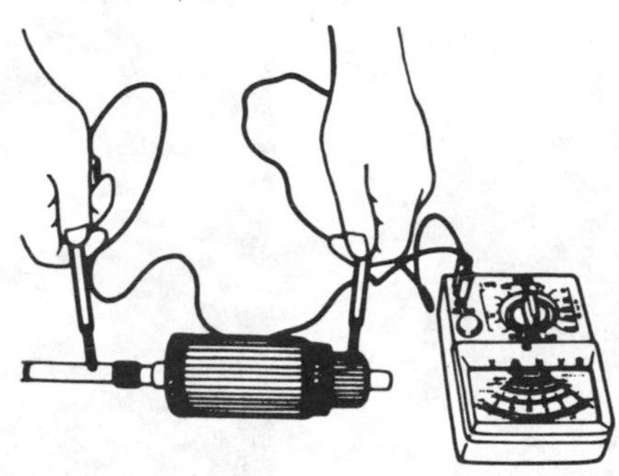

Fig. 10.14 Testing starter armature insulation (Sec 11)

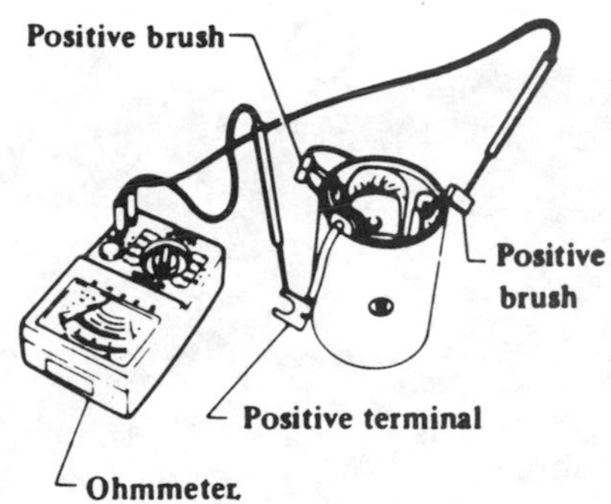

Fig. 10.15 Testing starter field coil for continuity (Sec 11)

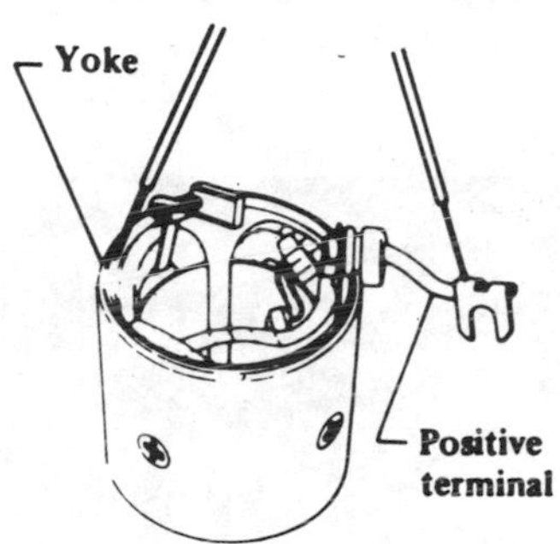

Fig. 10.16 Testing starter field coil insulation (Sec 11)

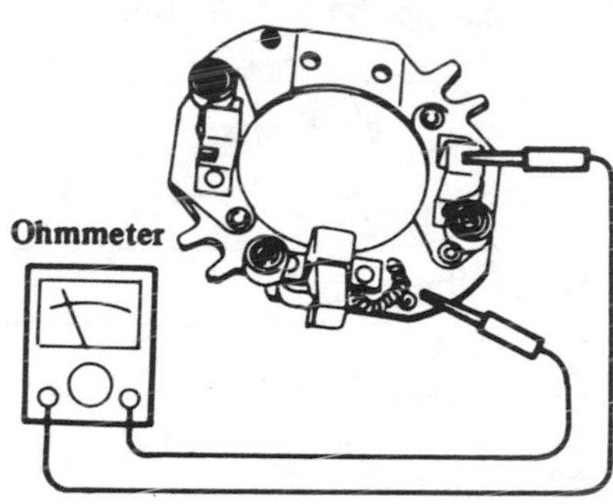

Fig. 10.17 Testing starter brush holder insulation (Sec 11)

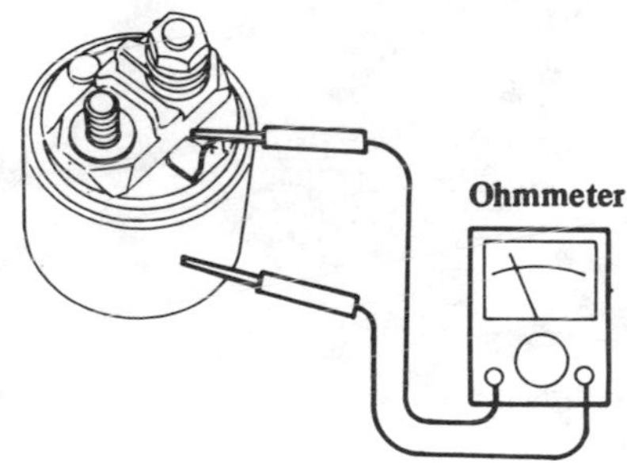

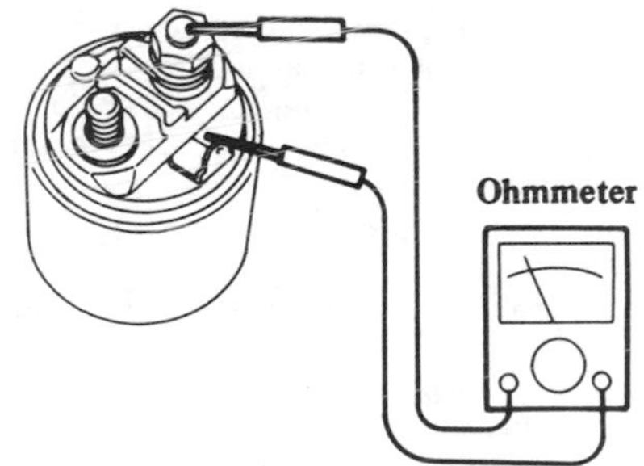

Fig. 10.18 Testing starter solenoid switch for continuity (Sec 11)

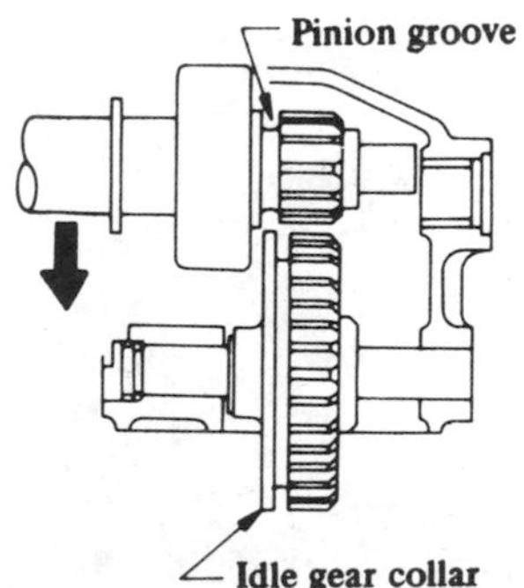

Fig. 10.19 Starter pinion-to-idler gear relationship – automatic transmission type (Sec 11)

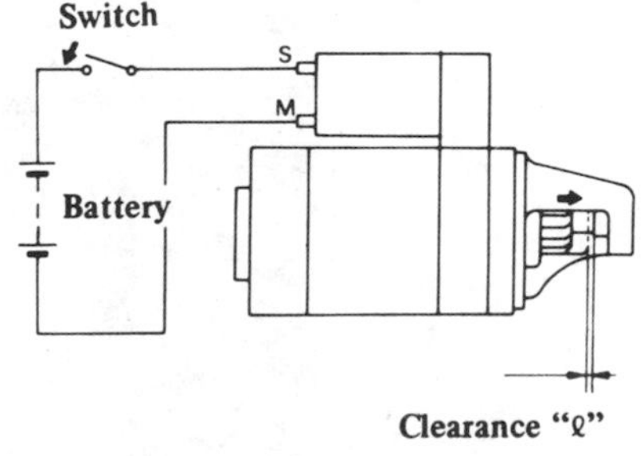

Fig. 10.20 Starter pinion setting diagram – manual transmission type (Sec 11)

Clearance = 0.3 to 2.5 mm (0.012 to 0.098 in)

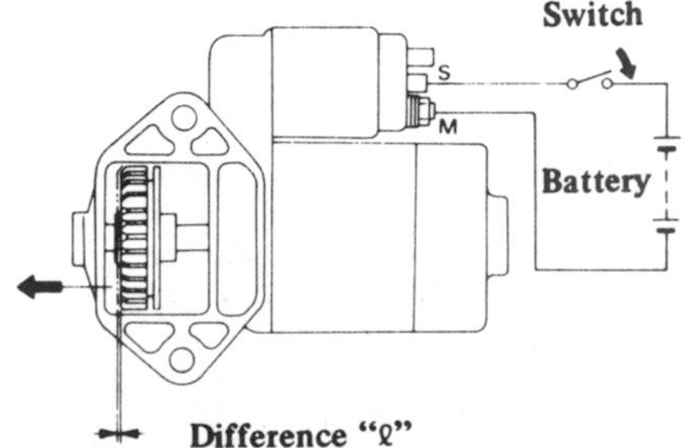

Fig. 10.21 Starter pinion setting diagram – automatic transmission type (Sec 11)

Difference = 0.3 to 2.5 mm (0.012 to 0.098 in)

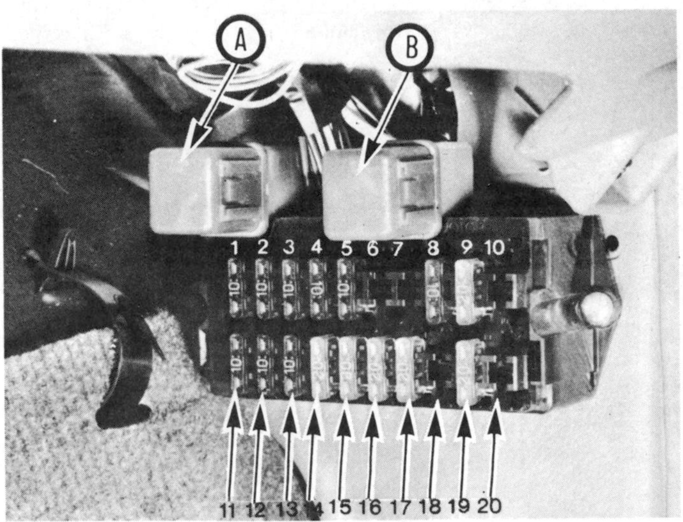

12.1 Fuse block

A Ignition relay *B Accessory relay*

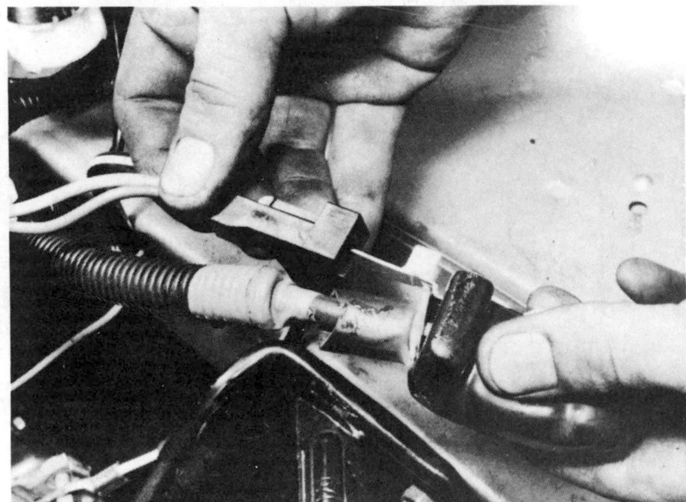

12.7 Fusible link connection at battery terminal

12 Fuses, fusible links and relays

Fuses

1 The fusebox (photo) is located inside the vehicle under the right-hand side of the facia panel.
2 Place the fingers under the fusebox cover and pull it off.
3 The fuses are of 10 to 20A rating according to the circuit which is protected.
4 A blown fuse can be detected visually and should be renewed with one of similar amperage.
5 If the new fuse blows immediately, suspect a short circuit, probably faulty insulation, which should be rectified at once.
6 Never substitute a fuse of higher amperage, or a piece of wire or foil as a means of preventing a fuse blowing, this could lead to a fire or severely damage the components of the circuit.

Fusible links

7 These are designed to melt in the event of a short in a major current carrying circuit (photo).
8 The links must never be taped up or placed in contact with adjacent wiring, plastic or rubber parts.
9 Before renewing a melted fusible link, rectify the cause or have a thorough check carried out on the vehicle wiring harness.

10 Fusible links are colour coded for ease of identification:

Green	*Ignition switch*
Red	*Power supply*
Brown	*Emission control (Californian and MPG models)*

Relays

11 The number and purpose of the relays fitted depends upon the particular model vehicle and its equipment.
12 All models have a direction indicator relay and a hazard warning relay located under the facia panel, adjacent to the steering column (photo).
13 All models also have an ignition and an accessory relay mounted just above the fuse block (see photo 12.1).
14 At the front corners of the engine compartment relays may be located which actuate the following:

Air conditioner
Air conditioner condenser fan
Horn
Headlamp dimmer
Rear foglamp
Automatic choke
Transmission switch

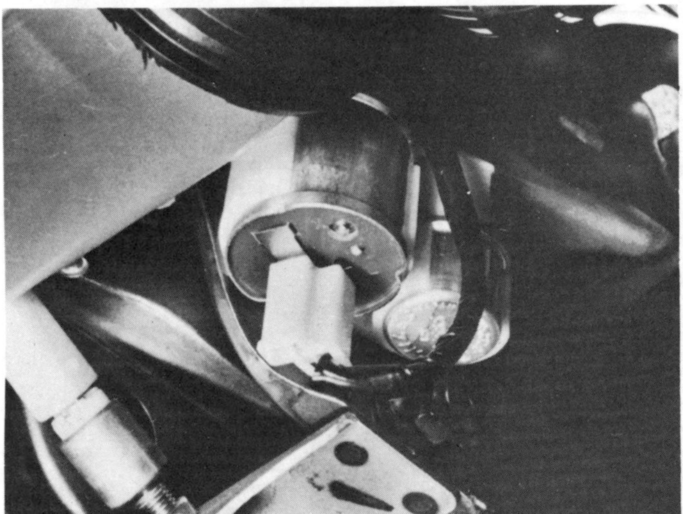

12.12 Direction indicator and hazard warning relays

12.15 Windscreen (intermittent) relay

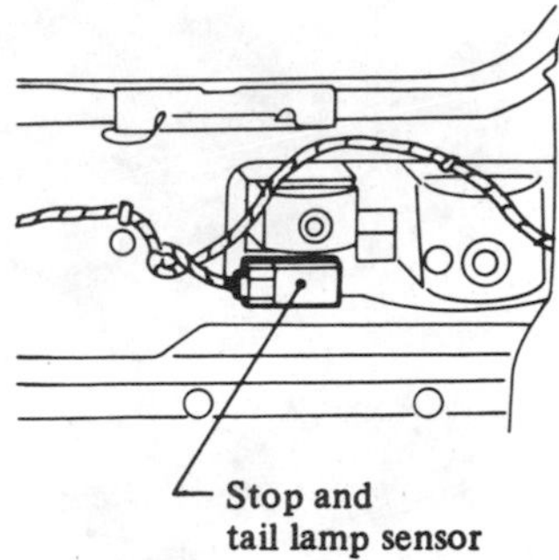

Fig. 10.22 Typical stop/tail lamp sensor (Sec 12)

15 On the engine compartment rear bulkhead a relay may be located which actuates the following:

Windscreen wiper (intermittent)

16 An anti-theft system warning buzzer (see Section 30) on certain models is located adjacent to the hazard warning and direction indicator relays.
17 A resistor for the tachometer (where fitted) is located on the engine compartment rear bulkhead.
18 On certain models, a stop/tail lamp sensor is located close to these lamps to indicate to the driver any failure of the bulbs.
19 On North American models relays are also included in the emission control system.

13 Steering column combination switch – removal and refitting

1 Remove the steering wheel, as described in Chapter 11. Remove the column shrouds.
2 Slacken the screw at the bottom of the left-hand side of the switch.
3 Withdraw the switch from the column (photo) and disconnect the wiring plugs as it moves up the column (photo).
4 Refitting is a reversal of removal.

14 Horn switch

1 The horn switches are located in the steering wheel spokes on Saloon models and at the hub of the wheel on Coupe and Estate models.
2 The switches are accessible once the spoke covers have been removed by extracting the screws from their rear faces, refer to Chapter 11 Section 13.

15 Courtesy lamp switch – removal and refitting

1 The courtesy lamp switch is not located, as is the usual practice, between the door front edge and the body pillar, but is fitted on the door closure face of the body (photo).
2 To remove the switch, extract the screw and pull the switch with leads from its hole.
3 If the leads are to be disconnected, tape them to the body panel to prevent them from slipping inside the body cavity.
4 Smear the switch contacts and plunger with petroleum jelly before fitting as an aid to preventing corrosion.

16 Facia panel mounted switches – removal and refitting

1 These switches are held in position by plastic tabs.
2 Reach up behind the switch and compress the tabs. Withdraw the switch far enough to be able to disconnect the wiring plug and remove the switch.
3 Refitting is a reversal of removal.

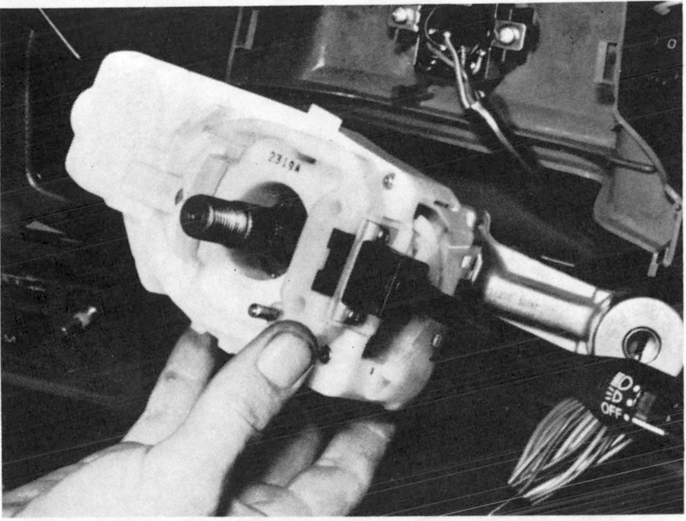

13.3A Withdrawing steering column switch

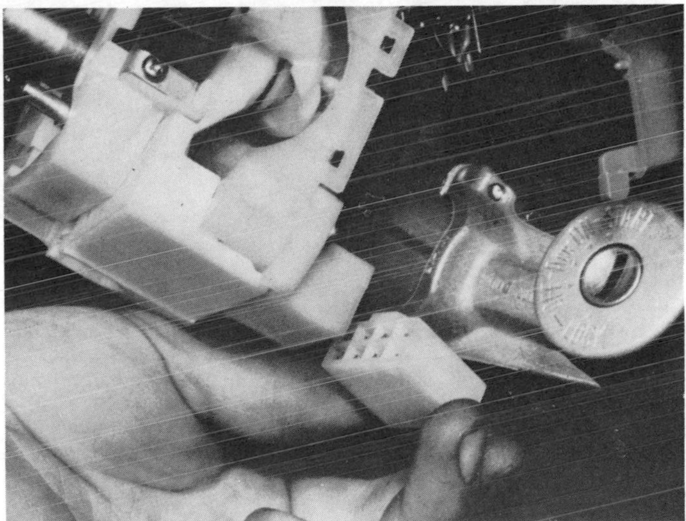

13.3B Disconnecting steering column switch wiring plug

15.1 Courtesy lamp switch

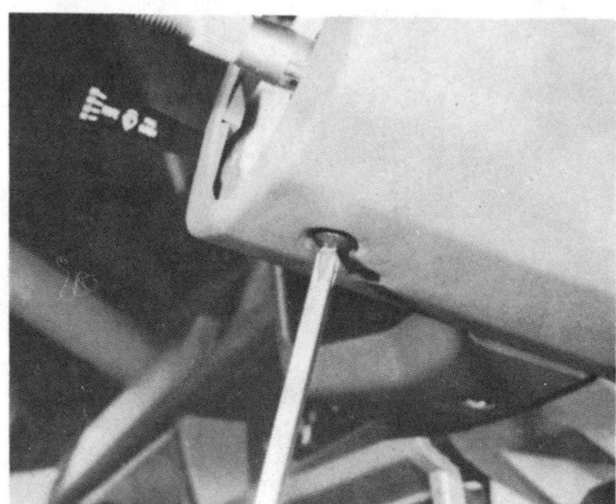
17.2A Removing steering column shroud screw

17.2B Hazard warning switch on underside of steering column upper shroud

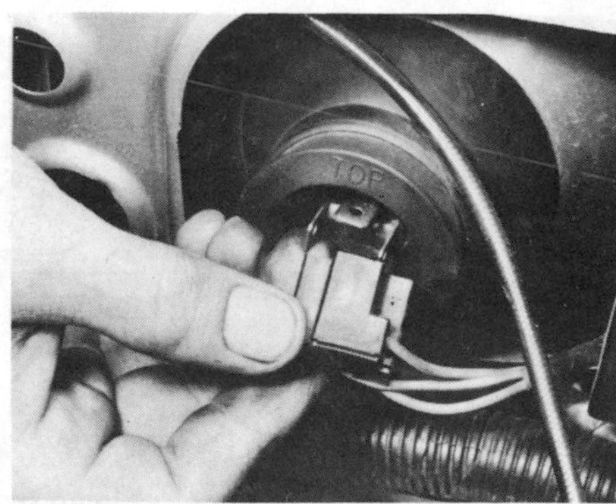
18.4 Headlamp bulb connecting plug

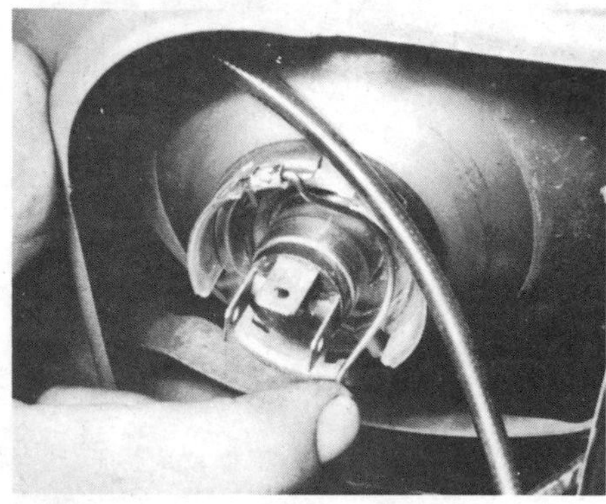
18.5 Removing headlamp bulb holder dust excluder

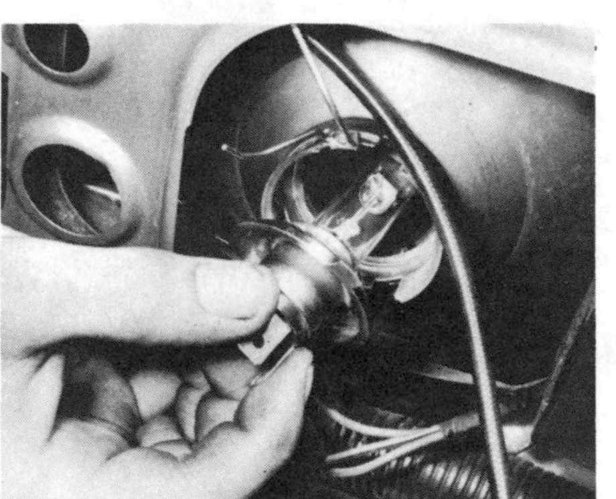
18.6 Removing headlamp bulb

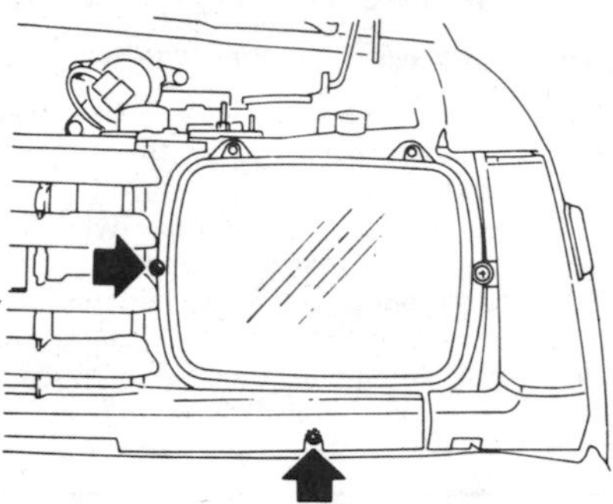
Fig. 10.23 Typical sealed beam type headlamp alignment adjusting screws (Sec 19)

17 Hazard warning switch – removal and refitting

1 The hazard warning switch is located on the steering column upper shroud.
2 Extract the retaining screw from the lower shroud (photo) and lift off the upper shroud to expose the switch mounted on its underside (photo).
3 Extract the two screws and remove the switch.
4 When refitting the switch do not overtighten the fixing screws.

18 Headlamp sealed beam unit or bulb – renewal

Sealed beam unit

1 Extract the two screws which hold the front sidelight in position, pull the lamp away.
2 Release the headlamp retaining screws, pull the headlamp forward and remove the wiring plug from the rear of the lamp.
3 Fit the new sealed beam unit by reversing the removal operations. Provided that the adjuster screws are not touched, the beam alignment will not have been altered.

Bulb type

4 Open the bonnet, pull the wiring connector from the rear of the headlamp (photo).
5 Peel off the rubber dust excluder (photo).
6 Prise back the spring clips and withdraw the bulb (photo).
7 With halogen type bulbs, avoid touching the glass of the bulb with the fingers, as any residual grease will shorten their life.
8 Refit by reversing the removal operations.

19 Headlamp beam alignment

1 It is recommended that this work is left to your dealer or a service station with the necessary optical beam setting equipment.

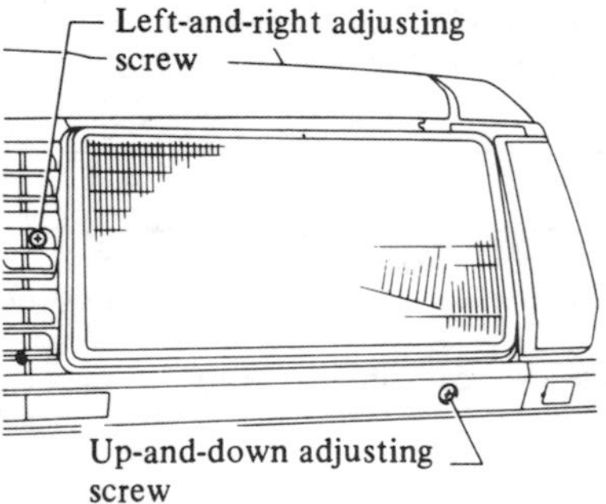

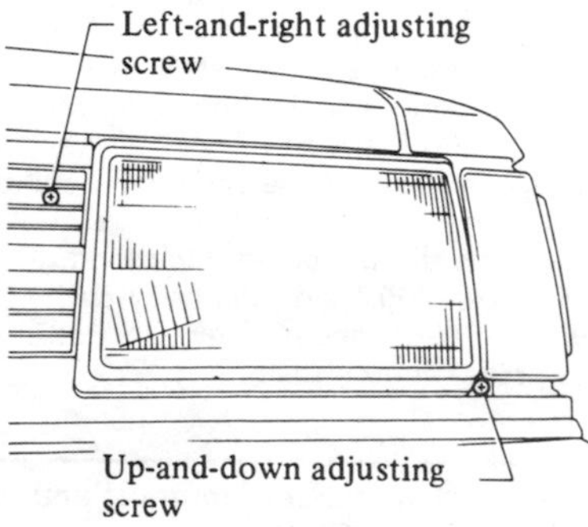

Fig. 10.24 Typical bulb type headlamp beam adjusting screws (Sec 19)

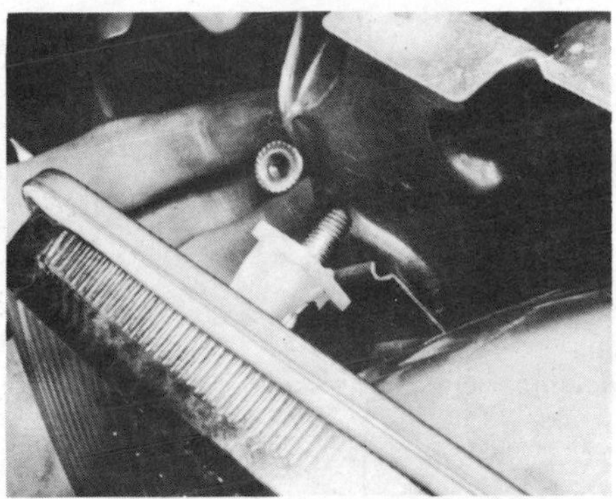
20.3 Headlamp body retaining stud and nut

20.4 Headlamp retaining fork and adjuster screw

21.1A Front sidelight screw (lower)

21.1B Front sidelight screw (upper)

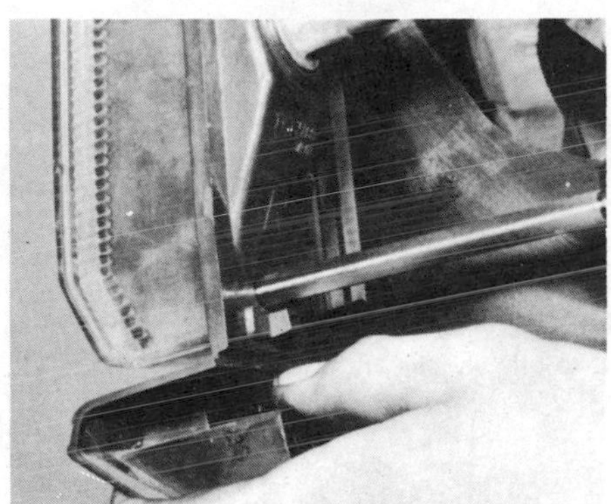
21.2 Extracting front sidelight lens screw

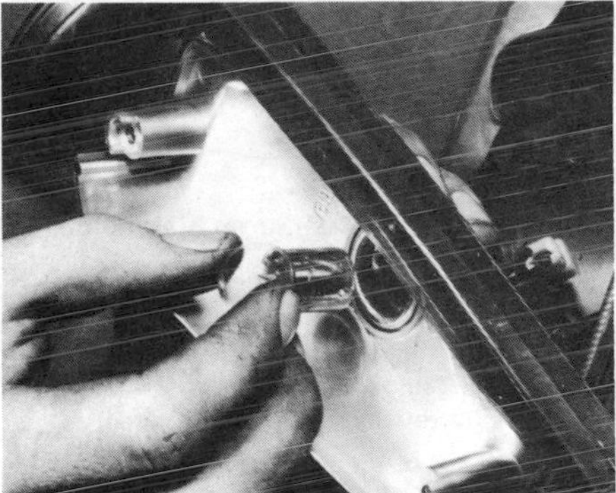
21.3 Front sidelight bulb

2 In an emergency the beams can be set in the following way.
3 Position the vehicle square to a wall or screen during the hours of darkness. The specified distance for vehicles with sealed beam headlamps is 7.6 m (25.0 ft) or for bulb type headlamps 5.0 m (16.0 ft).
4 Measure the height and separation of the centres of the headlamps and then transpose the measurements onto the wall.
5 Switch the headlamps to dipped beam and adjust the beam so that the upper edge of the brightest spot is level with the lamp centre mark on the wall.
6 Two beam adjusting screws are provided – one for vertical and the other for horizontal movement. The screws are accessible if a screwdriver is inserted through the end of the radiator grille and also through its lower slat (see Figs. 10.23 and 10.24).

20 Headlamp unit – removal and refitting

1 Disconnect the wiring plug from the bulb holder or sealed beam unit, according to type, as described in Section 18.
2 Unscrew and remove the radiator grille (Chapter 12).
3 Unscrew the nut from the upper outboard side of the headlamp unit (photo).
4 Swivel the headlamp so that its anchor fork slips out from under the head of the adjuster screw (photo). Disconnect the tension spring and lift the headlamp away.
5 Refit by reversing the removal operations. Provided the beam adjusting screws are not turned, the beam alignment should not have altered.

21 Exterior lamps – bulb renewal

Front sidelight

1 Remove the screws which hold the lamp in position. One screw is located at the base (photo) and the other either half-way up, or on top and slightly to the side, depending upon operating territory (photo).
2 Withdraw the lamp until the lens retaining screws on its reverse side can be extracted (photo).
3 Remove the bayonet type bulb from its holder (photo).
4 Fit the new bulb, and reassemble and refit the lamp by reversing the removal and dismantling operations.

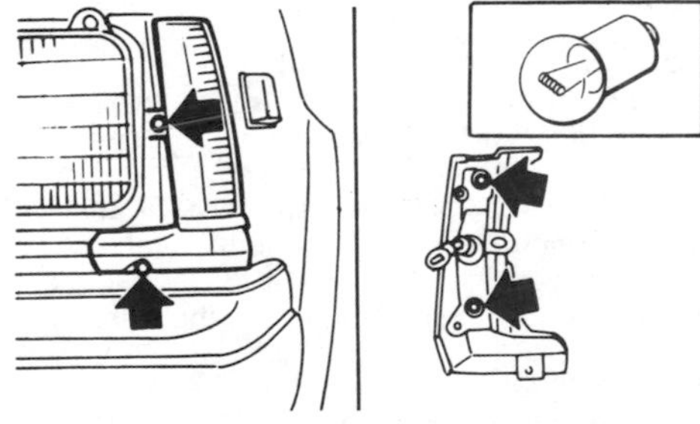
Fig. 10.25 Front sidelight retaining screws (Sec 21)

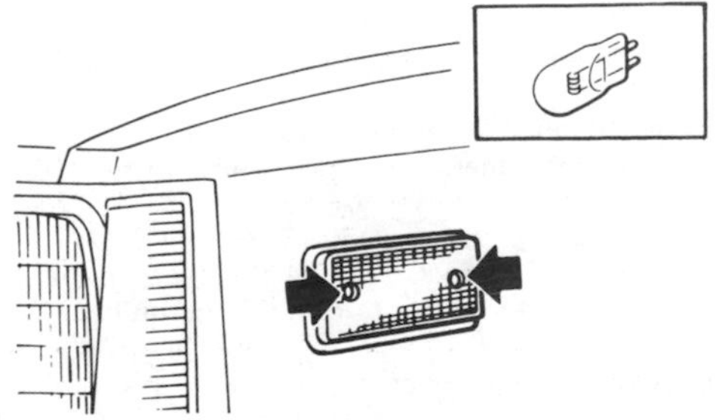
Fig. 10.26 Front side indicator lamp screws – North American (Sec 21)

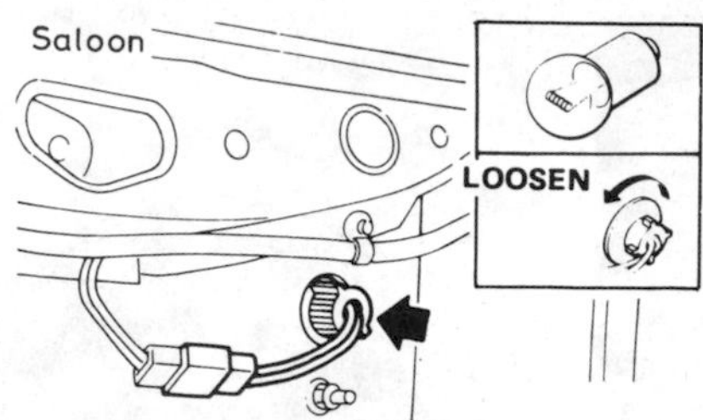

Fig. 10.27 Saloon number plate lamp – North American (Sec 21)

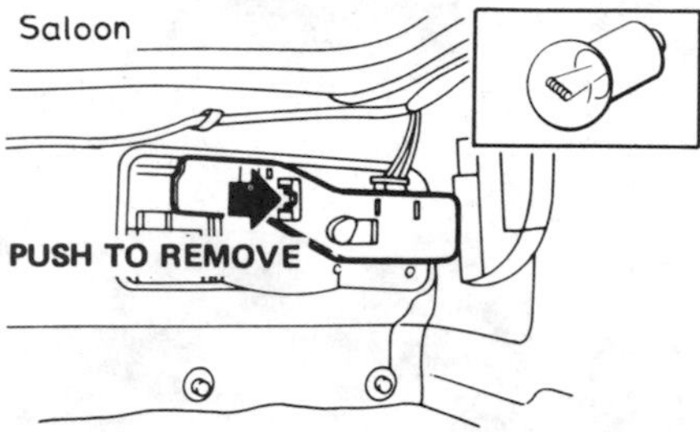

Fig. 10.29 Rear lamp bulb holder – Saloon (Sec 21)

Front direction indicator lamp

5 Remove the two lens fixing screws (photo), take off the lens and remove the bulb (photo)

6 Refit by reversing the procedure.

Front side indicator lamp

Except N America

7 Turn the lamp in an anti-clockwise direction and withdraw it. Twist the bulb holder to remove the bulb (photo).

N America

8 Remove the two lens fixing screws, take off the lens and remove the bulb.

9 Refit by reversing the procedure.

Rear side indicator lamp (N America)

10 Access to the bulb is obtained as for the similar type of front side indicator lamp.

Rear number plate lamp

Saloon (except N America)

11 Pull the lamp (against the resistance of its spring clips) out of the bumper.

12 Remove the screws from the rear face of the lamp (photo), separate the lens (photo) and remove the bulb (photo).

Saloon (N America)

13 Unscrew the knurled ring and then twist the bulb holder to remove it.

Estate

14 Raise the tailgate and remove the lens screws

Rear lamp cluster

Saloon

15 Push the plastic retaining clip and pull the lamp assembly from the luggage compartment rear panel. All the bulbs are of bayonet type (photo).

Coupe and Hatchback

16 Pull off the cover panels and twist the bulb holders to remove them.

Estate

17 Pull the lamp cover panel towards the rear of the vehicle and remove it. Twist the bulb holder to remove the bulb.

Rear foglamp

18 Located in the rear bumper, the bulb is accessible after removing the lens (two screws).

19 Refitting of all rear lamp bulbs is a reversal of removal.

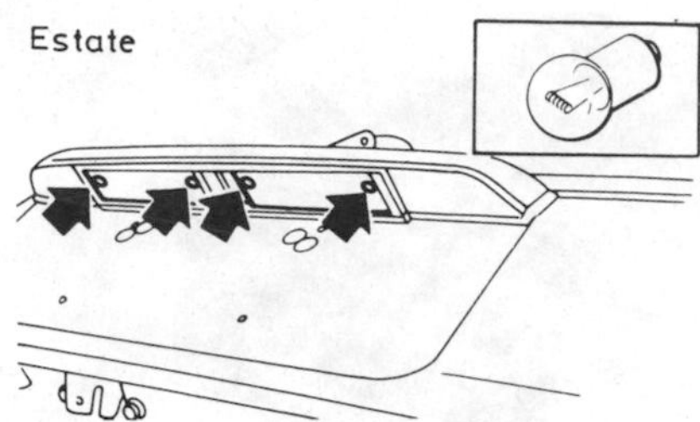

Fig. 10.28 Estate number plate lamp screws (Sec 21)

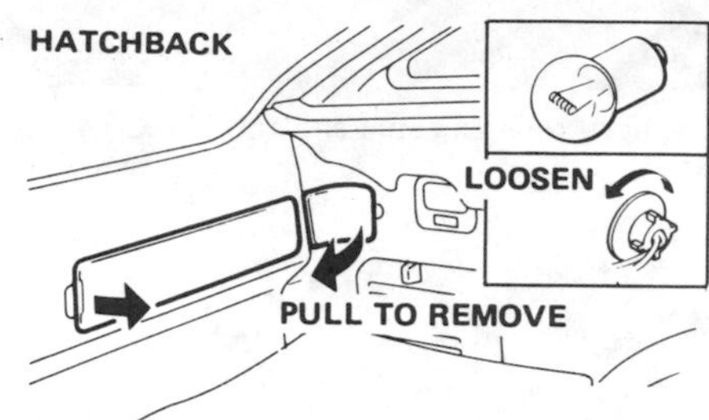

Fig. 10.30 Rear lamp bulb holder cover – Coupe and Hatchback (Sec 21)

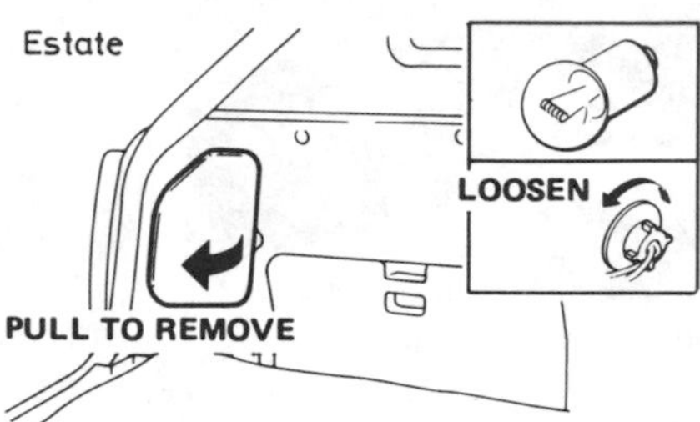

Fig. 10.31 Rear lamp bulb holder cover – Estate (Sec 21)

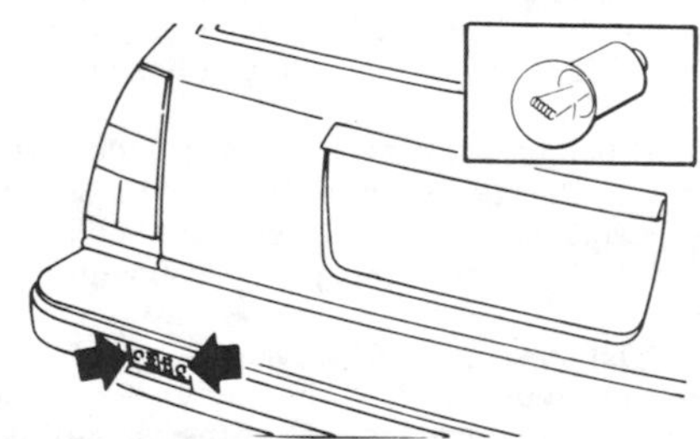
Fig. 10.32 Rear foglamp lens screws (Sec 21)

21.5A Removing front direction indicator lamp lens screw

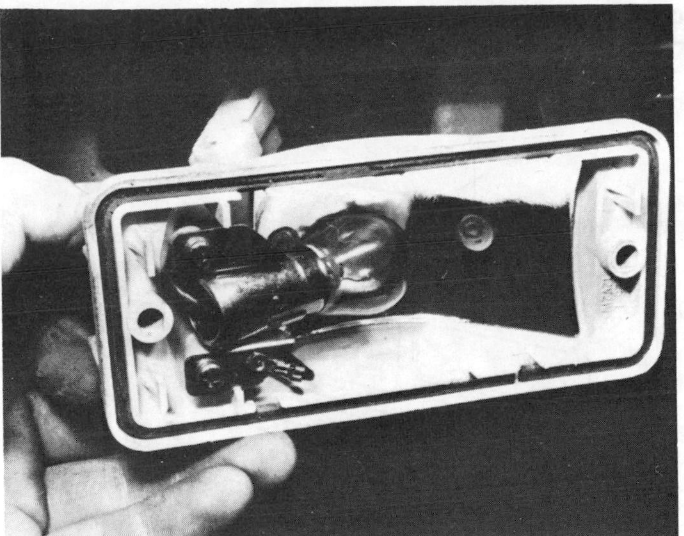

21.5B Front direction indicator lamp body and bulb

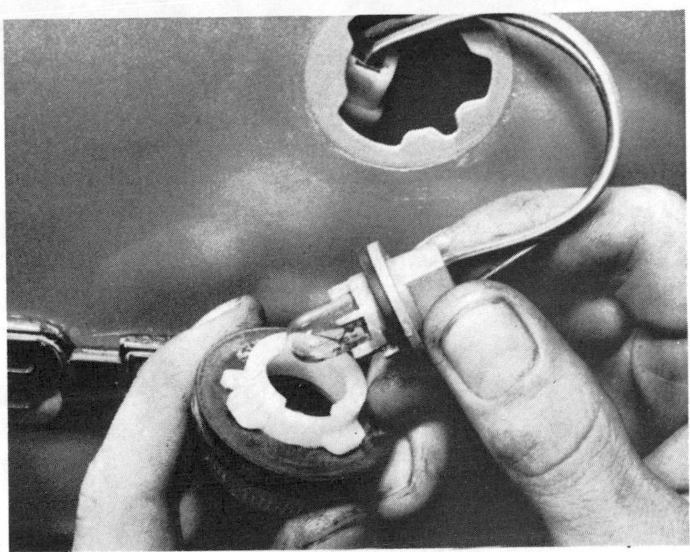

21.7 Side indicator lamp and bulb

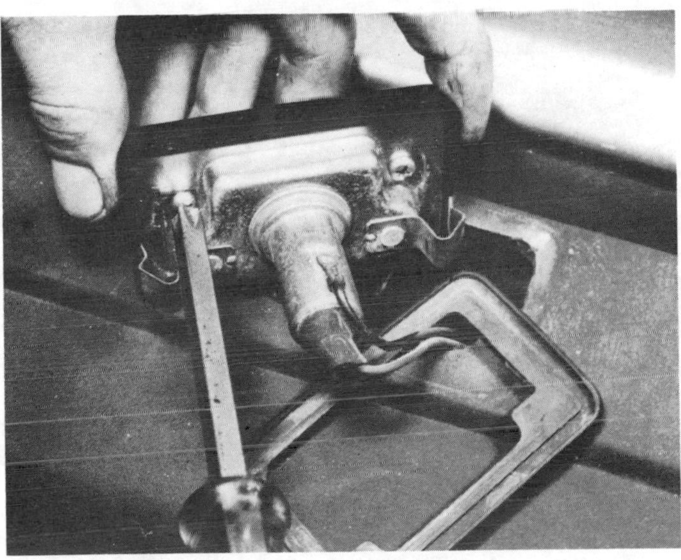

21.12A Removing rear number plate lamp lens screw

21.12B Separating rear number plate lamp lens

21.12C Rear number plate lamp bulb

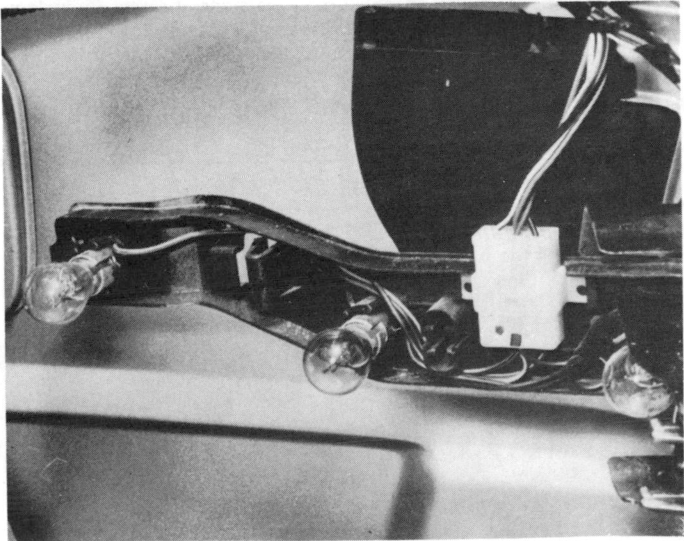

21.15 Rear lamp bulb holder (Saloon)

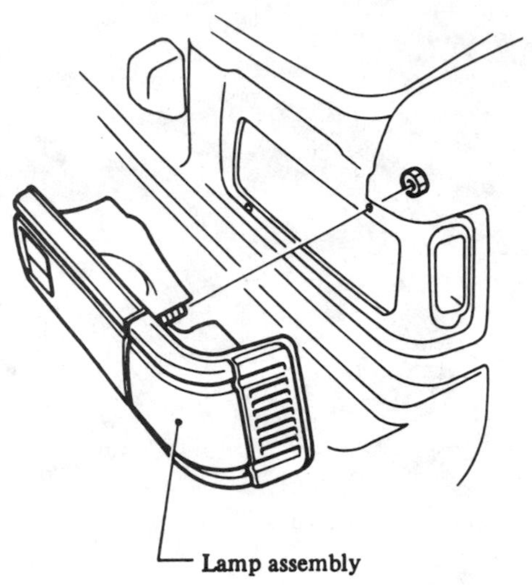

Fig. 10.33 Rear lamp lens (Saloon) – North American (Sec 22)

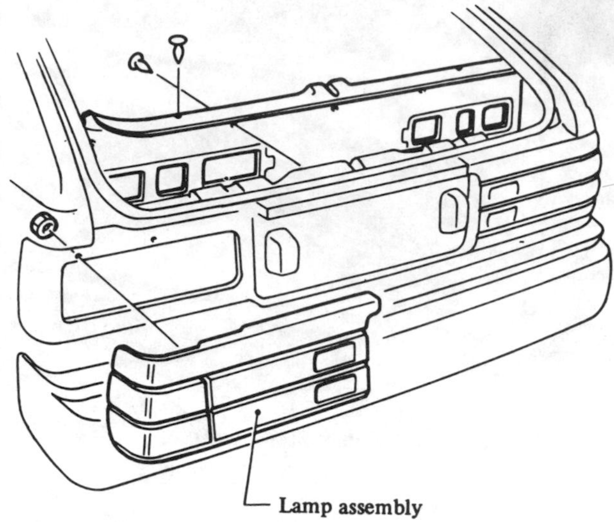

Fig. 10.34 Rear lamp lens (Coupe) – North American (Sec 22)

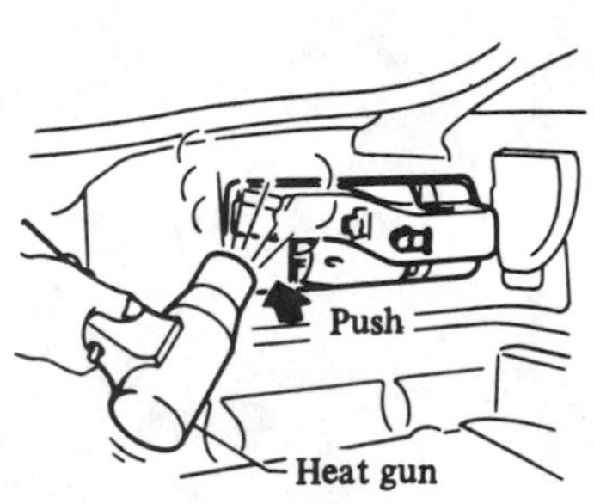

Fig. 10.35 Method of rear lamp lens removal (Sec 22)

23.1 Interior lamp lens

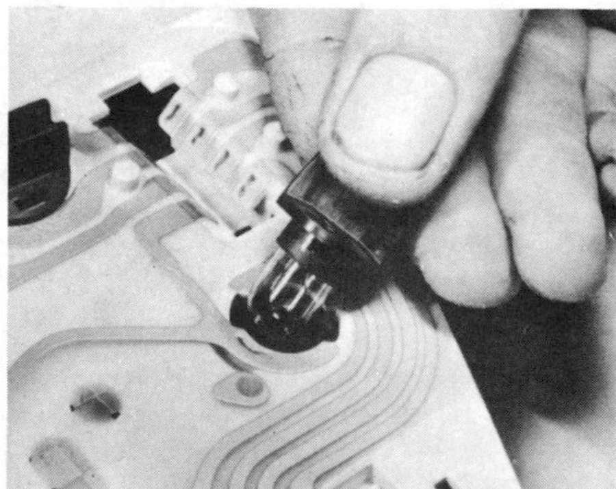

23.6 Warning/indicator lamp at rear of instrument panel

22 Rear lamp lens assembly (N America) – removal and refitting

1 On N American Saloon and Coupe versions the rear lamp lens clusters are sealed into the body with Butyl type sealant.
2 A heat gun is required to remove and refit this type of lamp by raising the temperature surrounding the lamp to just under 60°C (140°F). A single nut is used for positioning purposes.

23 Interior lamps – bulb renewal

Interior (roof) lamp

1 The lens is removed from the circular of lamp by twisting it in an anti-clockwise direction. The festoon bulb is then exposed for renewal (photo).
2 The rectangular type lamp lens is removed simply by pulling it from the lamp base.

Luggage compartment lamp

3 This is fitted into the luggage area of all models except the Saloon.
4 Remove the lens screws and the lens for access to the bulb.

Instrument panel warning and indicator lamps

5 The wedge type bulbs are accessible if the instrument panel is partially pulled from the facia panel, as described in Section 24.
6 The bulb holders can then be twisted out of the printed circuit and the bulbs renewed (photo).

24 Instrument panel – removal and refitting

1 Remove the two screws which secure the lower part of the instrument panel hood.
2 Tilt the hood upwards, release the retaining clips (photo) and remove the hood. At the same time disconnecting the switch and warning lamp wires from the lower section of the hood which is moulded to form a switch/indicator lamp panel.
3 Unscrew the two upper and two lower self-tapping screws from the instrument panel (photo).
4 Pull the panel towards you (photo) while an assistant eases the speedometer drive cable through its bulkhead grommet.
5 Reach behind the panel and disconnect the speedometer drive cable. Do this by squeezing the knurled part of the plastic connector.
6 Disconnect the wiring plugs at the rear of the panel (photo).
7 Remove the instrument panel from the facia (photo).
8 Refitting is a reversal of removal.

25 Windscreen wiper blades and arms – removal and refitting

1 The wiper blades should be renewed as soon as they cease to wipe the glass cleanly.
2 The complete blade assembly or just the rubber insert are available as replacements.
3 Pull the wiper arm from the glass until it locks.
4 Depress the small tab and slide the blade off the arm (photo).
5 Refitting is a reversal of removal.

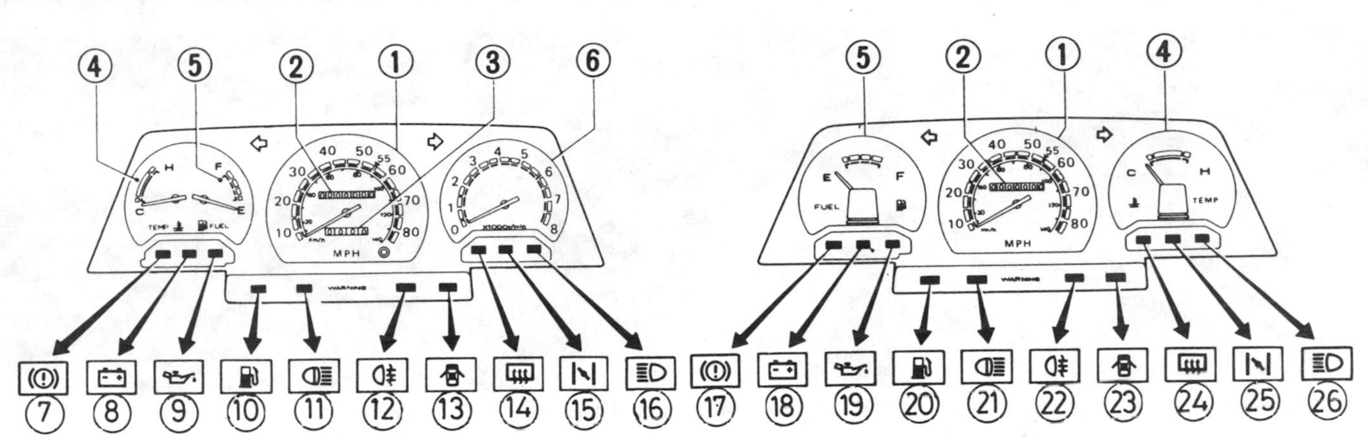

Fig. 10.36 Alternative types of instrument panel (Sec 24)

Type A
1 *Speedometer*
2 *Odometer (mileage recorder)*
3 *Mileage trip recorder*
4 *Coolant temperature gauge*
5 *Fuel gauge*
6 *Tachometer (rev counter)*
7 *Handbrake 'on' warning*
8 *Charge (ignition) warning*
9 *Oil pressure*
10 *Low fuel level*
11 *Stop/tail bulb warning*
12 *Rear fog*
13 *Anti-theft (door open, ignition on)*
14 *Heated rear window*
15 *Choke 'on' warning*
16 *Headlamp main beam*

Type B
1 *Speedometer*
2 *Odometer*
4 *Coolant temperature gauge*
5 *Fuel gauge*
17 *Handbrake 'on' warning*
18 *Charge (ignition warning)*
19 *Oil pressure*
20 *Low fuel level*
21 *Stop/tail bulb warning*
22 *Rear fog*
23 *Anti-theft (door open, ignition on)*
24 *Heated rear window*
25 *Choke 'on' warning*
26 *Headlamp main beam*

On N American models, an emission control service interval warning lamp is sometimes fitted

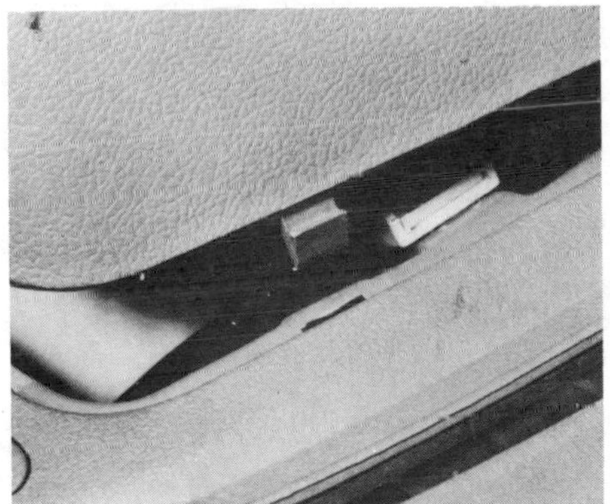
24.2 Releasing instrument panel hood clips

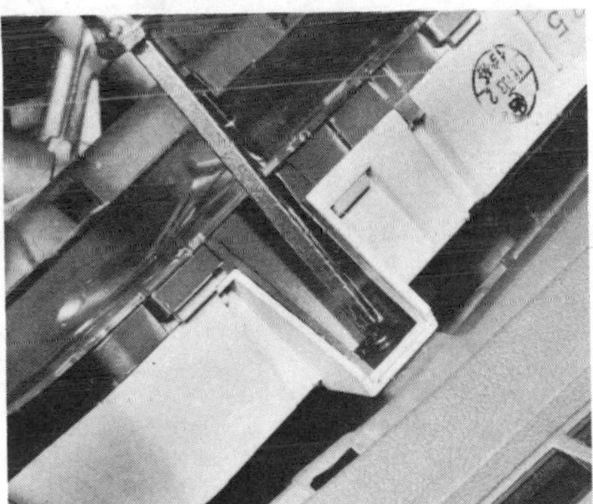
24.3 Removing instrument panel upper screw

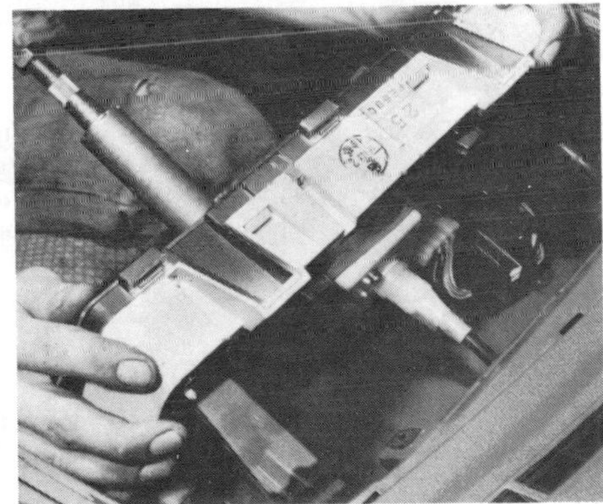
24.4 Withdrawing instrument panel

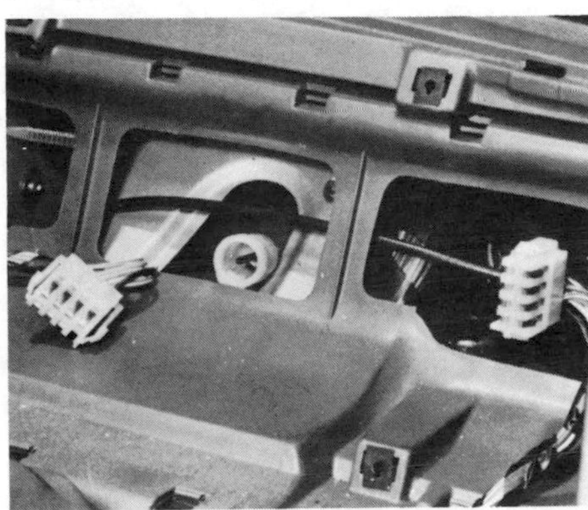
24.6 Instrument panel withdrawn, showing wiring plugs

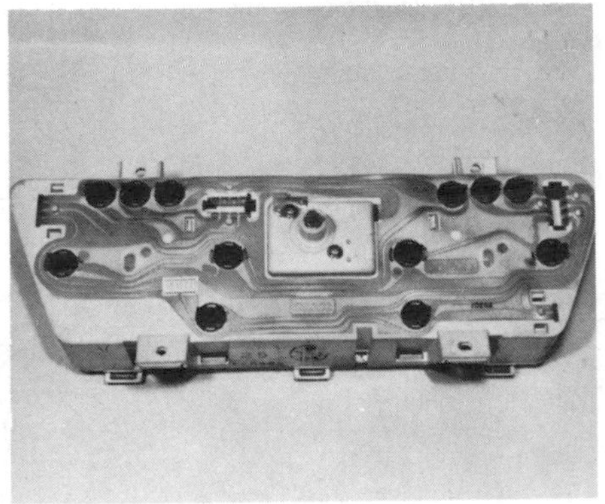
24.7 Rear view of instrument panel

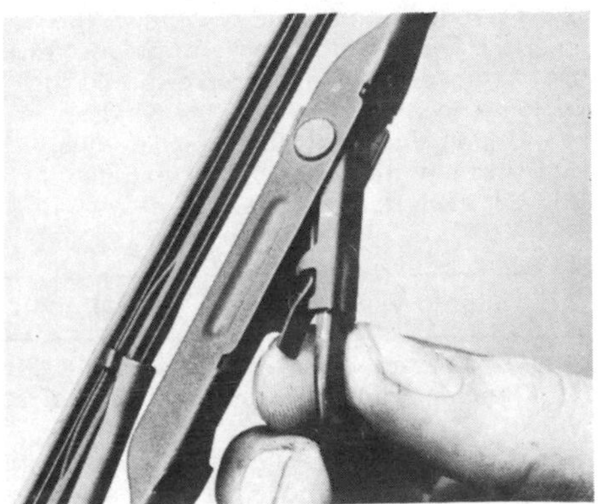
25.4 Disconnecting wiper blade from arm

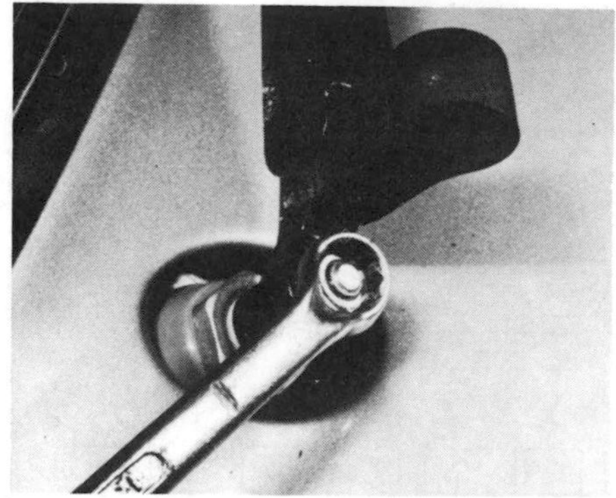
25.7 Unscrewing wiper arm nut

26.3 Heater air intake grille removed

26.5 Windscreen wiper motor

26.6 Windscreen wiper linkage

28.3 Washer pump

6 Before removing a wiper arm, it is worthwhile sticking a strip of masking tape on the glass against the edge of the wiper blade as a guide to wiper arm setting when refitting.
7 Lift up the cap to expose the nut which holds the wiper arm to the driving spindle (photo).
8 Unscrew the nut and pull the arm/blade assembly from the spindle splines.
9 Refit by reversing the removal operations.
10 Wet the glass and operate the wipers to check their arc of travel. If it is incorrect, remove the arm and move it a spline or two in the required direction.

26 Windscreen wiper motor/linkage – removal and refitting

1 Remove the wiper arms, as described in the preceding Section.
2 Open the bonnet and disconnect the wiper motor wiring. Disconnect the wiper motor crankarm by unscrewing the nut.
3 Remove the retaining screws and then pull the air intake grille, which is located in front of the windscreen, off its clips (photo).
4 Unbolt the wiper drive spindle units.
5 Unscrew the wiper motor mounting bolts (photo).
6 Lift away the motor and then withdraw the linkage (photo).

27 Tailgate wiper motor – removal and refitting

1 The tailgate wiper motor is of direct drive type, without linkages.
2 The wiper arm/blade is removed as described for the windscreen wiper in Section 25.
3 Open the tailgate and disconnect the wiper motor wiring.
4 Unscrew and remove the drive spindle nut.
5 Unbolt and remove the motor mounting bolts.
6 Refitting is a reversal of removal. Check the arc of travel of the wiper arm.

28 Washer system

1 All models are equipped with a windscreen washer.
2 The washer reservoir is located within the engine compartment.
3 On vehicles with a tailgate washer, the fluid reservoir with its electric pump serves both the windscreen and tailgate (photo).
4 Where a headlamp washer system is fitted, a separate fluid reservoir is used.
5 The windscreen wiper/washer is controlled by a stalk switch on the steering column.
6 The tailgate wiper/washer is controlled by a double action rocker switch.
7 The headlamp washer switch is of single action rocker type.
8 The washer jets which are located within the slats of the air intake grille are adjusted by inserting a pin in their nozzles and repositioning them to give a satisfactory spray pattern.

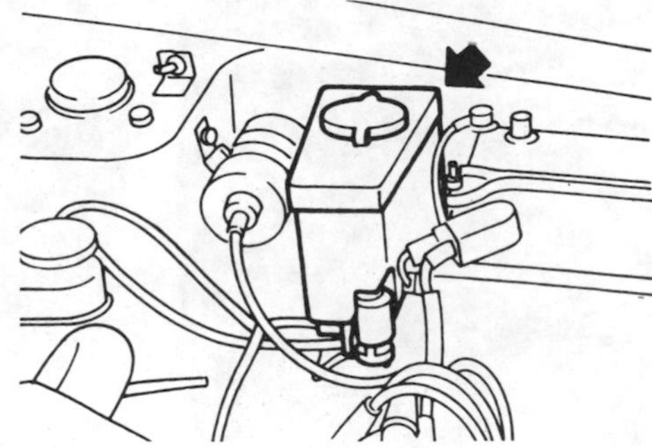
Fig. 10.37 Screen washer fluid reservoir (Sec 28)

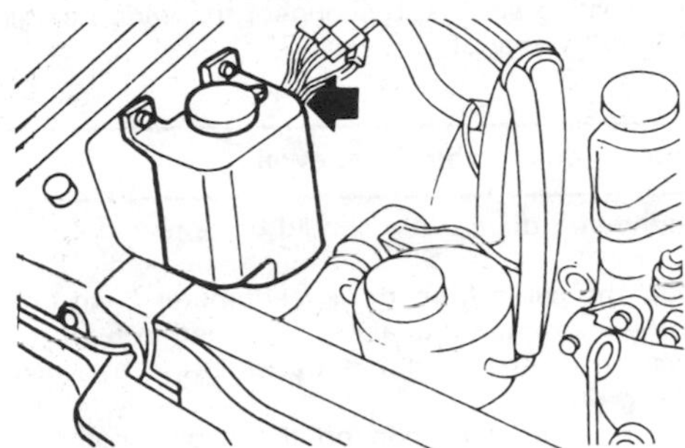

Fig. 10.38 Headlamp washer fluid reservoir (Sec 28)

29 Heated rear window

1 Care should be taken to avoid damage to the element for the heated rear window or tailgate.
2 Avoid scratching with rings on the fingers when cleaning, and do not allow luggage to rub against the glass.
3 Do not stick labels over the element on the inside of the glass.
4 If the element grids do become damaged, a special conductive paint is available from most motor factors to repair it.
5 Do not leave the heated rear window switched on unnecessarily as it draws a high current from the electrical system.

30 Anti-theft system

This system is fitted to some models as a device to prevent the vehicle being left unattended while the ignition key is in the lock.

A warning chime or buzzer sounds if the driver's door is opened while the ignition key is in the lock in the ACC, OFF or LOCK positions.

31 'Lights on' warning system

On certain Coupe models, a warning sound is given if the driver's door is opened and the iginition key removed while the lamps are on.

32 Seat belt warning system

On certain models the seat belt on the driver's side incorporates a visual and audible warning as a reminder that the belt is not connected when starting the vehicle.

The warnings are given for a six second period if the ignition key is turned to ON without the seat belt having been fastened.

33 Clock – setting, removal and refitting

1 To set the clock, depress the knob in the centre of the clock face and turn the knob.
2 To remove the clock carefully prise it from the facia panel against the resistance of its plastic retaining clips. Disconnect the wiring plug.
3 Refitting is a reversal of removal.

34 Radio – removal and refitting

1 A radio is fitted as standard equipment on all models.
2 Remove the ashtray.
3 Extract the single screw and remove the ashtray shield.
4 Remove the two screws from the underside of the radio.
5 Pull off the radio control knobs (photo).
6 Unscrew the control spindle bezel nuts and take off the washers (photos).
7 Prise the lower edge of the escutcheon panel upwards and then release the clips at the upper edge.
8 Withdraw the radio (photo) until the power, aerial and speaker leads can be disconnected.

34.5 Radio control knob

34.6A Radio control spindle bezel nut

34.6B Radio control spindle washer

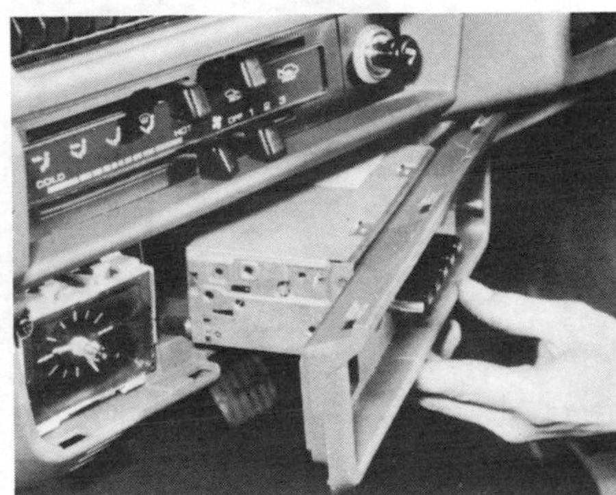

34.8 Removing the radio

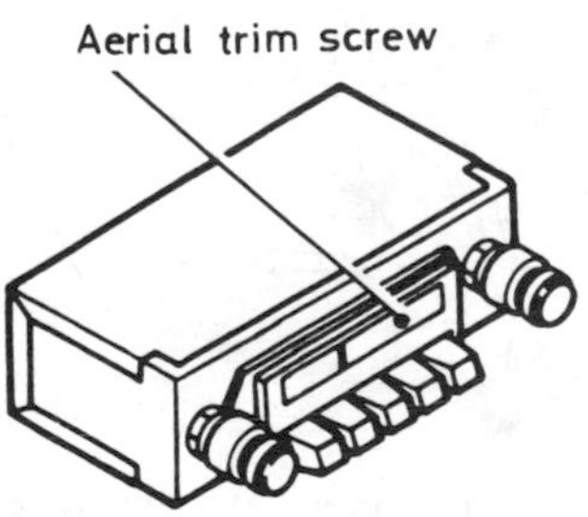

Fig. 10.39 Radio aerial trim screw (Sec 34)

9 Refitting is a reversal of removal, but, if a new receiver has been fitted, the aerial should be trimmed in the following way.
10 Extend the aerial fully, switch on the radio and turn to maximum volume.
11 Tune to a station which is barely audible and is found at around 1400 kHz.
12 Turn the trim screw in the front of the receiver until the signal is at its strongest.
13 The screw should not be turned more than one half turn in either direction.

35 Cassette player – removal and refitting

1 On B11 models remove the finisher and cover, which are held by clips.
2 Remove the mounting screws and disconnect the leads, not forgetting the earth connection.
3 On N12 models, remove the radio (Section 34) and then unscrew the cassette mounting screws. Disconnect the wiring plugs.
4 Refitting is a reversal of removal.

36 Speedometer drive cable – renewal

1 The speedometer drive cable should be renewed as an assembly if it breaks.
2 Disconnect the cable from the speedometer head after partially withdrawing the instrument panel, as described in Section 24.
3 Disconnect the cable from the transmission by unscrewing its knurled retaining ring.
4 Slip the cable out of its clip on the engine compartment rear bulkhead (photo) and then withdraw it, with its grommet, through the bulkhead.
5 Refit the new cable by reversing the removal operations.

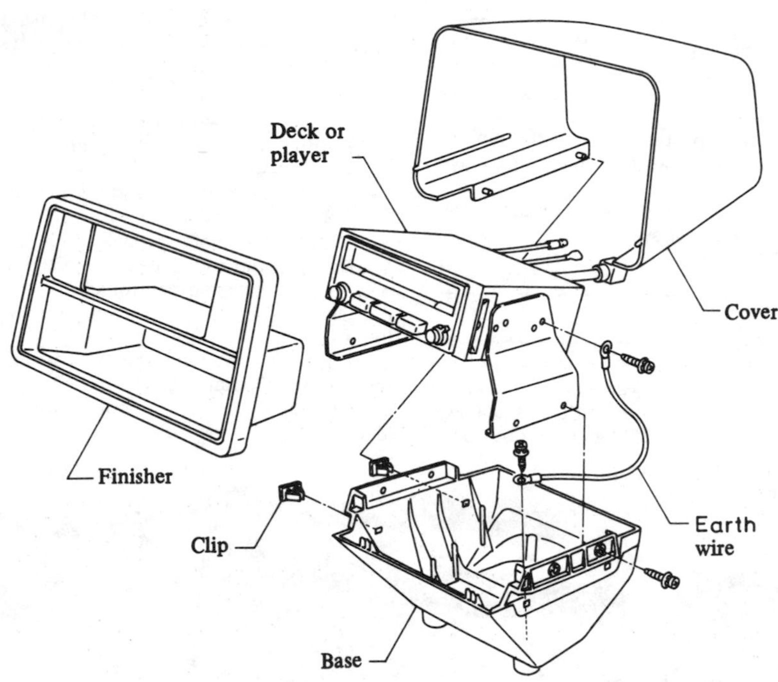

Fig. 10.40 Cassette player mounting components – B11 models (Sec 35)

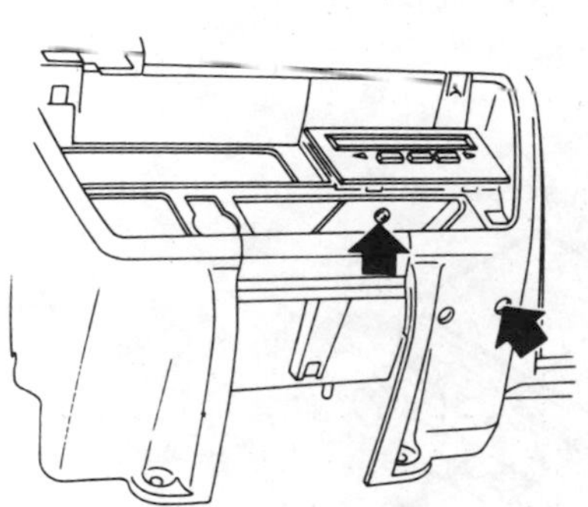

Fig. 10.41 Cassette player fixing screws – N12 models (Sec 35)

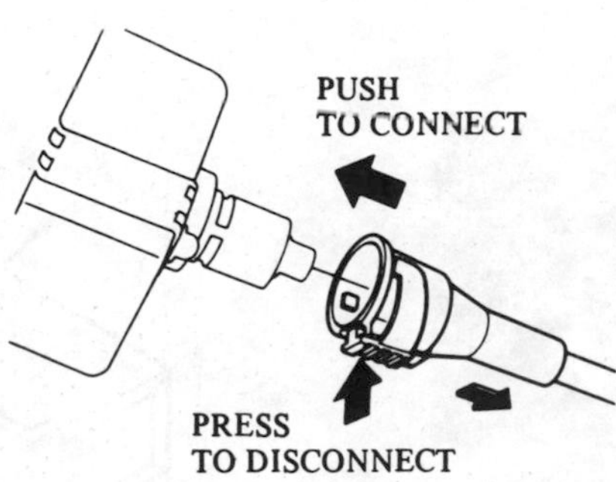

Fig. 10.42 Speedometer drive cable connection to instrument panel (Sec 36)

36.4 Speedometer drive cable at bulkhead

37 Fault diagnosis – electrical system

Symptom	Reason(s)
No voltage at starter motor	Battery discharged Battery defective internally Battery terminals loose or earth lead not securely attached to body Loose or broken connections in starter motor circuit Starter motor switch or solenoid faulty
Voltage at starter motor – faulty motor	Starter brushes badly worn, sticking, or brush wires loose Commutator dirty, worn or burnt Starter motor armature faulty Field coils earthed
Electrical defects	Battery in discharged condition Starter brushes badly worn, sticking, or brush wires loose Loose wires in starter motor circuit Starter motor pinion sticking on the screwed sleeve Dirt or oil on drivegear
Starter motor noisy or rough in engagement	Pinion or flywheel gear teeth broken or worn Starter drive main spring broken Starter motor retaining bolts loose
Alternator not charging*	Drivebelt loose and slipping, or broken Brushes worn, sticking, broken or dirty Brush springs weak or broken

**If all appears to be well but the alternator is still not charging, take the car to an automobile electrician for checking of the alternator*

Symptom	Reason(s)
Battery will not hold charge for more than a few days	Battery defective internally Electrolyte level too low or electrolyte too weak due to leakage Plate separators no longer fully effective Battery plates severely sulphated Drivebelt slipping Battery terminal connections loose or corroded Alternator not charging properly Short in lighting circuit causing continual battery drain
Ignition light fails to go out, battery runs flat in a few days	Drivebelt loose and slipping, or broken Alternator faulty

Failure of individual electrical equipment to function correctly is dealt with alphabetically below

Symptom	Reason(s)
Fuel gauge gives no reading	Fuel tank empty Electric cable between tank sender unit and gauge earthed or loose Fuel gauge case not earthed Fuel gauge supply cable interrupted Fuel gauge unit broken
Fuel gauge registers full all the time	Electric cable between tank unit and gauge broken or disconnected
Horn operates all the time	Horn push either earthed or stuck down Horn cable to horn push earthed
Horn fails to operate	Blown fuse Cable or cable connection loose, broken or disconnected Horn has an internal fault
Horn emits intermittent or unsatisfactory noise	Cable connections loose Horn incorrectly adjusted
Lights do not come on	If engine not running, battery discharged Light bulb filament burnt out or bulbs broken Wire connections loose, disconnected or broken Light switch shorting or otherwise faulty
Lights come on but fade	If engine not running, battery discharged
Lights give very poor illumination	Lamp glasses dirty Reflector tarnished or dirty Lamps badly out of adjustment Incorrect bulb with too low wattage fitted Existing bulbs old and badly discoloured Electrical wiring too thin not allowing full current to pass

Lights work erratically, flashing on and off, especially over bumps	Battery terminals or earth connections loose Lights not earthing properly Contacts in light switch faulty
Wiper motor fails to work	Blown fuse Brushes badly worn Wire connections loose, disconnected or broken Armature worn or faulty Field coils faulty
Wiper motor works very slowly and takes excessive current	Commutator dirty, greasy or burnt Drive to spindles bent or unlubricated Drive spindle binding or damaged Armature bearings dry or unaligned Armature badly worn or faulty
Wiper motor works slowly and takes little current	Brushes badly worn Commutator dirty, greasy or burnt Armature badly worn or faulty
Wiper motor works but wiper blades remain static	Linkage disengaged or faulty Drive spindle damaged or worn Wiper motor gearbox parts badly worn

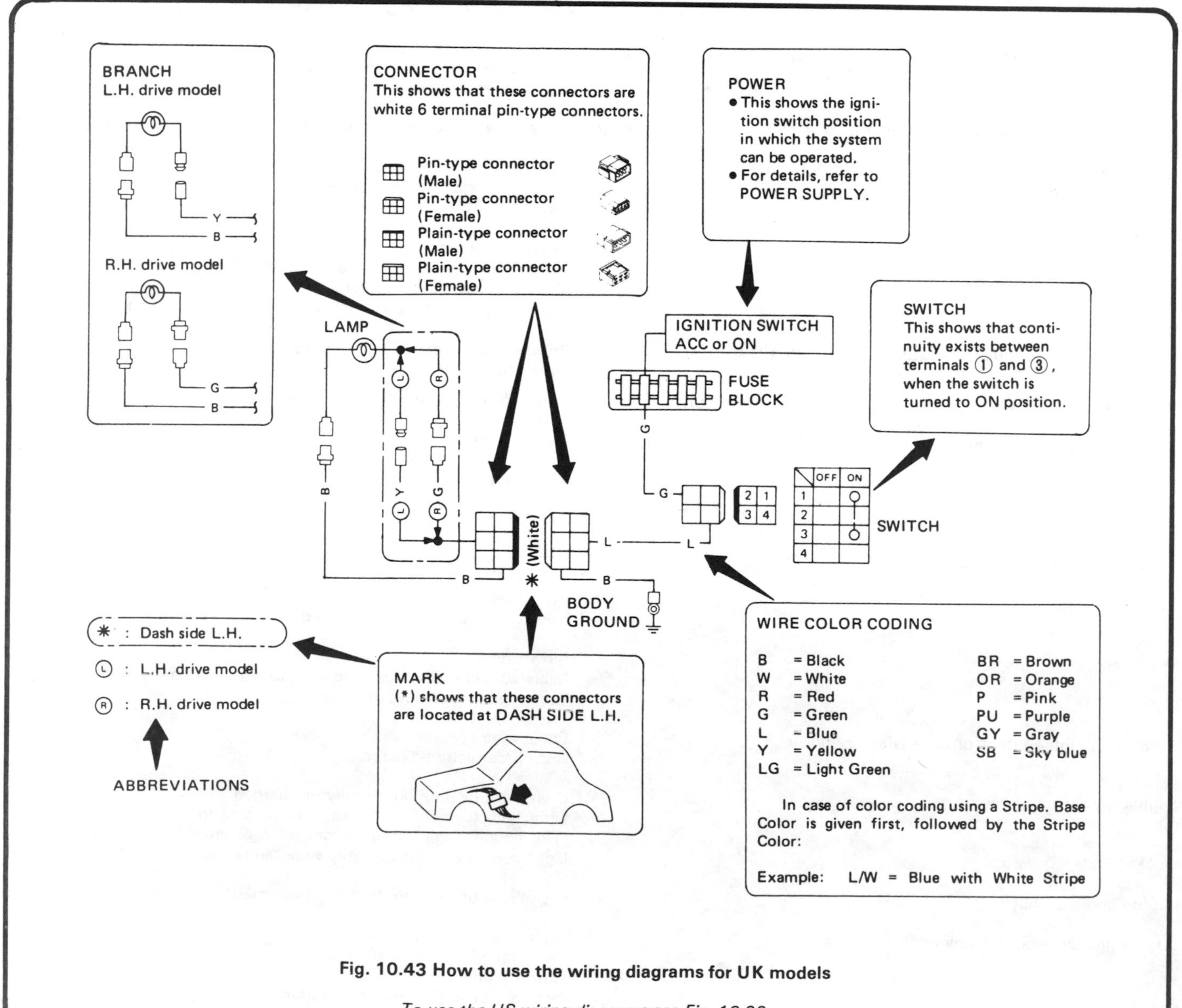

Fig. 10.43 How to use the wiring diagrams for UK models

To use the US wiring diagrams see Fig. 10.99

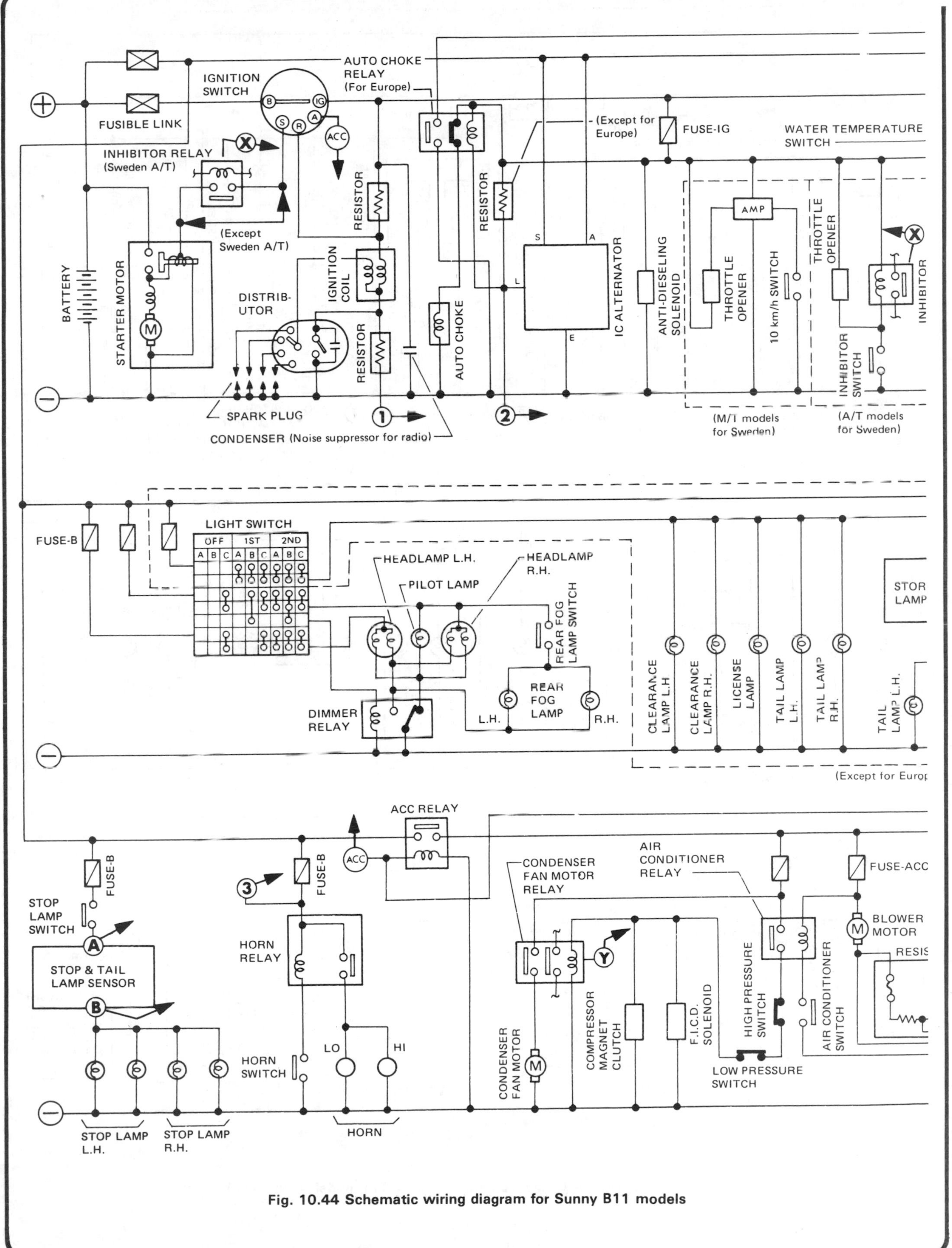

Fig. 10.44 Schematic wiring diagram for Sunny B11 models

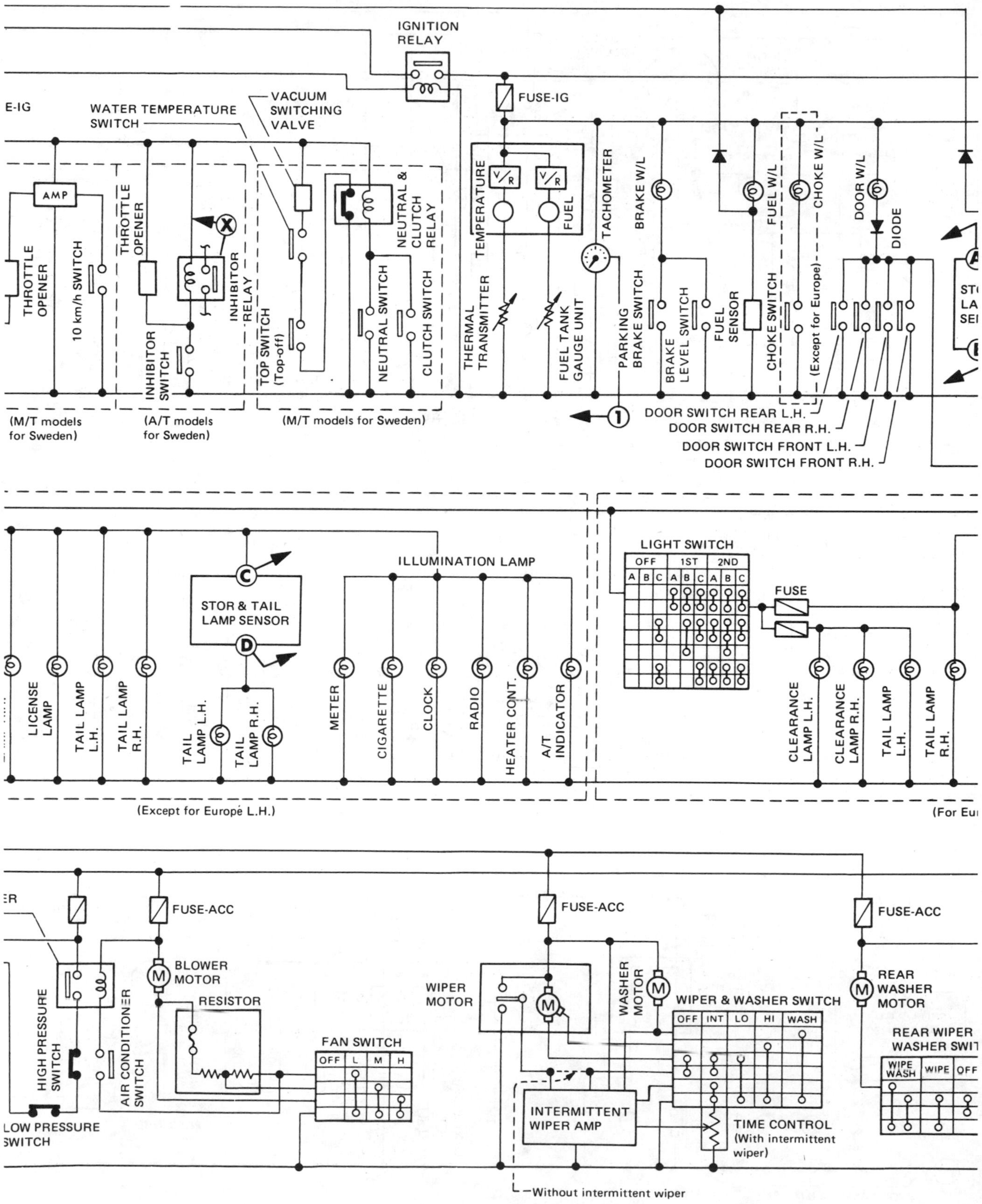

Fig. 10.44 Schematic wiring diagram for Sunny B11 models (continued)

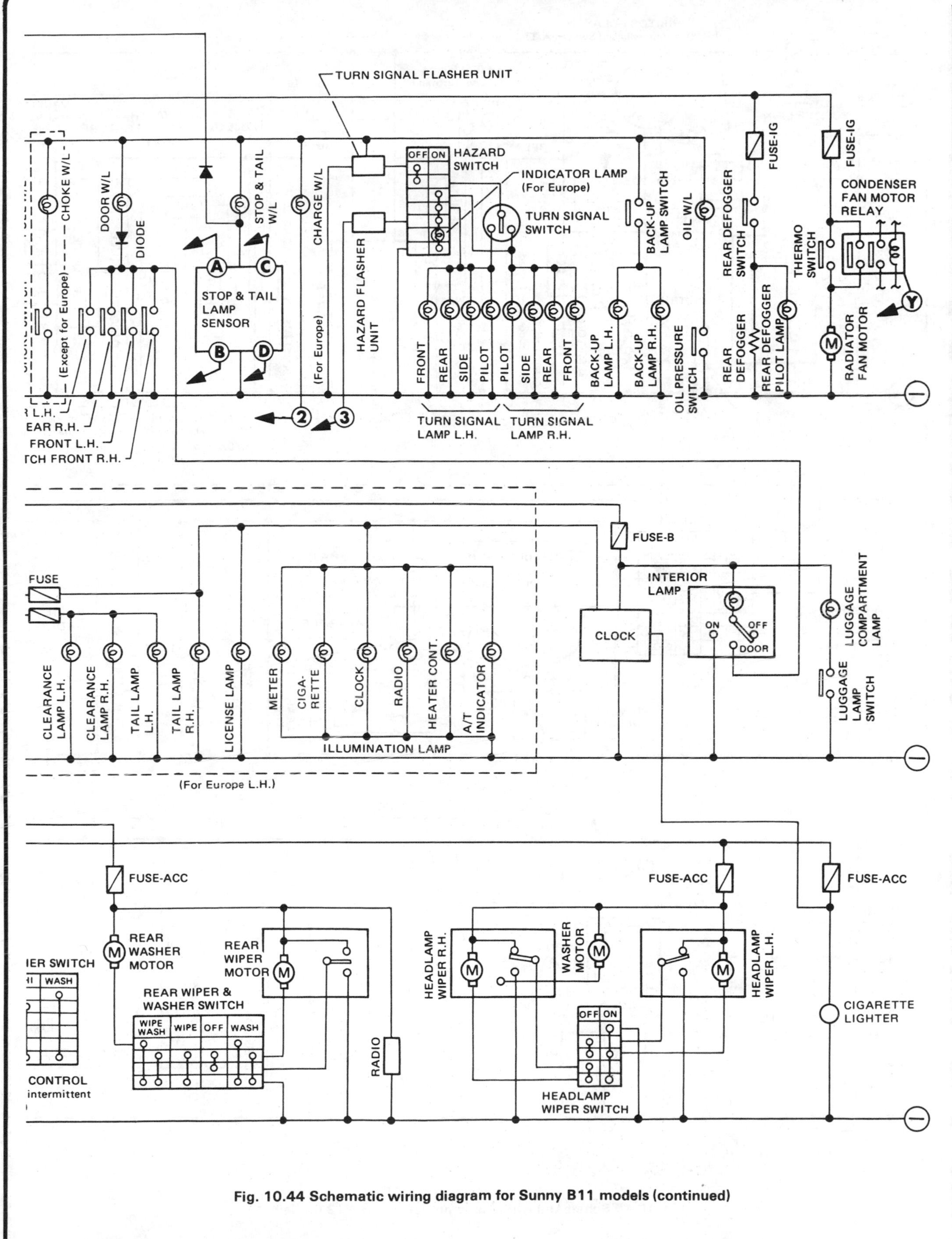

Fig. 10.44 Schematic wiring diagram for Sunny B11 models (continued)

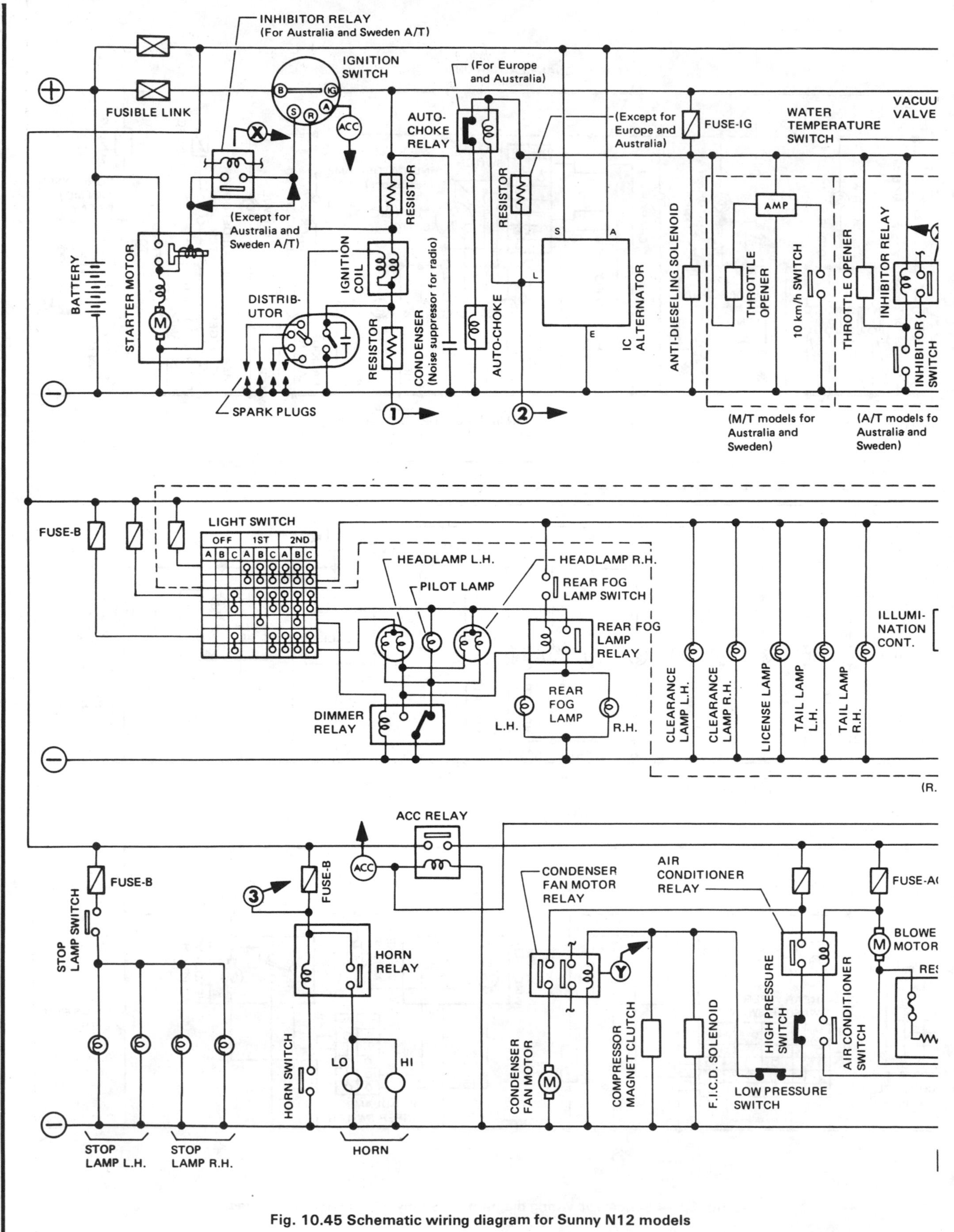

Fig. 10.45 Schematic wiring diagram for Sunny N12 models

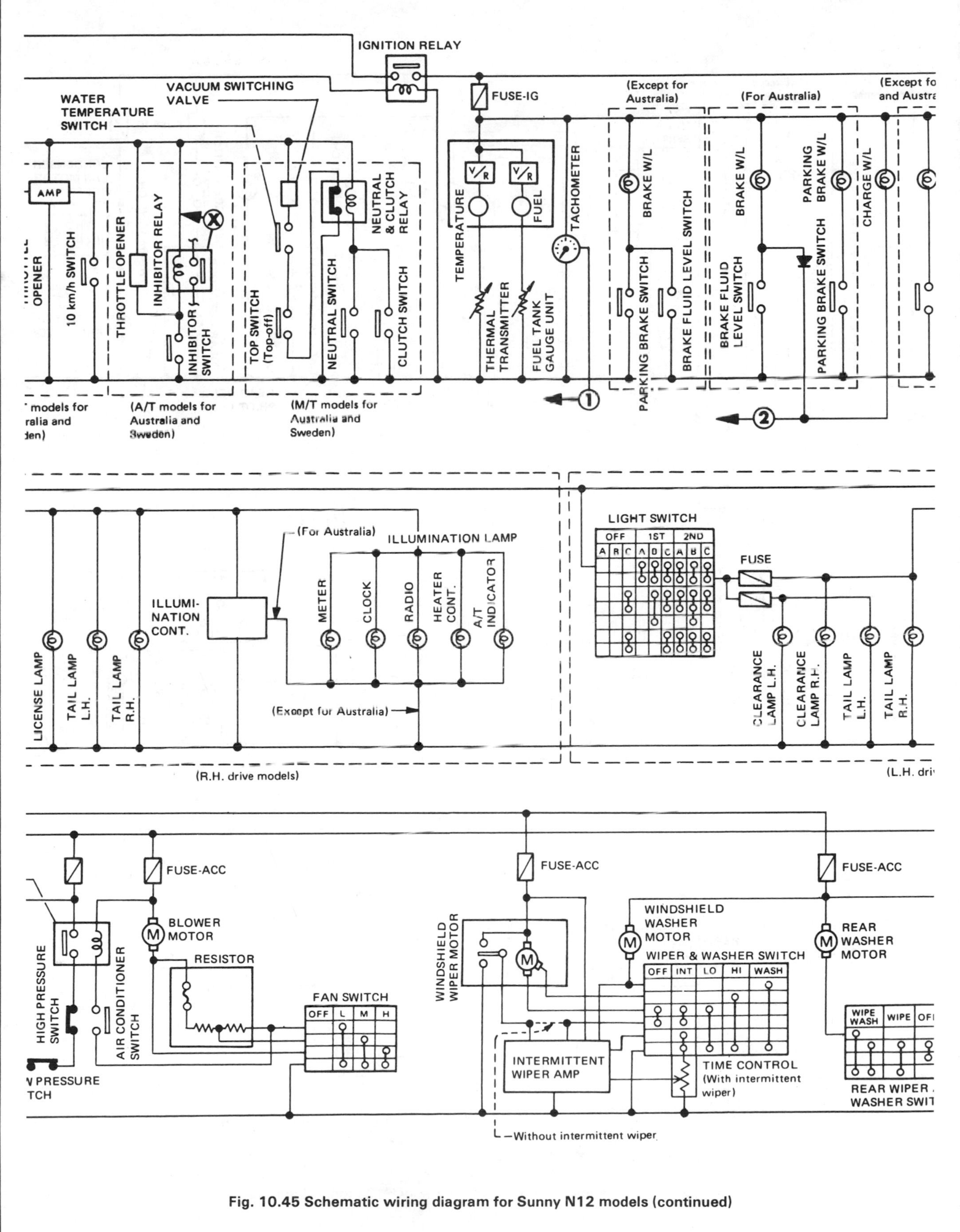

Fig. 10.45 Schematic wiring diagram for Sunny N12 models (continued)

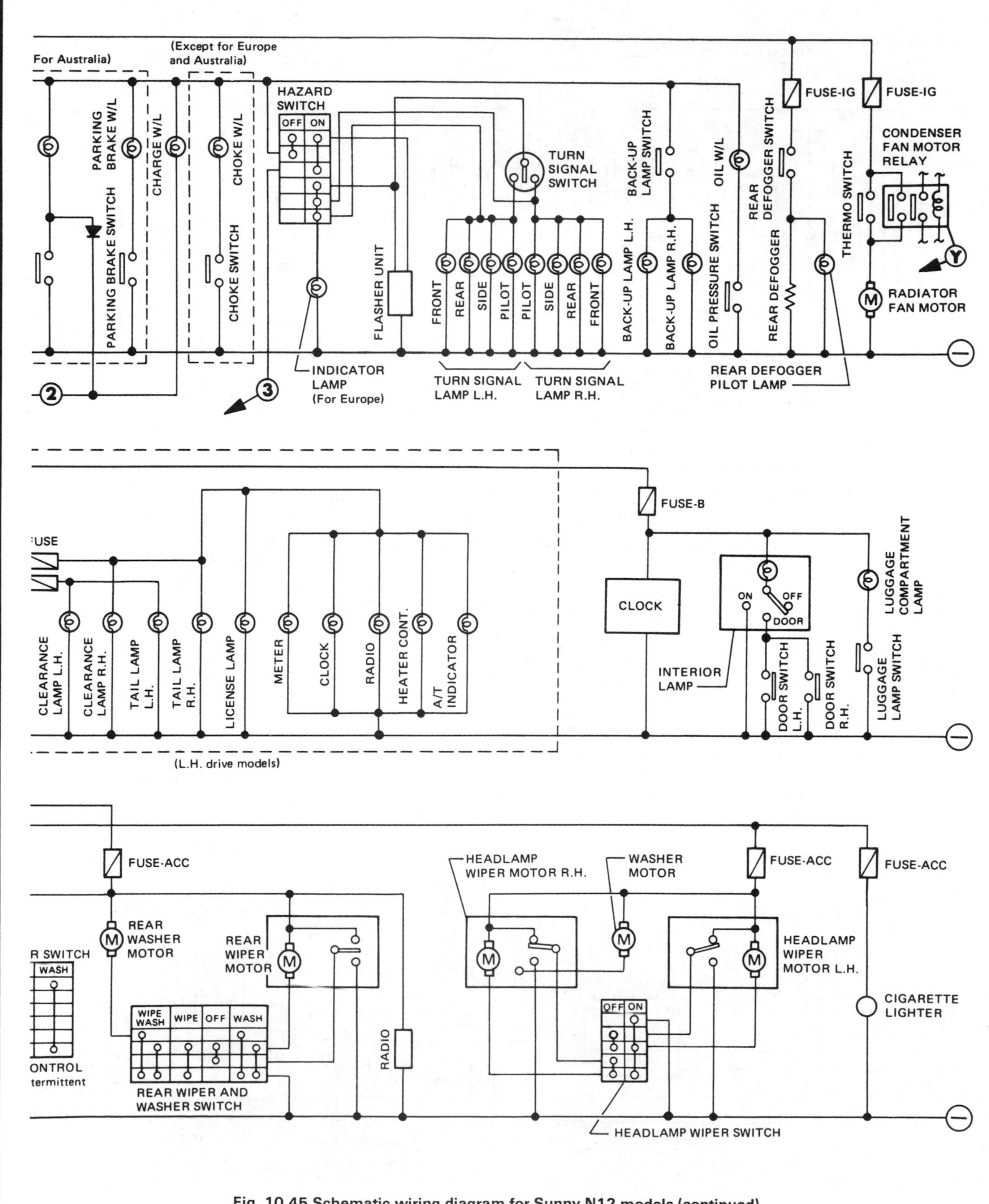

Fig. 10.45 Schematic wiring diagram for Sunny N12 models (continued)

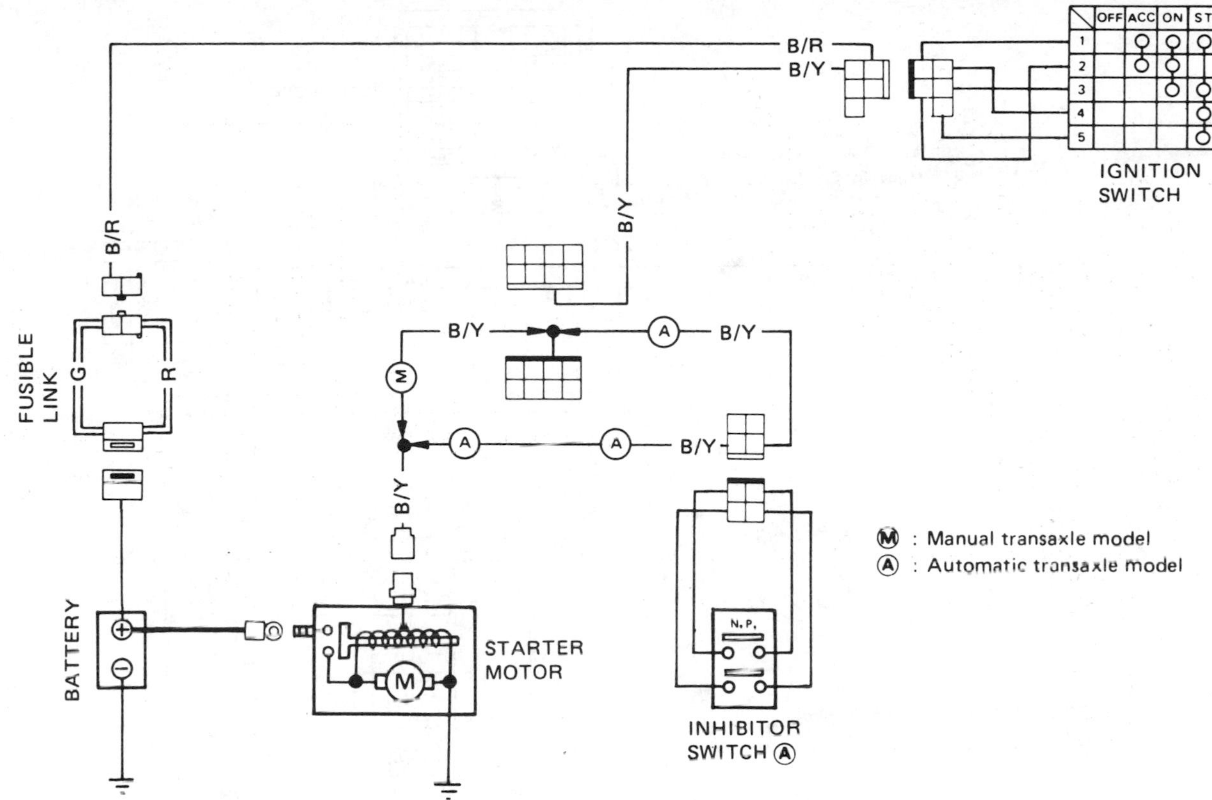

Fig. 10.46 Starter motor system (Sunny B11 models except Australia and Sweden)

For the colour code see Fig. 10.43

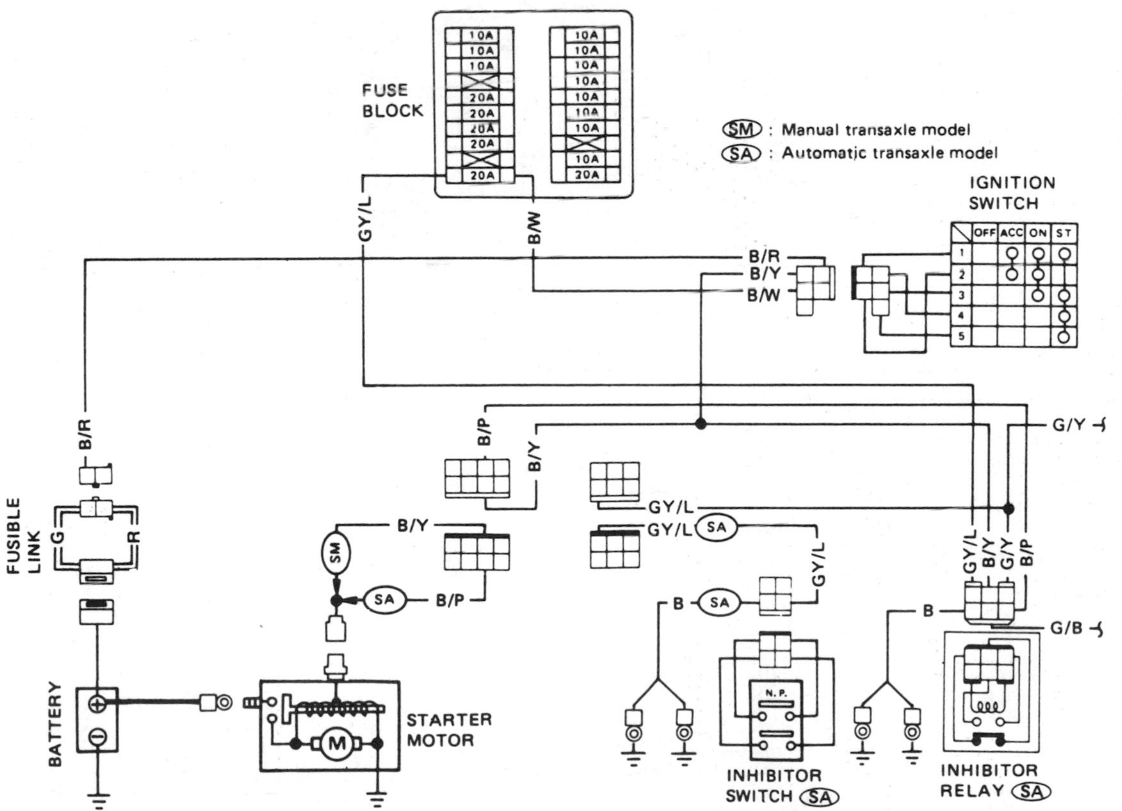

Fig. 10.47 Starter motor system (Sunny B11 models – Australia and Sweden)

For the colour code see Fig. 10.43

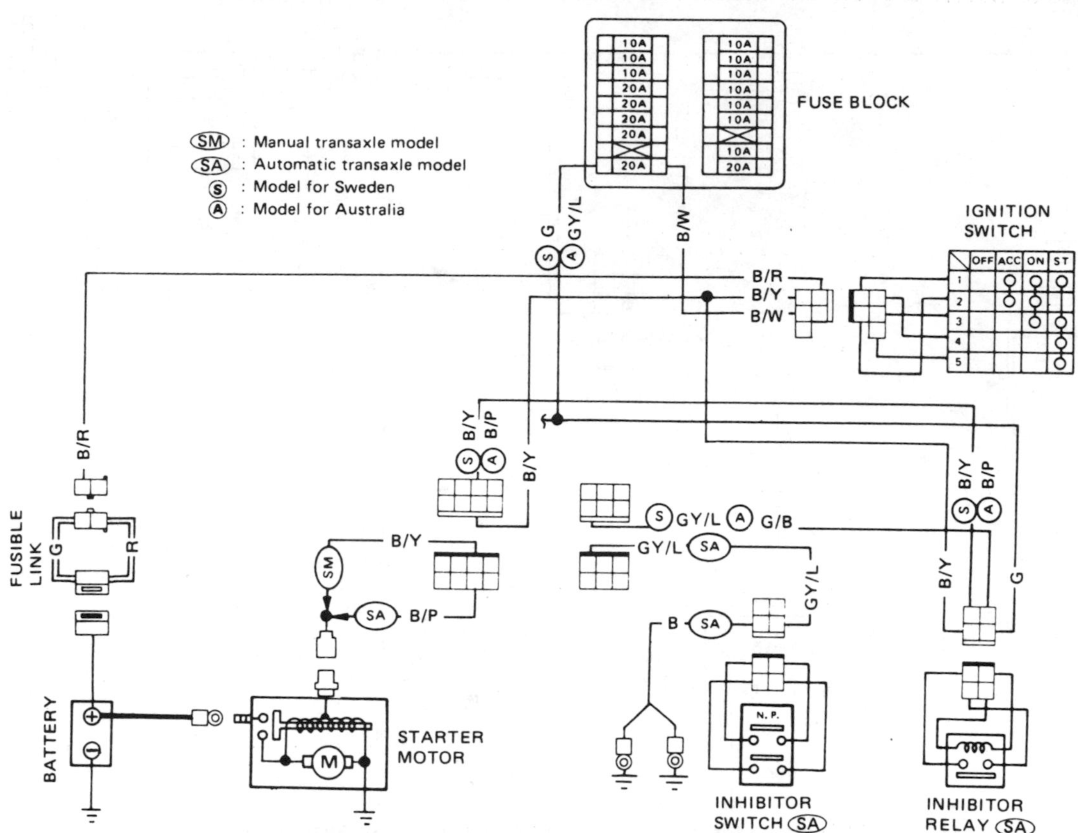

Fig. 10.48 Starter motor wiring diagram (Sunny N12 models)

For the colour code see Fig. 10.43

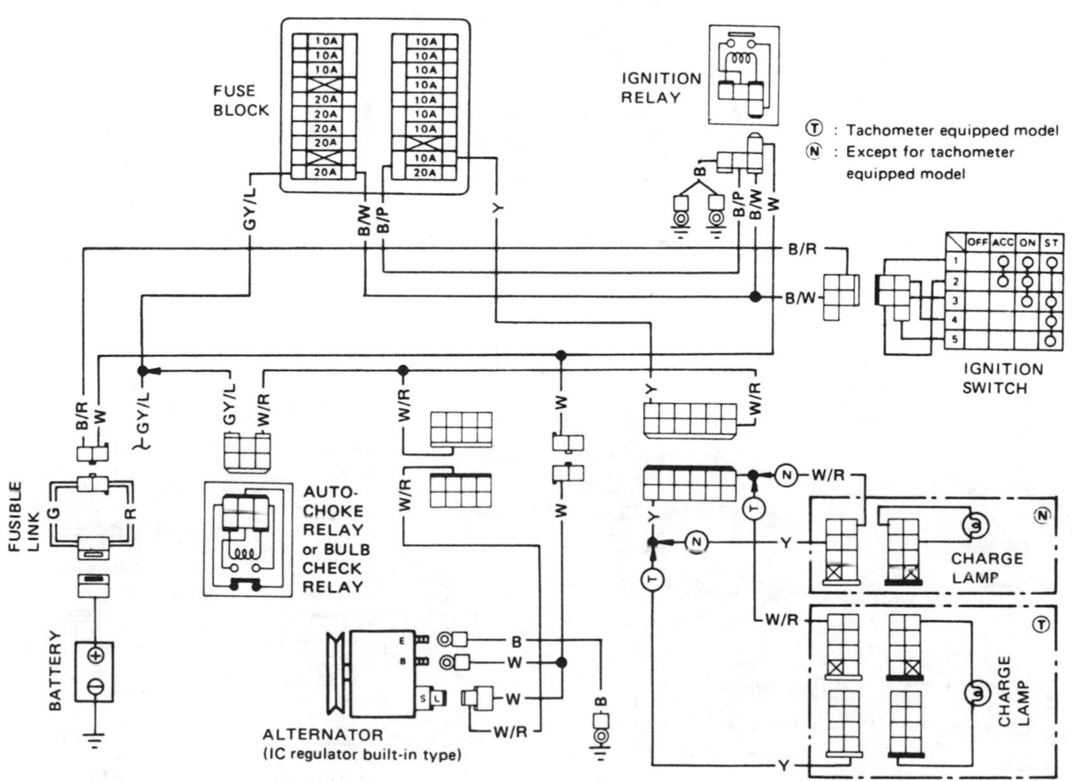

Fig. 10.49 Charging system (Sunny B11 models – left-hand drive, Europe and Hong Kong)

For the colour code see Fig. 10.43

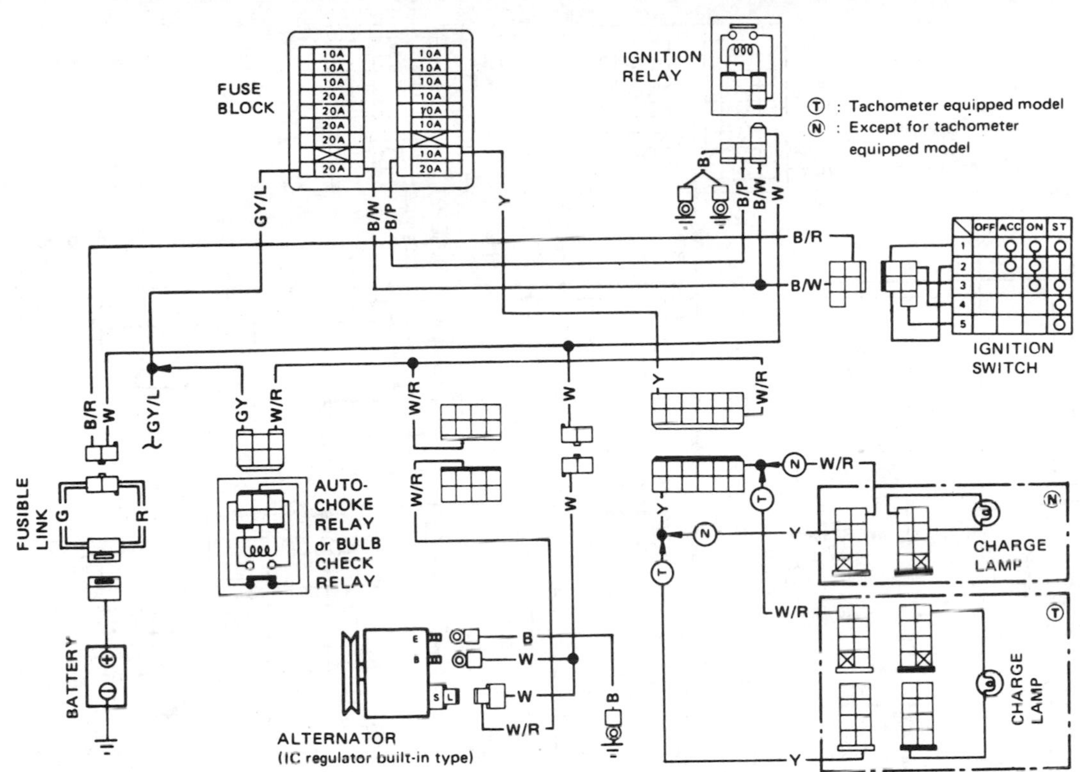

Fig. 10.50 Charging system (Sunny B11 models – right-hand drive except Europe)

For the colour code see Fig. 10.43

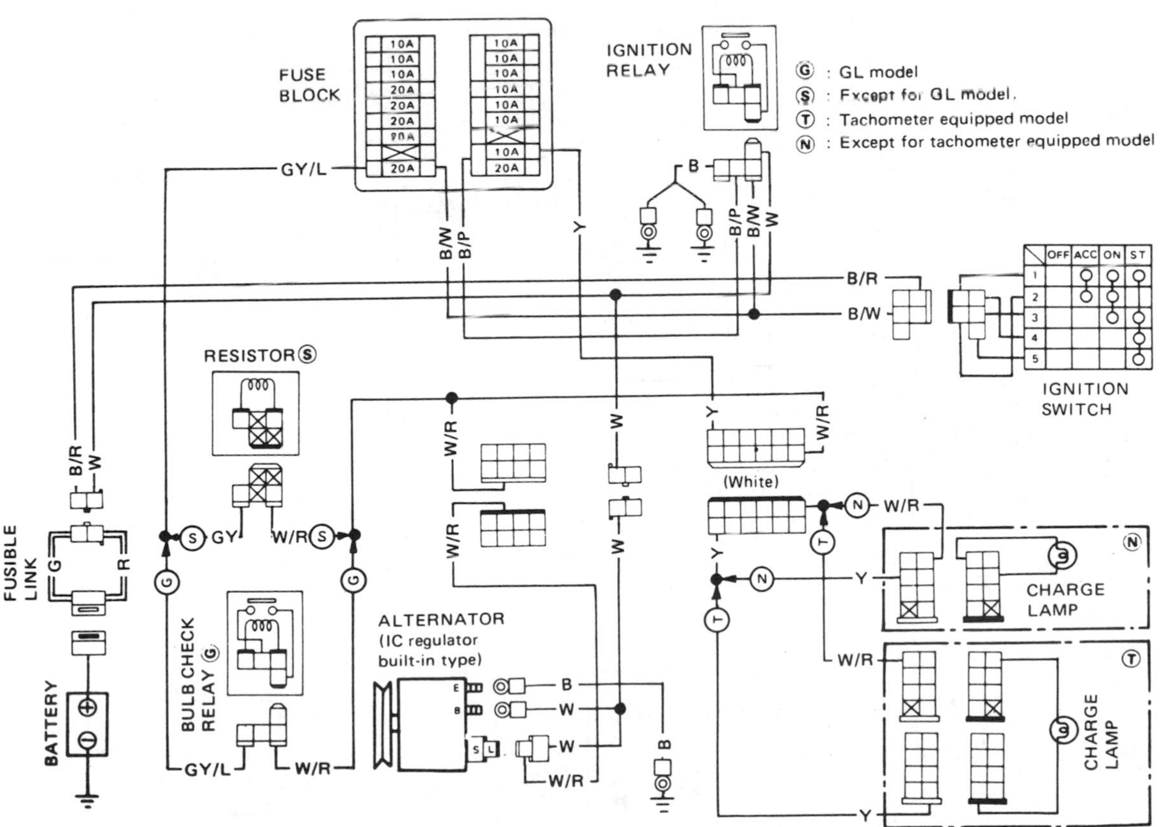

Fig. 10.51 Charging system (Sunny B11 models – left-hand drive except Europe and Hong Kong)

For the colour code see Fig. 10.43

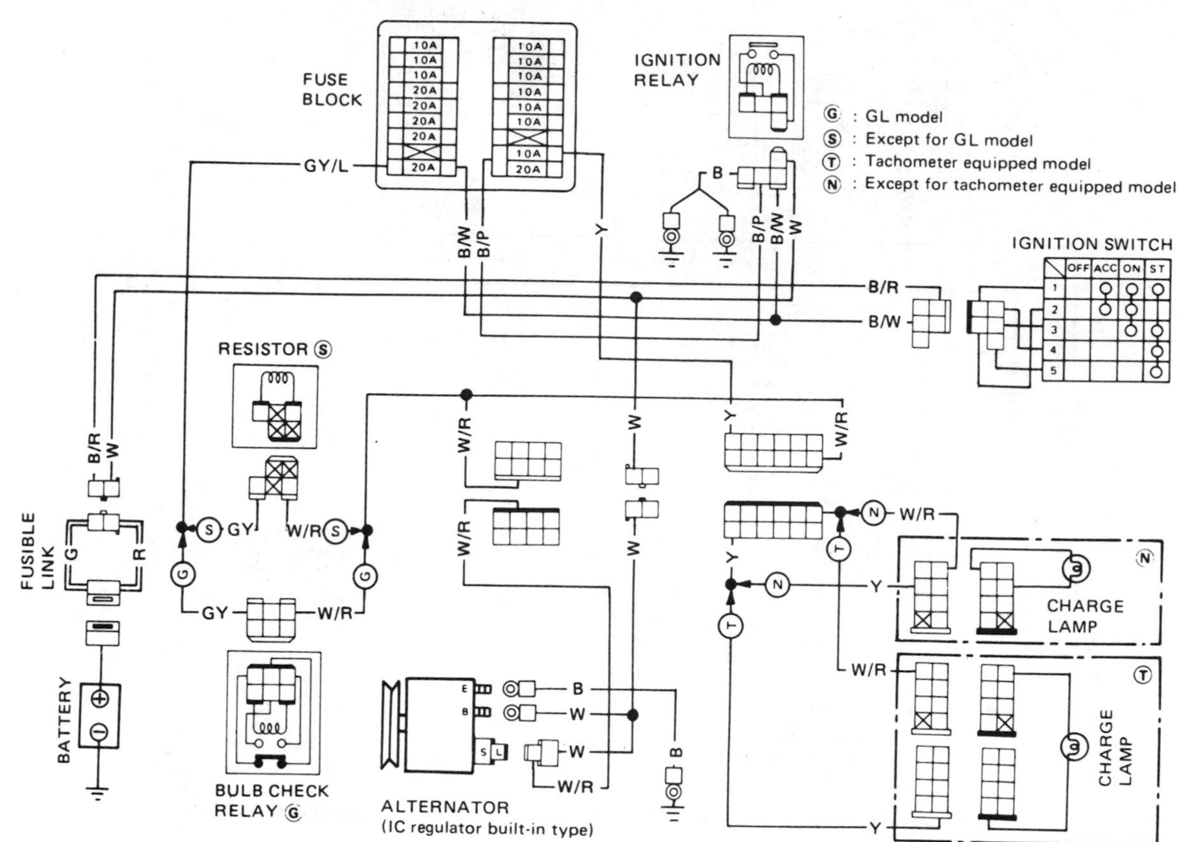

Fig. 10.52 Charging system (Sunny N12 models with autochoke)

For the colour code see Fig. 10.43

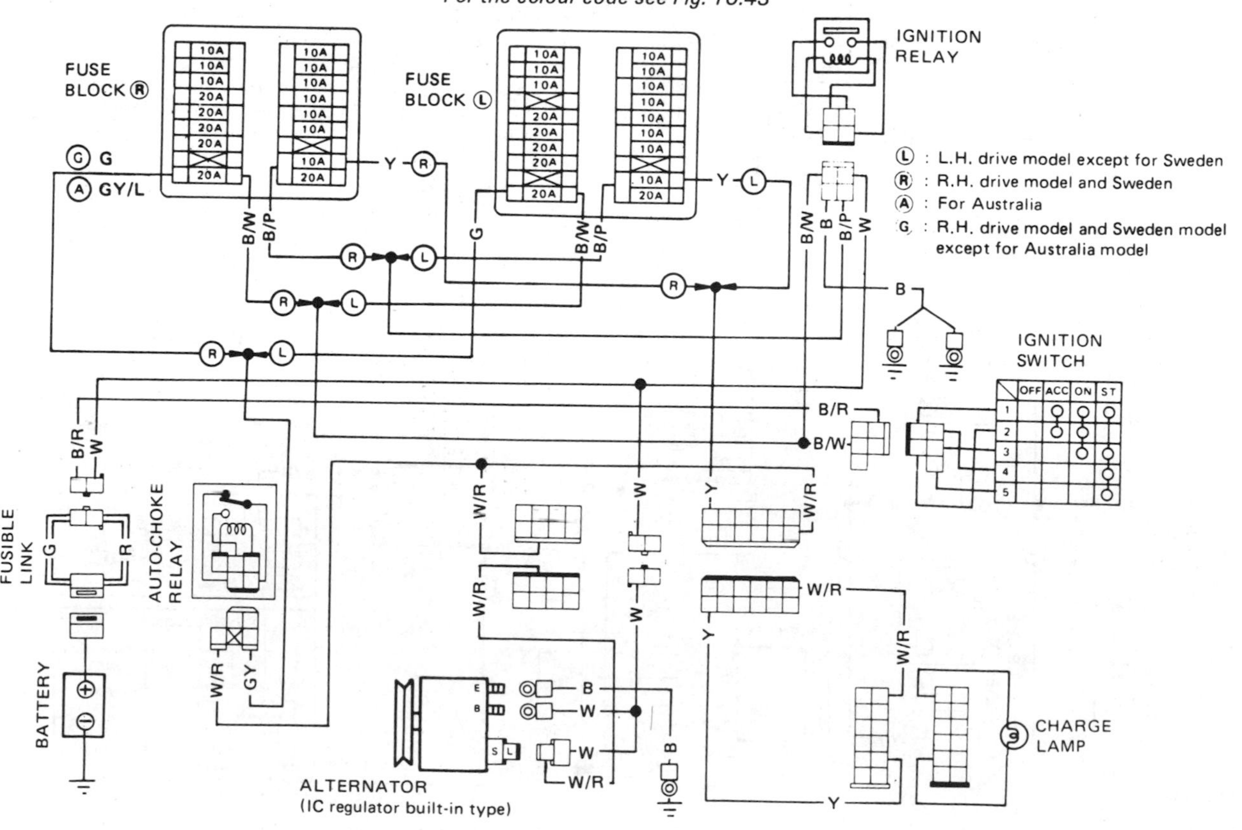

Fig. 10.53 Charging system (Sunny N12 models with autochoke)

For the colour code see Fig. 10.43

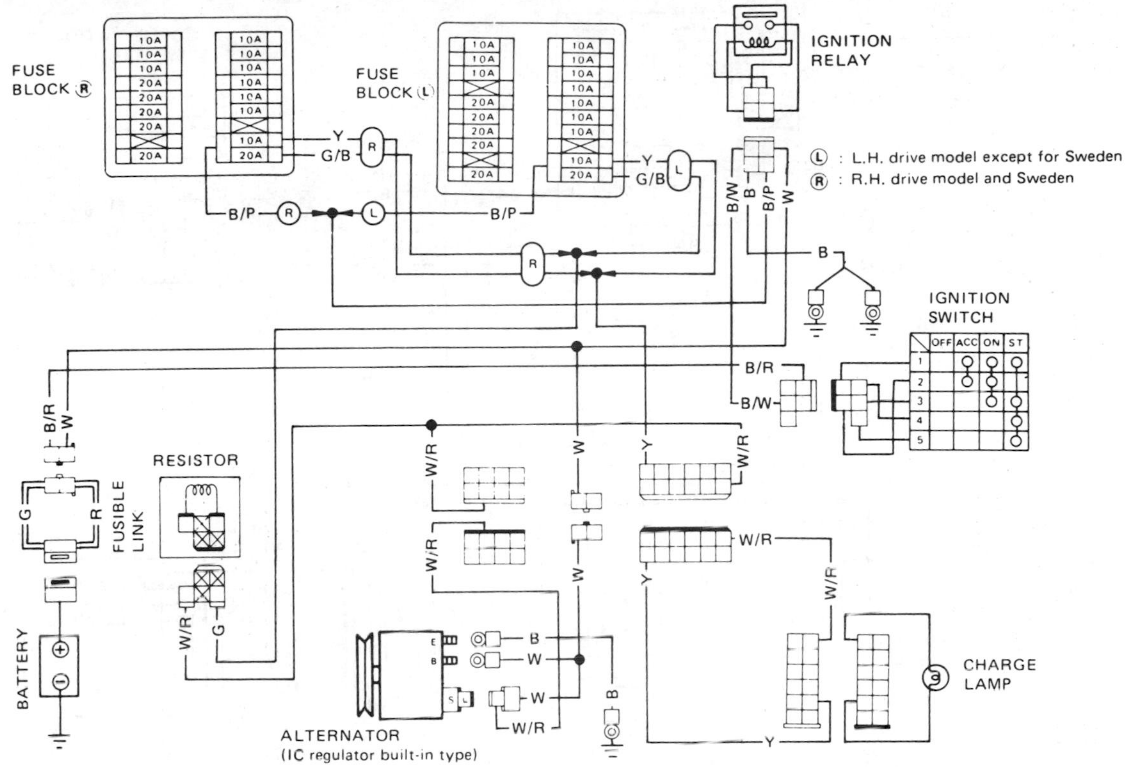

Fig. 10.54 Charging system (Sunny N12 models with manual choke)

For the colour code see Fig. 10.43

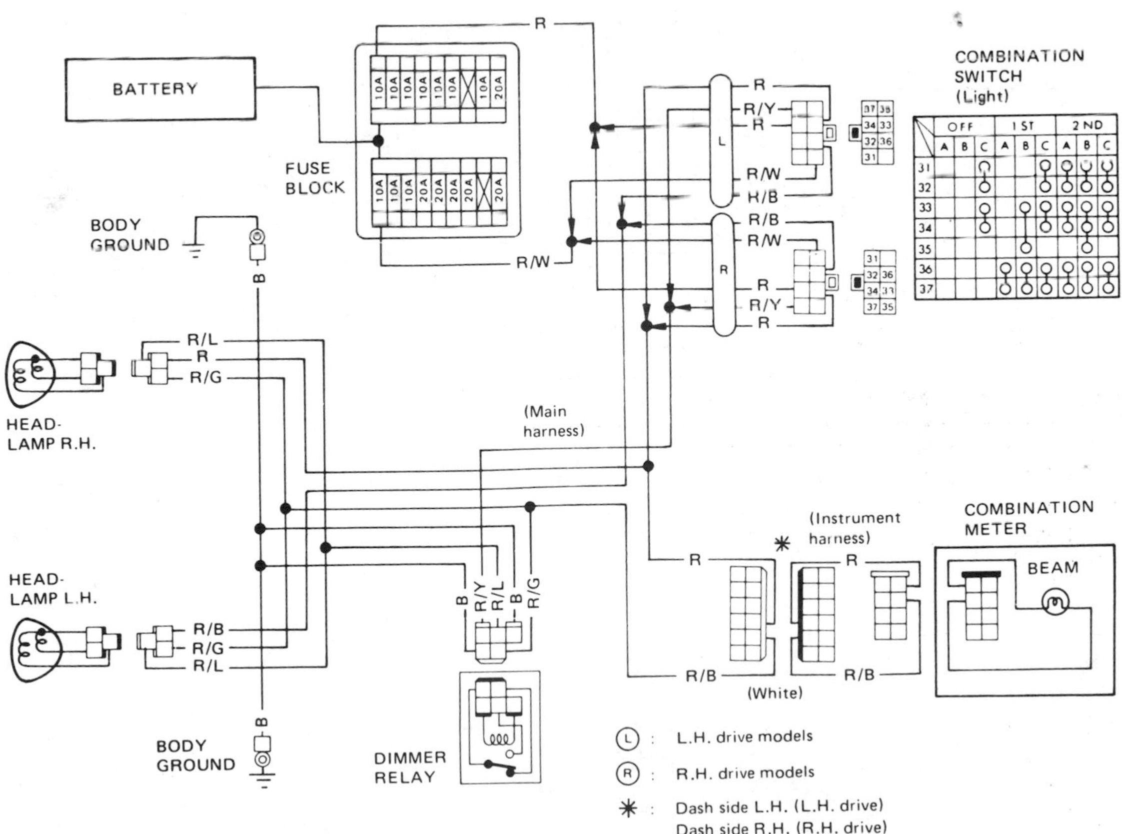

Fig. 10.55 Headlamp system (Sunny B11 models – except left-hand drive Europe)

For the colour code see Fig. 10.43

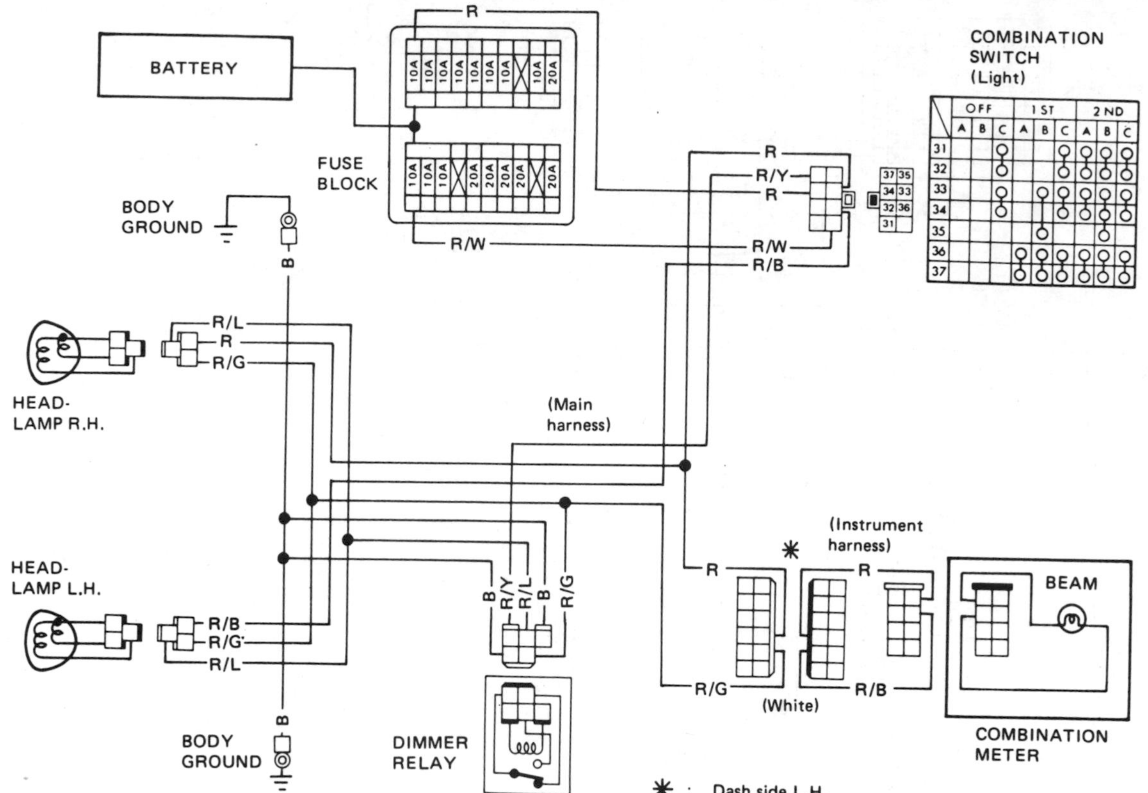

Fig. 10.56 Headlamp system (Sunny B11 models – left-hand drive Europe)

For the colour code see Fig. 10.43

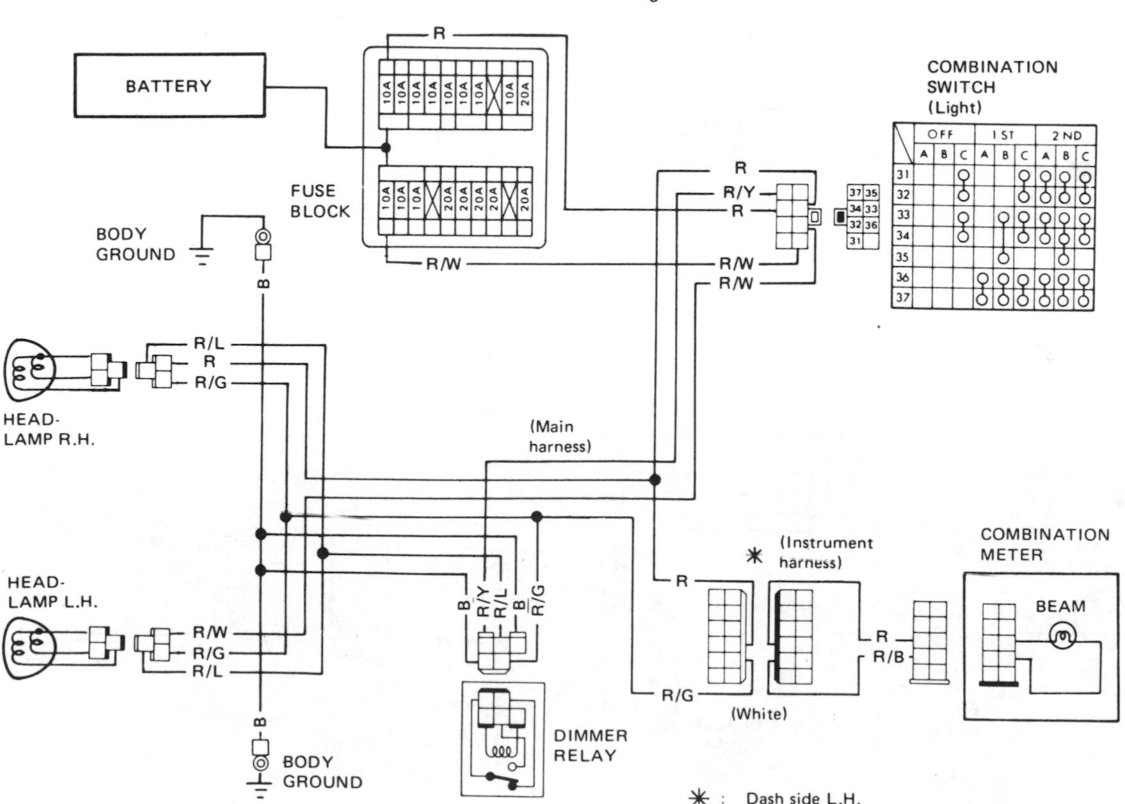

Fig. 10.57 Headlamp system (Sunny N12 models – left-hand drive Europe except Sweden)

For the colour code see Fig. 10.43

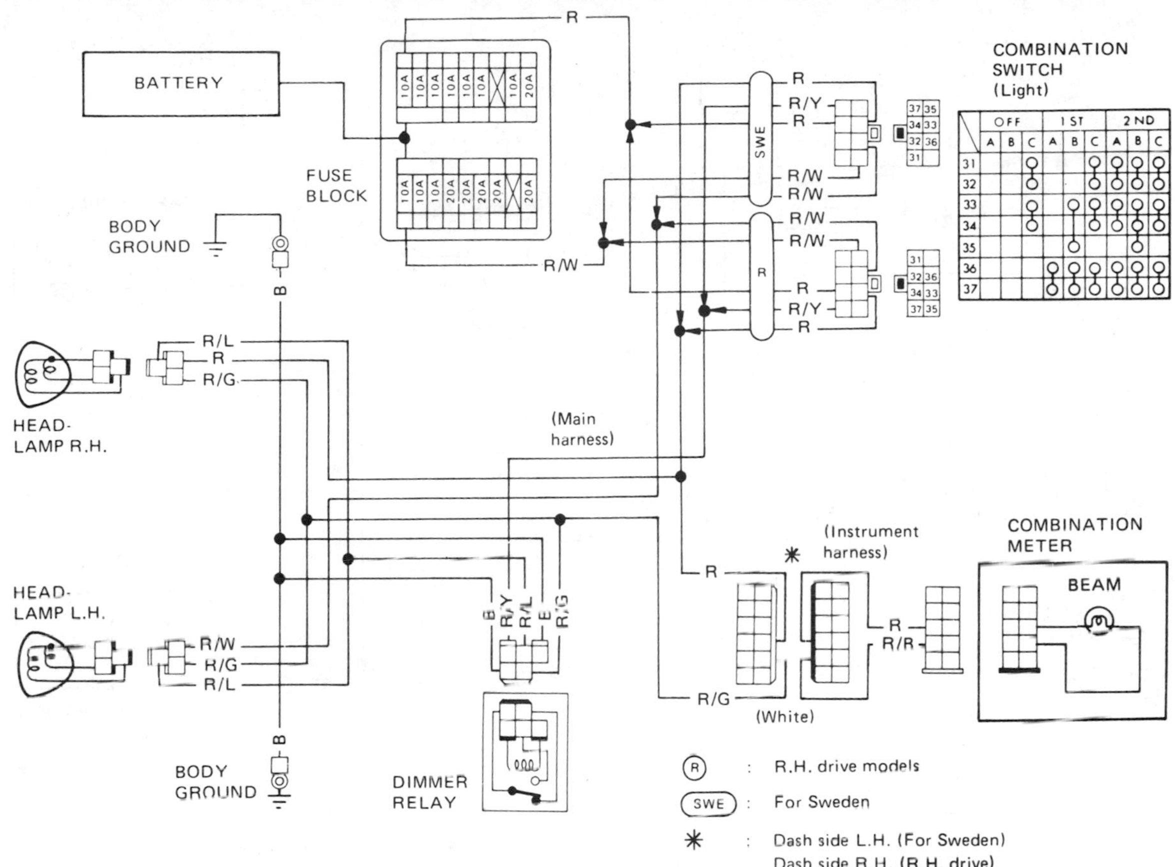

Fig. 10.58 Headlamp system (Sunny N12 models – right-hand drive and Sweden)

For the colour code see Fig. 10.43

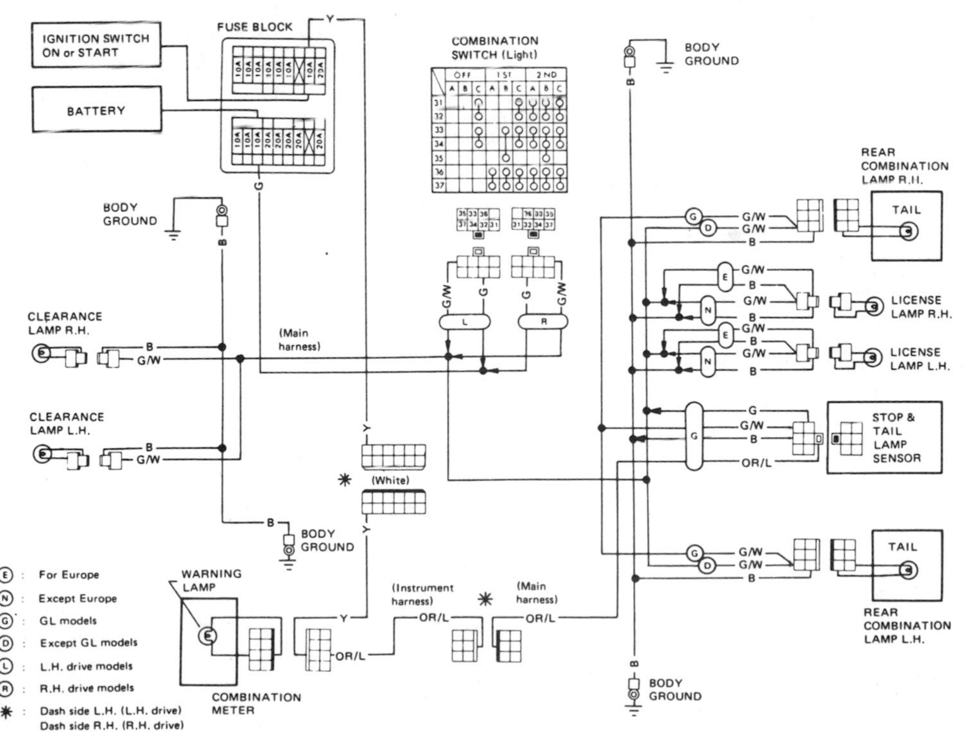

Fig. 10.59 Front sidelights, number plate light and tail lights (Sunny B11 models – except left-hand drive Europe)

For the colour code see Fig. 10.43

G/W
G/W
FUSE
BLOCK
L
COMBINATION
SWITCH (Light)
OFF 1 ST 2 ND
A B C A B C A B C
31
32
33
34
35
36
37
BODY
GROUND
REAR COMBINATION
LAMP R.H.
TAIL
G/W
B
BODY
GROUND
BATTERY
CLEARANCE
LAMP R.H.
B
G/W
L
W
LICENSE
LAMP R.H.
LICENSE
LAMP L.H.
CLEARANCE
LAMP L.H.
TAIL
REAR COMBINATION
LAMP L.H.
BODY
GROUND
BODY
GROUND

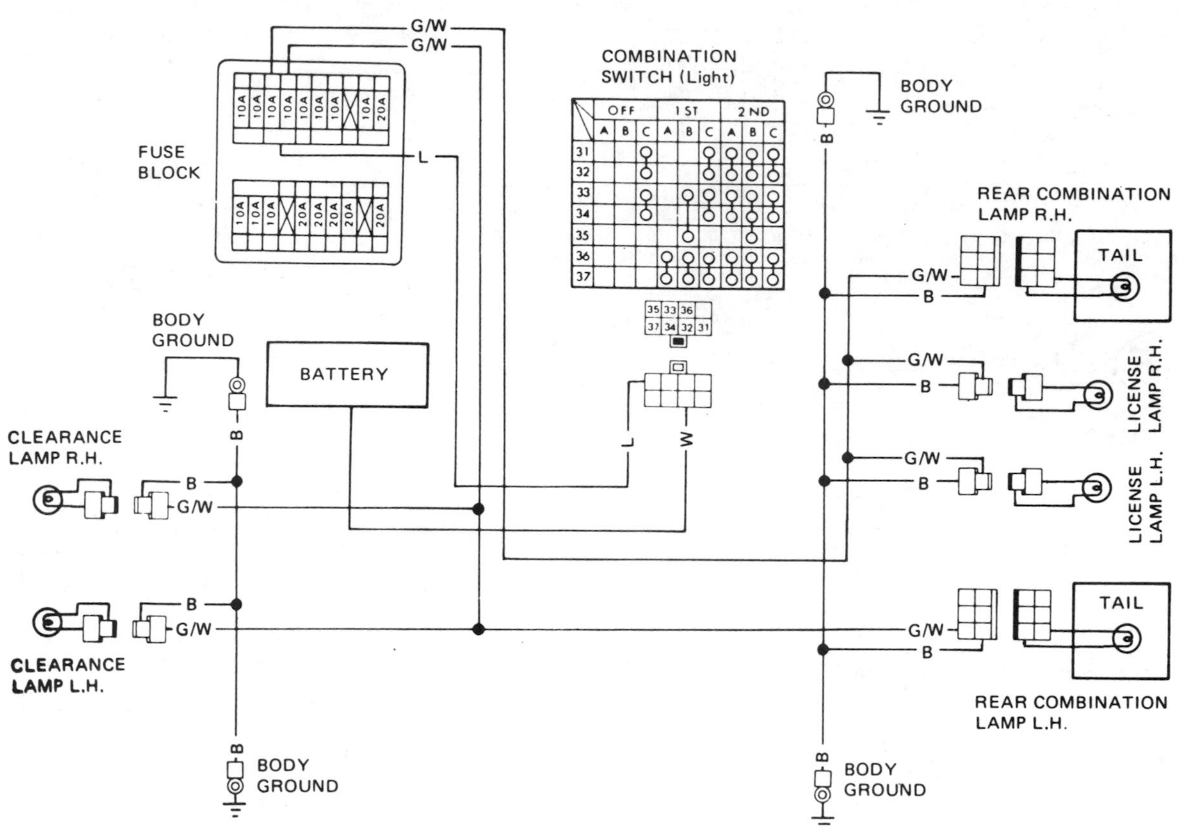

Fig. 10.60 Front sidelights, number plate light and tail lights (Sunny B11 models – left-hand drive Europe)

For the colour code see Fig. 10.43

Ⓖ : GL models
Ⓓ . Except GL models
Ⓟ : L.H. drive models for Europe
Ⓒ : Except L.H. drive models for Europe
✱ : Dash side L.H. (L.H. drive)
Dash side R.H. (R.H. drive)
IGNITION SWITCH
ON or START
BATTERY
Ⓟ
FUSE
BLOCK
STOP LAMP
SWITCH
BODY
GROUND
Y
LG
STOP
LG/B
B
REAR
COMBINATION
LAMP R.H.
BATTERY
IGNITION SWITCH
ON or START
Ⓒ FUSE
BLOCK
Without stop
lamp sensor
LG/R
OR/L
STOP
LAMP
SENSOR
STOP &
TAIL
LAMP
SENSOR
(White)
WARNING
LAMP
COMBINATION
METER
BODY
GROUND
STOP
REAR
COMBINATION
LAMP L.H.

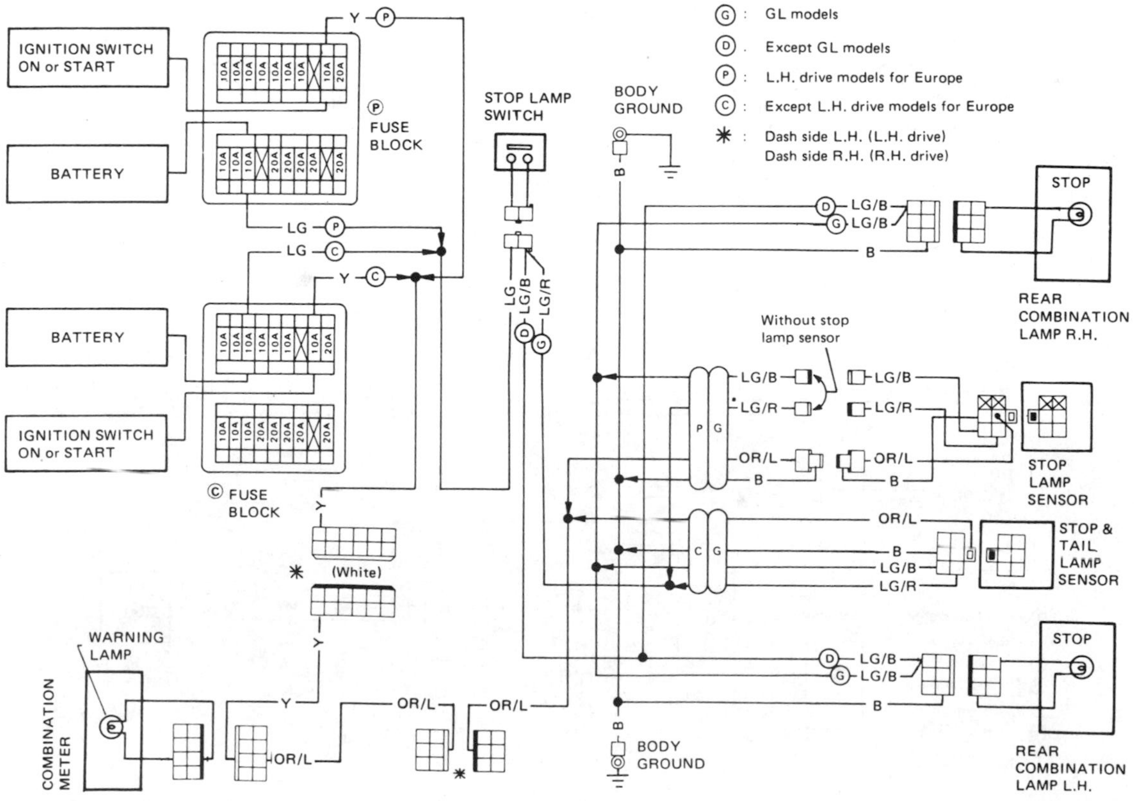

Fig. 10.61 Stop-lights (Sunny B11 models)

For the colour code see Fig. 10.43

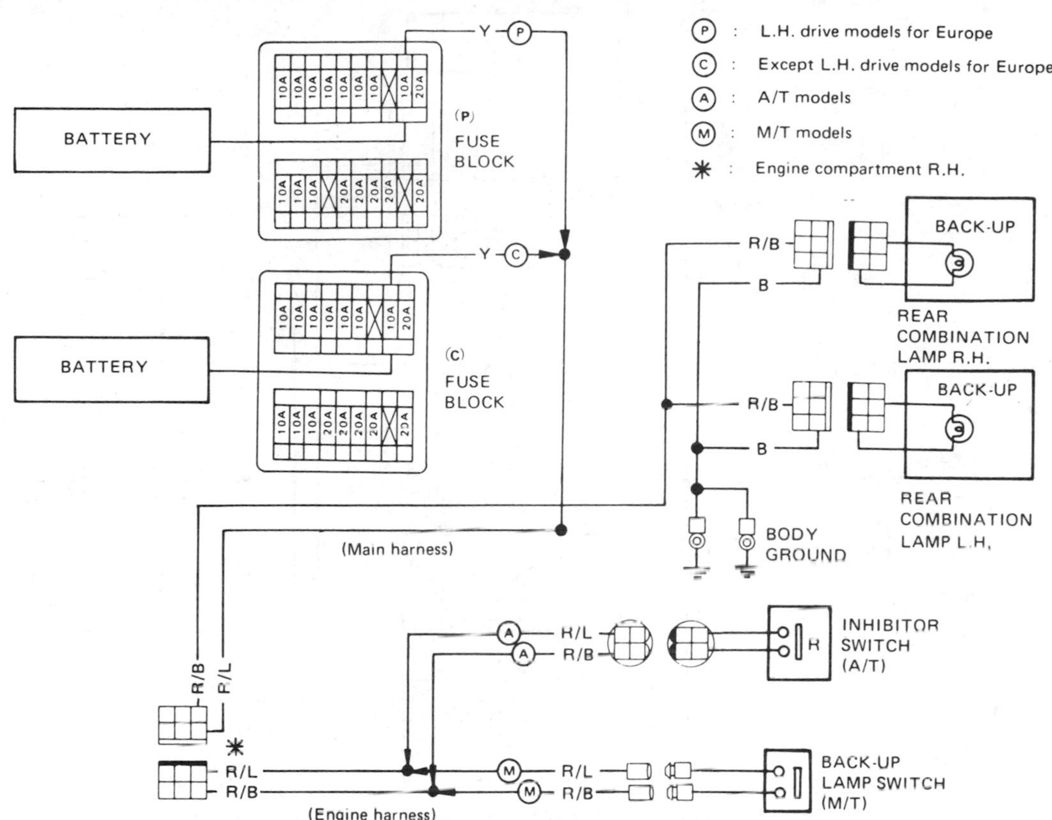

Fig. 10.62 Reversing lights (Sunny B11 models)

For the colour code see Fig. 10.43

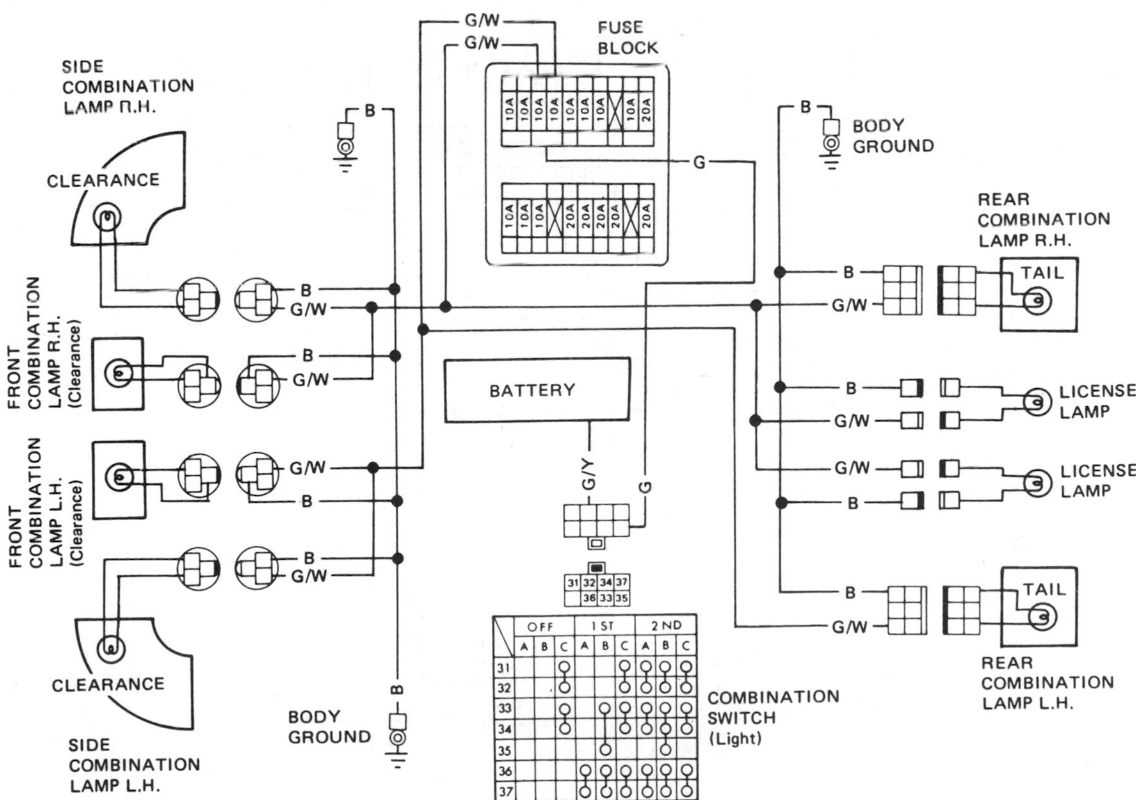

Fig. 10.63 Front sidelights, number plate light and tail lights (Sunny N12 models – left-hand drive except Sweden)

For the colour code see Fig. 10.43

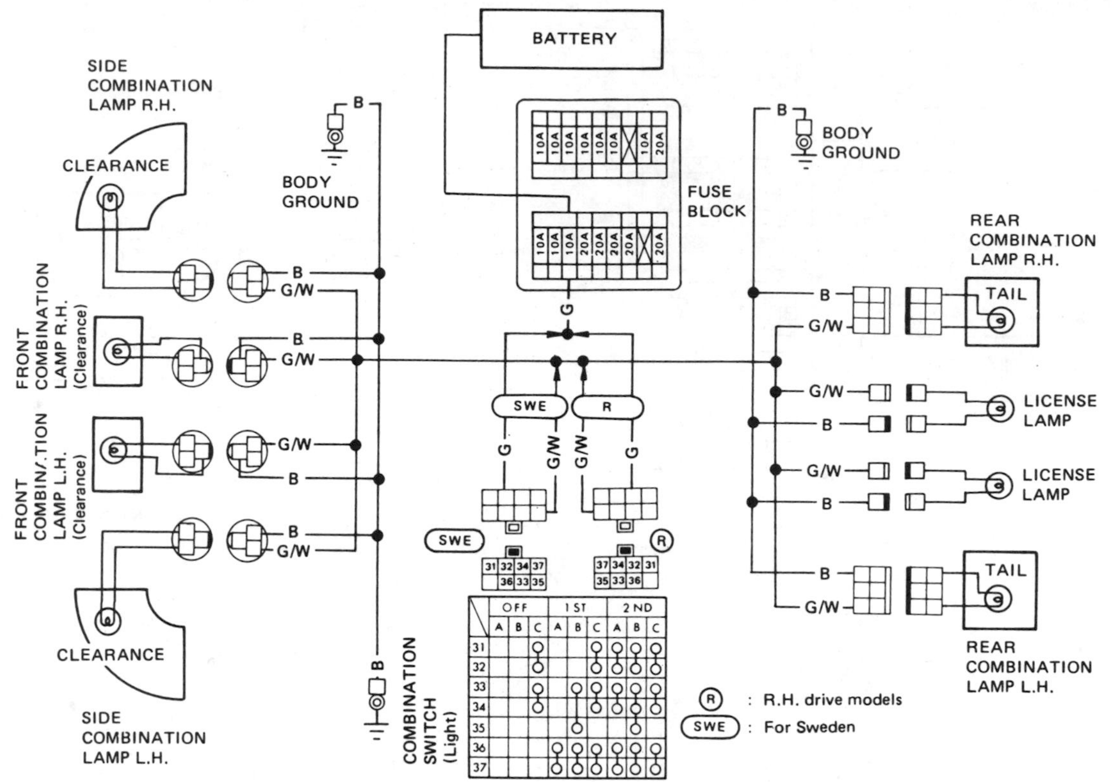

Fig. 10.64 Front sidelights, number plate light and tail lights (Sunny N12 models – right-hand drive and Sweden)

For the colour code see Fig. 10.43

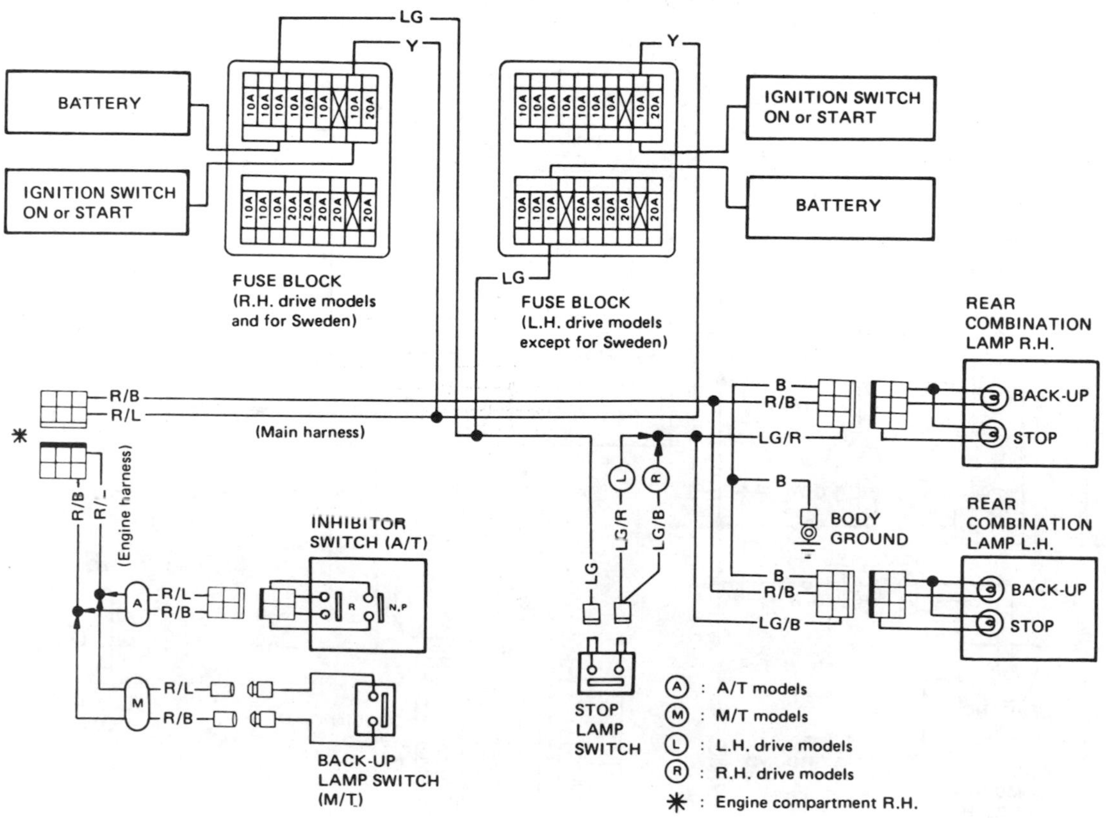

Fig. 10.65 Stop and reversing lights (Sunny N12 models)

For the colour code see Fig. 10.43

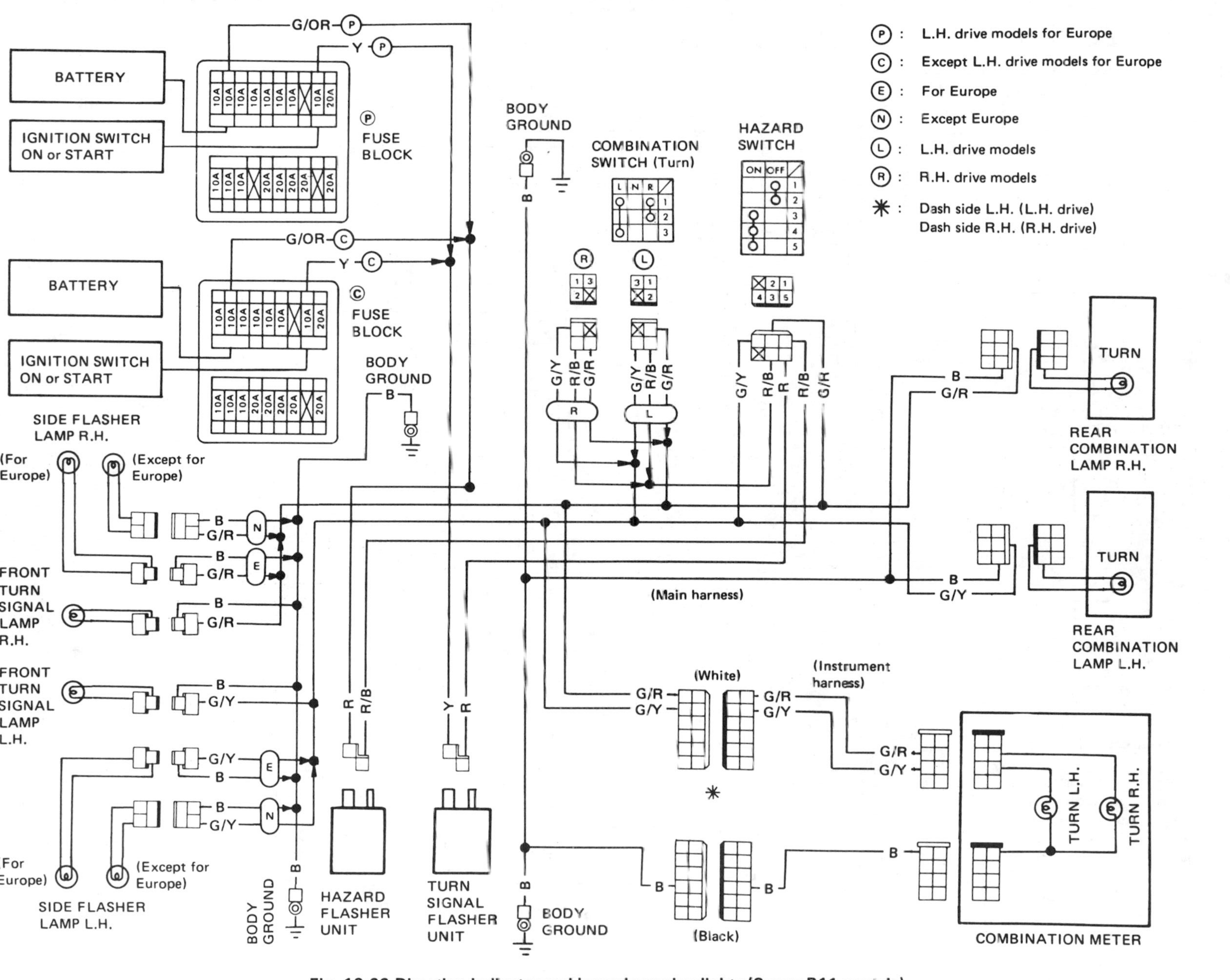

Fig. 10.66 Direction indicator and hazard warning lights (Sunny B11 models)

For the colour code see Fig. 10.43

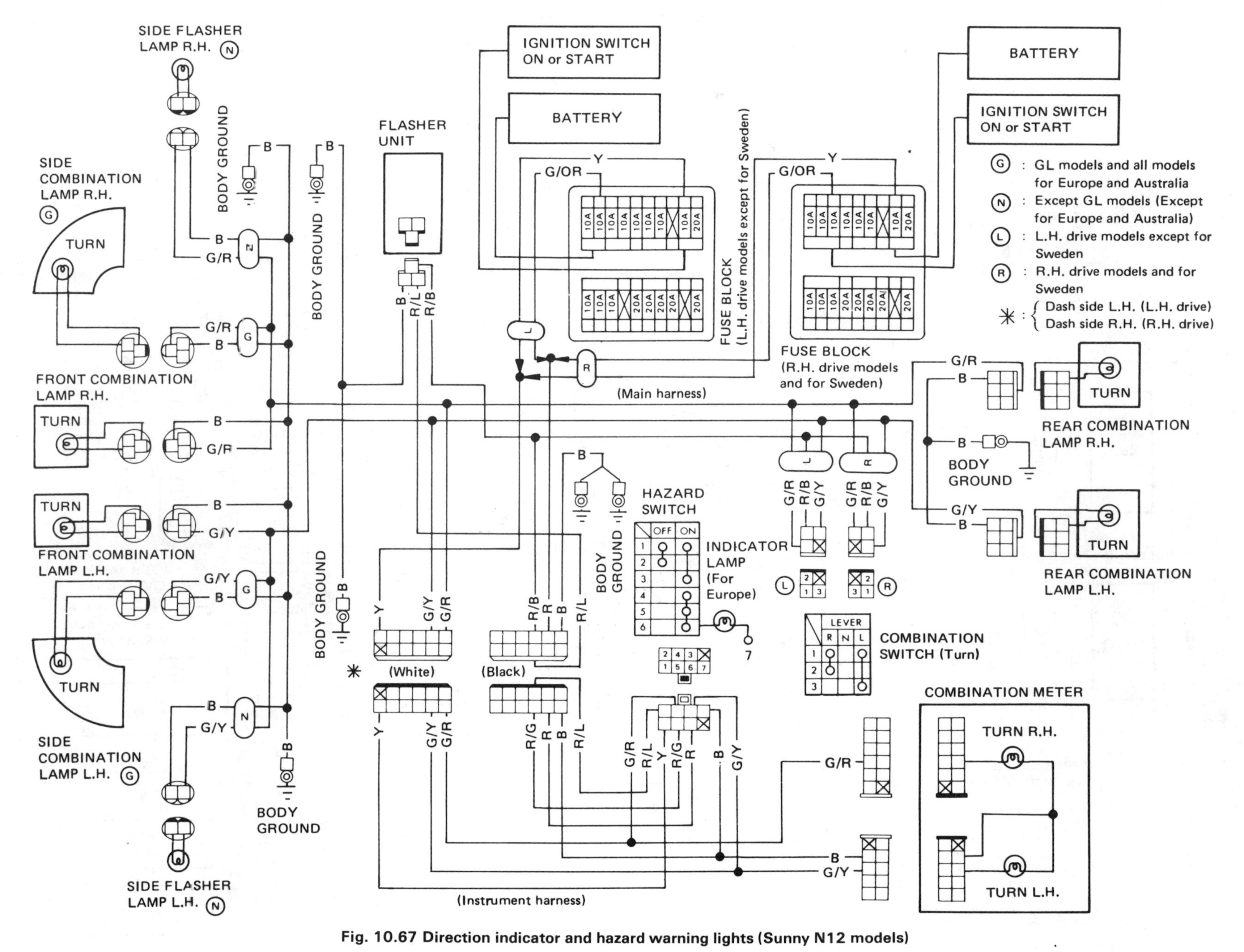

Fig. 10.67 Direction indicator and hazard warning lights (Sunny N12 models)

For the colour code see Fig. 10.43

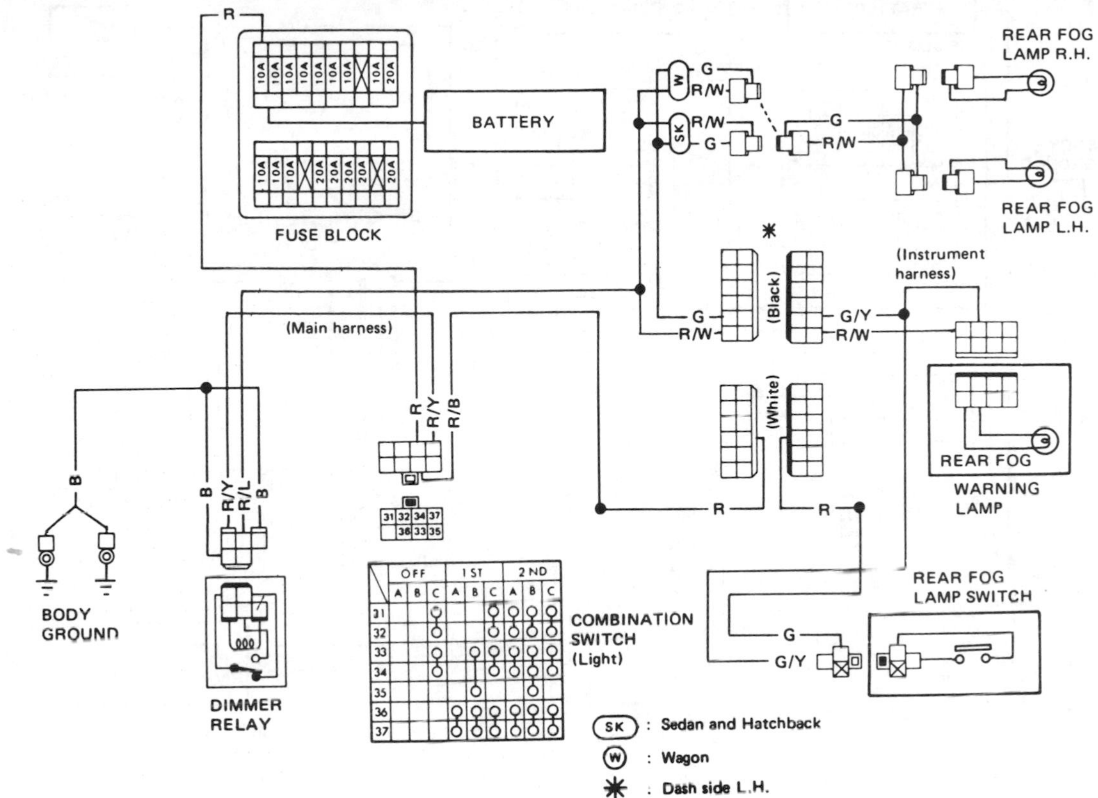

Fig. 10.68 Rear foglamps (Sunny B11 models – left-hand drive Europe)

For the colour code see Fig. 10.43

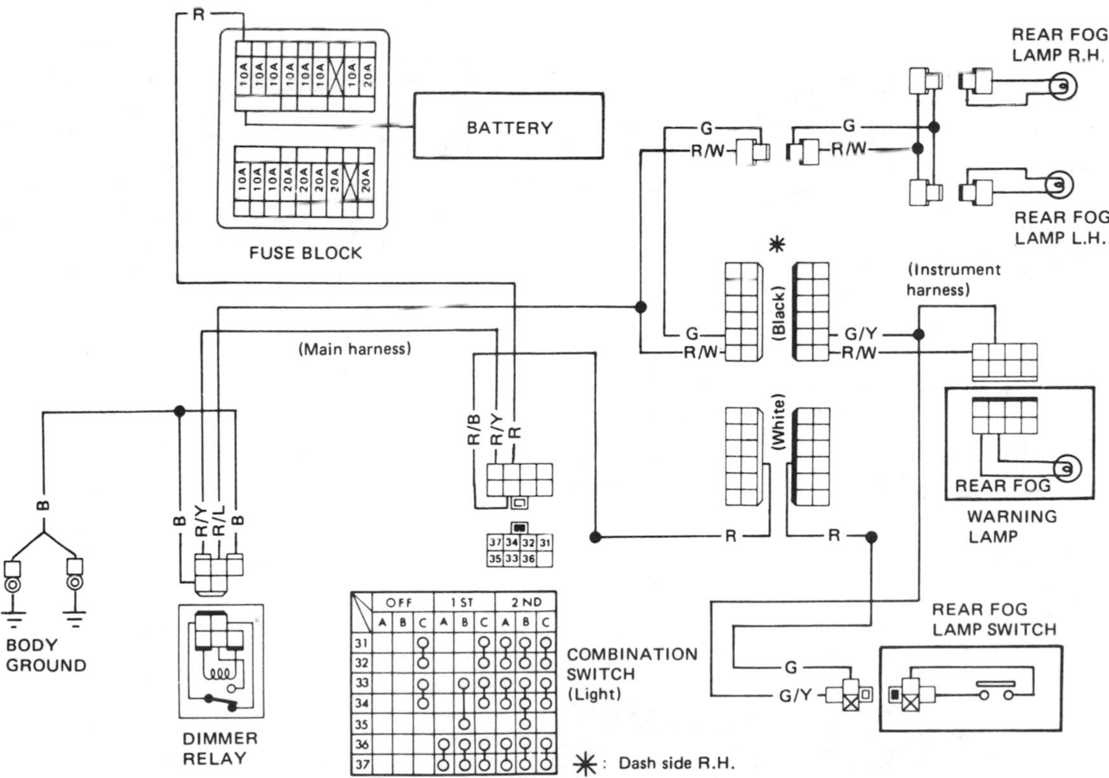

Fig. 10.69 Rear foglamps (Sunny B11 models – right-hand drive Europe)

For the colour code see Fig. 10.43

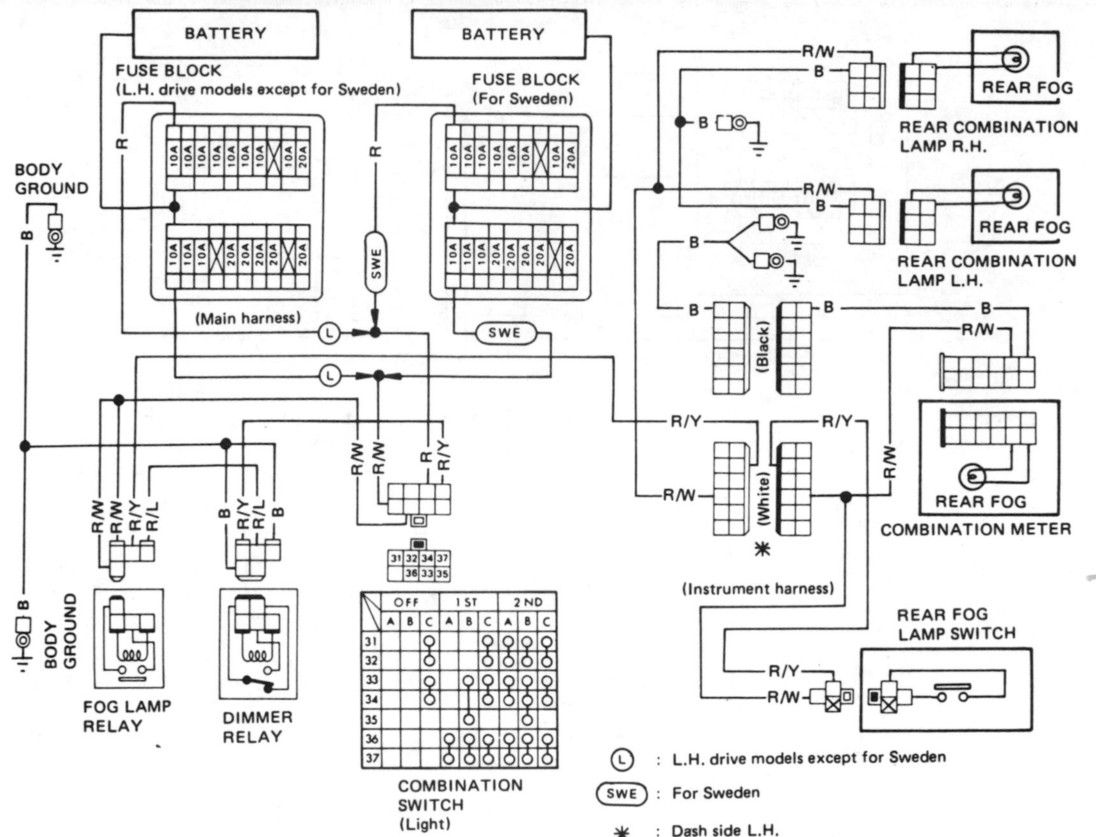

Fig. 10.70 Rear foglamps (Sunny N12 models – left-hand drive Europe)

For the colour code see Fig. 10.43

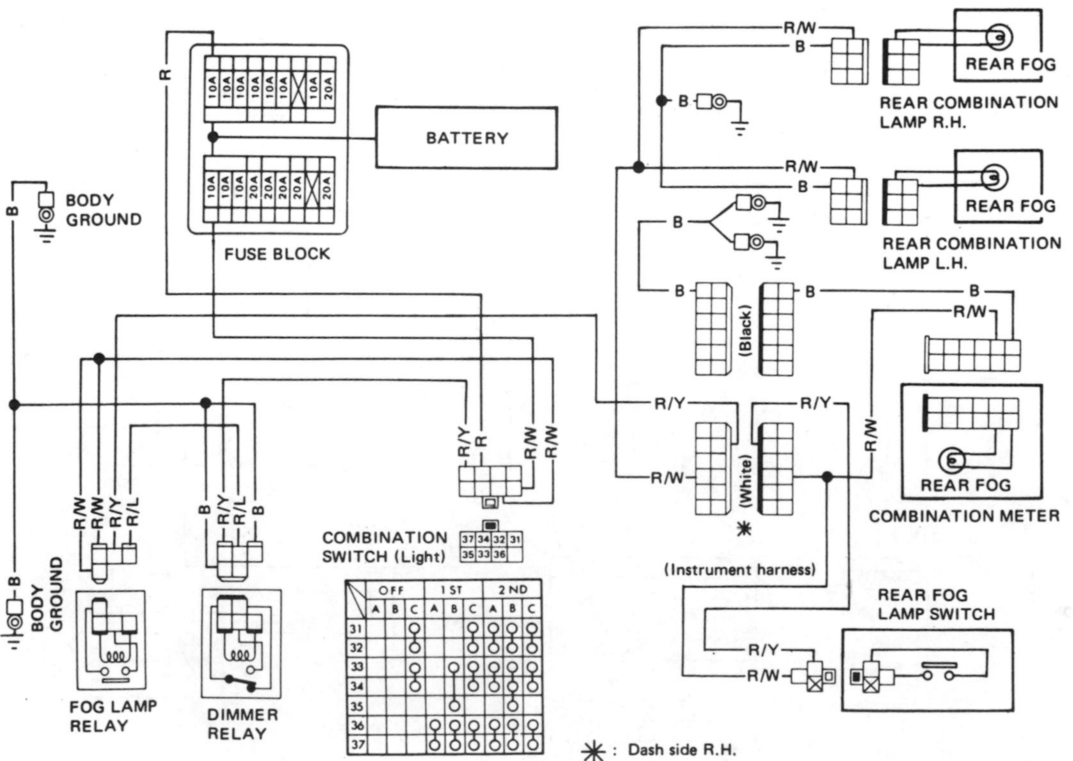

Fig. 10.71 Rear foglamps (Sunny N12 models – right-hand drive Europe)

For the colour code see Fig. 10.43

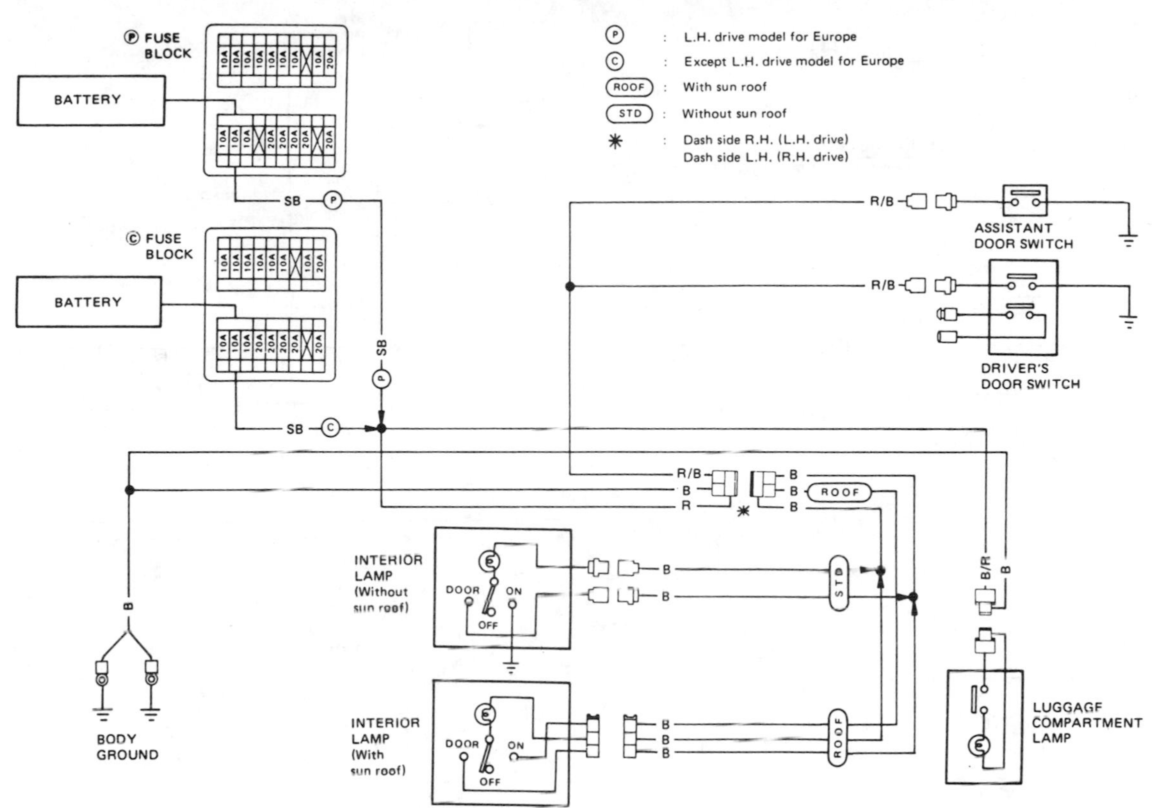

Fig. 10.72 Interior and luggage compartment lights (Sunny B11 models)

For the colour code see Fig. 10.43

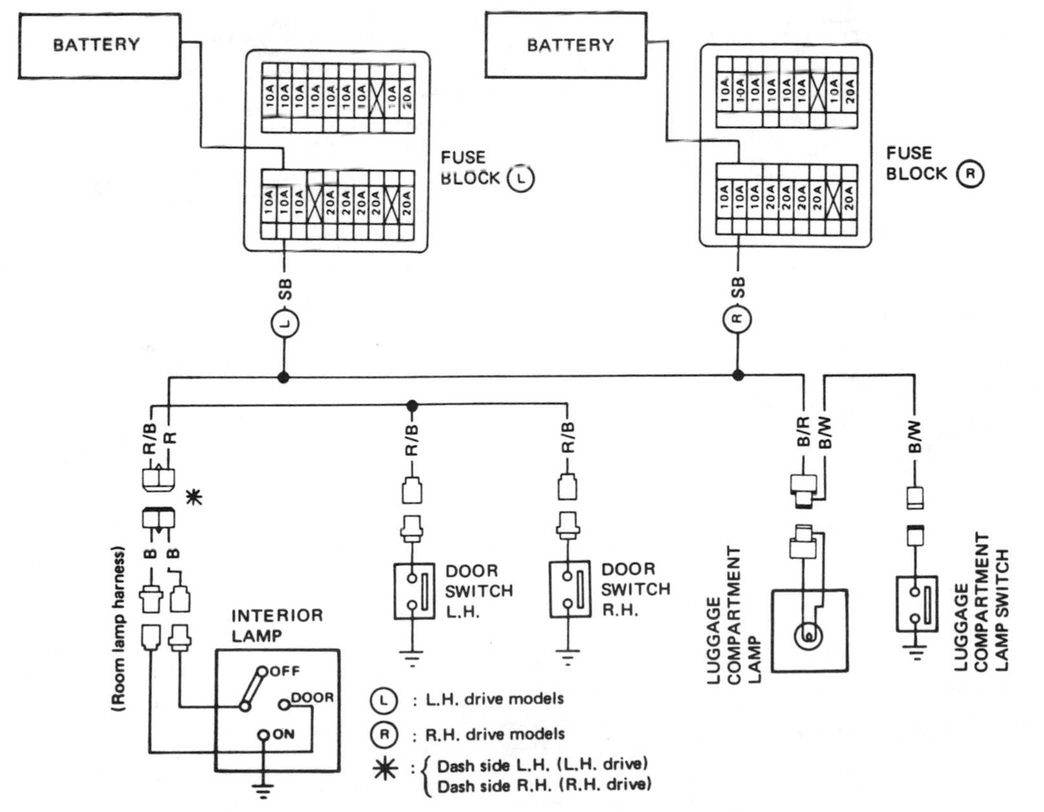

Fig. 10.73 Interior and luggage compartment lights (Sunny N12 models)

For the colour code see Fig. 10.43

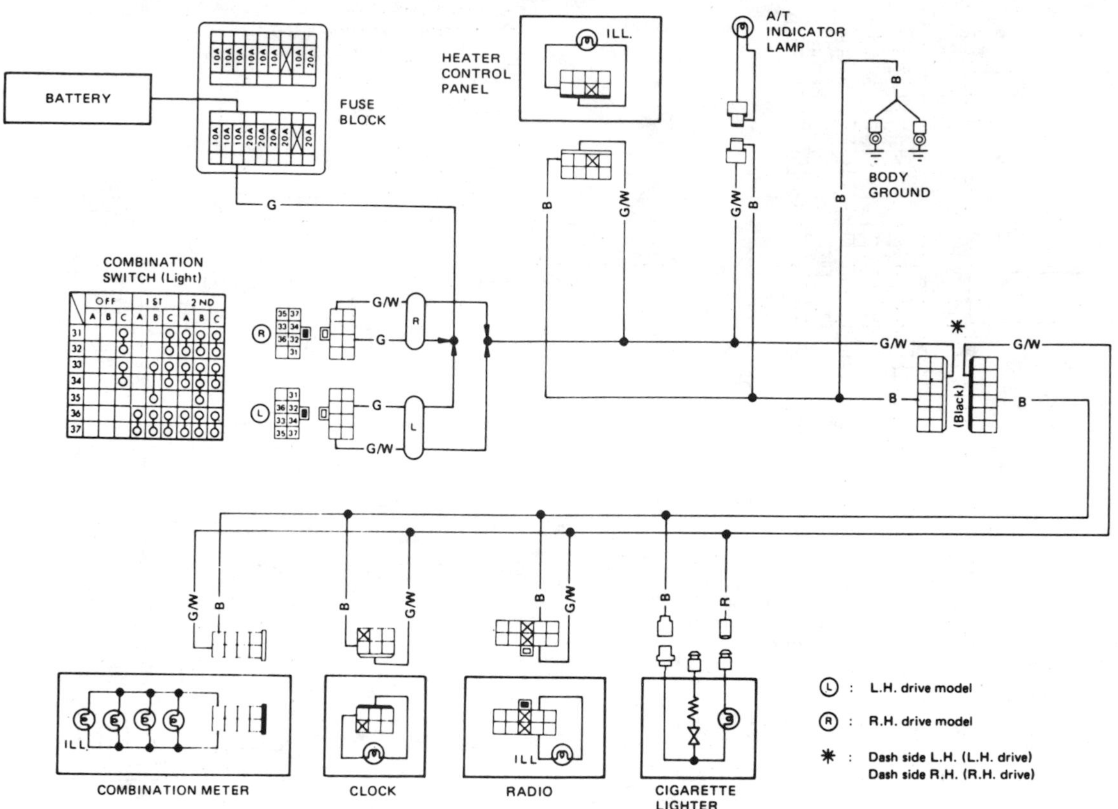

Fig. 10.74 Illumination for instruments and controls (Sunny B11 models – except left-hand drive Europe)

For the colour code see Fig. 10.43

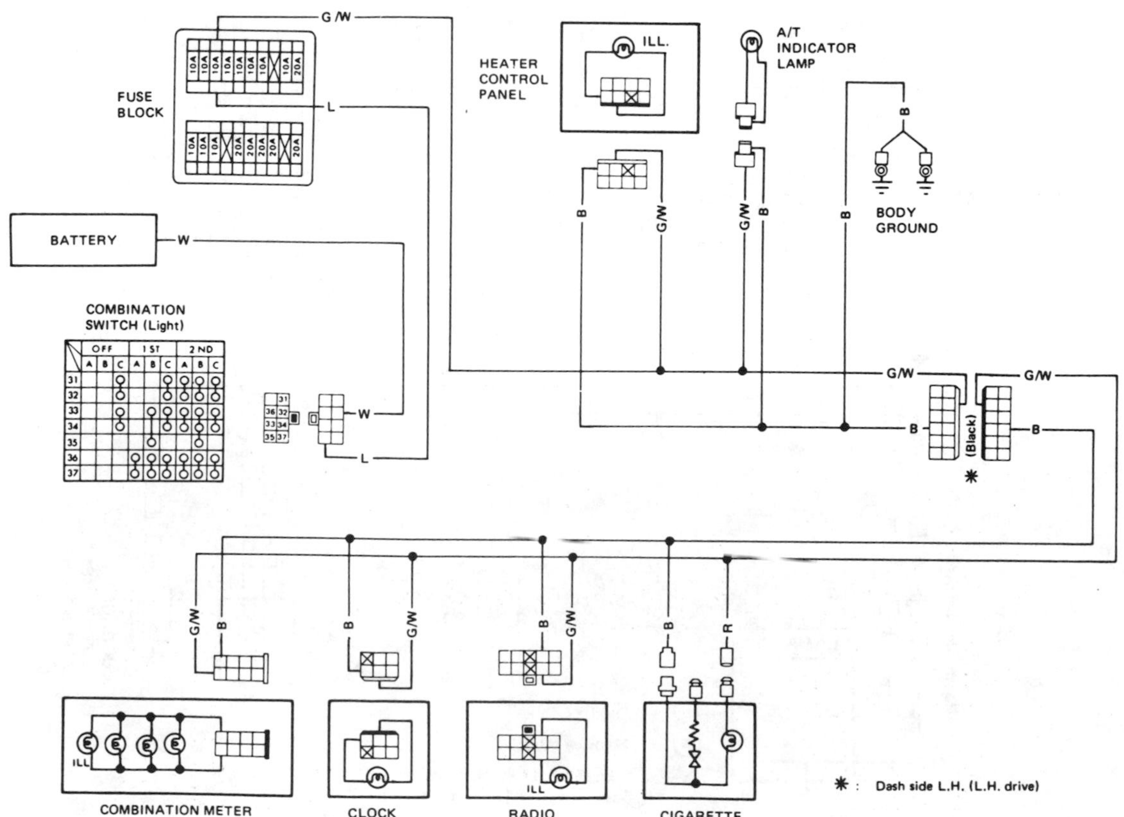

Fig. 10.75 Illumination for instruments and controls (Sunny B11 models – left-hand drive Europe)

For the colour code see Fig. 10.43

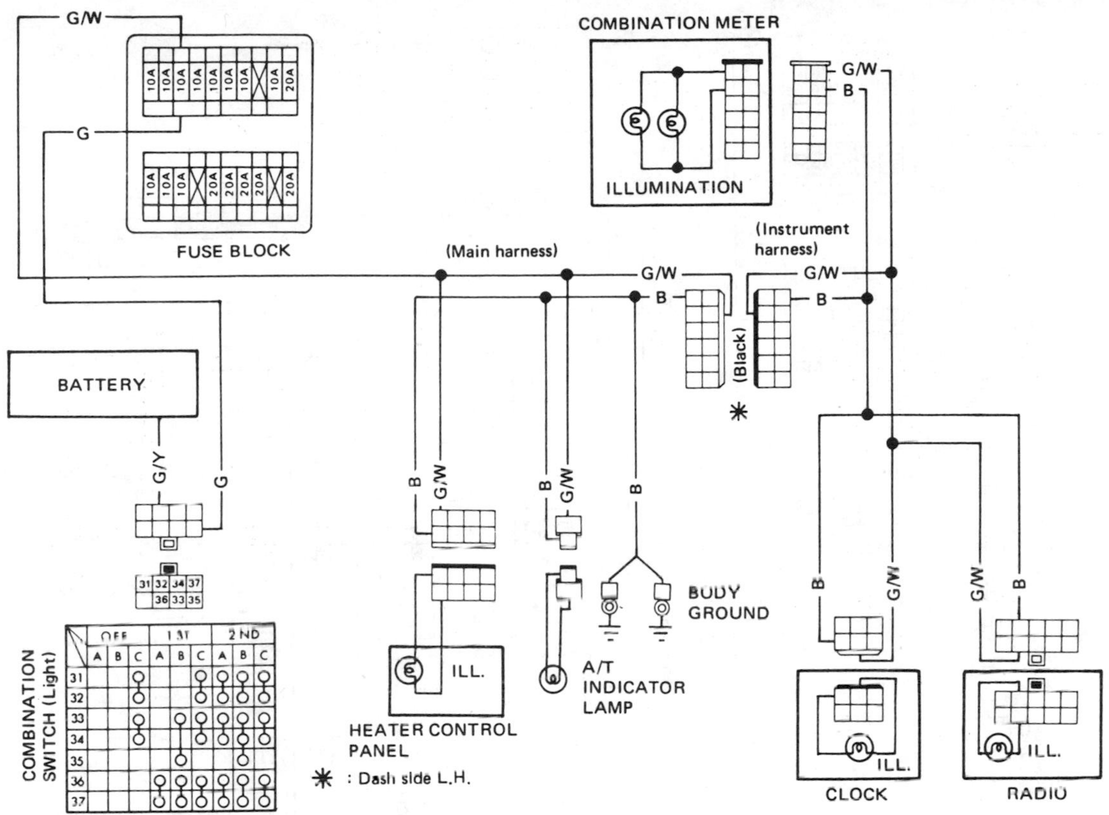

Fig. 10.76 Illumination for instruments and controls (Sunny N12 models – left-hand drive except Sweden)

For the colour code see Fig. 10.43

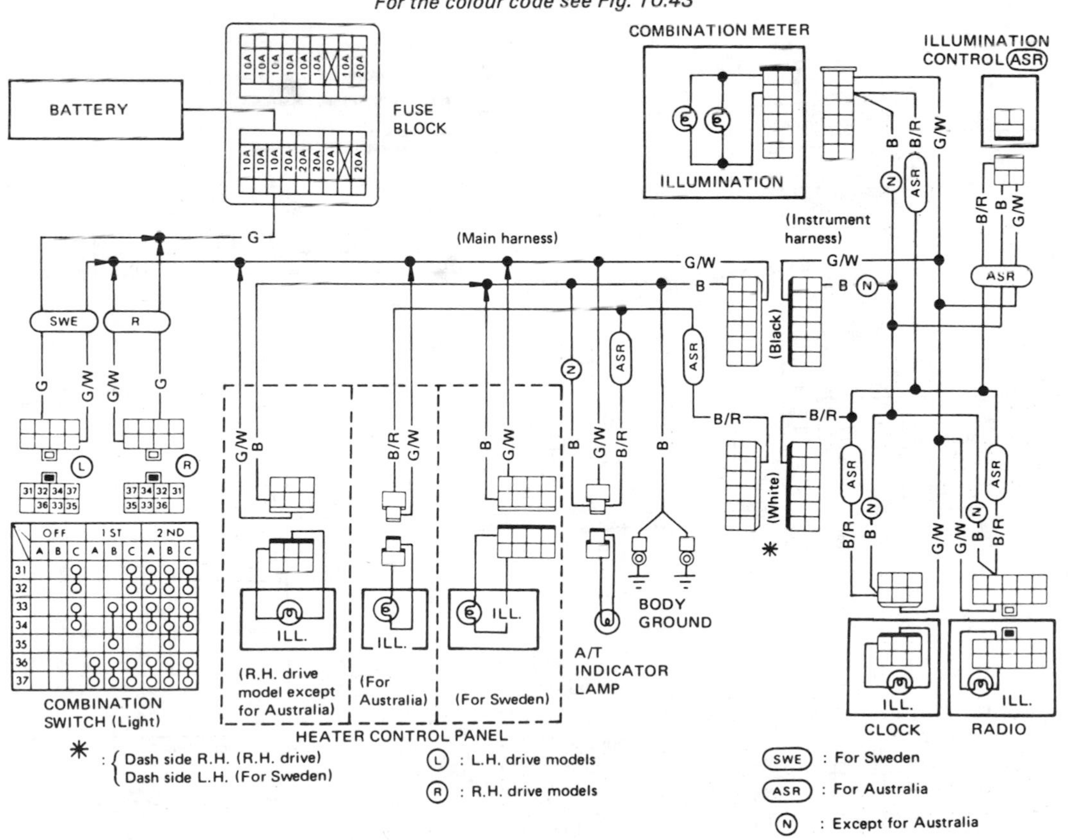

Fig. 10.77 Illumination for instruments and controls (Sunny N12 models – Sweden and Australia)

For the colour code see Fig. 10.43

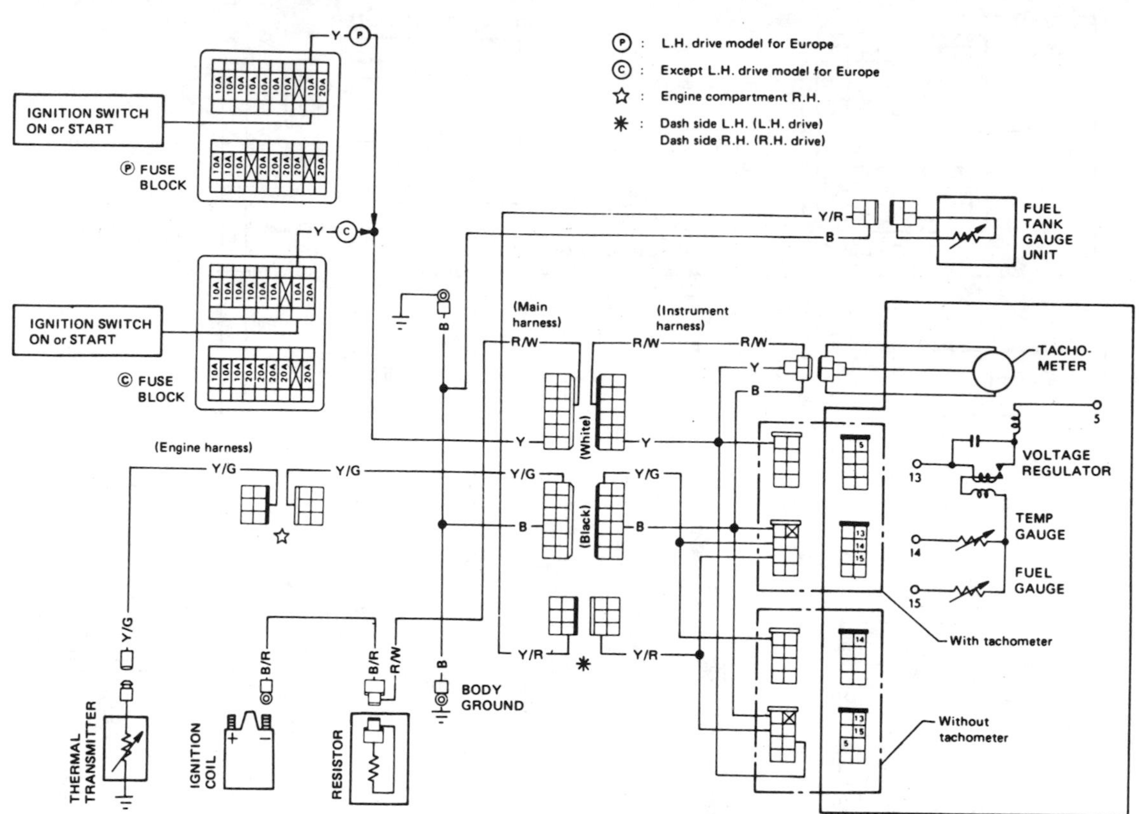

Fig. 10.78 Gauges and instruments (Sunny B11 models)

For the colour code see Fig. 10.43

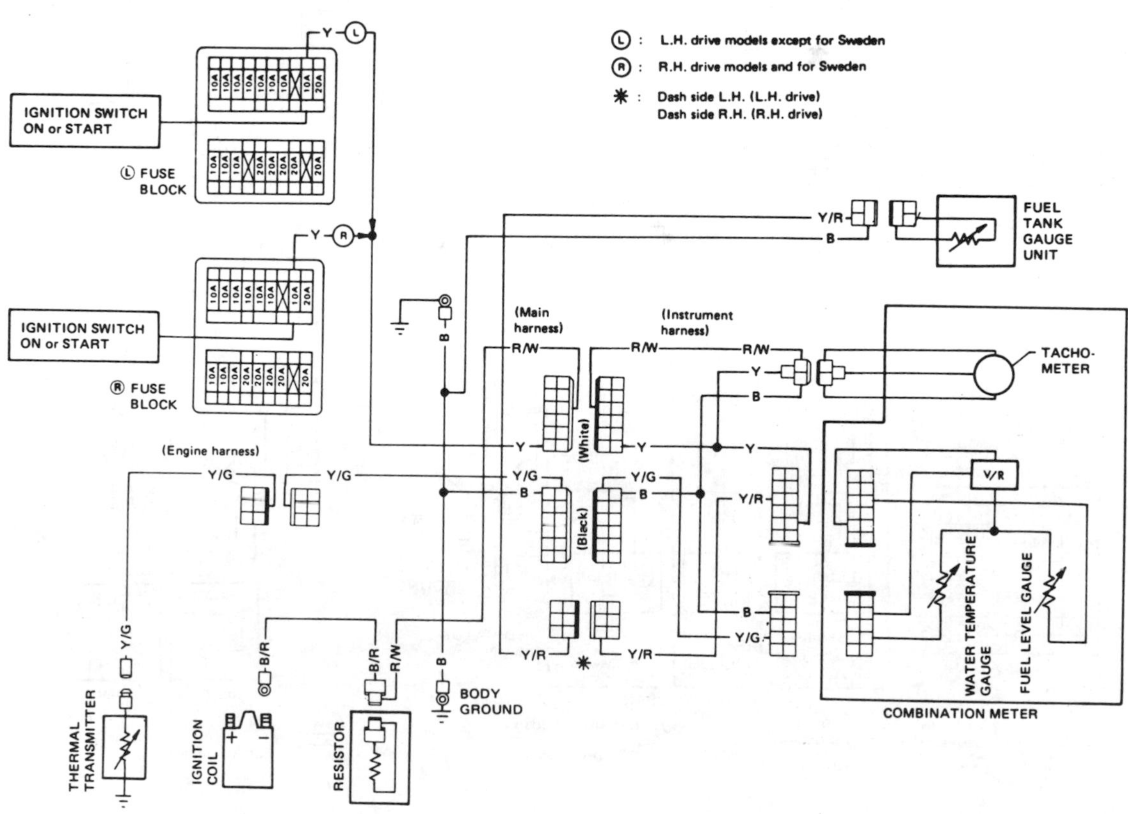

Fig. 10.79 Gauges and instruments (Sunny N12 models)

For the colour code see Fig. 10.43

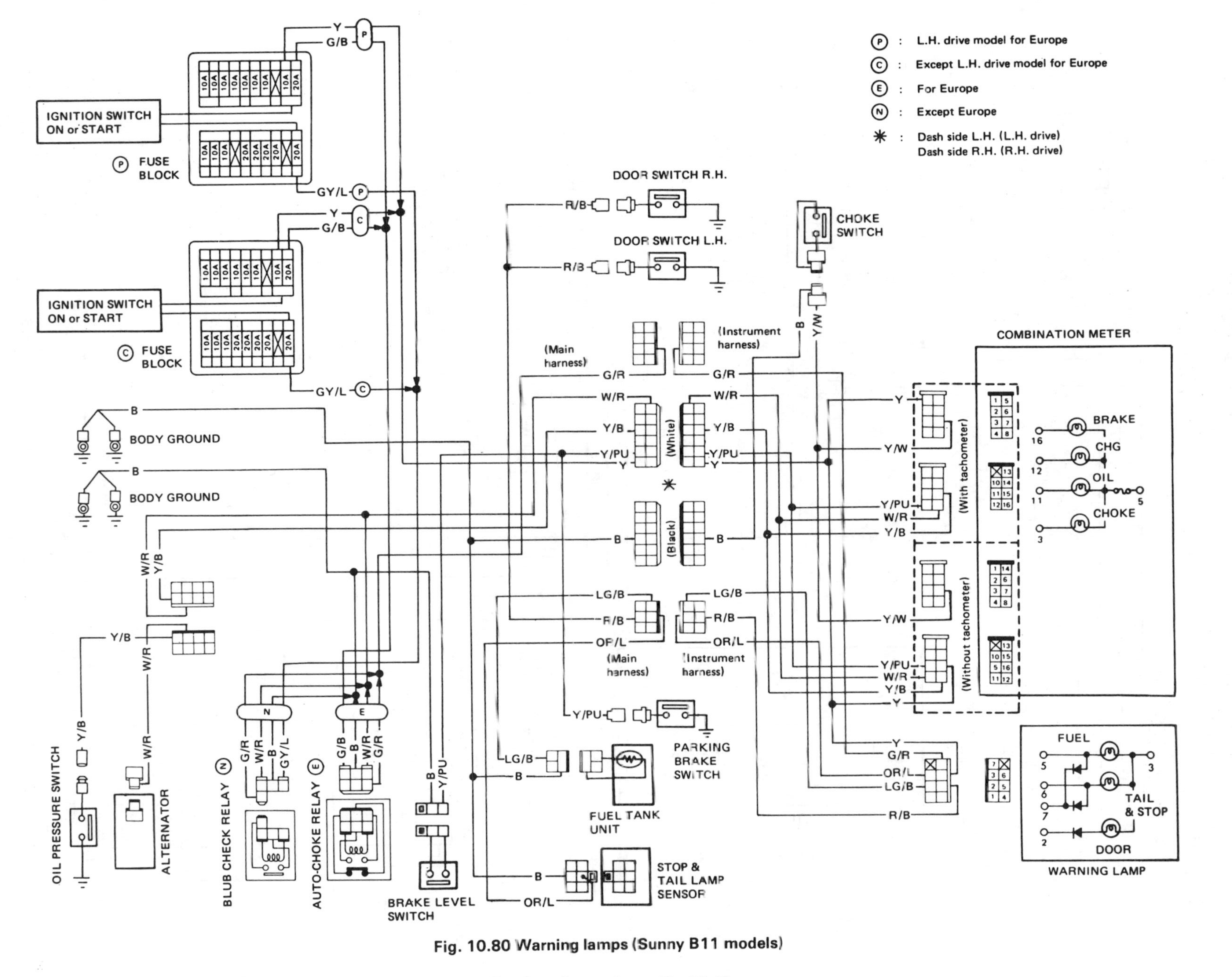

Fig. 10.80 Warning lamps (Sunny B11 models)

For the colour code see Fig. 10.43

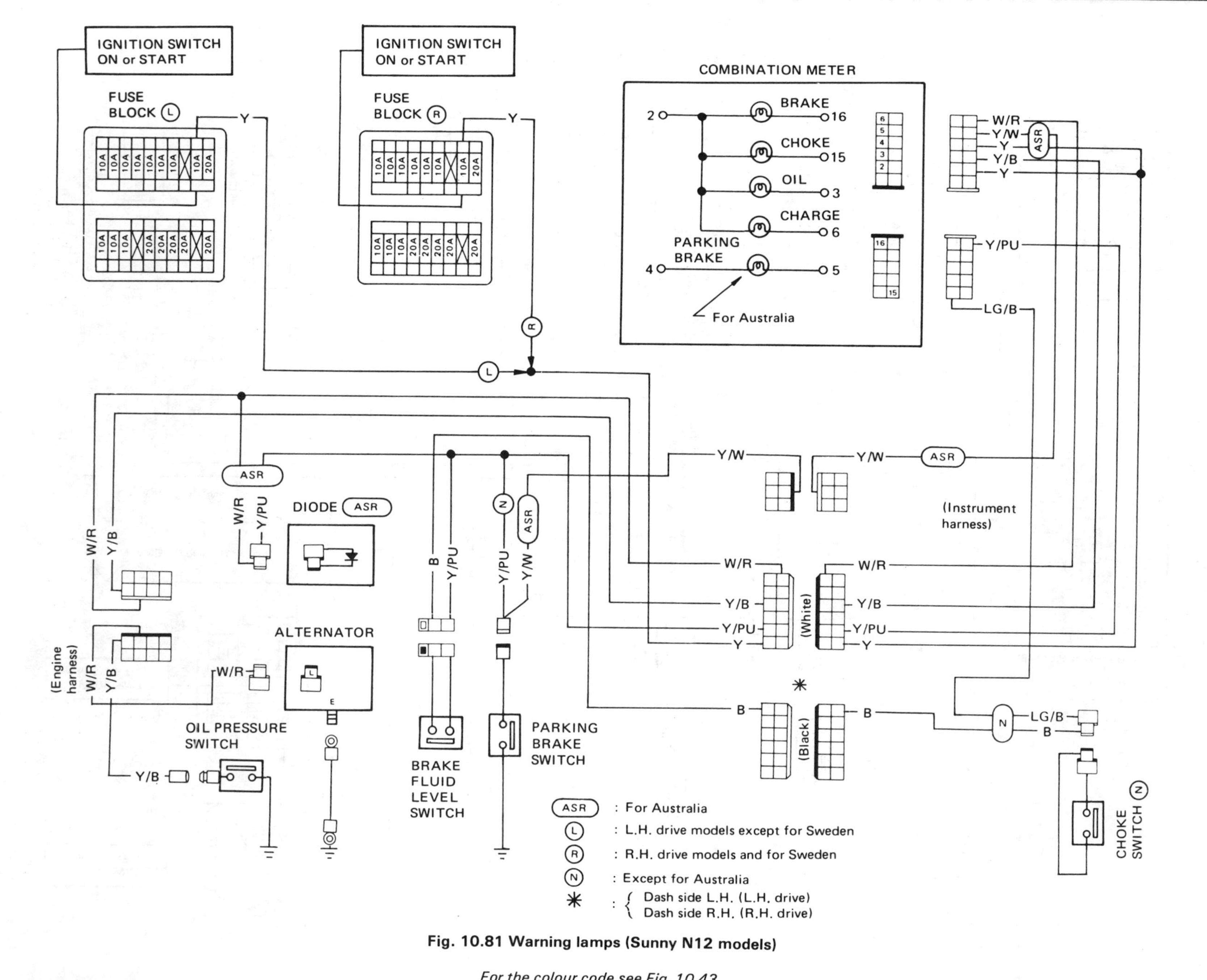

Fig. 10.81 Warning lamps (Sunny N12 models)

For the colour code see Fig. 10.43

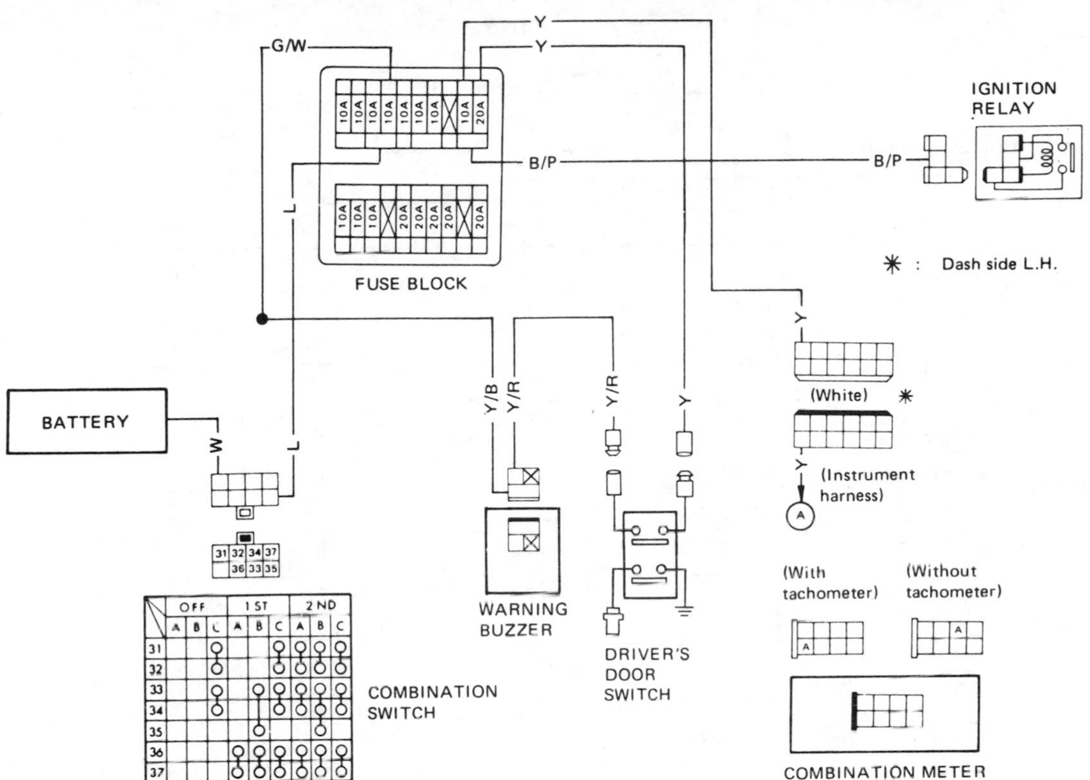

Fig. 10.82 Anti-theft buzzer (Sunny B11 models – left-hand drive Europe)

For the colour code see Fig. 10.43

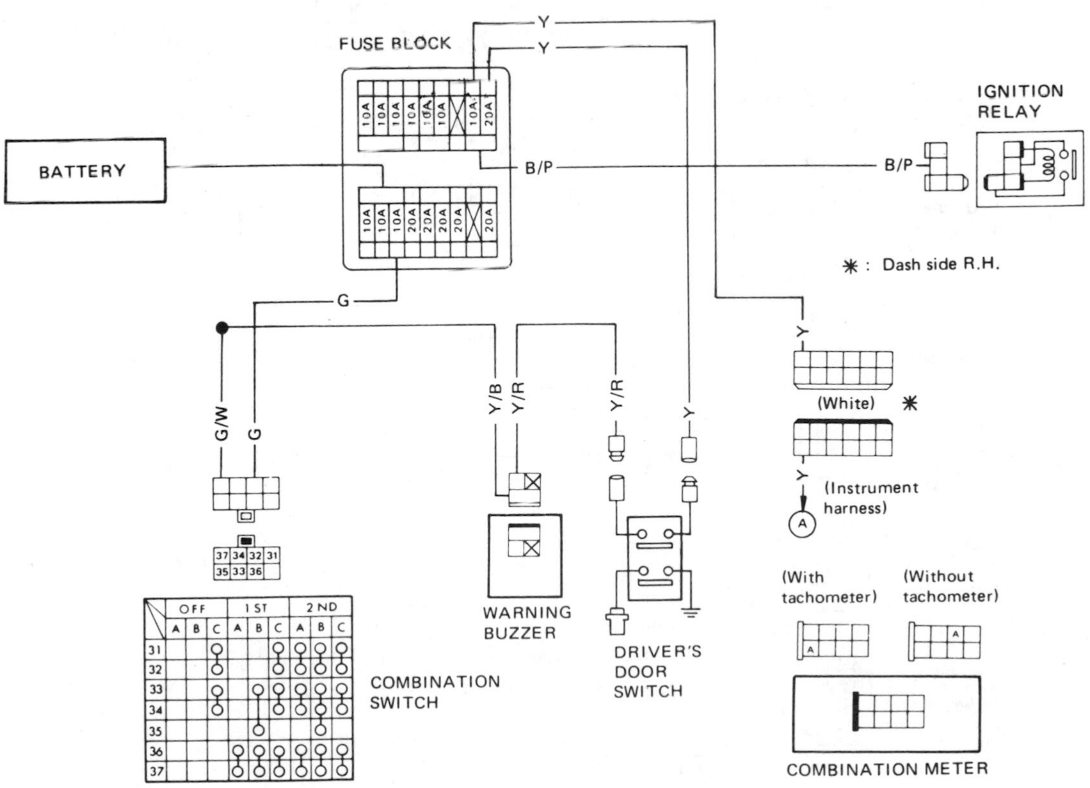

Fig. 10.83 Anti-theft buzzer (Sunny B11 models – right-hand drive Europe)

For the colour code see Fig. 10.43

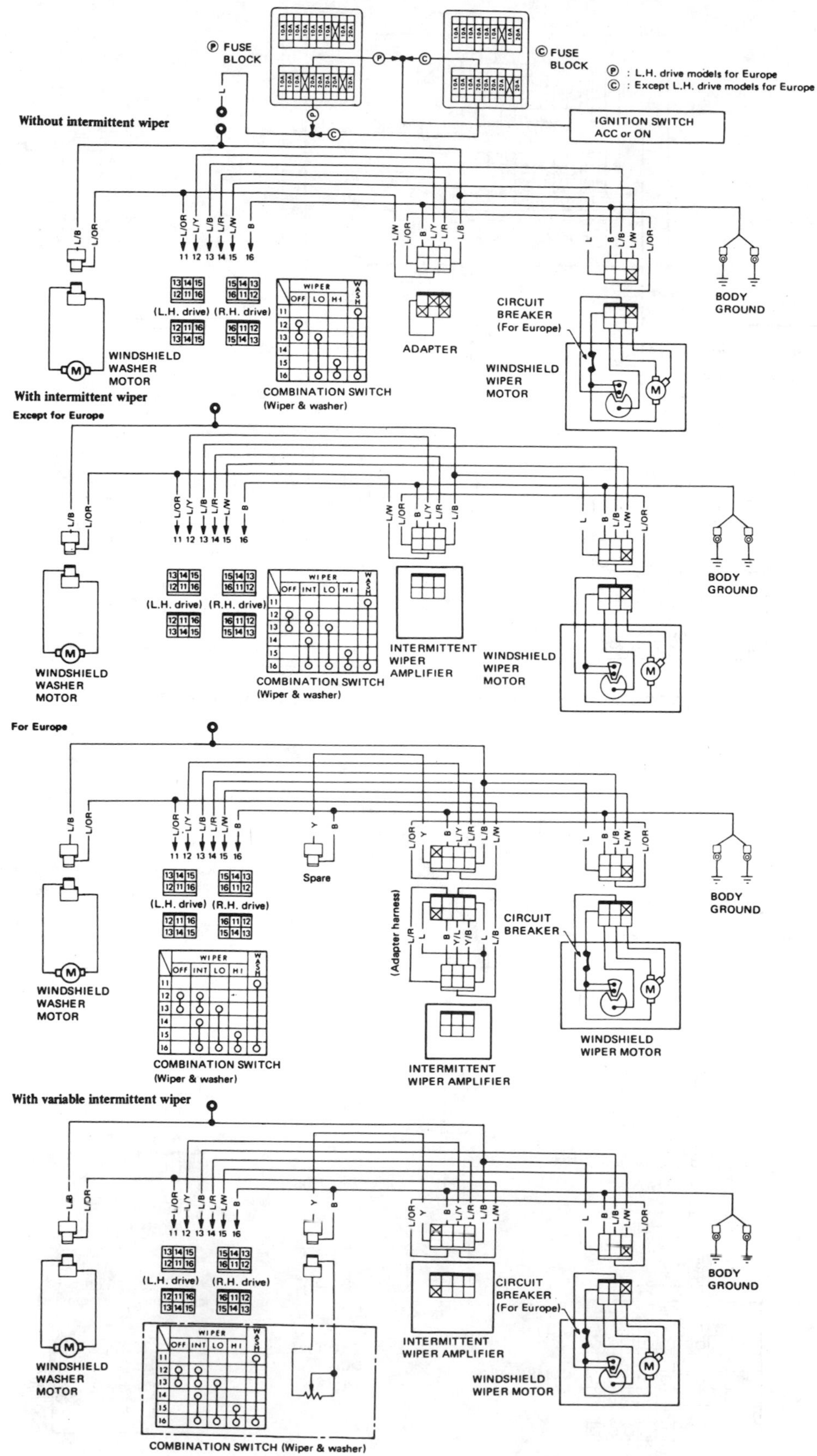

Fig. 10.84 Windscreen wiper/washer (Sunny B11 models)

For the colour code see Fig. 10.43

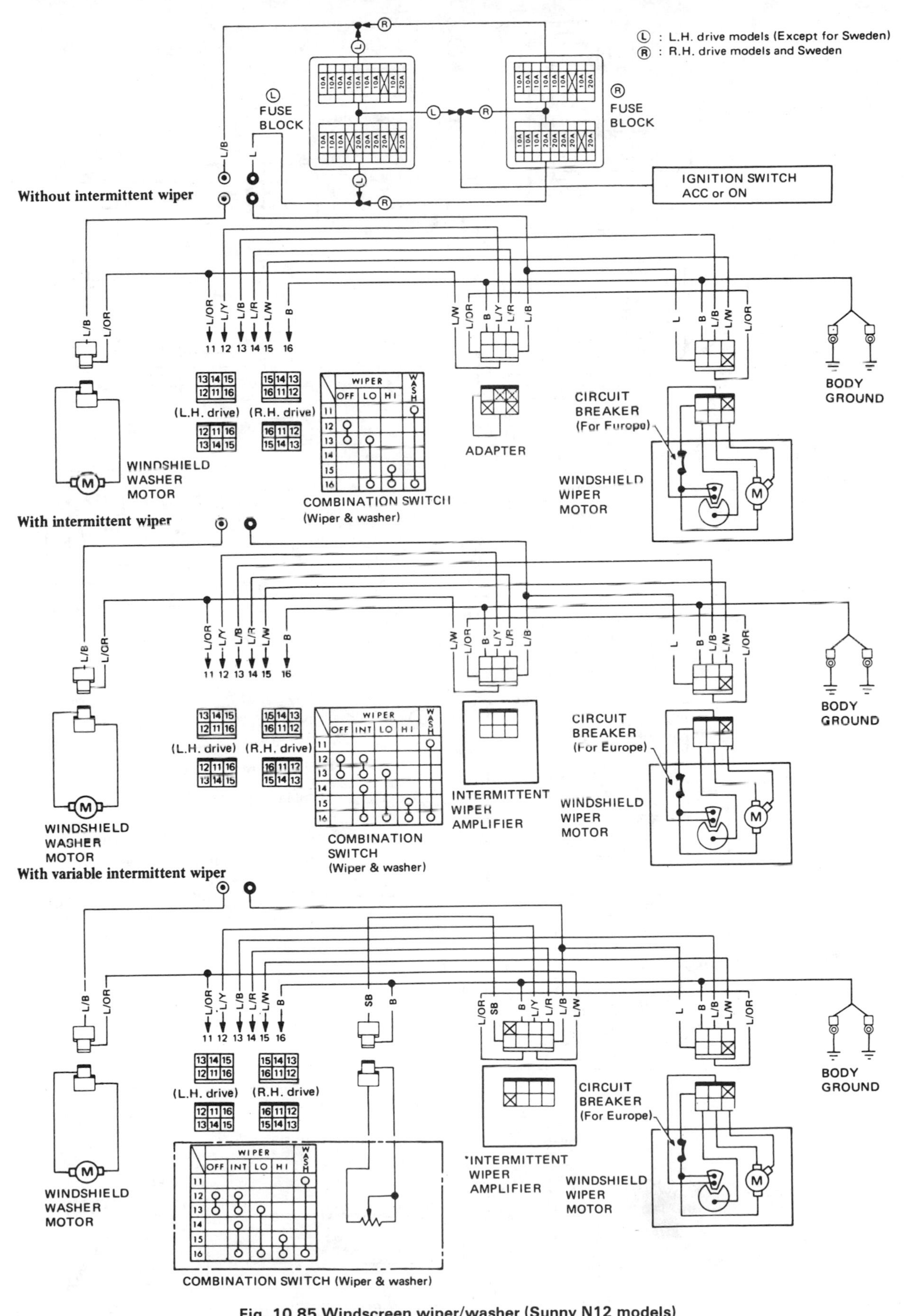

Fig. 10.85 Windscreen wiper/washer (Sunny N12 models)

For the colour code see Fig. 10.43

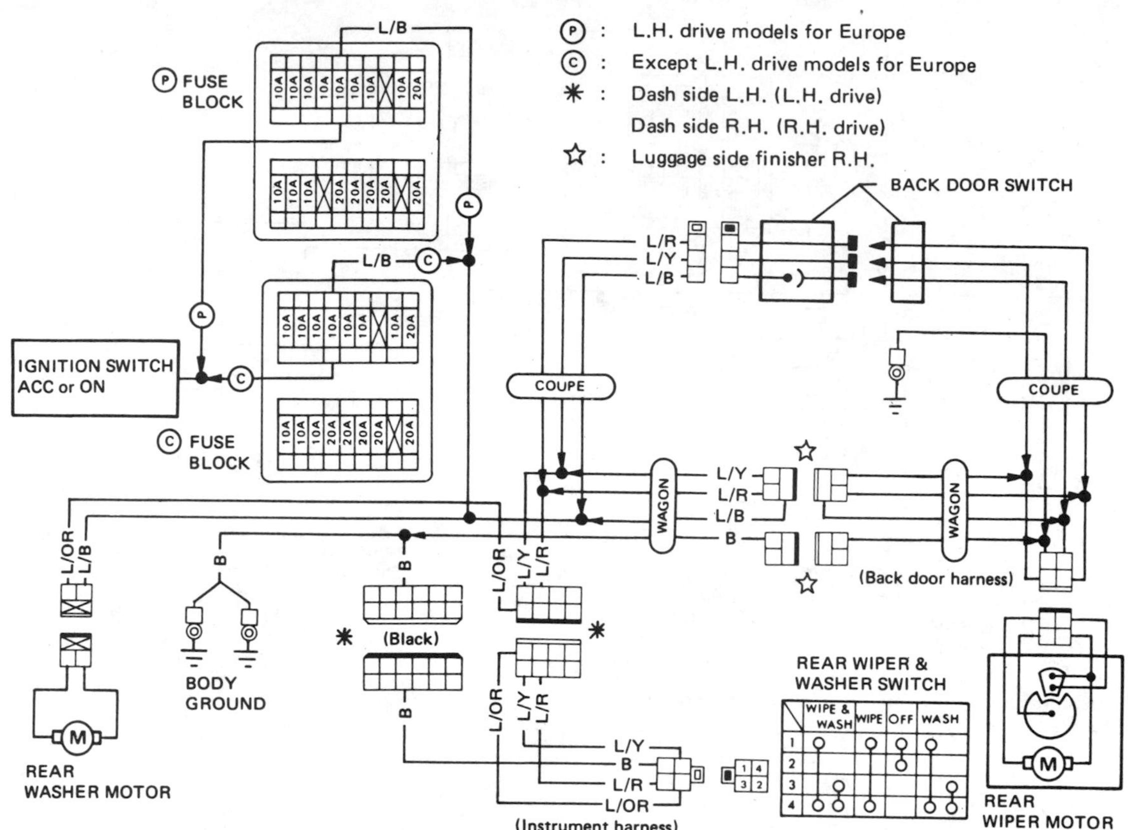

Fig. 10.86 Rear window wiper/washer (Sunny B11 models)

For the colour code see Fig. 10.43

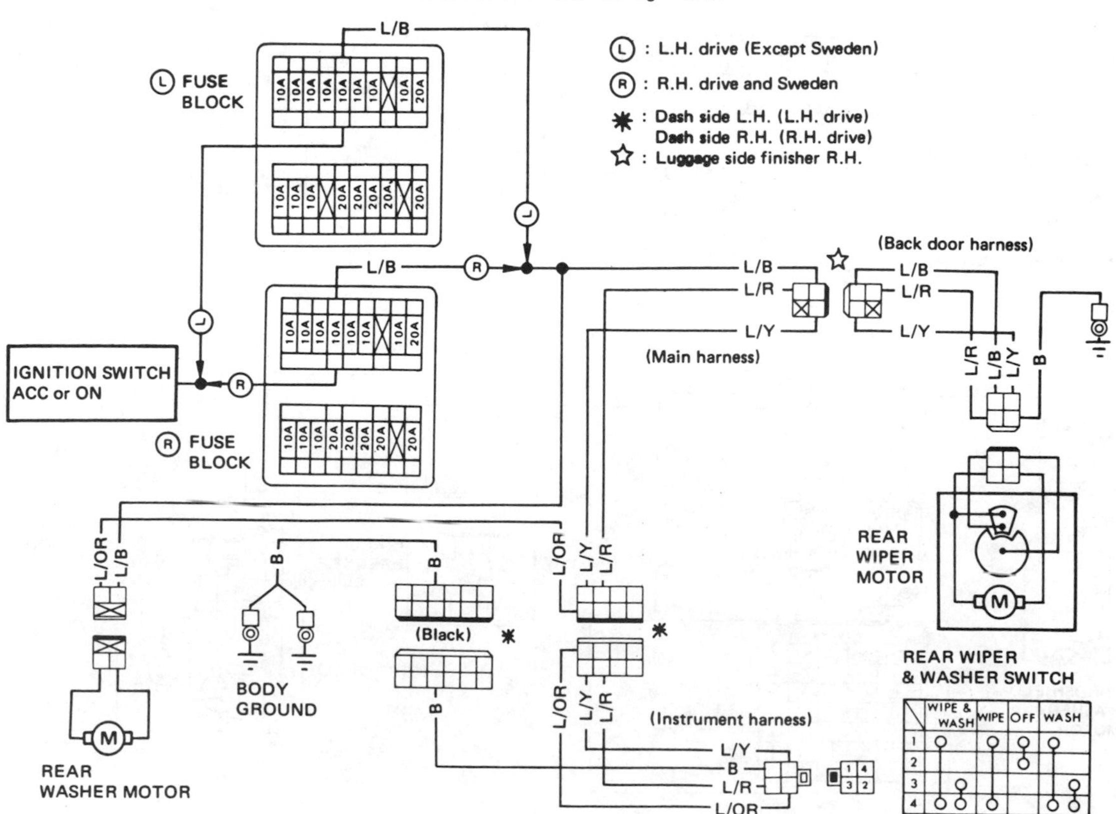

Fig. 10.87 Rear window wiper/washer (Sunny N12 models)

For the colour code see Fig. 10.43

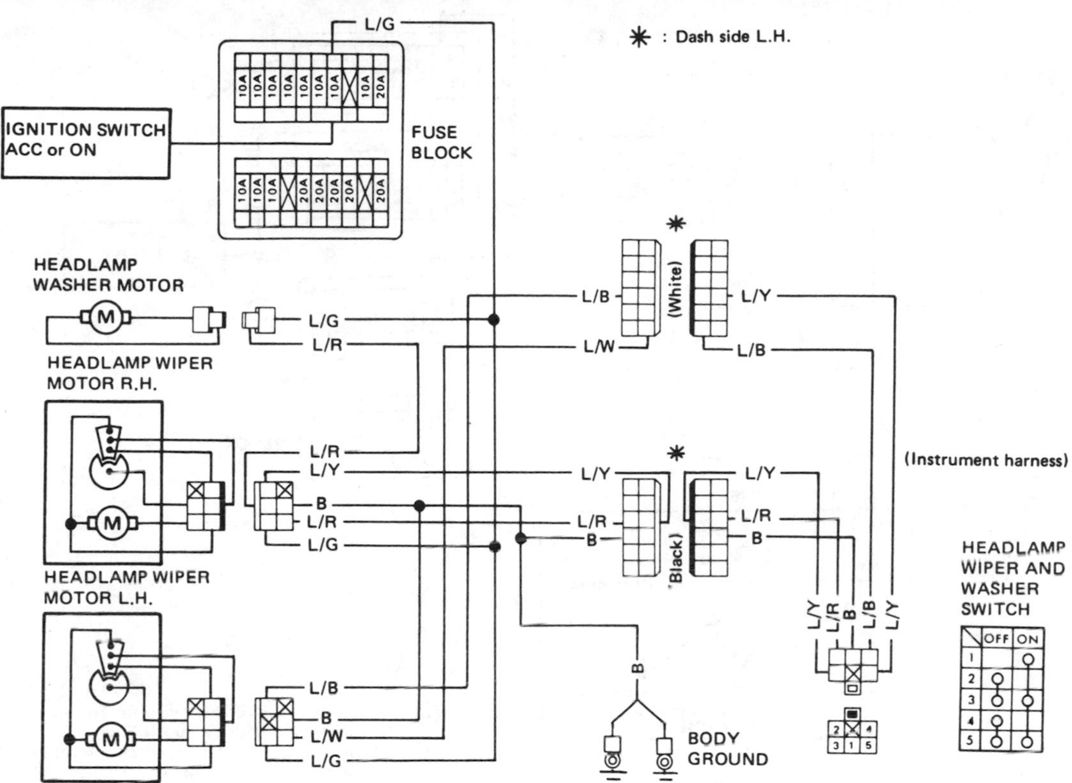

Fig. 10.88 Headlamp wash/wipe (Sunny B11 models)

For the colour code see Fig. 10.43

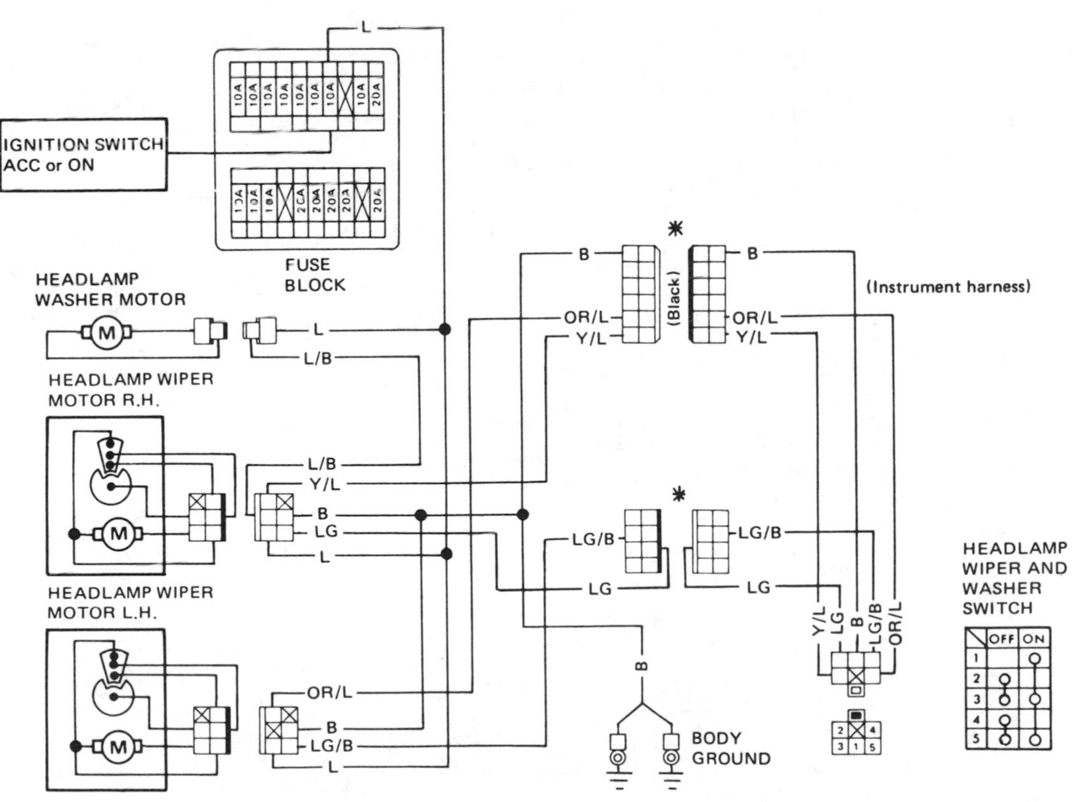

Fig. 10.89 Headlamp wash/wipe (Sunny N12 models)

For the colour code see Fig. 10.43

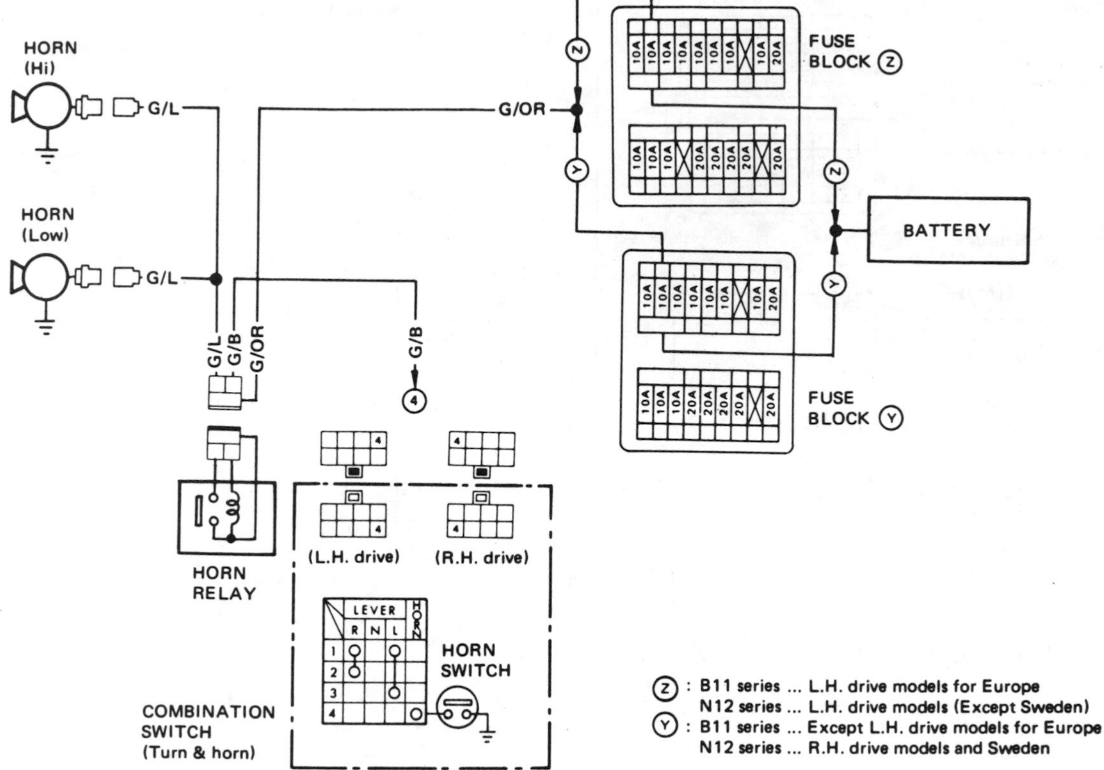

Fig. 10.90 Horn (all Sunny models)

For the colour code see Fig. 10.43

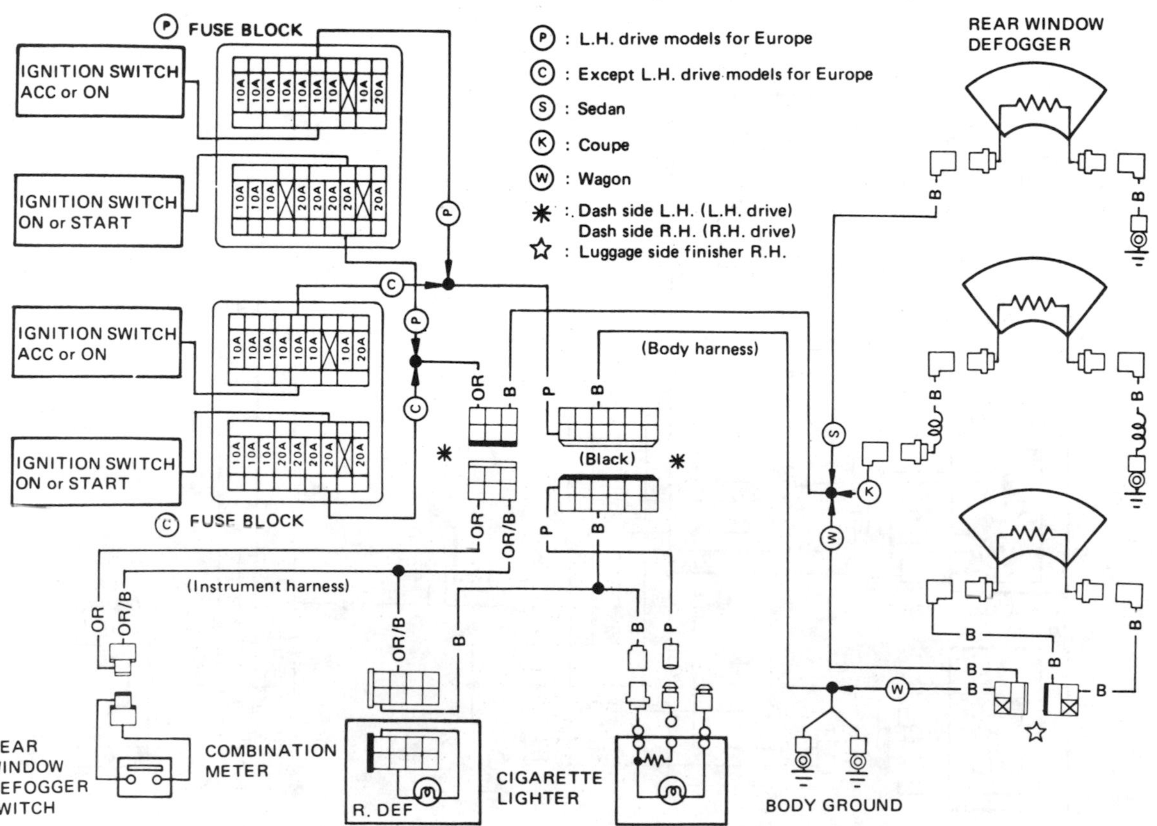

Fig. 10.91 Heated rear window and cigar lighter (Sunny B11 models)

For the colour code see Fig. 10.43

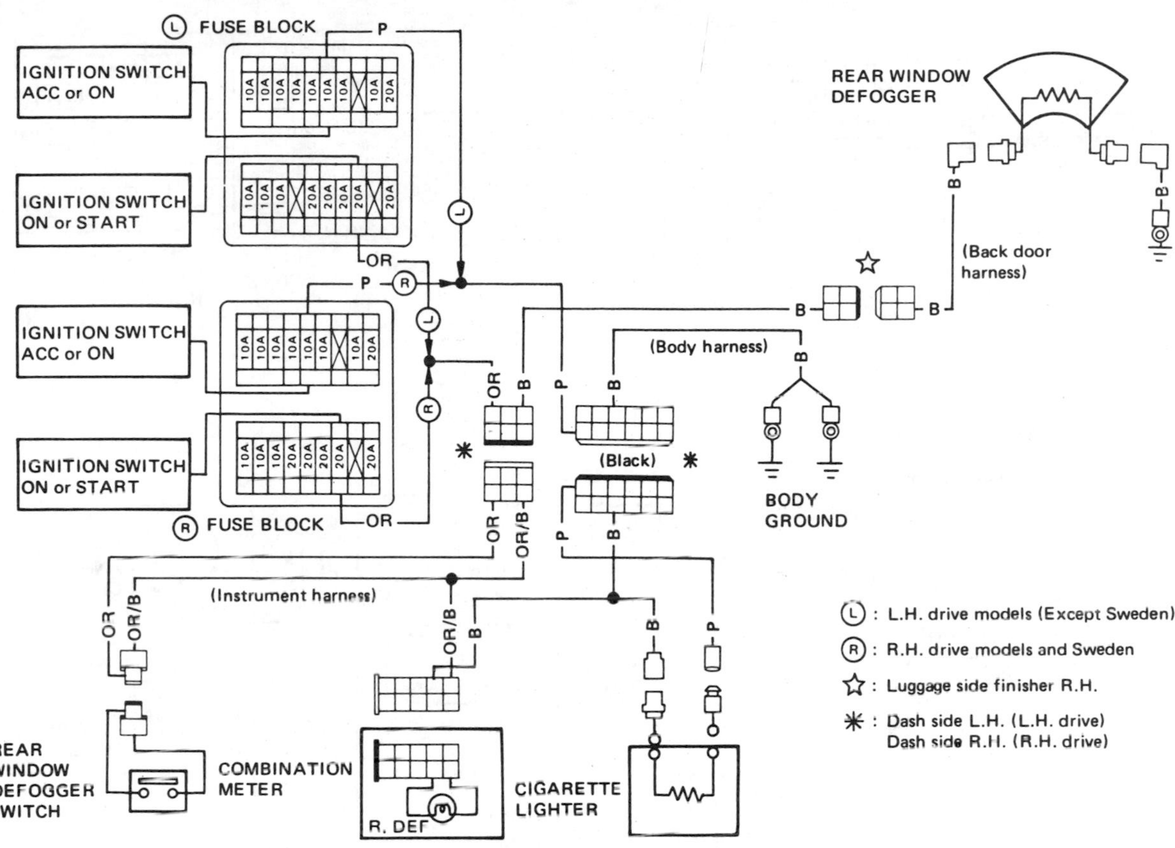

Fig. 10.92 Heated rear window and cigar lighter (Sunny N12 models)

For the colour code see Fig. 10.43

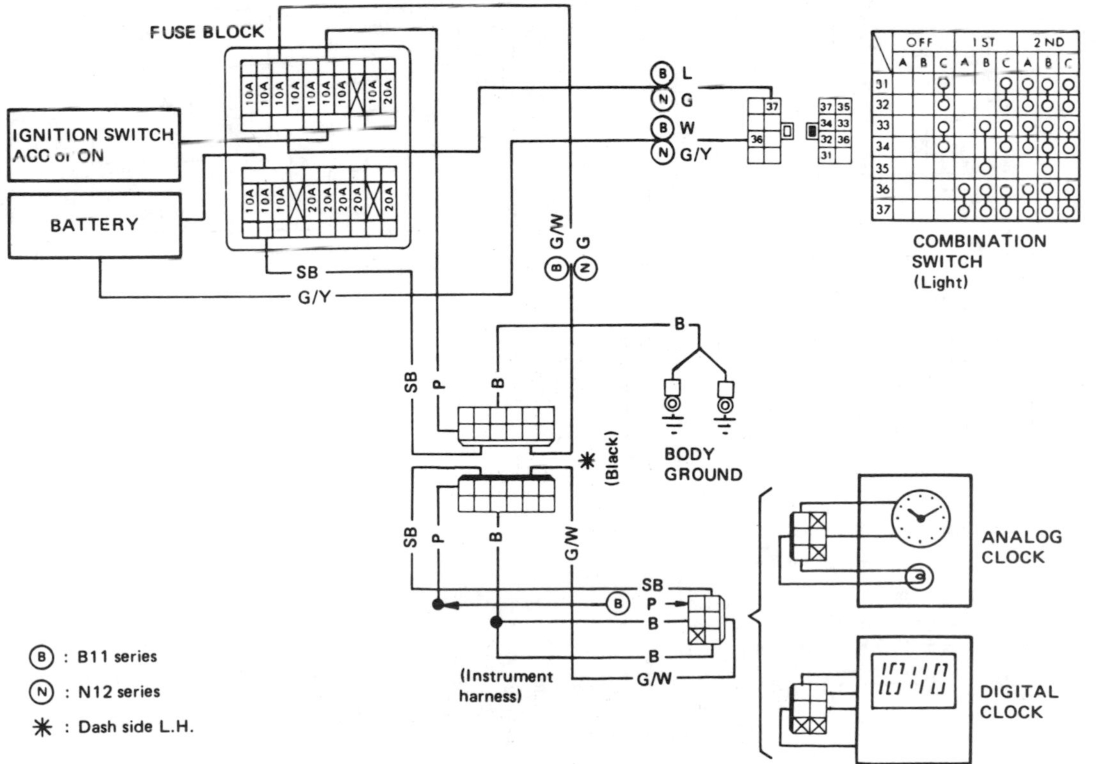

Fig. 10.93 Clock (all Sunny models – left-hand drive except Sweden)

For the colour code see Fig. 10.43

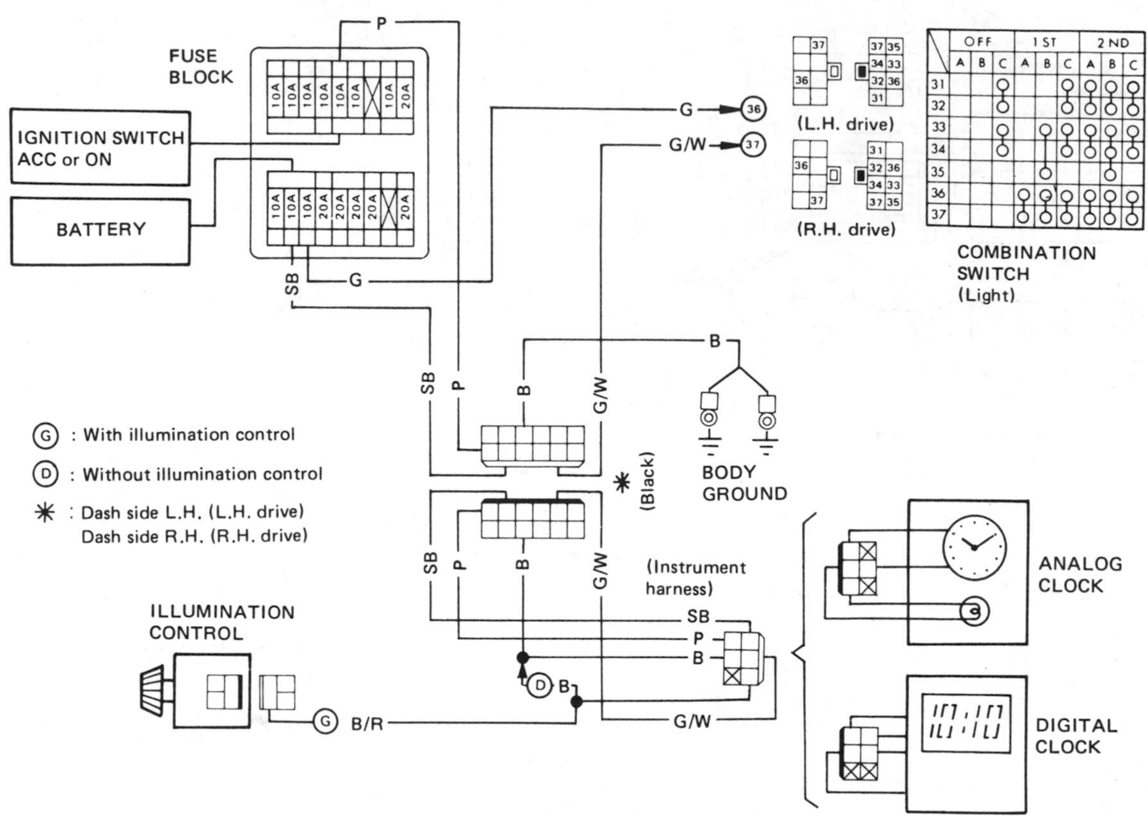

Fig. 10.94 Clock (all Sunny models – right-hand drive and Sweden)

For the colour code see Fig. 10.43

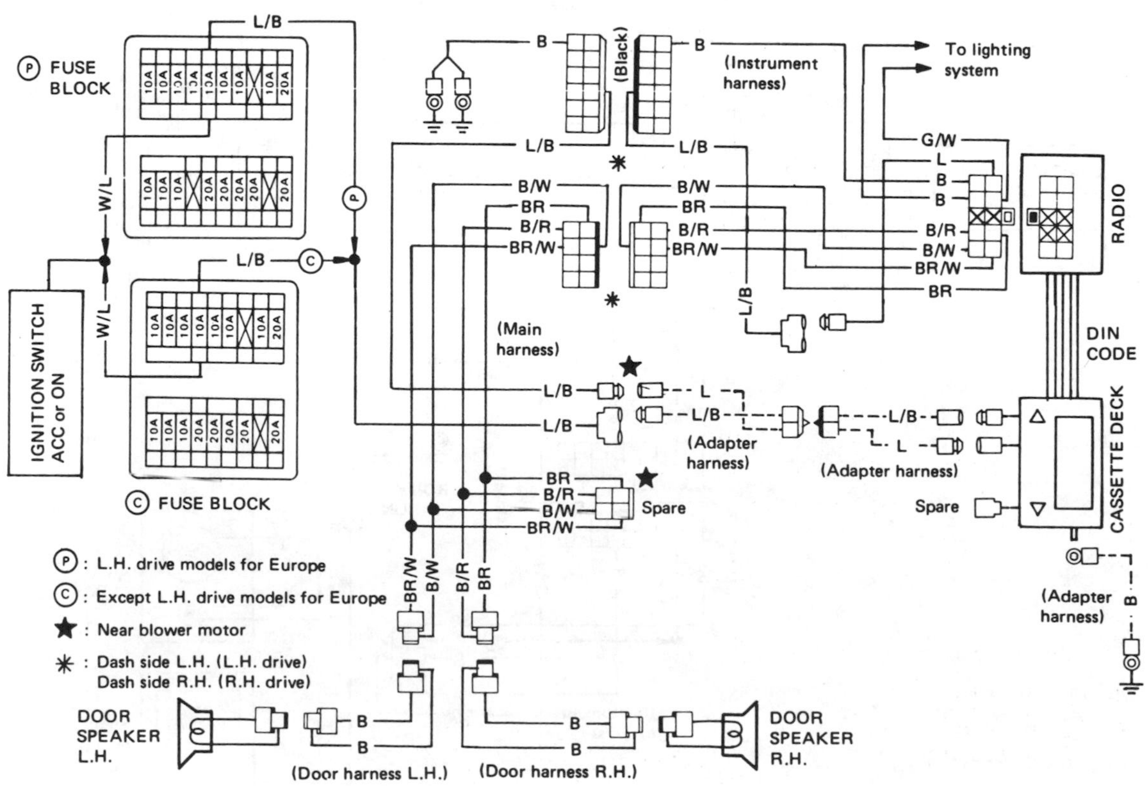

Fig. 10.95 Cassette player (all Sunny models – factory-fitted)

For the colour code see Fig. 10.43

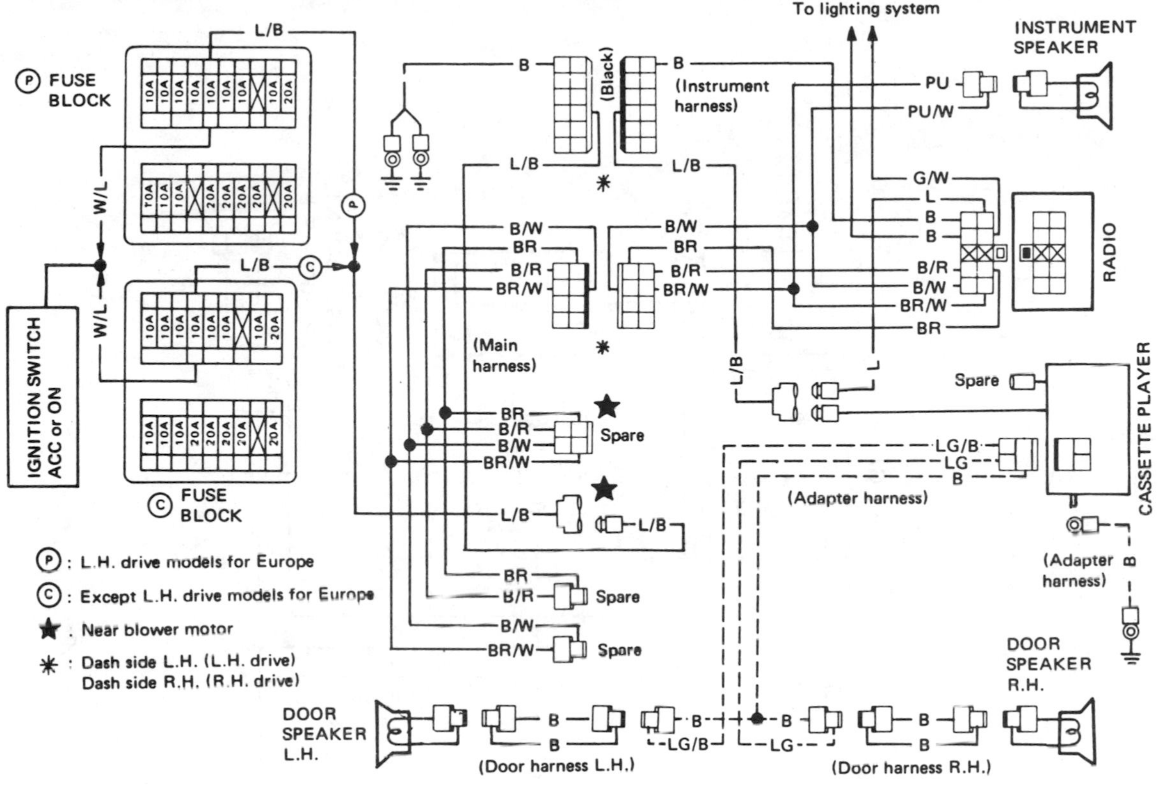

Fig. 10.96 Cassette player (all Sunny models – dealer fitted)

For the colour code see Fig. 10.43

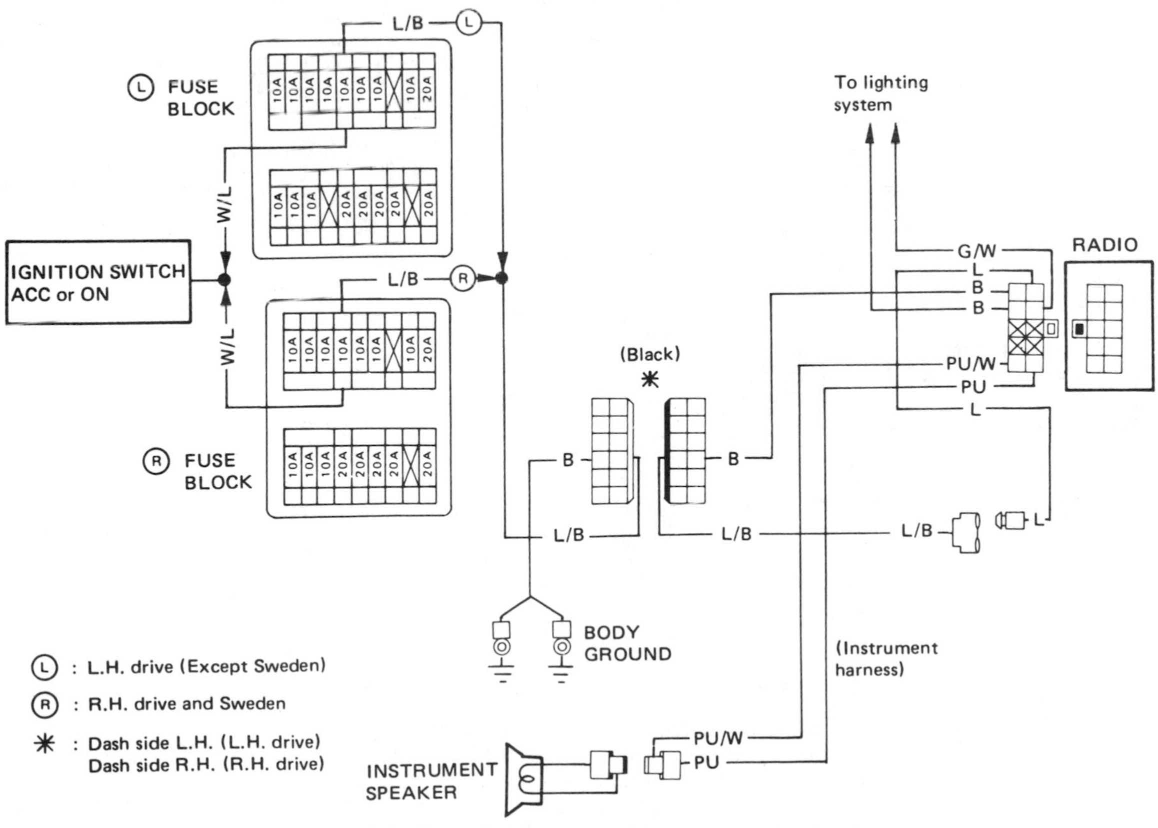

Fig. 10.97 Radio (all Sunny models – one speaker type)

For the colour code see Fig. 10.43

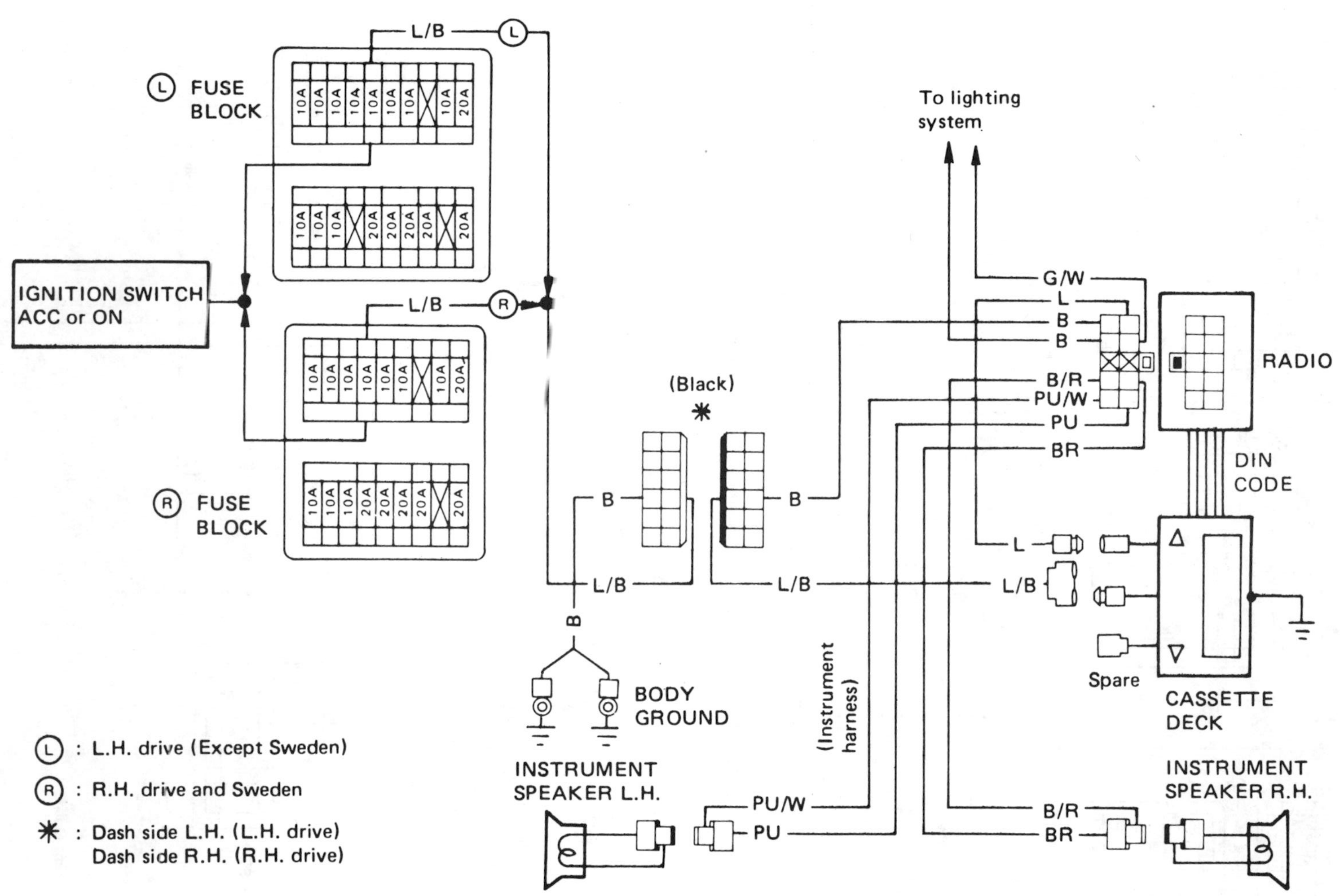

Fig. 10.98 Radio (all Sunny models – two speaker type)

For the colour code see Fig. 10.43

WIRE NUMBER:
For identification, all wires are numbered and generally, numbers are classified by system.

100 ~ 199 .... Engine electrical system
200 ~ 299 .... Headlamp system
300 ~ 399 .... Meter, gauges and Warning system
400 ~ 499 .... Signal system
500 ~ 599 .... Accessory system
600 ~ 899 .... Supplemental numbers
900 ~ 999 .... Ground wire (Earth)

COLOR:

W .... White
B ..... Black
R ..... Red
Y ..... Yellow
G ..... Green
L ..... Blue
BR .... Brown
LG .... Light green
OR ... Orange
P ..... Pink
PU .... Purple
GY ... Gray
SB .... Sky blue

In the case of two-tone color wires, the wire colors are indicated as follows.

B/R .... Black with Red stripe
L/OR ... Blue with Orange stripe

Indicates that No. 406 wire is found only in harness of GL models.

NISSAN

MAIN HARNESS

NO.	FROM	TO	REMARKS
203	HEADLAMP	INST H	
204	HEADLAMP	INST H	
406	HORN	408	GL
408	HORN	INST H	
910	HEADLAMP	INST H	

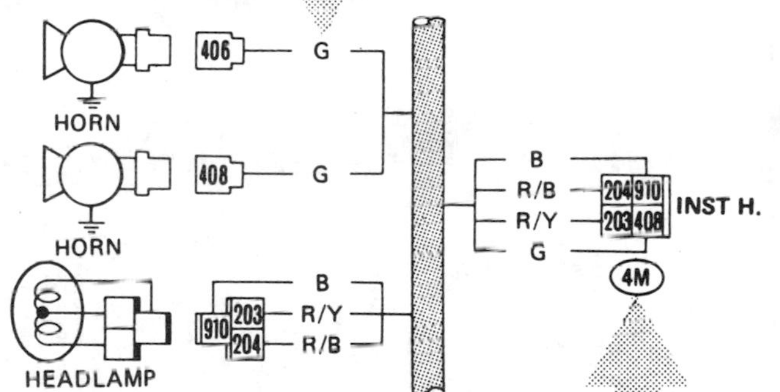

Indicates that No. 406 wire stems from the horn and is connected to No. 408 wire.

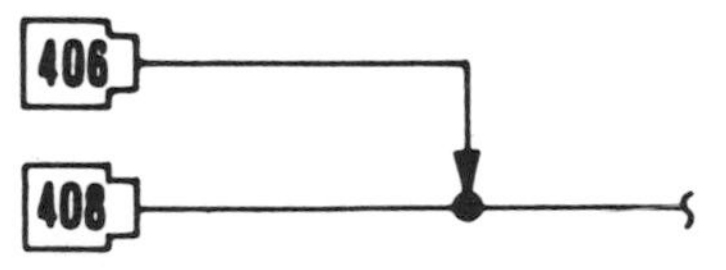

For easy identification, connectors indicated in the harness diagrams have the same code numbers as those used in the harness layout and system wiring diagram.

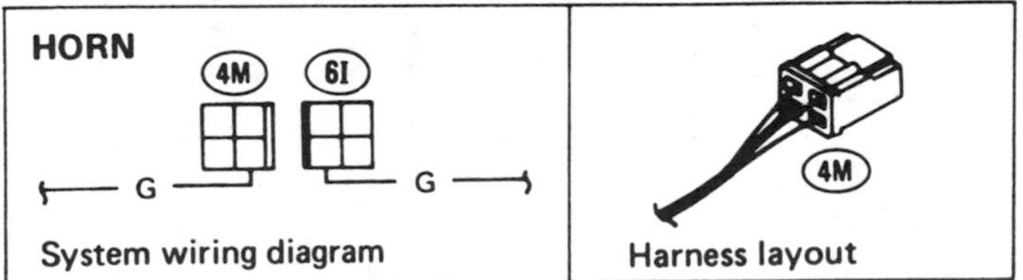

This harness diagram indicates harnesses and connectors to be used with all optional, as well as standard, equipment.

Fig. 10.99 How to use the wiring diagrams for US Sentra models

NO.	FROM	TO	REMARKS
100	ENGINE ELECTRICAL SYSTEM		
100	ENG H	FUSIBLE LINK	
106	FUSE BLOCK	100	
107	FUSE BLOCK	106	
108	ENG H	INST H	
109	ENG H	100	
110	FUSIBLE LINK	IGN SW	
111	FUSE BLOCK	IGN SW	
112	FUSE BLOCK	IGN SW	
114	ENG H	IGN SW	
115	INHIBIT RELAY	114	
116	INHIBIT RELAY	ENG H	
117	111	IGN COIL (+)	
118	IG RELAY	111	
119	IG RELAY	106	
120	IG RELAY	FUSE BLOCK	
121	ACC RELAY	112	
122	ACC RELAY	106	
123	ACC RELAY	FUSE BLOCK	
124	FUSE BLOCK	123	
125	FUSE BLOCK	111	
126	FUSE BLOCK	120	
127	FUSE BLOCK	112	
131	RESISTOR	IGN COIL (–)	
132	RESISTOR	INST H	
148	FUSE BLOCK	TANK UNIT	
160	AUTO CHOKE RELAY	165	
161	ENG H	AUTO CHOKE RELAY	
162	AUTO CHOKE RELAY	190	
163	AUTO CHOKE RELAY	108	
165	FUEL CUT RELAY	FUSE BLOCK	
166	FUEL CUT RELAY	SPEED AMP	
167	SPEED AMP	165	
168	INST H	SPEED AMP	
169	INST H	SPEED AMP	
170	FUEL CUT RELAY	165	
171	ENG H	FUEL CUT RELAY	
172	ENG H	165	
174	CLUTCH SW	165	
175	CLUTCH SW	176	
176	DIODE BOX	171	
177	DIODE BOX	WARM RELAY (1)	
179	ENG H	177	
180	WARM RELAY (1)	161	
181	WARM RELAY (1)	WARM RELAY (2)	
182	WARM RELAY (2)	165	
183	ENG H (TEMP SW)	WARM RELAY (2)	
184	ENG H (WARM SOL)	WARM RELAY (2)	
185	ENG H (WARM SOL)	DIODE BOX	
186	196	DIODE BOX	
187	FUEL CUT RELAY	195	
188	ENG H	VACUUM SW	
190	FUSE BLOCK	THERMO SW	
191	THERMO SW	RAD FAN MOTOR	
192	AIR CON H (B)	190	
193	AIR CON H (B)	191	
195	ENG H (MR SOL)	DIODE BOX	
196	ENG H (TEMP SW)	DIODE BOX	
197	INHIBIT RELAY	177	
200	LIGHTING SYSTEM		
200	COMB SW (LIGHT)	FUSE BLOCK	
201	COMB SW (LIGHT)	FUSE BLOCK	
202	COMB SW (LIGHT)	HEAD LAMP RH	
203	COMB SW (LIGHT)	HEAD LAMP LH	
204	COMB SW (LIGHT)	DIMMER RELAY	
205	DIMMER RELAY	HEAD LAMP RH	
206	DIMMER RELAY	HEAD LAMP RH	
207	HEAD LAMP LH	205	
208	HEAD LAMP LH	206	
209	INST H	202	
210	INST H	206	
220	COMB SW (LIGHT)	FUSE BLOCK	
222	COMB SW (LIGHT)	CLEARANCE LAMP RH	
223	CLEARANCE LAMP LH	222	
224	RR COMB LAMP RH	222	SED WAG
225	RR COMB LAMP LH	224	SED WAG
225	RR COMB LAMP LH	282	H/B
226	LICENSE LAMP	224	SED
226	LICENSE LAMP	281	H/B

NO.	FROM	TO	REMARKS
226	BACK DOOR H	224	WAG
227	LICENSE LAMP	226	
234	INST H	222	
236	A/T IND LAMP	234	
237	A/T IND LAMP	INST H	
238	FAN SW	234	
239	FAN SW	237	
251	ROOM LAMP H	545	
252	DOOR SW LH	ROOM LAMP H	
256	LUGGAGE ROOM LAMP	545	
271	SIDE MARKER LAMP RH	222	
272	SIDE MARKER LAMP LH	223	
273	RR SIDE MARKER RH	226	
274	RR SIDE MARKER LH	226	
281	STOP AND TAIL SENS	222	H/B
282	STOP AND TAIL SENS	RR COMB LAMP RH	H/B
300	METER, GAUGES AND WARNING SYSTEM		
301	INST H	FUSE BLOCK	
304	INST H	ENG H	
305	TANK UNIT	INST H	
320	INST H	324	
322	PARKING BRAKE SW	323	
323	INST H	BRAKE LEVEL SW	
324	AUTO CHOKE RELAY	DIODE	
325	323	DIODE	
327	TANK UNIT	INST H	
329	INST H	252	
330	DOOR SW RH	252	
334	STOP AND TAIL SENS	INST H	H/B
335	ENG H	INST H	
341	DIODE BOX	346	H/B
342	DIODE BOX	222	H/B
345	KEY SW	545	
346	DOOR SW LH	KEY SW	
347	DOOR SW LH	INST H	
355	SEAT BELT SW	INST H	
356	SEAT BELT SW	INST H	
390	CHECK CONNECTOR	301	
391	CHECK CONNECTOR	161	
392	CHECK CONNECTOR	195	
393	CHECK CONNECTOR	184	
394	CHECK CONNECTOR	ENG H	
400	SIGNAL SYSTEM		
401	T/SIGNAL F/UNIT	301	
402	T/SIGNAL F/UNIT	HAZARD SW	
403	COMB SW (TURN)	HAZARD SW	
404	COMB SW (TURN)	FR T/SIGNAL LAMP RH	
405	COMB SW (TURN)	FR T/SIGNAL LAMP LH	
406	SIDE FLASHER L	404	
407	SIDE FLASHER L	405	
408	RR COMB LAMP RH	404	
409	RR COMB LAMP LH	405	
410	INST H	404	
411	INST H	405	
420	HAZARD F/UNIT	431	
421	HAZARD SW	HAZARD F/UNIT	
422	HAZARD SW	404	
423	HAZARD SW	405	
431	FUSE BLOCK	HORN RELAY	
432	COMB SW	HORN RELAY	
433	COMB SW	432	
434	HORN RELAY	HORN	
435	HORN	434	
441	FUSE BLOCK	STOP LAMP SW	SED WAG
441	FUSE BLOCK	STOP LAMP SW	H/B
442	STOP LAMP SW	RR COMB LAMP RH	SED WAG
443	RR COMB LAMP LH	442	SED WAG
443	RR COMB LAMP LH	446	H/B
445	STOP LAMP SW	STOP AND TAIL SENS	H/B
446	RR COMB LAMP RH	STOP AND TAIL SENS	H/B
451	ENG H	301	
452	ENG H	RR COMB LAMP RH	
453	RR COMB LAMP LH	452	
500	ACCESSORY SYSTEM		
500	FUSE BLOCK	WIPER MOTOR	
502	WIPER MOTOR	COMB SW (WIPER)	
503	WIPER MOTOR	COMB SW (WIPER)	
504	WIPER AMP	WIPER MOTOR	H/B
505	WIPER AMP	COMB SW (WIPER)	H/B

NO.	FROM	TO	REMARKS
506	WIPER AMP	COMB SW (WIPER)	H/B
507	WIPER AMP	500	H/B
508	WIPER AMP	511	H/B
510	WASHER MOTOR	500	
511	WASHER MOTOR	COMB SW (WIPER)	
512	520	RR WASHER MOTOR	H/B WAG
513	INST H	RR WASHER MOTOR	H/B WAG
514	520	BACK DOOR SW	H/B
514	520	BACK DOOR H	WAG
515	INST H	BACK DOOR SW	H/B
515	INST H	BACK DOOR H	WAG
516	INST H	BACK DOOR SW	H/B
516	INST H	BACK DOOR H	WAG
517	COMB SW (WIPER)	WIPER AMP	H/B
520	FUSE BLOCK	INST H	
524	SPEAKER H RH	INST H	
525	SPEAKER H RH	INST H	
526	SPEAKER H LH	INST H	
527	SPEAKER H LH	INST H	
530	CONDENSER	117	
540	FUSE BLOCK	INST H (CIG)	
545	FUSE BLOCK	INST H (CLOCK)	
550	FUSE BLOCK	INST H (RR DEF)	
552	RR DEFOGGER	INST H (RR DEF)	SED H/B
560	FUSE BLOCK	BLOWER MOTOR	
562	FAN SW (H)	BLOWER MOTOR	
563	FAN SW (M)	RESISTOR	
564	FAN SW (L)	RESISTOR	
565	562	RESISTOR	
570	AIR CON H (A)	FUSE BLOCK	
571	AIR CON H (A)	560	
582	AIR CON H (A)	FAN SW	
900	GROUND		
900	BODY GROUND	BODY GROUND	
901	BODY GROUND	BODY GROUND	
910	INST H	BODY GROUND	
931	WARM RELAY (1)	900	
932	FUEL CUT RELAY	900	
933	AUTO CHOKE RELAY	900	
934	DIMMER RELAY	900	
935	INHIBIT RELAY	900	A/T
936	SIDE MARKER RH	900	
937	SIDE MARKER LH	900	
938	CHECK CONNECTOR	900	
939	ROOM LAMP H	901	
940	IG RELAY	901	
941	ACC RELAY	901	
942	SPEED AMP	901	
943	RR SIDE MARKER LH	901	
944	STOP AND TAIL SENS	901	H/B
945	LUGGAGE ROOM LAMP	901	H/B WAG
946	LICENSE LAMP	901	
947	LICENSE LAMP	901	
948	RR SIDE MARKER RH	901	
951	AIR CON H (B)	900	
952	VACUUM SW	900	
953	FR T/S LAMP RH	900	
954	CLEARANCE L RH	900	
955	CLEARANCE L LH	900	
956	FR T/S LAMP LH	900	
957	RAD FAN MOTOR	900	
958	BRAKE LEVEL SW	900	
959	WIPER MOTOR	900	
960	WIPER AMP	900	H/B
962	TANK UNIT	901	
963	RR COMB LAMP LH	901	
964	GROUND POINT	901	H/B
968	RR COMB LAMP RH	901	
971	DIMMER RELAY	900	
972	FAN SW	901	
973	COMB SW (WIPER)	901	
974	BACK DOOR H	901	WAG
975	INST H	901	

Fig. 10.100 Key to wiring diagram for the Sentra – USA models except MPG

For the colour code see Fig. 10.99

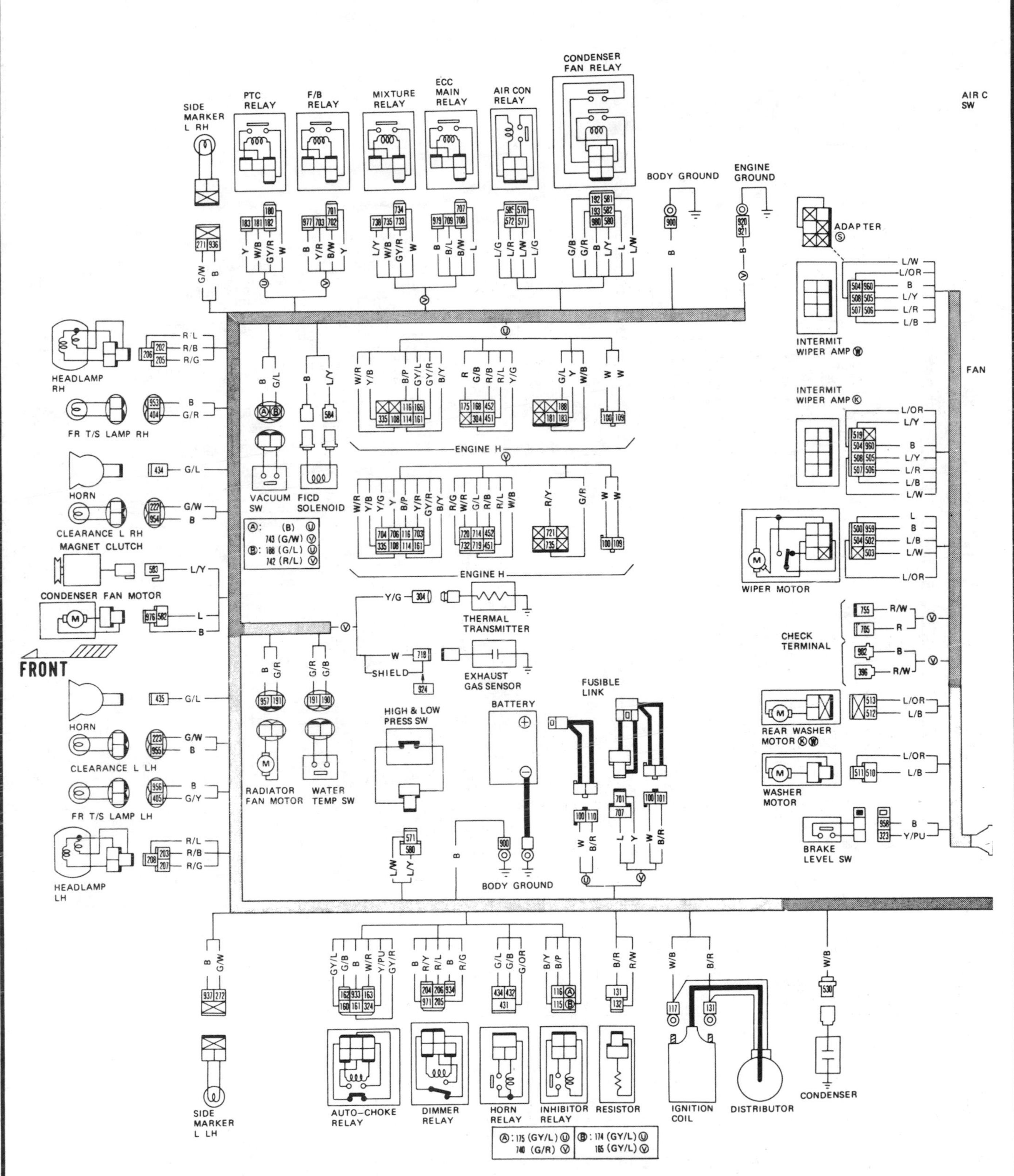

Fig. 10.101 Wiring diagram for the Sentra – USA models except MPG

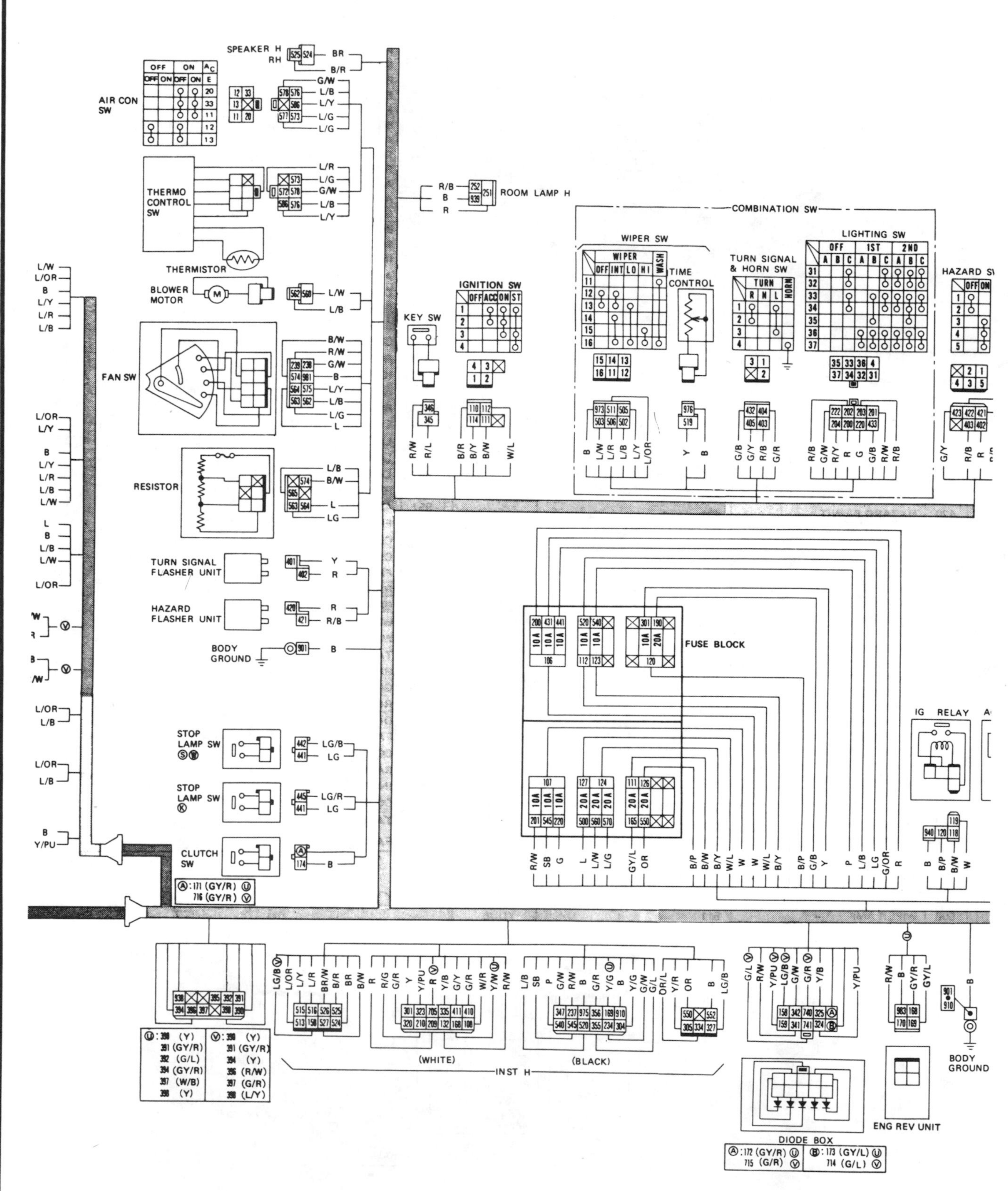

Fig. 10.101 Wiring diagram for the Sentra – USA models except MPG (continued)

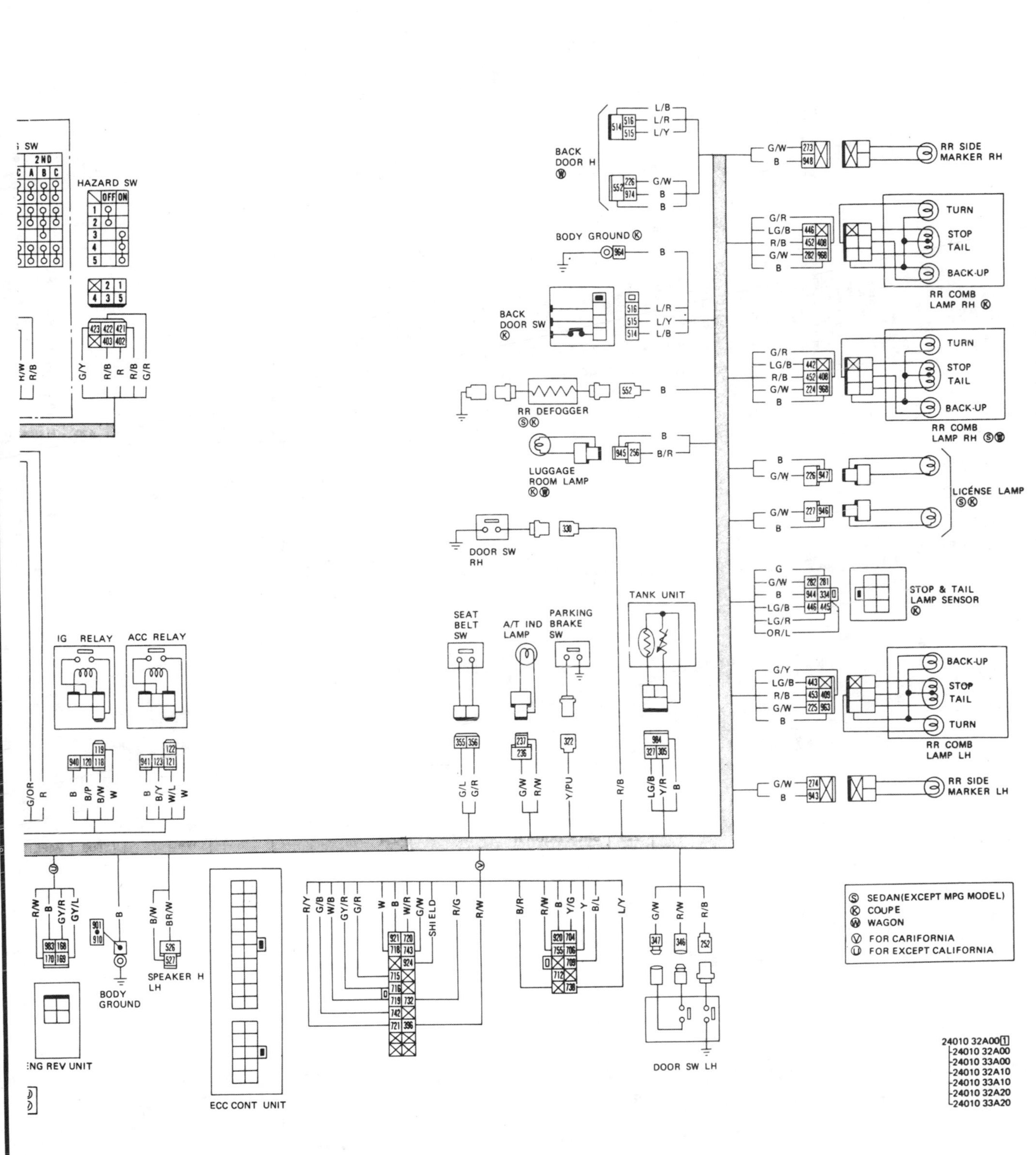

Fig. 10.101 Wiring diagram for the Sentra—USA models except MPG (continued)

NO.	FROM	TO	REMARKS
100	ENGINE ELECTRICAL SYSTEM		
100	ENG H	FUSIBLE LINK	
106	FUSE BLOCK	100	
107	FUSE BLOCK	106	
108	ENG H	INST H	
109	ENG H	100	
110	FUSIBLE LINK	IGN SW	
111	FUSE BLOCK	IGN SW	
112	FUSE BLOCK	IGN SW	
114	ENG H	IGN SW	
115	INHIBIT RELAY	114	
116	INHIBIT RELAY	ENG H	
117	111	IGN COIL ( )	
118	IG RELAY	111	
119	IG RELAY	106	
120	IG RELAY	FUSE BLOCK	
121	ACC RELAY	112	
122	ACC RELAY	106	
123	ACC RELAY	FUSE BLOCK	
124	FUSE BLOCK	123	
126	FUSE BLOCK	120	
127	FUSE BLOCK	112	
131	RESISTOR	IGN COIL (–)	
132	RESISTOR	INST H	
160	AUTO CHOKE RELAY	165	
161	ENG H	AUTO CHOKE RELAY	
162	AUTO CHOKE RELAY	190	
163	AUTO CHOKE RELAY	108	
165	FUSE BLOCK	ENG H	
170	INST H	165	
171	INST H	ENG H	
174	165	INHIBIT RELAY	
175	ENG H	INHIBIT RELAY	
180	MIXTURE RELAY	100	
181	MIXTURE RELAY	ENG H	
182	MIXTURE RELAY	161	
183	MIXTURE RELAY	ENG H	
190	FUSE BLOCK	WATER TEMP SW	
191	WATER TEMP SW	RAD FAN MOTOR	
192	AIR CON H (B)	190	
193	AIR CON H (B)	191	
200	LIGHTING SYSTEM		
200	COMB SW (LIGHT)	FUSE BLOCK	
201	COMB SW (LIGHT)	FUSE BLOCK	
202	COMB SW (LIGHT)	HEAD LAMP RH	
203	COMB SW (LIGHT)	HEAD LAMP LH	
204	COMB SW (LIGHT)	DIMMER RELAY	
205	DIMMER RELAY	HEAD LAMP RH	
206	DIMMER RELAY	HEAD LAMP RH	
207	HEAD LAMP LH	205	
208	HEAD LAMP LH	206	
209	INST H	202	
210	INST H	205	
220	COMB SW (LIGHT)	FUSE BLOCK	
222	COMB SW (LIGHT)	CLEARANCE L RH	
223	CLEARANCE L LH	222	
224	RR COMB LAMP RH	222	SED WAG
225	RR COMB LAMP LH	224	SED WAG
225	RR COMB LAMP LH	282	COU
226	LICENSE LAMP	224	SED
226	LICENSE LAMP	281	COU
226	BACK DOOR H	224	WAG
227	LICENSE LAMP	226	
234	INST H	222	
236	A/T IND LAMP	234	
237	A/T IND LAMP	INST H	
238	FAN SW	234	
239	FAN SW	237	
251	ROOM LAMP H	545	
252	DOOR SW LH	ROOM LAMP H	
256	LUGGAGE ROOM LAMP	545	
271	SIDE MARKER L RH	222	
272	SIDE MARKER L LH	223	
273	RR SIDE MARKER RH	226	
274	RR SIDE MARKER LH	226	
281	STOP AND TAIL SENS	222	COU
282	STOP AND TAIL SENS	RR COMB LAMP RH	COU
300	METER, GAUGES AND WARNING SYSTEM		
301	INST H	FUSE BLOCK	
304	INST H	ENG H	
305	TANK UNIT	INST H	
320	INST H	324	

NO.	FROM	TO	REMARKS
322	PARKING BRAKE SW	323	
323	INST H	BRAKE LEVEL SW	
324	AUTO CHOKE RELAY	DIODE	
325	323	DIODE	
327	TANK UNIT H	INST H	
329	INST H	252	
330	DOOR SW RH	252	
334	STOP AND TAIL SENS	INST H	COU
335	ENG H	INST H	
341	DIODE BOX	346	
341	DIODE BOX	346	
342	DIODE BOX	222	
342	DIODE BOX	222	
345	KEY SW	545	
346	DOOR SW LH	KEY SW	
347	DOOR SW LH	INST H	
355	SEAT BELT SW	INST H	
356	SEAT BELT SW	INST H	
390	CHECK CONNECTOR	301	
391	CHECK CONNECTOR	161	
393	CHECK CONNECTOR	171	
400	SIGNAL SYSTEM		
401	T/SIGNAL F/UNIT	301	
402	T/SIGNAL F/UNIT	HAZARD SW	
403	COMB SW (TURN)	HAZARD SW	
404	COMB SW (TURN)	FR T/S LAMP RH	
405	COMB SW (TURN)	FR T/S LAMP LH	
406	SIDE FLASHER L	404	
406	SIDE FLASHER L	404	
407	SIDE FLASHER L	405	
407	SIDE FLASHER L	405	
408	RR COMB LAMP RH	404	
409	RR COMB LAMP LH	405	
410	INST H	404	
411	INST H	405	
420	HAZARD F/UNIT	431	
421	HAZARD SW	HAZARD F/UNIT	
422	HAZARD SW	404	
423	HAZARD SW	405	
431	FUSE BLOCK	HORN RELAY	
432	COMB SW	HORN RELAY	
433	COMB SW	432	
434	HORN RELAY	HORN	
435	HORN	434	
441	FUSE BLOCK	STOP LAMP SW	SED WAG
441	FUSE BLOCK	STOP LAMP SW	COU
442	STOP LAMP SW	RR COMB LAMP RH	SED WAG
443	RR COMB LAMP LH	442	SED WAG
443	RR COMB LAMP LH	446	COU
445	STOP LAMP SW	STOP AND TAIL SENS	COU
446	RR COMB LAMP RH	STOP AND TAIL SENS	COU
451	ENG H	301	
452	ENG H	RR COMB LAMP RH	
453	RR COMB LAMP LH	452	
500	ACCESSORY SYSTEM		
500	FUSE BLOCK	WIPER MOTOR	
502	WIPER MOTOR	COMB SW (WIPER)	
503	WIPER MOTOR	COMB SW (WIPER)	
504	WIPER AMP	WIPER MOTOR	
505	WIPER AMP	COMB SW (WIPER)	
506	WIPER AMP	COMB SW (WIPER)	
507	WIPER AMP	500	
508	WIPER AMP	511	
510	WASHER MOTOR	500	
511	WASHER MOTOR	COMB SW (WIPER)	
512	520	RR WASHER MOTOR	COU WAG
513	INST H	RR WASHER MOTOR	COU WAG
514	520	BACK DOOR SW	COU
514	520	BACK DOOR H	WAG
515	INST H	BACK DOOR SW	COU
515	INST H	BACK DOOR H	WAG
516	INST H	BACK DOOR SW	COU
516	INST H	BACK DOOR H	WAG
519	COMB SW	WIPER AMP	
519	COMB SW	WIPER AMP	
520	FUSE BLOCK	INST H	
524	SPEAKER H RH	INST H	
525	SPEAKER H RH	INST H	
526	SPEAKER H LH	INST H	

NO.	FROM	TO	REMARKS
527	SPEAKER H LH	INST H	
530	CONDENSER	117	
540	FUSE BLOCK	INST H (CIG)	
545	FUSE BLOCK	INST H (CLOCK)	
550	FUSE BLOCK	INST H (RR DEF)	
552	RR DEFOGGER	INST H (RR DEF)	SED COU
560	FUSE BLOCK	BLOWER MOTOR	
563	FAN SW (M)	RESISTOR	
564	FAN SW (L)	RESISTOR	
565	562	RESISTOR	
570	AIR CON H (A)	FUSE BLOCK	
574	RESISTOR	FAN SW	
574	RESISTOR	FAN SW	
575	AIR CON H	FAN SW	
575	AIR CON H	FAN SW	
900	GROUND		
900	BODY GROUND	BODY GROUND	
901	BODY GROUND	BODY GROUND	
910	INST H	BODY GROUND	
933	AUTO CHOKE RELAY	900	
934	DIMMER RELAY	900	
936	SIDE MARKER RH	900	
937	SIDE MARKER LH	900	
938	CHECK CONNECTOR	900	
939	ROOM LAMP H	901	
940	IG RELAY	901	
941	ACC RELAY	901	
943	RR SIDE MARKER LH	901	
944	STOP AND TAIL SENS	901	COU
945	LUGGAGE ROOM LAMP	901	COU WAG
946	LICENSE LAMP	901	
947	LICENSE LAMP	901	
948	RR SIDE MARKER RH	901	
951	AIR CON H (B)	900	
953	FR T/S LAMP RH	900	
954	CLEARANCE L RH	900	
955	CLEARANCE L LH	900	
956	FR T/S LAMP LH	900	
957	RAD FAN MOTOR	900	
958	BRAKE LEVEL SW	900	
959	WIPER MOTOR	900	
960	WIPER AMP	900	
962	TANK UNIT	901	
963	RR COMB LAMP LH	901	
964	GROUND POINT	901	
968	RR COMB LAMP RH	901	
971	DIMMER RELAY	900	
972	FAN SW	901	
973	COMB SW (WIPER)	901	
974	BACK DOOR H	901	WAG
975	INST H	901	
976	COMB SW (WIPER)	901	COU
977	TANK UNIT	901	
978	FAN SW	901	

Fig. 10.102 Key to wiring diagram for the Sentra – Canadian models except MPG

For the colour code see Fig. 10.99

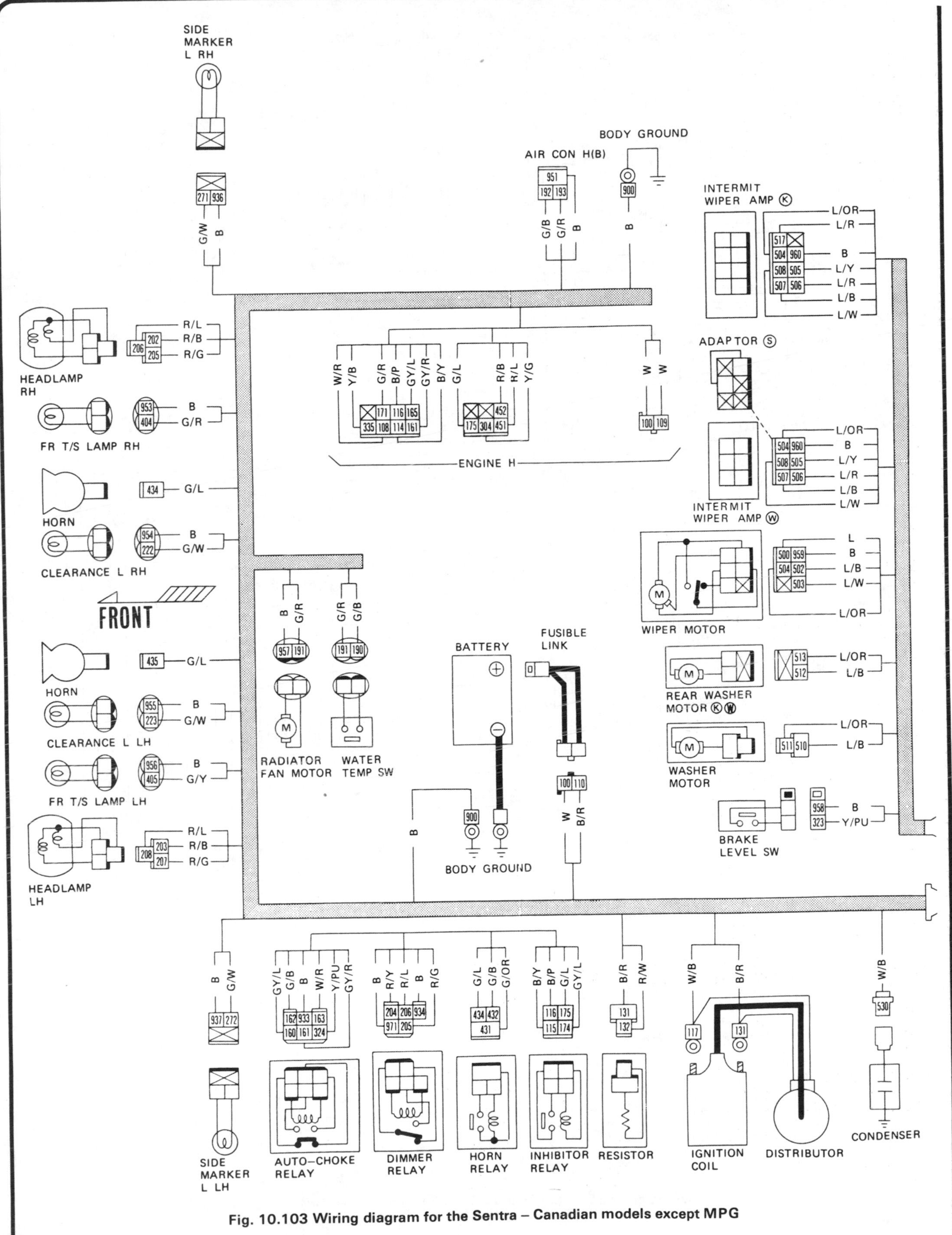

Fig. 10.103 Wiring diagram for the Sentra – Canadian models except MPG

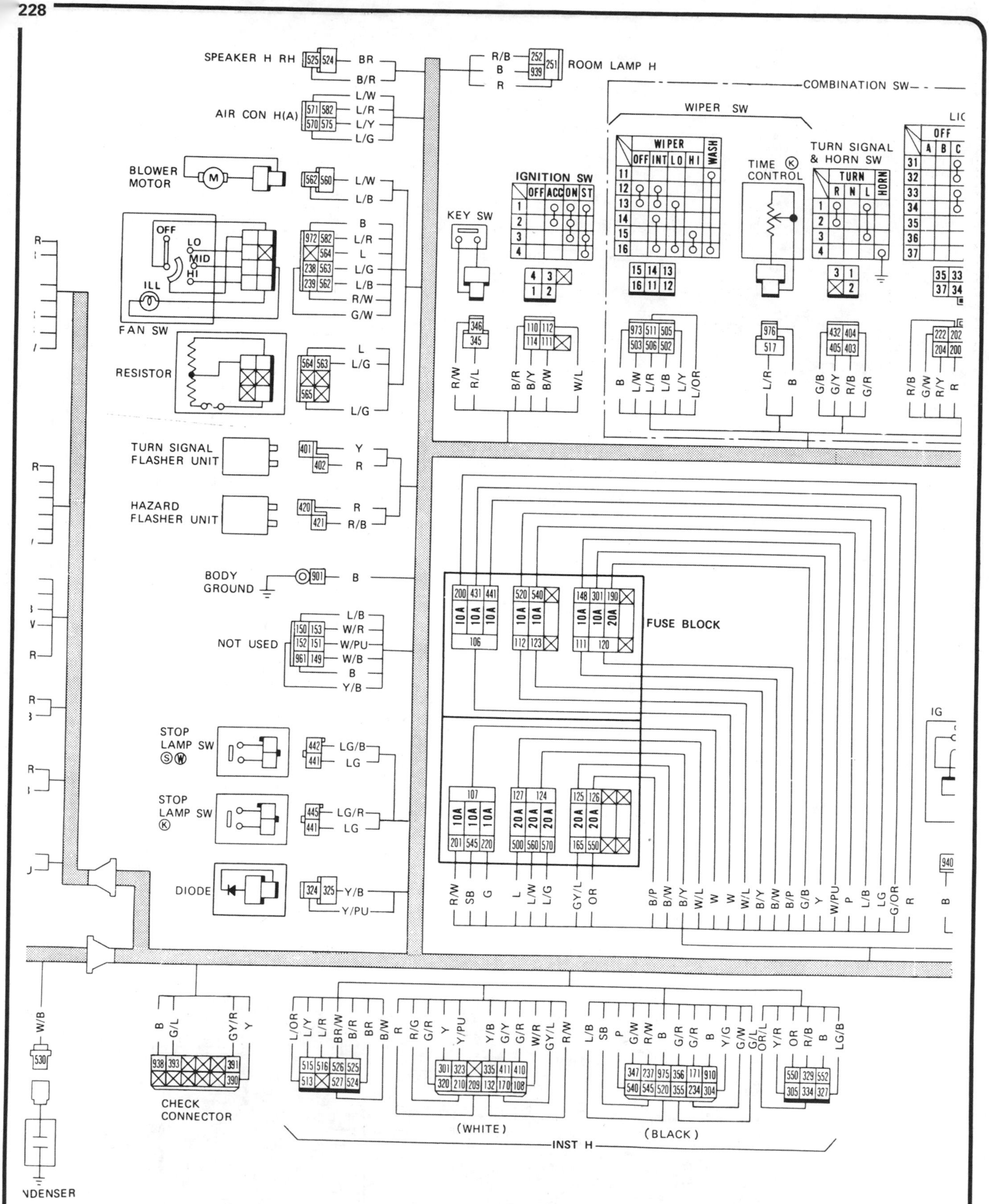

Fig. 10.103 Wiring diagram for the Sentra – Canadian models except MPG (continued)

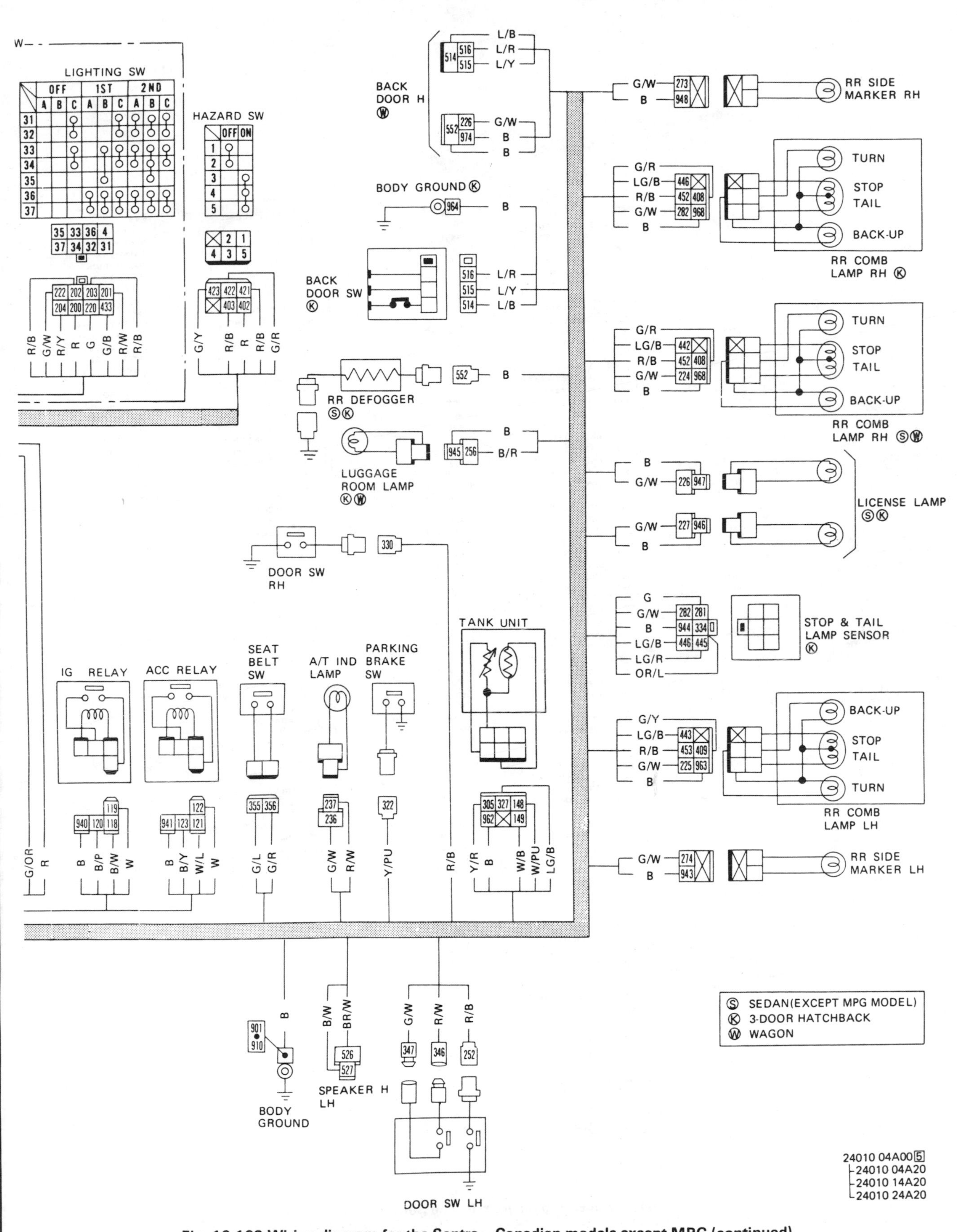

Fig. 10.103 Wiring diagram for the Sentra – Canadian models except MPG (continued)

NO.	FROM	TO
100	ENGINE ELECTRICAL SYSTEM	
100	ENG H	FUSIBLE LINK
106	FUSE BLOCK	100
107	FUSE BLOCK	106
108	ENG H	INST H
109	ENG H	100
110	FUSIBLE LINK	IGN SW
111	FUSE BLOCK	IGN SW
112	FUSE BLOCK	IGN SW
114	ENG H	IGN SW
117	111	IGN COIL (+)
118	IG RELAY	111
119	IG RELAY	106
120	IG RELAY	FUSE BLOCK
121	ACC RELAY	112
122	ACC RELAY	106
123	ACC RELAY	FUSE BLOCK
124	FUSE BLOCK	123
125	FUSE BLOCK	111
126	FUSE BLOCK	120
127	FUSE BLOCK	112
131	RESISTER	IGN COIL (−)
132	RESISTER	INST H
148	FUSE BLOCK	TANK UNIT
158	INST H	DIODE
159	324	DIODE
160	AUTO CHOKE RELAY	165
161	ENG H	AUTO CHOKE RELAY
162	AUTO CHOKE RELAY	190
163	AUTO CHOKE RELAY	108
165	FUSE BLOCK	WARM RELAY
190	FUSE BLOCK	WATER TEMP SW
191	WATER TEMP SW	RAD FAN MOTOR
192	AIR CON H (B)	190
193	AIR CON H (B)	191
200	LIGHTING SYSTEM	
200	COMB SW (LIGHT)	FUSE BLOCK
201	COMB SW (LIGHT)	FUSE BLOCK
202	COMB SW (LIGHT)	HEAD LAMP RH
203	COMB SW (LIGHT)	HEAD LAMP LH
204	COMB SW (LIGHT)	DIMMER RELAY
205	DIMMER RELAY	HEAD LAMP RH
206	DIMMER RELAY	HEAD LAMP RH
207	HEAD LAMP LH	205
208	HEAD LAMP LH	206
209	INST H	202
210	INST H	205
220	COMB SW (LIGHT)	FUSE BLOCK
222	COMB SW (LIGHT)	CLEARNCE L RH
223	CLEARANCE L LH	222
224	RR COMB LAMP RH	222
225	RR COMB LAMP LH	224
226	LICENSE LAMP	224
227	LICENSE LAMP	226
234	INST H	222
238	FAN SW	234
239	FAN SW	237
251	ROOM LAMP H	545
252	DOOR SW LH	ROOM LAMP H
256	LUGGAGE ROOM LAMP	545
271	SIDE MARKER LAMP RH	222
272	SIDE MARKER LAMP LH	223
273	RR SIDE MARKER RH	226
274	RR SIDE MARKER LH	226
300	METER, GAUGES AND WARNING SYSTEM	
301	INST H	FUSE BLOCK
304	INST H	THERMAL TRANS
305	TANK UNIT	INST H
320	INST H	324
322	PARKING BRAKE SW	323
323	INST H	BRAKE LEVEL SW
324	AUTO CHOKE RELAY	DIODE
325	323	DIODE
327	TANK UNIT	INST H
329	INST H	252
330	DOOR SW RH	252
335	ENG H	INST H
345	KEY SW	545
346	DOOR SW LH	KEY SW

NO.	FROM	TO
347	DOOR SW LH	INST H
355	SEAT BELT SW	INST H
356	SEAT BELT SW	INST H
390	CHECK CONNECTOR	301
391	CHECK CONNECTOR	161
392	CHECK CONNECTOR	706
393	CHECK CONNECTOR	735
396	CHECK TERMINAL	ECC CONT UNIT
400	SIGNAL SYSTEM	
401	T/SIGNAL F/UNIT	301
402	T/SIGNAL F/UNIT	HAZARD SW
403	COMB SW (TURN)	HAZARD SW
404	COMB SW (TURN)	FR T/S LAMP RH
405	COMB SW (TURN)	FR T/S LAMP LH
408	RR COMB LAMP RH	404
409	RR COMB LAMP LH	405
410	INST H	404
411	INST H	405
420	HAZARD F/UNIT	431
421	HAZARD SW	HAZARD F/UNIT
422	HAZARD SW	404
423	HAZARD SW	405
431	FUSE BLOCK	HORN RELAY
432	COMB SW	HORN RELAY
433	COMB SW	432
434	HORN RELAY	HORN
435	HORN	434
441	FUSE BLOCK	STOP LAMP SW
442	STOP LAMP SW	RR COMB LAMP RH
443	RR COMB LAMP LH	442
451	ENG H	301
452	ENG H	RR COMB LAMP RH
453	RR COMB LAMP LH	452
500	ACCESSORY SYSTEM	
500	FUSE BLOCK	WIPER MOTOR
502	WIPER MOTOR	COMB SW (WIPER)
503	WIPER MOTOR	COMB SW (WIPER)
504	WIPER MOTOR	ADAPTOR
505	COMB SW (WIPER)	ADAPTOR
506	COMB SW (WIPER)	ADAPTOR
507	ADAPTOR	500
508	ADAPTOR	511
510	WASHER MOTOR	500
511	WASHER MOTOR	COMB SW (WIPER)
520	FUSE BLOCK	INST H
524	SPEAKER H RH	INST H
525	SPEAKER H RH	INST H
526	SPEAKER H LH	INST H
527	SPEAKER H LH	INST H
530	CONDENSER	117
540	FUSE BLOCK	INST H (CIG)
545	FUSE BLOCK	INST H (CLOCK)
550	FUSE BLOCK	INST H (RR DEF)
552	RR DEFOGGER	INST H (RR DEF)
560	FUSE BLOCK	BLOWER MOTOR
562	FAN SW (H)	BLOWER MOTOR
563	FAN SW (M)	RESISTOR
564	FAN SW (L)	RESISTOR
565	562	RESISTOR
570	AIR CON H (A)	FUSE BLOCK
571	AIR CON H (A)	560
575	AIR CON H (A)	FICD
582	AIR CON H (A)	FAN SW
700	SUPPLEMENTAL NUMBERS	
701	FUSIBLE LINK	F/B RELAY
702	111	F/B RELAY
703	ENG H	F/B RELAY
704	ENG H	ECC CONT UNIT
705	CHECK TERMINAL	ECC CONT UNIT
706	ENG H	ECC CONT UNIT
707	FUSIBLE LINK	ECC MAIN RELAY
708	702	ECC MAIN RELAY
709	ECC CONT UNIT	ECC MAIN RELAY
712	131	ECC CONT UNIT
714	ECC CONT UNIT	ENG H
716	ECC CONT UNIT	CLUTCH SW
718	ECC CONT UNIT	EXHAUST GAS SENSOR
719	ECC CONT UNIT	ENG H
720	ECC CONT UNIT	ENG H

NO.	FROM	TO
721	ECC CONT UNIT	ENG H
732	ECC CONT UNIT	ENG H
733	161	WARM RELAY
735	ENG H	WARM RELAY
736	ENG H	ECC CONT UNIT
737	ENG H	165
738	ENG H	ECC CONT UNIT
740	ENG REV UNIT	165
741	ENG REV UNIT	132
742	ENG REV UNIT	ENG REV RELAY
743	740	ENG REV RELAY
744	ECC CONT UNIT	ENG REV RELAY
745	ECC CONT UNIT	ENG REV RELAY
755	INST H	CHECK TERMINAL
900	GROUND	
900	BODY GROUND	BODY GROUND
901	BODY GROUND	BODY GROUND
910	INST H	BODY GROUND
920	ECC CONT UNIT	ENG GROUND
921	ECC CONT UNIT	ENG GROUND
924	ECC CONT UNIT	EXHAUST GAS SENSOR
933	AUTO CHOKE RELAY	900
934	DIMMER RELAY	900
936	SIDE MARKER RH	900
937	SIDE MARKER LH	900
938	CHECK CONN	900
939	ROOM LAMP H	901
940	IG RELAY	901
941	ACC RELAY	901
943	RR SIDE MARKER LH	901
946	LICENSE LAMP	901
947	LICENSE LAMP	901
948	RR SIDE MARKER RH	901
949	F/B RELAY	900
950	ECC MAIN RELAY	900
951	AIR CON H (B)	900
953	FR T/S LAMP RH	900
954	CLEARANCE L RH	900
955	CLEARANCE L LH	900
956	FR T/S LAMP LH	900
957	RAD FAN MOTOR	900
958	BRAKE LEVEL SW	900
959	WIPER MOTOR	900
960	ADAPTOR	900
962	TANK UNIT	901
963	RR COMB LAMP LH	901
965	WARM RELAY	900
966	CHECK TERMINAL	900
967	CLUTCH SW	900
968	RR COMB LAMP RH	901
971	DIMMER RELAY	900
972	FAN SW	901
973	COMB SW (WIPER)	901
975	INST H	901
980	ENG REV UNIT	901

Fig. 10.104 Key to wiring diagram for the Sentra – MPG models

For the colour code see Fig. 10.99

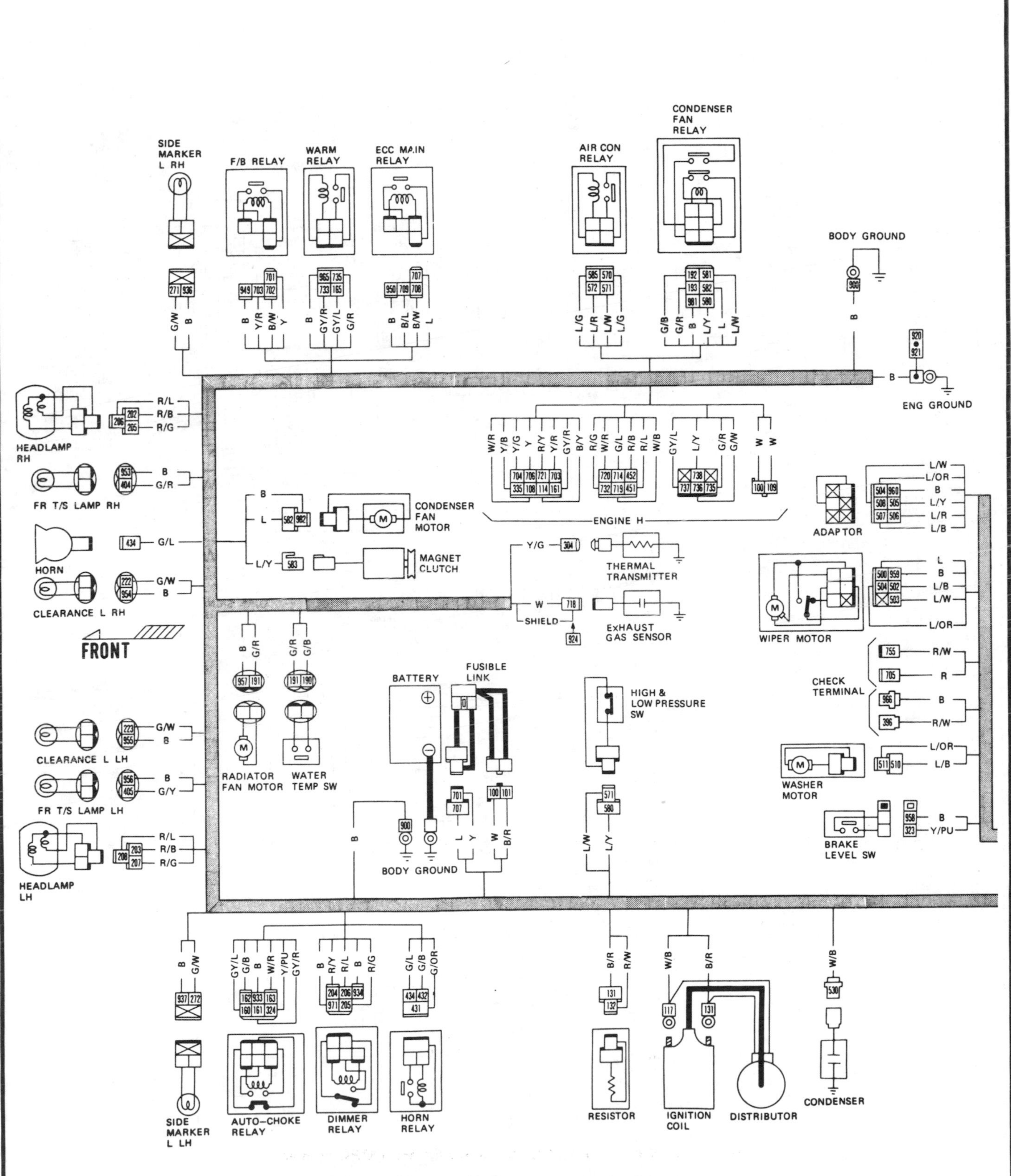

Fig. 10.105 Wiring diagram for the Sentra – MPG models

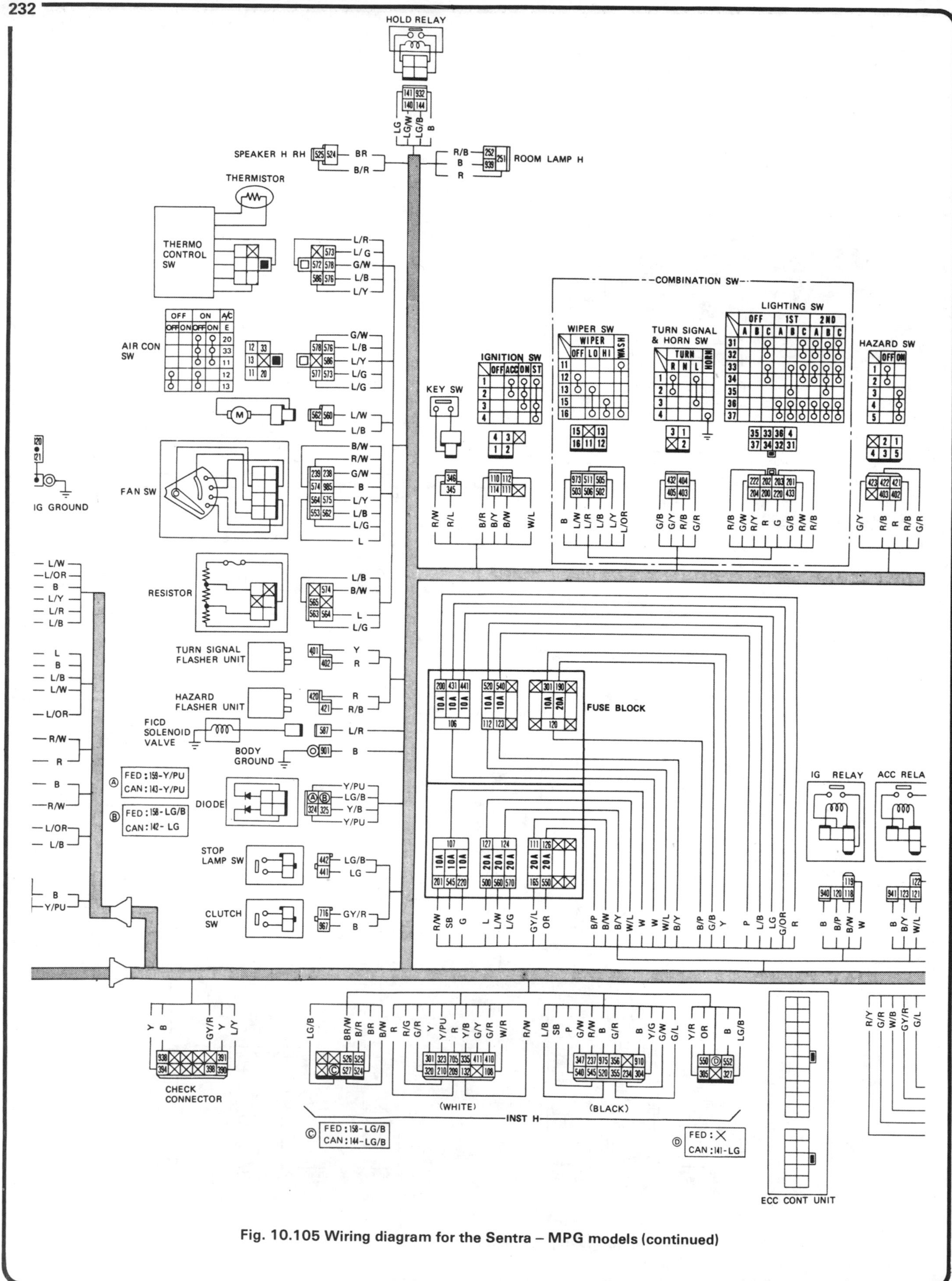

Fig. 10.105 Wiring diagram for the Sentra – MPG models (continued)

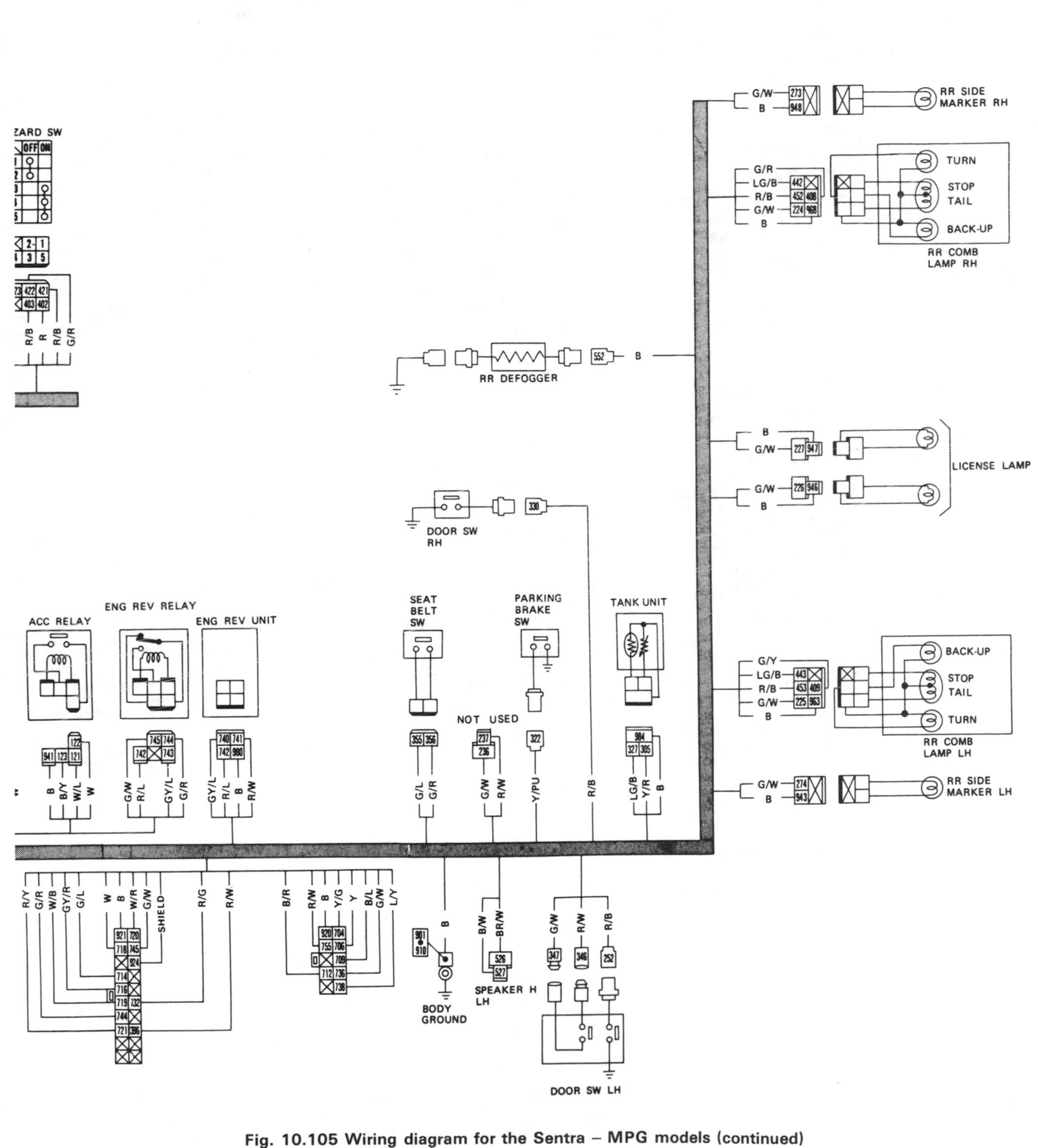

Fig. 10.105 Wiring diagram for the Sentra – MPG models (continued)

NO.	FROM	TO	REMARKS
100	ENGINE ELECTRICAL SYSTEM		
100	ALTERNATOR	MAIN H	
105	ALTERNATOR	100	
108	ALTERNATOR	MAIN H	
109	MAIN H	100	
114	MAIN H	ST MTR	M/T
116	MAIN H	ST MTR	A/T
161	CARB H	MAIN H	
171	VACUUM SW	MAIN H	
172	VACUUM SW	MAIN H	
173	VACUUM SW	CARB H	
178	172	N SW OR INHIBIT SW	
179	MAIN H	N SW OR INHIBIT SW	
183	WATER TEMP SW	MAIN H	
184	MAIN H	WARMING SOL	
185	MAIN H	WARMING SOL	CALIF
188	EGR CONT SOL	MAIN H	EXCEPT CALIF
189	EGR OR MR CONT SOL	172	
195	MAIN H	MR CONT SOL	CALIF
196	MAIN H	WATER TEMP SW	CALIF
198	WARMING SOL	WATER TEMP SW	EXCEPT CALIF
300	METER, GAUGES AND WARNING SYSTEM		
304	MAIN H	THERMAL TM	
335	OIL PRESS SW	MAIN H	
394	MAIN H	173	
400	SIGNAL SYSTEM		
451	MAIN H	B SW OR INHIBIT SW	
452	MAIN H	B SW OR INHIBIT SW	
900	GROUND		
913	ENG GROUND	BODY GROUND	
915	CARB H	BODY GROUND	
916	WATER TEMP SW	915	
917	WATER TEMP SW	915	

Fig. 10.106 Key to wiring diagram for the Sentra – engine components on all models except MPG

For the colour code see Fig. 10.99

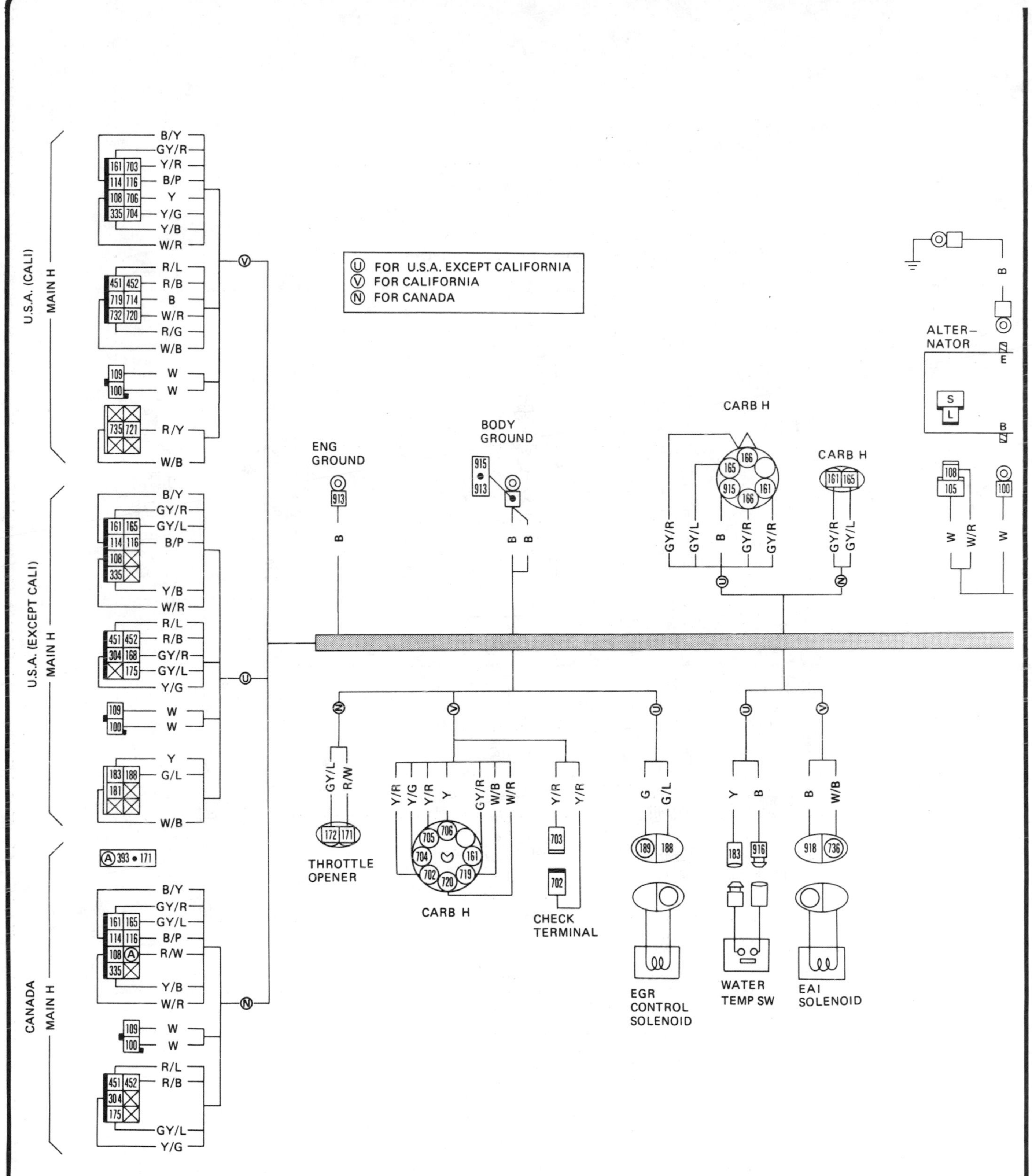

Fig. 10.107 Wiring diagram for the Sentra – engine components on all models except MPG

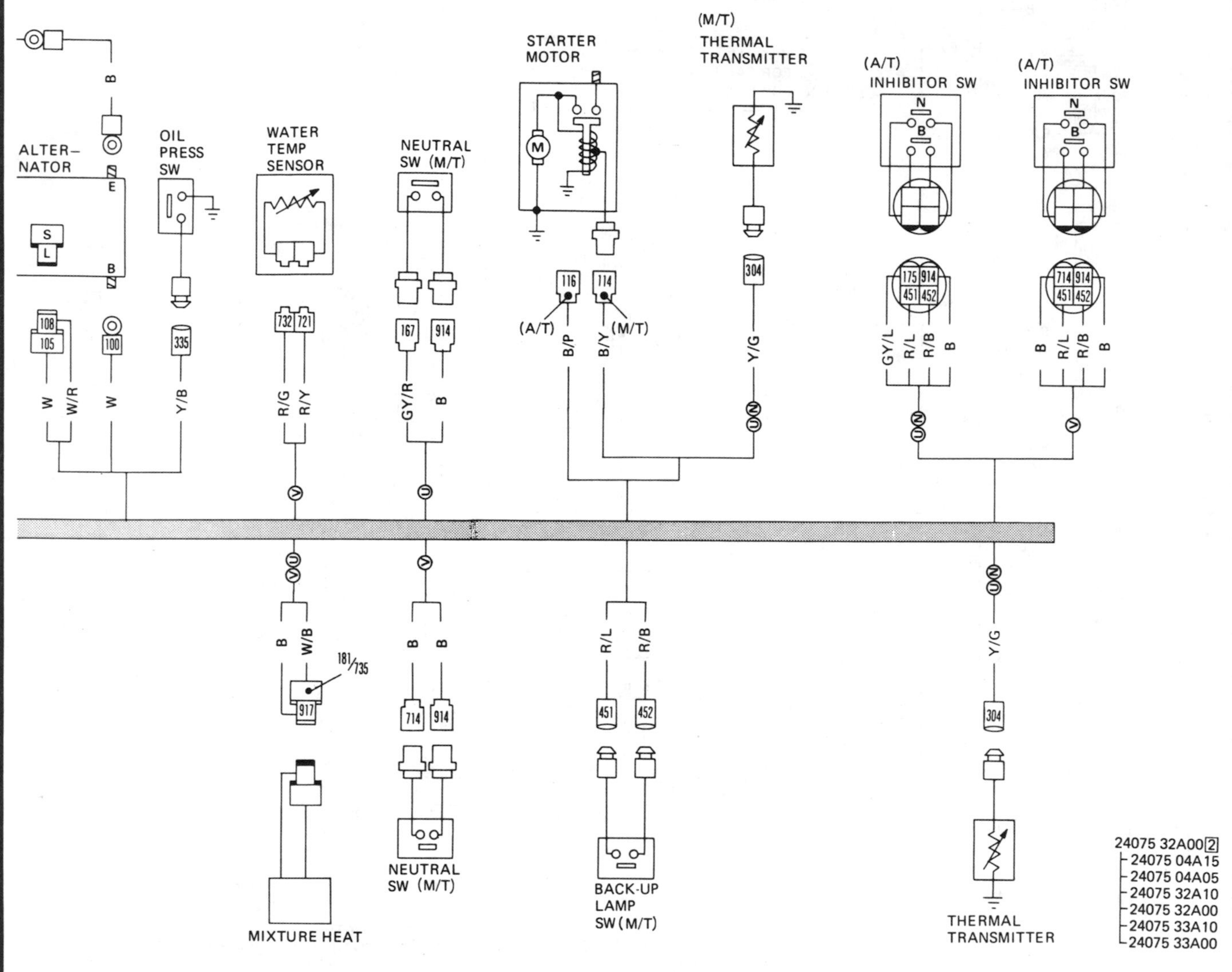

Fig. 10.107 Wiring diagram for the Sentra – engine components on all models except MPG (continued)

NO.	FROM	TO
100	ENGINE ELECTRICAL SYSTEM	
100	MAIN H	ALTERNATOR
105	ALTERNATOR	100
108	MAIN H	ALTERNATOR
109	MAIN H	100
114	MAIN H	ST MO
161	MAIN H	CARB H
300	METER, GAUGES AND WARNING SYSTEM	
335	MAIN H	OIL PRESS
400	SIGNAL SYSTEM	
451	MAIN H	BACK-UP L SW
452	MAIN H	BACK-UP L SW
700	SUPPLEMENTAL NUMBERS	
702	CHECK TERMINAL	CARB H
703	MAIN H	CHECK TERMINAL
704	MAIN H	CARB H
705	CARB H	703
706	MAIN H	CARB H
714	MAIN H	NEUTRAL SW
721	MAIN H	WATER TEMP SENSOR
732	MAIN H	WATER TEMP SENSOR
735	MAIN H	WARM SOL
736	MAIN H	WARM SOL
737	MAIN H	EAI SOL
738	MAIN H	EAI SOL
900	GROUND	
913	ENG GROUND	BODY GROUND
914	913	NEUTRAL SW

Fig. 10.108 Key to wiring diagram for the Sentra – engine components on MPG models

For the colour code see Fig. 10.99

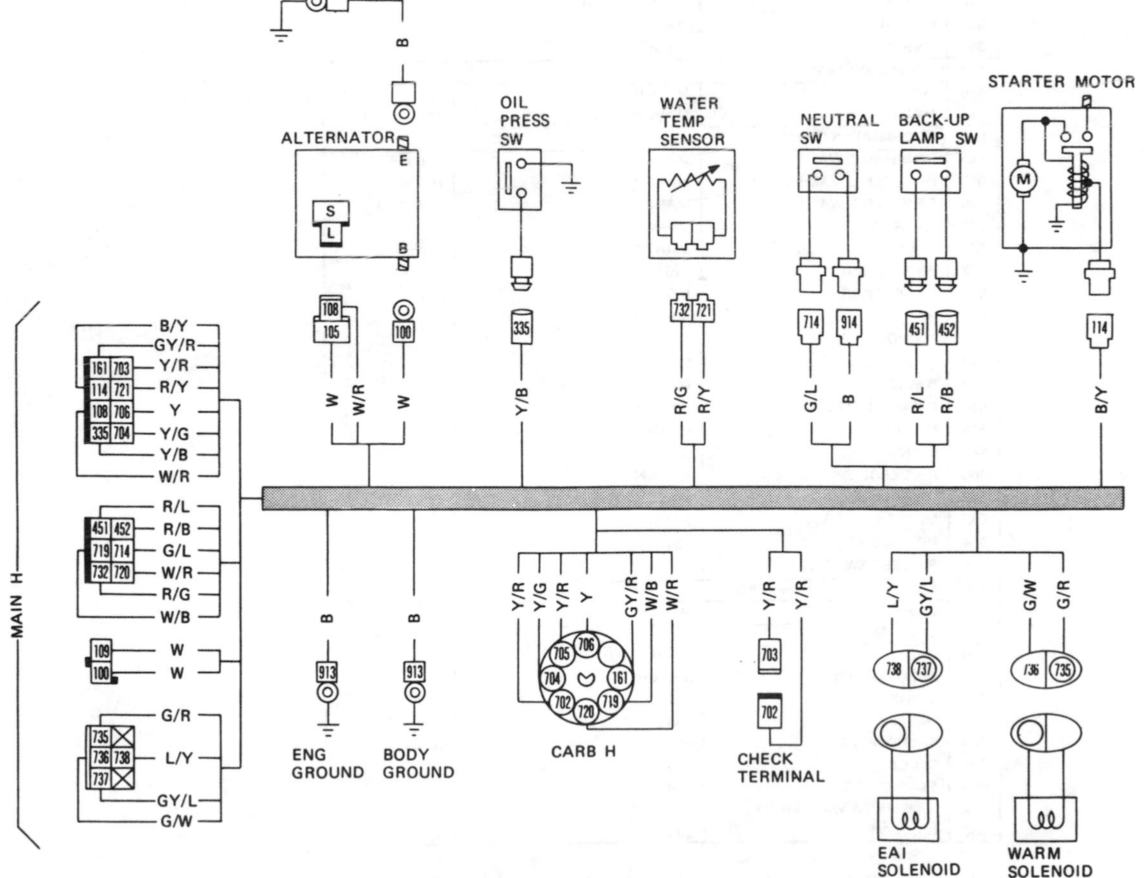

Fig. 10.109 Wiring diagram for the Sentra – engine components on MPG models

NO.	FROM	TO	REMARKS
100	ENGINE ELECTRICAL SYSTEM		
108	METER	MAIN H	
132	TACHO METER	MAIN H	USA H/B
133	TACHO METER	301	USA H/B
155	WARNING LAMP	301	MPG
156	WARNING LAMP	CHECK JOINT	MPG
157	METER (30000 MI SW)	CHECK JOINT	MPG
158	157	MAIN H	MPG
168	METER (SPEED SW)	MAIN H	USA
169	METER (SPEED SW)	MAIN H	USA
170	METER (10KM SW AMP)	MAIN H	CAN M/T
171	METER (10KM SW AMP)	MAIN H	CAN M/T
200	LIGHTING SYSTEM		
209	METER	MAIN H	
210	METER	MAIN H	
228	ILL CONT	234	
229	METER	234	
230	METER	235	
231	CIGAR LIGHTER	234	
232	RADIO	234	
233	RADIO	235	
234	CLOCK	MAIN H	
235	ILL CONT	CLOCK	
237	MAIN H	235	
300	METER, GAUGESAND WARNING SYSTEM		
301	METER	MAIN H	
304	METER	MAIN H	
305	METER	MAIN H	
320	WARNING LAMP	MAIN H	
321	WARNING LAMP	301	EXCEPT MPG
323	METER	MAIN H	
327	WARNING LAMP	MAIN H	EXCEPT MPG
334	WARNING LAMP	MAIN H	EXCEPT MPG
335	MAIN H	METER	
347	MAIN H	CHIME	
353	SEAT BELT SW	301	
354	METER	SEAT BELT SW	
355	MAIN H	354	
356	MAIN H	CHIME	
400	SIGNAL SYSTEM		
410	METER	MAIN H	
411	METER	MAIN H	
500	ACCESSORY SYSTEM		
513	RR WIPER & WASH	MAIN H	H/B WAG
515	RR WIPER & WASH	MAIN H	H/B WAG
516	RR WIPER & WASH	MAIN H	H/B WAG
520	JOINT (A)	MAIN H	
521	RADIO	JOINT (A)	
522	FR SPEAKER	526	
523	FR SPEAKER	527	
524	RADIO	MAIN H	
525	RADIO	MAIN H	
526	RADIO	MAIN H	
527	RADIO	MAIN H	
540	CIGAR LIGHTER	MAIN H	
545	MAIN H	CLOCK	
547	CLOCK	540	
550	RR DEFOG SW	MAIN H	
552	RR EFOG SW	MAIN H	
553	METER	552	
554	RR EFOG SW	234	
555	RR EFOG SW	235	
700	SUPPLEMENTAL NUMBERS		
705	WARNING LAMP	MAIN H	MPG
900	GROUND		
910	RADIO	MAIN H	
930	CIGAR LIGHTER	MAIN H	
931	CHIME	934	
932	METER	930	
933	TACHO METER	931	USA H/B
934	CLOCK	930	
938	SEAT BELT SW	934	
942	RR WIPER & WASHER SW	930	H/B WAG
960	ILL CONT	930	

Fig. 10.110 Key to wiring diagram for the Sentra – instruments

For the colour code see Fig. 10.99

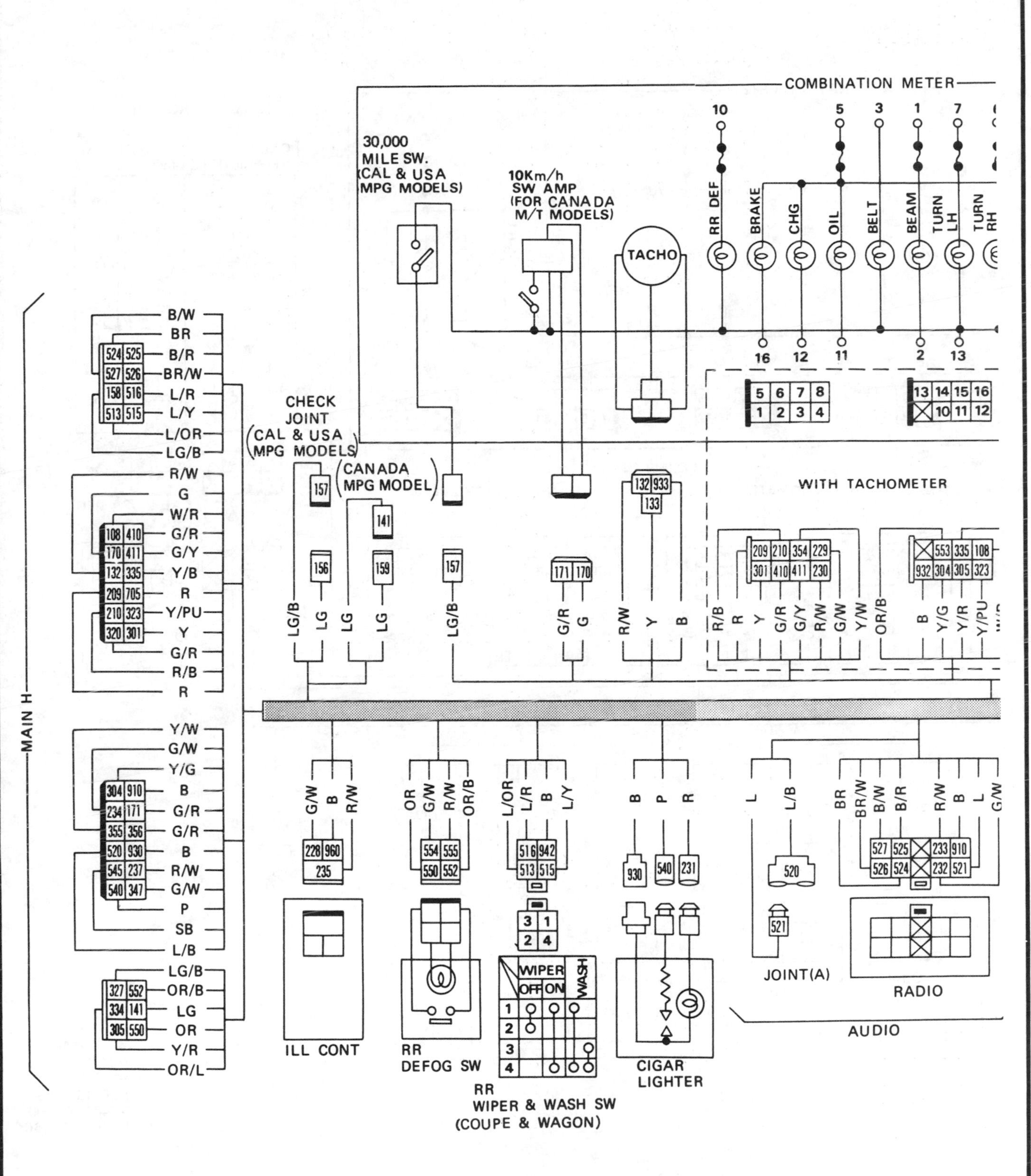

Fig. 10.111 Wiring diagram for the Sentra – instruments

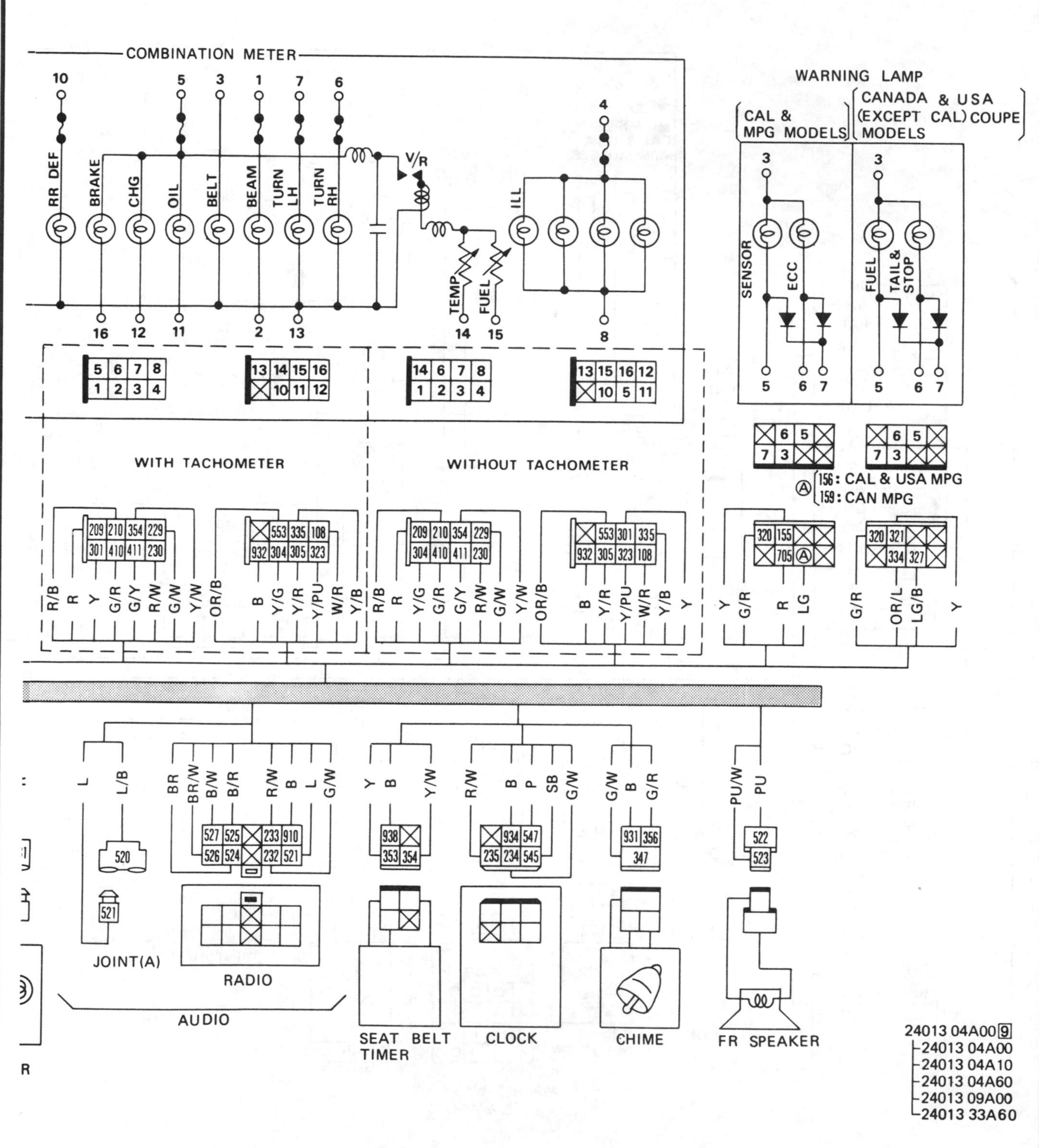

Fig. 10.111 Wiring diagram for the Sentra – instruments

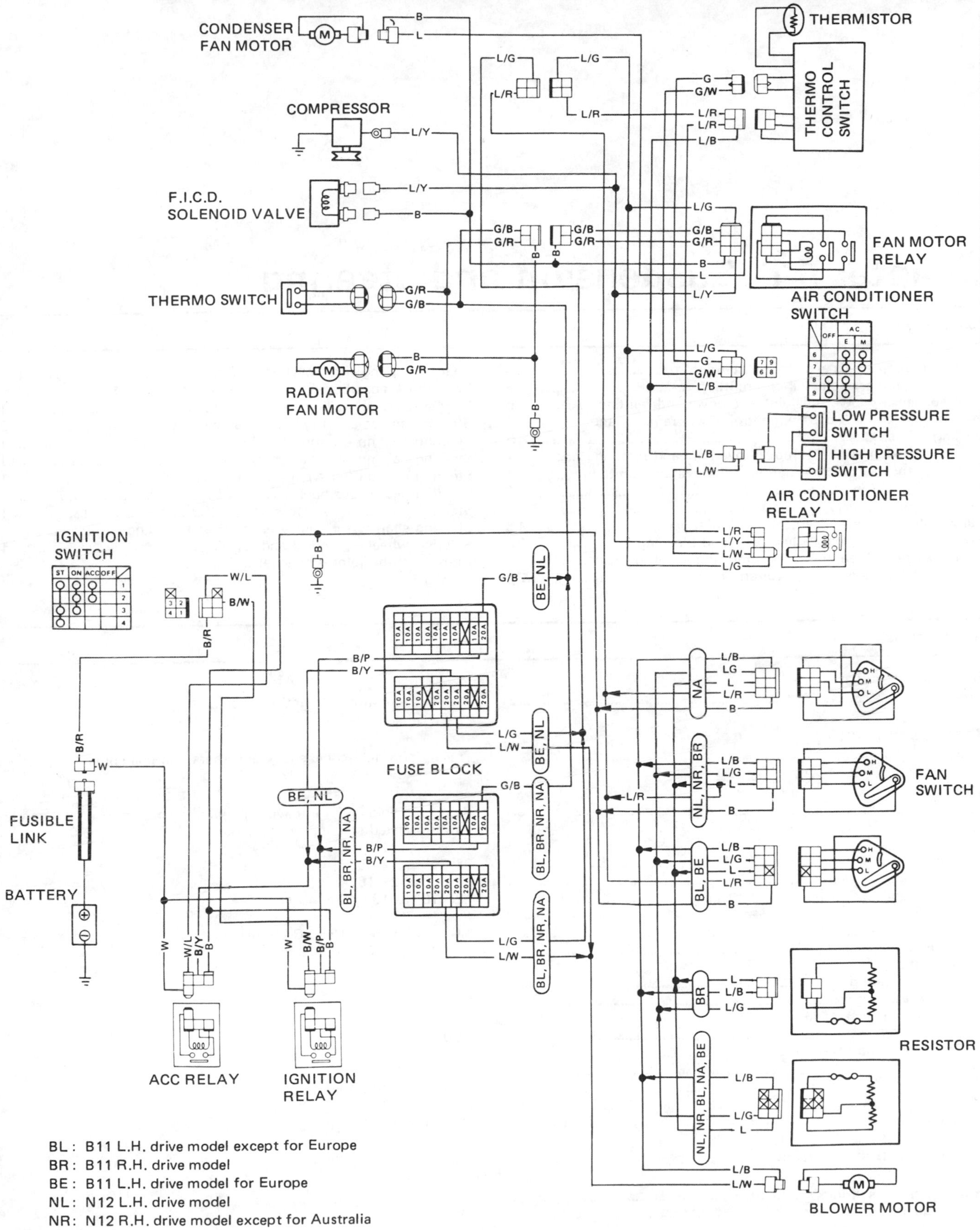

CONDENSER FAN MOTOR

COMPRESSOR

F.I.C.D. SOLENOID VALVE

THERMO SWITCH

RADIATOR FAN MOTOR

THERMISTOR

THERMO CONTROL SWITCH

FAN MOTOR RELAY

AIR CONDITIONER SWITCH

LOW PRESSURE SWITCH

HIGH PRESSURE SWITCH

AIR CONDITIONER RELAY

IGNITION SWITCH

FUSIBLE LINK

BATTERY

FUSE BLOCK

ACC RELAY

IGNITION RELAY

FAN SWITCH

RESISTOR

BLOWER MOTOR

BL: B11 L.H. drive model except for Europe
BR: B11 R.H. drive model
BE: B11 L.H. drive model for Europe
NL: N12 L.H. drive model
NR: N12 R.H. drive model except for Australia
NA: N12 R.H. drive model for Australia

Fig. 10.112 Wiring diagram for the Sentra – air conditioner

For the colour code see Fig. 10.99

Chapter 11 Suspension and steering

Contents

Specifications

Front suspension

Type	MacPherson strut with anti-roll bar

Rear suspension

Type	Trailing arm, telescopic shock absorbers and coil springs

Steering

Type	Rack and pinion with a universally-jointed column. A tilt column and power-assisted steering are optional
Steering angles	
Camber	0° 25′ to 1° 05′
Castor	0° 45′ to 2° 15′
Kingpin inclination	12° 10′ to 13° 40′
Toe-in:	
B11	3.0 to 5.0 mm (0.12 to 0.20 in)
N12	0 to 2.0 mm (0 to 0.079 in)
Steering ratio:	
Manual steering	21.55:1
Power-assisted steering	18.45:1
Number of turns lock to lock:	
Manual steering	3.90
Power-assisted steering	3.33
Turning circle	10.0 m (32.8 ft)
Wheelbase	2400.0 mm (94.5 in)
Front track	1395.0 mm (54.9 in)
Rear track	1375.0 mm (54.1 in)

Torque wrench settings

	Nm	lbf ft
Front suspension		
Strut piston rod self-locking nut	70	52
Strut upper mounting nuts	23	17
Strut to stub axle carrier	80	59
Lower balljoint to track control arm	61	45
Lower balljoint to stub axle carrier	48	35
Tie-rod balljoint taper pin nut	48	35
Track control pivot arm bolts	95	70
Track control arm support plate	95	70
Track control arm pivot nuts	110	81

Driveshaft nut:		
E13 engine	149	110
E15 and E16 engines	190	140
Disc-to-hub bolts	34	25
Caliper mounting bolts	61	45
Anti-roll bar clamp	12	9
Anti-roll bar end links	12	9
Rear suspension		
Shock absorber upper mounting	12	9
Shock absorber lower mounting	45	33
Trailing arm pivot bolt	65	48
Steering		
Steering wheel nut	50	37
Steering shaft lower joint pinch-bolt:		
M10	38	28
M8	28	21
Tilt lever bolt	11	8
Column mounting bracket	14	10
Steering gear mounting clamps	75	55
Fluid pump to bracket	25	18
Pump pulley nut	75	55
Pressure hose to gear housing	28	21
Pressure hose to pump	48	35

1 General description

The front suspension is of MacPherson strut type, having coil springs, a lower track control arm and an anti-roll bar.

The rear suspension is of trailing arm type with coil springs and telescopic shock absorbers.

The steering gear is of rack-and-pinion type with a universally-jointed steering column.

Power-assisted steering is available as a factory-fitted option.

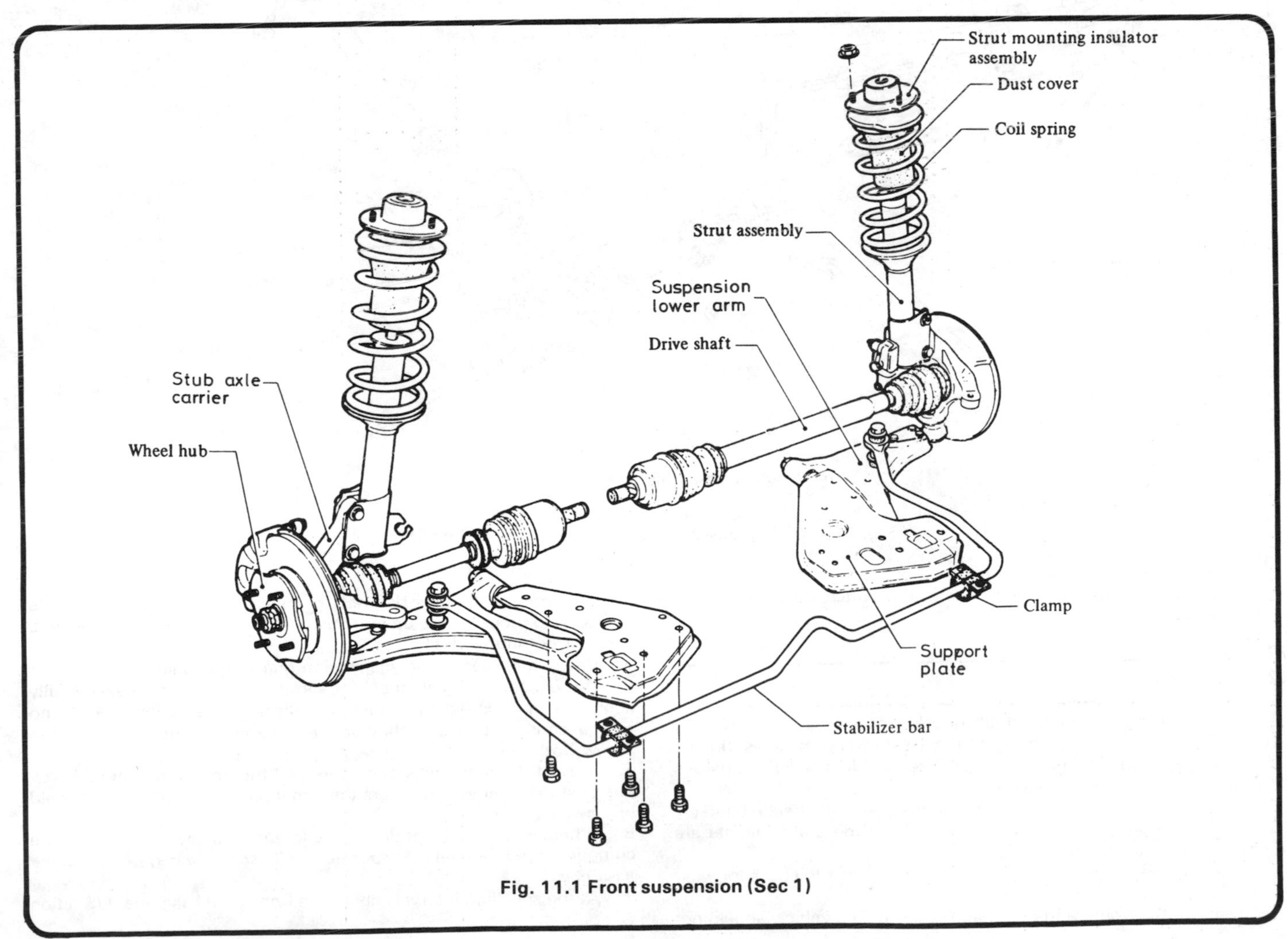

Fig. 11.1 Front suspension (Sec 1)

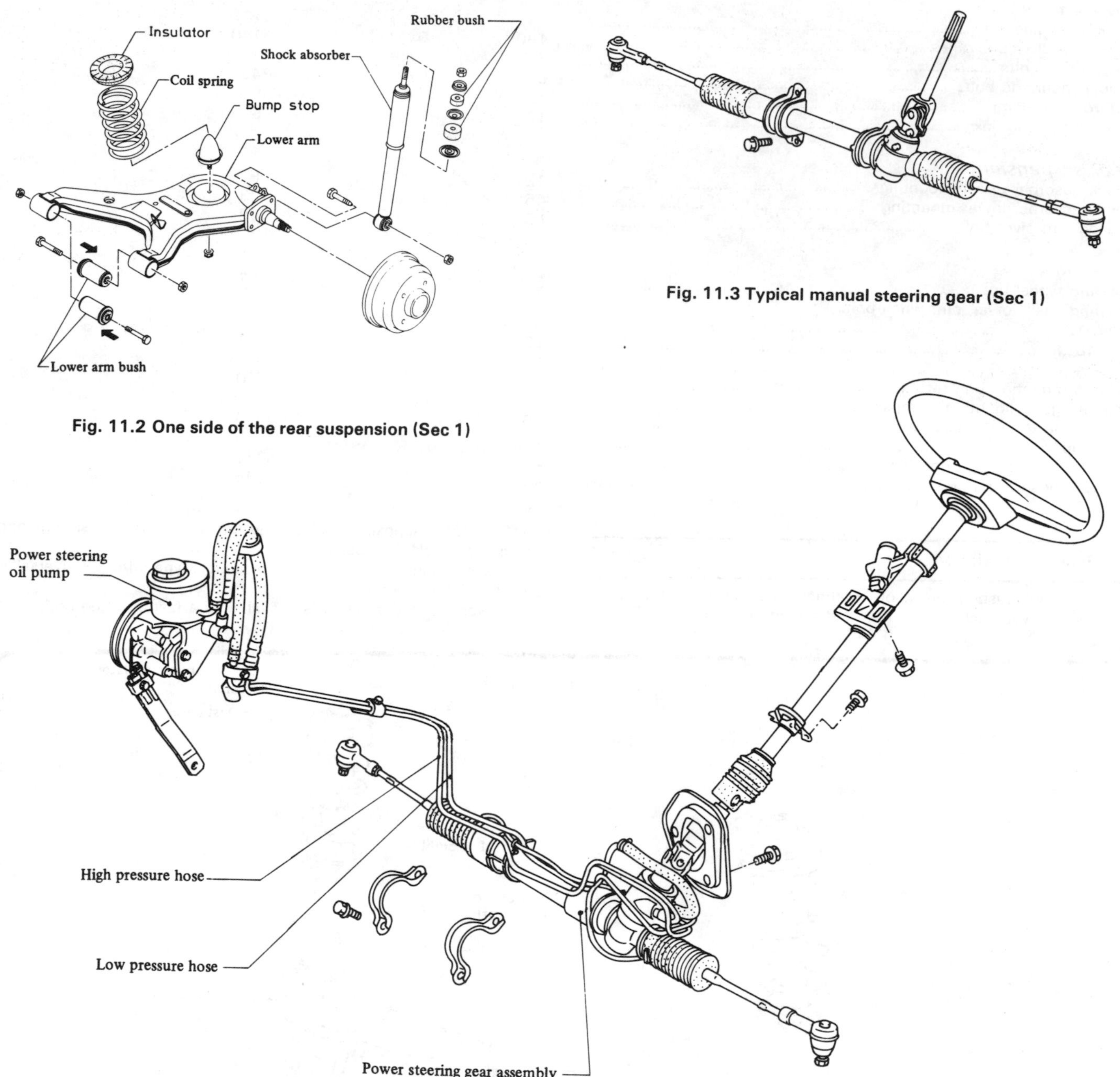

Fig. 11.2 One side of the rear suspension (Sec 1)

Fig. 11.3 Typical manual steering gear (Sec 1)

Fig. 11.4 Typical power-assisted steering gear (Sec 1)

Refer also to Chapter 8 for details of driveshafts, hubs and roadwheels.

2 Maintenance

1 At the intervals specified in Routine Maintenance check the condition of all balljoint gaiters and the steering rack bellows. If split, or in any way damaged, renew them or the complete balljoint if gaiters are not available separately.

2 With the help of an assistant, move the steering wheel repeatedly a few degrees in both directions while the tie-rod end balljoints are checked for lost motion and wear.

3 Using a lever, prise the stub axle carrier upwards to check for wear in the suspension lower balljoint.

4 Depress the front wing and then release it. The vehicle should not make several oscillations before becoming stationary as, if the struts are working properly, the up and down motion of the vehicle should be damped out immediately.

5 Check for wear in the suspension rear arm bushes.

6 Disconnect the rear shock absorber lower mountings and fully compress and extend the shock absorbers. If the action is jerky, no resistance is evident or if they are seized and will not compress then renew **both** units.

7 Inspect the rear shock absorbers and the front struts for oil leaks. The dust excluder which covers the upper part of the strut tube should be checked for damage.

8 Where wear is evident during the foregoing inspections, renew the component immediately. *Suspension units should always be renewed as a pair.*

9 At the specified intervals check the front wheel alignment (Section 23).

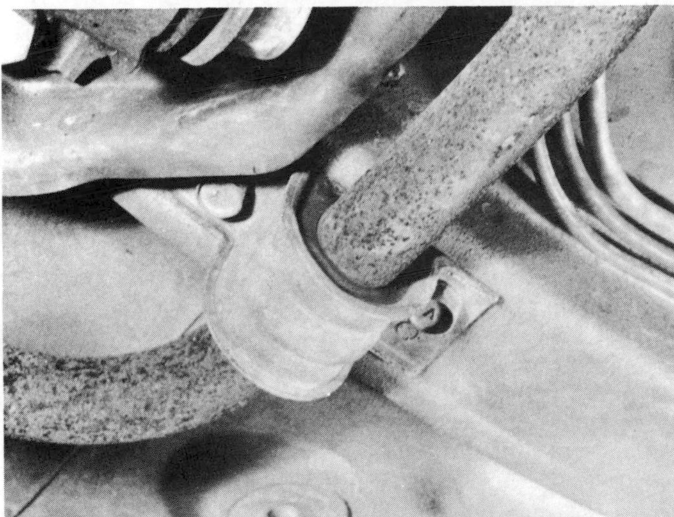
3.2A Front anti-roll bar clamp

3.2B Front anti-roll bar end link

3 Front anti-roll bar – removal and refitting

1 Disconnect the exhaust pipe front mounting bracket and the flexible mounting nearest the front expansion box.
2 Unscrew the anti-roll bar clamp to bolts (photo) and the end nuts (photo).
3 Withdraw the anti-roll bar.
4 Refitting is a reversal of removal, but if the vehicle was jacked up to remove the bar do not fully tighten the anti-roll bar nuts and bolts until the weight of the vehicle has been lowered onto the roadwheels.

4 Front suspension strut – removal, overhaul and refitting

1 Raise the front of the vehicle and support it securely on axle stands placed under the side-members.
2 Remove the roadwheel.

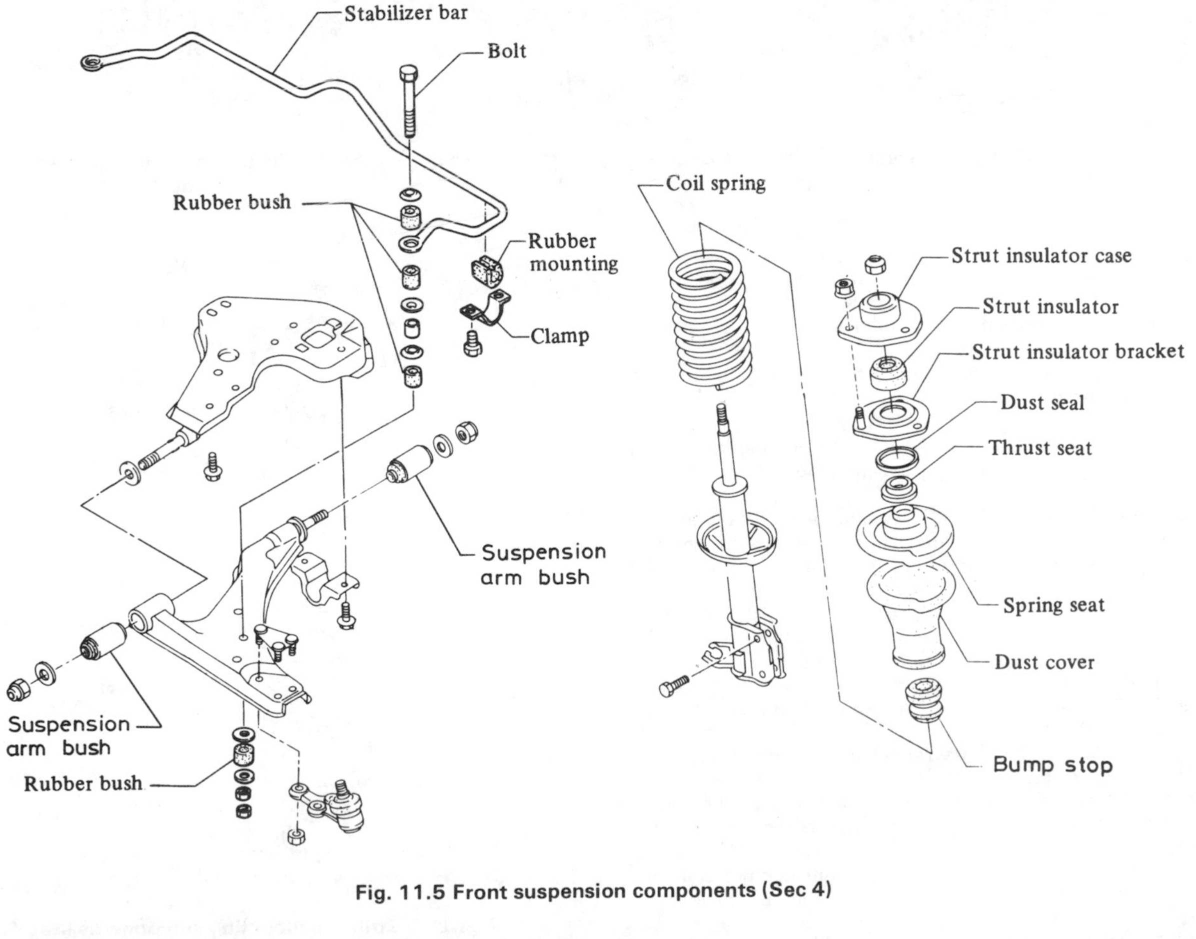

Stabilizer bar
Bolt
Rubber bush
Rubber mounting
Clamp
Suspension arm bush
Suspension arm bush
Rubber bush
Coil spring
Strut insulator case
Strut insulator
Strut insulator bracket
Dust seal
Thrust seat
Spring seat
Dust cover
Bump stop

Fig. 11.5 Front suspension components (Sec 4)

4.5 Stub axle carrier attachment to base of strut

4.6 Front suspension strut upper mounting

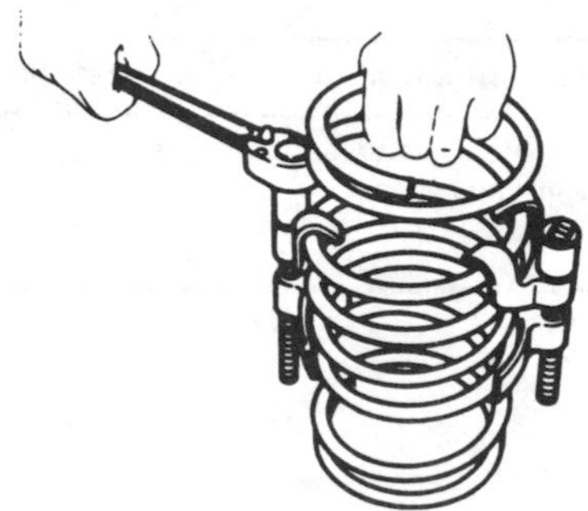

Fig. 11.6 Fitting coil spring compressors (Sec 4)

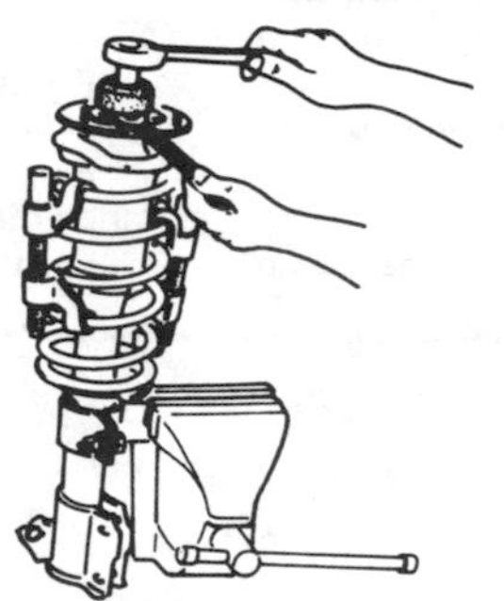

Fig. 11.7 Unscrewing strut piston rod locknut (Sec 4)

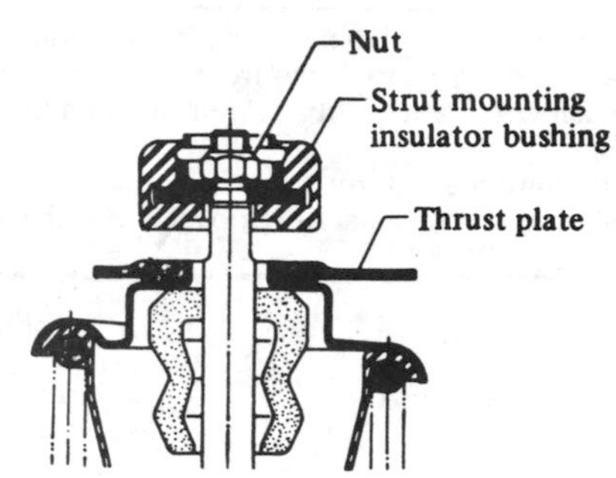

Fig. 11.8 Strut top mounting – in section (Sec 4)

3 Disconnect the hydraulic brake pipe from the suspension strut.
4 Support the suspension lower arm on a jack.
5 Unscrew the two pinch-bolts which hold the stub axle carrier to the base of the suspension strut (photo).
6 Working at the top of the inner wing within the engine compartment, unscrew and remove the three nuts which secure the strut top mounting (photo).
7 Support the strut assembly and withdraw it from under the wing.
8 Unless coil spring compressors are available do not carry out any further dismantling.
9 Where compressors are available (they can be purchased at most motor accessory stores) fit them to the strut coil spring and compress the spring just sufficiently to be able to turn the strut upper mounting insulator by hand.
10 Unscrew the self-locking nut from the top of the piston rod. Flats are machined on the rod so that an open-ended spanner can be used to prevent the rod rotating while the unit is unscrewed.
11 Take off the mounting insulator, the thrust seat, the dust seal, the spring upper seat, the rebound rubber, coil spring (with compressors) and the dust excluder.
12 Unless the coil spring is to be renewed, the compressors can remain on the spring for reassembly.
13 If the strut is distorted, leaking or has lost its damping qualities, then the strut tube must be renewed, no repair being possible. The renewal of both struts is advised.
14 Reassemble the strut by fitting the spring in its compressed state followed by the upper mounting components in their originally fitted sequence. Apply grease to the underside of the thrust plate.
15 Tighten the piston rod self-locking nut to the specified torque and

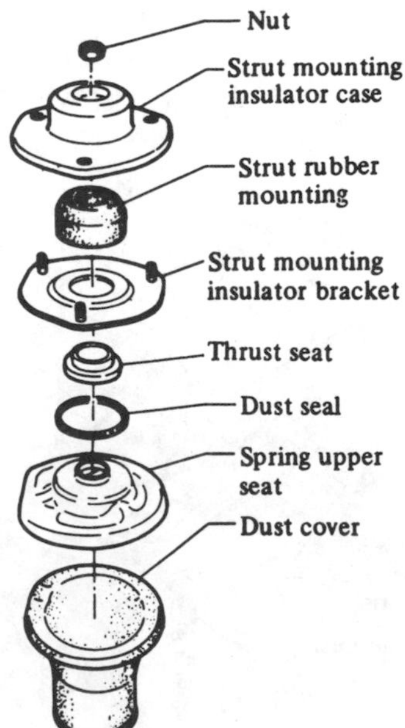

Fig. 11.9 Strut top mounting components (Sec 4)

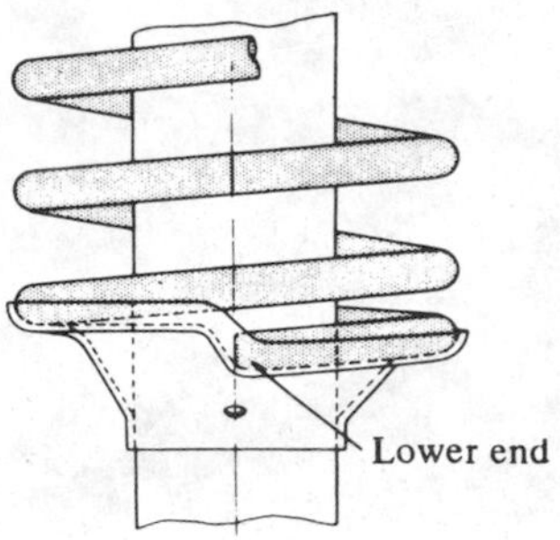

Fig. 11.10 Coil spring lower seat abutment (Sec 4)

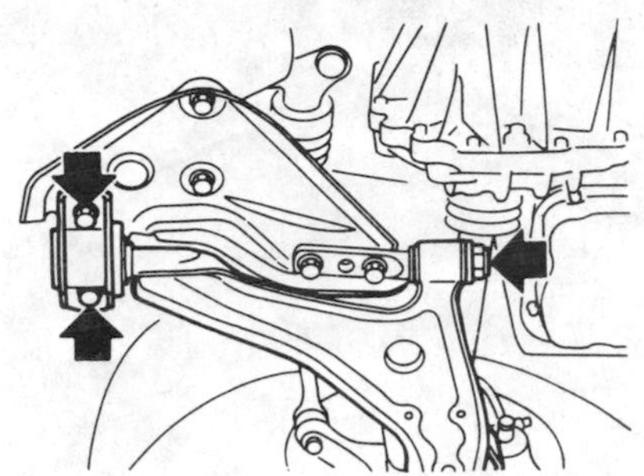

Fig. 11.11 Track control arm pivot bolts (Sec 5)

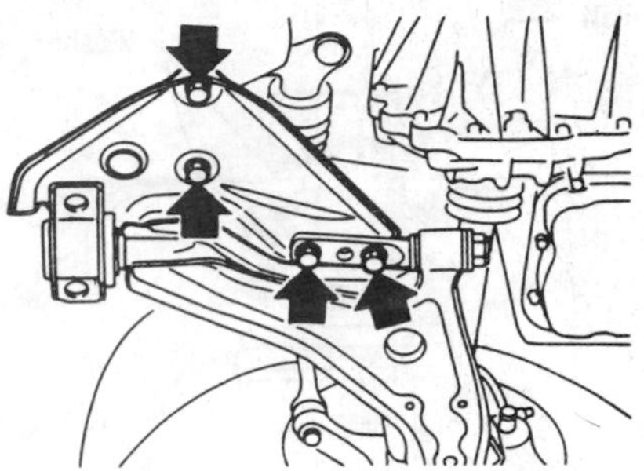

Fig. 11.12 Support plate and pivot arm bolts (Sec 5)

then gently remove the spring compressors. Make sure that the spring lower end is in full contact with the abutment on the lower seat.
16 Offer the strut to its mounting under the wing. Screw on the nuts finger tight.
17 Reconnect the base of the strut with the stub axle carrier.
18 Reconnect the brake pipe to the strut.
19 Refit the roadwheel and lower the vehicle.
20 Tighten all nuts and bolts to the specified torques.

5 Front suspension lower track control arm – removal and refitting

1 Raise the vehicle and support on axle stands placed under the side-members.
2 Remove the roadwheel.
3 Remove the anti-roll bar (see Section 3).
4 Disconnect the suspension lower balljoint from the track control arm by unscrewing the three securing nuts. It is recommended that these nuts are renewed at reassembly.
5 Working at the inboard end of the control arm, unbolt the pivot rod clamp and pivot end nut (photo). Remove the control arm.
6 Unbolt and remove the support plate, if required, by unscrewing the fixing bolts.
7 The flexible bushes may be renewed. Do this by pressing them out or by drawing them out using a bolt, nut, washers and tubular spacers. Smear the new bushes with hydraulic fluid to make fitting easier.
8 Refit the support plate and the control arm by reversing the removal operations.
9 Do not fully tighten the nuts and bolts to the specified torques until the weight of the vehicle is on the roadwheels.

6 Front suspension lower balljoint – removal and refitting

1 In order to obtain access to the balljoint fixing nut the driveshaft must first be removed, as described in Chapter 8.
2 Unscrew the balljoint nut and then, using a suitable balljoint extractor tool, disconnect the balljoint from the stub axle carrier.
3 Unscrew the three nuts which hold the balljoint to the track control arm and remove the balljoint. It is recommended that new nuts are used at reassembly.
4 Refitting is a reversal of removal, tighten all nuts and bolts to the specified torque. Do not apply any grease to the balljoint taper pin or eye before connecting. It is sometimes found that when tightening the taper pin nut the balls turns in the joint socket rather than the nut tightening. Should this happen, raise a jack under the balljoint in order to seat the taper pin more firmly in the eye of the stub axle carrier.

7 Front suspension stub axle carrier – removal and refitting

1 The operations are described in Chapter 8, in connection with renewal of the hub bearings.

5.5 Front suspension track control arm

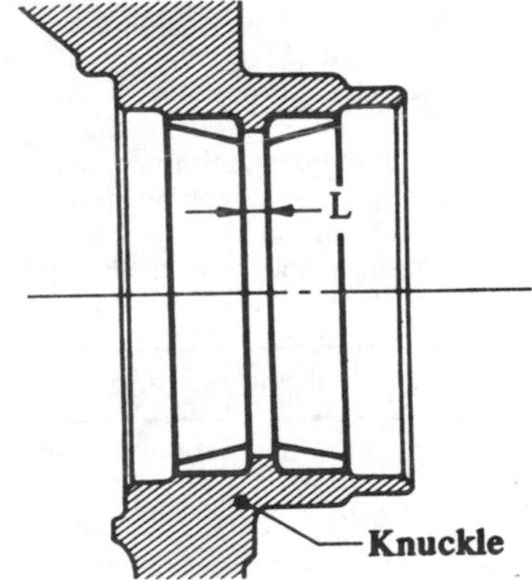

Fig. 11.13 Front hub outer bearing track space – L (Sec 7)

2 If a new stub axle carrier has been fitted then the original bearing spacer will have to be changed.
3 To calculate the thickness of the new spacer, measure the distance (L) between the two hub bearing outer tracks (see Fig. 11.13). From this figure subtract 0.09 mm (0.0035 in) and the remainder will be the thickness of the spacer required to obtain a satisfactory preload.
4 Spacers are available in eighteen increments, and your dealer's parts department will be able to supply the correct spacer once they know the dimension which resulted from your calculation.

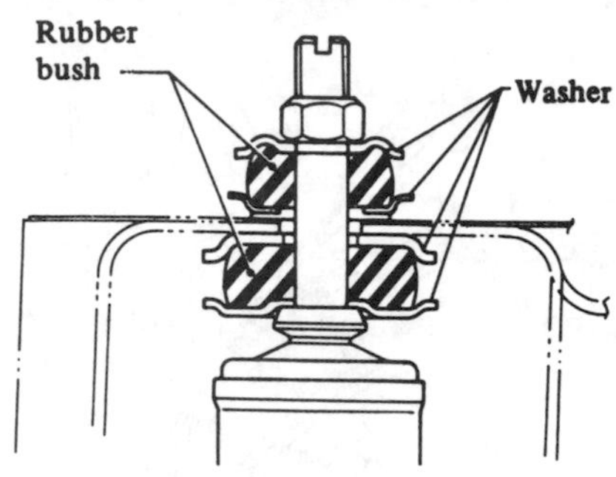

Fig. 11.14 Rear shock absorber upper mounting components (Sec 8)

8.1 Rear shock absorber upper mounting

8.2 Rear shock absorber lower mounting

9.4 Rear coil spring

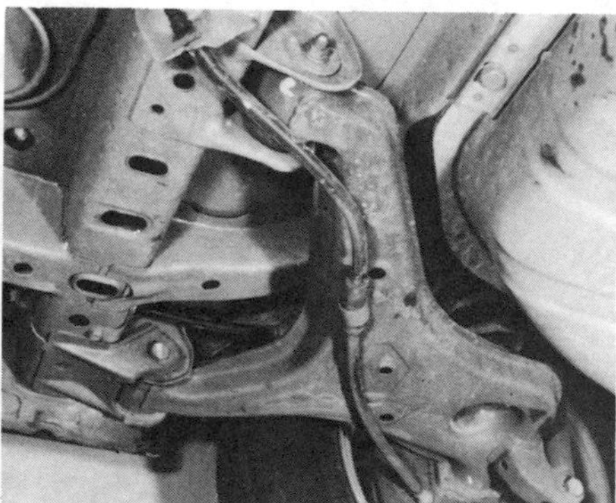

10.5 Rear suspension trailing arm

Fig. 11.15 Rear suspension arm pivot bolts (Sec 10)

8 Rear shock absorber – removal and refitting

1 Working within the boot, pull the protective cap from the shock absorber upper mounting stud on the rear wing inner arch (photo). Unscrew the nut and take off the seats and rubber cushions.
2 Working inside the vehicle, disconnect the shock absorber lower mounting (photo) and withdraw the shock absorber from under the wing.
3 Refitting is a reversal of removal, but make sure that all the rubber bushes and cushions are in good condition and make sure that the upper mounting components are located in their correct sequence.
4 Tighten the mounting nuts and bolts to the specified torque.

9 Rear coil spring – removal and refitting

1 Raise the rear of the vehicle and support it securely. Remove the roadwheel.
2 Support the suspension trailing arm on a jack.
3 Disconnect the shock absorber lower mounting.
4 Lower the jack under the suspension arm until the coil spring is free and can be removed (photo).
5 Refitting is a reversal of removal, but make sure that the rubber insulator is in good condition and that the flattened end of the spring engages correctly with the insulator.

10 Rear suspension trailing arm – removal and refitting

1 Remove the coil spring, as described in Section 9.
2 Unscrew the union and disconnect the rigid brake pipe from the flexible hose. Cap the end of the rigid pipe with a bleed screw dust cap, or similar, to reduce fluid loss.
3 Bend back the clamp and release the handbrake cable from the suspension arm.

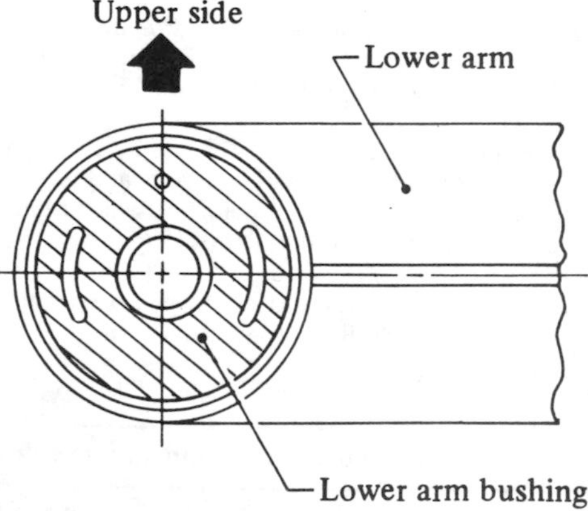

Fig. 11.16 Positioning of the rear suspension arm flexible bushes (Sec 10)

4 Refer to Chapter 9 and remove the brake drum, shoes, wheel cylinder and brake backplate.
5 Unbolt and remove the suspension arm pivot bolts (photo). Withdraw the suspension arm from the vehicle.
6 If the suspension arm flexible bushes are worn they can be renewed using a press or a bolt, nut, washers and tubular distance pieces. Before the bushes can be removed, however, the metal flange will first have to be ground off.
7 When fitting the new bushes, align their cut-outs as shown in the diagram (Fig. 11.16).
8 Refit the suspension arm by reversing the removal operations but do not tighten the nuts and bolts to the specified torque settings until the weight of the vehicle is on the roadwheels.
9 Bleed the brake circuit, as described in Chapter 9.

11.2 Typical balljoint splitter

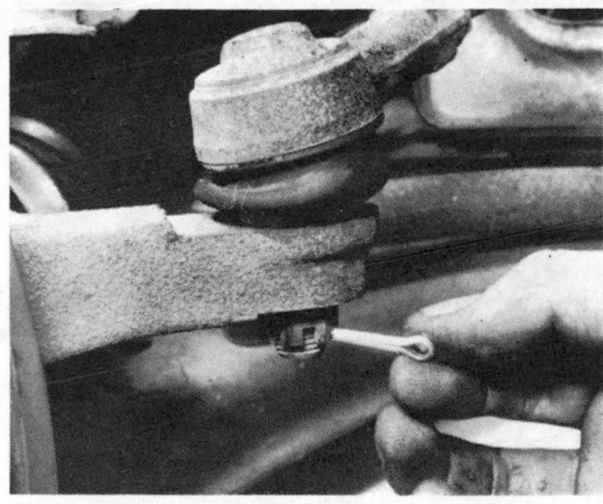

11.7 Fitting new split pin to balljoint taper pin

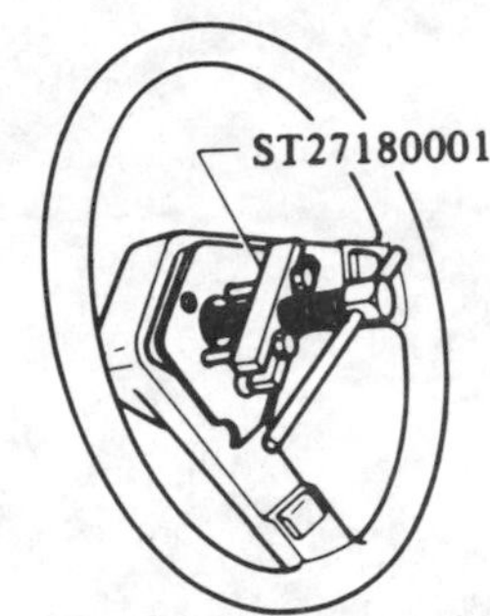

Fig. 11.17 Using extractor to pull off steering wheel (Sec 13)

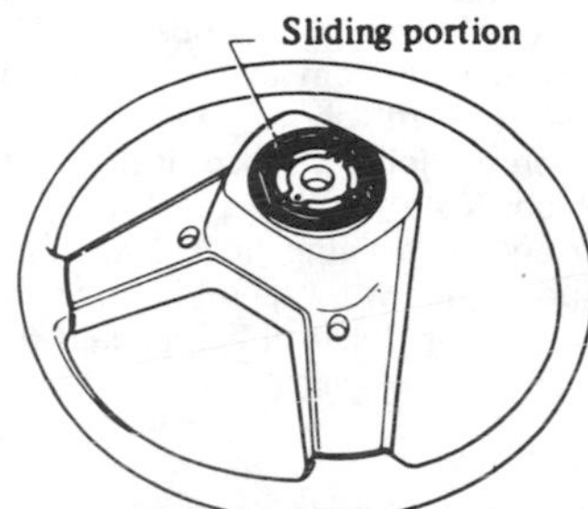

Fig. 11.18 Steering wheel sliding ring (Sec 13)

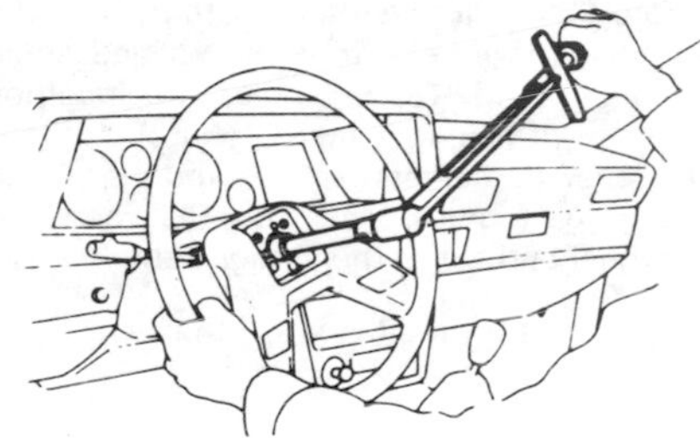

Fig. 11.19 Tightening steering wheel retaining nut (Sec 13)

11 Steering rack bellows – renewal

1 The steering rack bellows should be inspected periodically for splits. Have an assistant turn the steering to full lock while doing this, otherwise the split will not be immediately apparent.

2 Unscrew the nut from the balljoint taper pin and, using an extractor, separate the balljoint from the eye of the steering arm (photo).

3 Release the locknut and then unscrew the balljoint from the tie-rod, counting the number of turns required to remove it.

4 Release the bellows securing bands and pull the bellows from the rack housing and off the tie-rod.

5 If the bellows have been split for some time and dirt has entered, wipe away all the old lubricant and smear the rack (extended) and the rack end balljoint with a suitable grease. Even if the bellows are not being renewed it is recommended that the bellows are removed at the intervals specified in Routine Maintenance and fresh grease smeared onto the rack and rack end balljoint as they do tend to become dry after a high mileage.

6 Slide on the new bellows and fit the securing bands.

7 Screw the balljoint onto the tie-rod by the same number of turns as was recorded at removal and tighten the locknut. Reconnect the balljoint to the steering arm of the stub axle carrier, use a new split pin (photo).

8 Check the front wheel alignment by referring to Section 23.

12 Tie-rod end balljoint – renewal

1 The removal and refitting of a balljoint is covered in the preceding Section.

2 Always check the front wheel alignment after having fitted a new balljoint – refer to Section 23.

13 Steering wheel – removal and refitting

1 Set the front roadwheels in the straight-ahead position, disconnect the battery.

2 Prise out the cover from the centre of the steering wheel (photo). The steering wheel retaining nut can now be unscrewed, but better access to the nut can be provided if the horn switch cover is removed by extracting the two screws which are located on the rear face of the

13.2A Steering wheel hub cover plate

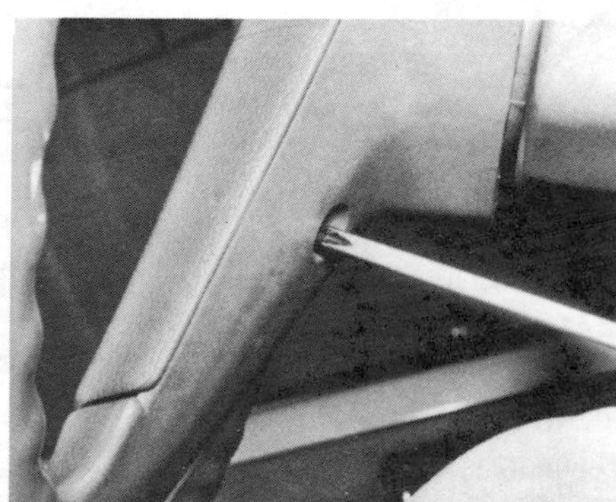

13.2B Extracting steering wheel spoke cover screw

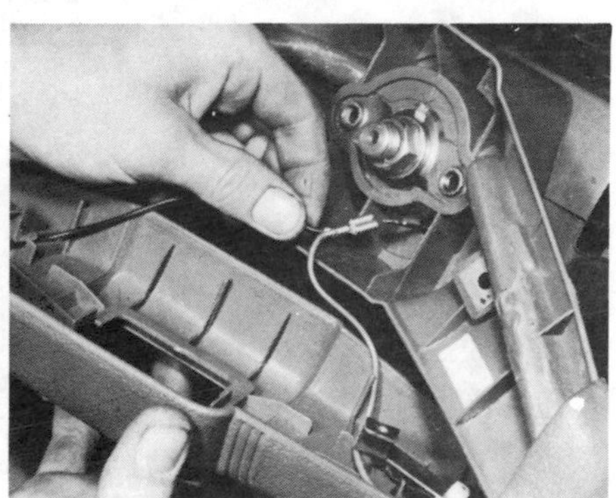

13.2C Removing spoke cover and disconnecting the horn switch wire

13.2D Steering wheel nut lock washer

13.4 Fitting the steering wheel

14.2 Steering shaft lower coupling

steering wheel spokes (photos). Remove the spring washer (photo).

3 If anything more than a gentle thump with the palms of the hands is required to remove the wheel from the splined steering shaft, a puller will have to be used. Tapped holes are incorporated in the steering wheel hub for attaching a puller (photo).

4 Apply a little grease to the shaft splines and the sliding ring before fitting the steering wheel (photo). Make sure that the spokes are in the lower half of the wheel and set in the straight-ahead position. Tighten the nut to the specified torque.

5 Fit the hub cover and horn switch cover as appropriate.

14 Steering shaft lower joint – removal and refitting

1 To provide better access remove the steering column aperture dust excluding cover from the bulkhead. Set the steering in the straight-ahead position.

2 Unscrew the pinch-bolts from both universally-jointed couplings, prise the jaws of the couplings open just enough to be able to withdraw the lower joint from the upper coupling and then from the steering gear pinion shaft (photo).

3 When refitting the joint, connect it first to the upper coupling and then to the pinion. Note that the pinch-bolt cut-out must be aligned with the upper coupling clamp jaws and that the jaws of the lower coupling must be aligned with the mark on the steering pinion housing.

4 Tighten the pinch-bolts to the specified torque.

15 Steering column – removal and refitting

Non-tilt type

1 Remove the steering wheel (Section 13).

2 Remove the shaft lower joint (Section 14).

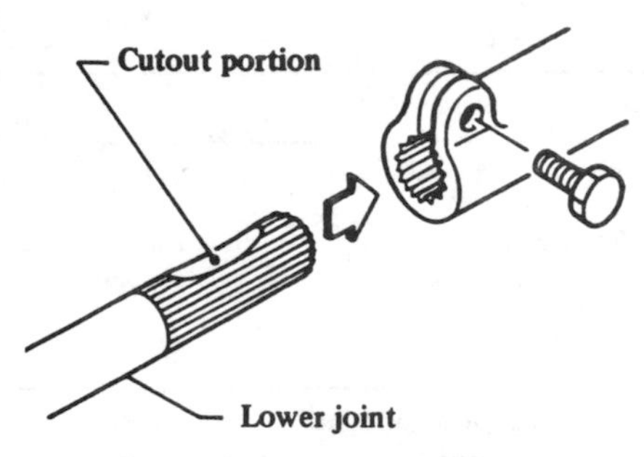

Fig. 11.20 Pinch-bolt cut-out (Sec 14)

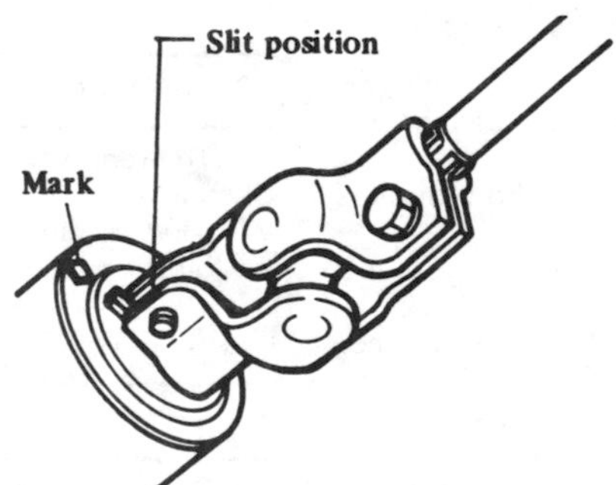

Fig. 11.21 Lower joint alignment marks (Sec 14)

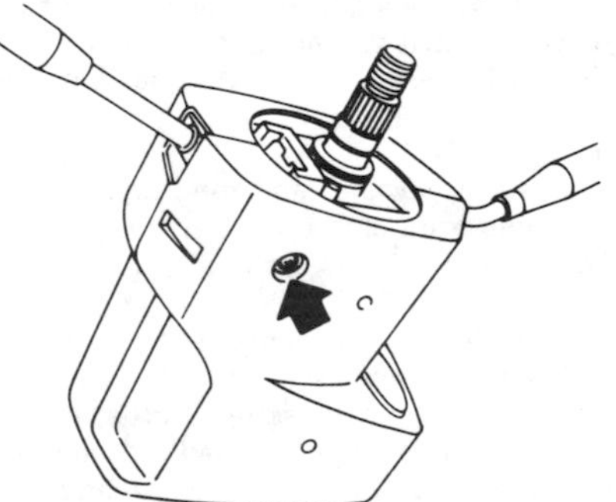

Fig. 11.22 Steering column shroud retaining screw (Sec 15)

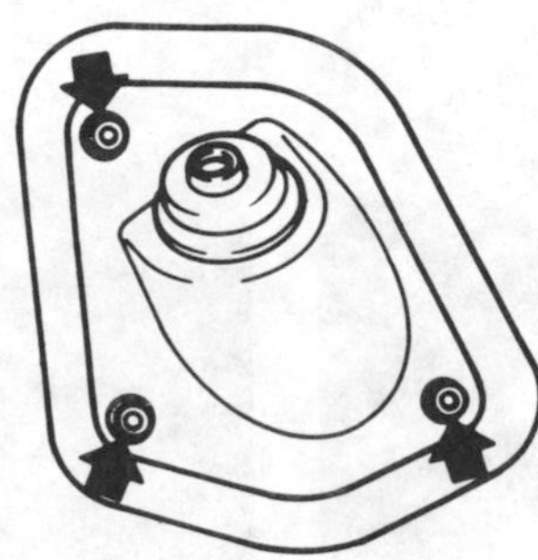

Fig. 11.23 Steering column dust excluder at bulkhead (Sec 15)

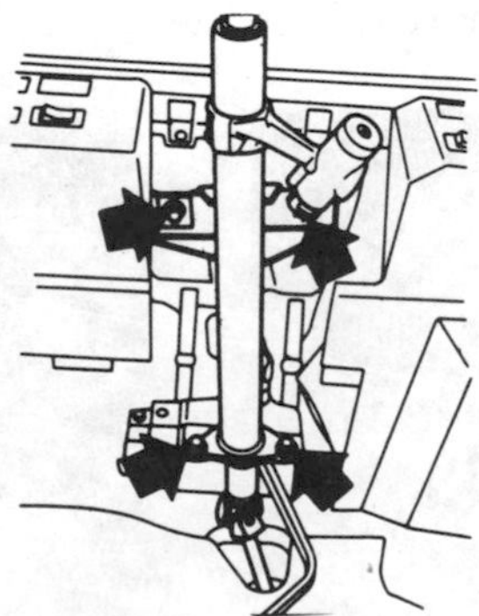

Fig. 11.24 Steering column bracket bolts (Sec 15)

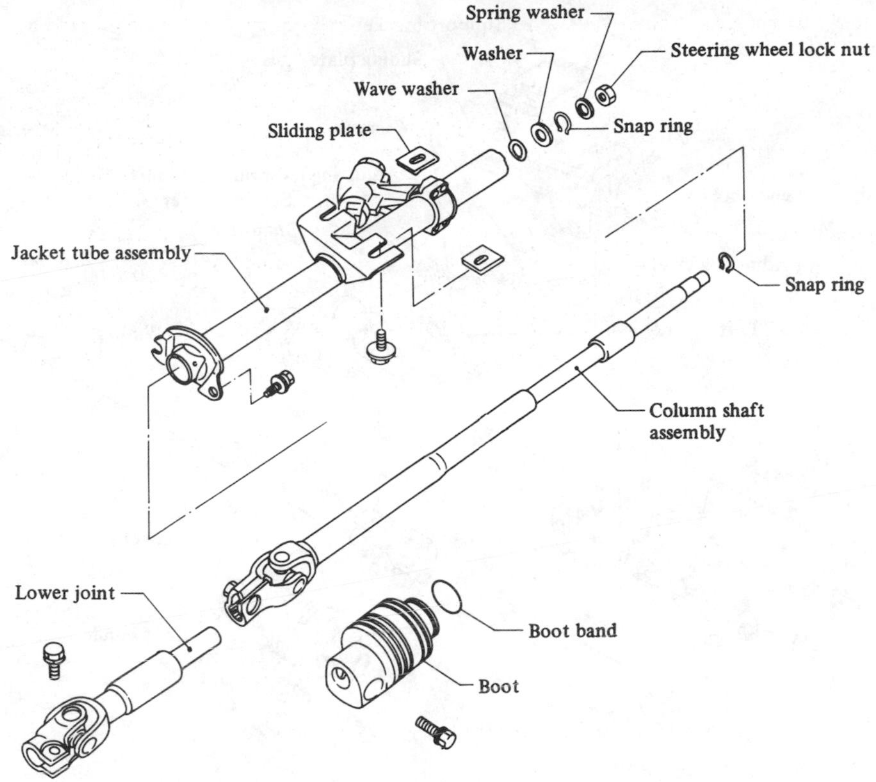

Fig. 11.25 Steering column components – non-tilt type (Sec 15)

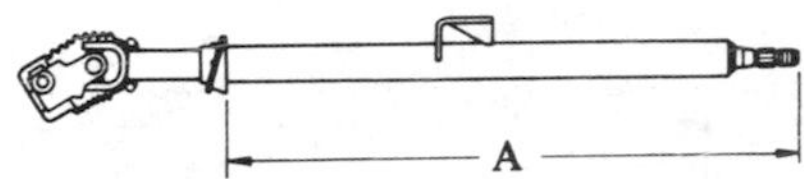

Fig. 11.26 Steering column length – non-tilt type (Sec 15)

A = 481.3 to 484.3 mm (18.95 to 19.07 in)

3 Remove the lower shroud from the upper steering column. Disconnect the battery.
4 Extract the screws, disconnect the wiring harness plugs and remove the steering column switch.
5 Remove the heater ducts (Chapter 2).
6 Remove the nuts from the column dust excluder on the bulkhead.
7 Unscrew the upper and lower column retaining bolts and withdraw the column from under the facia panel. Check the column length A (Fig. 11.26). If it does not conform, renew the assembly.

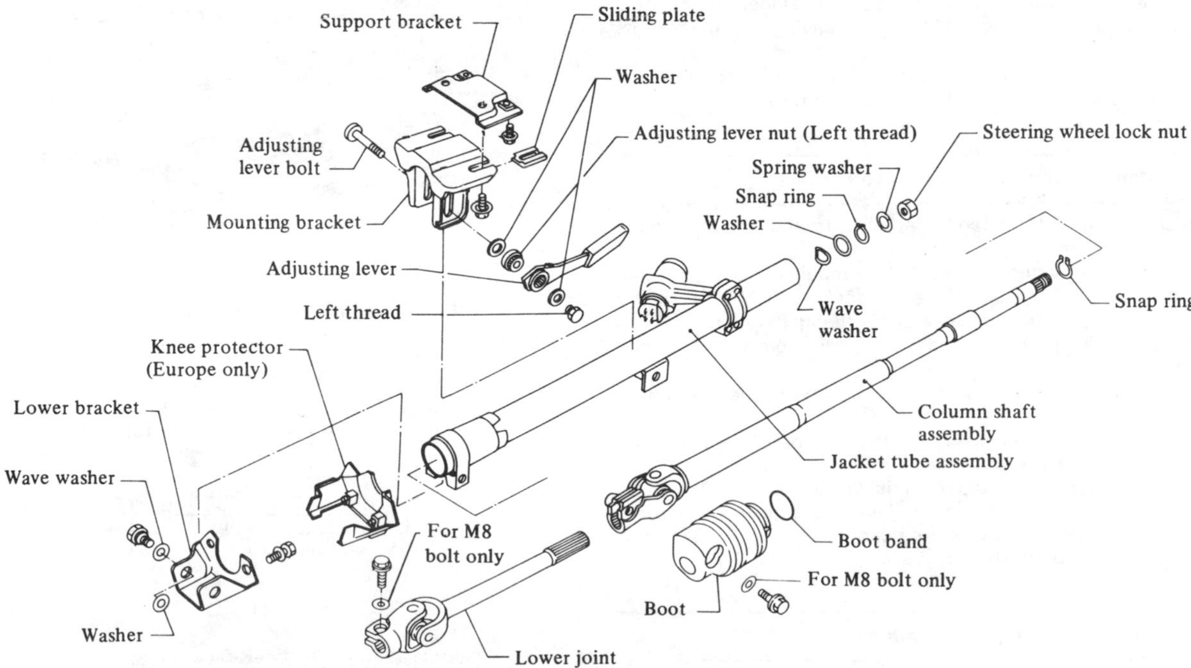

Fig. 11.27 Steering column components – tilt type of FKK make (Sec 15)

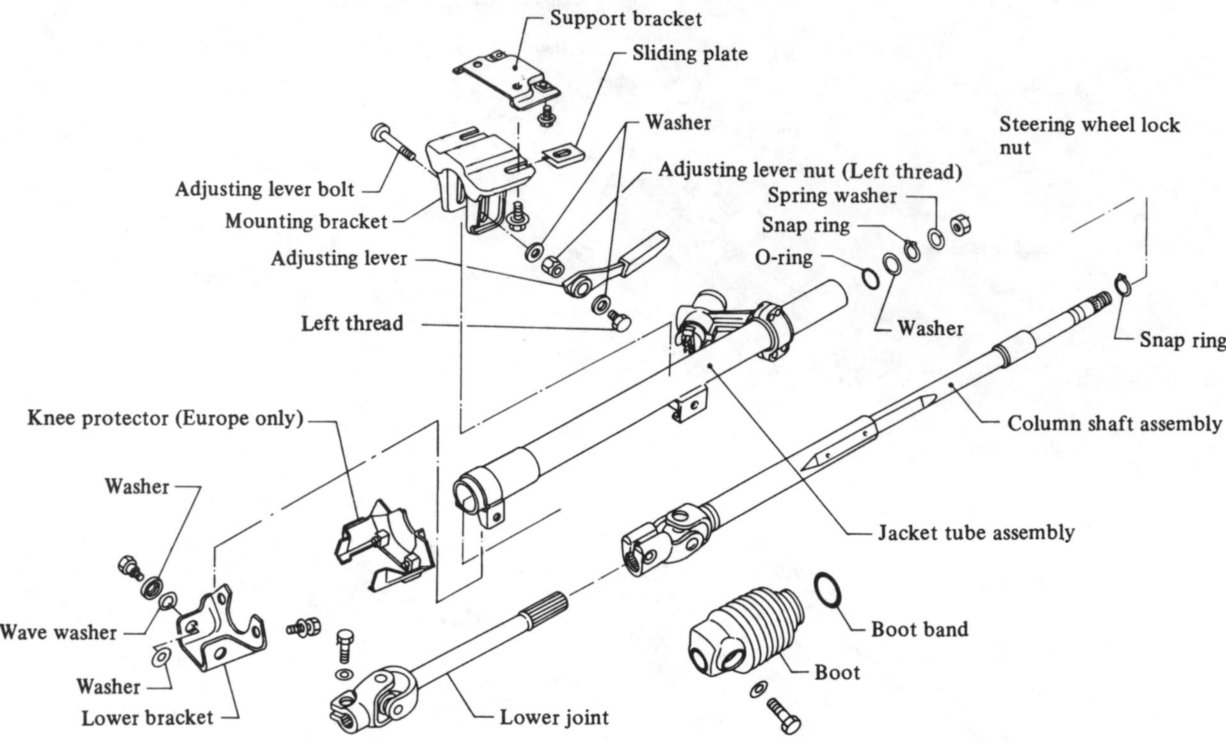

Fig. 11.28 Steering column components – tilt type of NSK make (Sec 15)

Tilt type

8 The operations are very similar to the non-tilt type, except for the tilt lever components at the upper end of the column which are shown in Figs. 28 and 29. Check the column length A (Fig. 11.29). If it does not conform, renew the assembly.

Refitting – all types

9 Offer the column into position making sure that the sliding plate is correctly located. Fit the bolts finger tight at this stage.
10 Fit the lower joint (Section 14), again leaving the pinch-bolts finger tight.
11 Check that none of the brackets or couplings are under stress and then tighten the column bolts to the specified torque.

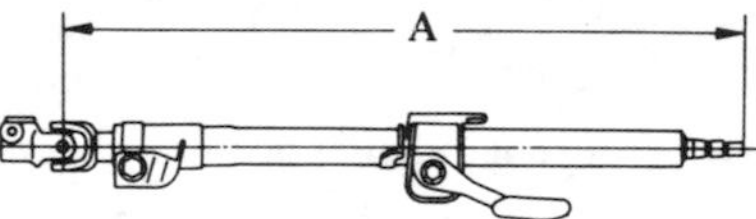

Fig. 11.29 Steering column length – tilt type (Sec 15)

A = 593.6 to 595.2 mm (23.37 to 24.43 in)

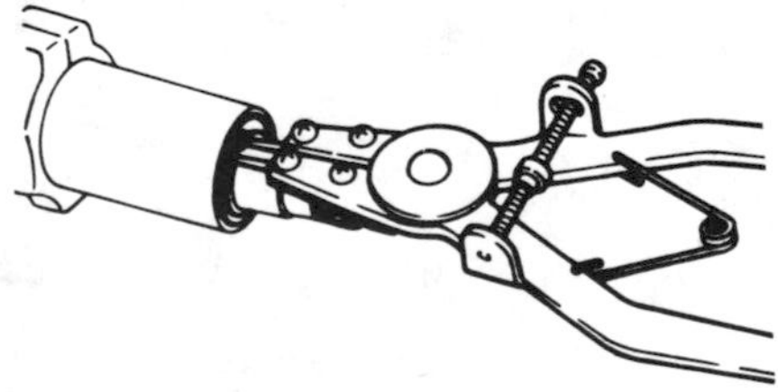

Fig. 11.30 Removing steering column circlip (Sec 16)

16 Steering column (non-tilt type) – overhaul

1 The steering column shaft can be removed from the column jacket tube if the bearings require greasing. If the bearings are worn a new jacket tube, complete with bearings, will be required.
2 Remove the steering column, as described in the preceding Section, and unlock the steering lock using the ignition key.
3 With a pair of circlip pliers, extract the circlip from the upper end of the column.
4 Remove the plain and wave washers and then pull the shaft out of the jacket tube.
5 Grease the bearings and bushes, push the shaft into the jacket tube and locate the wave washer followed by the plain washer.
6 Make sure that the circlip which is located below the upper bearing, and the one which is to be fitted above the plain washer both have their rounded edges towards the bearing (see Fig. 11.31). New circlips should always be used at reassembly.

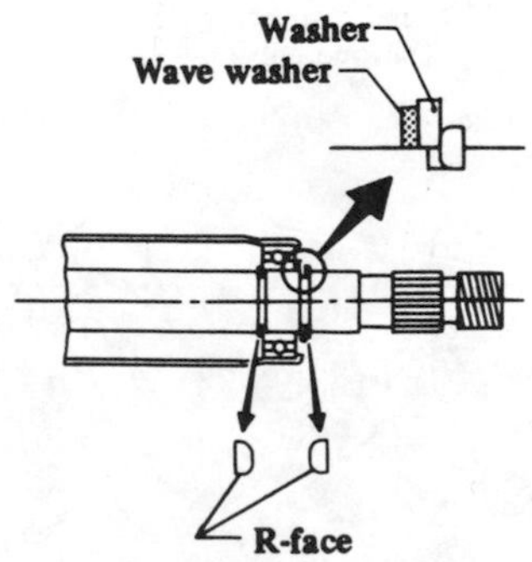

Fig. 11.31 Circlip positioning with washers at top of steering column – non-tilt type (Sec 16)

17 Steering column (tilt type) – overhaul

1 The operations are similar to those described in the preceding Section, but there are slight differences in detail between the two different makes of column. At the upper end of the FKK column a wave

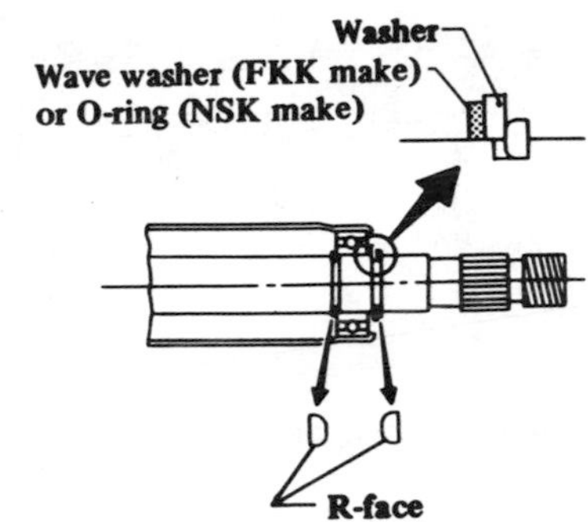

Fig. 11.32 Circlip positioning with washers or O-ring on steering column – tilt type (Sec 17)

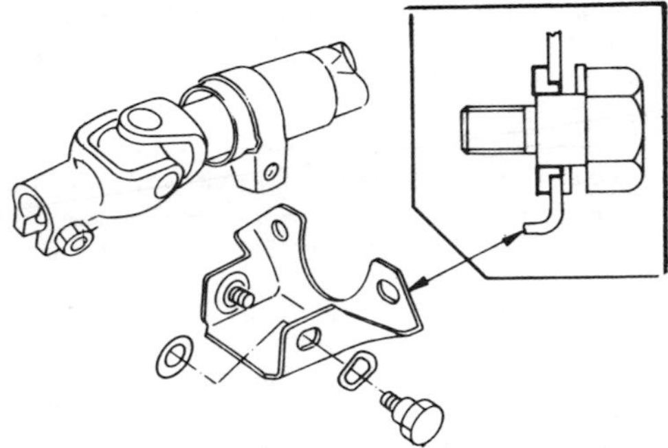

Fig. 11.33 Column lower mounting – FKK tilt-type (Sec 17)

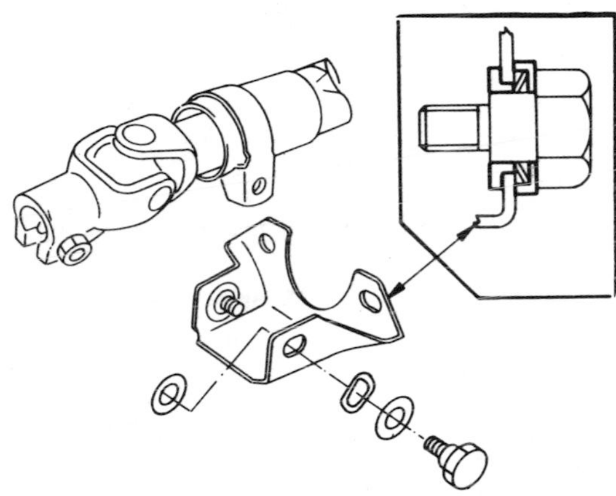

Fig. 11.34 Column lower mounting – NSK tilt type (Sec 17)

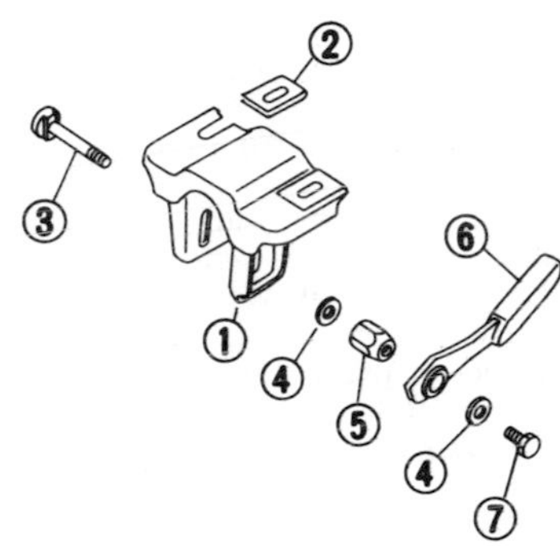

Fig. 11.35 Steering column tilt mechanism (Sec 17)

1 *Bracket*
2 *Sliding plate*
3 *Adjusting lever bolt*
4 *Washer*
5 *Nut (left-hand thread)*
6 *Adjusting lever*
7 *Bolt (left-hand thread)*

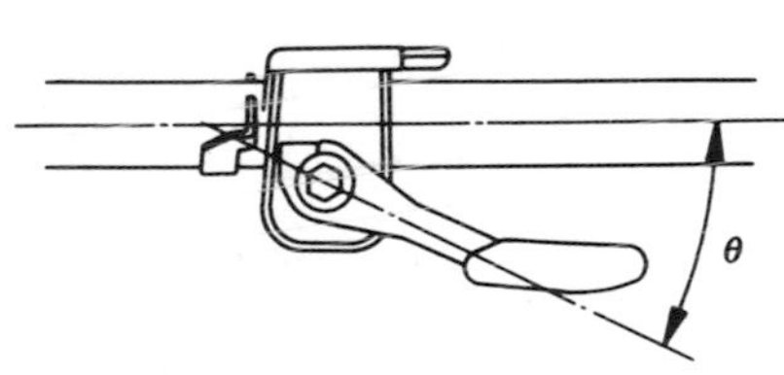

Fig. 11.36 Tilt lever setting angle (Sec 17)

θ = 20° to 30°

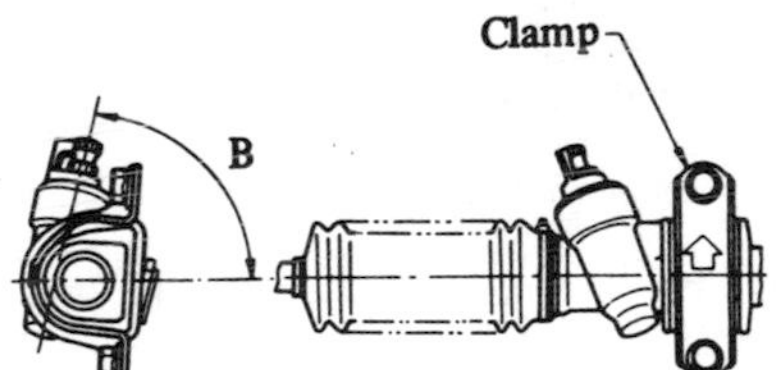

Fig. 11.37 Manual steering gear mounting diagram (Sec 18)

B = 76.5°

washer is used, as on non-tilt types, while on NSK columns an O-ring is fitted.

2 Make sure that the column lever mounting bracket is correctly assembled according to column make.

3 The sequence of fitting of the components of the tilt mechanism is important and a little grease should be applied to the sliding surfaces. The adjusting lever nut and bolt have *left-hand threads* and the nut must only be tightened while the tilt lever is held at between 20° and 30° to the centre-line of the column, as shown in Fig. 11.36.

18 Manual steering gear – removal and refitting

1 Raise the front of the vehicle and support it securely using axle stands under the side-members.

2 Disconnect both tie-rod balljoints from the steering arms on the stub axle carriers.

3 Remove the steering shaft lower joint, as described in Section 14.

4 Unscrew the rack housing mounting nuts and lift the steering gear from the bulkhead.

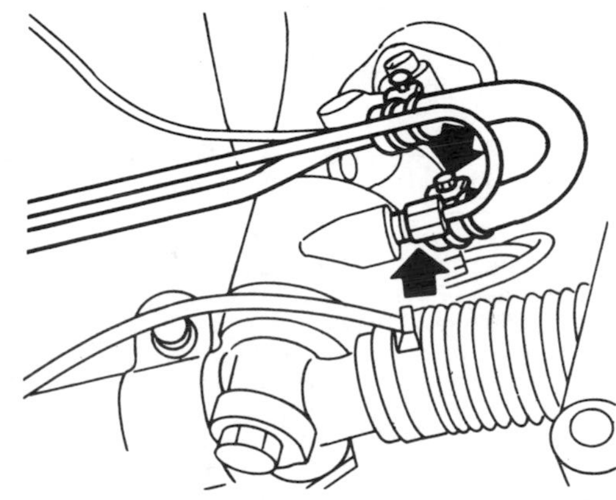

Fig. 11.38 Pressure and return line connections or power-assisted steering (Sec 18)

5 Refitting is a reversal of removal, but make sure that the arrows on the clamp housings point upwards in order to give the rack housing an inclination of 13.5° rearwards.
6 Tighten all nuts and bolts to the specified torques.

19 Power-assisted steering gear – removal and refitting

1 Raise the front of the vehicle and support it on axle stands by the side-members.
2 Disconnect the hydraulic hose clamp at the pinion housing on the steering gear to provide access to the union nut on the pipeline. Unscrew the union nut and allow the fluid to drain.
3 Extract the split pins and unscrew the castellated nuts from the tie-rod end balljoints. With a suitable tool, disconnect the balljoints from the steering arms on the stub axle carrier.
4 Support the transmission on a jack with a block of wood as an insulator.
5 Disconnect the exhaust downpipe from the manifold and also disconnect the exhaust support bracket just ahead of the steering gear.
6 Unbolt and remove the engine rear mounting.
7 Unscrew and remove the bolts from the steering gear mounting clamps.
8 Remove the steering shaft lower joint, as described in Section 14.
9 Withdraw the steering gear from under the front wing, rotating it in the direction of the arrows as shown in the diagram (Fig. 11.40).
10 Refitting is a reversal of removal, but make sure that the arrows on the mounting clamps are pointing upwards in order to give the rack housing an inclination of 19.3°.
11 Fill and bleed the system, as described in Section 22.

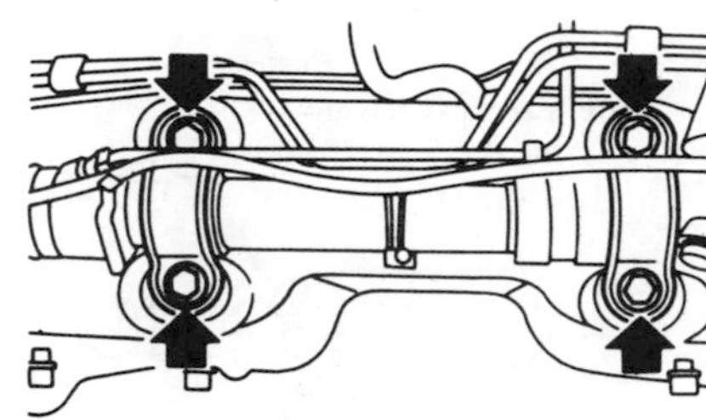

Fig. 11.39 Power steering gear mounting clamps (Sec 19)

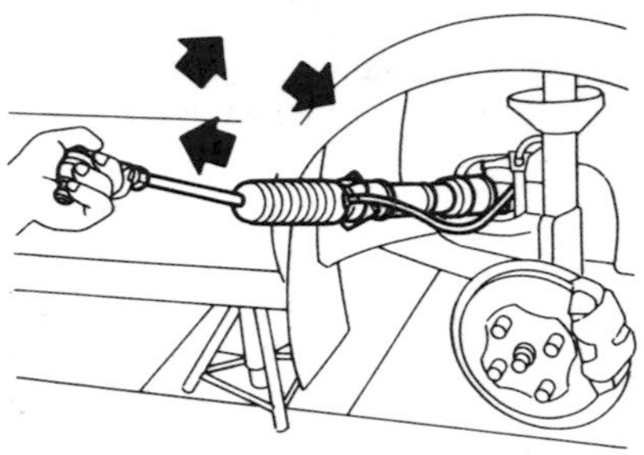

Fig. 11.40 Withdrawing power steering gear by rotating (Sec 19)

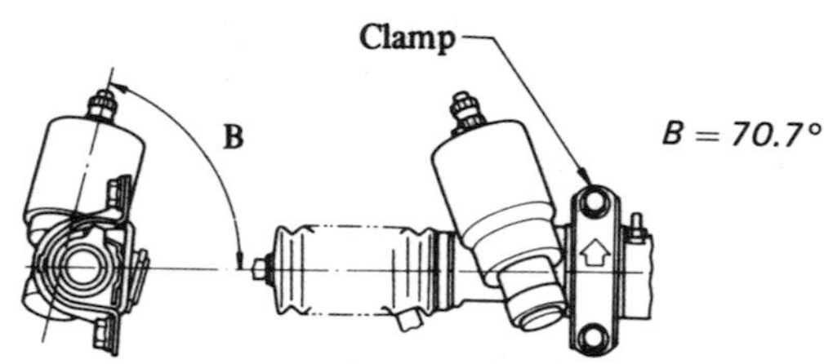

Fig. 11.41 Power steering gear mounting diagram (Sec 19)

20 Power steering pump – removal and refitting

1 Release the pump drivebelt adjuster link lockbolt and turn the adjuster bolt to release the tension on the belt. Slip the belt from the pulleys.
2 Disconnect the pressure hose from the pump by unscrewing the banjo union bolt. Allow the fluid to drain.
3 Take off the return hose clamp.
4 Unbolt and remove the pump.
5 If the connecting lines are to be removed, unscrew the union nuts and hose clips.
6 Refitting and reconnection are reversals of disconnection and removal.
7 Tension the pump drivebelt, as described in Chapter 2.
8 Fill and bleed the system, as described in Section 22.

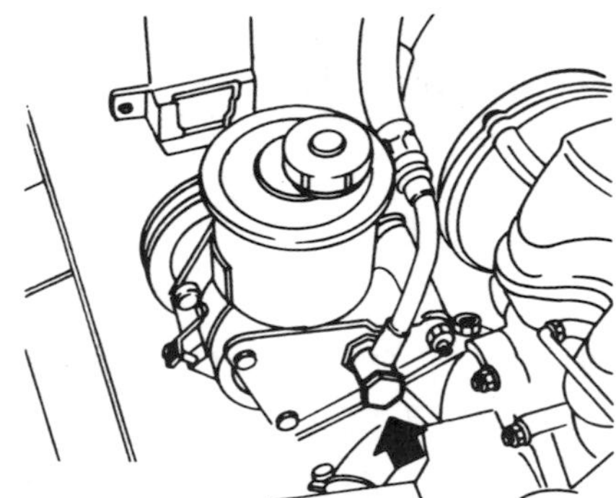

Fig. 11.42 Pressure line connection at power steering pump (Sec 20)

21 Steering gear – overhaul

1 It is not recommended that the manual or power-assisted steering gear or the power steering pump are overhauled.
2 Due to the precise nature of the assembly work and the need for special tools for measuring turning torque, it is preferable to purchase a new or factory-reconditioned unit when the original one becomes worn or develops a fault.

22 Power-assisted steering – fluid level and bleeding

1 At the intervals specified in Routine Maintenance unscrew the power steering pump filler cap when the engine and pump are cold and observe the level of fluid on the dipstick. Add fluid of the correct type to bring the fluid level between the low and high marks.
2 If the system pipelines have been disconnected or new components fitted then, after reassembly, the system must be bled.
3 Fill the pump reservoir with fluid.
4 Raise the front of the vehicle until the roadwheels are off the floor.
5 Turn the steering from lock to lock ten times and then top up the fluid in the reservoir so that it is at the correct level on the dipstick.
6 Start the engine and turn the steering wheel left and right lock until the fluid becomes hot to the touch (60 to 80°C – 140 to 176°F).
7 Switch off the engine and top up the reservoir, if necessary.
8 Start the engine and run for five seconds. Switch off and top up the fluid, if necessary.

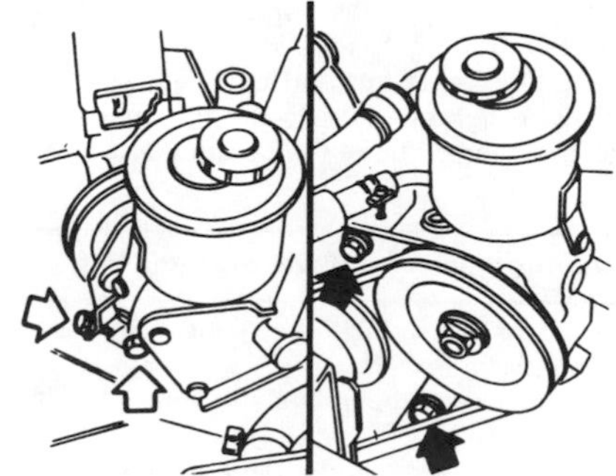

Fig. 11.43 Power steering pump mounting and adjuster bolts (Sec 20)

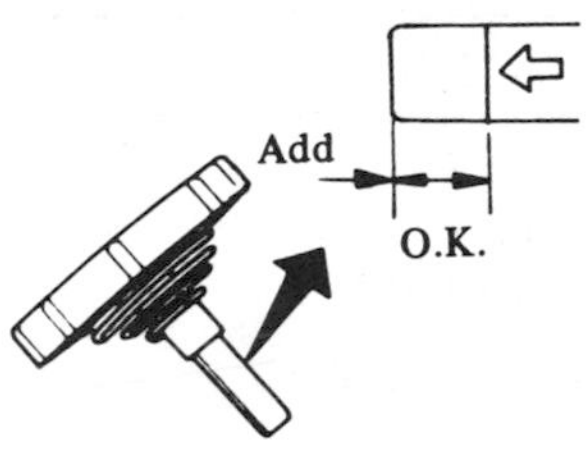

Fig. 11.44 Power steering fluid dipstick (Sec 22)

9 If air is still present in the system, which will be indicated by the steering wheel being stiff to turn, repeat the operations as previously described. When turning the steering from lock to lock during bleeding, do not hold it at full lock for more than fifteen seconds while the engine is running.

23 Steering angles and front wheel alignment

1 Accurate front wheel alignment is essential to good steering and for even tyre wear. Before considering the steering angles, check that the tyres are correctly inflated, that the front wheels are not buckled, the hub bearings are not worn or incorrectly adjusted and that the steering linkage is in good order, without slackness or wear at the joints.

2 Wheel alignment consists of four factors:

Camber, is the angle at which the roadwheels are set from the vertical when viewed from the front or rear of the vehicle. Positive camber is the angle (in degrees) that the wheels are tilted outwards at the top from the vertical.

Castor, is the angle between the steering axis and a vertical line when viewed from each side of the vehicle. Positive castor is indicated when the steering axis is inclined towards the rear of the vehicle at its upper end.

Steering axis inclination, is the angle, when viewed from the front or rear of the vehicle, between the vertical and an imaginary line drawn between the upper and lower front suspension strut mountings.

Toe, is the amount by which the distance between the front inside edges of the roadwheel rim differs from that between the rear inside edges. If the distance between the front edges is less than that at the rear, the wheels are said to toe-in. If the distance between the front inside edges is greater than that at the rear, the wheels toe-out.

3 Due to the need for precision gauges to measure the small angles of the steering and suspension settings, it is preferable that checking of camber and castor is left to a service station having the necessary equipment. Camber and castor are set during production of the vehicle, and any deviation from the specified angle will be due to accident damage or gross wear in the suspension mountings.

4 To check the front wheel alignment, first make sure that the lengths of both tie-rods are equal when the steering is in the straight-ahead position. The tie-rod lengths can be adjusted for length if necessary by releasing the locknuts from the balljoint ends and rotating the rods. Flats are provided on the rods in order to hold them still with an open-ended spanner when the locknut is undone.

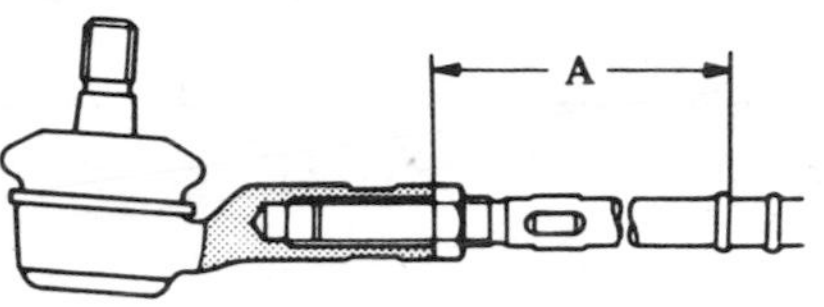

Fig. 11.45 Tie-rod setting to equalise their length (Sec 23)

A = 175.9 mm (6.93 in)

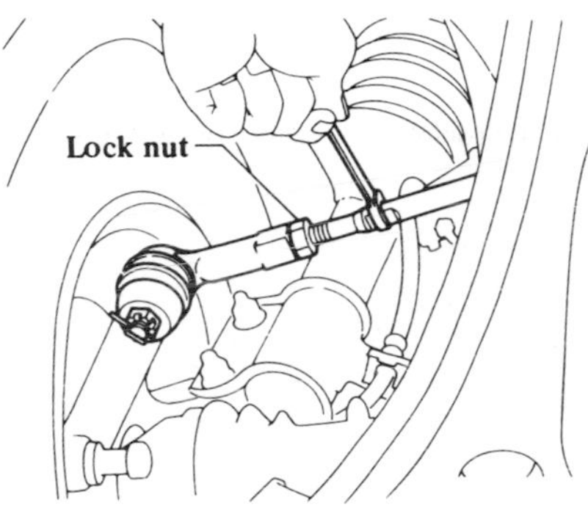

Fig. 11.46 Adjusting toe-in (Sec 23)

5 Obtain a tracking gauge. These are available in various forms from accessory stores, or one can be fabricated from a length of steel tubing suitably cranked to clear the sump and bellhousing and having a setscrew and locknut at one end.

6 With the gauge, measure the distances between the two wheel inner rims (at hub height) at the rear of the wheel. Push the vehicle forward to rotate the wheel through 180° (half a turn) and measure the distance between the wheel inner rims, again at hub height, at the front of the wheel. This last measurement should differ from the first by the appropriate toe-in which is given in the Specifications. The vehicle must be on level ground.

7 Where the toe-in is found to be incorrect, release the tie-rod balljoint locknut and turn the tie-rods equally. Only turn them a quarter of a turn at a time before re-checking the alignment. Do not grip the threaded part of the tie-rod during adjustment, but use an open-ended spanner on the flats provided. It is important not to allow the tie-rods to become unequal in length during adjustment, otherwise the alignment of the steering wheel will become incorrect and tyre scrubbing will occur on turns.

8 On completion, tighten the locknuts without disturbing the setting. Check that the balljoint is at the centre of its arc of travel.

Fault diagnosis overleaf

24 Fault diagnosis – suspension and steering

Symptom	Reason(s)
Front suspension	
Vehicle wanders	Incorrect wheel alignment Worn front control arm balljoints
Heavy or stiff steering	Incorrect front wheel alignment Incorrect tyre pressures
Wheel wobble or vibration	Roadwheels out of balance Roadwheel buckled Incorrect front wheel alignment Faulty strut Weak coil spring
Excessive pitching or rolling on corners or during braking	Faulty strut Weak or broken coil spring
Tyre squeal when cornering	Incorrect front wheel alignment Incorrect tyre pressures
Abnormal tyre wear	Incorrect tyre pressures Incorrect front wheel alignment Worn hub bearing
Rear suspension	
Poor roadholding and wander	Faulty shock absorber Weak coil spring Worn or incorrectly adjusted hub bearing Worn trailing arm bush
Manual steering gear	
Stiff action	Lack of rack lubrication Seized tie-rod end balljoint Seized suspension lower balljoint
Free movement at steering wheel	Wear in tie-rod balljoint Wear in rack teeth
Knocking when traversing uneven surface	Incorrectly adjusted rack slipper
Power-assisted steering gear	
The symptoms and reasons applicable to manual steering gear will apply, plus the following:	
Stiff action or no return action	Slipping pump drivebelt Air in fluid Steering column out of alignment Castor angle incorrect due to damage or gross wear in bushes and mountings
Steering effort on both locks unequal	Leaking seal in steering gear Clogged fluid passage within gear assembly
Noisy pump	Loose pulley Kinked hose Clogged filter in fluid reservoir Low fluid level

Chapter 12 Bodywork and fittings

Contents

1 General description

The bodywork on all versions is of welded steel, unitary construction. In the interests of economical repair, the front wings are readily detachable, but other body panels are not.

The vehicles are protected against corrosion by dipping and also by the provision of stone guards under the front wings.

All models in the range are well-equipped and certain factory-fitted options are also available.

2 Maintenance – bodywork and underframe

1 The general condition of a vehicle's bodywork is the one thing that significantly affects its value. Maintenance is easy but needs to be regular. Neglect, particularly after minor damage, can lead quickly to further deterioration and costly repair bills. It is important also to keep watch on those parts of the vehicle not immediately visible, for instance the underside, inside all the wheel arches and the lower part of the engine compartment.

2 The basic maintenance routine for the bodywork is washing – preferably with a lot of water, from a hose. This will remove all the loose solids which may have stuck to the vehicle. It is important to flush these off in such a way as to prevent grit from scratching the finish. The wheel arches and underframe need washing in the same way to remove any accumulated mud which will retain moisture and tend to encourage rust. Paradoxically enough, the best time to clean the underframe and wheel arches is in wet weather when the mud is thoroughly wet and soft. In very wet weather the underframe is usually cleaned of large accumulations automatically and this is a good time for inspection.

3 Periodically, it is a good idea to have the whole of the underframe of the vehicle steam cleaned, engine compartment included, so that a thorough inspection can be carried out to see what minor repairs and renovations are necessary. Steam cleaning is available at many garages and is necessary for removal of the accumulation of oily grime which sometimes is allowed to become thick in certain areas. If steam cleaning facilities are not available, there are one or two excellent grease solvents available which can be brush applied. The dirt can then be simply hosed off.

4 After washing paintwork, wipe off with a chamois leather to give an unspotted clear finish. A coat of clear protective wax polish will give added protection against chemical pollutants in the air. If the paintwork sheen has dulled or oxidised, use a cleaner/polisher combination to restore the brilliance of the shine. This requires a little effort, but such dulling is usually caused because regular washing has been neglected. Always check that the door and body sill drain holes

2.4A Door drain hole

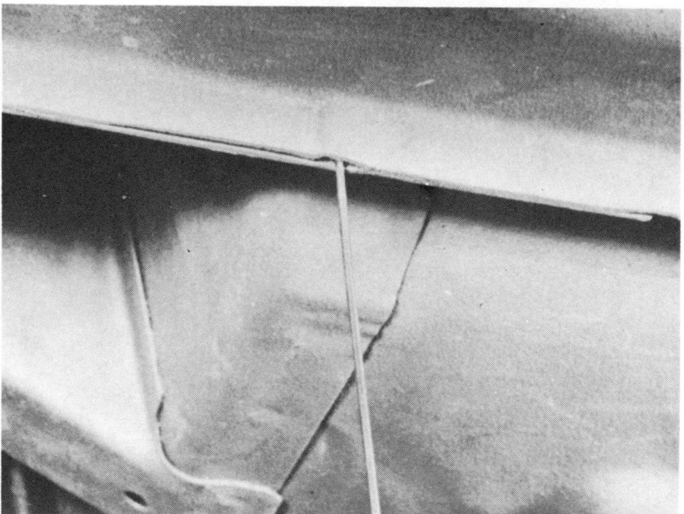
2.4B Sill drain hole

and pipes (photos) are completely clear so that water can be drained out. Bright work should be treated in the same way as paintwork. Windscreens and windows can be kept clear of the smeary film which often appears, by adding a little ammonia to the water. If they are scratched, a good rub with a proprietary metal polish will often clear them. Never use any form of wax or other body or chromium polish on glass.

3 Maintenance – upholstery and carpets

1 Mats and carpets should be brushed or vacuum cleaned regularly to keep them free of grit. If they are badly stained remove them from the vehicle for scrubbing or sponging and make quite sure they are dry before refitting. Seats and interior trim panels can be kept clean by wiping with a damp cloth. If they do become stained (which can be more apparent on light coloured upholstery) use a little liquid detergent and a soft nail brush to scour the grime out of the grain of the material. Do not forget to keep the headlining clean in the same way as the upholstery. When using liquid cleaners inside the vehicle do not over-wet the surfaces being cleaned. Excessive damp could get into the seams and padded interior causing stains, offensive odours or even rot. If the inside of the vehicle gets wet accidentally it is worthwhile taking some trouble to dry it out properly, particularly where carpets are involved. *Do not leave oil or electric heaters inside the vehicle for this purpose.*

4 Minor body damage – repair

The photographic sequences on pages 262 and 263 illustrate the operations detailed in the following sub sections.

Repair of minor scratches in bodywork

If the scratch is very superficial, and does not penetrate to the metal of the bodywork, repair is very simple. Lightly rub the area of the scratch with a paintwork renovator, or a very fine cutting paste, to remove loose paint from the scratch and to clear the surrounding bodywork of wax polish. Rinse the area with clean water.

Apply touch-up paint to the scratch using a fine paint brush; continue to apply fine layers of paint until the surface of the paint in the scratch is level with the surrounding paintwork. Allow the new paint at least two weeks to harden: then blend it into the surrounding paintwork by rubbing the scratch area with a paintwork renovator or a very fine cutting paste. Finally, apply wax polish.

Where the scratch has penetrated right through to the metal of the bodywork, causing the metal to rust, a different repair technique is required. Remove any loose rust from the bottom of the scratch with a penknife, then apply rust inhibiting paint to prevent the formation of rust in the future. Using a rubber or nylon applicator fill the scratch with bodystopper paste. If required, this paste can be mixed with cellulose thinners to provide a very thin paste which is ideal for filling narrow scratches. Before the stopper-paste in the scratch hardens, wrap a piece of smooth cotton rag around the top of a finger. Dip the finger in cellulose thinners and then quickly sweep it across the surface of the stopper-paste in the scratch; this will ensure that the surface of the stopper-paste is slightly hollowed. The scratch can now be painted over as described earlier in this Section.

Repair of dents in bodywork

When deep denting of the vehicle's bodywork has taken place, the first task is to pull the dent out, until the affected bodywork almost attains its original shape. There is little point in trying to restore the original shape completely, as the metal in the damaged area will have stretched on impact and cannot be reshaped fully to its original contour. It is better to bring the level of the dent up to a point which is about $\frac{1}{8}$ in (3 mm) below the level of the surrounding bodywork. In cases where the dent is very shallow anyway, it is not worth trying to pull it out at all. If the underside of the dent is accessible, it can be hammered out gently from behind, using a mallet with a wooden or plastic head. Whilst doing this, hold a suitable block of wood firmly against the outside of the panel to absorb the impact from the hammer blows and thus prevent a large area of the bodywork from being 'belled-out'.

Should the dent be in a section of the bodywork which has a double skin or some other factor making it inaccessible from behind, a different technique is called for. Drill several small holes through the metal inside the area – particularly in the deeper section. Then screw long self-tapping screws into the holes just sufficiently for them to gain a good purchase in the metal. Now the dent can be pulled out by pulling on the protruding heads of the screws with a pair of pliers.

The next stage of the repair is the removal of the paint from the damaged area, and from an inch or so of the surrounding 'sound' bodywork. This is accomplished most easily by using a wire brush or abrasive pad on a power drill, although it can be done just as effectively by hand using sheets of abrasive paper. To complete the preparation for filling, score the surface of the bare metal with a screwdriver or the tang of a file, or alternatively, drill small holes in the affected area. This will provide a really good 'key' for the filler paste.

To complete the repair see the Section on filling and re-spraying.

Repair of rust holes or gashes in bodywork

Remove all paint from the affected area and from an inch or so of the surrounding 'sound' bodywork, using an abrasive pad or a wire brush on a power drill. If these are not available a few sheets of abrasive paper will do the job just as effectively. With the paint removed you will be able to gauge the severity of the corrosion and therefore decide whether to renew the whole panel (if this is possible) or to repair the affected area. New body panels are not as expensive as most people think and it is often quicker and more satisfactory to fit a new panel than to attempt to repair large areas of corrosion.

Remove all fittings from the affected area except those which will act as a guide to the original shape of the damaged bodywork (eg headlamp shells etc). Then, using tin snips or a hacksaw blade, remove all loose metal and any other metal badly affected by corrosion. Hammer the edges of the hole inwards in order to create a slight depression for the filler paste.

Wire brush the affected area to remove the powdery rust from the surface of the remaining metal. Paint the affected area with rust inhibiting paint; if the back of the rusted area is accessible treat this also.

Before filling can take place it will be necessary to block the hole in some way. This can be achieved by the use of zinc gauze or aluminium tape.

Zinc gauze is probably the best material to use for a large hole. Cut a piece to the approximate size and shape of the hole to be filled, then position it in the hole so that its edges are below the level of the surrounding bodywork. It can be retained in position by several blobs of filler paste around its periphery.

Aluminium tape should be used for small or very narrow holes. Pull a piece off the roll and trim it to the approximate size and shape required, then pull off the backing paper (if used) and stick the tape over the hole; it can be overlapped if the thickness of one piece is insufficient. Burnish down the edges of the tape with the handle of a screwdriver or similar, to ensure that the tape is securely attached to the metal underneath.

Bodywork repairs – filling and re-spraying

Before using this Section, see the Sections on dent, deep scratch, rust holes and gash repairs.

Many types of bodyfiller are available, but generally speaking those proprietary kits which contain a tin of filler paste and a tube of resin hardener are best for this type of repair. A wide, flexible plastic or nylon applicator will be found invaluable for imparting a smooth and well contoured finish to the surface of the filler.

Mix up a little filler on a clean piece of card or board – measure the hardener carefully (follow the maker's instructions on the pack) otherwise the filler will set too rapidly or too slowly.

Using the applicator apply the filler paste to the prepared area; draw the applicator across the surface of the filler to achieve the correct contour and to level the filler surface. As soon as a contour that approximates to the correct one is achieved, stop working the paste – if you carry on too long the paste will become sticky and begin to 'pick up' on the applicator. Continue to add thin layers of filler paste at twenty-minute intervals until the level of the filler is just proud of the surrounding bodywork.

Once the filler has hardened, excess can be removed using a metal plane or file. From then on, progressively finer grades of abrasive paper should be used, starting with a 40 grade production paper and finishing with 400 grade wet-and-dry paper. Always wrap the abrasive paper around a flat rubber, cork, or wooden block – otherwise the surface of the filler will not be completely flat. During the smoothing of the filler surface the wet-and-dry paper should be periodically rinsed in water. This will ensure that a very smooth finish is imparted to the filler at the final stage.

At this stage the 'dent' should be surrounded by a ring of bare metal, which in turn should be encircled by the finely 'feathered' edge of the good paintwork. Rinse the repair area with clean water, until all of the dust produced by the rubbing-down operation has gone.

Spray the whole repair area with a light coat of primer – this will show up any imperfections in the surface of the filler. Repair these imperfections with fresh filler paste or bodystopper, and once more smooth the surface with abrasive paper. If bodystopper is used, it can be mixed with cellulose thinners to form a really thin paste which is ideal for filling small holes. Repeat this spray and repair procedure until you are satisfied that the surface of the filler, and the feathered edge of the paintwork are perfect. Clean the repair area with clean water and allow to dry fully.

The repair area is now ready for final spraying. Paint spraying must be carried out in a warm, dry, windless and dust free atmosphere. This condition can be created artificially if you have access to a large indoor working area, but if you are forced to work in the open, you will have to pick your day very carefully. If you are working indoors, dousing the floor in the work area with water will help to settle the dust which would otherwise be in the atmosphere. If the repair area is confined to one body panel, mask off the surrounding panels; this will help to minimise the effects of a slight mis-match in paint colours. Bodywork fittings (eg chrome strips, door handles etc) will also need to be masked off. Use genuine masking tape and several thicknesses of newspaper for the masking operations.

Before commencing to spray, agitate the aerosol can thoroughly, then spray a test area (an old tin, or similar) until the technique is mastered. Cover the repair area with a thick coat of primer; the thickness should be built up using several thin layers of paint rather than one thick one. Using 400 grade wet-and-dry paper, rub down the surface of the primer until it is really smooth. While doing this, the work area should be thoroughly doused with water, and the wet-and-dry paper periodically rinsed in water. Allow to dry before spraying on more paint.

Spray on the top coat, again building up the thickness by using several thin layers of paint. Start spraying in the centre of the repair area and then, using a circular motion, work outwards until the whole repair area and about 2 inches of the surrounding original paintwork is covered. Remove all masking material 10 to 15 minutes after spraying on the final coat of paint.

Allow the new paint at least two weeks to harden, then, using a paintwork renovator or a very fine cutting paste, blend the edges of the paint into the existing paintwork Finally, apply wax polish.

5 Major body damage – repair

This should be left to your dealer or a specialist body repairer. Special jigs and gauges will be required to check for body and underframe distortion. This must be corrected if the original steering and roadholding characteristics are to be retained.

6 Bonnet – removal and refitting

1 Open the bonnet and have an assistant support its weight.

2 Mark the position of the hinges on the underside of the bonnet with a soft pencil.

6.3 Bonnet hinge

3 Unscrew the hinge bolts (photo) and then lift the bonnet from the vehicle.

4 Refitting is a reversal of removal, but before fully tightening the bolts, gently close the bonnet and check its alignment. Adjust as necessary before fully tightening the bolts.

5 Now close the bonnet. If it does not shut smoothly and positively adjust the bonnet lock and striker, as described in Section 8.

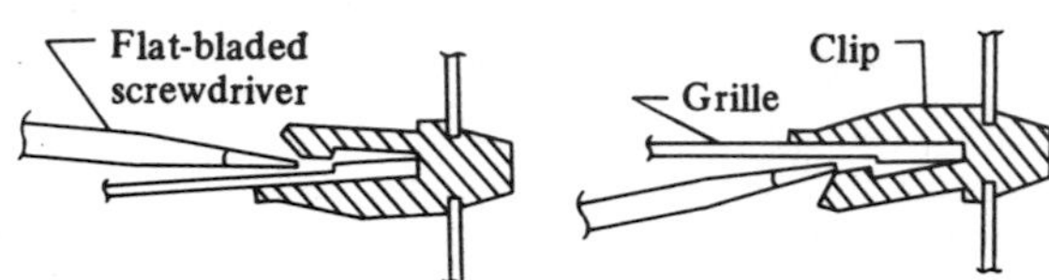

Fig. 12.1 Radiator grille clips – N12 models (Sec 7)

7.2 Releasing a radiator grille clip (B11 models)

7 Radiator grille – removal and refitting

1 Remove the sidelamps, as described in Chapter 10.
2 On B11 models, turn the square-headed plastic fixing screws through 90° (photo).
3 On N12 models release the clips by prising them open with a screwdriver (Fig. 12.1).
4 Remove the grille.
5 Refitting is a reversal of removal.

8 Bonnet lock and release assembly – removal, refitting and adjustment

1 Open the bonnet and support it on its strut.
2 Remove the radiator grille, as described in the preceding Section.
3 Unscrew the three lock retaining bolts (photo), pull the lock from its mounting bracket and unhook the release cable from it.
4 The control lever (photo) and cable may be removed after unscrewing the lever fixing screws under the facia panel and withdrawing the cable through its bulkhead grommet.
5 Refitting is a reversal of removal, but set the lock (bolts finger tight) so that when the bonnet is closed the striker enters the lock slot centrally.
6 Close the bonnet and check that there is no up and down movement when the front of the bonnet is depressed with the hand. If there is, move the lock downwards to eliminate any free play. Fully tighten the lock fixing bolts.

9 Front wing – removal and refitting

1 Raise the front end of the vehicle and support it securely, placing axle stands under the side-members. Remove the roadwheel.
2 Remove the radiator grille (Section 7).
3 Remove the headlamp (Chapter 10).
4 Open the bonnet and remove the row of fixing bolts from the top edge of the wing.
5 Working under the wing, disconnect the wing stay (photo).
6 Remove the bumper and screws.
7 Remove the screws from the lower edge of the wing.
8 Open the front door fully and, working between the hinges, extract the wing fixing screws.
9 Extract the retaining screws and clips and remove the plastic under-wing protective shield.
10 Disconnect the electrical leads from the side indicator lamp.
11 Using a sharp knife, cut along the mastic seal all round the wing sealing edge.
12 Remove the wing. If necessary, remove the indicator assembly.
13 Before fitting the new wing, clean the mating flange on the body and apply a new bead of mastic.
14 Offer the wing into position and fit the retaining screws.
15 Seal the joint between the front of the wing and the front apron.
16 Apply underseal to the underneath of the wing and refinish the outside to match the vehicle paintwork.
17 Fit the plastic undershield.

10 Bumpers – removal and refitting

Sunny models

1 The bumper bars on these models are mounted on brackets which are bolted to the body.
2 The impact resistant cover is fixed to the bumper bar by screws. Screws also locate the ends of the bumper to the wing.
3 Before removing the bumper, disconnect the leads from the front direction indicator lamps and, where applicable, from the rear number plate lamps.

Sentra models

4 The bumper bars on these models are mounted on telescopic, hydraulic shock absorbers. The shock absorbers can be unbolted from

8.3 Bonnet lock

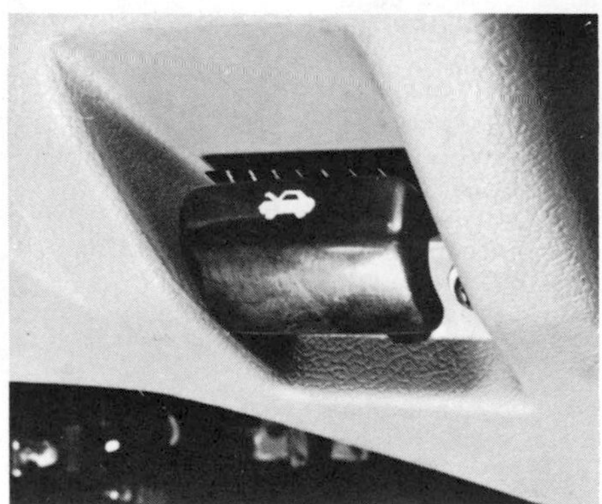
8.4 Bonnet release handle

9.5 Front wing stay and plastic under-shield

Bracket
Bar
Cover

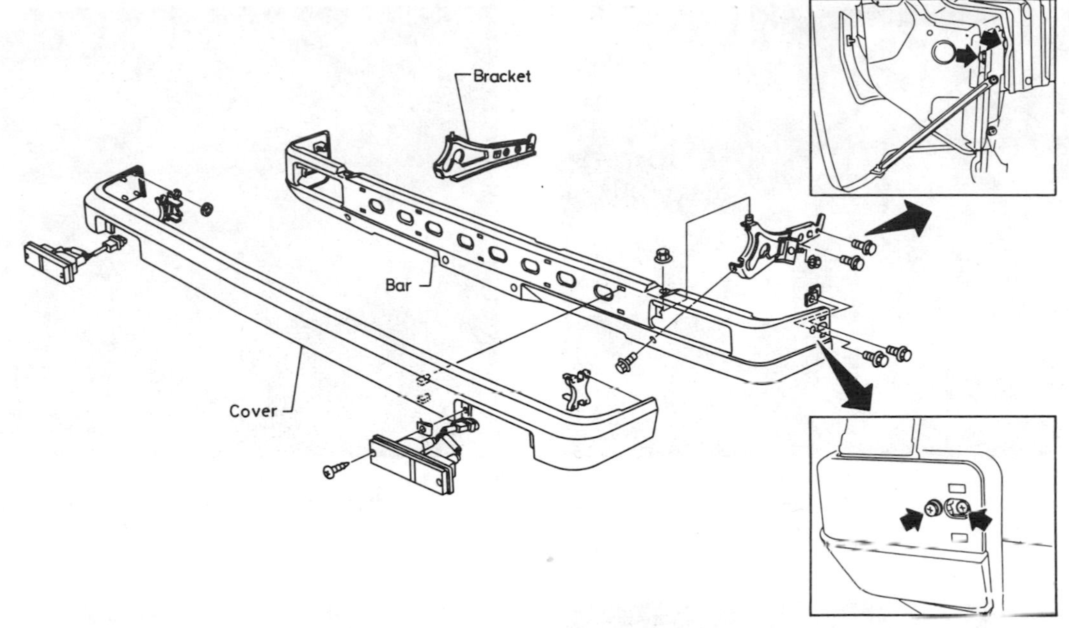

Fig. 12.2 Typical front bumper – except North American (Sec 10)

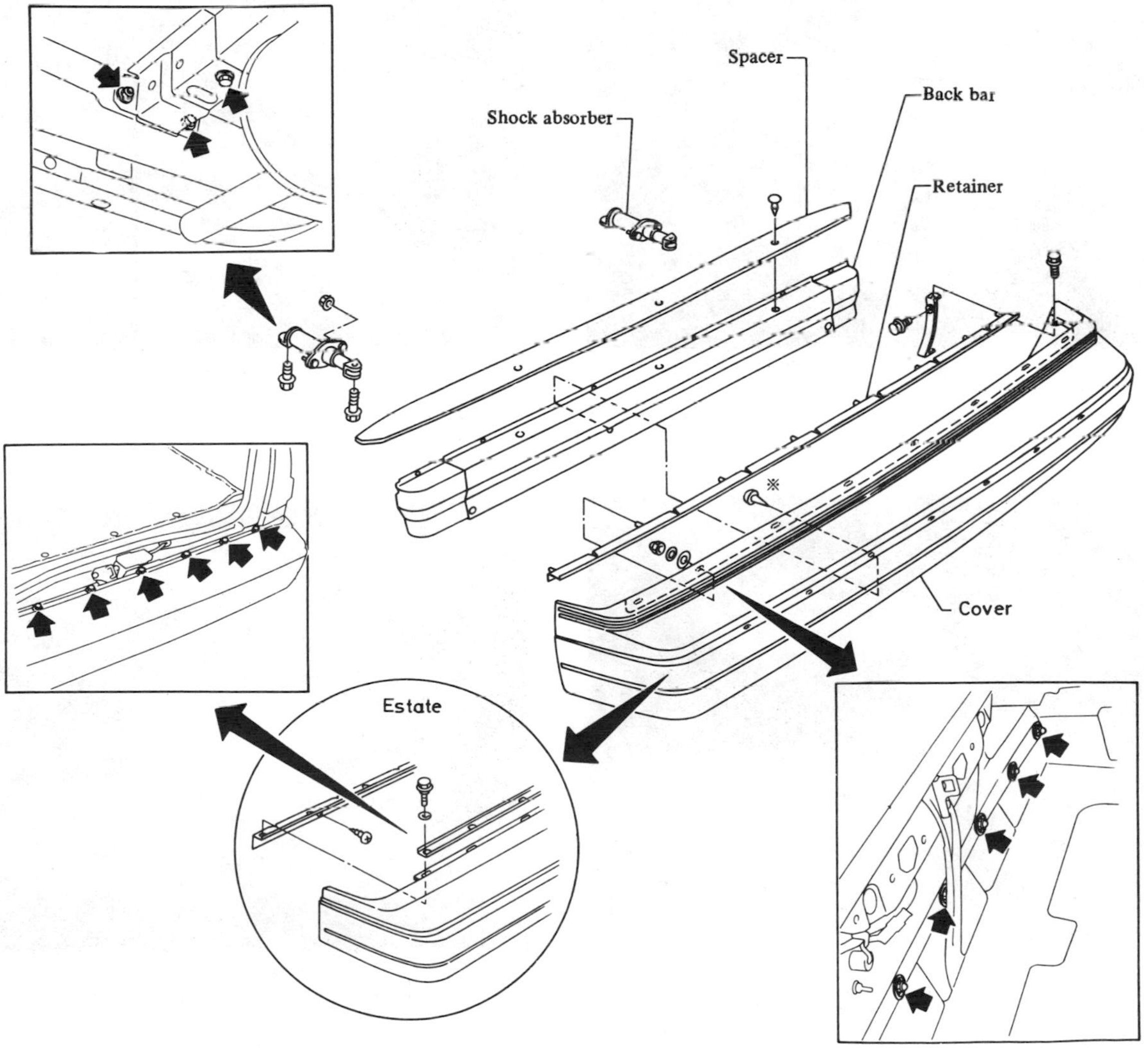

Spacer
Back bar
Shock absorber
Retainer
Cover
Estate

Fig. 12.3 Typical rear bumper – North American (Sec 10)

This sequence of photographs deals with the repair of the dent and paintwork damage shown in this photo. The procedure will be similar for the repair of a hole. It should be noted that the procedures given here are simplified – more explicit instructions will be found in the text

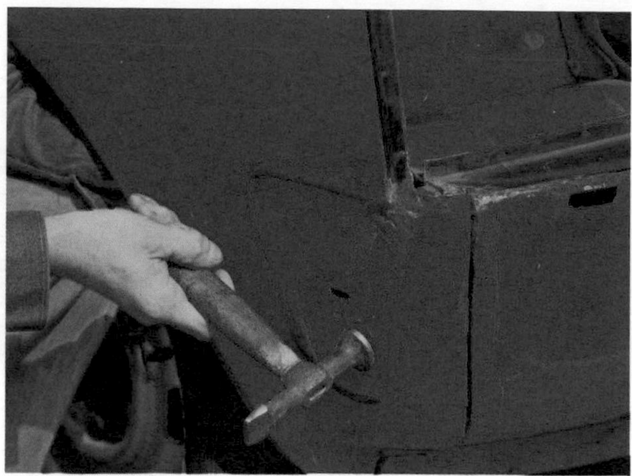

In the case of a dent the first job – after removing surrounding trim – is to hammer out the dent where access is possible. This will minimise filling. Here, the large dent having been hammered out, the damaged area is being made slightly concave

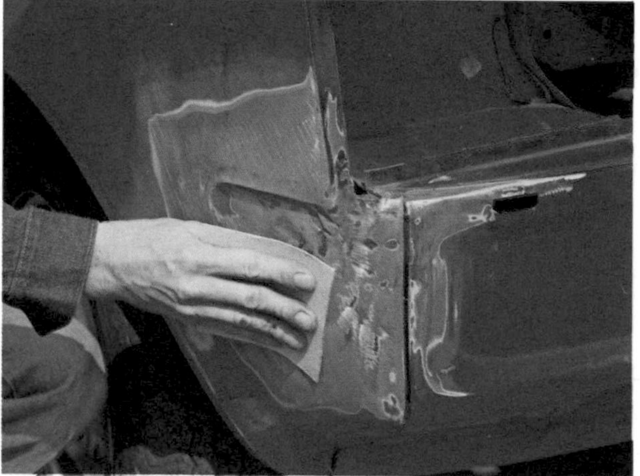

Now all paint must be removed from the damaged area, by rubbing with coarse abrasive paper. Alternatively, a wire brush or abrasive pad can be used in a power drill. Where the repair area meets good paintwork, the edge of the paintwork should be 'feathered', using a finer grade of abrasive paper

In the case of a hole caused by rusting, all damaged sheet-metal should be cut away before proceeding to this stage. Here, the damaged area is being treated with rust remover and inhibitor before being filled

Mix the body filler according to its manufacturer's instructions. In the case of corrosion damage, it will be necessary to block off any large holes before filling – this can be done with aluminium or plastic mesh, or aluminium tape. Make sure the area is absolutely clean before ...

... applying the filler. Filler should be applied with a flexible applicator, as shown, for best results; the wooden spatula being used for confined areas. Apply thin layers of filler at 20-minute intervals, until the surface of the filler is slightly proud of the surrounding bodywork

Initial shaping can be done with a Surform plane or Dreadnought file. Then, using progressively finer grades of wet-and-dry paper, wrapped around a sanding block, and copious amounts of clean water, rub down the filler until really smooth and flat. Again, feather the edges of adjoining paintwork

The whole repair area can now be sprayed or brush-painted with primer. If spraying, ensure adjoining areas are protected from over-spray. Note that at least one inch of the surrounding sound paintwork should be coated with primer. Primer has a 'thick' consistency, so will find small imperfections

Again, using plenty of water, rub down the primer with a fine grade wet-and-dry paper (400 grade is probably best) until it is really smooth and well blended into the surrounding paintwork. Any remaining imperfections can now be filled by carefully applied knifing stopper paste

When the stopper has hardened, rub down the repair area again before applying the final coat of primer. Before rubbing down this last coat of primer, ensure the repair area is blemish-free – use more stopper if necessary. To ensure that the surface of the primer is really smooth use some finishing compound

The top coat can now be applied. When working out of doors, pick a dry, warm and wind-free day. Ensure surrounding areas are protected from over-spray. Agitate the aerosol thoroughly, then spray the centre of the repair area, working outwards with a circular motion. Apply the paint as several thin coats

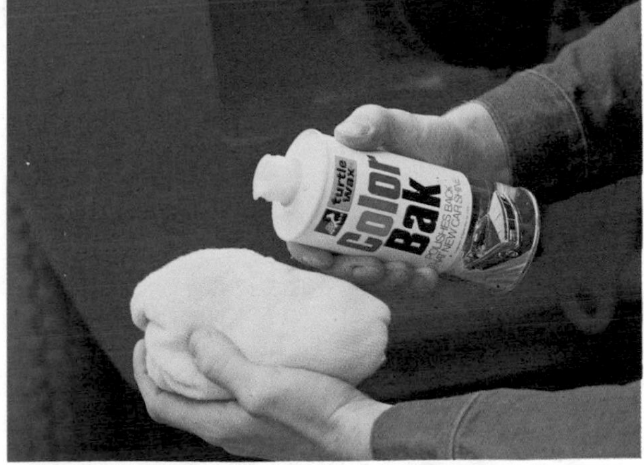

After a period of about two weeks, which the paint needs to harden fully, the surface of the repaired area can be 'cut' with a mild cutting compound prior to wax polishing. When carrying out bodywork repairs, remember that the quality of the finished job is proportional to the time and effort expended

the body and the bumper bar unbolted from the end of the shock absorber.

5 The efficiency of the bumper shock absorbers may be checked by placing the vehicle square to a wall and then, using a jack placed between the wall and the bumper, compressing the bumper by at least 10.0 mm (0.39 in). Retract the jack and check that the bumper returns to its original position. If it does not, or any fluid leaks are observed from the shock absorber body, renew the unit.

11 Door trim panel – removal and refitting

1 Open the door, extract the two retaining screws and remove the armrest (photo).

2 Extract the screw from the door lock remote control escutcheon plate (photo). Remove the plate (photo).

3 Push the panel away from the rear of the window regulator handle and, using a piece of wire with a hook at its end, extract the handle retaining spring clip (Fig. 12.4) and remove the handle.

4 Insert the fingers or a wide blade between the trim panel and the door and release the panel clips. A jerking movement will more readily overcome the resistance of the clips (photo).

5 Remove the trim panel and carefully peel away the waterproof sheet (photo).

6 Refitting is a reversal of removal, but with the window wound fully up, set the regulator handle 30° from the vertical towards the front of the car (Fig. 12.5). If the handle clip is fitted as shown (Fig. 12.6) simply bang the handle onto its splined shaft with the palm of the hand.

12 Door lock – removal and refitting

1 Remove the trim panel, as described in the preceding Section.

2 Unscrew the lock plunger knob and the screws which hold the lock assembly to the door edge (photos).

3 Disconnect the control rods from the lock and withdraw the lock through the aperture in the door inner panel.

4 The door exterior handle can be removed by unscrewing its two fixing nuts by passing a tool through the hole in the upper part of the

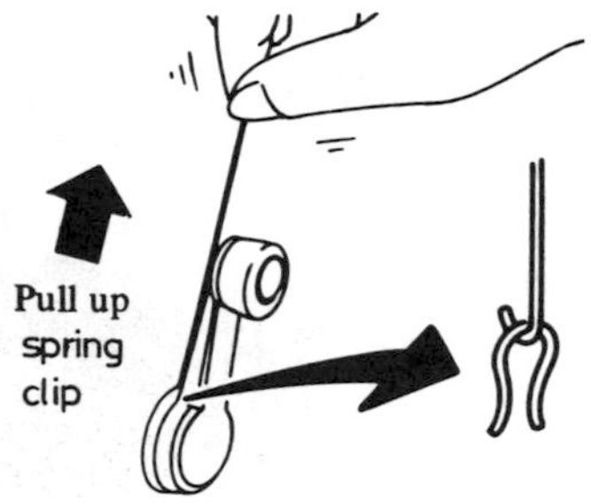

Fig. 12.4 Window regulator handle clip (Sec 11)

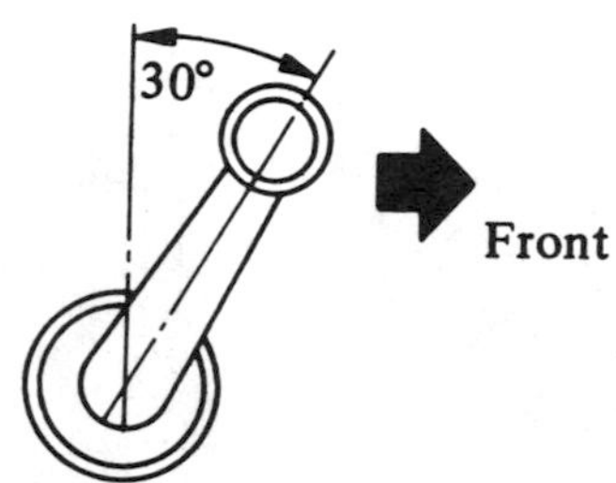

Fig. 12.5 Regulator handle fitting angle (Sec 11)

Fig. 12.6 Regulator handle and clip ready for fitting to shaft (Sec 11)

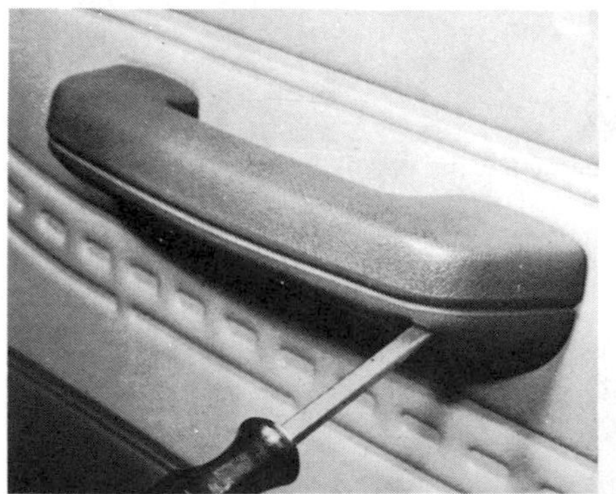

11.1 Removing the armrest screws

11.2A Removing the screw from the remote control lock escutcheon plate

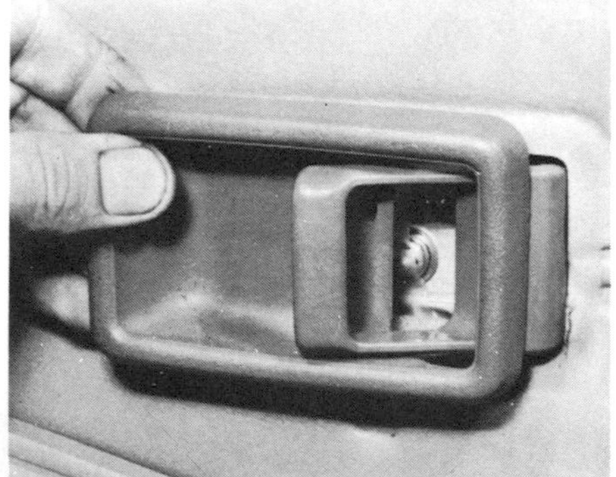

11.2B Removing remote control handle escutcheon plate

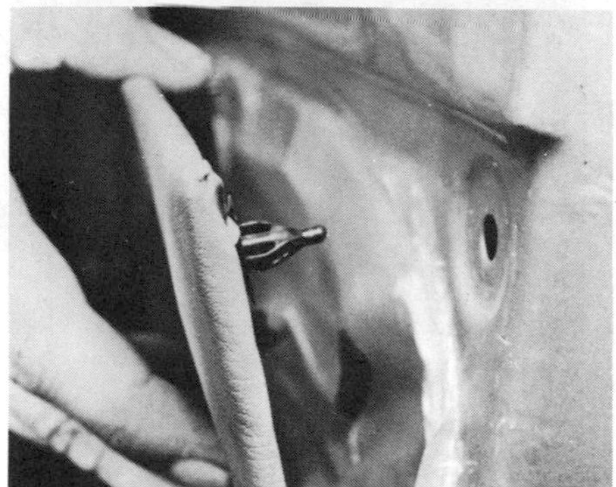

11.4 Trim panel clip

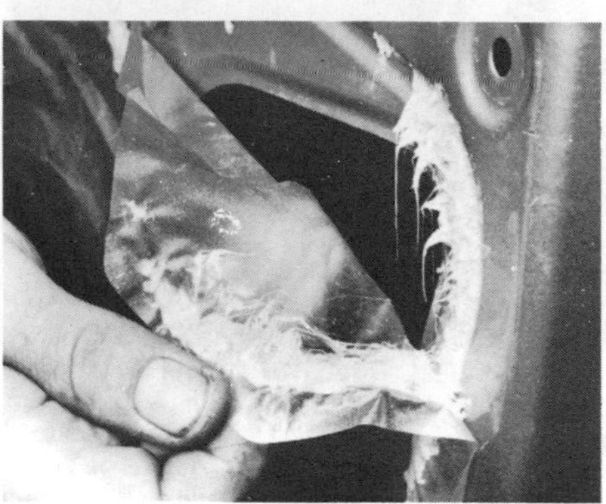

11.5 Door waterproof sheet and sealant

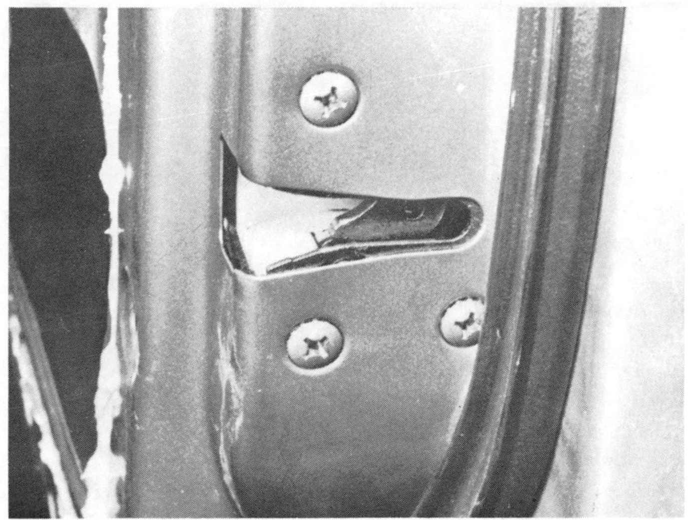

12.2A Door lock screws (front door)

12.2B Door lock screws and childproof catch (rear door)

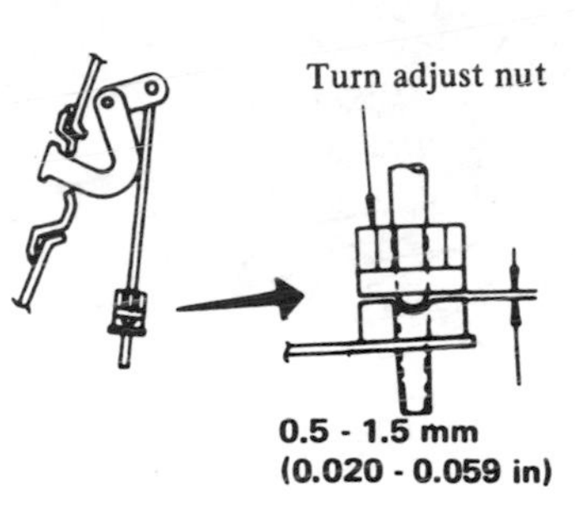

Fig. 12.7 Door exterior handle control rod adjuster – B11 models (Sec 12)

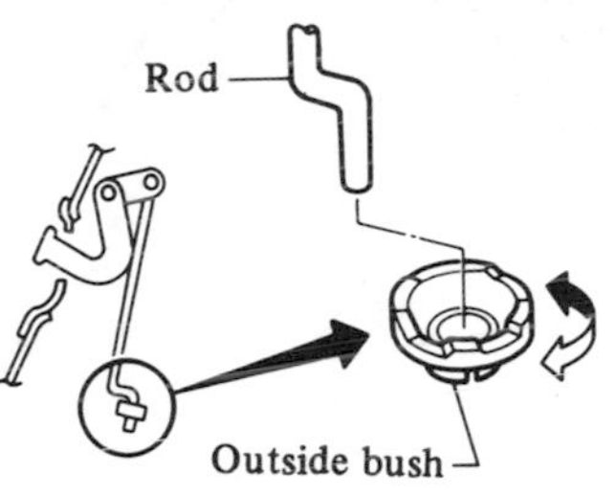

Fig. 12.8 Door exterior handle control rod adjuster – N12 models (Sec 12)

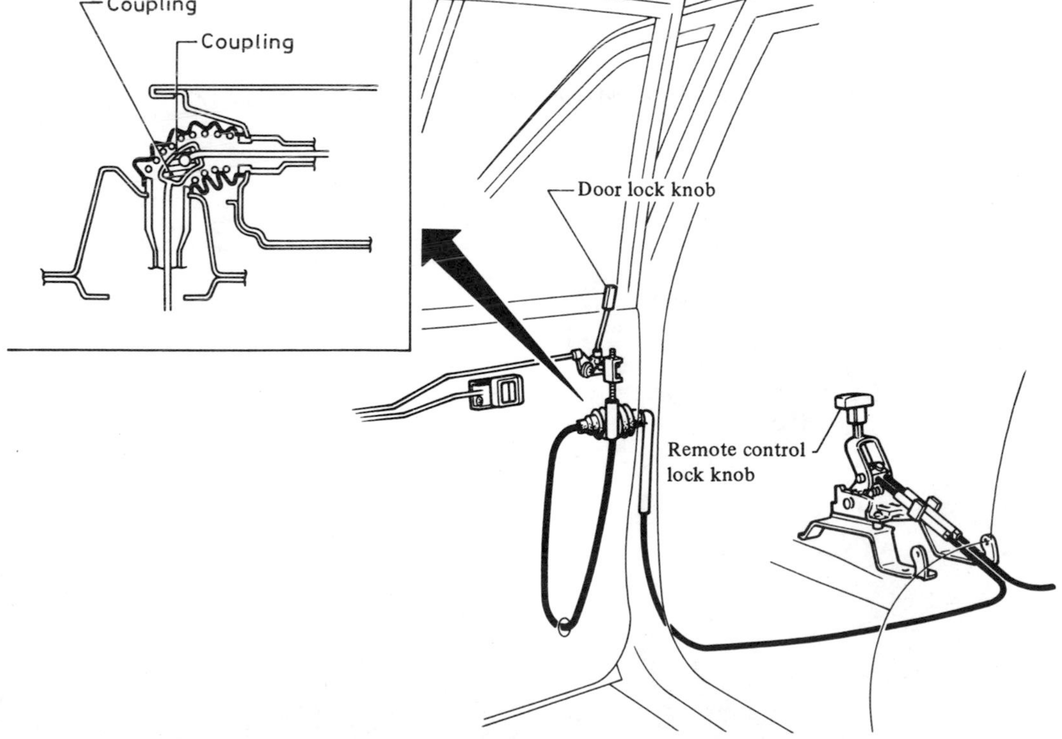

Fig. 12.9 Rear door lock remote control – B11 models (Sec 12)

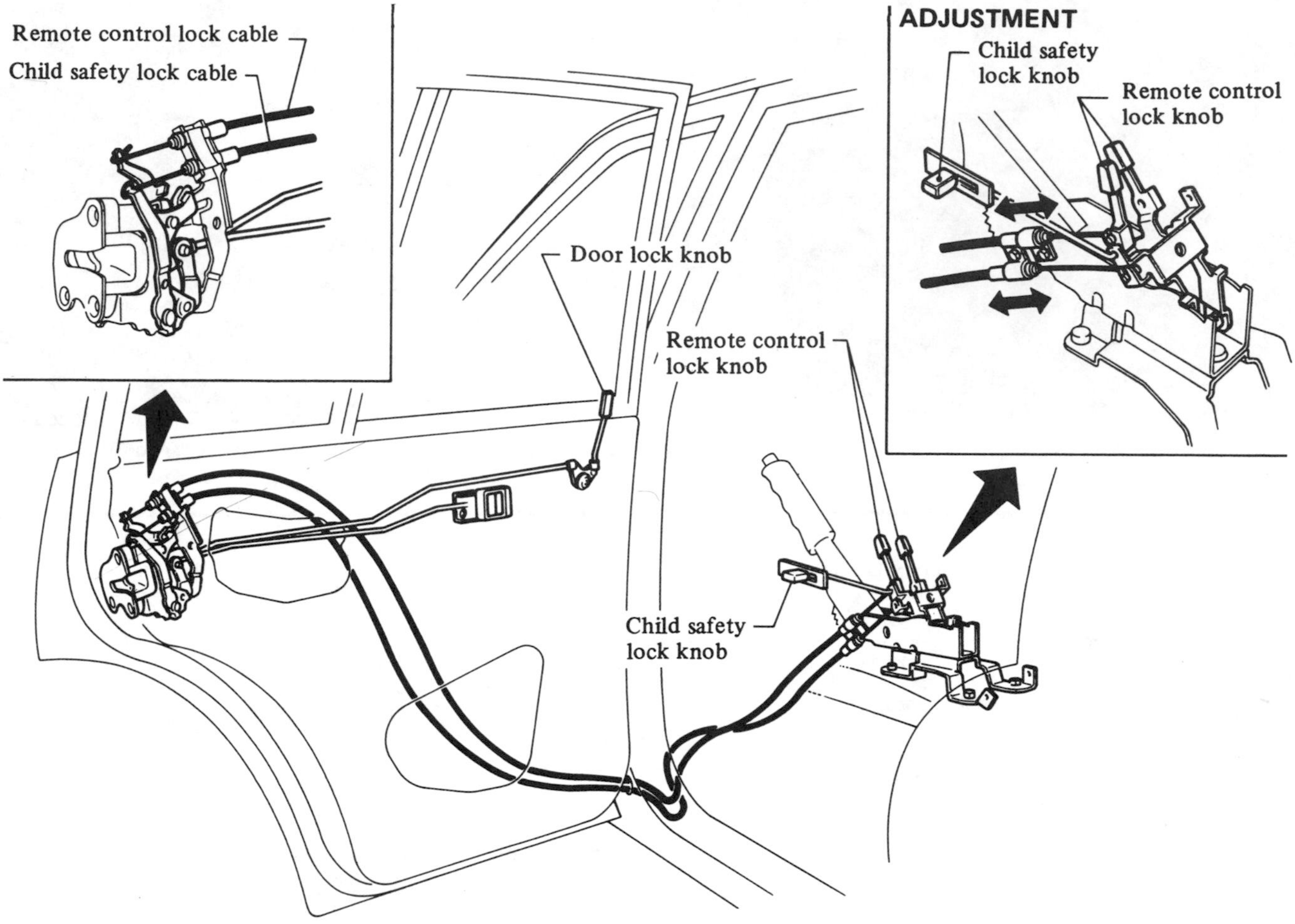

Remote control lock cable
Child safety lock cable

ADJUSTMENT
Child safety lock knob
Remote control lock knob

Door lock knob
Remote control lock knob
Child safety lock knob

Fig. 12.10 Rear door lock and child safety lock remote control (Sec 12)

12.4 Lock cylinder viewed from door interior

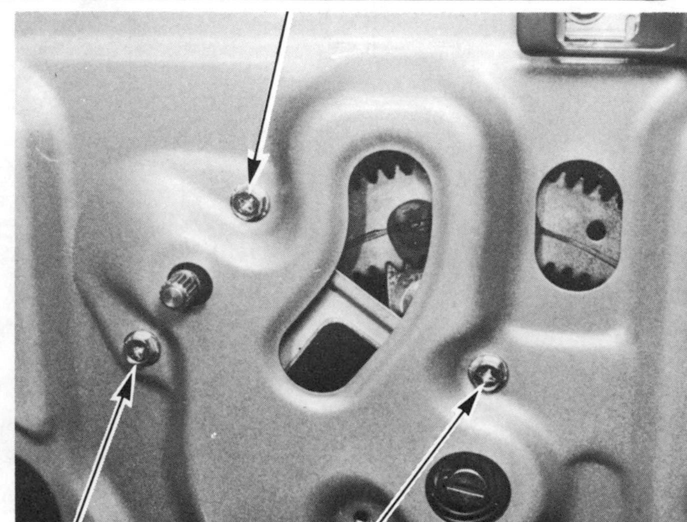

13.2A Window regulator fixing screws (arrowed)

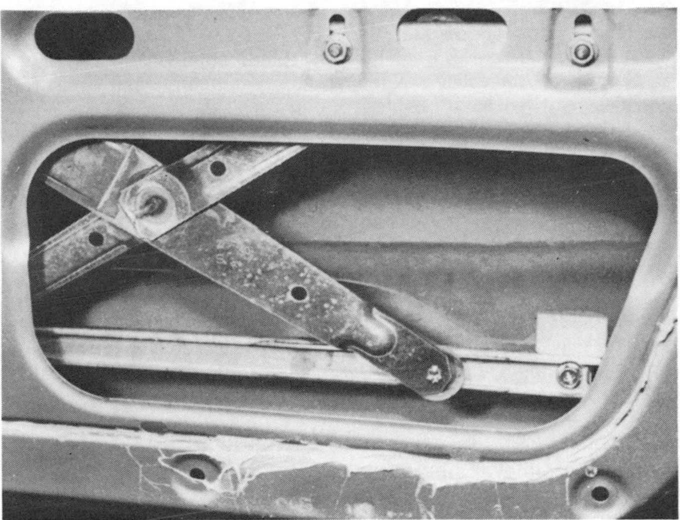

13.2B Door window regulator arms and channel

door inner panel. The lock cylinder can be removed after prising out its retaining clip (photo).

5 Refitting is a reversal of removal, but adjust the door exterior handle by turning the control rod nut to give a setting as shown in Fig. 12.7. On N12 models, a bush is used for the adjustment (Fig. 12.8).

B11 and N12 models

6 On certain versions a remote cable-operated rear door lock and child safety lock are fitted.

13 Front door window – removal and refitting

1 Remove the door trim panel, as previously described (Section 11).

2 Unscrew the window regulator fixing screws (photo). Lower and swivel the regulator and release its lifting arms from the channel at the base of the glass (photo).

3 Release the screws from the glass guide channel.

4 Lower the glass fully and remove the two weatherseal strips from the glass slot. These are held by spring clips.

5 Pull the glass upwards, tilt it and remove it from the door.

6 If a new window is being fitted, tap the base channel onto it using a wooden or plastic-faced hammer.

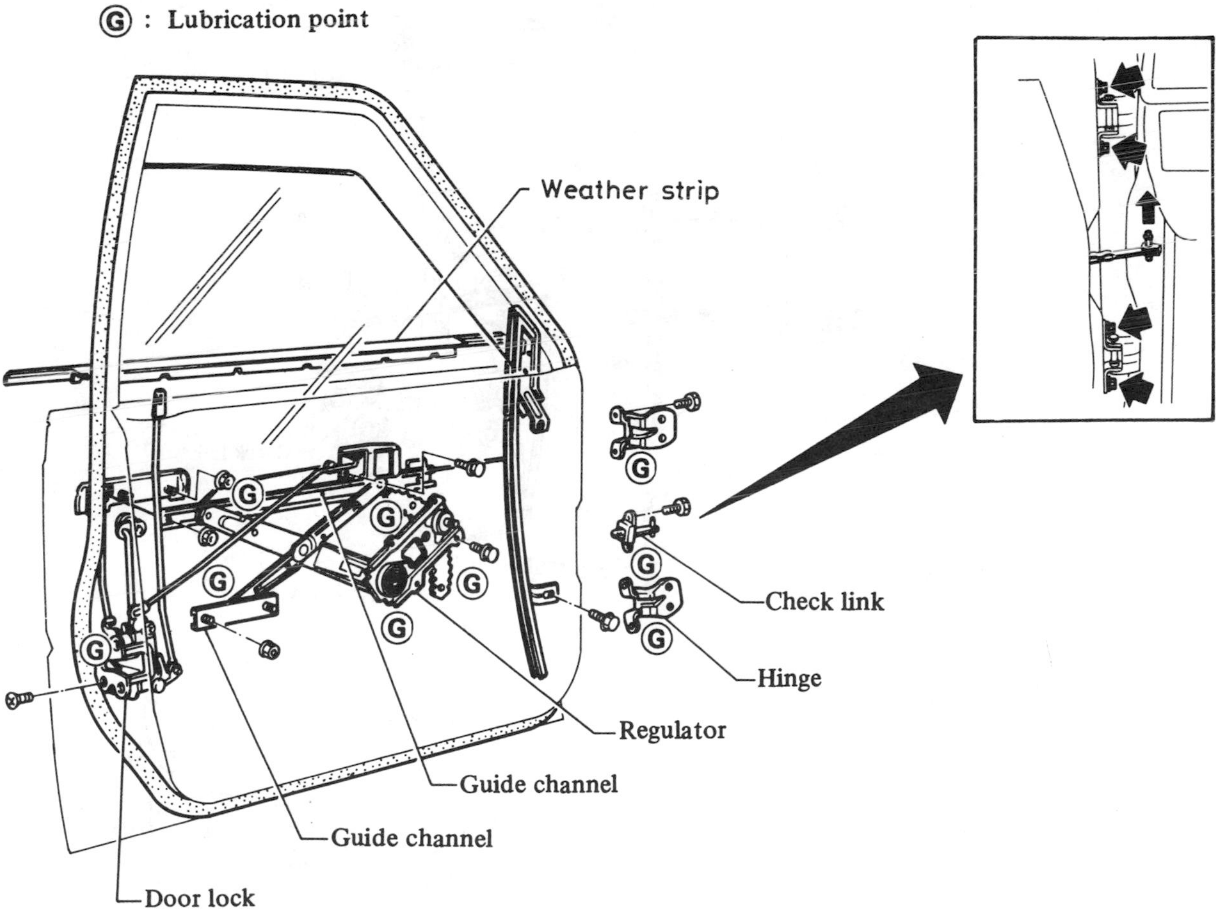

G : Lubrication point
Weather strip
Check link
Hinge
Regulator
Guide channel
Guide channel
Door lock

Fig. 12.11 Front door lock and window regulator components (Sec 13)

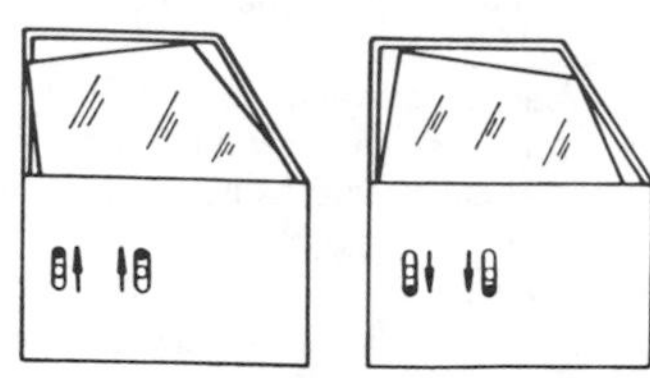

Fig. 12.2 Method of removing door window (Sec 13)

7 Refit by reversing the removal operations. Adjust the position of the glass guide channel before tightening its screw so that the window moves up and down smoothly.

14 Rear door window – removal and refitting

B11 models

1 On these models, the window regulator is of cable-operated type.
2 Remove the door trim panel and then extract the window regulator fixing screws.
3 Lower the glass, disconnect the cable drive from the channel at the base of the window.
4 Release the screws from the glass guide channel.
5 Lower the glass fully and remove the two weatherseal strips from the glass slot. These are held by spring clips.
6 Extract the screw from the top of the glass divider channel and tilt the channel until the quarter light can be removed by pulling it with its rubber weatherseal out of the door frame.
7 Raise the main window, tilt it and remove it from the door.
8 Refitting is a reversal of removal, adjust the glass guide channel and the cable drive attachment at the base of the glass to give smooth operation.

N12 models

9 The rear door window regulator on these models is of gear type. Apart from this, removal of the glass is as described in earlier paragraphs.

15 Door – removal and refitting

1 The door hinges are of bolt-on type (photo).
2 Open the door wide and support its lower edge on jacks or blocks with pads of rag to prevent damage to the paintwork.

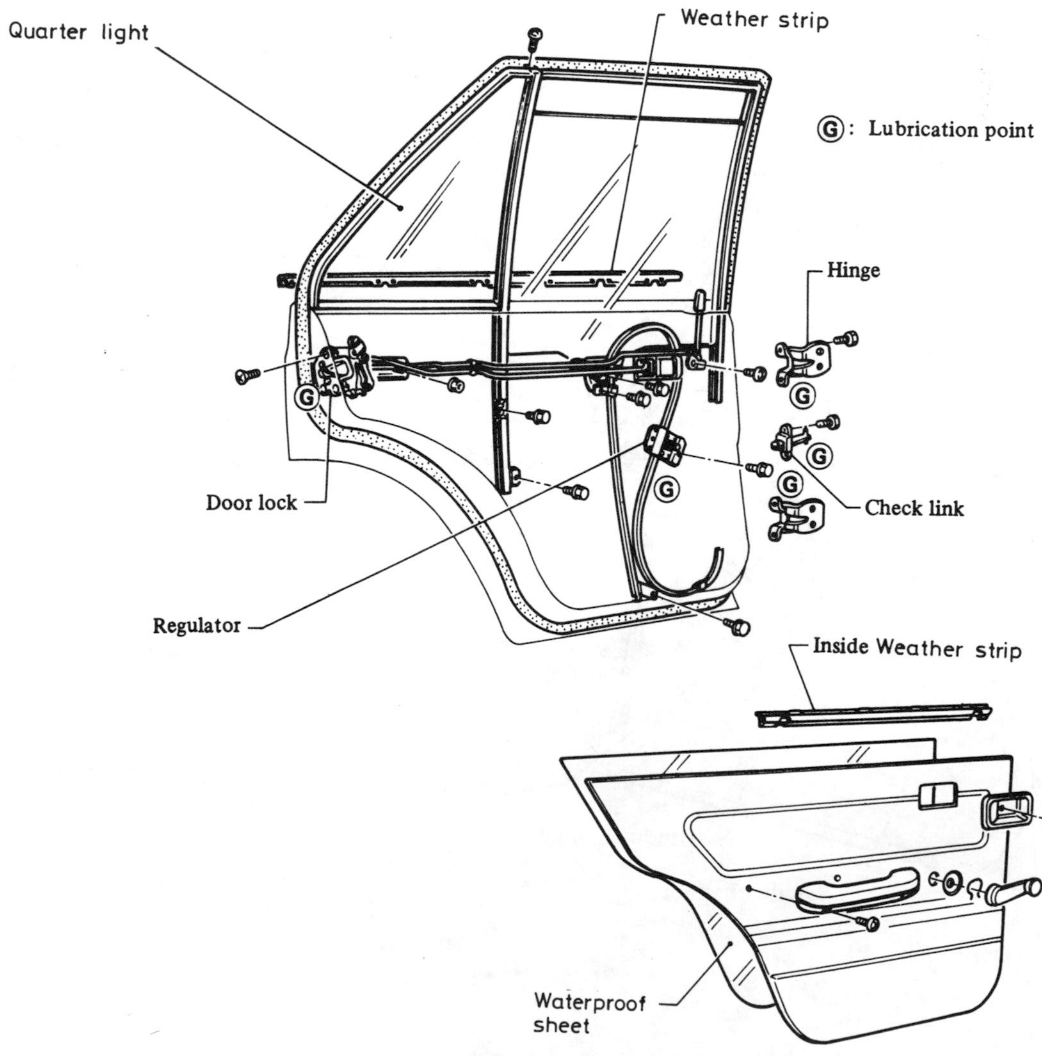

Quarter light
Weather strip
G: Lubrication point
Hinge
Door lock
Check link
Regulator
Inside Weather strip
Waterproof sheet

Fig. 12.13 Rear door lock and window regulator components – B11 models (Sec 14)

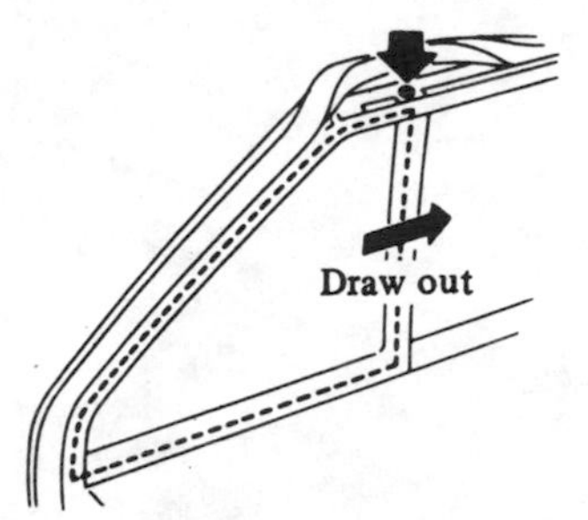

Fig. 12.14 Rear door quarter light removed (Sec 14)

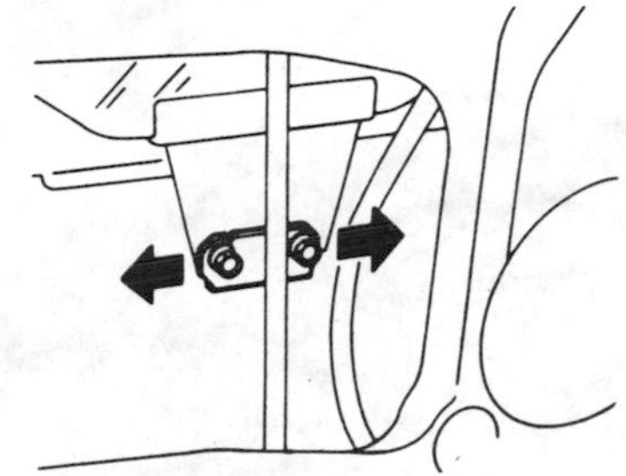

Fig. 12.15 Cable drive attachment at base of rear door window (Sec 14)

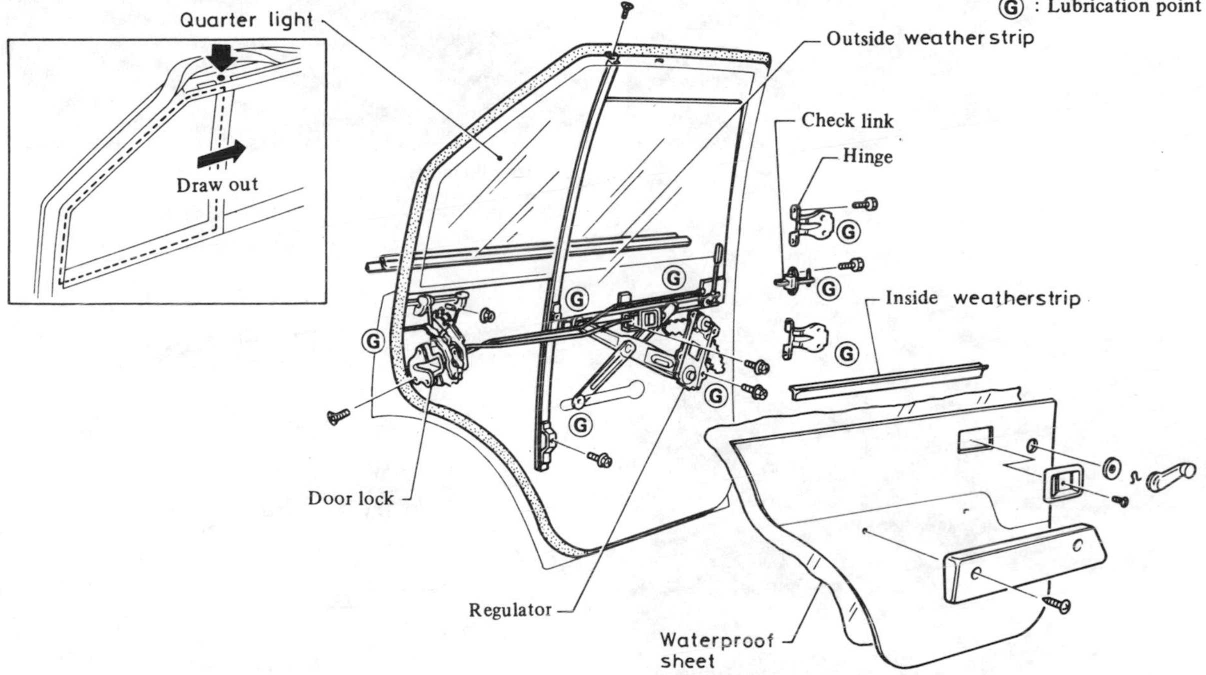

Fig. 12.16 Rear door lock and window regulator components – N12 models (Sec 14)

15.1 Door hinge

15.3 Door check link roll pin (arrowed)

15.7 Door striker

3 Disconnect the check link either by removing the fixing screws or by driving out the roll pin (photo).
4 Mark the position of the hinges on the door edge with a soft pencil and then support the weight of the door and remove the hinge bolts.
5 Lift the door from the vehicle.
6 Refitting is a reversal of removal. Provided the hinges are positioned within their original marked areas the door should close satisfactorily. Adjustment may be carried out by releasing the hinge bolts and moving the door.

7 The striker on the door pillar may also be adjusted to ensure smooth, positive closure (photo).

16 Boot lid – removal and refitting

1 Open the lid and unbolt the lock (photo).
2 Mark the position of the hinges on the underside of the lid.

16.1 Boot lid lock and cable

16.5 Boot lid hinge

16.8 Boot lid remote control lever

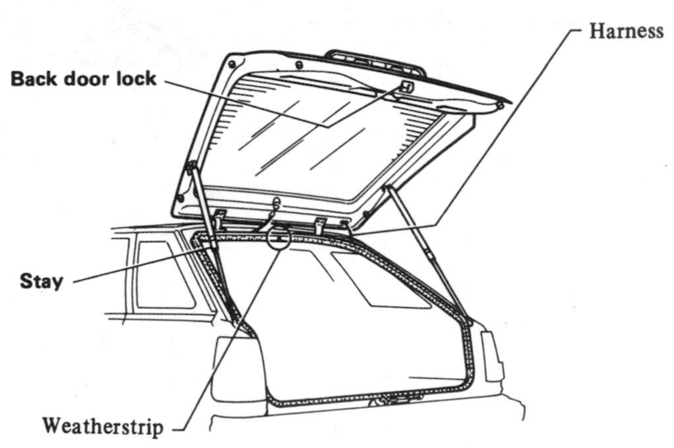

Fig. 12.17 Tailgate – B11 Estate (Sec 17)

3 With the help of an assistant, support the lid and unscrew the hinge bolts.
4 Remove the lid from the car.
5 On B11 models the hinges can be unbolted and removed (photo). *Do not dismantle the hinge,* as the spring may cause damage or injury if released.
6 On N12 models, torsion rods are used to counterbalance the boot lid and they should be released gently with a suitable lever before attempting to unbolt the hinges from the body.
7 Refitting is a reversal of removal. If adjustment is required, release the hinge bolts and move the boot lid to align it. Adjust the position of the striker to ensure smooth positive closure.
8 The boot remote control release lever is at the side of the driver's seat (photo).

17 Tailgate – removal and refitting

1 Removal of the tailgate from Coupe, Hatchback, and Estate models is similar .
2 Open the tailgate fully and disconnect the leads from the window heater element.
3 With an assistant supporting the tailgate, mark the position of the hinges on the body and then disconnect the gas-filled struts from the tailgate.
4 Unbolt the hinges from the body and lift the tailgate away.
5 Refit by reversing the removal operations. Adjust, if necessary, by releasing the hinge bolts and moving the tailgate to give correct alignment within the body.
6 Adjust the remote control mechanism and striker with reference to the next Section.

18 Boot lid or tailgate remote control assembly – removal, refitting and adjustment

1 The cable-operated lock can be removed from the edge of the boot lid or tailgate after removing its fixing bolts.
2 The cable can be renewed once its end fittings have been slipped out of the lock and hand control lever.
3 When refitting, adjust the cable by means of the control lever on N12 Hatchback models and at the lock on B11 Saloon, B11 Estate and N12 Coupe models. On B11 Coupe models, no adjustments are required, other than to the lock latch – within the limits of its elongated bolt holes.

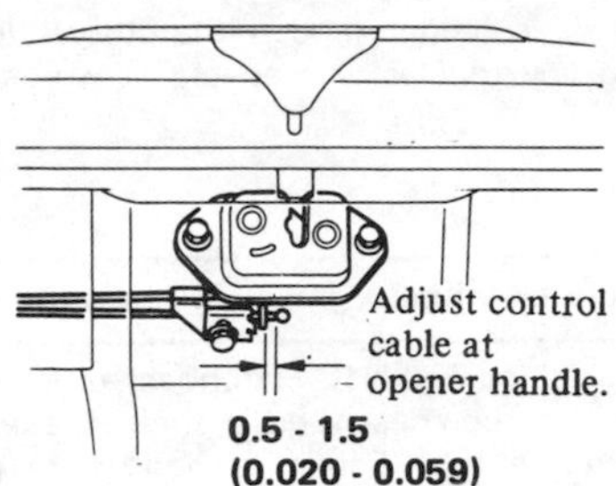

Fig. 12.18 Tailgate lock adjustment – N12 Hatchback (Sec 18)

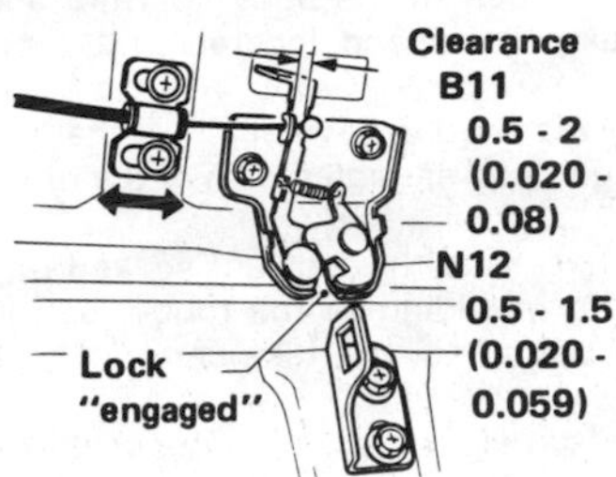

Fig. 12.19 Boot (B11 Saloon) and tailgate (N12/Coupe) lock adjustment (Sec 18)

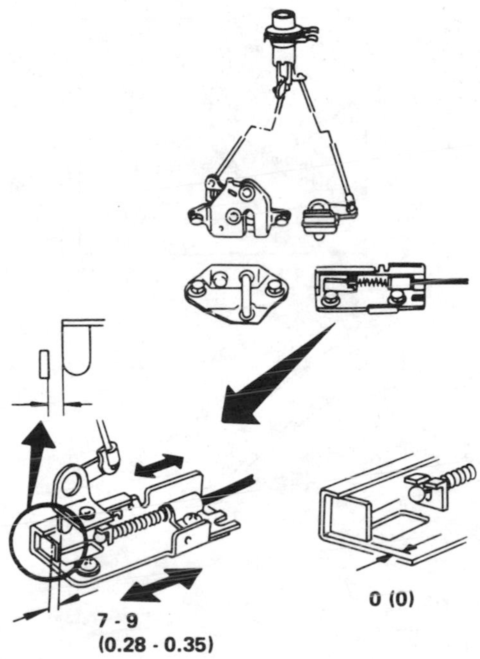

Fig. 12.20 Tailgate lock adjustment – B11 Estate (Sec 18)

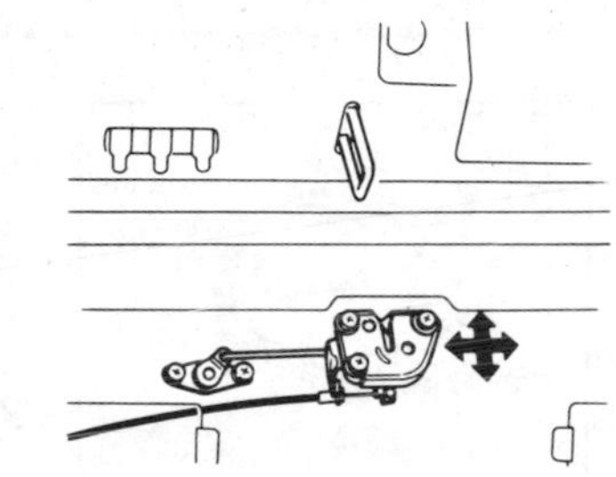

Fig. 12.21 Tailgate lock arrangement – B11 Coupe (Sec 18)

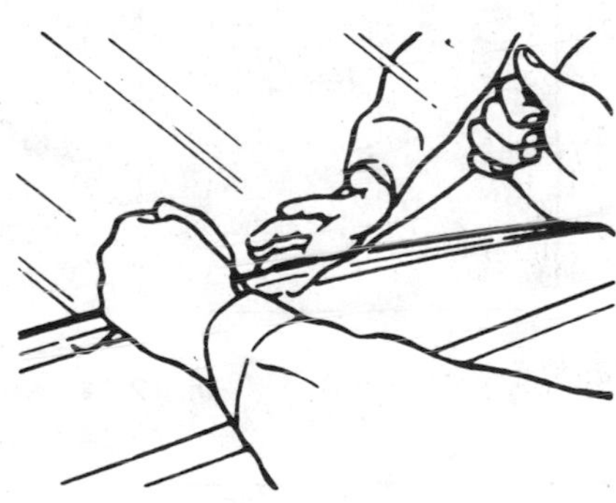

Fig. 12.22 Using a cord to fit a windscreen (Sec 19)

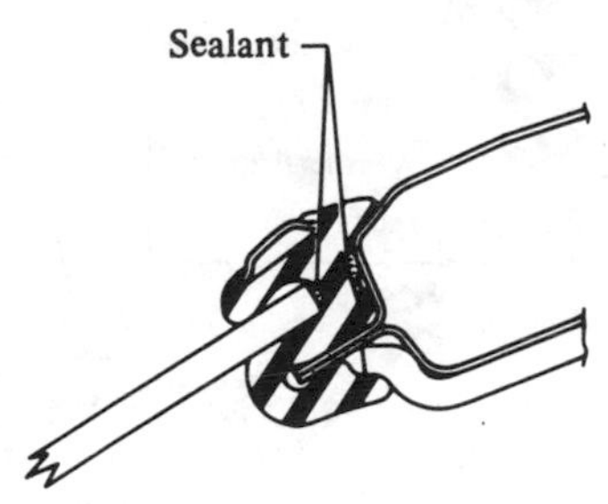

Fig. 12.23 Sectional view of windscreen/body joint (Sec 19)

19 Windscreen – removal and refitting

B11 models

1 If the windscreen is to be removed and/or replaced for any reason, it is a job which is better left to an auto glass replacement specialist. They will do the job in half the time and most important, ensure that it is correctly fitted with no leakages around the surround rubber. However, if you wish to do it yourself proceed as follows.

2 Where a windscreen is to be replaced due to shattering, the facia air vents should be covered before attempting removal. Adhesive sheeting is useful to stick to the outside of the glass to enable large areas of crystallised glass to be removed.

3 Where the screen is to be removed intact, or is of laminated type, an assistant will be required. First release the rubber surround from the bodywork by running a blunt, small screwdriver around and under the rubber weatherstrip both inside and outside the car. This operation will break the adhesive of the sealant originally used. Take care not to damage the paintwork or catch the rubber surround with the screwdriver. Remove the windscreen wiper arms and interior mirror and place a protective cover on the bonnet. Salvage your tax disc.

4 Prise out the trim strip from the rubber surround.

5 Have your assistant push the inner lip of the rubber surround off the flange of the windscreen body aperture. Once the rubber surround starts to peel off the flange, the screen may be forced gently outward by careful hand pressure. The second person should support and remove the screen complete with rubber surround.

6 Fit a new rubber weatherseal to the glass and ensure that all old sealant is removed from the body flange. Scrape it away and then clean the flange with a suitable solvent.

7 Apply a bead of sealant to the body flange all round the windscreen aperture.

8 Cut a piece of strong cord greater in length than the periphery of the glass and insert it into the body flange locating channel of the rubber surround.

9 Offer the windscreen to the body aperture and pass the ends of the cord, previously fitted and located at bottom centre, into the vehicle interior.
10 Press the windscreen into place, at the same time have an assistant pull the cords to engage the lip of the rubber channel over the body flange.
11 Remove any excess with a solvent-soaked rag.
12 Refit the bright moulding to the rubber surround. A special tool will facilitate this operation, but take care not to tear the lips of the rubber.
13 Refit the windscreen wipers, the interior mirror and the tax disc.

N12 models

14 The windscreen glass on these models is bonded into the bodyframe using a primer and Butyl sealant kit (Nissan Part No 72891-V7425). It is recommended that the fitting of this type of screen is left to your dealer or a specialist windscreen replacement company.

20 Rear window or tailgate glass – removal and refitting

1 The glass in Saloon and N12 Hatchback models is removed as for the B11 type windscreen,described in the preceding Section.
2 The glass in the B11 Estate is bonded in position, and it is recommended that removal and refitting is left to your dealer or a glass replacement specialist.
3 On B11 Coupe models, the glass cannot be removed – the tailgate must be renewed complete with glass.

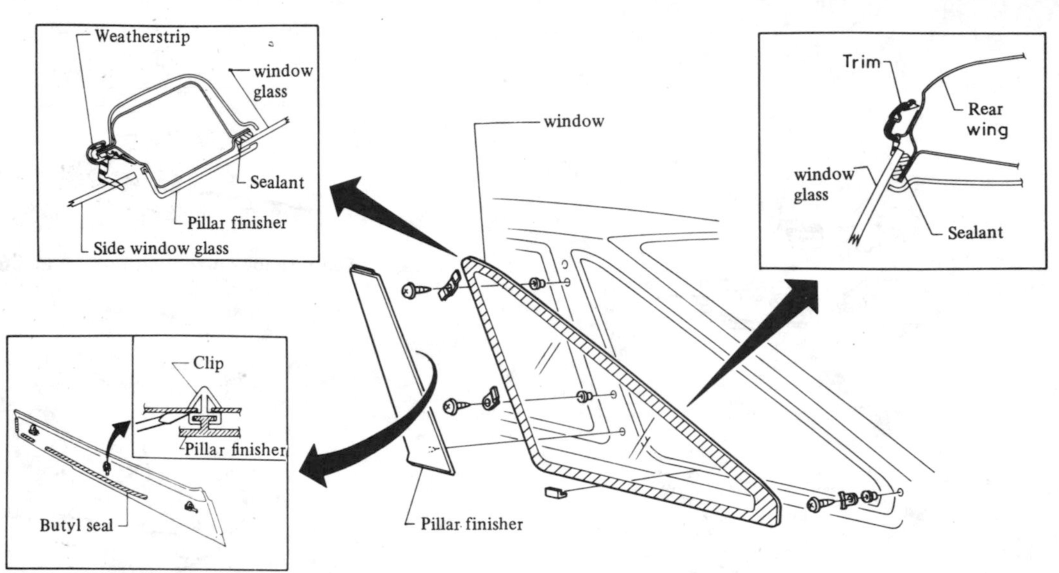

Fig. 12.24 Rear fixed quarter window – B11 Coupe (Sec 21)

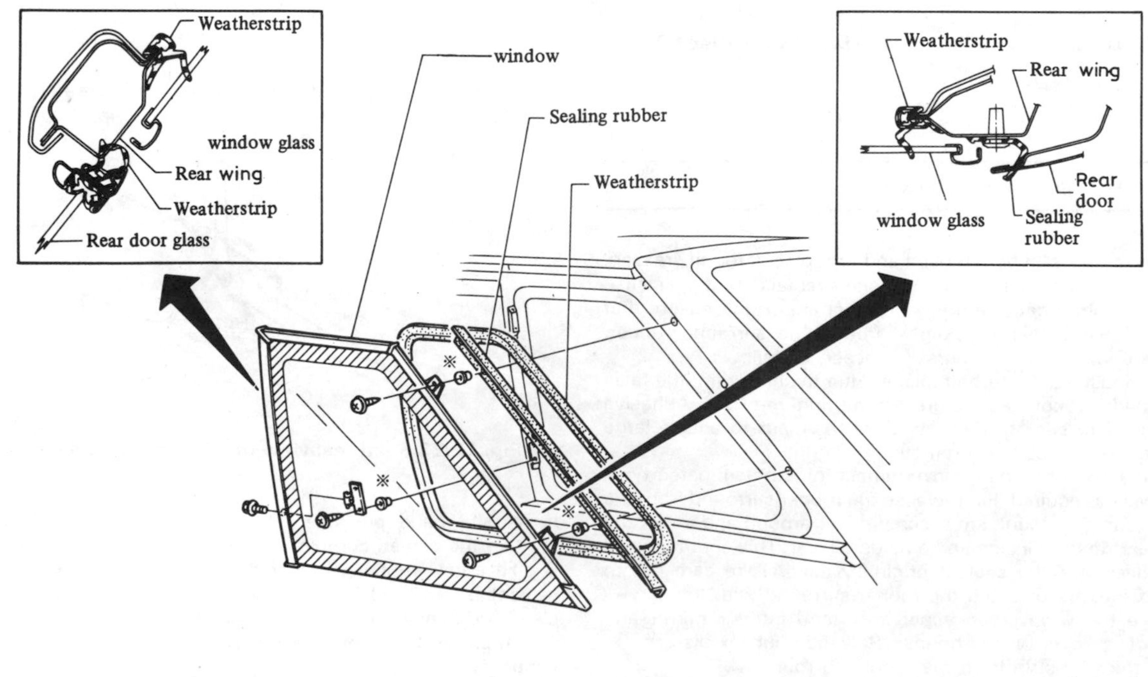

Fig. 12.25 Rear fixed quarter window – B11 Estate (Sec 21)

21 Fixed rear quarter window – removal and refitting

Coupe

1 The glass is bonded into the body with Butyl sealant, as for the N12 type windscreen (Section 19).

Estate

2 The glass can be removed once the fixing screws have been extracted from underneath the sealing rubber.

22 Opening rear quarter window – removal and refitting

B11 Coupe

1 Remove the screw from the opening handle.
2 Open the window and extract the screws from the pivot plates.
3 Remove the frame, rubber surround and glass.

N12 Hatchback

4 Extract the screws from the toggle type catch.

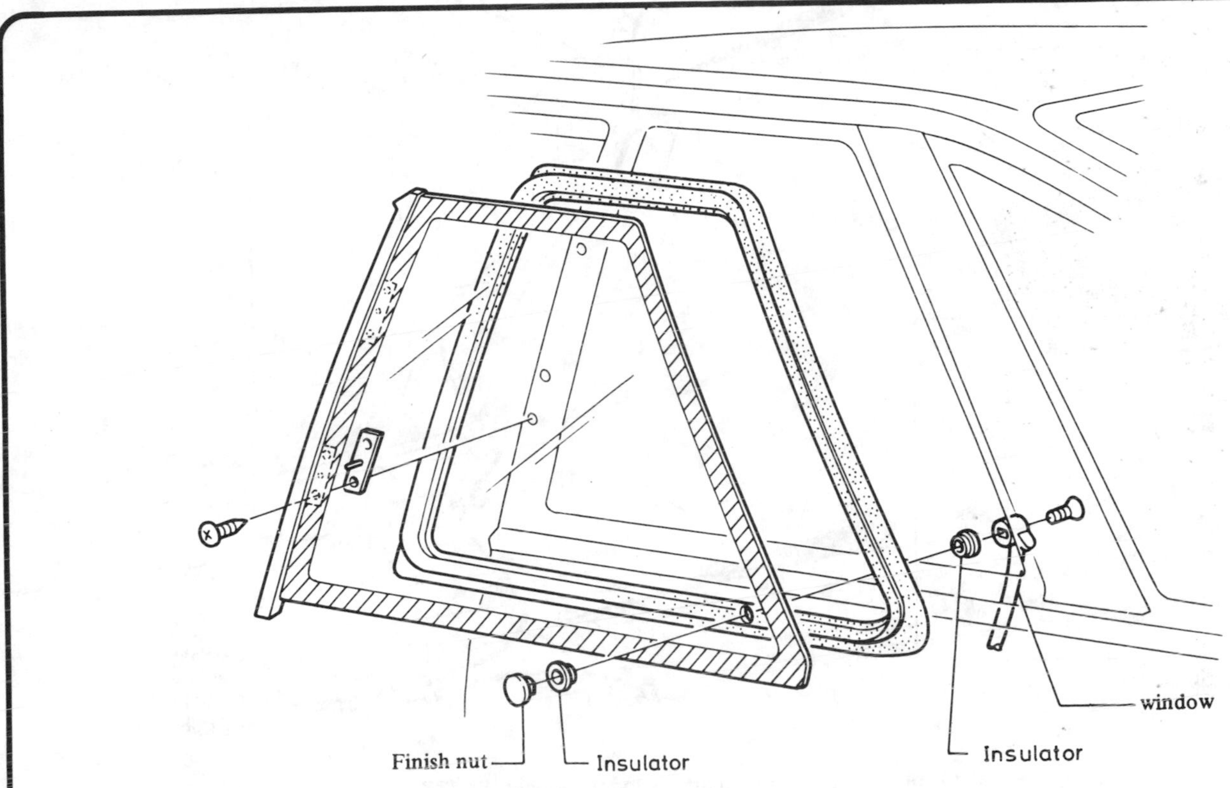

Fig. 12.26 Opening rear quarter window – B11 Coupe (Sec 22)

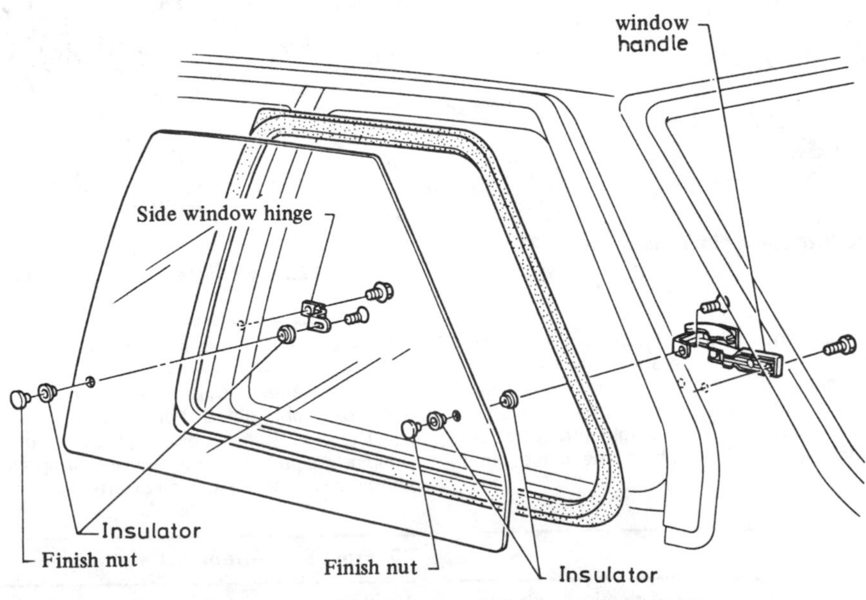

Fig. 12.27 Opening rear quarter window – N12 Hatchback (Sec 22)

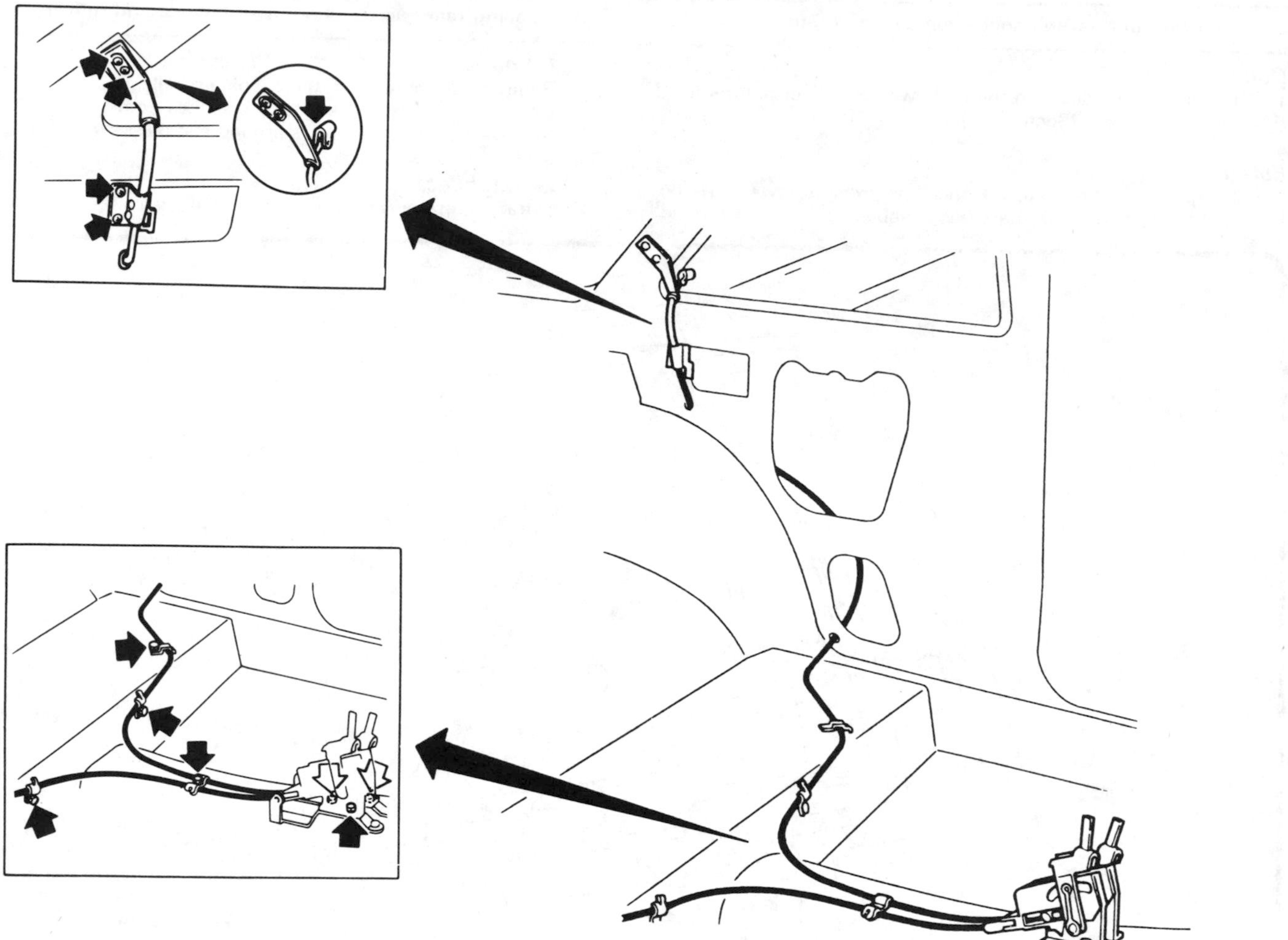

Fig. 12.28 Remote control quarter window opener (Sec 22)

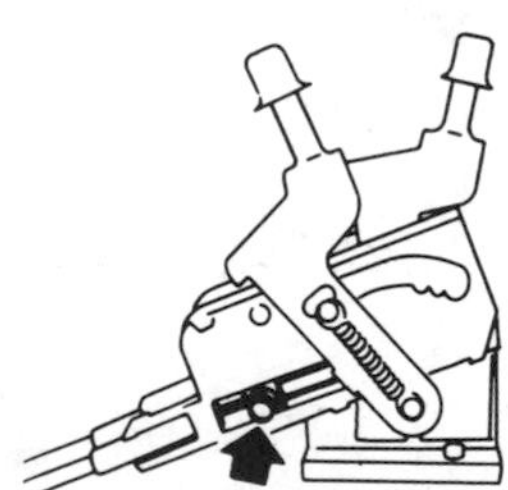

Fig. 12.29 Remote control cable pinch screw (Sec 22)

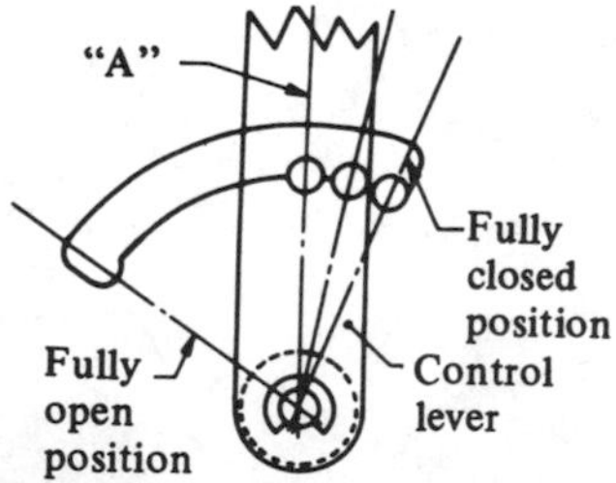

Fig. 12.30 Remote control lever set in position A (Sec 22)

5 Open the window until the hinges can be slid out of their slots.
6 Some models are fitted with cable-operated remote control catches. If necessary, adjust in the following way. Release the cable pinch screw at the control lever end. Set the control lever in position A (Fig. 12.30) and close the window so that it lightly touches the weatherseal. Without moving the settings, tighten the cable pinch screw.

23 Interior trim and mouldings

1 Most of the interior trim and mouldings are of plastic construction and care should be exercised when removing or refitting it.
2 Clips are used extensively to fix the trim, with self-tapping screws in certain positions.

24 Exterior trim and mouldings

1 The exterior body trim is either clipped in position or held by pop rivets or double-sided tape.
2 The side guard mouldings are secured by double-sided tape. To remove a side moulding, the use of an electrically-operated heat gun will be found to be the most effective.

25 Front seat – removal and refitting

1 Push the seat fully to the rear and unscrew the bolts which hold the seat runners to the floor (photo).
2 Now push the seat fully forward and unscrew the bolts from the rear of the runners (photo).

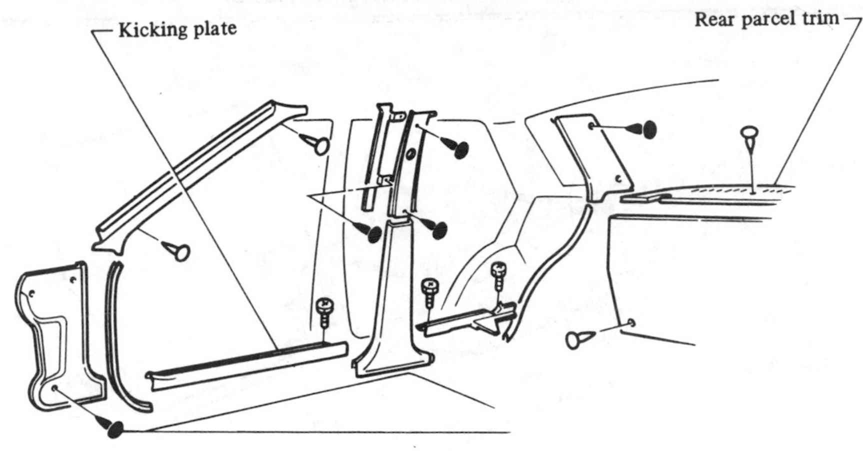

Fig. 12.31 Typical interior trim – Saloon (Sec 23)

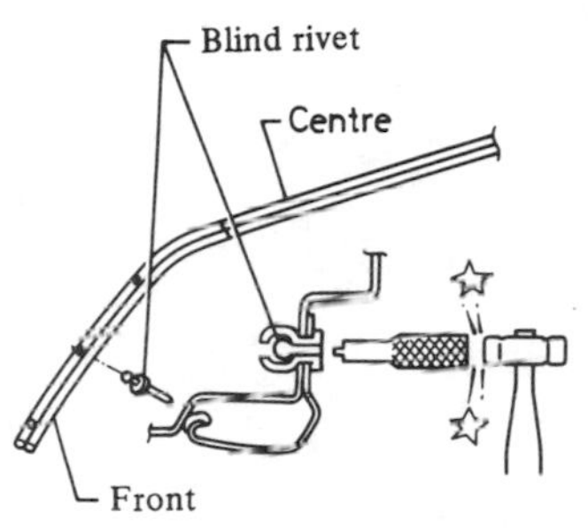

Fig. 12.32 Front door edge trim attachment (Sec 24)

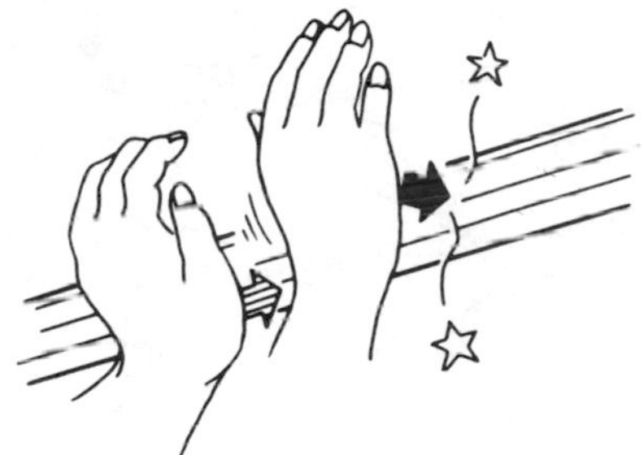

Fig. 12.33 Roof gutter trim attachment (Sec 24)

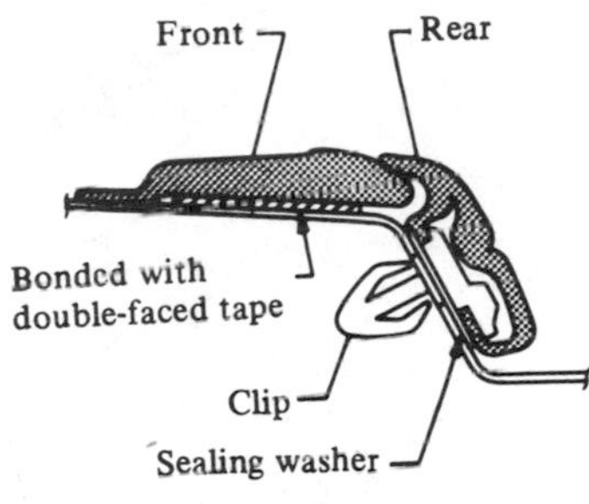

12.34 Rear wing trim attachment – Estate (Sec 24)

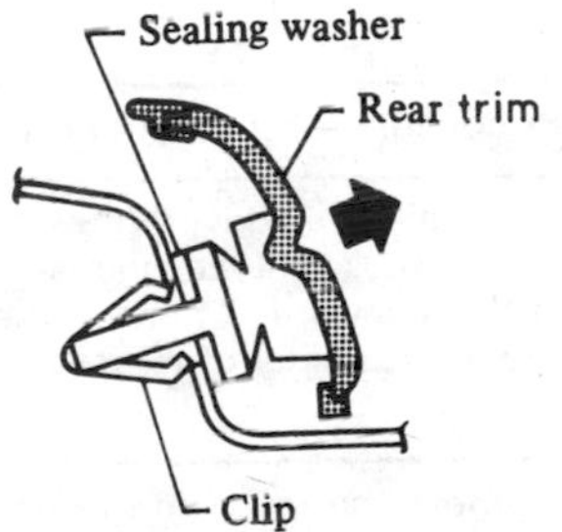

Fig. 12.35 Rear fixed quarter window trim – Estate (Sec 24)

Fig. 12.36 Heat gun applied to side guard moulding (Sec 24)

25.1 Front seat runner fixing bolt (rear)

25.2 Front seat runner fixing bolt (front)

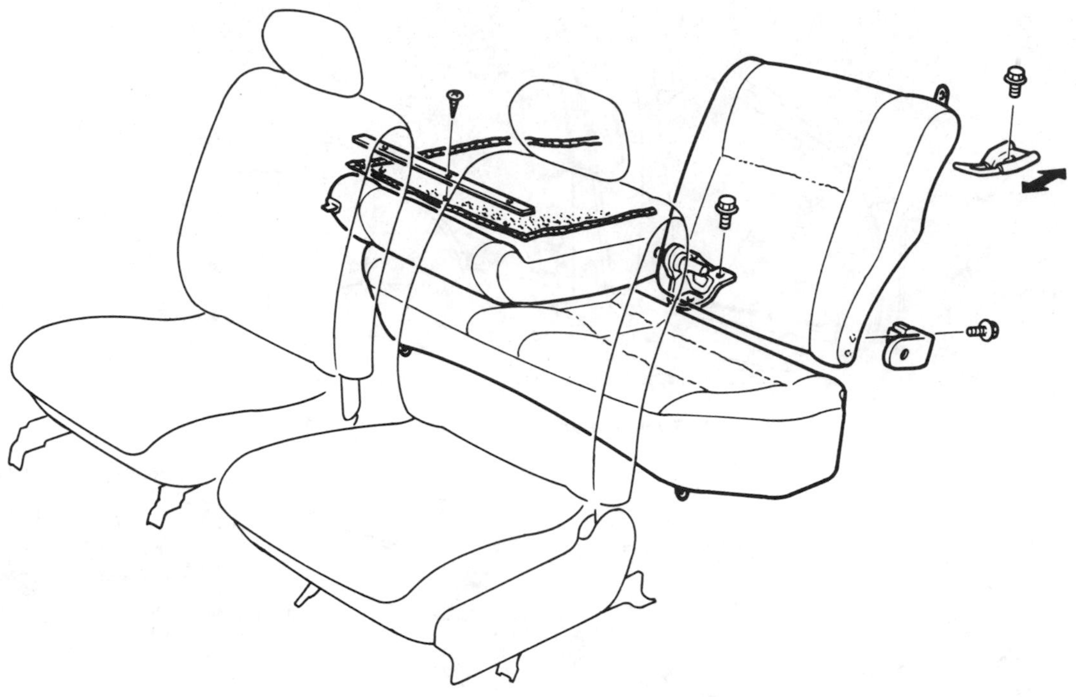

Fig. 12.37 Rear seats – B11 Coupe, Estate and N12 Hatchback (Sec 26)

3 Remove the seat from the vehicle.
4 Refitting is a reversal of removal.

26 Rear seat – removal and refitting

Saloon – removal

1 Grip the front edge of the seat cushion and pull it upwards to release it from its clips (photos). Remove the cushion.
2 Extract the screws from the base of the seat back (photo), lift the seat back upwards and release it from its hooks.

Coupe, Hatchback and Estate – removal

3 Remove the seat cushion as described in paragraph 1.
4 Tip the seat back forward and unscrew the pivot brackets.

Refitting

5 Refitting on all models is a reversal of removal.

27 Centre console – removal and refitting

1 Using a small screwdriver, prise out the small cover panels from the console to expose the console securing screws (photos).
2 Extract the screws and remove the centre console.
3 Refitting is a reversal of removal.

28 Facia panel – removal and refitting

1 Remove the instrument panel, as described in Chapter 10.
2 Disconnect the check control cable.
3 Disconnect the heater controls and remove the control panel.
4 Disconnect the leads and remove the clock.
5 Disconnect the power lead, the aerial and loudspeaker leads and the earth lead, and remove the radio.
6 Remove the facia panel fixing screws. There are two screws at the ends (photos), two at the centre (photo) and two at the top which are

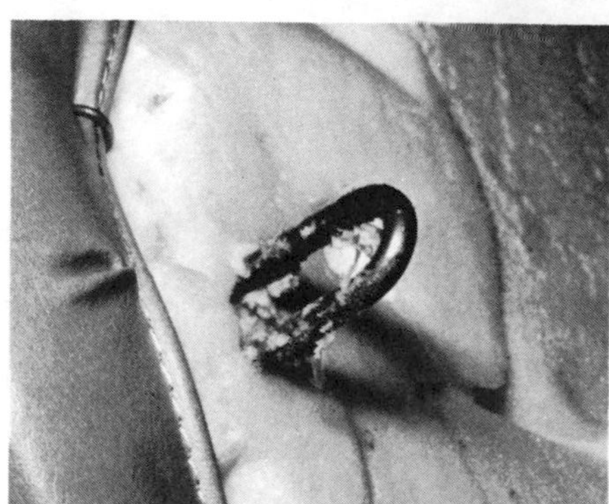

26.1A Rear seat cushion locating tongue

26.1B Rear seat cushion tongue recess

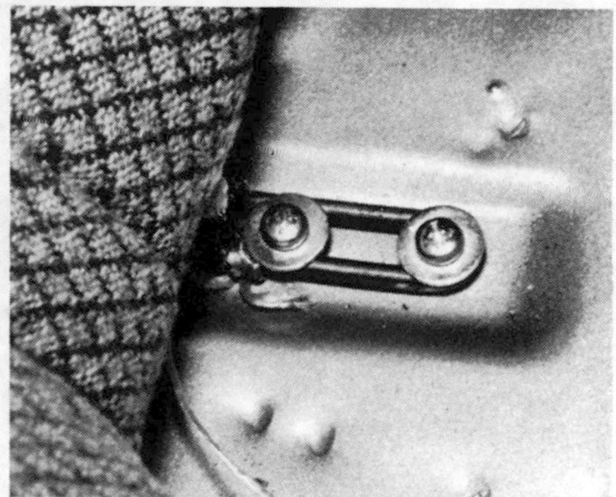

26.2 Rear seat back lower fixing

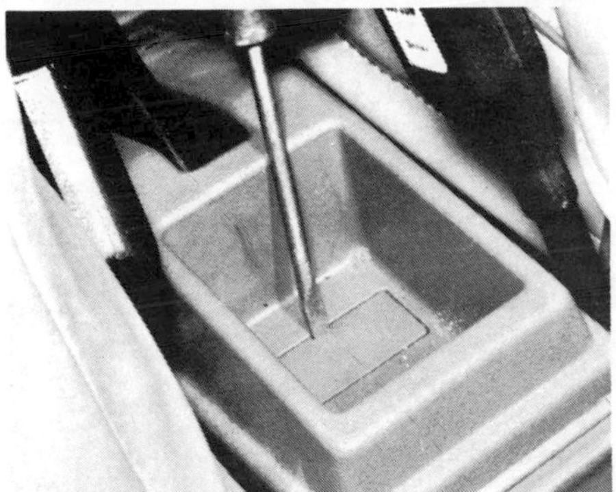
27.1A Prising the cover panel from the centre console

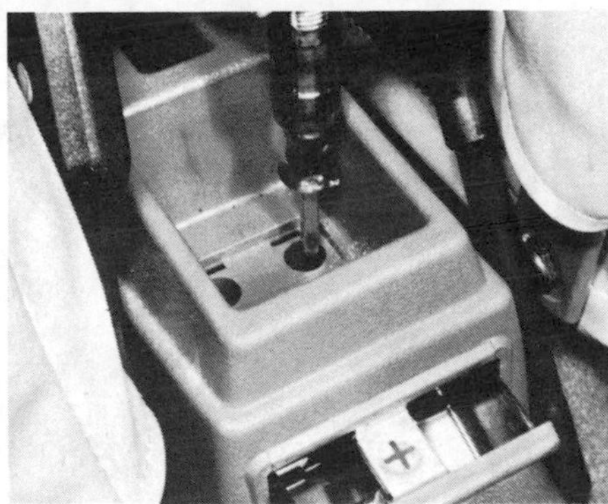
27.1B Unscrewing a centre console fixing screw

28.6A Facia fixing screw

28.6B Facia lower end screw

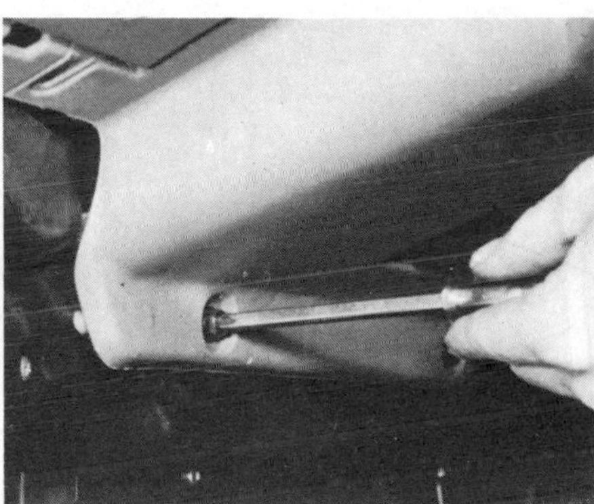
28.6C Facia centre screw

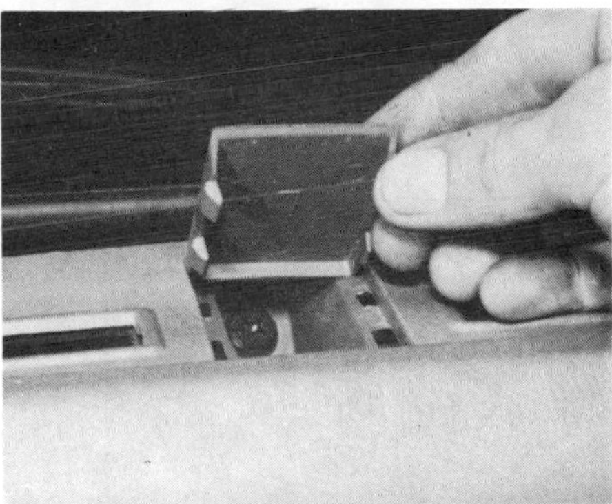
28.6D Facia top screw and cover panel

hidden under small square blanking panels which must be prised out to expose the screws (photo).
7 As the facia is pulled forward, disconnect the wiring connector plugs and the heater, demister and fresh air ducts.

29 Sunroof and shade plate – removal and refitting

The following operations should never be carried out while the vehicle is in motion.
1 To open the roof, pull the handle down to unlock the rear of the roof. Now push the handle fully upwards. To close the roof, pull the handle forward and push fully up.
2 To remove the sunshade plate, hold the plate while unscrewing the retaining bolts. Pull the hooks of the plate out of their holders.
3 To remove the sunroof (always having first removed the sunshade plate), slide the safety catch knob to the left-hand side.
4 Tilt the roof and push in the two buttons on the handle while pushing the sunroof upwards.
5 Remove the roof from outside the vehicle.
6 While removed, store the sunroof in the cover provided or, on Estate versions, on top of the spare wheel under the floor.
7 To refit the roof, tilt the air deflectors forward while inserting the front hinges in their holders.
8 Engage the handle linkage and close the roof, then slide the safety catch fully to the right-hand side.
9 To refit the sunshade plate, engage the two hooks on the front of the plate in their holders.
10 Align the two bolts on the rear edge of the plate with the nuts and then fully tighten the bolts.

Fig. 12.38 Sunroof opening method (Sec 29)

Fig. 12.39 Sunroof closure method (Sec 29)

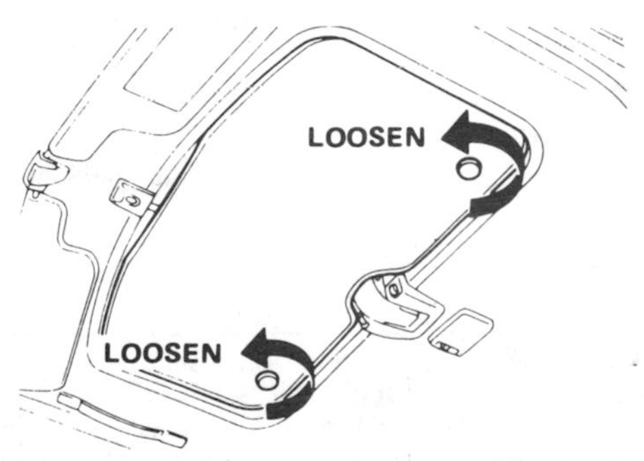

Fig. 12.40 Sunshade plate bolts (Sec 29)

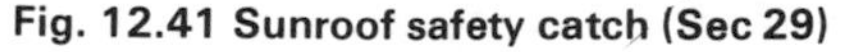
Fig. 12.41 Sunroof safety catch (Sec 29)

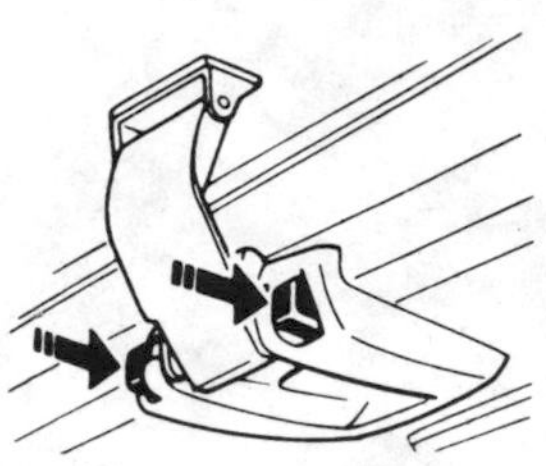
Fig. 12.42 Sunroof handle release buttons (Sec 29)

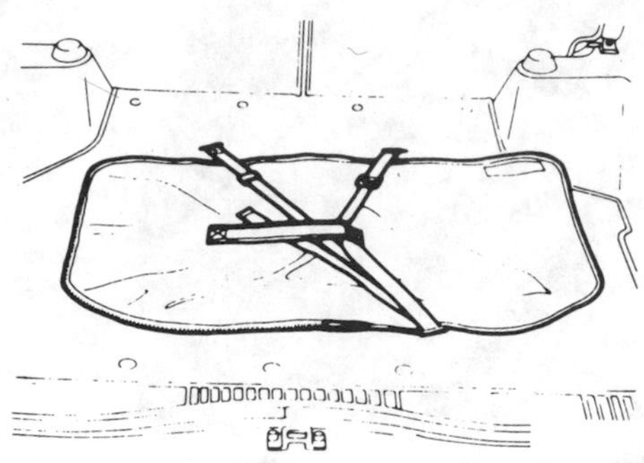
Fig. 12.43 Sunroof panel storage bag (Sec 29)

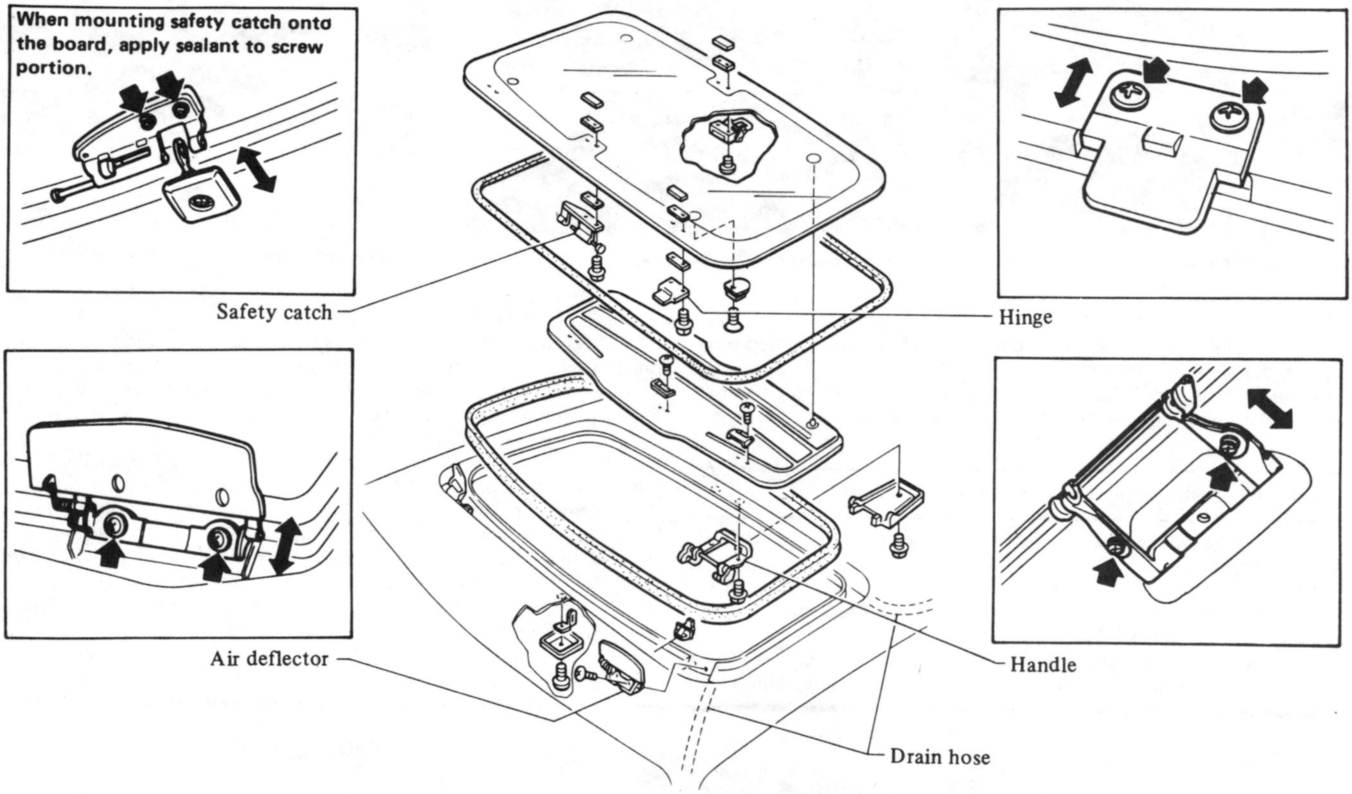

When mounting safety catch onto the board, apply sealant to screw portion.

Safety catch

Hinge

Air deflector

Handle

Drain hose

Fig. 12.44 Sunroof components – North American (Sec 29)

30 Seat belts

1 Regularly check the condition of the seat belts. If they are frayed or cut, they must be renewed.

2 Clean the webbing by wiping it with warm water and a mild detergent only. Leave the belts unretracted until quite dry.

3 Never alter the attachment points of the belts (photos) and, if removed, make quite sure that the original sequence of fitting of the anchor bolt, spacers, washers and connecting plate is retained.

4 On North American vehicles, a warning chime sounds for a six second period if the driver's seat belt is not fastened when the ignition is switched on.

31 Rear view mirrors – removal and refitting

Interior mirror

1 One of two types of interior mirror may be used, depending upon vehicle model. One type of mirror has a sprung base, while the other has a base designed to collapse on impact.

2 Both types of mirror are screwed to the roof rail.

Door mirror

3 To remove the mirror, extract the screw and take off the mirror positioning control knob.

4 Prise off the cover plate to expose the mirror mounting screws.

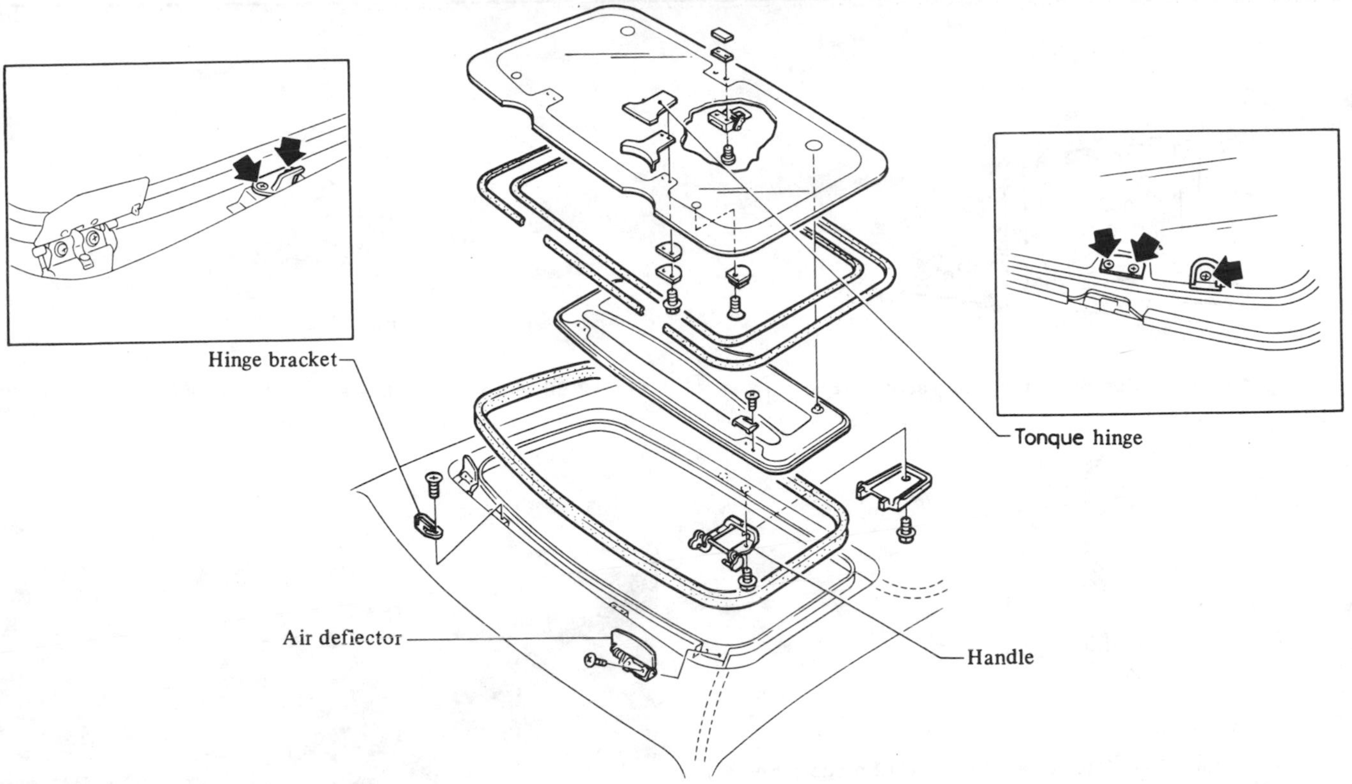

Hinge bracket

Tonque hinge

Air deflector

Handle

Fig. 12.45 Sunroof components – except North American (Sec 29)

30.3A Seat belt sill anchor bolt

30.3B Seat belt pillar anchor bolt

30.3C Seat belt stalks

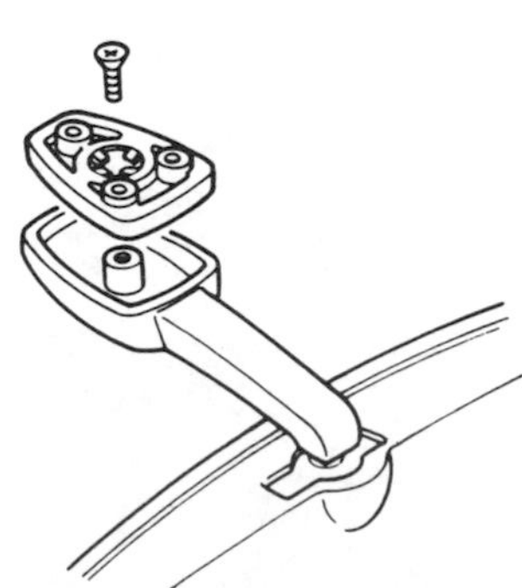

Fig. 12.46 Sprung base type interior mirror (Sec 31)

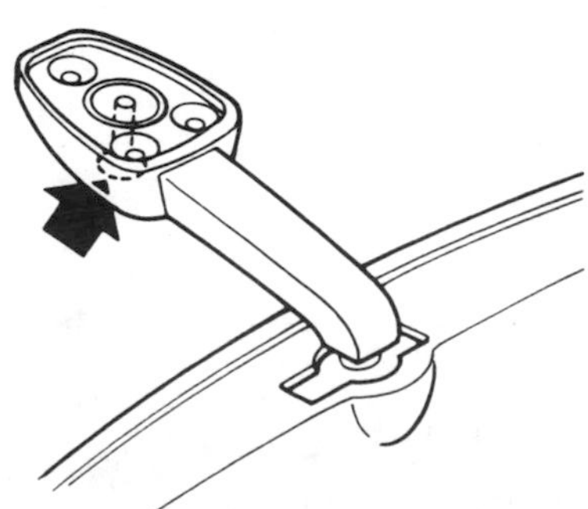

Fig. 12.47 Collapsible base type interior mirror (Sec 31)

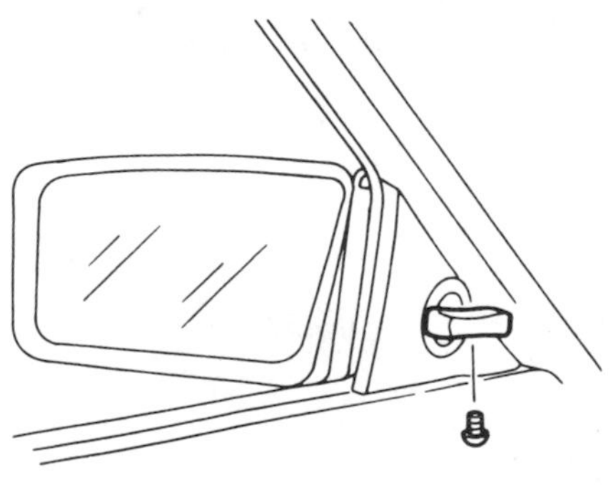

Fig. 12.48 Exterior mirror positioning handle screw (Sec 31)

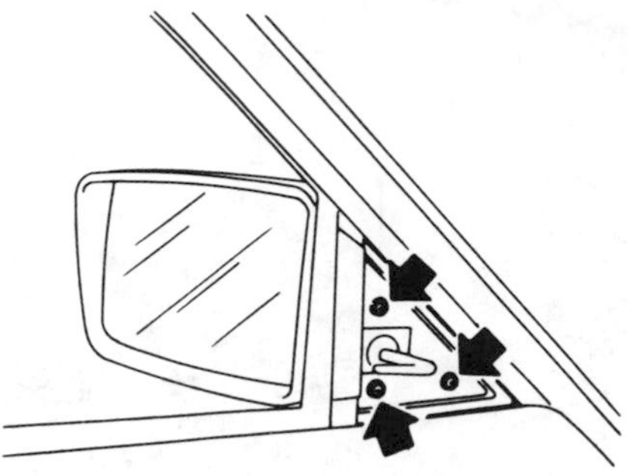

Fig. 12.49 Exterior mirror mounting screws (Sec 31)

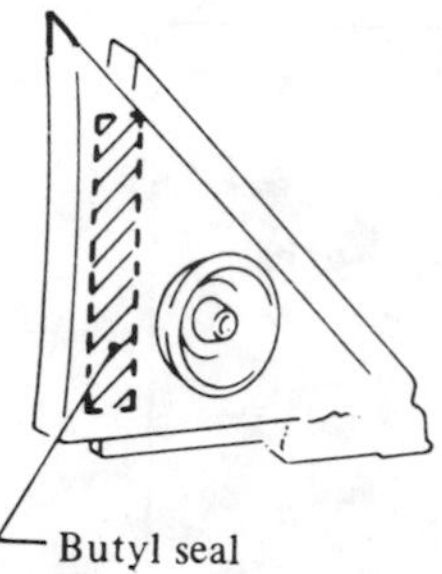

Fig. 12.50 Mirror cover plate sealant bead – B11 models (Sec 31)

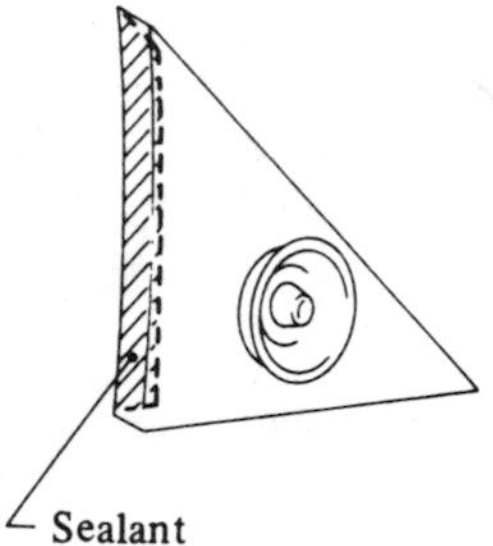

Fig. 12.51 Mirror cover plate sealant bead – N12 models (Sec 31)

5 Remove the screws and the mirror.
6 Refitting is a reversal of removal, but apply a bead of RTV type sealant to the cover plate when fitting it.

32 Interior grab handle – removal and refitting

1 Using a small screwdriver prise back the screw covers.
2 Extract the screws (photo) and remove the handle.
3 Refitting is a reversal of removal. The screw cover snaps into place.

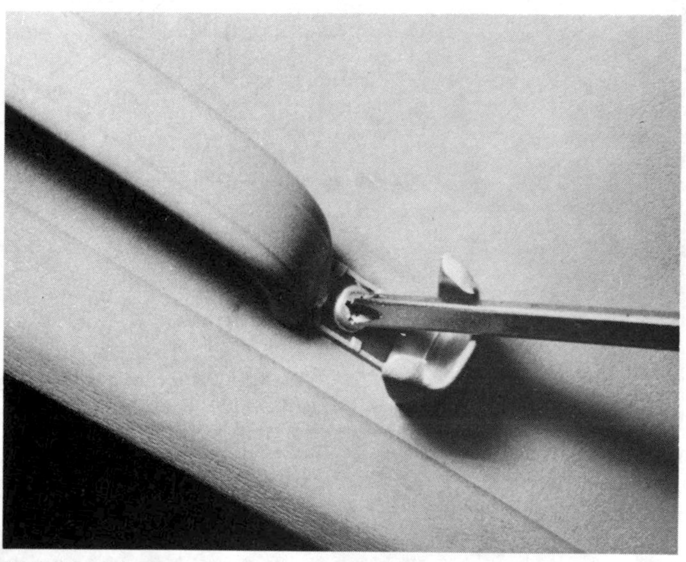

32.2 Extracting a grab handle screw

Chapter 13 Supplement: Revisions and information on later models

Contents

1 Introduction

The purpose of this Supplement is to provide information on the Nissan Sunny (UK/European model) and/or Sentra (N. American model) built from 1984 through 1986. The material in the first 12 Chapters of this manual still applies unless amendments are given in this Chapter. Therefore, owners of vehicles manufactured between the above years should refer to this Chapter before using the information in the original Chapters of this manual.

A notable change in the North American Sentra is the coolant passage added to the intake manifold and carburetor assembly. The brake system now uses only the larger of the two rotors in use earlier. A remolded version of the master cylinder is now in use on both models. Also, a new starter is used on North American models. Various other minor changes have been noted within this Chapter. **Note:** *Owners of UK/European Sunny models should be aware that many systems, components and features of earlier North American models were incorporated into 1984 through 1986 UK/European models. If you own such a vehicle, and this Supplement contains no information to the contrary, refer to the information pertaining to early North American models in the appropriate Chapter.*

2 Specifications

Engine

General		
Compression ratio — E15	9.5:1	
Jackshaft and camshaft pulley distance "A" from bolt to pulley	1mm (0.04 in)	
Crankshaft		
Crankpin diameter	39.961 to 39.974 mm (1.5745 to 1.5750 in)	
Big-end bearing clearance — E13	0.023 to 0.080 mm (0.0009 to 0.0031 in)	
Torque wrench settings	**Nm**	**lb ft**
Cylinder head tightening sequence		
step 1	29	22
step 2	69	51
step 3	Loosen all bolts completely in reverse order	
step 4	29	22
step 5 (or angles below)	69 to 74	51 to 54
If using an angle wrench	A = 45°, B = 55°, C = 40° (see text)	

Fuel system

Carburetor injection pump	
Plunger lift	0.94 ± 0.03 mm (0.0370 ± 0.0012 in)
Fast idle speed — E13 and E15	
UK/Europe manual transmission	2000 to 2400 rpm
UK/Europe automatic transmission	2200 to 2600 rpm

Fuel system (continued)

Torque wrench settings	Nm	lb ft
Camshaft pulley bolt	9 to 12	7 to 9
Jack shaft pulley bolt	9 to 12	7 to 9
Fuel cut solenoid	20 to 25	14 to 18
Injection pump drive pulley nut	59 to 69	43 to 51
Injection nozzle to engine	59 to 69	43 to 51
Injection to tube flare nut	22 to 25	16 to 18
Injection pump to bracket nut	13 to 18	9 to 13
Injection pump to bracket bolt	31 to 37	23 to 27
Spill tube nut	39 to 49	29 to 36
Oil filter adapter bolt	16 to 21	12 to 15
Plug bolt	14 to 20	10 to 14
Tensioner nut	16 to 21	12 to 15
Dust cover bolt	3 to 5	2.2 to 3.6

3 Engine

Oil filter adapter

1 An oil filter adapter has been added to reduce engine noise on automatic transmission equipped models in UK/Europe. In the future all E series engines will be fitted with the adapter.

Pulley fasteners

2 For improved performance, the washers for the jack shaft and camshaft pulley bolts have been modified. The modification has changed the bolts and tightening torque; see Specifications.

3 When changing the washer and bolts on the pulleys it is necessary to inspect the new washers and bolts by tightening the bolts temporarily to the shaft without a washer. Check the dimension "A" (Fig. 13.2b). If dimension "A" is less than 1 mm (0.04 in) the new type washer and bolts cannot be used and the former bolts and washers will have to be refitted.

Cylinder head — tightening sequence

4 The cylinder head gasket material has been modified and washers for the cylinder head bolts have been added. This affects all former E series engines.

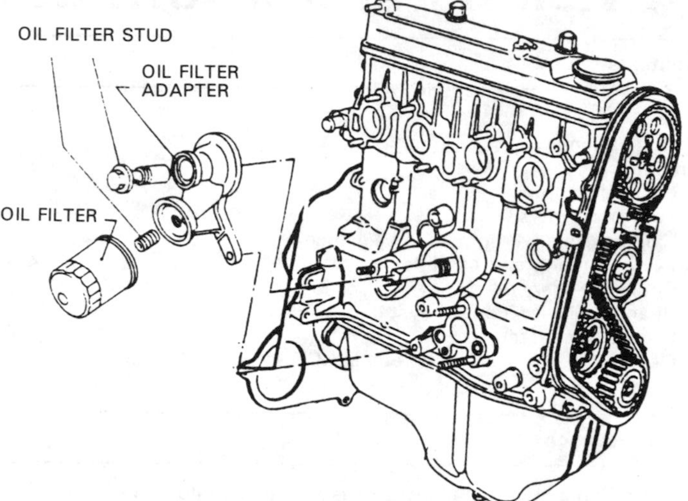

Fig. 13.1 An oil filter adapter has been added on E series engines equipped with an automatic transmission

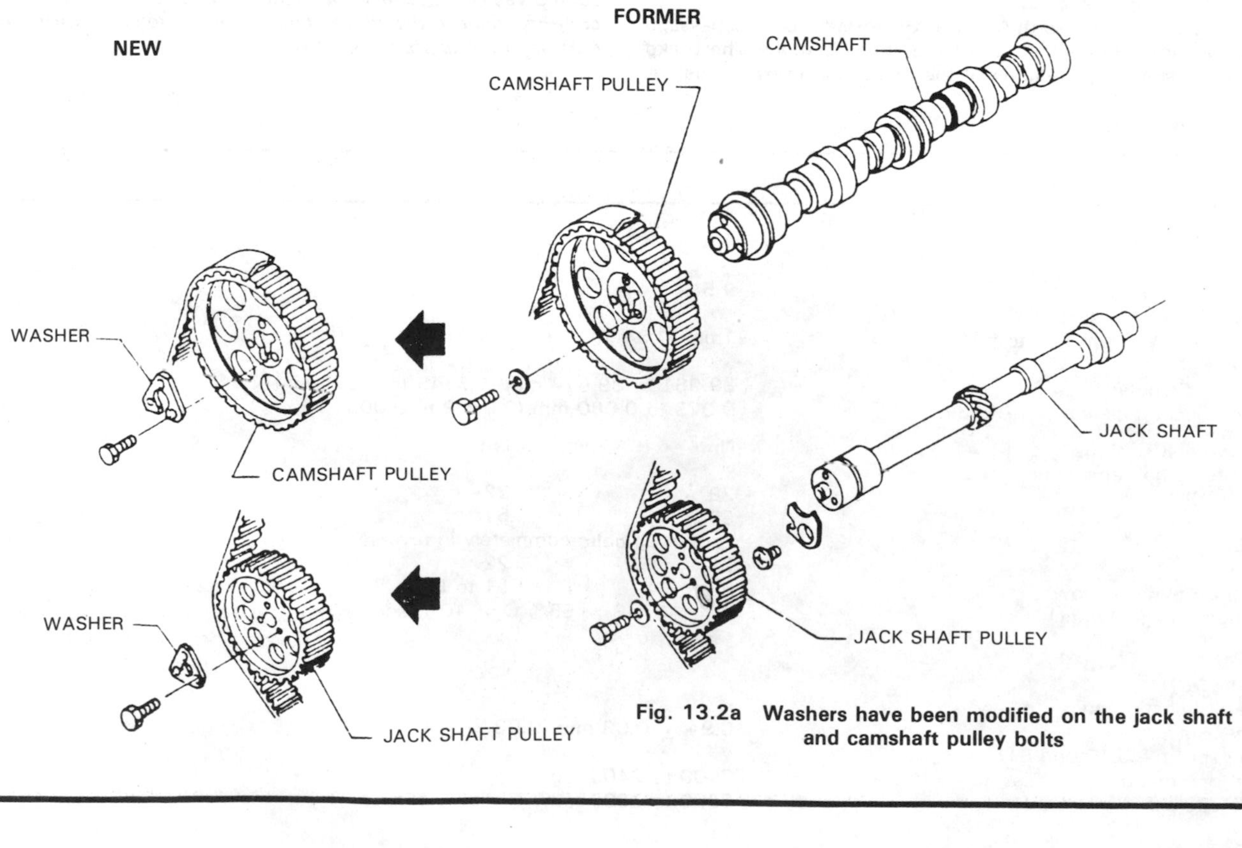

Fig. 13.2a Washers have been modified on the jack shaft and camshaft pulley bolts

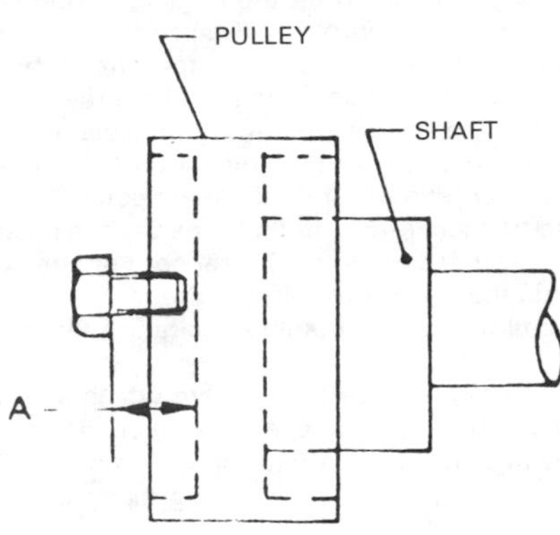

Fig. 13.2b Inspect the washer and bolt dimension A and if not acceptable to specifications the new washers and bolts cannot be used

5 Step 28 in Section 4 has been changed and the proper cylinder head tightening sequence is as follows:

a) Tighten all the bolts in the sequence shown (Fig. 13.3) to the amount shown in Specifications (step 1).
b) Tighten all the bolts to specification as shown in step 2 of Specifications.
c) Loosen all bolts by reversing the tightening sequence.
d) Repeat step "a".
e) Refer to step 5 in Specifications and tighten all bolts in sequence. If you have an angle wrench, turn each bolt clockwise the specified number of degrees (Fig. 13.4).

4 Cooling, heating and air conditioning

Cooling — general

1 On 1986 North American models a cooling passage running through the intake manifold flows coolant through a passage in the carburetor (Fig. 13.5).

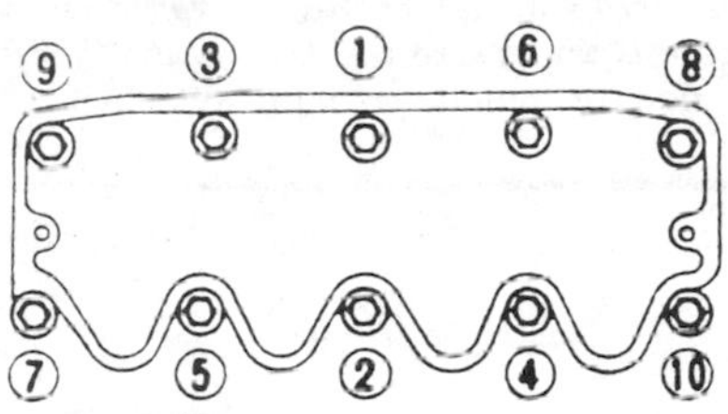

TIGHTEN IN NUMERICAL ORDER

Fig. 13.3 Tighten all cylinder head bolts in the sequence shown

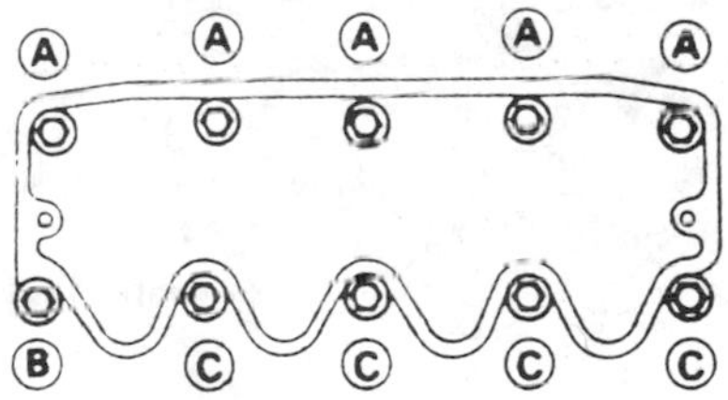

Fig. 13.4 If you have an angle wrench, turn each bolt clockwise the specified number of degrees in order to reach final torque (in place of step 5 in specs)
A = 45°, B = 55°, and C = 40°

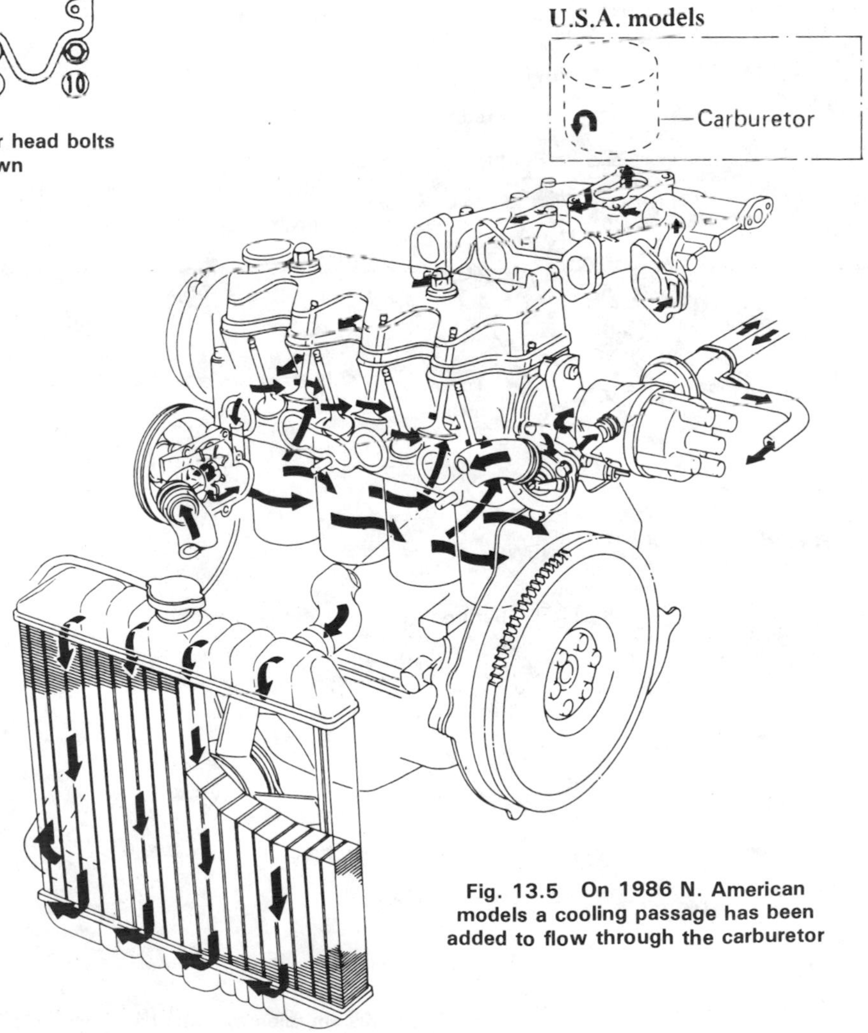

U.S.A. models

Carburetor

Fig. 13.5 On 1986 N. American models a cooling passage has been added to flow through the carburetor

5 Fuel and emission control systems

Fuel return system

1 Early in 1984 some of the E13 and E15 European model emission systems incorporated a fuel return system (Fig. 13.6) to improve engine performance at high temperatures.

Electronic Controlled Carburetor (ECC)

2 In 1984 some North American models received an electronically controlled carburetor (Fig. 13.7). Instead of the choke valve and fast idle cam (FIC) of a conventional carburetor, this carburetor system utilizes a duty-controlled solenoid valve for fuel enrichment and an idle speed control actuator (ISCA) as the basic controls. These devices are controlled according to the engine speed. Also, the air/fuel ratio and ignition timing are controlled according to the engine water temperature, atmospheric pressure, vehicle speed, and transaxle gear position. In addition, the system controls ignition timing and idle speed according to applied electrical loads, thereby achieving better emission control, driveability and fuel economy.

3 There are two methods of controlling the air/fuel ratio. Either through a method called open loop control or closed loop control. The system switches back and forth by the signal sent by the water temperature, engine rpm, battery voltage, exhaust gas sensor and vacuum manifold pressure sensor.

4 In the open loop method, the air/fuel ratio is determined by the ECC unit, corresponding to the information it receives from the sensors. This method is used when starting the engine, during cold start, hot restarting, deceleration, driving at high speeds and at full throttle.

5 The closed loop system is designed to control the air/fuel ratio precisely to the stoichiometric point so that the three-way catalyst can minimize emissions. The system employs an exhaust gas sensor located in the exhaust manifold to give an indication of whether the air/fuel ratio is richer or leaner than the stoichiometric point. The sensor sends pulses of voltage to the control unit that receives the pulse and adjusts feedback pulse width according to the sensor voltage so the mixture ratio will be within the narrow window of the three-way catalyst. This system opens until the sensor reaches operating temperature during warm up.

6 The air/fuel ratio control solenoid valve which is attached to the carburetor body, opens or closes repeatedly every 65 msec. Under the closed loop control, the percentage of opening time and closing time feedback is controlled by the ECC unit being triggered by the exhaust gas sensor.

ECC control system — component description

7 The ECC control unit is a microcomputer with electrical connectors for receiving input signals. The control unit controls the feedback pulse width and fuel shutoff operation, etc. A barometric pressure sensor is installed in order to correct the mixture according to the elevation.
Caution: *If your Nissan is equipped with the ECC unit, use of a radio transmitter (not a radio receiver) may interfere with unshielded electronic controls and cause the ECC to malfunction.*

8 An important component in this system is the oxygen sensor. This

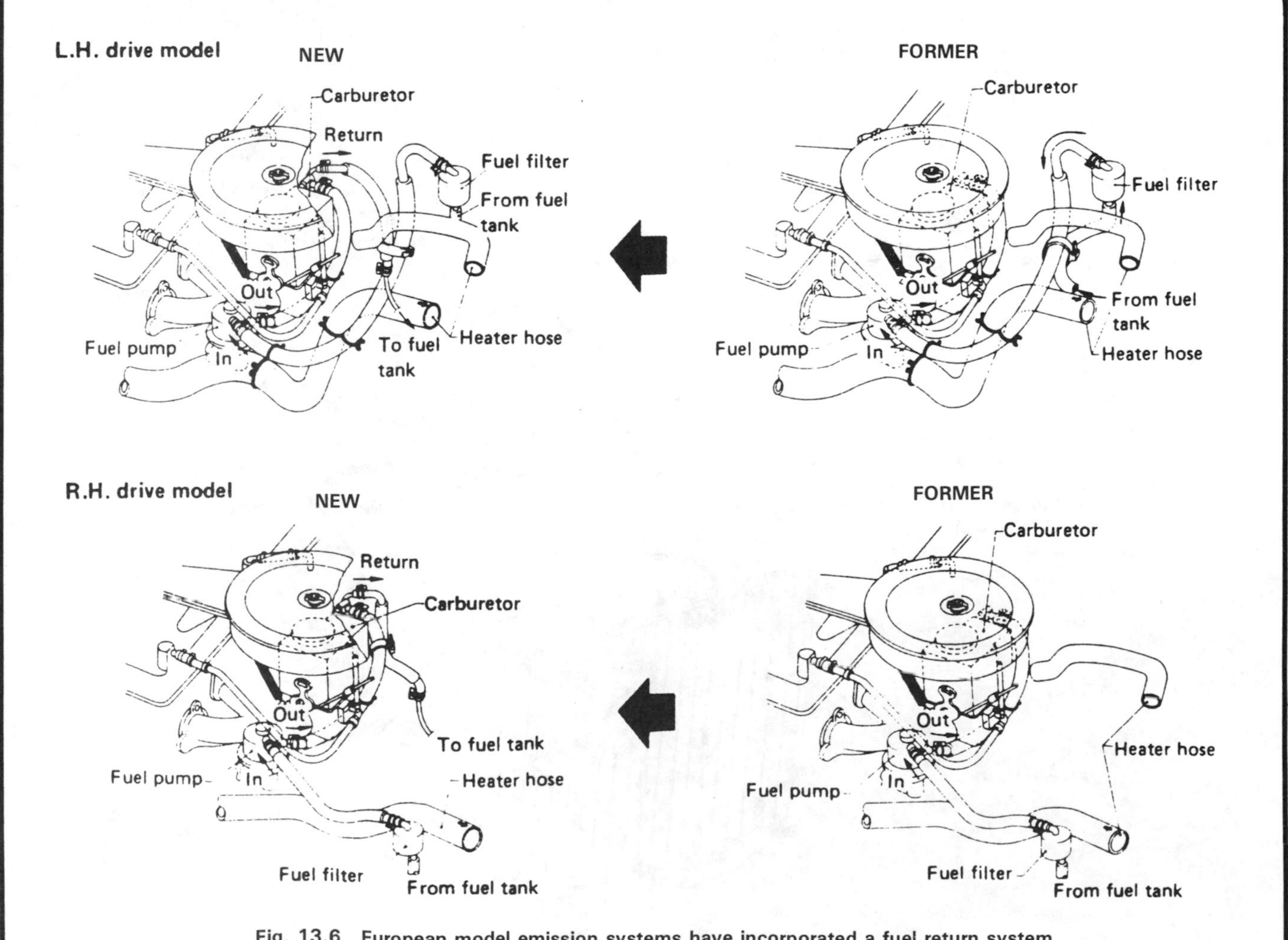

Fig. 13.6 European model emission systems have incorporated a fuel return system

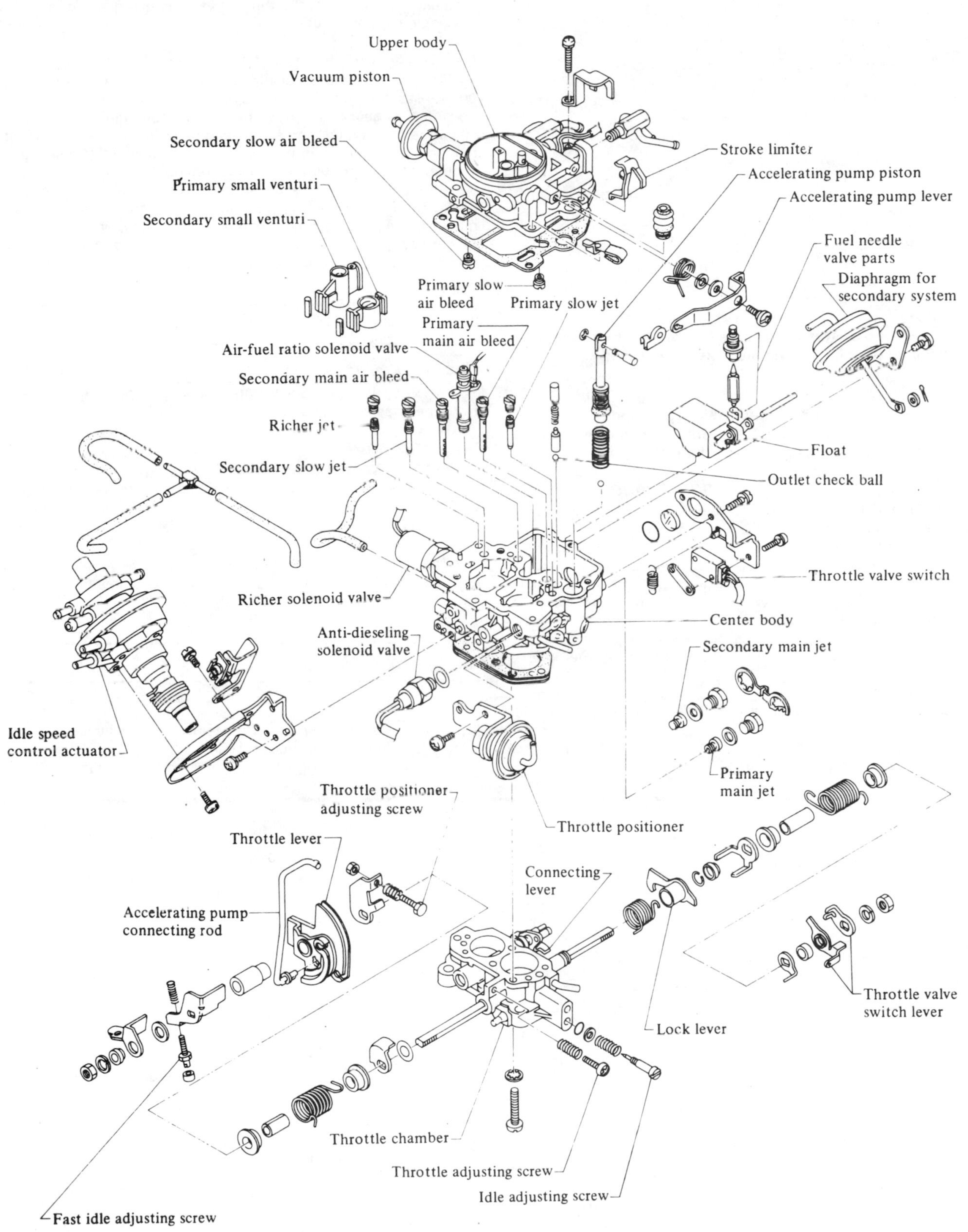

Fig. 13.7 The updated carburetors found on some North American models are electronically controlled and have replaced the choke valve with an idle speed control actuator

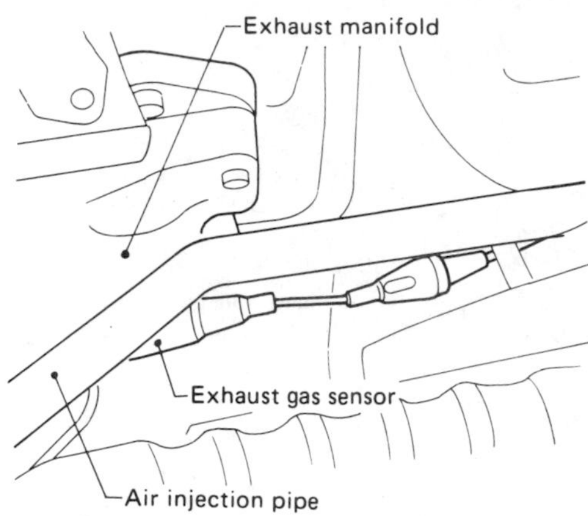

Fig. 13.8 An exhaust gas sensor is incorporated into the exhaust manifold to monitor oxygen content

sensor is built into the exhaust manifold (Fig. 13.8) and monitors the density of oxygen in the exhaust gas. This information is used by the control unit to determine pulse feedback duration.

ECC cold enrichment system — description

9 While the engine is cranking, the air/fuel ratio is controlled mainly by the cold enrichment solenoid valve (Fig. 13.9). From the moment of ignition, the air/fuel ratio is controlled by the vacuum piston and richer solenoid valve. After the engine starts, in accordance with the time elapsed and warm up condition of the engine, the air/fuel ratio is controlled by the richer solenoid valve, and the engine speed is controlled by the idle speed control actuator.

10 The throttle positioner keeps the throttle valve in the proper position while the engine is cranking and does not operate after the engine starts.

11 The richer solenoid valve, which is controlled by the ECC unit, controls the fuel feed under the secondary throttle valve and the air/fuel ratio during warm up.

12 After the engine starts the vacuum piston controls the air to the richer solenoid, regulating the air/fuel ratio.

13 The idle speed actuator is controlled by the vacuum control modulator and controls the throttle valve opening in accordance with the engine warm up condition.

Idle speed control system — basic operation

14 The idle speed is under the direction of the ECC control unit. The unit senses the idle condition and determines the appropriate idle speed according to gear position, water temperature and connection of the air conditioner switch and so on, and provides the electric signal corresponding to the difference of best idle and actual idle speed to the vacuum control modulator. The vacuum control modulator transforms electrical current into a vacuum signal. The idle speed control actuator controls the idle speed by vacuum signal from the vacuum control modulator. A fail safe system is incorported and is activated when any of the vacuum hoses connecting the idle control actuator with the vacuum control modulator is disconnected or cut off due to an accident.

6 Brakes

Rear brake drum

1 In 1985, the brake shoe anti-rattle spring seat has been removed from the assembly on all models.

Master cylinder

2 In 1984, North American models were equipped with an updated master cylinder (Fig.13.10). The changes were mainly in the reservoir design.

Front brake caliper

3 The front caliper has been changed slightly on some models (Fig. 13.11). The new design has added inner shims to the pads. Pad and caliper replacement remains the same.

7 Electrical system

Wiring diagrams

1 Electrical wiring diagrams for later models are included at the end of this Chapter. If a particular circuit is not shown here, it can be assumed that the wiring has not changed from earlier models.

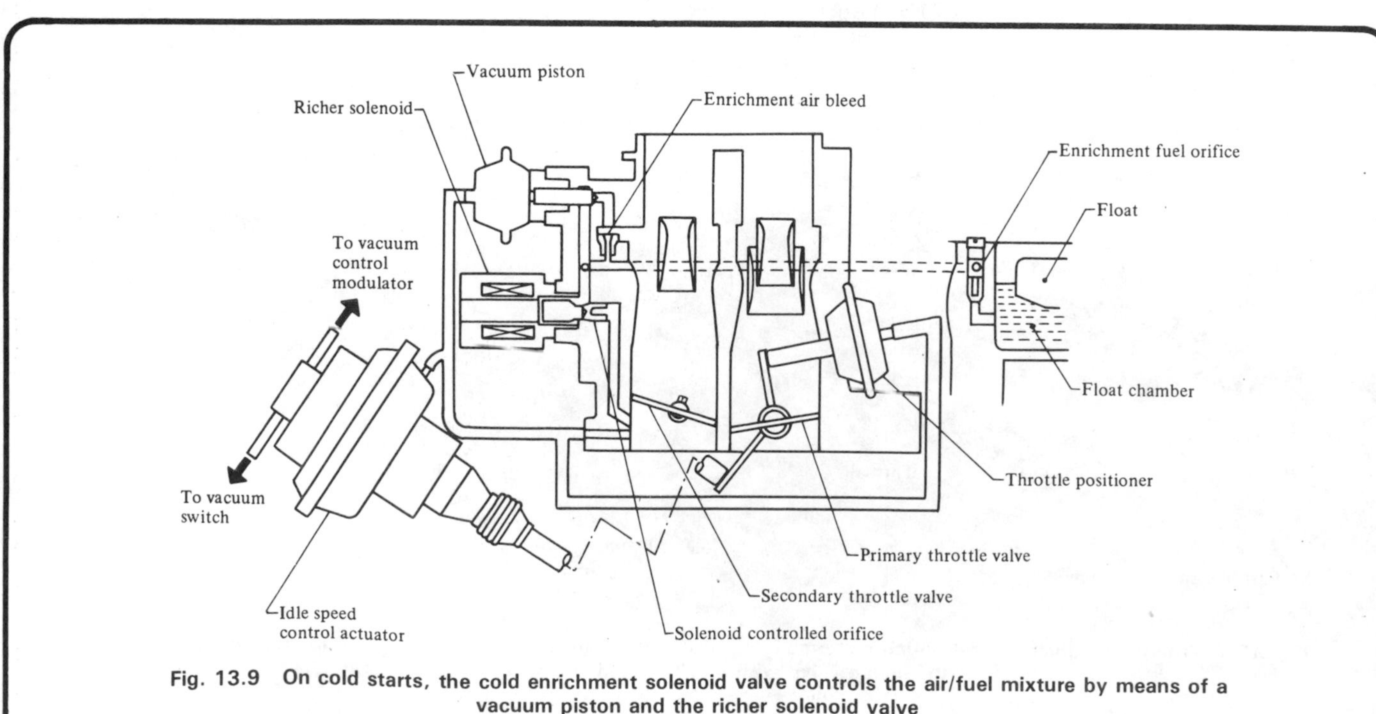

Fig. 13.9 On cold starts, the cold enrichment solenoid valve controls the air/fuel mixture by means of a vacuum piston and the richer solenoid valve

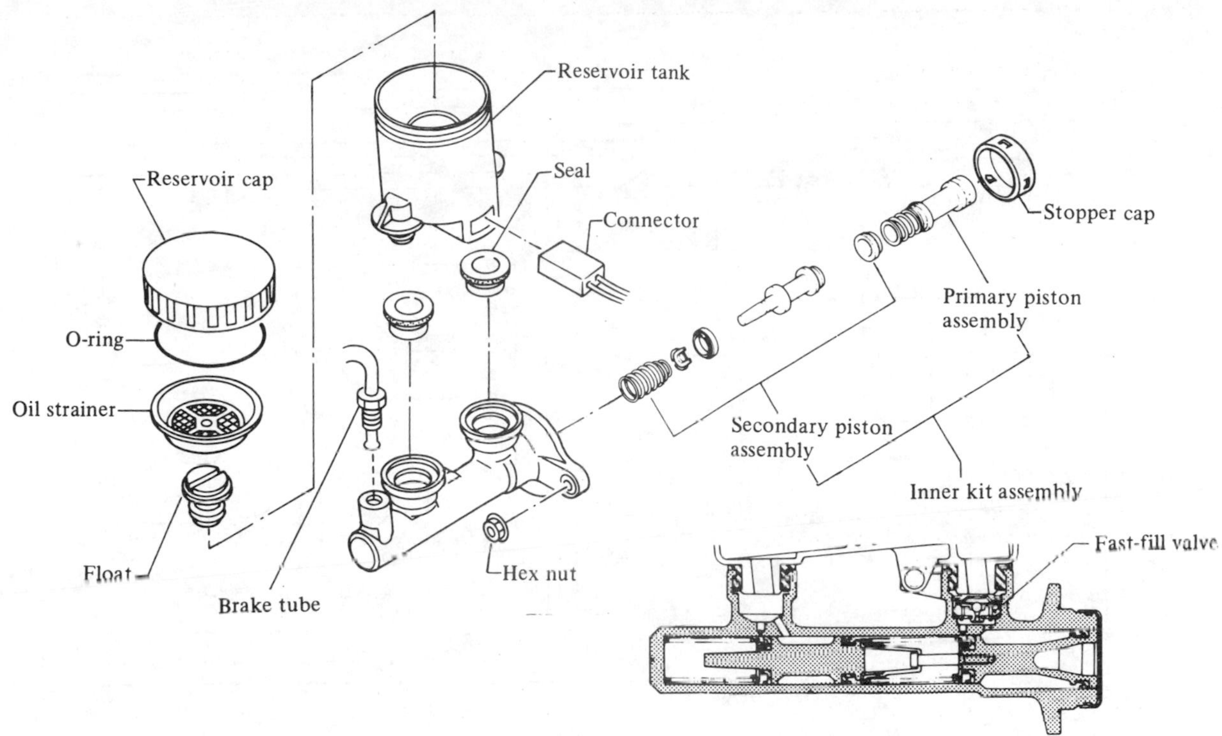

Fig. 13.10 Minor changes have occurred in the design of the master cylinder

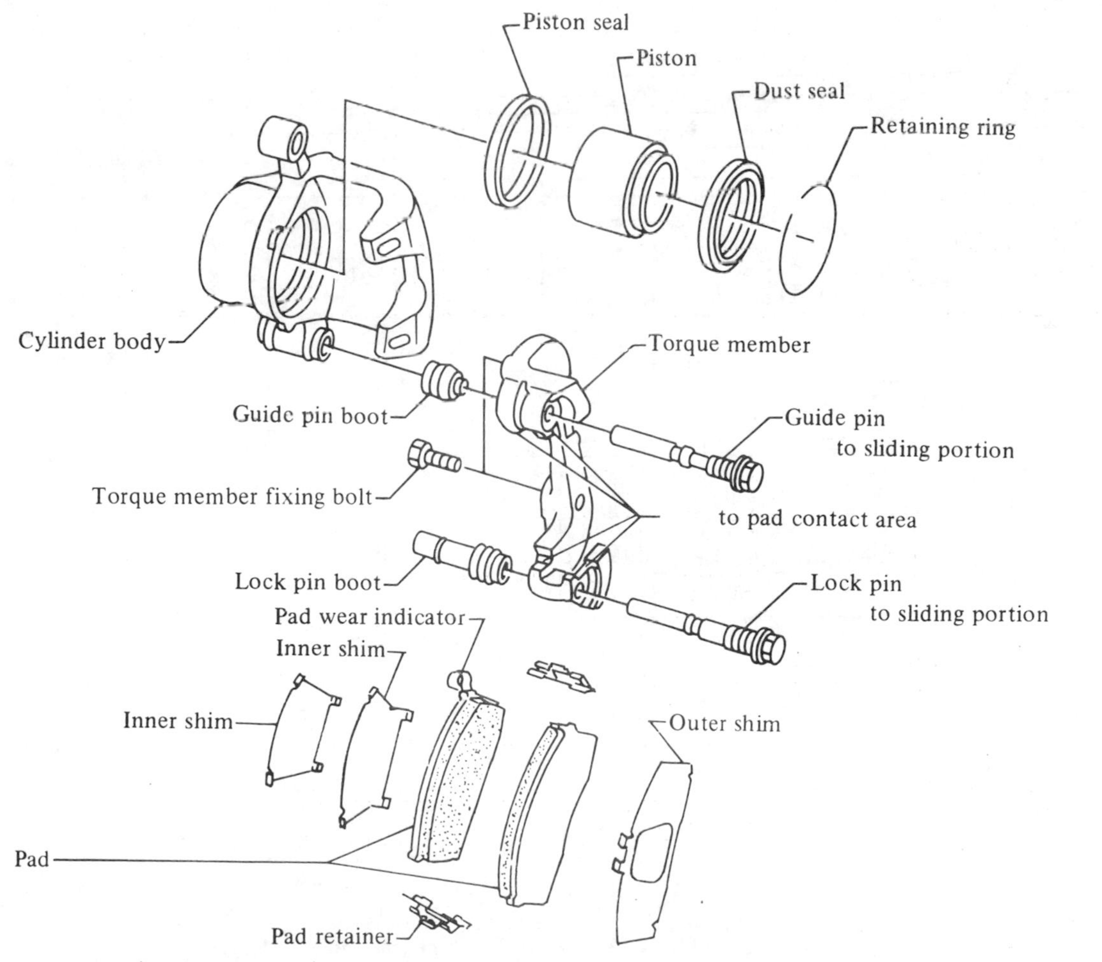

Fig. 13.11 Inner shims have been added to the front caliper pads

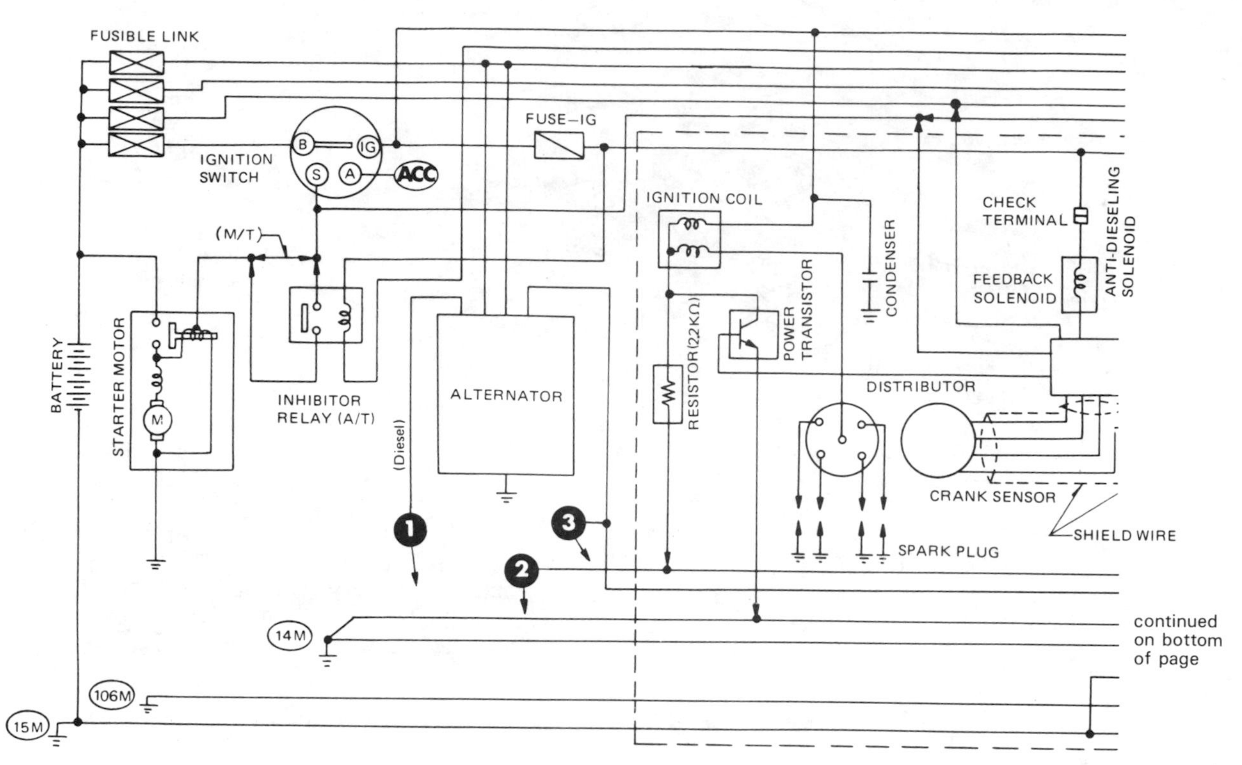

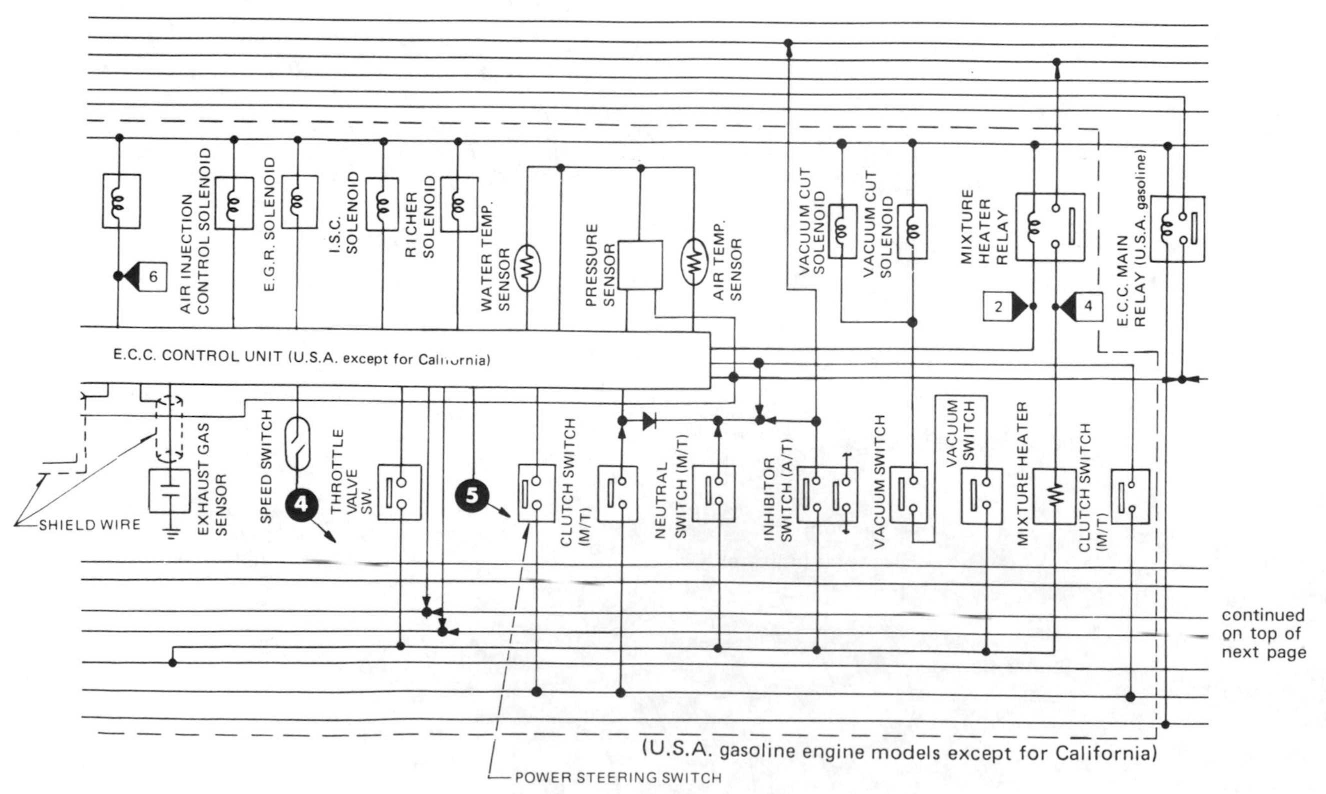

Wiring diagram for 1984 thru 1986 N. American models (1 of 7)

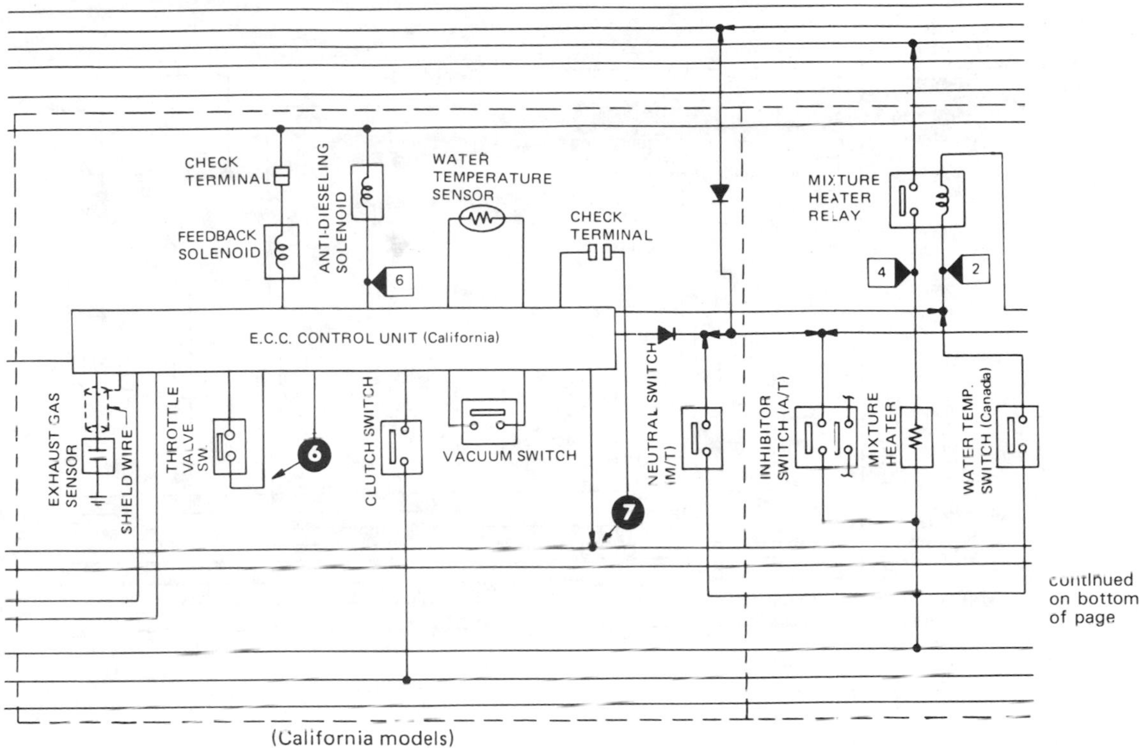

continued on bottom of page

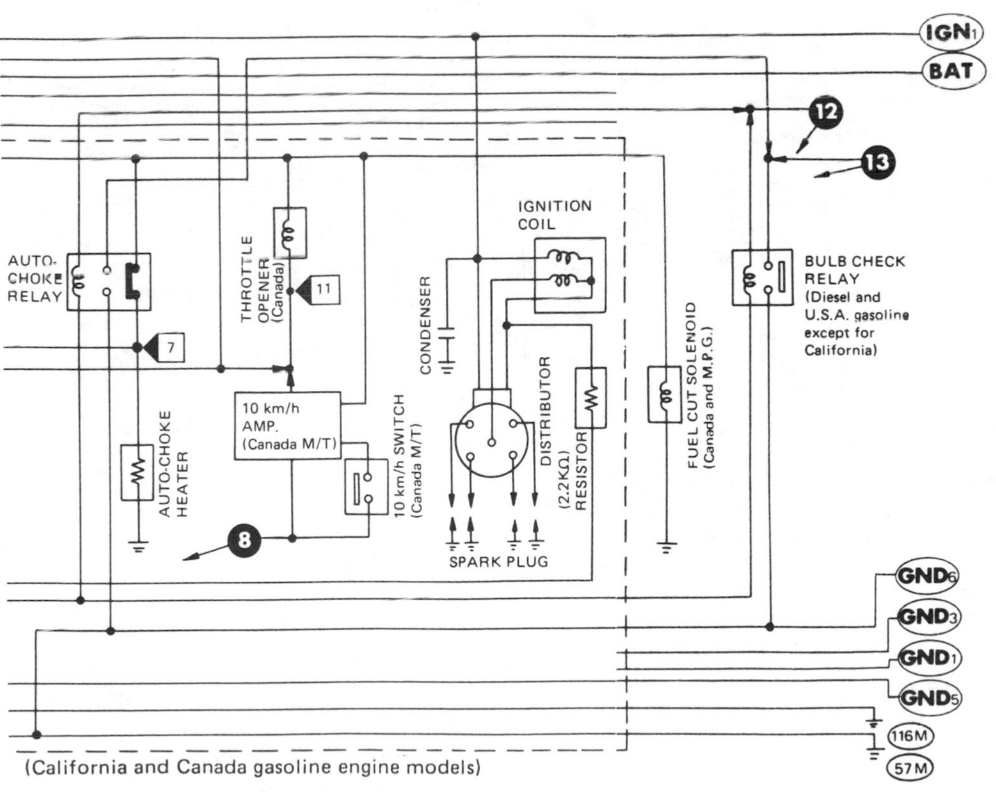

Wiring diagram for 1984 thru 1986 N. American models (2 of 7)

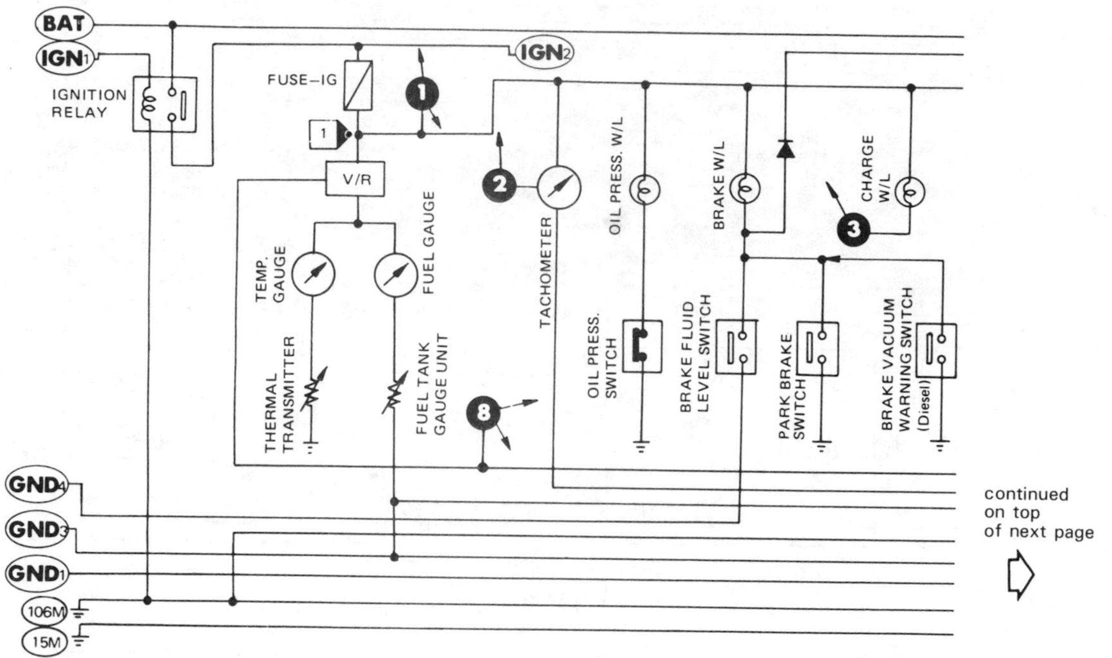

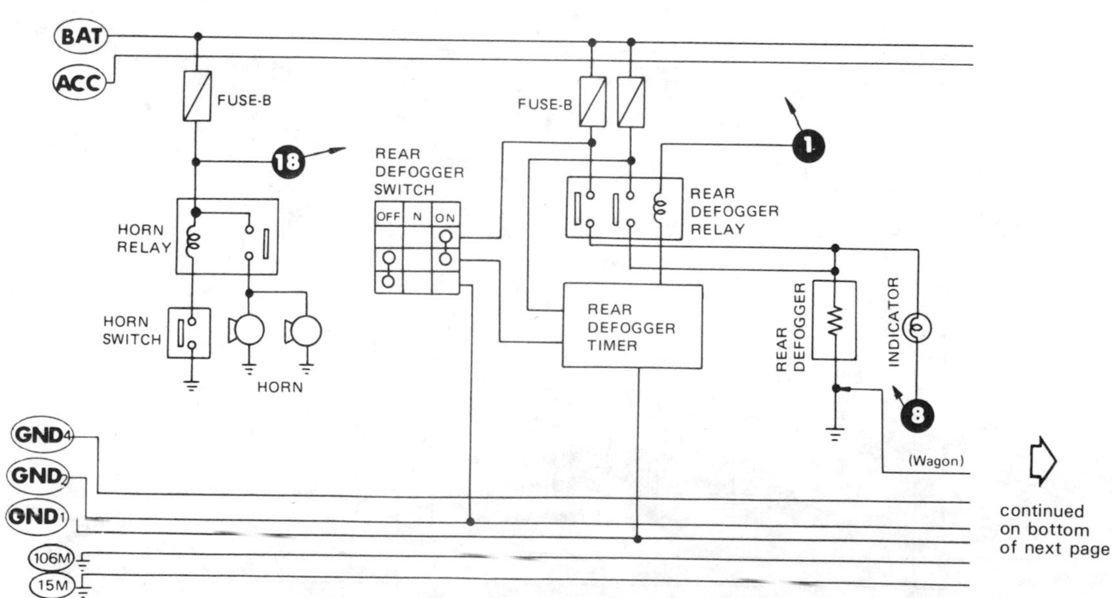

Wiring diagram for 1984 thru 1986 N. American models (3 of 7)

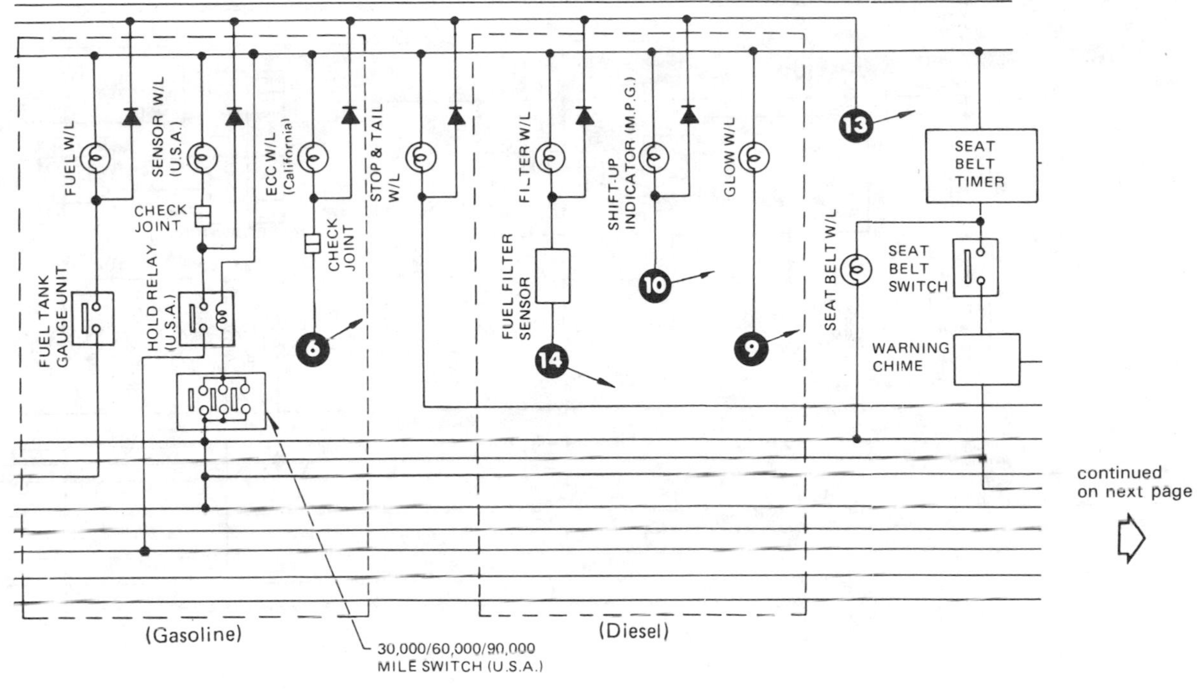

continued on next page

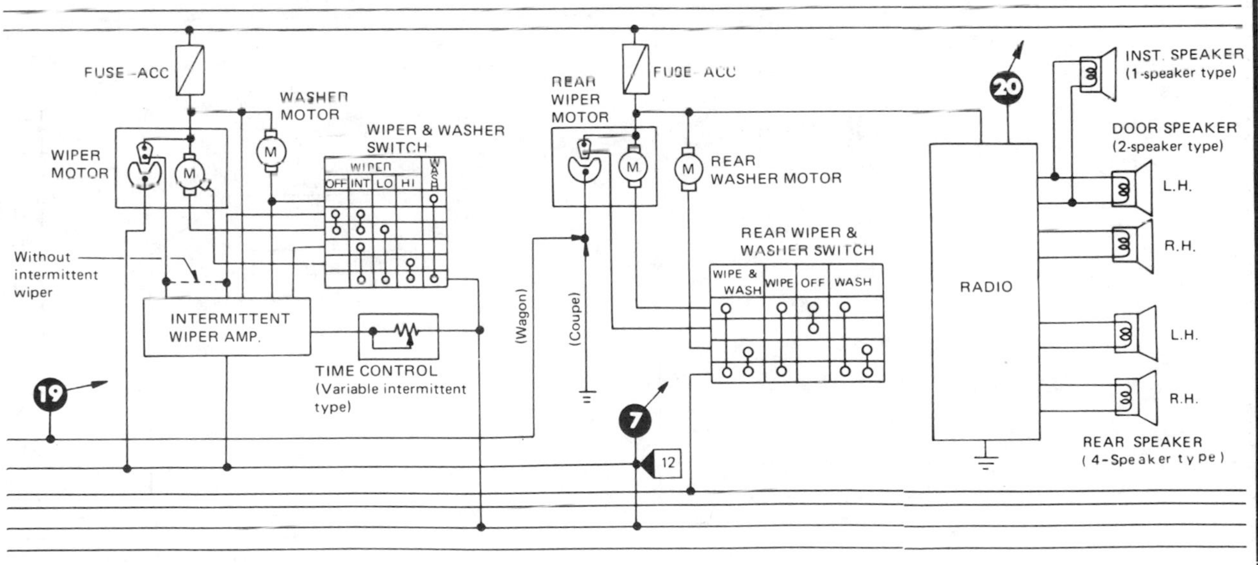

continued on next page

Wiring diagram for 1984 thru 1986 N. American models (4 of 7)

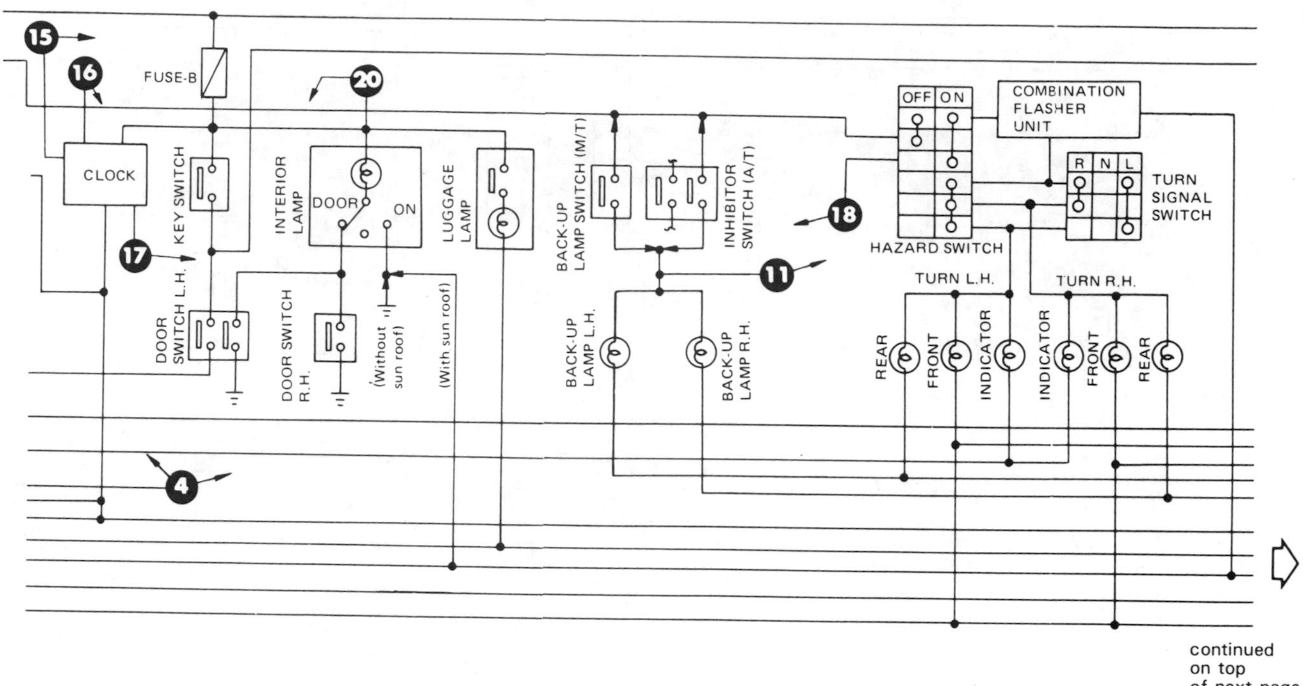

continued on top of next page

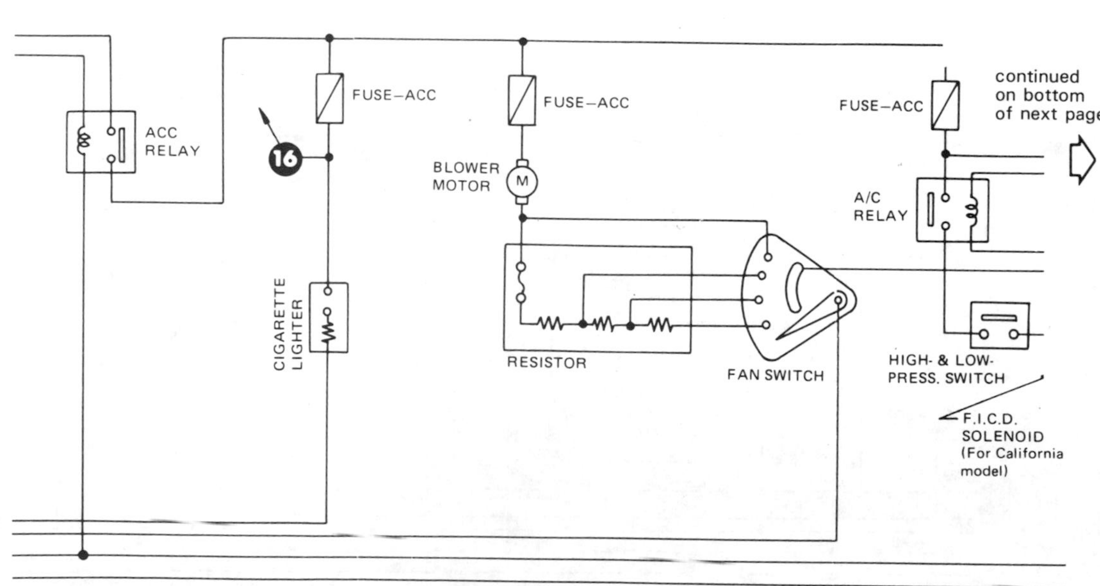

continued on bottom of next page

Wiring diagram for 1984 thru 1986 N. American models (5 of 7)

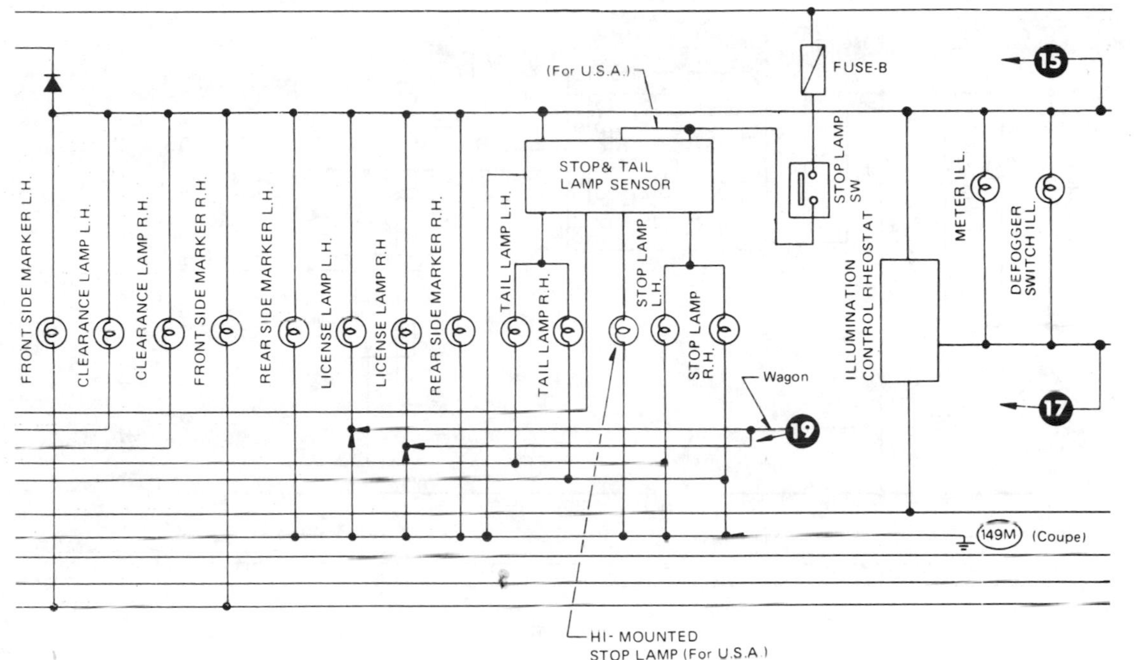

continued on next page

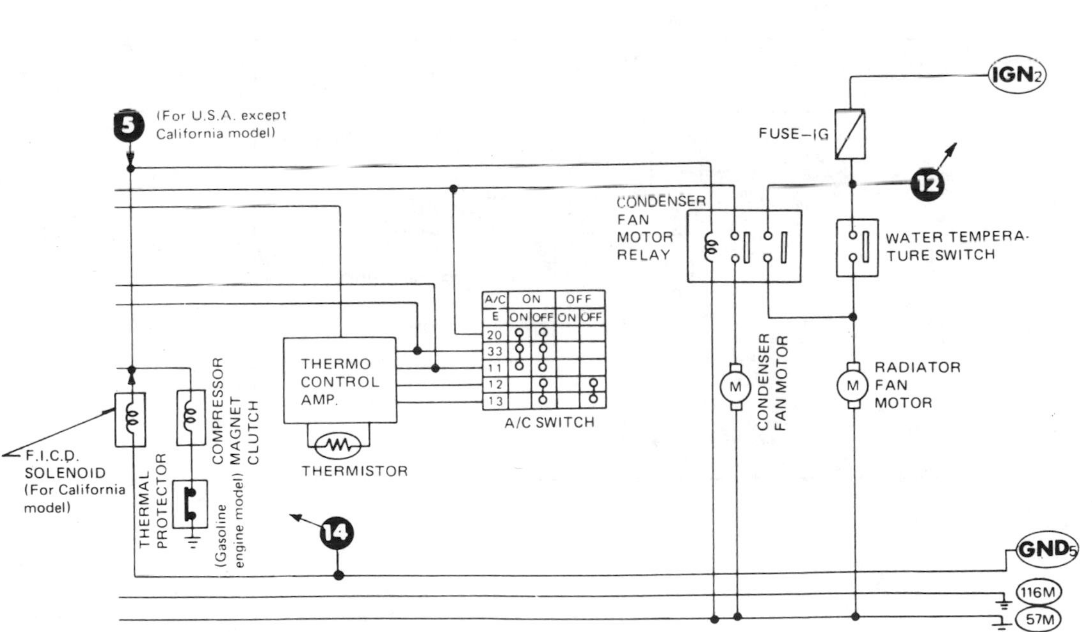

Wiring diagram for 1984 thru 1986 N. American models (6 of 7)

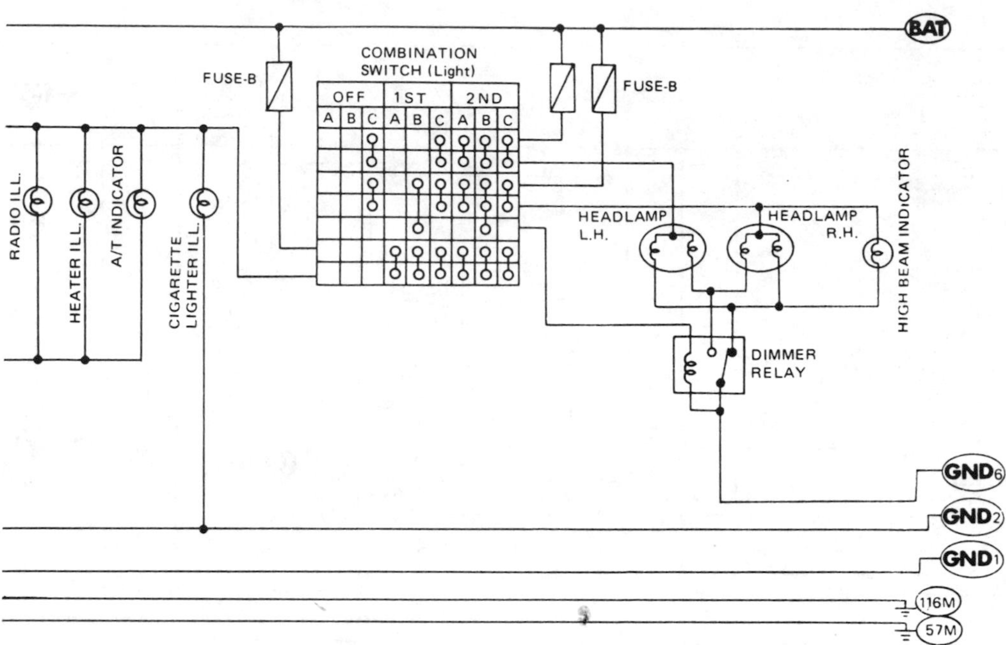

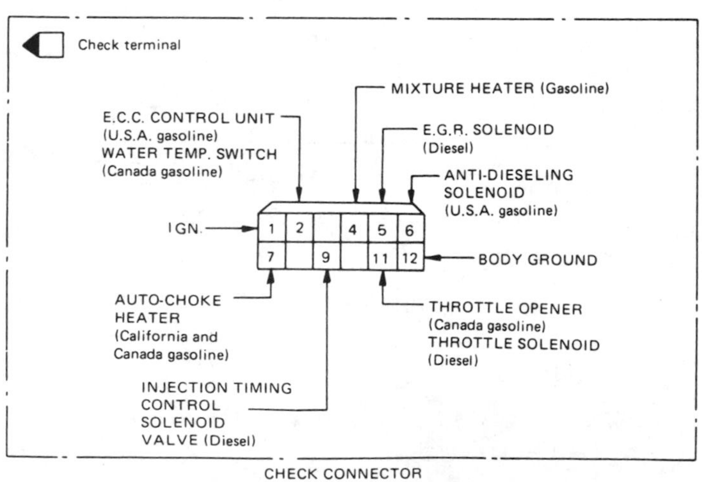

CHECK CONNECTOR

Wiring diagram for 1984 thru 1986 N. American models (7 of 7)

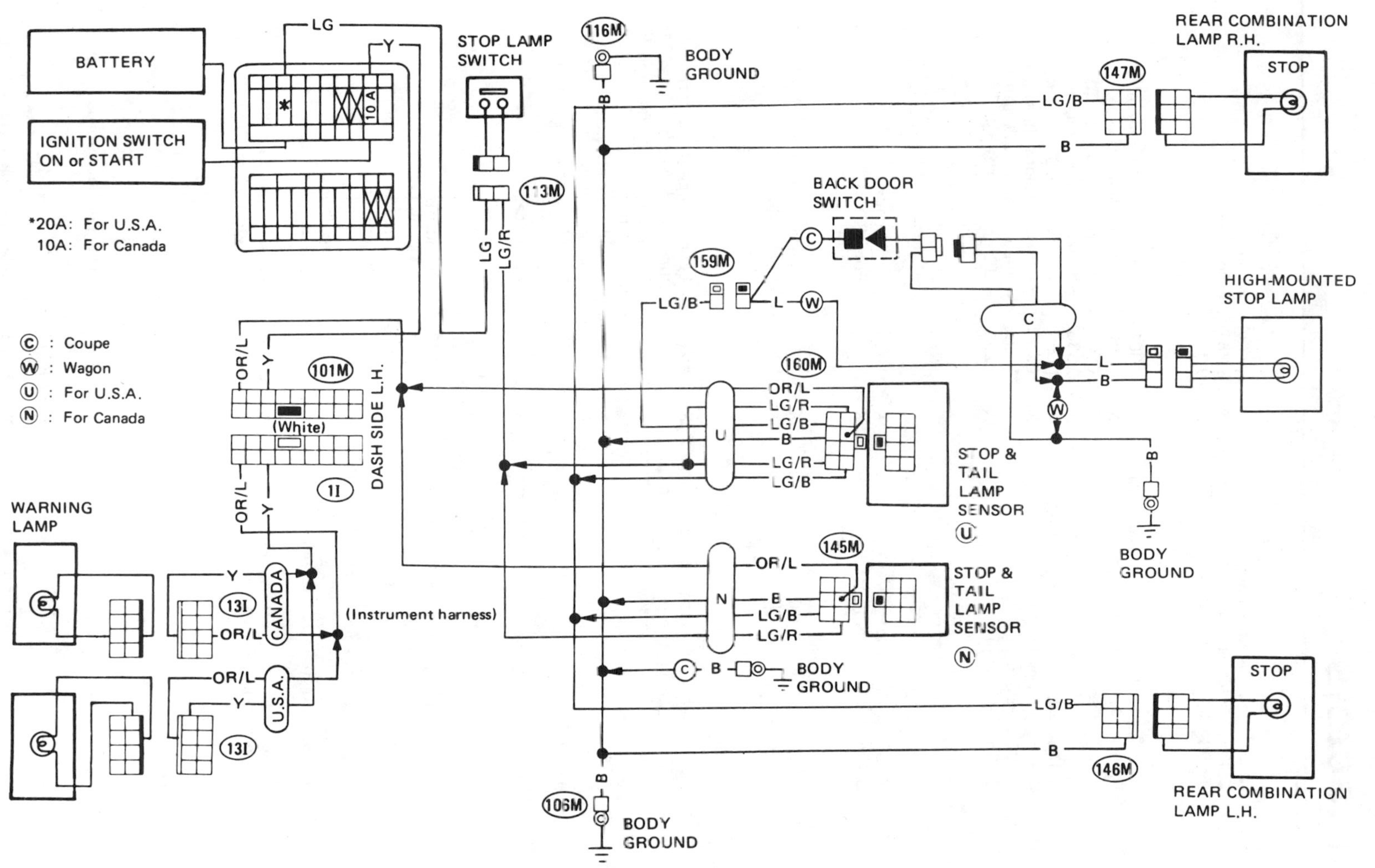

Wiring diagram for warning and stop lamps on N. American models

Conversion factors

Length (distance)					
Inches (in)	X 25.4	= Millimetres (mm)	X	0.0394	= Inches (in)
Feet (ft)	X 0.305	= Metres (m)	X	3.281	= Feet (ft)
Miles	X 1.609	= Kilometres (km)	X	0.621	= Miles
Volume (capacity)					
Cubic inches (cu in; in^3)	X 16.387	= Cubic centimetres (cc; cm^3)	X	0.061	= Cubic inches (cu in; in^3)
Imperial pints (Imp pt)	X 0.568	= Litres (l)	X	1.76	= Imperial pints (Imp pt)
Imperial quarts (Imp qt)	X 1.137	= Litres (l)	X	0.88	= Imperial quarts (Imp qt)
Imperial quarts (Imp qt)	X 1.201	= US quarts (US qt)	X	0.833	= Imperial quarts (Imp qt)
US quarts (US qt)	X 0.946	= Litres (l)	X	1.057	= US quarts (US qt)
Imperial gallons (Imp gal)	X 4.546	= Litres (l)	X	0.22	= Imperial gallons (Imp gal)
Imperial gallons (Imp gal)	X 1.201	= US gallons (US gal)	X	0.833	= Imperial gallons (Imp gal)
US gallons (US gal)	X 3.785	= Litres (l)	X	0.264	= US gallons (US gal)
Mass (weight)					
Ounces (oz)	X 28.35	= Grams (g)	X	0.035	= Ounces (oz)
Pounds (lb)	X 0.454	= Kilograms (kg)	X	2.205	= Pounds (lb)
Force					
Ounces-force (ozf; oz)	X 0.278	= Newtons (N)	X	3.6	= Ounces-force (ozf; oz)
Pounds-force (lbf; lb)	X 4.448	= Newtons (N)	X	0.225	= Pounds-force (lbf; lb)
Newtons (N)	X 0.1	= Kilograms-force (kgf; kg)	X	9.81	= Newtons (N)
Pressure					
Pounds-force per square inch (psi; lbf/in^2; lb/in^2)	X 0.070	= Kilograms-force per square centimetre (kgf/cm^2; kg/cm^2)	X	14.223	= Pounds-force per square inch (psi; lbf/in^2; lb/in^2)
Pounds-force per square inch (psi; lbf/in^2; lb/in^2)	X 0.068	= Atmospheres (atm)	X	14.696	= Pounds-force per square inch (psi; lbf/in^2; lb/in^2)
Pounds-force per square inch (psi; lbf/in^2; lb/in^2)	X 0.069	= Bars	X	14.5	= Pounds-force per square inch (psi; lbf/in^2; lb/in^2)
Pounds-force per square inch (psi; lbf/in^2; lb/in^2)	X 6.895	= Kilopascals (kPa)	X	0.145	= Pounds-force per square inch (psi; lbf/in^2; lb/in^2)
Kilopascals (kPa)	X 0.01	= Kilograms-force per square centimetre (kgf/cm^2; kg/cm^2)	X	98.1	= Kilopascals (kPa)
Torque (moment of force)					
Pounds-force inches (lbf in; lb in)	X 1.152	= Kilograms-force centimetre (kgf cm; kg cm)	X	0.868	= Pounds-force inches (lbf in; lb in)
Pounds-force inches (lbf in; lb in)	X 0.113	= Newton metres (Nm)	X	8.85	= Pounds-force inches (lbf in; lb in)
Pounds-force inches (lbf in; lb in)	X 0.083	= Pounds-force feet (lbf ft; lb ft)	X	12	= Pounds-force inches (lbf in; lb in)
Pounds-force feet (lbf ft; lb ft)	X 0.138	= Kilograms-force metres (kgf m; kg m)	X	7.233	= Pounds-force feet (lbf ft; lb ft)
Pounds-force feet (lbf ft; lb ft)	X 1.356	= Newton metres (Nm)	X	0.738	= Pounds-force feet (lbf ft; lb ft)
Newton metres (Nm)	X 0.102	= Kilograms-force metres (kgf m; kg m)	X	9.804	= Newton metres (Nm)
Power					
Horsepower (hp)	X 745.7	= Watts (W)	X	0.0013	= Horsepower (hp)
Velocity (speed)					
Miles per hour (miles/hr; mph)	X 1.609	= Kilometres per hour (km/hr; kph)	X	0.621	= Miles per hour (miles/hr; mph)
Fuel consumption*					
Miles per gallon, Imperial (mpg)	X 0.354	= Kilometres per litre (km/l)	X	2.825	= Miles per gallon, Imperial (mpg)
Miles per gallon, US (mpg)	X 0.425	= Kilometres per litre (km/l)	X	2.352	= Miles per gallon, US (mpg)

Temperature

Degrees Fahrenheit = (°C x 1.8) + 32

Degrees Celsius (Degrees Centigrade; °C) = (°F - 32) x 0.56

**It is common practice to convert from miles per gallon (mpg) to litres/100 kilometres (l/100km), where mpg (Imperial) x l/100 km = 282 and mpg (US) x l/100 km = 235*

Index

A

B

C

D

E

F

T

V

W